American Public Policy

An Introduction

TENTH EDITION

CLARKE E. COCHRAN
Covenant Health System
Texas Tech University (Emeritus)

LAWRENCE C. MAYER
Texas Tech University

T.R. CARR
Southern Illinois University at Edwardsville

N. JOSEPH CAYER
Arizona State University

MARK J. McKENZIE
Texas Tech University

LAURA R. PECK
Arizona State University

WADSWORTH
CENGAGE Learning

Australia • Brazil • Japan • Korea • Mexico • Singapore • Spain • United Kingdom • United States

WADSWORTH
CENGAGE Learning

American Public Policy: An Introduction, Tenth Edition
Clarke E. Cochran, Lawrence C. Mayer, T.R. Carr, N. Joseph Cayer, Mark J. McKenzie, and Laura R. Peck

Senior Publisher: Suzanne Jeans

Executive Editor: Carolyn Merrill

Development Editor: Lauren Athmer/LEAP Publishing Services, Inc.

Assistant Editor: Laura Ross

Editorial Assistant: Nina Wasserman

Marketing Manager: Lydia LeStar

Marketing Communications Manager: Heather Baxley

Content Project Management: PreMediaGlobal

Art Director: Linda Helcher

Print buyer: Fola Orekoya

Rights Acquisitions Specialist: Shalice Shah-Caldwell

Production Service: PreMediaGlobal

Cover Designer: LouAnn Thesing

Cover Image: Malven/istockphoto; JimLarkin/istockphoto; Mastahlphoto/istockphoto

For product information and technology assistance, contact us at **Cengage Learning Customer & Sales Support, 1-800-354-9706**

For permission to use material from this text or product, submit all requests online at **www.cengage.com/permissions**. Further permissions questions can be emailed to **permissionrequest@cengage.com.**

Library of Congress Control Number: 2010941586

ISBN-13: 978-1-111-34288-3

ISBN-10: 1-111-34288-1

Wadsworth
20 Channel Center Street
Boston, MA 02210
USA

Cengage Learning is a leading provider of customized learning solutions with office locations around the globe, including Singapore, the United Kingdom, Australia, Mexico, Brazil and Japan. Locate your local office at **international.cengage.com/region**

Cengage Learning products are represented in Canada by Nelson Education, Ltd.

For your course and learning solutions, visit **www.cengage.com**.

Purchase any of our products at your local college store or at our preferred online store **www.cengagebrain.com**.

Instructors: Please visit **login.cengage.com** and log in to access instructor-specific resources.

Printed in the United States of America
2 3 4 5 6 7 14 13 12

To
Anne
Etta
Lucy
Matt
Bob, Gret, Robbie, and Scarlett
Brad

Contents

Preface

American Public Policy is an introductory undergraduate text that focuses on the substantive issues of public policy. Most texts stress methods of policy analysis, models of policy, or the policymaking process. Although these topics are important, their dominance at the introductory level often makes the subject too abstract to engage students' imaginations. In our own teaching, we have found that an interest in more rigorous analysis grows most naturally out of a lively classroom discussion of specific policy debates—for example, welfare, abortion, tax reform, immigration, or crime control. *American Public Policy* is unique in its emphasis on such issues, combining history and description with presentation of alternative solutions.

This text is intended for the first undergraduate course in public policy, either a one-semester course or part of a two-semester sequence that includes both political institutions and public policy. We do not assume any prior knowledge of public policy on the student's part, although we do presume an understanding of the structure of American government. Therefore, we present the policy material step by step, building a picture of existing policy that students can use to evaluate alternatives.

Most chapters follow the same outline for easy access and comparison. The first section, "Issue Background," provides information the reader needs to know about the background of the particular topic, including descriptions of early policy actions. The second, "Contemporary Policy," outlines the evolution of present-day governmental policy. The section on "Policy Evaluation" presents an in-depth discussion of the principal successes and failures of policy relating to the particular issue under study. Finally, the "Future Alternatives" section evaluates possible alternatives to existing policy. Each chapter includes a list of helpful books and websites for further study. Each chapter compares a wide range of perspectives—from conservative to liberal to radical—but *American Public Policy* does not take a single ideological position. Instead, this approach challenges students to develop their own evaluations of the alternatives proposed in contemporary controversies.

This book does not neglect the state and local dimensions of policy issues, but the focus is primarily on national policy and national policy debate. Cross-national comparisons of policies and their impacts are presented when relevant.

We have made a variety of changes for the tenth edition of *American Public Policy*. Having completed this edition in the fall of 2010, we have tried to keep our text current with the issues most prominent in the political debate, particularly the dynamics leading up to the 2010 mid-term election, without simply focusing on "current events." Some issues, such as the outcome of the war in Afghanistan, finance reform, immigration reform, and increased attention on global climate change, were not clear in their full effects at the time of writing. We have expanded the chapter on foreign policy for a more comprehensive examination of the Iraq War, the Middle East, terrorism, and nuclear proliferation. The chapter on crime considers the continued decline in crime rates and the reasons for them. Chapter 8 covers the major changes in health policy, especially the 2010 Patient Protection and Affordable Care Act (PPACA). Immigration has become a topic of intense passions, which are covered in Chapter 11.

Chapter 1 introduces the study of public policy. Major policy concepts are defined, illustrated, and explained. Chapter 2 focuses on the contexts in which contemporary public policy operates—institutional, economic, demographic, cultural, and ideological. This chapter continues the structural introduction of Chapter 1. Each succeeding chapter examines an individual policy arena.

Chapter 3 gives attention to economic theory, economic regulation, changes in the economy, and international competition, leaving the entirety of Chapter 4 for macroeconomic policy, including the federal budget, taxes, and spending. Chapter 5 deals with environmental and energy policy, highlighting the important interaction between these two policy areas.

Chapter 6 considers fluctuation in rates of crime, including speculation about the causes of crime. This chapter evaluates the impact of policies specifying an individual's constitutional rights: confessions and the right to counsel, the exclusionary rule and search and seizure, and capital punishment. It considers alternative methods of responding to crime, including gun control, capital punishment, and sentencing reform.

Chapter 7 looks at the bifurcated nature of social welfare policy by considering the definition of poverty and the evolution of the U.S. welfare state. This chapter examines the distinction between social insurance and social assistance and describes the various programs and policies that make up the U.S. system, concluding with an assessment of effectiveness and shortcomings.

Chapter 8 discusses the nation's health care as a kind of double bind, one of unlimited needs but limited resources. Special attention is given to the prospects for reform in the future with a focus on Medicare reform, national health insurance, and the effects of new research into the building blocks of life itself.

Chapter 9 shows the tradition of free public education in the United States to be in jeopardy. This chapter considers such problems as poor student achievement, teacher competence, inequities resulting from the system of local control, and the role of the federal government in education. The idea of equality, both legal and social, is discussed in Chapter 10. Programs of the 1960s and 1970s—those aimed at achieving equality in the schools and in employment—are now questioned seriously. Chapter 11 is then devoted to the issue of immigration and the various responses that the American government has made over time to its challenges. Chapter 12 describes the challenges to American foreign policy. Chapter 13 focuses on issues involving strong moral content—abortion, freedom of speech and censorship, the right to die, the role of religion in society and politics, and feminism and family values.

American Public Policy may be used in a variety of ways. Instructors may choose to consider all of the policy areas presented or to select a group of them for special emphasis. Chapters 1 and 2 should be read first, but the rest of the chapters can be assigned in any sequence the instructor prefers. Supplementary readings focusing on particular issues may be conveniently added, or the text may be used in conjunction with other texts focusing on political institutions or the policy process. Cengage Learning also offers an eBank Instructor's Manual with Test Bank (ISBN-10: 111134289X | ISBN-13: 9781111342890) that provides suggestions for class discussions, writing assignments, Internet and research projects, and exam questions to make course preparation easier.

Rebecca C. Harris, Washington and Lee University; and Christine H. Rossell, Boston University, shared with us helpful comments on this and earlier editions. Richard Riley, Baylor University; Timothy Sherratt, Gordon College; John Lofton, Arkansas State University; Kim Spiezio, Cedar Crest College; Justin Halpern, Northeastern State University; and Gary Klass, Illinois State also provided feedback on earlier editions. Evie Selberg and Matthew Young provided help on tables and figures. Kate MacLean of Cengage Learning and Lauren Athmer of LEAP Publishing Services, Inc., provided invaluable editorial assistance. Our thanks to all of them.

Clarke E. Cochran
Lawrence C. Mayer
T.R. Carr
N. Joseph Cayer
Mark J. McKenzie
Laura R. Peck

About the Authors

Clarke E. Cochran is Vice-President of Mission Integration at Covenant Health System in Lubbock, Texas. He is Professor Emeritus of Political Science at Texas Tech University, where he specialized in religion and politics, political philosophy, and health care policy. Dr. Cochran received his Ph.D. from Duke University in 1971 and taught at Texas Tech from 1970 to 2007. He is the author of four books and numerous journal articles. Dr. Cochran held the position of Research Fellow in the Erasmus Institute at the University of Notre Dame (1998–1999) and the Shannon Chair in Catholic Studies at Nazareth College (Spring 2001). His research interests include religious institutions and health care policy, Catholic social theory and health care reform, church and state controversies, and liberalism and religious participation in politics.

Lawrence C. Mayer is Professor of Political Science at Texas Tech University specializing in Comparative Politics and the Politics of Advanced Western Democracy, in addition to American Public Policy. In addition to *American Public Policy: An Introduction*, he is the author of *Comparative Political Inquiry*, *The Politics of Industrial Societies*, *Redefining Comparative Politics: Promise versus Performance*, *Comparative Politics: Nations and Theories in a Changing World*, *Comparative Politics: The Quest for Theory and Explanation*, *Conflicting Perspectives in Comparative Politics: A Reader*, and *The Emerging Politics of Identity in Advanced Western Democracies* (forthcoming). His current research is on the determinants of tolerance in western societies.

T.R. Carr is Professor and Department Chair of Public Administration and Policy Analysis at Southern Illinois University, Edwardsville. He teaches primarily in the areas of quantitative methods and policy analysis. In addition to *American Public Policy*, he has published chapters and articles focusing on public management issues. He is active in academic and professional associations and has served in numerous offices in state and local chapters of the American Society for Public Administration. He also serves as mayor of Hazelwood, Missouri, and is engaged in activities sponsored by the National League of Cities and state and local municipal leagues.

N. Joseph Cayer is Frank and June Sackton Professor of Public Administration at Arizona State University. He received his Ph.D. from the University of Massachusetts, Amherst, and a B.A. and MPA from the University of Colorado, Boulder. He also has taught at Lamar University, the University of Maine, Orono, and Texas Tech University. He is the author or coauthor of seven books and numerous chapters and articles on public management and policy, with an emphasis on issues of human resources management in the public sector. Books he has authored or coauthored include *Public Administration: Social Change and Adaptive Management, American Public Policy: An Introduction, Managing Human Resources, Handbook of Training and Development for the Public Sector,* and *Supervision for Success in Government.*

Mark J. McKenzie is an Assistant Professor of Political Science at Texas Tech University. He specializes in judicial politics, public opinion, and campaigns and elections. Dr. McKenzie received his Ph.D. in government from the University of Texas at Austin in 2007 and a Doctor of Jurisprudence from the University of Texas School of Law in 1998. Between 1998 and 2001, he practiced general litigation in Texas at the law firm of Ross & Matthews. He has published articles in such journals as *Judicature, Justice System Journal, Politics & Policy,* and *American Politics Research.*

Laura R. Peck is a tenured Associate Professor at the Arizona State University School of Public Affairs where she also serves as Associate Dean for Barrett, The Honors College. She earned her Ph.D. from New York University's Robert F. Wagner Graduate School of Public Service. Now Dr. Peck regularly teaches research methods, public policy analysis, and program evaluation. Her research focuses on the effects of U.S. social policy on the well-being of children and families, and on research methods and program evaluation. In addition to her contributions to this *American Public Policy* text book, Professor Peck has 20 peer-reviewed publications in journals such as *Policy Studies Journal, Journal of Policy Analysis and Management* and *Evaluation Review.* Dr. Peck serves as the Associate Editor for the *American Journal of Evaluation.*

Chapter 1

Public Policy: An Introduction

Public policy affects each citizen in hundreds of ways, some of them familiar and some unsuspected. Citizens directly confront public policy when they are arrested for speeding, but they seldom remember that the advertising on the television shows they watch is regulated by the Federal Communications Commission and the Federal Trade Commission. Many citizens who complain loudly at tax time about government bureaucracy and overregulation have forgotten the fire and police protection or the paved streets those revenues provide. Indeed, public policy in America affects a vast range of activities, from nuclear warheads to bathroom plumbing, from arresting lawbreakers to providing medical care for the elderly. Indeed, the expanding reach of government and the threatened dominance of the public sector over the private sector with accompanying record budget deficits for the national government constituted a major political issue toward the end of the first year of the Obama administration. This book aims to clarify key dimensions of this ubiquitous influence on American life and to introduce the debates swirling around its major controversies. It takes an *issue-oriented approach* to the beginning study of public policy.

STUDYING PUBLIC POLICY

What Constitutes Public Policy?

Even though examples of public policy come readily to mind, defining public policy in clear and unambiguous terms is not easy. Political scientists have devoted considerable attention to the problem without reaching a consensus.[1] In this text, the term *public policy* refers to a set of actions by the government that includes, but is not limited to, making laws and is defined in terms of a common goal or purpose. For example, a policy to stimulate economic growth in a time of economic stagnation may include tax cuts for business, increased spending to put money into the economy, or actions by the Federal Reserve System to increase the money supply. A policy to secure the country from possible terrorist attacks may include a law, such as the USA Patriot Act, which enables the government to listen to the phone conversations of potential terrorists; an invasion of putative terrorist strongholds in Iraq and Afghanistan; encouraging dissidents in Iran to effect regime change; or searching prospective passengers boarding airplanes. Making policy requires choosing among goals and alternatives, and choice always involves intention. The federal government under President Obama, for example, chose to pursue a wholesale restructuring of our system of delivering health care. The intention is supposedly to have everyone insured, including the 15 percent or so that is, or chooses not to be, insured. Policy is not a single action, but is a set of actions coordinated to achieve a goal. Such an action may be manifested in laws, public statements, official regulations, or widely accepted and publicly visible patterns of behavior, such as the vigorous implementation of existing laws to control and deter crime. Public policy, however, is ultimately rooted in law and in the authority and coercion associated with law. (The terms *public policy* and *policy* will be used interchangeably.)

Three qualifications are necessary, however, for this definition of public policy. First, the idea of an intentional course of action includes decisions made *not* to take a certain action. For example, Congress voted in 1993 not to continue funding for the Superconducting Supercollider Project. Second, the requirement that official actions be sanctioned by law or accepted custom is necessary because public officials often take courses of action that step outside public policy—for example, they sometimes take bribes or exceed their legal authority. Such deeds should not be considered public policy—that is, unless they are openly tolerated in a particular political system. Third, laws or official regulations should not be mistaken for the whole realm of policy; nor does policy always meet intended goals. Lawmaking is not enough to establish a policy; the implementation, interpretation, enforcement, and impact of policies are also part of the policymaking process. Moreover, as we shall see later in this chapter, quite often there are unintended consequences to public policies. What actually happens when policy is put into effect or *implemented* is called policy impact. Although some political scientists argue that these unintended impacts are part of the policy, we believe that it is conceptually clearer to consider policy and its impacts separately. Below, we shall consider the strategies and factors that make it more or less likely that the impact of a policy will be what the policymakers intended.

Why Study Public Policy?

Students of political science and public administration have several reasons for studying public policy. The first is *theoretical*: Political scientists seek to understand and explain the world of politics—that is, they attempt to develop and test explanatory generalizations about the political behavior of individuals and institutions. Because public policy is a part of politics, political scientists are concerned with how it is related to such things as political party structure, interest groups, inter-party competition, electoral systems, and executive-legislative relations.

Political scientists who seek explanation call for the discipline to develop and test policy theory.[2]

A second reason for studying public policy is *practical*. Political scientists and students of policy apply knowledge to solve practical problems. Public policy has become increasingly pervasive over time as measured by such data as the percent of the gross domestic product (GDP: the value of all the goods and services produced in the U.S. in a year) that is spent by the federal government. This figure has risen from about five percent at the turn of the century to about a quarter of the GDP in 2010. With the heavy indebtedness and an expensive health care bill passed at the end of the first year of the Obama administration, the percent of the gross domestic product in the public sector is predicted to reach 35 percent. This indicates that the government, and the federal government in particular, do more things; hence, citizens are continually confronted with impact of public policy on their lives and well-being.

A third reason for studying public policy, related to the second, is *political*. Debate and controversy over public policy in America are not new, but today the range of issues over which serious disagreement occurs is far greater than in the past. This is due in large part to the spread of education, which is strongly related to political involvement and to the mobilization of the population through the mass media. Participation and awareness of government and its policies are greater than any time in our history. The Tea Party movement of 2010 exemplifies the extent to which more people are involved with politics and policy than ever before. It makes sense to channel this new mobilization of the population into paths guided by understanding and information. The emphasis of this book is on the second and third reasons for studying policy—the practical and political—but it draws on the first as well, for intelligent policy selection depends on the analysis and understanding developed by the theoretical findings of political science.

Reasons for the Growing Pervasiveness of Public Policy

The growing pervasiveness of public policy alluded to above is primarily a consequence of modernization. Modernization entails the development of technology and knowledge and the consequent role specialization and division of labor. This makes us all interdependent. The pioneer could erect a log cabin without outside assistance, but the erection of a modern dwelling requires the expertise of a cement contractor, a carpenter, an electrician, a plumber, a bricklayer, a roofer, etc. We can rely on the competence and performance of these tradesmen whose work we are not qualified to judge because they are given their credentials by an agency of the state. We are usually even more unqualified to independently judge the work of professionals such as physicians or attorneys. Whenever new technology is developed, we need a new agency to regulate it.

Modernization requires the concentration of a workforce that was not needed in an agrarian society. This means an urbanization of modern society, with its concomitant issues of traffic, public health and sanitation, sewage and garbage disposal, crime, and the myriad ways in which the choices that people make affect others in patterns of close interaction.

This expansion of the role of public policy is frustrating to many because each new regulation emanating from a government agency circumscribes our freedom to some extent. The needs and desires of each person must be balanced against the needs and desires of others with whom one interacts. Hence, government treats people according to impersonal principles and rules that may offend one's sense of justice for one particular case.

Because of this frustration with an expanding public sector, many people feel that government has become too big and too intrusive. The 2009–2010 Tea Party movement that mobilized large numbers of ordinary people in demonstrations against big government, which they saw as allegedly out of touch with ordinary folk, exemplifies this frustration. Some people yearn for a return to the seemingly simpler times of the good old days. Yet, in many ways "the good old days" were not so good. Life tended to be shorter and less comfortable and convenient. Opportunities for travel and communication were significantly fewer. To return to an era of a much smaller public sector, we would have to "un-invent" much of the technology that has made life longer and more enjoyable.

Policy Impact: The Frequent Failure
of Public Policies to Achieve Their Goals

Americans are by and large an optimistic people who tend to believe that for every identified problem there must be a solution if we simply have the will to find it.

Yet despite the growing pervasiveness and expansion of government, the actual impact of policies—what actually happens when the policy is put into effect—is all too frequently not what those who formulated the policy intended. This frequent failure of policies to achieve their intended impact is due to the following factors.

First, there is disagreement about the issues of society and what constitutes a social or political problem that must be addressed by policymakers. One of the core issues dividing the social and political left from the right regards the imperatives of social justice. Does the fact that some people have a great deal more than others, either through inheritance, hard work, creativity, or just luck, constitute a problem that must be rectified? What are one's entitlements in one's society? The subprime lending crisis of 2009–2010 was a result of elevating homeownership to an entitlement. Does social justice require that we "spread the wealth" around?

Second, for some issues there is no plausible scenario on which the contending parties conceivably agree. For example, the attempts to engineer a two-state solution to the tensions in the Middle East between the Israelis and the Palestinian Arabs have resulted in failure despite continued efforts for over sixty years because the conflict is not about borders or what lands will be set aside for Palestinian statehood. The Arab leaders were formally offered such a state on five separate occasions (see Chapter 12 for details) and they eschewed the offer each time. Clearly, their ultimate goal is not just statehood. The Arab leaders have reiterated over and over that they will never accept the existence of Israel as a Jewish state. Obviously, one's extermination is not a scenario to which one will ever agree as a result of negotiation. Hence, no plausible resolution to the conflict exists to which both parties might possibly agree upon.

Third, no solution that is socially acceptable may exist for a problem. Assume, for example, that society agrees that greater socioeconomic equality must be engineered. One should then address the causes of such inequality. The strongest predictor of one's ultimate socioeconomic well-being is academic achievement. Each step up the academic ladder brings significantly greater lifetime earnings, regardless of one's academic specialty. One should therefore engineer greater equality of academic achievement, as with President George W. Bush's policy of "no child left behind." This policy assumes that everyone is educable. An important massive study of the causes of educational achievement, the Coleman Report, found that the best single predictor of educational achievement is the academic achievement level of one's parents. Thus, to best engineer equality of educational achievement, the state would have to specify that only educated people would be allowed to reproduce. Obviously, no reasonably free society is going to specify who can or cannot have children. Hence, the solution to our hypothetical problem may theoretically exist, but would be socially unacceptable.

Fourth, policies and the laws that they produce are usually ambiguous enough to permit various interpretations of them. The more actors that are involved in the process of implementation, the more that the original intended meaning of the law or policy will be distorted. In this technologically advanced society, lawmakers are frequently generalists. As an example, consider the lawyers or business people who lacked the technical expertise to determine how much of which emissions could be allowed to protect air quality, so they set up an Environmental Protection Agency (EPA) to make those rules. Appointed bureaucrats, selected according to the standard of specialization and division of labor, are more likely to have such expertise. Accordingly, the politically accountable parts of the government—Congress and the presidency—pass general authorizations to some agencies of the civil service to actually make the specific decisions about who gets how much of what, where, and why. But the civil service or public bureaucracy—the administrative branch of government—is set up to implement policy, not to make it.

The attributes of the administrative sector that make it effective in implementing policy are undesirable attributes for policymaking. The attributes of the civil service or public bureaucracy are a hierarchical structure; specialization and the division of labor; an elaborate set of impersonal rules, which enhance predictability but stifle creativity and adaptability; and tenure of office, which insulates the bureaucrats from the public. Moreover, the discretion that bureaucrats inevitably have in interpreting the law means that the intent of the original policymakers will likely be changed in the implementation process.

DEFINING MAJOR CONCEPTS

People acquire interests out of the roles that they play in the social and economic system. These interests often come into conflict. For example, what is good for the blue-collar working class may not be good for the entrepreneurs who employ them. The interests of people who live in one geographical setting may conflict with the interests of people in another setting. The point is that the distinction between "the special interests" and the good of "the people" is a false one. All interests are special because no one can rise completely above his/her socioeconomic role to promote the "general interests."

Because interests conflict, policies that benefit some will harm or impede others. This idea that because the resources of society are *finite*, one cannot allocate values to some groups without taking them from others, is known as a *zero-sum society*. Hence, it seems laudable to place members of underrepresented groups in desired roles that they otherwise would not have attained, such as admission to medical school or a place in corporate management. However, for each individual so placed, another individual who otherwise would have attained the coveted role is excluded. Thus, in a zero-sum society, the allocation of values to members of one underrepresented group requires that members of other groups will have to pay the costs. This of course increases the intensity of partisanship.

Some values, such as clean, unpolluted air, are at first glance good for everyone. These are known as *public goods*. These are values that are shared by everyone concerned; they cannot be allocated according to some criterion of merit or justice. But the costs of such values are not equally shared. The owner of a factory who cleans up its emissions at considerable cost has paid a disproportionate share of the costs of the clean air; however, he or she does not get a disproportionate amount of that air to breathe. It would thus be rational for that factory owner to not clean up the emissions.

Private rationality, when pursued by all the members of a collectivity, can lead to disaster for that collectivity. California, for example, requires that each motor vehicle have a catalytic converter attached to the exhaust system. When most people began to obey that requirement, the air quality over the state's cities greatly improved. However, the converter lowers the performance of the vehicle and increases its fuel consumption. It would therefore be rational for any one motorist to have the device removed; however, if everyone did that, the cities would again be enveloped in smog. This is a case when private rationality conflicts with public necessity. In such cases, government may step in to coerce people to violate private rationality for the public good.

Private goods are the opposite. These are goods that can be divided and given to some persons, but not others. Most distribution and redistribution policies fall into this classification. Some persons qualify for food stamps; others do not. Some students qualify for admission to a selective state university; others may be admitted to second-tier colleges or to junior colleges. Liberals, conservatives, and other ideological groups strongly disagree about the range of private goods that it is appropriate for government to distribute.

Models of the Policy Process

Making public policy is extraordinarily complex. It involves public opinion, media attitudes, expert ideas, active citizens, business and labor leaders, elected representatives, presidents and governors, judges, and bureaucrats. Policymaking calls on political resources, economic conditions, popular cultural attitudes, and international conditions. When political scientists do research attempting to understand public policy, they try to reduce the complexity of the policymaking process to a manageable degree by creating *models of policymaking* that summarize the primary forces at work. None of these models is complete; none captures all of the relationships that are important. It is indeed the purpose of such models to simplify aspects of the reality they represent. No one model best describes the features of policymaking in every area. Although the chapters that follow do not adhere strictly to any of these models, they draw upon the primary qualities of some political science models.

Features of the *institutional model* appear in the description of the institutional context of public policy in Chapter 2. This model stresses the opportunities and constraints on policy that are part of the very structure of the American constitutional order: judiciary, bureaucracy, executives, legislatures, separation of powers, federalism, and so forth. A variant of the institutional model is *historical institutionalism*, which combines the institutional focus with the effect of long-term patterns of development. Here there is recognition that early policy decisions carry large effects through time, so that policies become *path dependent*. The cost of changing policy direction increases over time. Once, for example, a state legislature takes a get-tough approach to crime by building more prisons, these very prisons become institutional forces that prevent different approaches in the future. What would the state do with empty prisons if it decided on a different approach?[3]

The *elite model* focuses on the influence over policy exercised by powerful individuals or groups to maximize their own interests at the expense of competing groups. Scholars who claim this model describes American society paint a scenario in which the country is controlled by a single coherent elite sharing a distinct set of values.[4] Members of this elite possess similar attributes (white, male, and mostly Protestant), come from the same background (prestigious prep school, Ivy League university), and move from one leadership role to another (from corporate boards of directors, to academia at our most prestigious universities, to the highest ranks in the military).

This model contrasts with the *pluralist model*, which stresses that many elites with competing interests bargain with one another to affect policy. Generally no one group gets all of what they want; hence, policy is an impersonal outcome of the bargaining process. Each of these group's interests and ideas must be taken into account. Both of these models picture these individuals and groups being active and influential across many policy areas. The *group* or *subgovernment model* is similar to the pluralist model, but recognizes that different policy areas (for example, crime, health, transportation) are important to different actors. Legislators, bureaucrats, experts, and interest groups that are active in one area are often quite different from those active in a different policy arena. These groups form advocacy coalitions that are active in particular policy areas, but not in others. Under these conditions, policy networks develop webs of lobbyists, committee staff members, and policy administrators all deeply involved in a particular policy domain, but not active in other policy areas.

Some political scientists model policy as a rational process. Policymakers in the *rational-comprehensive model* take account of all information about the policy problems and of all policy options, then select the options that best fulfill the policymaker's goals. The *public choice model* thinks of those active in policymaking as actors attempting to choose options that maximize their self-interest. They select policy options that help them realize their interests. Game models are a variation of this idea, focused on situations of policy choice with options that cannot be compromised.[5]

Policy Analysis

Policy analysis is principally concerned with describing and investigating how and why particular policies are proposed, adopted, and implemented. This is the theoretical side of policy studies. A policy option must be evaluated in the light of what policy analysis reveals about its chances of being adopted, the probable effectiveness or impact of the option, and the difficulties of implementation. A proposal for increased spending for high school education, for example, would need to be tested against data from the Coleman Report, which concluded, it will be recalled, that increased spending had no significant impact on student achievement levels and other analyses that temper the findings. Advocates of the fundamental restructuring of the health care system, such as that adopted in May 2010, needed to take into account the difficulty in determining the costs of such a large and untried enterprise.

Policy analysis is not, however, value neutral. Policy analysts want to discover which policy proposals best fulfill important public values.[6] Thus, policy analysis invokes such principles as freedom, equality, justice, decency, and peace. Indeed, politics often concerns debates about the very meaning of these terms.

Those who would sharply separate policy analysis from fundamental social values make a grave mistake. Policy analysis without awareness of ethical perspectives is incomplete. This is particularly true when evaluating the impact of policy. Ethical principles must be brought to bear on the discovery of the good and bad effects of policy. Such principles not only measure success and failure; they also provide insight into consequences that otherwise would not be revealed.

Policy analysis carried out by political scientists can be distinguished from *policy advocacy* by politicians, partisans, or interest groups. Advocacy differs from analysis, because advocacy begins with a commitment to economic interests or to principles as interpreted by specific ideological systems, such as liberalism, conservatism, and environmentalism. Analysis should better equip policymakers to make policy choices while advocacy attempts to impose such choices on others. Nevertheless, both advocacy and analysis draw upon similar principles and goals, and the two intertwine in the real world of politics. Although ideological commitments can bring important overlooked values to policy analysis, policy advocates are more concerned to advance their ideology than to understand the policy process, which is the goal of policy analysis. The following chapters will discuss different ideological perspectives on policy at some length because the policy debates are often framed by ideology.

Stages of Policy Development

Political scientists often use a model of the policymaking process that focuses on the stages through which ideas and proposals move before becoming public policy. Some political scientists criticize these models as overly rigid and rational. That is, they argue that politics does not follow the clear lines and divisions of the stages model. Windows of opportunity for policy creativity open many times in unexpected ways, so that policy entrepreneurs have to be ready at any time to jump or to move through stages of the process rapidly. Multiple streams of policy proposals and political forces can converge and overwhelm careful policy deliberation.[7] Moreover, these models have not generated important theoretical insights into policymaking.[8] Despite the importance of these criticisms, the stages model is a suggestive tool; that is, it isolates various aspects of public policy and helps to focus attention on them. Some of these aspects are widely recognized and need to be part of any introduction to public policy.[9] Different scholars label the stages differently and place different emphasis on them, but the terms in Figure 1.1 are common.

The development of a public policy begins with a public belief that a problem exists. The three *pre-policy stages* are (1) problem definition or issues formation, (2) policy demands, and (3) agenda formation.

Before a policy issue is defined or adopted, a problem of public concern must be perceived. Ethical and ideological perspectives play an important role during this problem perception stage because different perspectives will see and define problems differently. For example, imagine how the same social phenomenon, the pornography industry, might be viewed by people of differing moral values. Some might view sexually explicit literature as a manifestation of a socially open and healthy attitude toward sexuality. Others might see it as a symptom of an unhealthy obsession with sex and a rejection of higher values. Due to the contrasting opinions of the two groups, different formulations of the issue will result. Similarly, people with different values might disagree as to whether socioeconomic

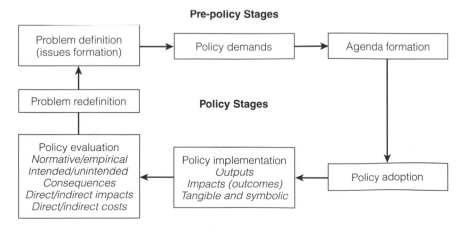

FIGURE 1.1 Stages of the Policy Process

inequality violates the concept of social justice and is therefore a problem that must be rectified.

Thus, the issues formation stage leads to the next stage, policy demands: Opposing demands are now made for government action. For example, some people want the smut shops closed down and the owners thrown in jail. Others want the authorities to keep out of what they see as the private business of individual citizens (a demand for government nonaction). Gradually, this social give-and-take may coalesce into a perception that policymakers must deal with this problem, and it competes with other problems for the attention of policymakers. Some problems fail to sustain attention in this competition; others rise to prominence. That is, some make it and some fail to make it onto the policy agenda. The various demands and perspectives create an agenda of alternative proposals for dealing with the issue. Some proposals and demands never make it to the agenda; others are put on the agenda in altered form.

Agenda-setting is always a political process; that is, groups struggle for power to control the agenda. Because all legislative and executive bodies are limited in the issues they can address at any given time, the power to have attention paid to "your" issue on the agenda is invaluable. Therefore, ideological and interest groups compete to broaden the agenda to include their issues or to narrow it by excluding issues that they do not want considered. Such groups may be elected officials, bureaucrats responsible for policy administration, public interest groups, or groups directly affected by particular policies. The following chapters call attention to groups active in the problem definition, policy demand, and agenda formation stages.

Following the pre-policy stages, the next major stage in the development of a public policy is deliberation and *policy adoption*. From the policy agenda, decision makers, with the input of interest groups, policy experts, and constituents, debate and bargain over alternative policy formulations, settling on an alternative or a combination of alternatives to respond to the problem. Decisions are made; policies are formulated; and policy statements are issued, taking such forms as orders, regulations, or laws. Clearly, the same kinds of considerations of power as in the policy agenda stage are relevant here. Also important is the constitutional and statutory structure of the institution that makes the policy decision. Structure often determines which outcomes have a greater chance of success in the political struggle.

Policy statements and lawmaking are not the whole of policymaking. Policy decisions must be implemented—a concept defined earlier in the chapter as putting the policy into effect. Policy *implementation* means money spent, laws enforced, employees hired, and plans of action formulated. A law against theft would hardly be a policy if no public resources were devoted to preventing thefts and apprehending thieves. In implementation, the intent of the policymakers is often distorted. Even programs involving little conflict can be difficult to implement if there are numerous participants with differing perspectives and if many particular decisions have to be made before the policy is fully implemented.[10] The more complex the implementation process, the more likely that the intent of the policy will become distorted or lost. Successful achievement of policy goals depends upon the tractability of the problem being addressed by the policy; that is, how possible is it really to make a change. Implementation depends as well upon the clarity of the law, the talents and financial resources available to those administering it, and a variety of political factors, such as public support, media attention, socioeconomic conditions, and the attitudes and resources of groups affected by the policy.[11]

Policy implementation produces impacts. Policy impact, it will be recalled, refers to what actually happens when the policy is implemented. The impact of a policy may be unforeseen as in the case of busing for racially balanced schools (discussed in detail in Chapter 10). Whites were usually able to avoid having their children being bused by simply moving to the suburbs, which often meant a different school district. This "white flight" left the cities and their schools more racially unbalanced than before busing.

Policy impact is a major component of an important focus of this text, the evaluation of public policy. Policy evaluation focuses principally on the impact of policy, because it is largely from the performance and consequences of policy that we assess its success or failure. This is the question of impact. Evaluation attempts to assess the outcomes of policies (the effects on society) in order to compare the outcomes with the policies' intended goals while balancing the actual benefits of a policy with its cost. It asks whether the goals have or have not been met, with what costs, and with what unintended consequences. For example, policy evaluation asks whether the welfare reforms legislated in 1996 did in fact reduce poverty, increase work, or improve the lives of low-income persons. With regard to the Vietnam War, it was not enough to show that we would be better off with a pro-Western government in South Vietnam. The question was whether that benefit was worth the cost of blood and treasure it would require to achieve it. A policy can be evaluated only after those benefits and costs are known. Moreover, evaluation leads back to issue formation and policy deliberation in a (nearly) endless loop. Evaluations of policy inevitably produce advocates for change and other advocates for maintaining the policy. The social problems that stimulate policy responses can seldom be completely fixed. "Policy is more like an endless game of Monopoly than a bicycle repair."[12]

Aspects of Policy Evaluation

Policy evaluation thus involves collecting and analyzing information about the efficiency and effectiveness of policies. The purpose is to determine whether goals of policy have been achieved and to improve policy performance. Evaluating policy has both normative and empirical dimensions. The *normative dimension* refers to values, beliefs, and attitudes of society as a whole, of particular groups and individuals in society, and of the policy evaluators themselves. Persons of different values and ideologies use different normative concepts to evaluate policy. For example, if one can assume the right to produce and publish material with strong sexual content leads to greater sexual promiscuity, then that would be a cost for social conservatives. It may be less of a problem for social liberals, however. Evaluation, therefore, is always political. Progressives, conservatives, socialists, feminists, and anarchists differ fundamentally in their understanding of such concepts and in their ranking of them. Conservatives, for example, believe that free competition and protection of private property are fundamental values to be pursued by economic policy. Socialists, however, see just distribution of the social product as the principal value. Different policy evaluators and different political groups, then, will evaluate public policy differently. Normative perspectives come into play, not only in assessing the goals of policy but also in analyzing how well policy accomplishes the desired goals.

Normative evaluation, however, is not enough. The *empirical dimension*—that is, understanding the facts—must precede judgment. Before praising or damning the Supreme Court's freedom-of-the-press decisions, one must examine the actual decisions and attempt to assess what difference, if any, they have made or are likely to make in the day-to-day operations of the press. And before criticizing welfare fraud, one should obtain the most accurate statistics available on money lost through fraudulent claims. Policy evaluation without empirical analysis of policy content, output, and impact is like voting for a baseball all-star team without information on players' batting, earned-run, or fielding averages.

Specifically, policy evaluation is used to:

1. Determine which goals are being met and to what degree (including unintended consequences)
2. Identify reasons for success and failure
3. Allocate (or reallocate) resources
4. Make changes to improve policies or decide to end policies that are not working

Through these efforts, policymakers can make sure that policies accomplish what they are intended to and are responsive to the public and elected leaders. Moreover, a glance at Table 1.1 suggests the multiple factors involved in a public policy. Complex social problems, such as crime, the economy, health care, and foreign policy, have multiple dimensions requiring multiple approaches. The various dimensions and the many policy initiatives required to address them mean that major public problems will never have single policy solutions. There is no "one policy fits all" for responding to terrorism, for example. Border security, electronic and human intelligence, military action, disaster preparedness, and many other initiatives are required. This means as well that any major policy issue requires choices and trade-offs. There are limited resources of time, money, and attention. Spending more on border security may leave less for intelligence gathering, not to mention less for education or crime policy. As suggested by the concept of the zero-sum society discussed above, scarce resources demand, in turn, careful policy evaluation to make sure that assets are being used most effectively.

Policy evaluation may be required by the legislation creating the policy or by more general legislation, such as *sunset laws*. Sunset laws are statutes that require each program to be terminated at some specific time (five or ten years, for example), unless an evaluation leads to a decision to continue it. Administrative

TABLE 1.1   Con

Concept		
Implementation		
Outputs		
Impacts (outcomes)		
Direct		
Indirect (externalities)		
Intended		
Unintended		
Short-term	Ou ... ~~shortly~~ after policy is implemented	Changes in crime rate during the year after a policy change
Long-term	Outcomes evaluated after policy has been in place for a longer time	Changes in crime rate over 10 years
Policy evaluation	Process of assessing impacts of a policy	Assessment of effectiveness of a program intended to reduce crime rate
Empirical dimension	Evaluation by policy's measurable outputs and outcomes	Crime statistics; prison statistics; conviction rates
Normative dimension	Evaluation by policy's effect on values, beliefs, and attitudes	Effect of policy on freedom, justice, security, and family stability
Cost–benefit analysis	Compares benefits of a program with costs of implementing it	Money spent; crime rate reduction
Direct	Costs and benefits from allocation of resources and impact on other than intended population	Prison costs; reimprisonment rate of persons released from prison
Indirect (externalities)	Costs and benefits from allocation of resources and impact on other than intended population	Economic prosperity in communities housing new prisons; public assistance costs

rules or executive orders also may requi
grams also include a requirement that
The evaluation determines whether
provements should be made in it
mance management, the ong
Evaluation goes beyond p
tematic process of data
over a particular per
gram evaluation
higher level o
to this eval
as to sp

e evaluation. Most grant-in-aid pro-
the program being funded be evaluated.
the program should continue or what im-
Public administrators are responsible for *perfor-*
ing review of accomplishments and problems.
rformance management reviews and involves a sys-
collection and analysis of a program's goal achievement
od of time. This text cannot accomplish the detailed pro-
escribed here for the policies it discusses. Its evaluation is at a
generality. However, the same considerations and concepts apply
ation of general policies (such as Medicare or criminal justice policy)
cific programs.
valuations may be process (often called formative) or outcome (often called
mmative) evaluations. Process evaluation assesses the activities and structures of
the policy implementation. The processes may include, for example, whether a
community policing program follows procedure, how many police are assigned
to the program, or what kind of patrol is practiced. Outcome evaluations focus
on the impact of the policy or program. Thus, outcome evaluation of a community policing policy would examine whether there was an impact on crime in
the neighborhood, such as reduction in burglaries or muggings. Both forms of
evaluation are necessary for a complete assessment of the policy.[13] It would not
make much sense, for example, to know that community policing was not
working, but not know why. Thus, it would be important to know that it is
not working (outcome) and what processes led to the failure so that the processes
can be corrected.

In order to conduct an evaluation, it is necessary to plan ahead. As in writing a research paper, it goes much smoother if a plan is developed in advance.
Thus, it is necessary to decide what purpose the evaluation serves. Is it to focus
on process or outcome? What is the goal of the policy or program? What does
the evaluation need to determine? What assumptions are being used? How
much money, time, and people resources are available for the evaluation?
What indicators or measures are going to be used? How will the information
be collected? How will unexpected circumstances be handled? What is the
schedule for completion? What use will be made of the results? These essential
questions need to be thought through before beginning the evaluation. Once
they have been addressed, the evaluator needs to decide on the evaluation
method or tool to use.

We have already introduced the technique, *cost-benefit analysis,* with reference to the Vietnam War. This technique compares the benefits or outcomes
of the program with the costs of implementing it. The benefits and costs may
be stated in dollar terms, thus allowing for determining how much the outcomes
cost. While on the surface, it may seem easy to determine costs and benefits, it is
much more complicated. *Direct costs* and *benefits* may be easy to determine. However, *indirect costs* and *benefits* are another matter.

Direct costs and benefits relate to the specific allocation of resources and the
impact on the intended population. Thus, a plan to develop a light rail system in

an urban area presumably would be designed to improve commuting. It might also have the goals of reducing pollution and decreasing the need for roads and highways. The amount of money spent on the system and the disruption to residents and businesses along the route are direct costs. Indirect costs might include the loss of business to areas not served by the light rail line and the increase in time needed for delivery of goods to businesses along the lines because of more limited access. The increase in the value of property along the route may be an indirect benefit to owners of the property but a negative, indirect impact on those who rent the property. These indirect costs and benefits are also called *externalities,* or *spillover effects.* So, in evaluating a program or policy, it is necessary to consider all the costs and benefits, not just the obvious direct costs and benefits.

Policies also have long-term effects and short-term impacts. Both need to be considered in evaluation. Similarly, some policies have symbolic importance. The decision to build a new football stadium for a professional team may have great symbolic importance to the residents of a city. The stadium project may have been justified in part on the basis of making a world-class city and thus would be an intended symbolic benefit. Unintended and long-term costs can be illustrated by the Iraq War. With one out of six soldiers who served in Iraq suffering some degree of post-traumatic stress disorder or major health problem, likely long-term increases in health care costs, drug abuse, family violence, suicide, mental illness, and crime must be considered long-term costs.

Costs and benefits of some programs are difficult to measure. How do we measure the benefit of *public goods,* such as clean air? Businesses may want to measure it in one way: the cost to them. Clean air advocates, however, may want to measure it in terms of the incidence of medical problems in the communities affected by the quality of the air near a manufacturing plant. Still others may focus on the aesthetics of the community and the presence or absence of a brown cloud over the area. As the administration of President George W. Bush demonstrated, business sometimes has a great deal of influence over what is examined and what use is made of the information. Business was successful in influencing the Bush administration to discount much of the evaluation on environmental issues, and the administration reversed many environmental policies because of their perceived negative impact on business. Similarly, debates over whether to facilitate embryonic stem cell research or to make a morning-after birth control pill available over the counter illustrate the interweaving of political reasons with scientific data in the adoption and evaluation of policies.

Program evaluation is conducted by various agencies or officials. At the national level, the Government Accountability Office (GAO) conducts evaluation of federal government programs, usually at the request of members of Congress, as it is an agency of Congress. GAO may initiate evaluations on its own, and many of the evaluations required in the legislation setting up programs are its responsibility. The Congressional Budget Office and Congressional Research Office also conduct many evaluations. Most states have an auditing agency responsible for evaluation or have legislative committees with such responsibilities. Local governments use a variety of similar agencies. Governments often also contract with independent contractors to conduct evaluations. The result of all of them is the evaluation report. It then is the responsibility of managers and policymakers to make effective use of the evaluations. Politics affects how they do so.

Policies do not go on forever (though some appear to). Policies change over time. For example, welfare policy changed fundamentally in the 1990s. Policies sometimes are terminated. Their reason for being passes, and legislatures end them. The processes involved in changing and terminating policies are the same as those involved in policymaking: problem definition, agenda-setting, adoption, and evaluation.

APPROACHES TAKEN BY THIS BOOK

This text covers areas that are of permanent major interest and controversy. Though other issues occasionally rise to prominence, the issues we discuss—welfare, health, education, economic regulation, foreign and defense policy—are issues of long-range interest and controversy.

Chapter Plan

The chapters that follow present the major policy issues in American politics. Each chapter (except Chapters 2 and 13) follows a similar pattern. This pattern assumes that students need to know the history of policies and the most fundamental facts about them before evaluation is possible. Also vital is an understanding of the ways the policies work (or don't work). Then it is possible to speculate intelligently about possible modifications that the future will present.

Issue Background.   Each chapter discusses the basic issue, problem, or dilemma toward which public policy is directed, that is, the general background. Policies do not arise in a vacuum, as we have already noted, but, rather, grow in response to developments that the public, or some part of it, perceives as requiring government action.

Contemporary Policy.   Each chapter describes the evolution of present public policies in their areas of concern. They sketch in detail the major features of substantive public policies, as adopted and implemented. The principal goals and target populations intended by the policymakers are also outlined, and some of the political factors surrounding adoption are described. Although absolute neutrality and objectivity are impossible, we have tried to be as unbiased as possible.

Policy Evaluation.   The third section of each chapter evaluates policy outputs and impacts empirically and normatively. Here our concern centers on the major successes and failures of policy in responding to the dilemmas specified. We focus on the ability of existing policies to reach their goals and to have maximum beneficial effect, and we discuss the main differences of opinion on the good and bad effects of the policies. Our level of analysis is the general shape of the policy and its alternatives, not the detailed cost–benefit or other evaluation analysis discussed previously.

Future Alternatives.   Each chapter lists the major policy alternatives and their supporting arguments as specifically as possible. Here again, we present different values, different definitions of the issue, and different predictions for policy options. The authors do not put forth their own proposals but, rather, attempt to help the reader make sense of the welter of policy proposals, statistics, and competing values. The arguments of conservatives, radicals, and liberals, as well as a variety of other interested parties, find their way into the following pages in order to illustrate the range of alternatives from which policy selections may be made.

Finally, each chapter ends with a list of books and websites to assist study and reflection. To facilitate study and reference, a glossary of major terms and concepts from each chapter appears at the end of the book.

National Focus

Although the chapters on education and the section on intergovernmental relations discuss state and local government activity extensively, our attention will be on the national arena, for the issues at stake on the state and local level, given the tremendous variation in their social, political, and economic climates, are less clear and less easily presented than those at the national level. Therefore, although state and local policies are obviously important, here they are discussed as they relate to national policies.

Comparative Information

Many chapters discuss comparable policies in other modern industrial nations. Noting international trends is essential to evaluate U.S. public policy properly.[14] To discuss American health care policies as though they were the best possible policies would be like discussing American wine as though France and Germany grew no grapes. Moreover, issues of crime, employment, economic stagnation, immigration, social welfare spending, and cultural change have begun to affect other advanced nations in ways similar to those occurring in the American context. But the focus of this book is on *American* public policy.

ENDNOTES

1. James E. Anderson, *Public Policymaking: An Introduction*, 6th ed. (Boston: Cengage, 2005).
2. For example, Kim Quaille Hill, "In Search of Policy Theory," *Policy Currents*, 7 (April 1997): 1–9.

3. See Jacob S. Hacker, *The Divided Welfare State: The Battle over Public and Private Social Benefits in the United States* (New York: Cambridge University Press, 2002), Chapter 1, for a summary of the model and its application to social policy.

4. C. Wright Mills, *The Power Elite* (New York: Oxford University Press, 1956).

5. For a convenient summary of models and their development, see James P. Lester and Joseph Stewart, Jr., *Public Policy: An Evolutionary Approach*, 2nd ed. (Belmont, CA: Wadsworth, 2000), Chapters 4–9.

6. See Robert A. Heineman et al., *The World of the Policy Analyst: Rationality, Values, and Politics* (Chatham, NJ: Chatham House, 1990); Deborah Stone, *Policy Paradox: The Art of Political Decision Making*, 3rd. ed. (New York: Norton, 2002); and Henry J. Aaron et al., eds., *Values and Public Policy* (Washington, DC: Brookings Institution, 1994).

7. See the influential work of John W. Kingdon, *Agendas, Alternatives, and Public Policies*, 2nd ed. (New York: Longman, 2003).

8. See Stone, *Policy Paradox*, especially pp. 5–14; Paul A. Sabatier, "Toward Better Theories of the Policy Process," *PS: Political Science & Politics*, 24 (June 1991): 147–156; and Paul A. Sabatier, ed., *Theories of the Policy Process* (Boulder, CO: Westview Press, 1999).

9. More detailed discussion of these stages can be found in Anderson, *Public Policymaking*. See also Charles L. Cochran and Eloise F. Malone, *Public Policy: Perspectives and Choices* (New York: McGraw-Hill, 1995), 38–57.

10. See the pioneering study by Jeffrey L. Pressman and Aaron Wildavsky, *Implementation*, 3rd ed. (Berkeley: University of California Press, 1984).

11. Paul A. Sabatier and Daniel Mazmanian, "The Implementation of Public Policy: A Framework for Analysis," in Stella Z. Theodoulou and Matthew A. Cahn, eds., *Public Policy: The Essential Readings* (Englewood Cliffs, NJ: Prentice Hall, 1995), 153–173.

12. Stone, *Policy Paradox*, p. 261.

13. Blaine Worthen, James Sanders, and Jody Fitzpatrick, *Program Evaluation* (New York: Longman, 1997).

14. See Richard Rose, *Lesson-Drawing in Public Policy: A Guide to Learning across Time and Space* (Chatham, NJ: Chatham House, 1993); and Arnold J. Heidenheimer, Hugh Heclo, and Carolyn Teich Adams, *Comparative Public Policy*, 3rd ed. (New York: St. Martin's Press, 1990).

RESOURCES

Books

Aaron, Henry J., Mann, Thomas E., and Taylor, Timothy, eds. *Values and Public Policy.* Washington, DC: Brookings Institution, 1994.

Adolino, Jessica R., and Blake, Charles H. *Comparing Public Policies: Issues and Choices in Six Industrialized Countries.* Washington, DC: CQ Press, 2001.

Anderson, James E. *Public Policymaking: An Introduction*, 6th ed. Boston: Houghton Mifflin, 2006.

Bardach, Eugene. *A Practical Guide for Policy Analysis: The Eightfold Path to More Effective Problem Solving.* New York: Chatham House, 2000.

Chelimsky, Eleanor. *Evaluation for the 21st Century: A Handbook.* Thousand Oaks, CA: Sage, 1997.

Ellis, Ralph D. *Just Results: Ethical Foundations for Policy Analysis.* Washington, DC: Georgetown University Press, 1998.

Kingdon, John W. *Agendas, Alternatives, and Public Policies,* 2nd ed. New York: Longman, 2003.

Kraft, Michael E., and Furlong, Scott R. *Public Policy: Politics, Analysis, and Alternatives.* Washington, DC: CQ Press, 2004.

McCool, Daniel C. *Public Policy Theories, Models, and Concepts: An Anthology.* Englewood Cliffs, NJ: Prentice Hall, 1995.

Munger, Michael C. *Analyzing Policy: Choices, Conflicts, and Practices.* New York: Norton, 2000.

Pressman, Jeffrey L., and Wildavsky, Aaron. *Implementation,* 3rd ed. Berkeley: University of California Press, 1984.

Stone, Deborah. *Policy Paradox: The Art of Political Decision Making,* rev. ed. New York: Norton, 2002.

Theodoulou, Stella Z., and Matthew A. Cahn, eds. *Public Policy: The Essential Readings.* Englewood Cliffs, NJ: Prentice Hall, 1995.

U.S. General Accounting Office. *Managing for Results: Emerging Benefits from Selected Agencies' Use of Performance Agreements.* Washington, DC: U.S. Government Printing Office, 2000.

Weiss, Carol. *Evaluation.* Upper Saddle River, NJ: Prentice Hall, 1997.

Websites

Association for Public Policy Analysis and Management: **www.appam.org**

Congressional Budget Office: **www.cbo.gov**

FedStats (Government statistics): **www.fedstats.gov/index.html**

Government Accountability Office (GAO): **www.gao.gov**

New York Times: **www.nytimes.com**

Project Vote Smart: **www.vote-smart.org/**

Public Agenda: **www.publicagenda.org/**

Statistical Abstract of the United States: **www.census.gov/compendia/statab/**

Washington Post: **www.washingtonpost.com**

Chapter 2

Contexts of Public Policy

Public policymaking takes place within the general social, political, and economic environment of the nation. It takes place as well within contexts specific to each policy area. Substantive chapters will outline these specialized influences, but first we examine some general factors that will influence all policy areas in the next decade. This chapter describes those trends in U.S politics, culture, and society that will determine the framework for policy debates in a wide variety of issue areas. Five contexts are particularly important: institutional (especially intergovernmental relations), economic, demographic, ideological, and cultural.

THE INSTITUTIONAL CONTEXT

The unique features of the American political system, its basic structures—federalism, the party system, the power of the presidency, and the system of checks and balances—will shape policy as they always have. Policy in the area of civil rights, for example, will continue to be determined substantially by the federal courts because of the constitutional system of government and the courts' power of judicial review.

In addition to lasting features of the American political system, however, a serious distrust of institutions, particularly political ones, is now endemic in the American electorate. This is not the simple distrust of government that is a constant in American history, but a deep cynicism and anger about government, politics, and politicians, even to the point of violence (most shockingly in the Oklahoma City Federal Building bombing in April 1995, but also in the attacks on members of Congress and their offices in the wake of their votes on health care reform in 2010). The statistics illustrate the American public's lackluster response to the political process: The percentage of the eligible population voting in presidential and congressional elections declined substantially after 1960, with barely half of voting-age Americans now voting for president, little more than one-third for Congress in nonpresidential years, and far fewer voting for state and local offices. Polls on confidence in leadership reveal substantial decline in the trust the public holds for leadership in all areas of life. The popularity of politician and incumbent bashing on talk radio testifies to distrust of politics and politicians generally.

The trend among young Americans is uneven. In the early 1970s, about half of eighteen- to twenty-nine-year-olds voted in presidential elections. Rates reached a low of 39.6 percent in 1996 and 51.1 percent in 2008. While many lament that young people are more and more disengaged from the civic and political life of society, and that their knowledge of politics and world events is substantially lower than that of their elders, they often participate at about the same rate as their elders.[1]

We need not go far to seek the sources for the decline in trust of government.[2] The Vietnam War, the protests and social divisions it spawned, and its tragic impact on many veterans, put American foreign policy leadership under a cloud; the leadership had only partially emerged from this cloud before the Iraq War began creating similar scenarios that have been perpetuated by the war in Afghanistan. Findings of corruption and illegality at the highest levels of government have fed distrust. Such revelations have included the Watergate conspiracy during the Nixon administration, criminal investigations of major Reagan administration officials, and the revelation of corruption at the highest levels of the CIA and FBI in the Aldrich Ames and Robert Hanssen cases in the mid-1990s. "Monicagate" and the impeachment trial of President Clinton kept the scandal pot at boiling point in the 1990s. In the 2000s, the major scandal involved lobbyist Jack Abramoff, with a number of congresspersons indicted and convicted of bribery and abuses of office. Discovery of corruption and lawlessness in politics is nothing new, but these abuses were so serious and widespread and occurred in such rapid sequence that public trust in the ability and willingness of public officials to produce policy in the public interest eroded. Gridlock within Congress from 2007–2010 further eroded people's trust and confidence in government. In mid-2010, only 26 percent of people said they were "satisfied with the way the nation is being governed."[3]

"Monicagate" manifested distrust and cynicism about politics as well as the increasingly partisan and rancorous atmosphere in Congress and many state legislatures. The scandal involved not only the sexual behavior of President Clinton but also the almost visceral hatred of many Republicans for the president, his wife, and all that they represented that is wrong in America from the conservative point of view. By the time of the 2004 and 2006 elections, many Democrats felt the same instinctive hatred of President Bush and his view of America and the world. Similarly, the election of Barack Obama in 2008 stirred passions from the other side, resulting in complete rejection of anything Obama advocated by many conservatives. This mutual antipathy accounted for the high degree of rancor, smear charges, and vicious attack ads of the 2004 election campaign. The passions also are reflected in the strong partisanship and resistance to compromise found in Congress since the 1990s and 2000s. The immigration policy debate of 2007 and health care reform debate of 2010 demonstrate the strong partisan divisions that now make it difficult to pass legislation addressing major national issues.

At the same time that public distrust has grown, the presence of the federal government in economic, cultural, and social life has expanded as a product of modernization and technology. Federal regulations and federal spending increase each year. Suspicion that such growth is inevitable no matter which party is in power, that neither party has an interest in halting it, and that such growth produces no noticeable or dramatic improvement in the quality of life contributes to distrust in government. It also contributes to substantial resistance to new policy initiatives in health, education, and consumer protection, to cite only a few cases. Suspicion is growing among the public that the national government has been captured by corporate and other interest groups who use it for private benefit rather than for public good. In the technocratic age, leadership, responsibility, and accountability seem divorced from ordinary citizens. At the same time, as Americans become more cynical, they become less interested in, and less informed about, politics and policy.[4] Some speculated that the "war on terror" and revived patriotic fervor would check the spread of government distrust and restore some measure of legitimacy to an active federal government. Public anger at the outcome of the war in Iraq, the financial bailout of Wall Street and automobile companies, the inept response to Hurricane Katrina, a perceived lack of urgency in response to the 2010 *Deepwater Horizon* oil spill in the Gulf of Mexico, and the 2010 health care debate suggest the opposite result.

Intergovernmental Relations

The United States' political system is based in part on a separation of responsibilities among different units of government. Problems that must be addressed by government, however, do not respect jurisdictional boundaries. *Intergovernmental relations* refer to the links between the national government, the states, and local governments, as well as the interactions between and among states and local governments. Because approaches to contemporary policy issues often involve controversies about which level or levels of government are most appropriate to address them, we devote considerable attention in the present chapter to this particular context of public policy.

Because most intergovernmental relations are vertical, with the federal government above and state and local governments below, most discussions in this text involve vertical relations. Some forms of intergovernmental relations are referred to as horizontal intergovernmental relations because they involve relationships between or among units at the same level. *Interstate compacts* are examples of horizontal intergovernmental relations. States enter into formal agreements to deal with issues that cross state lines and cannot be dealt with effectively by individual states. The Education Commission of the States, the New York and New Jersey Port Authority, the Delaware River Basin Compact, and the Colorado River Authority are examples of interstate compacts that deal with specific issues of mutual concern. Local governments also often enter into agreements to deal with common concerns. Mass transit authorities in metropolitan areas are results of interlocal government agreements. Such agreements deal with air and water pollution, airports, community colleges, and public safety services. Compacts between states and tribal governments regarding casino gambling are examples of special intergovernmental compacts.

Another form of cooperative relationships involving all levels of government has emerged as political leaders attempt to integrate the variety of activities that are important to the resolution of problems. For example, thirty-seven states now have fully operational Rural Development Councils.[5] These efforts recognize that many agencies and governments offer services and programs that have an impact on development activities. By collaborating, they hope to reduce duplication and conflicting policies and services.

The federal system established by the U.S. Constitution ensured both the need for interaction among governmental units and flexibility in those interactions. Federalism is a middle ground between a unitary system of government and a confederation. In a unitary system, the central governmental unit controls the system's operation and the distribution of powers. Although the central government may delegate certain powers to local governments, the national level may change those powers or take them away without the consent of the local units. Great Britain is an example of a unitary system.

In a confederation, the local, or constituent, units control the fate of the government. Specifically, the constituent units have the final power to make and enforce laws over their own subjects, a concept called *sovereignty*. In such a system, the other governmental units create the central government. The local units define the powers of the central government. The United Nations is a confederation made up of nations. Our government under the Articles of Confederation was such a system, and the weaknesses of that experiment led to the creation of the federal system. In *federalism*, the powers are distributed between a central government (national) and constituent units (states) and the power relationship cannot be changed except by action of both levels.

Issues in a Federal System.   The principal issue in federalism is what role each level of government should assume. The authors of the Constitution were wary of too strong a central government and cognizant of the problems of one too weak. They felt that it was necessary to have a national government that could reasonably coordinate the actions of the states, but they also wanted to give the states the autonomy to deal with their own concerns. Generally, the states were relatively strong from the beginning of the Republic until the 1930s. After the 1930s, the national government assumed greater and greater responsibility until 1980. President Ronald Reagan, elected in 1980, strove to reduce the influence of the national government, an effort that most national leaders continue to espouse to this day. It is now a settled issue that, by virtue of the supremacy clause in Article VI of the Constitution, the powers of the national government are not limited by any specific state power. However, since 1992, the Supreme Court has been limiting national power relative to state autonomy, thus restricting the reach of the national government. After passage of health care reform in 2010, several states joined to sue over federal mandates such as requiring people to buy insurance and some states passed legislation to opt out of the law. The courts will have to sort the issues out, but most experts believe the states will be unsuccessful.

Intergovernmental relations raise numerous questions. Should governmental units work together on common problems? Should the national government deal through the states to work with local units of government? Questions also arise as to whether the national government should only help other levels of government deal with their problems or whether it should also implement its own programs at the state and local levels.

Yet another concern is who should control program implementation. If the national government's money is used in programs, it is not surprising that the national government wants control over how the money is spent. Without such control, the national government would take the blame for raising tax revenue but would have no say in how it is spent. Those responsible for raising money usually are not willing to give up that say. On the other hand, state and local officials wish to retain as much discretion as possible and do not want to be told by federal bureaucrats how to conduct their business, because they believe they can better address their own differing needs and situations.

Opponents of national government effort usually argue that state and local governments can deliver needed programs more efficiently. On the other hand, many programs may be developed on the national level that would not get off the ground if left to the lower levels, such as programs that require tremendous capital and other resources available only to the national government or that require consistent application throughout the nation.

Many national government programs are created to stimulate states or local units to take action in areas in which they have been reluctant to do so. They also may be applied where there are great inequities among the states or localities. For example, intergovernmental programs may be created to eliminate inequity in education, health, or welfare programs. Other programs may stimulate states to improve transportation, the environment, or work safety when they would not be so inclined without federal government prodding. Of course, critics argue that federal programs reduce the initiative and creativity of local or state units. If left to themselves, without the carrot of federal monies, they might experiment more and develop innovative approaches to solving problems. Innovative approaches often have difficulty getting by the federal bureaucracy. On the other hand, various groups believe that state experimentation can take the nation in the wrong direction. Controversies discussed in subsequent chapters over same-sex marriage, crime, public assistance, immigration, and health care illustrate these conflicting viewpoints.

Forms of Funding.   Most federal funding has been in the form of *categorical* grants in which money is provided for a specific project with stipulations on exactly how the money can be used. A grant to develop a program for gifted children is an example.

Advocates of fewer restrictions support *block grants*, which give money to state or local units for general purposes instead of a specific project. For example, instead of grants for a program for gifted students, a state may receive an education block grant. The state then determines how best to use the education funds. Debates over the structure of Temporary Assistance to Needy Families and the State Children's Health Insurance Program illustrate the differences between advocates of categorical and block grants.

General revenue sharing, which refers to the transfer of money from one level of government to another with little or no restriction on its use, was another popular form of national intergovernmental policy in the 1970s. A formula is used to determine how much money each jurisdiction is entitled to receive.

Unfunded mandates of the national government have become common and are the source of much complaint by state and local officials. Unfunded mandates are requirements imposed on state and local governments with no national government funding to implement them. For example, national government requirements on reducing air pollution or attaining a certain standard in drinking water system quality are mandates without funding that must be paid for by the state or local governments. State and local governments become especially upset with the fact that they are under pressure to operate with less revenue and, at the same time, the federal government develops policies requiring them to engage in new initiatives without providing money for those activities. States have even gone to court to attempt to reverse some of the mandates or to require the federal government to provide resources, but such efforts so far have been unsuccessful.

Participants in Intergovernmental Relations

Numerous groups or special interests affect intergovernmental policies. Congress is the main actor in that it passes the legislation that fosters intergovernmental activities. Congress also tends to want to impose conditions on programs it funds and is the focal point for broad national policy development, which often results in particular mandates on state and local government.

The executive branch, particularly the president, often takes the lead in pushing particular policy agendas. Many of those agendas have intergovernmental implications. In addition to the executive leadership, the bureaucracy is part of the executive branch and has the responsibility for implementing policies developed by Congress and the president. In the implementation process, the administrative agencies often impose their own restrictions and conditions, particularly regarding how the policy is to be administered. Much of the federal government red tape complained about is the result of agency action. Administrators who make their concerns about policies known also influence Congress and the president; thus, they also are involved in policymaking processes.

The courts have become significant actors in intergovernmental relations as well.[6] Since the 1960s, courts have mandated state and local governments to take particular actions, especially in school desegregation, school funding, and management of corrections. They even have required local governments to impose taxes. Some courts have assumed administrative responsibility for schools and prison systems. Since the 1990s, the courts have sided more with the states, but their intrusion into state activities remains significant.[7]

The national government's actions are affected by the concerns of state and local governmental officials. The mayors and governors, through their conferences and organizations, make pronouncements on those national government policies that affect them. Within their own parties, they also attempt to influence the direction of national leaders on relevant issues.

The recipients of services under intergovernmental programs often voice their feelings. For example, when aid to education is slated for change or reduction, teachers and school administrators are likely to make entreaties to Congress and the president. Similarly, changes in welfare programs bring reactions from welfare advocates. Other groups that might not benefit directly from a program may also participate in intergovernmental policy development; a program to develop a recreational lake is likely to stimulate environmental or chamber of commerce groups to take a stand on the issue. Of course, the taxpayer is another interested party, to whom political candidates often appeal in their efforts to reduce federal government spending. The main contention is that federal government involvement creates unnecessary administrative expenses that taxpayers have to absorb.

Contemporary Intergovernmental Realities

During the first century and a half, the United States federal system changed gradually. Because the nation was essentially rural and society relatively uncomplicated, the responsibilities of the national government and the states were easy to define. Although there were major controversies, as illustrated by states' rights conflicts, for the most part the powers of the national government were interpreted to be rather narrowly defined. Citizens dealt primarily with state and local jurisdictions. Overriding the separation-of-powers concept was the general philosophy that government at all levels should be restricted in scope.

In the late nineteenth century, intergovernmental relationships began to develop more formally. In 1862, for example, the Morrill Act provided federal land grants for agricultural education programs; the land grant universities are the result of this program. Hatch Act grants for establishing agricultural experiment stations beginning in 1887 were the first actual cash transfers from the national government to the states for specific program development. Still, intergovernmental activities grew gradually until the 1930s. Thereafter, changes occurred much more rapidly.

Forms of Intergovernmental Interaction

Because money provided by the national government is a major source of funding for intergovernmental activity, the emphasis in intergovernmental relations is often on fiscal relationships, but there are other forms of interaction as well, such as regulations and voluntary cooperative efforts.

In 1984, the then Advisory Commission on Intergovernmental Relations identified four types of *regulations* that are part of intergovernmental relations: direct orders, cross-cutting requirements, crossover sanctions, and partial preemption.[8]

Direct orders either prohibit or mandate state and local government actions. For example, equal employment opportunity legislation prohibits discrimination in employment by state and local government. The Safe Drinking Water Act requires water providers to reach and maintain certain standards in the drinking water they supply. *Preemption* is a form of direct order that has concerned many state and local officials, especially as they have become more prevalent, partly in response to September 11, 2001.[9] An example is the Real ID Act of 2005 that imposed requirements on states for "smart" driver's licenses, which are standardized licenses with enhanced security making them tamperproof. They also required a standard set of documents establishing identity to obtain. Opposition by state government officials effectively stopped implementation of the law, and Congress has been considering a watered down version called Pass ID. Other examples are the preemption (prohibition) of sales taxes on some Internet services in the Internet Tax Freedom Act of 1998 and the Controlled Substances Act of 1970 that prohibits states from permitting sale of certain drugs.

Cross-cutting requirements are those in which a condition in one law is applied to all programs using federal funds. Thus, the Civil Rights Act of 1964 requires that jurisdictions not discriminate against people on the basis of race, color, national origin, gender, or disability status where federal funds are used. The Drug Free Workplace Act of 1988 and the Cash Management Improvement Act of 1990 are other examples.

Crossover sanctions are sanctions applied to one area or activity for failure to comply with certain conditions in another area. For example, federal highway funds can be withheld from states that fail to enforce air quality standards.

Partial preemption refers to situations in which the national government requires or permits states to administer policies as long as the states meet federal criteria for the program. If the states do not meet the federal criteria, the federal government may administer the program directly. Examples include the Clean Air Act Amendments of 1990, Hazardous and Solid Waste Amendments of 1984, and the provisions of the Health Care and Education Reconciliation Act of 2010 relating to states developing insurance pools for the uninsured.

These regulatory processes engender much criticism from state and local government officials. Generally, the policies reflected in these regulations are in response to the desire by some elements of society to further their vision of the public good. Congress often is supportive because, essentially, they represent good public policy. Imposing the requirements without having to provide funding for implementation (unfunded mandates) allows Congress to satisfy strong interests without having to raise the revenue to fund them. Of course, state and local governments then have to find the revenue, thus raising the ire of officials at those levels. Ironically, state mandates have resulted in the same types of complaints from local governments, which feel that they have excessive costs imposed upon them by states. The complaints of local governments appear to have had an impact; state mandates did decline, at least in some states.[10] The national government, even with the passage of the Unfunded Mandate Reform Act of 1995, continued to impose new mandates on state and local governments (see Table 2.1).[11] The Unfunded Mandates Reform Act of 1995 requires federal funding for mandates costing more than $50 million and requires federal agencies to assess impacts of their new rules and regulations on state and local governments. In every session of Congress, bills are introduced, but not passed, to require reimbursement by the national government of any direct cost to state and local governments resulting from federal mandates.

Changing Intergovernmental Relations

Complaints about the intergovernmental system usually have focused on the growth of the national government at the expense of state and local autonomy. We shall encounter these arguments in later chapters, particularly with respect to economic regulation, education, and public assistance. State and local governments have grown as the national government has expanded its involvement in domestic policy issues. The result has been more and more intergovernmental activities and a more complex web of relations. Of course, the intention of most advocates of reform of the system is to reverse that complexity and lighten the hand of the national government in the affairs of state and local governments.

Administrative Problems.   One of the most common complaints about the federal government is that it imposes too much red tape on the state and local recipients of aid. State and local administrators complain about the amount of paperwork in applying for and administering grants. The paperwork increases the costs to the recipients and delays the project's completion. Much of the difficulty arises because the regional administrators of federal agencies cannot make the final decisions on most grants. Instead, they advise the central agency office, which in turn makes the final decision. Disputes in interpreting program criteria and rules and regulations take a long time to resolve, and conflicting rules and regulations and duplication of effort only compound the problem. Even more difficult for the state and local agencies is the need for clearance from numerous agencies from local officials on up to federal agency managers.

These requirements lead to inflexibility in the categorical programs. Local officials feel that their needs cannot be met; rather, the program requirements appear to be oriented more to the needs of the federal agency. Additionally, many of the categorical programs are so narrowly defined that it becomes difficult to fit them to the particular needs of the state and local governments.

Block grants and general revenue sharing were supposed to eliminate some of the administrative problems previously noted. Giving state and local officials more discretion in the structure of their programs would subject the money to fewer restrictions. Although block grants generally begin with such aspirations, state program administrators seem to recategorize them as part of their actual implementation. Conflicts develop within the state block grant administrative agencies. Program specialists fight for funds for their programs, and the funds end up being allocated on a program basis. The result is that after they reach the state level, the block grants often begin to look again like categorical grants. Additionally, national government policy seems to reimpose conditions.

T A B L E 2.1   Sample Enactments and Statutory Amendments Regulating State and Local Governments

Title	Regulatory Type*
Age Discrimination in Employment Act Amendments of 1986	DO
Americans with Disabilities Act of 1986	CC/DO
Asbestos Hazard Emergency Response Act of 1986	DO
Cash Management Improvement Act of 1990	CC
Child Abuse Amendments of 1984	CO
Civil Rights Restoration Act of 1987	CC
Clean Air Act Amendments of 1990	PP
Commercial Motor Vehicle Safety Act of 1986	CO
Controlled Substances Act of 1970	DO
Drug-Free Workplace Act of 1988	CC
Education of the Handicapped Act Amendments of 1990	CO
Emergency Planning and Community Right-to-Know Act of 1986	PP
Fair Housing Act Amendments of 1988	DO
Family and Medical Leave Act of 1993	DO
Handicapped Children's Protection Act of 1986	CO
Hazardous and Solid Waste Amendments of 1984	PP
Health Care and Education Reconciliation Act of 2010	PP
Highway Safety Amendments of 1984	CO
Internet Tax Freedom Act of 1998	DO
Lead Contamination Control Act of 1988	DO
National Voter Registration Act of 1993	CC/DO
No Child Left Behind Act of 2001	DO
Ocean Dumping Ban Act of 1988	DO
Older Workers Benefit Protection Act of 1990	DO
Public Health Security and Bioterrorism Preparedness and Response Act of 2002	DO/PP
Real ID Act of 2005	DO
Safe Drinking Water Act Amendments of 1986	DO/PP
Sarbanes-Oxley Act of 2002	PP
Social Security Amendments of 1983	DO
Surface Transportation Assistance Act of 1982	DO
USA PATRIOT Act of 2001	DO/PP
Voting Accessibility for the Elderly and Handicapped Act of 1984	DO
Water Quality Act of 1987	CC/DO/PP

*Key: CC = Cross-Cutting Requirement; CO = Crossover Sanction; DO = Direct Order; PP = Partial Preemption
SOURCE: *Intergovernmental Perspective*, 18, No. 4 (Fall 1992): 8, provides the original concept and pre-1990 enactments. Newer enactments are added.

For example, general revenue sharing was found to contain the compliance requirements of fifteen different federal agencies just four years after its adoption as federal aid without strings.[12]

Related to administrative problems is monitoring by federal agencies. In granting money to other units of government, the national government tries to see that the money is used properly and for beneficial programs. Federal agencies and many state and local governments recognize the need for coordination. Typically, a regional council of governments or a regional planning commission is responsible for reviewing and commenting on grant applications. Additionally, the request usually faces review by some statewide agency before going to the federal agency. These requirements should reduce overlapping projects and ensure that one project does not work at cross-purposes to another. The end result should be cost savings to the taxpayer and more efficient use of grant monies, but there is no hard evidence that such objectives are met.

There is no question that the review process has many beneficial effects in generating greater cooperation among governments in a region. Nonetheless, the instrument has not been entirely successful. Because the regional councils of governments and the like are made up of representatives of the area's jurisdictions, they each pursue their own interests in making decisions.

Granting agencies also monitor recipients of a grant. Most federal agencies have so many programs and grants to monitor that it is impossible to do a complete job of monitoring, so recipient governments may find ways to get around or ignore compliance with impunity. And when an agency decides to take action against a unit, the affected government has many options at its command to lessen the agency's ability to do so. Because the agencies rely on congressional support to continue their activities, the affected government can turn to members of Congress to put pressure on the granting agency. The agency also depends on its clientele, the recipient units of government, to ensure support for its programs. Thus, agency administrators usually see the advantage of working things out with the state or local units rather than fighting with them.

Finances.   The financial relationships between governmental units are among the most significant interactions. Because the national government increased the numbers of funded programs during the mid-twentieth century, intergovernmental transfers of funds became significant (see Figure 2.1). The problem with providing federal funds lies in who controls the use of those funds. With categorical grants, the national government clearly established criteria for using the money. With block grants and general revenue sharing, the expectation was that the national government would loosen its control. Recent domestic policy has focused on loosening restrictions and cutting domestic spending. The Personal Responsibility and Work Opportunity Reconciliation Act of 1996, which reformed the welfare system (see Chapter 7), is a good example of devolving responsibility to the states and, in the process, controversy about levels of financial support for the program.[13]

With grants, state and local levels are never certain what amount of money is going to be available from year to year. This uncertainty in the level of funding makes it more difficult for them to plan their own activities and budgets.

Another irritating aspect of most federal grants for the recipient units is the *maintenance of effort* requirement, which means that state and local governments cannot use federal money to replace their own spending on the affected program. The receiving governments are locked into spending patterns if they wish to receive the grants with such requirements. For example, Community Development Block Grants cannot be used to reduce the amount of money that the local government spends on redevelopment. Instead, the program requires a government to continue to spend at previous levels or it cannot continue to receive Community Development funds.

Block grants and general revenue sharing combined with cuts in domestic spending have had several effects on state and local governments. State and local units are faced with absorbing the costs of many programs if they are to continue to provide services, especially social and human services. Studies of the effects of block grants so far have indicated that the state replacement of lost federal funds has been relatively low.[14] The principal question is whether state and local governments wish to continue programs and whether they have the resources to do so. The shift to block grants increased the internal competition for funds in state governments. Another feature of the funding shift has been to show the states how they can influence local units to a greater degree. And the states are themselves now using the block grant approach to fund many programs.

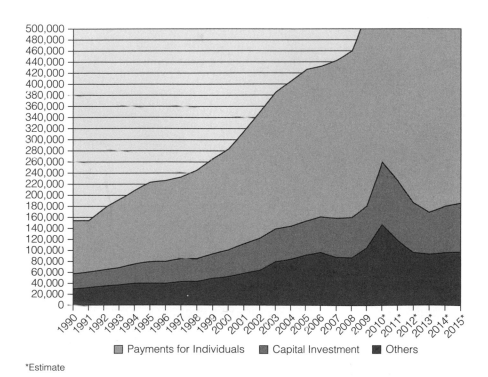

*Estimate

F I G U R E 2.1 Federal Grants to State and Local Government (outlays)

SOURCE: Executive Office of the President, Office of Management and Budget, Budget of the United States Government, FY 2011, Historical Tables, pp. 249–250, www.gpoaccess.gov/usbudget/fy11/pdf/hist.pdf; Accessed June 3, 2010.

Whither Federalism?

Federalism continues to evolve as differing demands are made on the political system. Political scientists Parris Glendening and Mavis Mann Reeves characterized the federal system as a pragmatic one, adapting to changing conditions and assuming new forms to accommodate political, economic, and social realities.[15] Similarly, Martha Derthick notes that American federalism was built upon ambiguity in the relationship of the national government and the states and that change in that relationship also will always be characterized by ambiguity.[16] Thus, it is safe to say that there will be changes in federalism, but the directions of those changes are subject to debate.

Issues in the debate revolve around which levels of government have particular powers and how those powers are exercised. The argument about which level has what powers arises as the national government adopts policies or implements decisions on any number of issues. The trend in the courts until the 1990s had been a centralizing one in which national government authority expanded. Since the 1990s, however, the U.S. Supreme Court has reversed the trend. While some argue that it has favored the states over the national government, others argue that it just has slowed the trend. Analysis of the Court's decisions suggests that the Court sees itself as setting a balance. It slowed federal expansion of power in some cases, but sanctioned it in others.[17]

The National Governors Association, the Conference of State Legislatures, and the American Council on Intergovernmental Relations believe that the roles of the national government and states can be better defined. The problem is in determining exactly which functions should be the responsibility of the national government and what should be the responsibility of state and local units. Commonly, suggestions are made that the national government assume all responsibility for health and income support programs and shift the responsibility for all other social programs to the states. Governors occasionally call upon the national government to assume all responsibility for funding welfare programs, in return for the states picking up other programs, such as education and transportation. Again, the primary emphasis is on turning over many functions to the state and local governments while reducing federal involvement, but there is little agreement on exactly how the division should be made. For example, in 1995 and 1996, many governors suggested devolving Medicaid more fully to the states. By 2004, many governors wanted responsibility for the program to remain national, as many states were overwhelmed by the financial demands of the Medicaid system. Governors keep asking the federal government to provide more funding.

The process of dividing responsibility suggests a view of federalism in which functions can be neatly separated. But history has suggested that such neat divisions are unrealistic. Since most policy activities affect more governments than one, it is unrealistic to leave such activities exclusively under the control of any one government. Therefore, it is improbable that any system could be devised that abolished sharing and cooperation. Nonetheless, proponents of this view continue to expound these objectives. There has been continuing pressure for shifting the balance to the states. With governors and mayors putting pressure on the federal government and with a sympathetic Congress, shifts are likely to continue. The fact that Presidents Clinton and Bush were governors also led them to be sympathetic, thus fostering cooperative efforts with greater discretion for the states, in such areas as health care, welfare, and economic development. The Obama administration seems to be taking the position that states can complement federal power, as in the decision to allow California to establish emission standards more strict than federal rules.

Opponents of the shift of responsibility to the states argue that states are not able to assume that responsibility. States are not likely to have the resources to fund the programs adequately. As noted, states may not always be inclined to continue such programs. Opponents of these proposals see the administrative complexity of fifty states administering programs, such as under block grants, as inefficient and burdensome. There are also concerns that some states will be less sensitive to issues such as equity, fairness, and civil rights in developing and implementing programs. Concerns also arise over which groups have access to decision makers with many arguing that the poor and powerless bear the greatest burden of these reforms.

Those favoring the centralization of programs also are concerned about the complexity of the problems facing American society. They see problems as being so complex that only the national government can possibly marshal the resources to address them and provide a coordinated effort. The terrorist attacks of September 11, 2001, led many to argue that centralization of functions was necessary in dealing with terrorism, for example.[18] Similarly, Arizona's SB2010 law on immigration led to many concerns that it would lead to a violation of civil rights, create a patchwork of laws, and preempt national responsibility for a single policy for the country.

The advocates of change are not likely to see their proposals realized completely, but some shuffles are certain. It appears certain that fiscal changes will continue: The trend toward fewer real dollars in grants is not likely to be reversed, especially with the renewed federal deficit pressures. As a result, there will be fewer dollars for state and local units to share. Competition for those dollars is bound to increase, and some analysts suggest that changes in political coalitions of public interest groups would result, as they now oppose one another, rather than work together, on grant requests.[19] With fewer dollars available, fiscal relationships are likely to give way to cooperative efforts in other ways and to the national government's attempts to regulate activities of states and local governments through general policy. Such general policy is likely to increase the costs of state and local government through unfunded mandates without providing federal monies to cover those costs.

It is hard to predict what will happen with the block grants. These programs appear to be popular with the general public and with state officials because they imply few strings. However, the general public is ineffective in pressuring Congress to sustain these programs. Categorical grants most likely will continue to be the most significant element of the fiscal relationship, because the interests affected by them often are strong and can influence Congress when cuts are contemplated. Even with the consolidation of programs into block grants, there has been little effect on the number of categorical grant programs. There were approximately 500 federal grant programs in 1978 and over 750 in 2002. More significantly, categorical grants account for about 90 percent of grant funds.

THE ECONOMIC CONTEXT

The 1980s added a new specter to the usual worries about unemployment, recession, and inflation—a federal budget deficit that grew more rapidly during the Reagan presidency than at any time before (see Chapter 4). Programs as diverse as arts funding and health care reform became hostage to the budget debate during that decade. The economy grew steadily in the 1990s, but wages stagnated for families in the middle and bottom of the distribution, and Americans had to work harder to keep pace. The economy turned down again in 2001, entering into recession; another recession that lasted from 2007 well into 2009 was the longest in U.S. history. Budget deficits that were eliminated at the end of the 1990s returned in the early 2000s and reached record size in 2004 and again in 2010, setting off new rounds of program cutbacks. At the same time, the globalization of economic activity poses significant challenges to American economic prosperity and political stability. The outsourcing of jobs to other nations by American companies became an electoral issue as did efforts to bail out stressed corporations. Corporate downsizing and the growth of temporary and part-time employment are simply the most dramatic symptoms of a rapidly changing economy. Economic uncertainties shape new policy initiatives and cause the reevaluation of old ones.

Confidence has waned that the economic pie is indefinitely expanding, and the question of how to manage scarce resources and to distribute them fairly occurs more frequently. The changing family income structure illustrates this concern. Median family income in inflation-adjusted terms, which increased steadily from the 1950s through the early 1970s, did not grow substantially in the 1980s or 1990s and started falling after 2000. The need to absorb millions of new workers, the decline in family size, trends in divorce, and the movement toward two-wage earner families all produced an economic squeeze on the lower and middle classes. Inflation-adjusted income declined in recent decades for the poorest 40 percent of families and expanded only modestly for the middle 40 percent, while growing substantially for the richest 20 percent. Young males and single females, young families, and older blue-collar workers face a highly uncertain economic future.

Later chapters more fully discuss these matters, especially economic policy (Chapters 3 and 4) and income maintenance (Chapter 7), but it is important to recognize here that these economic trends have an impact well beyond strictly economic issues. Budget deficits, fear of sending jobs overseas if too much regulation affects corporations, and changing job requirements have influenced education, health policy, and foreign policy, for example. New spending initiatives for programs other than defense and homeland security have had great difficulty in Congress. Economically challenging times also have exacerbated racial tensions and affected the controversies over affirmative action and immigration considered in Chapters 10 and 11.

THE DEMOGRAPHIC CONTEXT

The generational, racial, and residential characteristics of a nation's population change constantly, reflecting new trends in birthrates, life expectancy, job opportunities, and migration patterns. Some of these trends directly affect policymaking.

The children born during the "*baby boom*" after World War II reach Social Security retirement age in 2012, placing pressure on social insurance policies. The proportion of the population under age twenty-five, which rose until the mid-1970s, declined until the mid-1990s, when it leveled off briefly. Such changes in the number of young people not only seriously affect education policy, but other areas as well. For example, persons between the ages of fourteen and twenty-five commit a highly disproportionate number of violent crimes (see Chapter 6). Economic performance from 1960 to 1985 was substantially affected by the need to absorb millions of new, young workers.[20] The aging of the population raises the question of where to find younger workers to sustain a productive economy.

The proportion of the population sixty-five and older, now about 12.8 percent, is increasing at twice the national population rate and is likely to be 20 percent by 2030 (see Figure 2.2). Those over eighty-five will reach over 4 percent of the population by 2050. Because only a small proportion of persons in this age group work full-time and because their health care requirements exceed those of the rest of the population, pressure on Social Security and Medicare will be intense. Moreover, because life expectancy for women is significantly higher than for men, many of those over sixty-five are widowed women, living alone or in some kind of institution, such as a nursing home or apartment complex for the elderly. It is possible that the working population will come to resent supporting such a large number of retired persons. On the other hand, because the elderly vote more regularly than the young do, the aged themselves have become a large and powerful political force for the protection of their own interests. These generational considerations were much in evidence during the 2005 debates over Social Security reform (see Chapter 7) and the 2010 health care reform (see Chapter 8).

Immigration continues to change the shape of the American population and present challenges to federal and state policy. Legal immigration set a record of more than 1.5 million persons in 2010. Immigration now accounts for more than half of U.S. population growth. These immigrants, primarily of Asian and Hispanic descent, present both opportunities for dynamic expansion of the

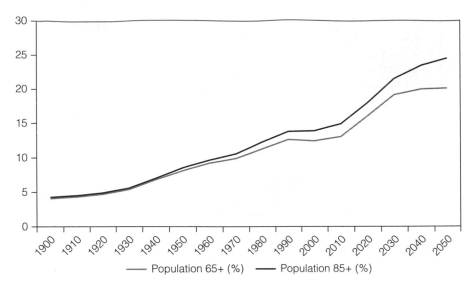

FIGURE 2.2 Population Aging

Note: 2010 to 2050 are projections.

SOURCE: http://www.aoa.gov/aoaroot/aging_statistics/future_growth/docs/By_Age_Total_Population.xls; Accessed June 3, 2010.

economy and challenges for services in housing, schools, jobs, and health care. Moreover, the impact of immigration is not spread evenly across the country. Over 70 percent of the new residents settle in Texas, California, Florida, New York, Illinois, and New Jersey, placing a critical assimilative burden on these states (see Chapter 11).

Public policy in a number of areas will also have to respond to changes in the racial mix of the population. Non-Hispanic whites made up 90 percent of the population in 1955. By the turn of the century, the proportion had declined to just fewer than 70 percent. Because of illegal immigration and the younger average age of the Spanish-surname population, the Hispanic proportion of the population has increased rapidly, surpassing the African American proportion. By 2008, Hispanic Americans constituted about 15.4 percent of the population; they accounted for 6 percent in 1980. By the middle of the twenty-first century, one-quarter of Americans will be of Hispanic background, and the white percentage will be about half (see Figure 2.3). Though they share many problems with African Americans, poverty and racial discrimination being the most important, Hispanics also bring with them a different language and culture. Historically, combinations of simultaneous racial change and economic uncertainty have been volatile. The passage of anti-immigration California Proposition 187 in 1994, as well as the polarization of voters (young and white male voters moving increasingly to the Republican Party, with older and African American voters staying Democratic), were symptoms of this kind of volatility, as was passage of federal immigration reform policy in 1996 and the acrimonious debate over immigration in 2006–2007. Lack of national government action on immigration frustrated many states, especially those along

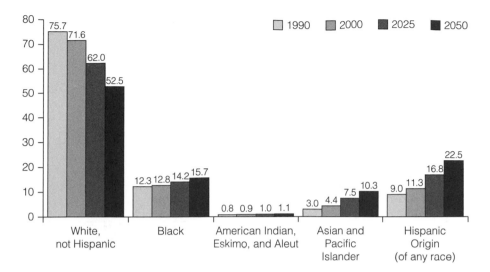

FIGURE 2.3 Racial Groups as Percent of Population
SOURCE: http://www.census.gov/population/www/pop-profile/natproj.html, Accessed June 3, 2010.

the border with Mexico. This resulted in state legislation such as Arizona's SB1070 placing state penalties on immigrants being in the state illegally. Thus, the issue became contentious in the 2010 elections once more.

Changes in marriage and family life have had a major impact on policy. The increasing percentages of working women, the high divorce rate, and the high rates of illegitimate births and of single-parent families affect labor policy, welfare expenditures, child care, schools, and gender equality policies (see Figure 2.4). Moreover, married households with children now constitute less than a quarter of all households. Marriage and family life increasingly are chosen by the college-educated and affluent, with lower-income working families choosing to live together and have children out of wedlock. This pattern has contributed to widening income inequality in the United States.[21] Although the divorce rate declined in the 1990s, these trends produced the "feminization of poverty," closely linking women's issues with income maintenance and health care policies.[22] Nearly 50 percent of all children born in the late 1970s experienced family breakup at some time prior to their sixteenth birthday. Currently, over one-quarter of children under age eighteen live in single-parent, mostly female-headed, homes for some part of each year. African American families are most strongly affected by these demographic trends. Today, over two-thirds of African American children are born out of wedlock, and over half live in female-headed, single-parent families. Poverty, race, and changes in family life create an economic and demographic prison, a situation discussed in Chapter 7. Policy must also focus on child care for working parents and on health care and income support for children in poverty. These facts, and disagreements about their meaning, intensify the politics of culture and morality described in the next two sections and in Chapter 13.

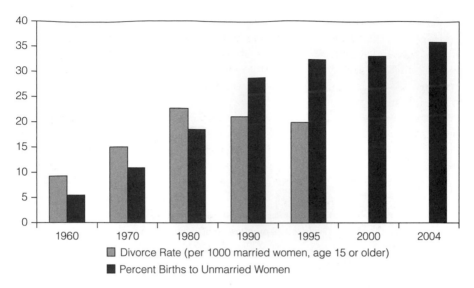

FIGURE 2.4 Divorce and Out-of-Wedlock Births

SOURCE: Statistical Abstract of the United States: 1985 (Tables 94 & 120), 1996 (Table 146), and 2007 (Tables 84), www.census.gov/compensia/statab/vital_statistics/; Accessed July 24, 2007.

Finally, the declining population of such large urban centers as New York, Baltimore, Chicago, and Cleveland and the rising population of rural, suburban, and small urban areas, especially in the South and Southwest, continues to influence a broad range of policies. Controversies rage over how the federal government should allocate its grant-in-aid money for urban rehabilitation, jobs, housing, education, unemployment assistance, water and sewer projects, and many other needs. Between 1980 and 2000, the North and Northeast lost and the South and West gained forty seats, or nearly one-tenth of Congress. The division between "red states" and "blue states" in their partisan loyalties and voting patterns partly reflects these demographic changes.

THE IDEOLOGICAL CONTEXT

Public policy is a field of debate over the meaning of basic values and principles. Defining policy problems, according to political scientist Deborah Stone, is fundamentally about the conceptual and symbolic terms that we use to describe them. The numbers, symbols, and discussions of causality in the following chapters occur in the context of ideological debate over their meaning and significance. Conservatives, feminists, liberals, and socialists fight over the very goals of public policy, such as equity, efficiency, security, and liberty.[23]

Ideological perspectives on American public policy have always ranged along a spectrum—including extreme positions at either end, such as communists on the Left and militia groups on the Right. Historically, however, *conservatism* and *liberalism* have dominated policymaking and evaluation in America. The majority of Americans, including policymakers, are some variety of liberal or conservative, despite small and periodically powerful numbers of adherents to other ideologies. Although liberals and conservatives in America share a great many commitments to abstract ideals, such as freedom, democracy, the market system, and individualism, they disagree on the principles to be used in making and evaluating policy. First, they disagree over the meaning of freedom and its limits: Conservatives tend to value civil and personal freedoms less and are more willing to limit them. They often favor censorship of sexually explicit materials, for example. Liberals are more ready to limit economic freedom, for example, by placing restrictions on advertisers. Liberals have a deeper commitment to equality than do conservatives. Conservatives are committed to tradition and authority, which is balanced by liberal commitment to change and individual choice in moral and social behavior. Liberals tend to have faith in the power of government to make the world better; conservatives are more pessimistic about such a prospect. These disagreements affect policy debates in all areas, because government itself and the extent to which market forces may be relied on for economic and social health are central issues.

Traditional conservatism and liberalism have fragmented in recent years, with new ideological viewpoints surfacing from the two mainstream movements. *Neo-conservatives* and the *New Right* have competed for influence within the Republican Party. In domestic policy, neo-conservatives are critical of the government's regulation of business enterprise and suspicious of government action to correct past injustices, such as affirmative action, when there is basic disagreement about the goals of such policies. They are not, however, as opposed to government economic action as traditional conservatives or libertarians, who also form part of the right end of the ideological spectrum. The New Right, on the other hand, directs most of its attention to social issues. It opposes abortion, same-sex marriage, feminism, pornography, and what it sees as government interference in religious expression. Included in the New Right are the evangelical religious groups, such as the Christian Coalition, that became a prominent part of electoral politics in the early 1980s. The Tea Party movement of 2009 and 2010 is also associated with conservatives.

Movements on the Left of the spectrum are harder to define and classify, as they are more fragmented and less prominent than the Right in recent decades. Communists and socialists stress fundamental change in the social and economic system, government control of the basic means of production, and equal distribution of most income. Such groups have lost virtually all influence in American politics. Other groups on the Left that take a predominantly economic approach to policy stress democratic control of the means of production through worker self-management and local, direct democracy.

Because the term *liberal* has declined in popularity, often being used as a term of disparagement in political campaigns, many on the left call themselves *progressives*. This term is meant to suggest willingness to improve society and to discard old restrictive attitudes and rules. The remaining chapters employ both the older "liberal" and the newer "progressive" to designate this part of the ideological spectrum. Other groups often classified on the left focus primarily on social or environmental issues. Moreover, they contain within themselves more and less extreme varieties. The less extreme ones make up an important part of contemporary liberalism and of the Democratic Party politically. These are groups defined by feminism, environmental protection, or gay equality. These movements view public policy primarily through a particular lens. *Feminists* evaluate policy according to its impact on women. Liberal feminists strive to make sure that men and women are treated equally and that women have the opportunity to achieve success in all areas of political, economic, and social life. More radical variants of feminism seek to challenge the traditional structures of society. Similarly, more liberal elements of the gay and lesbian community seek to integrate homosexual persons into the fabric of society by guaranteeing the same rights and responsibilities (job access and military service, for example) as heterosexuals. Some gay activists, on the other hand, wish to weave a very different fabric of society, by challenging, for example, the definition of marriage and sexuality. These splits within newer ideological movements and their uneasy relationship with more traditional progressives have made the Left and the Democratic Party highly fractious in recent decades. The early stages of the 2008 election campaign revealed these divisions in the very mixed reaction among the party faithful to the way some Democratic candidates worked to appeal to religious groups, in order to counter the role of the New Right within the Republican Party. The divisions erupted again as some believed that the Obama administration was not aggressive enough in championing their causes such as eliminating "don't ask, don't tell" in military service and in not supporting the public option or single payer system in health care reform.

Still other groups are more difficult to classify. Although environmentalists are most often counted as part of the liberal coalition, there are many traditional conservatives who value and participate in environmental groups that stress conservation of natural resources and respect for the physical environment. This fact gives some environmental policy issues broad political support. *Libertarians* combine a conservative economic agenda with a liberal social agenda. Although usually classified on the right, libertarians support abortion rights, oppose restrictions on sexually explicit speech, and favor keeping government out of the bedroom as well as out of the boardroom.

In the late twentieth century, a movement known as *communitarianism* received national attention. Prominent communitarians, such as political scientist William Galston, have held important positions in the Clinton and second Bush administrations. Communitarians focus on the interconnection between rights and responsibilities. Their policy attention concentrates on revitalizing local neighborhood and city institutions, on community policing, family restoration, character formation, and education reform.

Issue definition is not a neutral, apolitical process. The ideological perspectives just described affect how issues appear on the policy agenda. The definition of a policy problem is always a matter for disagreement among people of competing beliefs and principles. Poverty, for example, was not seen as a problem to be solved until the 1930s. Before that, it was held to be an inevitable social condition. Conservatives still tend to view it, at least partially, in this way. Radicals, on the other hand, view poverty as a requirement of capitalist society; from this standpoint, public assistance policy becomes simply a device used by capitalism to maintain itself, not a response to a neutral problem. Even the statistics used to illustrate the dimensions of an issue will frequently vary depending on the perspective from which the issue is being defined. For example, as we shall see in Chapter 7, liberals and conservatives cite the same poverty statistics but draw opposite conclusions from them. Care must be exercised in using and interpreting statistics—even those presented in this book!

Particularly significant in the ideological context is the continuing growth of support for conservatism, the New Right, and the Republican Party. Republican dominance of the presidency and Congress in the early 2000s produced policy changes more favorable to free markets, to social conservatism, and reduction of economic regulations. However, the unpopularity of the war in Iraq, combined with the continuing public strength of progressive attitudes, produced strong Democratic victories in 2006 and 2008 and attempts to roll back some of these conservative gains. Yet voters continue to suspect both Democratic and Republican politicians of self-interest, and they do not trust most interest and ideological groups. Many citizens certainly *perceive* a failure in domestic policy programs, and this perception supports conservative politics. Yet, at the same time, Americans value the benefits that government programs bring them, their cities, and their employers. This commitment points toward more liberal policies. Moreover, ideology is very much involved in the cultural changes sweeping American society. The meaning of our connections with each other, the definition of the family and its responsibilities, and acceptable forms of sexual expression all create considerable turmoil within and among ideological groups, making it hard to achieve policy consensus.

THE CULTURAL CONTEXT

During the 1980s, it became increasingly clear that many policy issues were caught up not only in passionate ideological disputes but also in a cultural conflict of increasing dimensions. Culture refers to the patterns of fundamental beliefs, principles, traditions, and social assumptions that characterize a society. There is frequently a dominant culture and one or more subcultures. Political conflict challenges which fundamental values dominate American life.

Demographic changes discussed earlier, particularly those affecting the family, directly affect culture. As family life changes, other parts of culture come into question. The family is one of the primary ways of passing on moral understandings, but clearly standards of morality with respect to sexuality, competition, money, material goods, and work, to name just a few, are hotly debated today.

Ideology is inextricably bound to attitudes toward culture. Among many, especially conservatives, there is a perception that something is wrong with the fabric of national life, starting with the family, but also reflected in crime, economic noncompetitiveness, political and social corruption, and greed. Communitarians also articulate these themes. According to conservatives, television and movies portray and advocate ways of life at odds with traditional American values. Abortion, pornography, and sexual promiscuity are increasingly acceptable. Public schools do not permit prayer, and the educational system fails hundreds of thousands of young people. The role of women in the workplace and in public life also raises questions about the meaning of traditional cultural values, as does recognition and acceptance of homosexual behavior. Moral crusades have always been part of American history, though their targets and political consequences vary substantially.[24]

Progressives, no less than conservatives, recognize fundamental changes in gender, sexual, and cultural roles of all kinds. Rather than fearing these changes, liberals tend to accept most. They support legislation protecting the right to abortion. They want fundamental political, social, and economic rights available to all persons, regardless of gender or sexual orientation. To the extent that traditional family life oppresses women and children, liberals accept necessary change in family structures.[25] Because these controversies often pertain to the role of religion in public life and the strong divide between religiously observant and secular voters, the Constitution's First Amendment receives a great deal of attention.

Cultural conflict thus runs through many of the policy issues that appear in the following chapters. Chapter 13 directly addresses this conflict. Cultural issues were significant in each of the presidential elections of the last two decades since 1980.

ENDNOTES

1. William A. Galston, "Civic Education and Political Participation," *Philosophy & Public Policy Quarterly*, 25 (Winter/Spring, 2005): 18–21; and Kei Kawashima-Ginsberg, Amanda Nover, and Emily Hoban Kirby, "State Election Law Reform and Youth Voter Turnout," *Circle Fact Sheet*, The Center for Information & Research on Civic Learning & Engagement, July 2008, http://www.civicyouth.org/PopUps/FactSheets/State_law_and_turnout_Final.pdf; Accessed May 4, 2010.

2. E. J. Dionne, Jr., *Why Americans Hate Politics* (New York: Simon & Schuster, 1991).

3. Gallup Poll, May 05, 2010, http:www.gallup.com/poll/110456/trust-government-remains-low.aspx; Accessed May 5, 2010.

4. See Richard Morin, "They Only Know What They Don't Like," *Washington Post National Weekly Edition*, October 3–9, 1994, p. 37; and Richard Morin, "Tuned Out, Turned Off," *Washington Post National Weekly Edition*, February 5–11, 1996, pp. 6–8.

5. Beryl Radin, *Intergovernmental Partnerships and Rural Development Councils: Profiles of Twenty-nine State Rural Development Councils* (Washington, DC: Government Printing Office, 1995); John DeWitt, Donald F. Kettl, Barbara Dyer, and

W. Robert Lovan, "What Will New Governance Mean for the Federal Government?" *Public Administration Review*, 54 (March/April 1994): 170–175; and National Rural Development Partnership, *2006 Report to Congress*, www.rurdev.usda.gov/nrdp/ NRDP_Report_2006_Final.pdf; Accessed May 6, 2010.

6. Brady Baybeck and William Lowry, "Federalism Outcomes and Ideological Preferences: The U.S. Supreme Court and Preemption Cases," *Publius*, 30, No. 3 (Summer 2000): 73–97; Matthew H. Bosworth, "'An Innate Sense of Fairness': State Responses to the U.S. Supreme Court's Sovereign Immunity Decisions," *Publius*, 36, No. 3 (2006): 393–420; "The Federal Courts: Intergovernmental Umpires or Regulators," *Intergovernmental Perspective*, 18 (Fall 1992): 12–15; Susan Mezey Gluck, "The U.S. Supreme Court's Federalism Jurisprudence: *Alden v. Maine* and the Enhancement of State Sovereignty," *Publius*, 30, Nos. 1 & 2 (Winter/Spring 2000): 31–38; David H. Rosenbloom, Rosemary O'Leary, and Joshua Chanin, *Public Administration and Law*, 3rd ed. (New York: CRC Press, 2010), Chapter 1; and Charles R. Wise, "The Supreme Court's New Constitutional Federalism: Implications for Public Administration," *Public Administration Review*, 61, No. 3 (May/June 2001): 343–358.

7. Christopher Banks and John Blakeman, "Chief Justice Roberts, Justice Alito, and New Federalism Jurisprudence," *Publius*, 38 (2010): 576–600; Baybeck and Lowry, "Federalism Outcomes and Ideological Preferences"; Bosworth, "An Innate Sense of Fairness"; John Dinan and Shama Gamkhar, "The State of American Federalism 2008–2009: The Presidential Election, the Economic Downturn, and the Consequences for Federalism," *Publius*, 39, No. 3 (2009): 369–407; Gluck, "The U.S. Supreme Court's Federalism Jurisprudence"; Bert Waisanen, "Federalism: Watchdog for States," *State Government News*, 40, No. 2 (March 1997): 12–15; and Carol S. Weissert and Sanford F. Schram, "The State of American Federalism," *Publius*, 26, No. 3 (Summer 1996): 1–26.

8. U.S. Advisory Commission on Intergovernmental Relations, *Regulatory Federalism: Policy, Process, Impact, and Reform*, Vol. 2 (Washington, DC: U.S. Government Printing Office, 1984).

9. Joseph F. Zimmerman, "Congressional Preemption During the George W. Bush Administration," *Publius*, 37, No. 3 (2007): 432–452; Joseph F. Zimmerman, "The Nature and Political Significance of Preemption," *PS: Political Science & Politics* (July 2005): 360–362.

10. Beverly A. Cigler, "State-Local Relations: A Need for Reinvention?" *Intergovernmental Perspective*, 20 (Spring 1994): 20–23; Lawrence J. Grossback, "The Problem of State-Imposed Mandates: Lessons from Minnesota's Local Governments," *State and Local Government Review*, 34, No. 3 (Fall 2002): 183–197; Susan A. McManus, "Mad About Mandates: The Issue of Who Should Pay for What Resurfaces," *Publius*, 21 (Summer 1991): 59–76; Joseph F. Zimmerman, "State Mandate Relief: A Quick Look," *Intergovernmental Perspective*, 20 (Spring 1994): 28–30; and David B. Walker, *The Rebirth of Federalism: Slouching Toward Washington* (Chatham, NJ: Chatham House, 1995), 264–267.

11. U.S. General Accounting Office, *Unfunded Mandates: Analysis of Reform Act Coverage* (Washington, DC: U.S. General Accounting Office, May 2004).

12. Lawrence D. Brown and Bernard Frieden, "Guidelines and Goals in the Model Cities Program," *Policy Sciences*, 7 (December 1976): 488; and Bruce A. Wallin, *From

Revenue Sharing to Deficit Sharing: General Revenue Sharing and Cities (Washington, DC: Georgetown University Press, 1998), Chapter 4.

13. Weissert and Schram, "The State of American Federalism." Also see Steven D. Gold, "Issues Raised by the New Federalism," *National Tax Journal*, xlix, No. 2 (June 1996): 213–287; Rosemary O'Leary and Paul Weiland, "Regulatory Reform in the 104th Congress: Revolution or Evolution?" *Publius*, 26, No. 3 (Summer 1996): 27–44; and John M. Quigley and Daniel L. Rubinfell, "Federalism and Reductions in the Federal Government," *National Tax Journal*, xlix, 2 (June 1996): 289–302.

14. John L. Palmer and Isabel V. Sawhill, *The Reagan Experiment* (Washington, DC: Urban Institute Press, 1982), chapter 6; Richard P. Nathan and Fred C. Doolittle and Associates, *The Consequences of Cuts* (Princeton, NJ: Princeton University Urban and Regional Research Center, 1983); and Shana Gamkhar and Wallace Oates, "Asymmetries in the Response to Increases and Decreases in Intergovernmental Grants: Some Empirical Findings," *National Tax Journal*, xlix, No. 4 (December 1996): 501–511.

15. Parris N. Glendening and Mavis Mann Reeves, *Pragmatic Federalism: An Intergovernmental View of American Government*, 2nd ed. (Pacific Palisades, CA: Palisades Publishers, 1984).

16. Martha Derthick, *Keeping the Compound Republic* (Washington, DC: Brookings Institution, 2001).

17. Christopher Banks and John Blakeman, "Chief Justice Roberts, Justice Alito, and New Federalism"; Matthew H. Bosworth, "An Innate Sense of Fairness"; John Dinan and Shama Gamkhar, "The State of American Federalism 2008–2009"; Charles R. Wise, "The Supreme Court's New Federalism."

18. John Kincaid and Richard L. Cole, "Issues in Federalism in Response to Terrorism," *Public Administration Review*, 62, Special Issue (September 2002): 181–192.

19. George E. Hale and Marian Lief Palley, *The Politics of Federal Grants* (Washington, DC: Congressional Quarterly Press, 1981), 169–171.

20. John E. Schwarz, America's Hidden Success: A Reassessment of Public Policy from Kennedy to Reagan, rev. ed. (New York: Norton 1988), 116ff.

21. Blaine Harden, "First Comes Love, Then What?" *Washington Post National Weekly Edition*, March 12–18, 2007: 31.

22. The data in Figure 2-4 for divorce end in 1995 because the Census Bureau ceased collecting data in this form after that date. Other Census Bureau data, collected in a different form, show a continued slow decline in divorces since 1995. The decline may be a function of two factors: fewer married couples divorcing but also growing cohabitation without marriage.

23. Deborah Stone, *Policy Paradox: The Art of Political Decision Making*, 3rd. ed. (New York: Norton, 2002).

24. James Morone, *Hellfire Nation: The Politics of Sin in American History* (New Haven, CT: Yale University Press, 2003).

25. For broad discussion of cultural conflict and of the policy issues directly involved, see James Davison Hunter, *Culture Wars: The Struggle to Define America* (New York: Basic Books, 1991); Raymond Tatalovich and Byron W. Daynes, eds., *Social Regulatory Policy: Moral Controversies in American Politics* (Boulder, CO: Westview

Press, 1988). Political scientists disagree about how extensive these cultural differences are and about how polarized the electorate is around these differences. See, for example, Morris P. Fiorina, *Culture War? The Myth of a Polarized America* (New York: Pearson, 2005); Mark D. Brewer and Jeffrey M. Stonecash, *Split: Class and Cultural Divides in American Politics* (Washington: CQ Press, 2007).

RESOURCES

Books

Barrales, Ruben. "Federalism in the Bush Administration." *Spectrum: The Journal of State Government*, 74, No. 3 (Summer 2001): 5–6.

Berman, David. *State and Local Politics*, 9th ed. Armonk, NY: Sharpe, 1999.

Brewer, Mark D., and Stonecash, Jeffrey M. *Split: Class and Cultural Divides in American Politics*. Washington: CQ Press, 2007.

Derthick, Martha, *Keeping the Compound Republic: Essays in American Federalism*. Washington, DC: Brookings Institution, 2001.

Dinan, John, and Krane, Dale. "The State of American Federalism, 2005: Federalism Resurfaces." *Publius*, 36, No. 3 (2006): 327–274.

Fix, Michael, and Kenyon, Daphne A., eds. *Coping with Mandates*. Washington, DC: Urban Institute Press, 1990.

Gerston, Larry N. *American Federalism*. Armonk, NY: Sharpe, 2007.

Hunter, James Davison. *Culture Wars: The Struggle to Define America*. New York: Basic Books, 1991.

Morone, James A. *Hellfire Nation: The Politics of Sin in American History*. New Haven, CT: Yale University Press, 2003.

O'Toole, Laurence J., Jr. *American Intergovernmental Relations*, 4th ed. Washington, DC: CQ Press, 2006.

Stephens, G. Ross, and Wikstrom, Nelson. *American Intergovernmental Relations: A Fragmented Federal Polity*. New York: Oxford University Press, 2007.

Tatalovich, Raymond. *Moral Controversies in American Politics*. Armonk, NY: Sharpe, 1998.

Wald, Kenneth D., and Calhoun-Brown, Allison. *Religion and Politics in the United States*, 5th ed. Lanham, MD: Rowan & Littlefield, 2007.

Zimmerman, Joseph F. "Congressional Preemption During the George W. Bush Administration." *Publius*, 37, No. 3 (2007): 432–452.

Zimmerman, Joseph F. *Interstate Cooperation: Compacts and Administrative Agreements*. Westport, CT: Praeger, 2002.

Websites

American Council on Intergovernmental Relations:
http://govinfo.library.unt.edu/amcouncil/index.html

The Institute for Communitarian Policy Studies:
www.gwu.edu/~ccps/index.html

Council of State Governments: **www.csg.org/**

Family Facts: **www.familyfacts.org/**

National Association of Counties: **www.naco.org**

National League of Cities: **www.nlc.org/**

New York Times: **www.nytimes.com**

The Pew Forum on Religion & Public Life: **http://pewforum.org/**

Public Agenda: **www.publicagenda.org/**

Urban Institute: **www.urban.org/**

Washington Post: **www.washingtonpost.com**

Chapter 3

The Economy: Changing Government–Business Relationships

A merican government has always been preoccupied with economic activities. During its first century, the country's main concern was preserving the property of citizens. Although property rights still hold a high place in American values, other economic concerns—such as economic growth, level of employment, international competition, and the scarcity of natural resources—gradually replaced preservation of property rights as a major focus of government. Yet one factor has remained constant over the years: Government and economic activity are inextricably intertwined; therefore, activity in one sector automatically has major consequences for the other. At the same time, quality of life and the relationship of economic development to the environment and to social issues represent current concerns for economic policy.

ISSUE BACKGROUND: KEY CONCEPTS IN ECONOMICS

Economic systems produce and distribute wealth among people in the form of goods and services. Different systems perform these functions in different ways. In theory, a market system operates according to the concept of supply and demand—that is, it responds to people's demands by supplying what they want, for a profit. The key to understanding the market system is that both prices and the allocation of goods and services are determined impersonally. That is, they are not set by any actor or institution according to some rational criterion, but rather are produced by the interaction of the impersonal forces of supply and demand. This simplified view of economic systems assumes that there will be a balance between supply and demand and that the economic actors have essentially equal ability to bargain with one another. In reality, however, people vary in the economic power they have, and other factors affect the supply–demand relationship. As economist John Kenneth Galbraith noted, people band together in organizations to acquire power.[1] These organizations often serve their own economic self-interest, not that of society. Because some individuals and organizations have more money, property, or political access than others, imbalances in the distribution of wealth develop. Governments often intervene to protect the interests of those with power or to rebalance the system; economic policy deals with these governmental efforts.

The Free-Enterprise System

Industrialized nations are characterized by a variety of economic systems. They can, however, be divided roughly between two extreme alternatives of economic organization: *market capitalism* (or *free enterprise*) and *socialism* (or public ownership). Although each existing economy more closely approximates one of these two extremes, most combine elements of free enterprise and government control. One may actually conceptualize three types of economic systems. *Free-enterprise capitalism* implies both the market system and the private ownership of the major means of production, distribution, and exchange, with these means run for the profit of their owners. *Socialism* involves the public or governmental ownership and control of these major means of production, distribution, and exchange, run for the public interest. In this system, prices and the allocation of goods and services are planned by government agents according to rational considerations. Between these polar opposites is the system practiced in most industrial democracies, a type called *welfare-state capitalism*. In this system, the allocation of goods and services, and frequently prices, are to a large extent planned, but the major means of production are still in private hands and run for profit.

The major systems champion economic development and industrialization, but they favor different methods for achieving them. Proponents of free-market capitalism justify it on the grounds that the private ownership of firms provides incentives for production. They believe the state should refrain as much as possible from interfering with the conduct of economic activity. In the socialist approach, on the other hand, the political system plays a major role in the conduct of economic activity. Such a system is based on the assumption that economic wealth should be fairly equally distributed among the population and that such distribution improves social welfare. Socialists reject the assumptions that underlie the market system. From the socialist perspective, capitalist societies are dominated by a few wealthy owners and managers of private enterprise, policymakers who are neither chosen by, nor responsible to, the people as a whole. Proponents of capitalism see the same problems in a socialist economy, namely, that government officials concentrate economic power along with political and social power in their own hands, but capitalists view this as a threat to individual liberty.

In socialist economies, such as those in the pre-1989 Soviet Union, the formerly communist countries of Eastern Europe, and China, government ownership predominated. Thus, government controlled economic activity through its normal decision-making processes. Even within such societies, however, there were variations, and some had more mixed economies than others. Eastern European nations, in particular, permitted private enterprise, particularly in agriculture, to coexist with the state-owned economic entities. East Germany, Yugoslavia, and Czechoslovakia diverged from total government ownership, often at the expense of incurring Soviet enmity and sometimes intervention. Relatively independent of Soviet dominance, Yugoslavia, for example, because of the decentralization of its productive mechanisms, had most of its prices determined by market forces. The Solidarity labor movement in Poland also demonstrated that socialist governments cannot always maintain total control over economic activities. Even in China, where communism still exists, a market economy constantly grows.

With the failure of communism in 1989 and the dissolution of the Soviet Union and its control over Eastern Europe, these socialist, or command, economies collapsed. As a result, the development of the free-market system accelerated. Although they face immense challenges, these countries are developing mixed economies reflecting elements of command and free-market systems.

In most industrialized nations—such as the United States, France, Germany, Italy, Sweden, and Japan—a capitalist approach dominates, but it is inevitably a mixture of private ownership and public control that characterizes such systems.[2] Government monopolies invariably run postal services and, in many nations, other economic activities, such as telephone and telegraph services and transportation. These activities (sometimes called natural monopolies) often are viewed as being so basic to the maintenance of society that government monopoly is justified.

What differentiates capitalist and socialist economies for purposes of government-economic interaction is that socialist states, as we have seen, have built-in controls through public ownership and operation of economic enterprise. Capitalist economies, on the other hand, utilize other kinds of intervention as a means of supporting, guiding, or controlling the activities of the private sector. Socialist states do not need the regulation or economic stimulation common in capitalist states as they exercise direct control; capitalist economies, on the other hand, use numerous methods to influence economic enterprise.

Among the industrial nations, the United States is one of the most purely capitalist in the way its economic activity is organized. It is especially distinguished by the extent to which it still relies on market forces. The majority of economic enterprise is privately operated, and few activities are totally publicly owned. Nonetheless, although economic activity is primarily privately owned, the United States does intervene in economic activity to a great extent. Thus, people in the United States, who pride themselves on having a nearly pure form of free-market capitalism, actually function within a regulated economy.

Economist Milton Friedman, probably the preeminent twentieth-century defender of the free-market system, suggested that a pure free-enterprise economy would be based on:

- A self-adjusting free market independent of any government intervention.
- Human beings who seek to maximize their own economic self-interest.
- Competition, stimulated by individual self-interest, that produces maximum benefits for all.
- Private ownership of the means of production and distribution, which leads to competition, which results in the best quality of product at the lowest price.[3]

Critics of Friedman's position argue that the free-market approach is based on several assumptions that simply are not valid, at least as the so-called free market is known in the United States. Free-market theory rests on the imperfect assumptions that:

- Human beings are motivated essentially by economic wants.
- People have perfect information on which to make rational economic choices.
- Demand is elastic (adjusts to changing prices).
- Production and price are elastic (producers can respond easily to shifts in demand).
- There is perfect competition.[4]

These assumptions frequently do not reflect real-life economics. The market often fails because human beings act on bases other than economic rationality. Producers, for example, often create demand through advertising—that is, they create artificial needs in people purely through the power of persuasive advertising and then fill these new needs at a profit to themselves.[5] Furthermore, people often do things because they enjoy doing them, even though there may be negative economic consequences. People do not have perfect information about goods and services and would probably not be able to assimilate and analyze all the information even if it were available. Time is limited, and choices must be made.

Nor is there perfect competition in the market. Instead, the economy is characterized by unevenness in the resources among producers. Some students of economic systems suggest that our economy actually is made up of two different groups of economic entities.[6] On one side are the large, powerful firms that are few in number but have the resources to persist and to influence other actors in the economy. Then there are many very small firms that find it difficult to compete because they lack the resources to keep up with technological innovations. They often are absorbed by the large firms or are forced out of existence because they are not competitive. Consumers, by the same token, have little ability to influence the powerful producers. The result is that little effective competition takes place in the economy, and therefore prices do not follow the supply-and-demand curve. What happens is that those with resources end up dominating the market, taking advantage of their power to further their own interests.

Finally, consumers' choices within the market may be limited. Even though the cost of gasoline may be very high, some people have no other way to get to work than by automobile and thus are limited in how much they can reduce consumption. Similarly, regardless of cost, a sick or injured person needs medical assistance.

Because of the failure of the free-market system to operate perfectly (*market failure*), many governments intervene to guide and control the economic system. Much government policy is based on the intent to protect citizens and consumers against fraud and abuse, to control monopolies (and thus help make the market truly free), and to protect against inequities and inefficiencies. On the other hand, if those with economic power also have political power, as is often the case, government policy also may be oriented toward protecting their interests. Still other goals of economic planners have been to keep the economy operating on a stable basis and to avoid constant sharp fluctuations between *inflation* with full employment and *recession* with unemployment. Such often-conflicting objectives have been difficult to pursue, and economic policy has been characterized by numerous unintended consequences and indirect impacts.

History of Government's Role

Many critics of government policies seem to mistakenly believe that the United States began with economic enterprise flourishing, free from intervention by the political system. Policies to influence economic activity have always been a part of the American political landscape. The American Revolution resulted, in part, from financial grievances of the colonists, who felt the British monarchy was unfairly impeding colonial development through its taxation policies. After the Revolution, policies affecting economic well-being continued to be a major concern. Witness the controversy surrounding the establishment of a national bank and its relationship to the national debt during George Washington's administration.

In its early history, the United States government stimulated the economy through public investment or attempts to create an environment in which the economy could prosper. The national government subsidized development through land grant programs to the railroad industry and to states to establish educational institutions that would, in turn, focus on supporting the agricultural economy. State governments set many precedents during this time in their attempts to spur economic growth. Roads and canals also were built with *government subsidy*, further illustrating government's efforts to stimulate development.

Although citizens became accustomed to government playing a supportive role in economic activity, they did not appear willing to accept government interference beyond that role. During the latter part of the nineteenth century, a very strong anti-government sentiment developed. The national government had begun to develop regulatory policies aimed at curbing some of the abuses of large corporate enterprises. Industry, however, was influential politically and was successful in convincing the political leadership to take a *laissez-faire* approach to economic activities.[7] It was not until the 1930s that government returned to an interventionist approach. The severe economic *depression* following the stock market crash of 1929 led people to accept a greater government role, but even then there was a great deal of hesitation about permitting government to become too deeply involved in private enterprise.

When the Great Depression first hit, the immediate response of President Herbert Hoover's administration was to raise taxes and try to balance the budget. Unfortunately, these actions exacerbated the problem. The nation, in no mood for half-measures, sought a new leader in Franklin D. Roosevelt, who quickly took another approach. He convinced Congress to create several new agencies and programs to address the extraordinary problems of unemployment and the slump in production. This whirlwind of legislative action was unprecedented; within the first 100 days of Roosevelt's first term, Congress

- passed the Emergency Banking Act, which was intended to put the banking industry back on a solid foundation;
- created the Civilian Conservation Corps, a public works program to hire the unemployed directly by government;
- funded state welfare programs through the Federal Emergency Relief Act;
- passed the National Industrial Recovery Act to regulate wages, collective bargaining, and work hours, and to permit business to organize combinations to eliminate waste and some forms of competition;
- created the Agricultural Adjustment Administration to support agricultural production and prices; and
- created the Securities and Exchange Commission to protect investors.

These measures represent only a few of the new programs; an era had begun in which governmental intervention in economic matters would grow immensely. It is important to note, however, that these programs maintained the tradition of government support for economic prosperity and that intervention was limited to rebuilding the economy through aid to particular enterprises. Later came government efforts to influence the private sector to perform in a particular way, sometimes against its will. These programs helped in curing the ills of the Depression, but they did not lead to complete prosperity for the economic system.

During the late 1930s, many leaders, including Roosevelt, became convinced that the free-market system could not regulate itself satisfactorily. The Depression had shown that some of the assumptions of free-market theory, discussed earlier, were not valid. Now it was recognized that, for a variety of reasons, sometimes severe fluctuations in the market economy were inevitable without government intervention. Influenced by the ideas of John Maynard Keynes, whose *General Theory of Employment, Interest, and Money* suggested new approaches to the relationship between government and the economy, Roosevelt and his administration began to modify public policy.[8] Not until the economic impact of World War II became apparent, however, was the immense power of the political system in influencing the economy recognized. Active government intervention began in virtually every aspect of the economy.

The wartime economy of the early 1940s, dictated in large part by the government, had clearly stimulated employment and economic growth. Recognition that government spending could create such dramatic effects created the foundation for sustained government action to influence desirable economic activity and to correct problems in the economy. It was, then, during the late 1940s that maintenance of prosperity became a major public issue. Today, this recognition remains one of the most, if not *the* most, important concerns of any national administration. The American people now expect the government to take action to resolve problems in the economy, but there are major differences of opinion on just what action will produce the desired results. The contrasts between the philosophies of Friedman and Galbraith outlined at the beginning of this chapter are examples of opposing perspectives on what the role of government should be.

Today, few argue that government has no appropriate role in the economic sector. Instead, controversy exists over where government should intervene, and for whom. We already have reviewed most of the areas of responsibility. Traditionally, one purpose of government economic policy has been to stimulate economic growth. In the 1970s, however, many economic policies also had to address problems of scarcity, particularly in energy and food. Another purpose of economic programs is protecting and supporting the private enterprise system through promoting full employment, protecting the well-being of citizens, and controlling the pressures of inflation and recession. Ultimately, economic policies also result in redistributing resources among the various groups in society. Government involvement in the economy supports both the prosperity goal and meeting the needs of people purposes of government.

Inflation and Recession

Inflation is a rise in price of goods and services, even though the actual value of those goods and services does not increase. Thus, although prices increase, production does not keep pace, resulting in a decline in the purchasing power of money—that is, each dollar purchases less than it did in the past.

Inflation may occur when the demand for goods and services grows at a faster rate than available supplies. Competing consumers drive up the prices for such goods. This type of inflation is known as *demand-pull inflation*. Another type, *cost-push inflation*, refers to an increase in the cost of a product, even though demand remains constant or drops. It occurs when prices are regulated in some way rather than impersonally set by supply and demand. A rise in oil prices, for example, can cause cost-push inflation, as do increases in wage rates without a corresponding rise in productivity. Normally during periods of demand-pull inflation, employment goes up, although this may not be true during times of cost-push inflation. We shall see in Chapter 4 why different remedies are appropriate to these different inflation forms. The inflation of the 1970s and early 1980s seemed to result from a combination of demand-pull and cost-push factors. The demand-pull inflation was clearly initiated by the attempt to fight the Vietnam War without a tax increase. Military spending pumps many additional dollars into the economy without generating a corresponding increase in consumer goods and services that those dollars can buy and is therefore the most inflation-ary kind of spending. Once this inflation is generated, the wage-price spiral of cost-push inflation perpetuates it.

Recessions are periods in which there is a decline in economic activity arising from a slump in effective demand for goods and services. An oversupply of goods and services may cause a drop in production, leading to increased unemploy-ment. Unemployed people are able to purchase less, thus further nourishing the recession. Most recently, recessions hit the United States from 1981 to 1982, 1991, and in 2001–2002. In 2007, another recession began, as foreclosures on mortgages surged and the economy lost many jobs. There is disagreement on whether it ended in early 2010 with the Federal Reserve seeming to indicate that it did in fact end and the National Bureau of Economic Research saying it ended in June of 2009. Prolonged recessions are called *depressions*.

Microeconomic Approaches

Government concerns about the economy fall into two groups, *microeconomic* and *macroeconomic policy*. Generally, microeconomic policy refers to government ac-tivities regarding particular firms and businesses, and macroeconomic policy refers to the overall management of the economy. Examples of microeconomic policy are regulation and subsidy programs. Macroeconomic policy includes monetary and fiscal policies. Microeconomic approaches are the primary subject of the rest of this chapter; macroeconomic approaches are examined in the next chapter.

Government intervention now extends to almost every aspect of our lives in efforts to protect the health, safety, welfare, and environment and to promote economic and social justice. The emphasis in this chapter, however, is on interven-tion that directly affects economic activity. Other chapters address government activities as they relate to other substantive areas, such as the environment, health, education, and equality of opportunity.

As noted earlier, the U.S. government has always intervened in economic activities. Early on, those activities were supportive and eventually gave way to a more regulatory approach. Today, we have a combination of the two. Regula-tion may be characterized as old style (economic) regulation or new style (social) regulation. Each has an impact on economic activity and the viability of eco-nomic enterprises.

Economic Regulation.   Old style, or economic, regulation, in the form of early antitrust laws, began as a way of controlling concentrations of wealth and power in large private-sector economic enterprises; the purpose was to ensure that private economic gain did not hurt the public interest. Guarding the public interest generally meant protection against economic abuse of citizens by prohi-biting such practices as charging unreasonable prices, engaging in anticompetitive activities, or selling products hazardous to the health and safety of the public. Basically, the regulators are meant to be watchdogs for the public. In addition to protecting the public interest, economic regulation had the objective of preserving competition and controlling natural monopolies.

Regulatory agencies normally have a fair degree of independence from other governmental institutions. In establishing regulatory agencies, legislative bodies delegate certain of their policymaking powers to them and try to protect them as much as possible against interference from the executive branch. An *independent regulatory commission*, such as the Federal Trade Commission (FTC), for example, is created by legislative action. The mandate that Congress gave to the FTC is somewhat vague: to regulate in the interest of ensuring competition and to prevent deceptive advertising by industry. Five commissioners serve staggered seven-year terms on this commission, with the provision that no more than three may be from the same political party. The president designates one member as chairperson. Once appointed by the president and confirmed by the Senate, a commissioner may not be removed by the president except under unusual circumstances. Other regulatory agencies are similarly created and members similarly appointed, although the number of commissioners varies from agency to agency. Much regulating also is carried out by units within regular operating departments of the executive branch that are, therefore, less independent of the president. One example is the Food and Drug Administration in the Department of Health and Human Services. The Department of Justice also regulates activities through its prosecution of parties for violation of laws and rules.

Congress often gives regulatory agencies relative independence from the president because partisan politics should have no place in regulation, and it does not want to surrender its powers to the executive branch. Another reason Congress delegates its powers is simply that it does not have the time, expertise, or other resources to carry out the specialized activities for which regulatory agencies are created. Ideally, the application of expertise and technical judgment is supposed to be free of politics. Though insulated from partisan political forces to the extent that board or commission members have fixed terms and ordinarily cannot be removed by the president, regulatory agencies have not escaped politics entirely. Rather, they are subject to many political pressures from interest groups, legislative committees, and the White House. For example, the Federal Communications Commission (FCC) became much more concerned with indecency on television after George W. Bush was elected in 2000 as he appointed a chair of the FCC who was concerned with the issue. After the infamous 2004 Super Bowl halftime wardrobe malfunction, in which Justin Timberlake exposed the breast of Janet Jackson as they were performing, television viewers and politicians brought pressure on the Commission to do something about it. The FCC eventually fined CBS $550,000 ($27,500 for each of the twenty CBS-owned stations). The FCC action has caused much self-censorship by television. Because Congress and the president have much to say about the budgets and, indeed, the very existence of regulatory agencies, the agencies pay attention to opinions from those sources as well.

In applying their expertise to problems, regulatory agencies give meaning to the general policies developed by legislative bodies. To do so, regulatory agencies adopt rules and regulations that have the force of law. Unlike legislative policymakers, however, regulatory agencies also enforce and serve as judges regarding policy. Thus, once they draw up a rule or regulation, they have the responsibility to see that the regulated party abides by the rules. They also decide whether a rule has been violated by an individual party and fashion a punishment appropriate for the violation.

Of course, a commission itself cannot do all the work of a regulatory agency and usually performs only the policymaking and judging functions. Commission policy is executed by its staff, although the staff also creates policy and does the major work in investigating and hearing evidence on cases in which violation of policy is charged. Once a hearing examiner (now called administrative law judge) has heard and evaluated the evidence, the examiner makes a recommendation on how the case should be decided. Normally, the commission accepts the examiner's recommendation, although changes may be made by the commission.

Social Regulation.   New style, or social, regulation attempts to correct problems in society through incentives or regulation to encourage or control various behaviors involving health, safety, welfare, and working conditions. Economic enterprises often are the vehicles for achieving social policy goals and thus are the objects of government intervention. Social regulation may be in the form of financial penalties, such as in emissions fees or fines for emitting pollutants into the air. Presumably, private enterprise will reduce emissions to avoid the financial penalties. An alternative approach is to encourage action by providing financial subsidies for conversion of polluting plants or bonuses for early compliance. Another alternative is to allocate permits for a specific level of emissions. By reducing emissions below its permitted level, a company could sell portions of its permit to others (*cap and trade*). Presumably, such a system would serve as an incentive to modernize equipment and reduce pollution or at least stop addition of more pollution. Policies that require contractors with the government to subcontract a certain portion of the contract with businesses owned by minorities or females represent another alternative for achieving a social goal.

Typically, social regulation occurs through already established executive departments, although there are exceptions as with the Equal Employment Opportunity Commission, which operates like the typical economic independent regulatory commission. Many social policies are implemented through contract compliance activities or through such departments as Labor and Commerce, although all departments have some role in such activities. State governments mirror many of the national regulatory activities and have many of their own regulatory agencies.[9]

Regulation of economic activity is an attempt to stabilize the economy and protect the interests of the general public. We already have looked at the most common form of regulation in the United States, agencies that create specific rules and regulations to control the behavior of economic enterprises or that provide incentives or penalties to encourage particular actions. Control of activities also is accomplished in several other ways. These methods include government ownership and the creation of government corporations. Ownership of public lands by the Department of the Interior is intended to control how the land is used. The U.S. Postal Service and the Federal Deposit Insurance Corporation are government-owned corporations that regulate and control many postal and banking activities. In addition, there are many programs and policies to protect particular economic interests. In agriculture, for example, many of the programs and policies subsidize particular economic entities and interfere with the free market. The case studies examined next demonstrate the different types of government intervention to support and control economic enterprises.

CONTEMPORARY POLICY: CASE STUDIES IN ECONOMIC INTERVENTION

In the following section, we examine how different forms of microeconomic intervention have been applied in influencing the economy through *antitrust policy* and subsidy of business activity, and old and new style regulation. Virtually every aspect of the economy is subject to some intervention by government, but to inventory them all here would be impossible. These case studies will illustrate pertinent approaches to today's economic policy.

The Federal Trade Commission: Traditional Economic Regulation

Around the close of the nineteenth century and the beginning of the twentieth, various energetic business entrepreneurs managed to acquire near monopolies on many American industries, including steel and the railroads. These concentrations of power in a few hands were accompanied by many abuses. Consumers were charged exorbitant prices, small companies were bullied into selling out or were ruined by the large firms, and local governments were pressured into making concessions. Workers in such monopolies, with almost no bargaining power, were exploited at will by ruthless employers. All of these factors led to the reaction, by the public and politicians alike, that concentration of economic power in a small number of enterprises was not in the public interest. A movement grew in the United States to regulate industry through antitrust policy (a trust is a combination of several companies, especially one that limits competition). In time, a series of laws was enacted that forms the framework of today's government controls over such economic concentration. Policies eventually went beyond antitrust to include other types of protection of the general public and to support corporate entities as well.

Antitrust policy is aimed at preventing one or a small number of firms from directly dominating all or most of a particular market. It also attempts to prevent private firms from agreeing among themselves to restrict competition. Thus, antitrust policy prohibits monopolies, as well as practices and agreements that fix prices, divide markets, or collude on bidding. To control monopolies and to dissolve those that had already come into being, Congress passed the Sherman Antitrust Act in 1890. The Federal Trade Commission Act of 1914 went further by creating the Federal Trade Commission to stem the development of monopolies and prevent practices that would lead to unfair competition. Because these laws were only partially successful, the policy was strengthened in 1950 with the Anti-Merger Act, which gave enforcement powers to administrative agencies. As part of its activities, the FTC has the responsibility to control anticompetitive and unfair trade practices and to protect consumers from unfair advertising.

Taken together, the antitrust laws give government a number of enforcement tools. The Sherman Act and subsequent legislation make illegal any action in restraint of interstate commerce. Government attorneys, currently the Antitrust Division of the Justice Department, can initiate criminal prosecution against companies charged with this violation. Additionally—and with greater effect—the Antitrust Division may initiate civil suits to obtain court orders requiring firms to cease practices that are found to be in restraint of trade. A similar proceeding may require a firm to break up into several units; the Standard Oil Corporation, for example, was divided into a number of companies in this way during the early part of the twentieth century. AT&T, which controlled 83 percent of the telephone market, was the object of antitrust litigation. Because the government's case was so strong, the company settled out of court in 1982 and agreed to dissolve, resulting in the current decentralized telephone service structure. Starting in 1995, the Antitrust Division charged Microsoft with anticompetitive practices and by 1997 sought orders to break up the company and to require it to desist from some practices. While Microsoft lost the case, it still has been slow to change its practices. Complaints about its software bundling practices, which force purchasers of Microsoft's operating system to buy other Microsoft software, continue to arise. In 2010, for example, Microsoft still owned more than 95 percent of the market in PC operating systems, but many experts suggest that development of smart phones will shift market share of computing devices overall away from Microsoft.

The Antitrust Division also has the authority to approve or disapprove *mergers*. In the 1980s, the Justice Department took essentially a hands-off approach leading to virtually uncontrolled mergers. The Clinton administration approach was mixed in that it looked more carefully at mergers, but most of the effort was in adjusting terms of the mergers to assure market competition rather than disallowing them. The Bush administration took a hands-off approach to mergers.[10] The Obama administration has signaled "reinvigorated antitrust enforcement," and began review of guidelines on mergers in 2009 and 2010 after being very critical of the hands-off approach of the Bush administration.

Another weapon that can be used is a suit by an individual who has been hurt by an antitrust violation. Current law permits court awards of triple the amount of damages suffered. But relying on such suits is not a very effective method of enforcing regulations: Both lack of interest and the large amount of time required of the litigants and courts in such procedures discourage victims from suing. It is not an efficient method of controlling behavior unless all the parties affected join in a class action suit. Nonetheless, the Recording Industry Association of America (RIAA) uses suits against those who download copyrighted music from the Internet to discourage the practice. RIAA first subpoenas the Internet Service Provider (ISP) for names and addresses of peer-to-peer file sharers and then selectively sues the users. RIAA hopes the threat of suit causes people to stop the sharing. Many universities have cooperated with RIAA to take away Internet access to anyone who is found to be illegally sharing files.

Class action suits are those in which an individual or individuals sue on behalf of all people who are in a similar situation. Thus, a female employee who has been discriminated against in pay and promotional opportunities may sue her employer for remedy and may include all other female employees who had worked for the employer during the same period of time. Those female employees would be part of the class on whose behalf litigation is initiated. Because of the large number of people who may be affected in such cases, and because courts usually have required litigants to demonstrate personal injury in order to be a party to a court action, class-action suits have been difficult to pursue. Also, courts often require the litigants to identify and notify all members of the class. This requirement can be difficult to meet because the people are hard to locate, and many may be too indifferent to respond. As a result, class action suits are not a major means of accomplishing regulation, although they are used on occasion.[11] In 2006, the Electronic Frontier Foundation filed a class action suit against AT&T for giving customer records to the National Security Agency (NSA) on calls overseas. NSA did this at the behest of the president as part of the anti-terror program. The suit alleged it was in violation of legislative and constitutional privacy rights of customers. The case was dismissed in 2009 because Congress passed the *Foreign Intelligence Act Amendments of 2008,* which granted telecommunications retroactive immunity for violations of the *Foreign Intelligence Act of 1978.* Federal courts have been reluctant to accept class action lawsuits; thus, state courts have handled most of them. Critics of class action lawsuits claim that lawyers shop around for states where the courts are most amenable to such suits. As a result, President Bush in 2005 pushed reform through Congress requiring most class action suits to be filed in federal courts, resulting in a decline in state courts and an increase in federal courts.

FTC Hearings. Until the late 1930s, antitrust legislation was not very effective because the Supreme Court was unsympathetic to such regulation. In particular, judges were hesitant to rule in favor of restrictions on the use of private property—owners were protected in their right to use their property as they saw fit. In its first decision regarding the Sherman Act, for example, the U.S. Supreme Court held that manufacturing was exempt from the act because it was not commerce.[12] Ironically, the Sherman Act became an ally of business because the court interpreted it to restrict labor unions as restraints of trade.[13] After 1937, however, the Supreme Court's receptivity to antitrust action grew, and the Federal Trade Commission became more active in pursuing antitrust violators. Cases have involved action against Exxon Oil Corporation; International Telephone and Telegraph; cereal companies; Heinz and Beech-Nut baby food companies; Kroger and Winn Dixie grocers; Coca-Cola and PepsiCo, along with five other soft drink companies; and many others. The FTC, however, has not always been very successful in these cases. The ironies of antitrust policy were evident in 1997 when the FTC approved the merger of Boeing and McDonnell Douglas, resulting in a single aircraft manufacturer in the United States. However, it opposed the merger of Staples and Office Depot, office supply retailers, on the basis that the merger would lead to control of too much of the market: it would result in Staples being the only such retailer in some local markets.

The Federal Trade Commission, like most regulatory agencies, has a small staff and budget compared to the corporations it confronts in its work. The opportunities for the regulated parties to delay or buy time are many, some the result of procedural protections required by the courts or the FTC's own rules. These requirements give FTC proceedings the aura of a courtroom process. Complaints are investigated by the staff and a formal hearing may ensue. The hearing requires notice to the parties involved, and each has the opportunity to present its case. Parties under investigation sometimes inundate the agency with volumes of testimonial material, considerably lengthening the time it takes for the investigation and hearing to be completed. Afterwards, the administrative law judge must evaluate the record before making a decision. With the record often comprising thousands of pages of very complex material, the examiner has a formidable task and needs time to reflect on the evidence.

Once the process is completed, a party to the case may appeal the decision of the administrative law judge. The full commission then hears the case as if it were a totally new proceeding. The same opportunity for delays exists here. After the commission makes its decision, the defendants in the case may appeal to the courts, and—given the high stakes in many cases—litigation can drag on for years, first through the appellate courts, then on to the Supreme Court. A case involving the makers of the diet supplement Geritol, for example, took thirteen years to resolve, although the FTC finally was successful in getting Geritol's ads—which claimed the product cured "tired blood" and "iron deficiency anemia"—removed from the air.[14] The amount of time and money expended caused many to question whether the whole process was worth it.

The FTC also is subject to political whims. Members of the commission are political appointees of the president and, of course, tend to reflect the president's political philosophy. Additionally, Congress controls the FTC's budget; thus, there is a tendency to be careful not to offend important members of Congress. During the 1960s, for example, Ralph Nader and his Center for the Study of Law in the Public Interest conducted a study of the Federal Trade Commission and castigated it for being timid and unresponsive to the consumer. A similarly critical report was issued by the American Bar Association in 1969. With the popularity of the consumer protection movement increasing in the 1960s and into the 1970s, members of Congress prodded the FTC to become aggressive in protecting the consumer. The agency responded and became active in pushing consumer rights.

By 1979, the commission had become so aggressive that many industries began to exert pressure on Congress to limit its activities. During 1979 and 1980, for example, the funeral industry, life insurance industry, and many professionals including doctors, dentists, and lawyers brought pressure on Congress to limit the authority of the FTC to regulate their business practices. Many members of Congress agreed with their complaints, and it appeared that the powers of the FTC might be severely limited. Although Congress ultimately did not adopt this policy, the prospect of such restrictions does illustrate the tenuous position of the agency. Created to protect the consuming public, the FTC often finds itself the object of intense political pressures to conform to industry's position on regulation. The election of Ronald Reagan as president in 1980 led to a swing entirely in the opposite direction from the consumer protection focus of the 1970s. During the 1980s, the FTC became a protector of private enterprise, and budgets and staff were severely slashed. After 1989, with the President George H. W. Bush's appointment of Janet D. Steiner to the chair, the FTC developed a balanced stance, and Clinton and second Bush administration appointees continued this approach with a little more assertiveness on the commission's part. It pursued price-fixing cases but placed little focus on mergers. The current position of the FTC appears to be that the free market can work, but that consumers have rights as well, and a balance between those interests is the best policy.

Mergers.   The role of the Justice Department's Antitrust Division in the Reagan administration led to an era of almost uncontrolled mergers. The Antitrust Division stopped challenging mergers except in rare cases. As a result, some very large mergers, which probably would not have been approved in any previous administration, were completed. The $20.3 billion Kohlberg Kravis and Roberts Company deal to buy RJR Nabisco attracted a lot of attention in 1988, as the most expensive to that date. There were many implications, not the least of which was that approval by the Justice Department signaled that mergers were not of much concern to it. The first Bush administration appeared to favor some regulation of mergers, and 1990 did witness a decline in the number and value of mergers. There was an upswing in mergers again in the 1990s, a sharp decline beginning in 2001, and gradual increase starting in 2004 (see Figure 3.1). The causes may be economic as much as policy-based, given the ups and downs of the economy. In December 2000, the FTC approved the merger of America Online, Inc. (AOL) and Time Warner Inc. in a deal worth $166 billion. In 2004, mergers included Comcast Corporation and Walt Disney Company, as well as J.P. Morgan Chase and Bank One Corporation. Cingular Wireless and AT&T merged in 2004 as well. Mergers in banking, health care, communications, airlines, and many other industries continued with little government

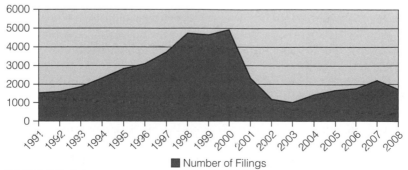

FIGURE 3.1

intervention. Since 2004, mergers have increased again. In 2007, Whirlpool acquired Maytag, meaning it would control about two-thirds of most household appliance manufacturing, and the government approved AT&T's acquisition of BellSouth, creating a dominant communications enterprise. In 2010, Continental Airlines and United Airlines announced plans to merge to become the largest airline in the world. Government regulators appear to be ready to approve the merger.

The courts have been less hostile to mergers as well in recent years. In the past, market share was a very important consideration in decisions on mergers. The FTC and the courts were likely to disallow any merger that increased market share of a corporation by even as much as 10 percent. In recent years, mergers have been allowed wherein market share was increased as much as 40 percent or, as in the case of Boeing and McDonnell Douglas, 100 percent of domestic production. The courts have sanctioned such mergers even when the FTC has been opposed.

Weaknesses in U.S. antitrust policy are the result of many factors. One is a lack of clarity about goals. Given the responsibility to restore competition and prevent deceptive advertising, the FTC and the Justice Department would seem to have easily understood objectives. However, these are rather ambiguous goals in terms of the precise actions that might be taken to achieve them. Another factor also explains sometimes erratic performance: The commission and the Justice Department have discretion as to which of these objectives they emphasize. As different presidents influence these regulators through their appointments, the perspectives of the agencies vary. Thus, uneven attention is given to enforcement of rules and regulations. Ambivalence about how strongly antitrust policy should be pursued also provides regulated industries with opportunities to articulate their positions. Industries have the resources and contacts to make their concerns known to regulators, who are often sympathetic in the first place. They are usually effective in mobilizing political forces to reduce the intensity of the enforcement efforts. With the increasingly globally competitive environment, there also are pressures to be more flexible with domestic corporations so that they can compete with foreign corporations.

Global Approaches to Antitrust.   Industrialized nations generally favor some form of control over *monopoly* and restraint of trade, although some nations, such as Italy, have virtually no antitrust or antimonopoly laws. Reflecting a different perspective, most Western European nations identify their policies as competition policies as opposed to antitrust policies, as they are named in the United States. Although many of the Western European nations use approaches similar to that of the United States, there are variations. Some countries have weaker policies. For example, in Great Britain the approval of Parliament is required before the Monopolies Commission can prevent mergers. This provision opens regulation much more directly to political pressures and thus lessens its effectiveness. So long as mergers are not found to be contrary to the public interest, they are not prohibited. Very seldom does British government find them to be harmful.

Germany represents the opposite end of the spectrum. There, government approval is required before mergers of large corporations can occur. More significantly, the German Cartel Office also has the authority to dissolve a corporation brought about by merger. Most European nations employ an approach somewhere between these two extremes.

Japan appears less enthusiastic about controlling competition. Nonetheless, after World War II, policy to break up monopolies was imposed upon Japan. Although enforcement has been weak, the law was strengthened in 1977, and efforts have been made to limit price fixing and protect consumers through communication about abuses.[15]

Globalization of the economy poses particular challenges for businesses and regulation. The merger of AT&T and BellSouth required approval of the FTC and three other countries because of its global implications. In 2007, Microsoft lost an appeal to the European Union's Court of First Instance, which upheld a 2004 European Commission antitrust decision against Microsoft. As a result, Microsoft has to sell an unbundled version of Windows and share information about its operating system with competitors so that they can interface with Windows. The European Commission continued to focus on Microsoft's business practices in 2008 and 2009, illustrating that regulation is complicated by global policy and trade.

Community Revitalization Issues: Merging Social and Economic Concerns

All levels of government face rapidly changing economic conditions and technology, thus requiring governments to engage in economic development. Economically depressed areas are fraught with many social problems, such as unemployment, crime, deteriorated housing, and limited tax bases. During the 1980s, the concept of *enterprise zones* was imported from Great Britain and implemented in many states.[16] The national government adopted the idea when the Clinton administration made enterprise zones a major part of its urban policy. Beginning with nine such zones nationwide, the number has grown to more than a thousand such designations by national and state governments.[17] The designations carry various names, including Renewal Communities, Brownfield Communities, Empowerment Communities, Enterprise Communities, and Enterprise Zones.

The zones target economic development geographically. They are partnerships in which government and the private and nonprofit sectors work together to attempt to stimulate economic development and to solve some of the social problems associated with economically depressed areas. The experiments are examples of how government supports business. The zones provide for such benefits as reduced taxes, tax credits, technical assistance, and reduction or elimination of regulations so that private-sector entities can develop innovative economic activities.

In addition to the economic incentives and push for economic development, these zones focus intensive governmental agency attention to such social problems as crime, lack of good housing, and high unemployment in the zones. As economic development occurs, many of the social problems are expected to recede in severity, but not all can be cured by economic development alone. Thus, federal agencies, in cooperation with state and local units as well as private and non-profit organizations, work together to apply resources to address social problems.

The experience so far suggests that the zones can have beneficial effects, although it is difficult to measure just how much improvement can be attributed to the zones themselves. States usually provide income tax credits and some allow property tax abatements as well as waivers of sales taxes in the zone. Businesses building in some zones also receive discounts on utility bills. Encompassing broader purposes, some enterprise zones have reinvested the tax revenues generated in the zones in the infrastructure of the zones to improve conditions even more. Job training programs have been developed for zone residents in some cases.

As economic development tools, these initiatives represent a politically popular notion. Given a political climate supportive of less government and letting the private sector operate with fewer restrictions, the enterprise zone provides one avenue for doing so. Theoretically, innovative approaches will flow from the decreased taxation and regulation. Government is a facilitator, not the owner, of the process. Business benefits and, in the process, so do residents of the zone as well as the general public, who presumably bear less expense resulting from crime and other social problems.

These efforts, however, may cause dislocation of residents with the attendant breakdown of a sense of community. Finding new housing for displaced residents is not easy, either. Sometimes the social problems only move to a new area that becomes overpopulated with the press of residents who have been displaced. Critics of these approaches also note that economic development activity is attracted from other areas that might become economically depressed, thus just moving the problem. The loss in tax revenue caused by the tax abatements and waivers also concerns some people.

As noted earlier, government always has provided support to private enterprise, and these revitalization programs represent one facet of such support. Critics, however, often suggest that government goes too far in supporting economic enterprises. In the debate over government spending, conservatives in Congress target personal welfare and liberals challenge them to look at corporate welfare. They cite subsidies to corporations such as McDonald's, Campbell's Soup, and others to advertise abroad or billions in subsidies for agriculture that goes primarily to corporate farm organizations. Similarly, they note that mining companies gain title to land for much less than it is worth and then do not pay royalties on what they extract. Others note state and local government subsidies of professional sports teams through building of facilities paid for by tax dollars. Obviously, the list of the various types of support provided corporations is a long one. Liberals challenge their conservative colleagues to look at those benefits as they try to find ways of reducing government spending and the deficit.

International Trade

International trade represents another aspect of the current economic environment. Most administrations in recent history have supported free trade in theory.

In reality, the United States often fosters barriers like tariffs, import quotas, or subsidies to industries that give them advantages over others. Other nations do the same thing.

NAFTA.   The *North American Free Trade Agreement (NAFTA)*, enacted by Congress in November 1993, created a free trade area among the United States, Canada, and Mexico. Theoretically, NAFTA would result in the United States being better able to sell goods in the Mexican market and stimulate economic development in Mexico as well. Immigration pressures on the United States presumably would be lessened as better economic opportunities developed for Mexican citizens. Critics of the agreement feared the migration of U.S. jobs to Mexico and the lessening of health, safety, and environmental standards.[18] NAFTA built upon the United States–Canada Free Trade Agreement of 1988 which provides virtually free trade between the two countries.

The Omnibus Trade Act of 1988 provides for the United States to impose such restrictions as tariffs or import quotas on any trading partner that imposed barriers on American access to their markets. The trade act was a product of rising concern over the nation's growing trade deficit, particularly the trade imbalance with Japan. The act required the president to identify those nations with unfair trade practices and a large American trade surplus as targets for trade negotiations. If the negotiation process failed, American trade restrictions would follow as retaliation. It also created a training program for American workers adversely affected by international trade practices. Promotion of American exports and training for American industry to enhance the likelihood of success internationally also were parts of the act. The act has been used against even Canada over importation of Canadian lumber into the United States. Similarly, the United States has attempted to limit importation of clothing from China using the law.

GATT.   A major debate in Congress in 1994 involved ratification of agreements under the *General Agreement on Tariffs and Trade (GATT)*. GATT, established after World War II, was designed to reduce national tariff barriers to international trade. It took almost a decade to negotiate the agreement, and it stirred emotions within the political establishment. The agreement reduces tariffs on manufactured goods an average of nearly 40 percent. Presumably, that would translate into lower prices for consumers. Opponents say that reduced U.S. collection of tariffs add to the federal deficit (see Chapter 4).

Supporters of GATT argued that it would lead to increased sales of U.S. products around the world, while opponents pointed to the increased sales of foreign goods in the United States, thus eliminating jobs and lowering wages for American workers. The agreement provides more protection against piracy of software and other copyrighted works throughout the world. Advocates of the agreement also indicated that new markets would be opened for U.S. construction firms and architects and engineers.

Perhaps the most controversial part of the GATT agreement was the creation of the *World Trade Organization (WTO)*. WTO is the successor to GATT. It attempts to settle disputes and monitor and crack down on unfair trade practices. While advocates applaud the provision as bringing pressure on others to comply with fair trade practices, opponents suggest that it weakens health, safety, and labor laws in the United States. Further, they argue that it makes state and local governments conform to WTO policies and standards. Any suggestion of a world organization impinging on U.S. sovereignty arouses heated debate. Although political posturing during the 1994 election and after was intense, Congress did ratify the agreement in December of 1994. The United States joined 123 other nations in an effort to eliminate trade barriers on many items. Opponents of WTO argue that it has the power to override federal and state laws on labor and environmental standards among others. WTO decisions have affected many United States industries from food to steel. Many countries target United States subsidies of farm exports, and their complaints to WTO have been sustained. As a consequence, the level of subsidies is being reduced. An interesting case in 2005 involved Internet gambling. Antigua and Barbuda complained that U.S. restrictions on Internet gambling were illegal. WTO ruled that the United States could restrict such activity under its Wire Communications Act of 1961, based on protecting public morals or maintaining public order. At the same time, WTO said that the United States must apply its Interstate Horseracing Act equally to domestic and foreign betting services. Thus, online betting must be open to international outlets, a position the United States opposed. In 2007, WTO affirmed its earlier decision while criticizing the United States for ignoring the earlier ruling. Thus, WTO has both positive and negative consequences for the United States.

Many of the arguments for and against the GATT accord are the same as those for and against NAFTA. Neither the grand promises of NAFTA's advocates nor the dire predictions of its detractors seem to have developed. There are indications of success, especially in export of American goods to Mexico, although Mexico's monetary crisis and devaluation of the peso in 1995 slowed progress. NAFTA supporters point to improved economic conditions in Mexico as evidence that it is working. Opponents highlight the poverty and low wages in Mexico as evidence that NAFTA is not working and is hurting U.S. workers who command higher wages.

European Union.   Another issue related to trade and the economy is the move by the European Economic Community (EEC) to develop an integrated economy. In 1985, member nations of the EEC developed a detailed plan to achieve a unified economic system by the end of 1992. Restrictions on trade, services, flow of capital, and labor supply would be eliminated. The goal of this plan is to create an environment that stimulates economic growth in member nations. The EEC along with other European organizations became the *European Union (EU)* in 1993. With twenty-seven nations in 2010, growth in numbers continues. Croatia, Turkey, and Macedonia have applied to join. Former members of the Soviet bloc make up many of the recently added members. In 2002, the EU substituted the Euro for national currencies in all but Denmark, Great Britain, Norway, and Sweden. By 2005, the Euro was competing heavily with the U.S. dollar for world currency domination; however, by 2010, concern over whether the Euro would survive surfaced because of economic and monetary crises in several EU nations.

Successful implementation of the EU economic system provides major economic competition for the United States in the global economy. The EU represents a potential market of over 300 million consumers with a significant commercial and industrial base. The United States has yet to develop a comprehensive economic policy to address the impact of this change in Europe.

POLICY EVALUATION: ENCOURAGING COMPETITION OR DISCOURAGING INNOVATION?

Deregulation

A clear trend since the mid-1970s has been the *deregulation* of industries that were previously heavily regulated. The Carter administration began the process gradually by examining individual regulatory agencies and the industries they regulated. The Reagan and first Bush administrations took a more sweeping approach to deregulation, reflecting a strong commitment to a market economy free of governmental constraints. Ideologically, conservatives have been strong supporters of deregulation.

Deregulation is promoted as a consumer-oriented policy that will result in more competition and lower prices. In the rush to deregulate in the late 1970s and early 1980s, there was little consideration of the social benefits of regulation. With deregulation came many benefits to consumers and some parts of industry. Some businesses also suffered economic reversals. In the airline industry, for example, consumers benefited from increased competition as airfares declined. In the long run, airfares increased again, but competition sustained many bargain fares. Service to smaller communities suffered on occasion, and bunching of departure times around peak travel hours has led to complaints of delays and inconvenience. However, the public seems to prefer the bargain fares over matters of scheduling and service. The terrorist attacks of September 11, 2001, and near misses since then have caused more support for regulations to improve safety.

Similarly, there have been many calls for increased regulation of company-sponsored investment programs and of accounting firms after the collapse of Enron in 2002, followed by disclosure of WorldCom's financial mismanagement. Many companies were caught manipulating their books to make themselves look more profitable than they were. Even one of the most trusted auditing firms, Arthur Andersen, went from worldwide dominance to going out of business because of collaboration with corporate crooks. These scandals led to the Securities and Exchange Commission (SEC) strengthening standards for financial reporting and auditing. Nonetheless, in 2008, new scandals arose and many banks and investment firms teetered on the edge of bankruptcy because of poor investment strategies and some outright fraud. As a result, Lehman Brothers, a global financial investment firm, went out of business and another, Goldman Sachs, faced charges of securities fraud and other crimes by the federal government.

The U.S. government bailed out numerous firms and banks as a result of high-risk investment schemes and the housing market collapsed due to mortgage fraud and risky loans. Again, Congress moved to develop new regulations for the financial market and for banks.

The benefits of regulation in protecting consumers from capricious action, ensuring a reasonable distribution of important services at a fair cost, and protecting the health and safety of the community are now reemerging concerns as the effects of deregulation are assessed. As with any policy, deregulation has resulted in both positive and negative consequences.

The relaxation of regulation has had broader implications. Republican administrations in the 1980s and from 2000–2008 deemphasized implementation of such policies as antitrust, equal employment opportunity, and labor relations. The business sector found the administrators of these programs willing to interpret policies in ways more sympathetic to business. Thus, the National Labor Relations Board and the federal courts changed the direction of much of labor law. They permitted the use of bankruptcy laws, for example, to release corporations from contract obligations under collective bargaining agreements, as happened with Continental Airlines and the Manville Corporation. One effect is that labor unions found it necessary to accept bargaining agreements that scaled back their earnings and benefits. Corporations thus clearly have had a stronger hand in controlling their own destiny. While the Clinton administration generally was more supportive of labor and consumers, its tendency was cautious in reinstituting regulation, especially in light of the public complaints about the overregulated society. The George W. Bush administration emphasized the interests of business in removing as much regulation as possible. Businesses continued to get approval for relaxing rules on such things as labor agreements and pension obligations when they sought bankruptcy protection. Delta, United Airlines, and U.S. Airways for example, won many such concessions in courts.

Similarly, antitrust policy became more flexible since the early 1980s. The Federal Trade Commission seemed less interested than ever in prohibiting mergers based on the size of the market controlled. Merger mania began in the late 1970s and accelerated in the 1980s as the Reagan administration relaxed rules. Many of these mergers were *hostile takeovers* in which entrepreneurs took over undervalued corporations. The managers of the takeover targets usually are the most resistant to takeovers, although many stockholders also question the long-term wisdom of such actions. Mergers continued at a high rate until the 2001 recession, with many high-profile mergers in the 1990s and early 2000s. After 2004, they again rose until 2008, when they dipped.

Free Trade

Yet another aspect of the current business environment is the policy regarding international trade. Although the Reagan and first Bush administrations strongly supported free trade as a stated policy, they did exert pressure on foreign competition. Other nations were pushed to agree to voluntary import quotas on such items as steel, textiles, and automobiles. The expectation was that import quotas would improve the prospects of domestic industry to sell its products. After the 1984 election, the administration lessened its efforts in maintaining voluntary quotas. Without the political pressures of an election, it was easier for the administration to act consistently with its free trade stance. However, as the Reagan administration left office, it became involved in a trade war with members of the European Economic Community, which banned U.S. beef that had been fed growth hormones. The administration retaliated with duties equal to 100 percent of the value of food imports from those nations. At the same time, a free trade agreement was reached with Canada. The Bush administration signed a free trade agreement with Mexico, but was less inclined to do so with Western Europe and others. In addition, the Bush administration entered into negotiations with Canada and Mexico and the member nations of GATT. Eventually, NAFTA and GATT were negotiated and ratified in 1993 and 1994, respectively, under the auspices of the Clinton administration. In 2007, Congress refused to approve renewal of the president's *fast track authority* (meaning that Congress has to vote up or down on a treaty with no opportunity to change it) in negotiating trade agreements, thus making agreements more difficult to reach. In every session of Congress, bills are introduced to reinstitute fast track authority (also called *trade promotion authority*), but so far they have not succeeded.

Assistance to Business

The efforts to support economic enterprise reflect some reaction to the increasing criticism of government intervention as a regulator of business activity. Thus, instead of being seen as an inhibitor of economic innovation, the effort is to support new approaches. Government provides the support and facilitation of efforts, but is not the controller of those activities. In the states that have used enterprise zones in the past, supporters usually point to impressive numbers, especially in job creation. However, critics note that many of those jobs would have been created in the absence of enterprise zones or other support. While development and job creation may not have occurred in the particular locales, they probably would have happened in other places. Evaluation of the programs then needs to take into account program objectives other than just economic development. For example, do they actually help solve social problems?

The evidence on success of enterprise zones certainly is difficult to assess partly because there are few formal studies of their impact. Those studies that have been done are inconsistent in their conclusions. A 1994 study in Indiana concluded that enterprise zones were very successful in achieving their goals, while a similar study in New Jersey in 1996 found "no evidence" that the program improved economic conditions.[19] A 2004 study of California and Florida enterprise zones concluded that the zones "had no measurable impact on the employment of residents."[20] Another study published in 2004 found that the incentives used in such programs produce minimal effect for the cost.[21]

The use of *risk subsidies* is yet another way government supports economic enterprise. The use of subsidies in agriculture is well known. While normally couched in terms of helping the family farm, such subsidies usually protect corporate farms from risks of the market and ensure profits. The subsidies to sugar producers and tariffs on sugar imports protect the producers from the realities of the marketplace. In health care insurance, many proposals suggest subsidies for premiums for low-income, high risk populations.[22] The state of Massachusetts includes such a feature in its mandatory health care insurance. Similarly, the increase in public deposit insurance guarantees in the 1980s led some financial institutions into high-risk investments that ultimately resulted in the savings and loan crisis and huge costs to the national government to pay off depositors and investors. In 2009, the bailout programs for financial institutions and insurance and auto industry giants represented a form of subsidy for private corporations.

All of these elements of policy are sympathetic to the business community. The theoretical effects of government intervention in the economy were examined at the beginning of this chapter, but actual outcomes do not always match the expected results. Critics of regulation note that although much regulation is justified as a means of promoting competition, it often actually tends to stifle that competition. By making entry into a market very difficult, for example, regulation often restricts competition. Competition also is reduced by price controls, as was true in the airline industry until the 1980s. Ironically, for this same reason many industries also defend regulation. Assured of a comfortable environment in which to do business, industry can count on a certain profit margin. Complete competition would make its situation less predictable. Consumers, or consumer advocates, object to this arrangement because it results in higher prices.

Effects of Regulation

One impact that industry often complains of is that government regulation interferes with its capacity to operate efficiently in a free society. According to this charge, regulatory agencies have become pervasive in all economic areas, and their red tape and complex regulations make compliance almost impossible. Many agencies make conflicting demands on industry, and paperwork has increased to the point that industry must employ people solely to deal with government regulation. Confusion abounds: Industries are firmly instructed not to consider race, sex, age, or religion in personnel decisions and, at the same time, are required to submit data on their workforce according to the same taboo categories. Moreover, many critics wonder whether regulations are developed to benefit society or simply to keep the wheels spinning so the agency will have something to do.

Regulation also may have unintended consequences in terms of its effects on innovation. Generally, regulated industries appear to be less inclined to adopt new technology and improve their methods of doing business than are nonregulated industries.[23] As a result, regulated industry is likely to be outmoded and less efficient. This is especially true when regulation guarantees a profit. The losers are consumers. Many critics raised this issue regarding British Petroleum's (BP) close relationship with the U.S. Minerals Management Service (MMS) after the *Deepwater Horizon* oil spill in the Gulf of Mexico in 2010. Evidence indicated that MMS allowed BP virtually regulation-free rein to operate.

Regulation also is criticized for contributing to the cost of doing business. Estimates in 2005 ranged from $34 billion to $1.1 trillion in costs to businesses and consumers for just ninety-one programs, a small portion of such programs.[24] Putting that kind of money into nonproductive efforts diverts it from productive ones. However, critics—though usually agreeing that regulation has become excessive—are also anxious that deregulation not go too far, that is, to the point of eliminating legitimate controls.

A common complaint of consumer-oriented critics is that regulation is dominated by the regulated industries themselves, which have the money and other resources to keep abreast of policy. Consumers, especially individuals, find access to regulatory agencies difficult because they lack knowledge of procedures and because of the costs associated with input into decision making. Due to the fact that regulators constantly deal with people from the regulated industries, they develop strong rapport with them. It is only natural that the regulators should consider their interests when making decisions. After all, the regulators would have no one to regulate if they did not help promote their survival! This close relationship often results in strong industry influence and sometimes control over regulators. The interests of consumers may be ignored.

Closely related to the access issue is the complaint that regulatory agencies are outside normal political activities and therefore are not answerable to anyone but themselves and the industries they regulate. It is unreasonable to expect agencies to respond to the major concerns of society if they do not have to answer to the political leadership produced by that society. Of course, regulatory agencies were created to be independent of direct political pressure so that they could consider a wider public interest. This criticism goes to the heart of the original reason for creating independent regulatory agencies in the first place. Independence has both benefits and costs.

It sometimes is argued that government is too involved in too many aspects of everyday life. Government seems to take the position that people need guidance in everything they do, and so virtually no activity is free of government intervention. The duplication of effort, red tape, and examples of bureaucratic bungling, which are constantly given coverage in the news media, reinforce negative images of regulation. Tax revolts and a rejection of governmental paternalism have led to serious questioning of regulatory efforts. As anti-government feelings seem to grow, regulatory agencies face major challenges to their activities.

A new twist to these regulatory processes is the effort of the Federal Trade Commission to keep state and local governments from interfering with competition in the marketplace. Most notable have been those cases in which the FTC has successfully sued municipalities to force deregulation of taxicab companies and their fares as a restraint of trade. This emphasis is a new use of antitrust law consistent with the pro-business, free trade stance that national elections in the mid- and late 1990s and early 2000s seemed to support. After the disclosures of business practices of banks and financial firms and their contribution to the economic crisis of 2008–2010 and the impact of lax regulation in the Gulf of Mexico oil spill in 2010, people once again debated the merits of regulation versus deregulation.

Changes in Regulation

Changes in economic regulation have been many, and the effects have varied greatly. For example, the effects of de-emphasis of antitrust policy are very difficult to assess. While the business world generally applauds the reduction of control over its activities, consumers are not so sure of the benefits. The rash of mergers and leveraged buyouts create impressive profits for many opportunists, but there are usually losers as well. Many employees, especially white-collar employees, lose their jobs and pensions (e.g., Sears and Kmart in 2005) as a result of the inevitable restructuring of the corporations that are merged. New and reorganized companies often pay lower wages and provide fewer benefits. For the consumer, of course, mergers can lead to less competition and eventually higher prices. Stockholders also are potential losers as total corporate debt increases, exceeding total corporate assets.

Much deregulation in the business sector reduced sensitivity to safety concerns that affect employees. Thus, the effect on employees has been negative. The 2010 West Virginia Massey Energy Company coal mine disaster that left 29 miners dead, and the *Deepwater Horizon* oil rig explosion that killed 11 people and injured many more the same year, illustrate the impact of lax regulation. Similarly, the elimination of regulations on product safety can benefit producers in the short run and hurt consumers. In the long run, producers may also be hurt as lawsuits over liability for death and injury create major financial setbacks.

Mergers themselves do not always work out well. Many of them are undone through divestiture or spinning off parts of the acquired companies. For example, Daimler-Benz and Chrysler merged in 1998; by 2007, the merged company, DaimlerChrysler, agreed to dissolve. Daimler-Benz paid $36 billion for Chrysler in 1998 and the merged company never was a success. So, in 2007, the company sold 80 percent of its assets for $8.9 billion, losing a lot of money. There are numerous examples of similar experiences in which neither party to the merger benefited. In recent years, many of those companies that had diversified have begun divesting in order to narrow their focus and concentrate on what they do best. In this scenario, competition increases in some areas. Among those splitting up and paring down are RCA Corporation, ITT, Gulf and Western, and Textron. Supporters of deregulation claim that this trend also is a result of the greater flexibility allowed by deregulation. At the same time, many of these newly separate companies merge with other similar companies (i.e., Mobil with Exxon and Texaco with Chevron).

Government economic intervention in the form of subsidies and supports for enterprise has raised serious questions as well. The federal government's efforts to stimulate and stabilize financial institutions through loans and loan guarantees, for example, have made them safe places for investors to place their money, but these supports have, at the same time, encouraged risky investments leading to bank and savings and loan failures. Similarly, the federal government provides loans and loan guarantees to homeowners, college students, farmers, and others; moreover, it guarantees other financial instruments, such as pensions. In 2007, many worried about the mortgage industry and government guarantees of credit in it as a possible source of more liability for government, only to see the collapse of the housing industry in 2009 because of mortgage credit abuses. Congress passed, and President Obama signed, financial regulatory reform legislation in 2010 in an effort to ensure that more such liabilities do not develop.

Even though there are questions about support for private enterprise, it always has been a part of American economic policy. Experiments utilizing the concept of enterprise zones are attempting to integrate economic and social issues in a comprehensive program focused on particular geographic areas, but experience is mixed. Many of the successes claimed in jobs created, industries enticed to open in the zones, and improvements in services in the area may have occurred without the enterprise zones. Nonetheless, the zones offer support in the form of subsidies, tax breaks, and technical assistance to business.

The globalization of the world economy and the emergence of the EU have created a new environment for the private sector as well, resulting in efforts by the national government to negotiate trade agreements whose primary emphasis is reducing the barriers to free trade as in NAFTA. Produce farmers claim that they have been hurt by lower production costs in Mexico and thus lower prices for their produce. The movement of industry to Mexico to take advantage of cheap labor has not increased to the extent the opponents of NAFTA had claimed. GATT and WTO represent another effort to reduce trade barriers and some industries are certain to be hurt. The textile industry, in particular, has been hurt because of the inexpensive labor in those industries in many countries, while high-tech and construction industries benefit. Regulators struggle to keep up with changing technology. Copyright enforcement faces challenges with Internet access to all forms of copyrighted material. The laws creating regulation did not anticipate the change that occurred in all areas of communication technology.

REFORMING THE RELATIONSHIP OF GOVERNMENT AND THE ECONOMY

There are many suggestions for reform in government's relationship to the economy. As indicated earlier, many of the recommendations deal with eliminating government's intervention in economic activity. Thus, creation of a free-market economy independent of government influence is seen as a means to stimulate economic enterprise toward more productivity and to restore the economy to a strong position. However, given the long history of government involvement, it is highly unlikely that such action is possible. As critics of Milton Friedman's ideas (noted earlier) suggest, a true free market is likely to produce a situation in which those groups with power dominate the system. There would not be freedom for all participants to compete equally.

Perhaps the most drastic reform proposal is that regulatory agencies be abolished.[25] Legislative bodies create regulatory agencies because of their own inability to regulate. Regulatory agencies became little legislatures of their own, enjoying independence from normal political controls. Advocates of reform want a return to citizen control through elected political leaders and believe that redistributing control over economic activities among the three branches of government would permit the public to influence the regulators' activity more effectively. A variation on this theme is that because much regulatory activity ends up in the slow-moving courts, regulatory agencies could be abolished and the courts could be assigned the responsibility in the first place. Although courts usually are viewed as inappropriate for regulation because of their slowness and lack of expertise, the increasing slowness of regulatory agencies tends to undermine the argument. Nonetheless, courts may only respond to cases brought to them, and they lack the ability to oversee constantly a particular economic activity.

Abolition of the regulatory agencies may appeal to many, but given the tendency of Congress to create more and more regulatory policies and the agencies to enforce them, it is unlikely that such proposals will enjoy much success. First, there are too many interests that oppose abolition, including the regulatory agencies themselves, their clientele, and the beneficiaries of agency regulation. Consider, for example, the obstacles faced by the Reagan administration in its first year as it whittled away at various regulators' powers but failed to dismantle completely all but a few. Second, another factor in opposing abolition is that regulatory policy is likely to have less visibility if placed in a regular administrative department. A particular regulatory policy then may have to compete with other agency priorities and—especially if controversial—may be buried by the agency's politics. Robbed of its independent status, the regulatory unit is likely to be less effective. Hence, for both political and practical reasons, completely abolishing regulatory agencies seems improbable.

Future Alternatives

Deregulation.   Deregulation, very popular among reformers, has enjoyed moderate success. We saw, for example, how the airline industry experienced a dramatic deregulation in pricing and, to a great extent, in the geographic areas its various companies could serve. But if some deregulation is good, does that automatically mean that total deregulation would be better? Again, consider the airline situation: Although some well-traveled markets prospered, other marginal areas suffered under partial deregulation. The failure of many airlines since deregulation raises concern, and concentration of the market in a few companies leads to decreasing competition. In 2005, major airlines began increasing fares, leading many to believe that the era of low fares resulting from deregulation was over. When the flying public resisted increasing fares, airlines instituted fees on everything from baggage to use of lavatories on the plane. The question becomes one of weighing costs against social objectives, such as the need to serve communities that cannot support the service on a purely economic basis. Regulation can have several objectives, whereas deregulation proposals often focus on only the economic factor.

Some of the effects of deregulation have generated suggestions for again regulating some industries, for example, the airline and trucking industries.

Representatives of America West Airlines (one of the airlines developed with deregulation that later merged with U.S. Airways) blamed chaotic market conditions for the company's financial troubles in the late 1990s and early 2000s and predicted disaster for the industry without some controls. Others are concerned that deregulation did not consider social costs and should do so.

Incentives.   A number of new ideas come from industries that would like to put some controls on what they see as overregulation. One alternative proposed by some is that regulatory policy should focus on results rather than on punishment for violations. If the intent of a policy is to improve safety for employees, for example, the most effective method of accomplishing such an objective might be to reward industries for good safety records.

Another idea is that new rules and regulations should include assessing their economic impact. Congress already considers the economic impacts of its policies. Regulators now are required to make such assessments. Congress appears to be strongly in support of identifying the costs up front.

Sunset Laws.   *Sunset laws* are yet another favored means of preventing excessive regulation. Sunset legislation requires that agencies and their programs be given specific periods of existence and be reviewed at the end of the time allotted. Thus, five years might be a common life span for an agency; at the end of that time it would have to justify its existence. The idea is that the regulatory agency would of necessity eliminate unneeded and nonconstructive activities in order to pass this five-year review. Similar state sunset laws exist. This evaluation can lead to better performance and to a careful consideration by the legislature of whether to continue a regulatory activity.

Nationalization.   At the polar opposite of deregulation and regulatory abolition lies *nationalization*. Nationalization of industry—for example, health care—would involve government bureaucracy in operating the economic enterprise directly. The criticisms often made of British railroads or the national health service—both nationalized institutions—generate serious opposition to this idea. Neither the American public nor its political leaders appear to feel that nationalization would lead to anything but more red tape and even less efficiency than regulation involves. Therefore, nationalization does not appear to be a viable alternative. With the move to get government out of business activities and the privatization of many government activities, the trend is clearly in the opposite direction. The opposition is reinforced by the fact that the British government is gradually denationalizing some industry. One exception is the safety screening at airports. After the September 11, 2001, terrorist attacks, Congress made airport passenger screening a national function within the Homeland Security Department.

Consumer Oversight.   Another controversial suggestion is to create consumer committees to evaluate economic activities and then make suggestions for change. This is known as direct consumer oversight. Industry tends to be hostile to this innovation, feeling that consumer groups often focus on one specific issue to the exclusion of the industry's general health. As a result, this proposal has not been accorded serious consideration.

Dramatic new economic proposals are often popular, but the realities of the political process must be faced. The parties with the resources to influence policy usually also have access to the regulatory and economic policymaking system. Thus, reform must confront them as well. The likelihood is that influential interests will prevail, and reform, if any, will continue to be gradual.

Community Revitalization.   The experiments with community revitalization, such as enterprise zones, will be watched carefully to determine whether they produce economic development. Enterprise and empowerment zones are likely to be given credit for any success there is in economic development in the targeted areas. Assessing the evidence will be the difficult part. Especially if they are viewed as helping to solve social problems, they are likely to spread.

Trade/Globalization.   Trade has accelerated the connectedness of the world in all aspects of society, meaning that globalization is a contemporary reality. Globalization refers to the international flow of trade, capital, technology, and information. With the constantly increasing strides in technology, transmission and accumulation of information affects all other aspects of society. Although some believe that globalization is an intentional effort of some powerful interests to enhance their own power and wealth, most people understand that it is an inevitable consequence of advances in technology and interchange in world society. Clearly, globalization provides many benefits to society such as enhancing economic output, increasing competition, and enhancing efficiency of economic systems; it also can have negative consequences for particular individuals and groups within a given society.

In American society, supporters of globalization point to the economic gains it creates for the American economy, estimated to be more than $1 trillion every year.[26] Opponents point to the increasing competition and its costs to workers and business owners in declining industries that are hurt. They also point to declining wages brought about by lower paid workers in other countries. Many perceptions lead to opposition, including the belief that foreign nations benefit from unfair trade practices and that globalization benefits only a select few, especially big businesses.[27] United States' policy alternates between promoting global opportunities for business and attempting to mitigate the negative effects. Initiatives for free trade usually favor economic enterprises and have been a staple of recent administrations. It is likely that free trade will continue to be controversial.

Some policies have focused on helping those within American society who are disadvantaged in the short run by globalization. Thus, programs for assistance for people dislocated by international competition include income support, job training, job search assistance, and relocation services. Wage insurance for older workers and tax credits for health insurance also are part of a program known as Trade Adjustment Assistance. There is much support for expanding this program, which is popular with Democrats, but is unlikely to get the support of the 2011 Republican majority in the House of Representatives.

Other policies include education assistance such as job training for skills needed in the new economy. Tax policy is advocated to address income distribution as a way to reduce resistance to globalization. Thus, earned income tax credits and tax credits for employer-sponsored health care benefits and other incentives have some advocates. Creation of high-wage jobs in the United States is also a common theme in discussions of how to deal with globalization. How to do so is a matter of debate. Of course, trade policy itself is addressed directly by many proposals. Many issues are addressed in trade negotiations with enforceable labor standards, working conditions, and collective bargaining being among them. The United States also focuses on unfair trade policies such as subsidies and predatory pricing of other nations in actions before the World Trade Organization. As we have seen, other nations accuse the United States of similar practices. Clearly, U.S. policy on globalization is grounded in serving the interests of the U.S. economy.

There are inevitably conflicting goals in public policy, and intervention in the economy is no exception. Agencies have to be concerned with protecting the general public, but they also have to be concerned with the health of the economic sectors with which they work. Therefore, they often get caught in the middle between advocates of their industries and consumer advocates. It is left to the elected policymakers to mediate these conflicts and to determine what is best for everyone.

ENDNOTES

1. John Kenneth Galbraith, *Economics and the Public Purpose* (New York: Signet, 1973), 3–4.
2. This discussion relies heavily on Richard L. Siegel and Leonard B. Weinberg, *Comparing Public Policies* (Homewood, IL: Dorsey Press, 1977), Chapter 4. Also see Richard Lehne, *Industry and Politics: United States in Comparative Perspective.* (Englewood Cliffs, NJ: Prentice Hall, 1992), especially Chapters 1 and 2; and Murray I. Weidenbaum, *Business and Government in the Global Marketplace*, 7th ed. (Upper Saddle River, NJ: Prentice Hall, 2004).
3. Milton Friedman, *Capitalism and Freedom* (Chicago: University of Chicago Press, 1962).
4. For an excellent critique of Friedman's position, see Rick Tilman, "Ideology and Utopia in the Political Economy of Milton Friedman," *Polity*, 8 (Spring 1996): 422–442.
5. John Kenneth Galbraith explores this and many of the following ideas in three of his books: *The Affluent Society* (Boston: Houghton Mifflin, 1958); *The New Industrial State* (Boston: Houghton Mifflin, 1968); and *Economics and the Public Purpose* (Boston: Houghton Mifflin, 1973).
6. The following position is taken by Robert Averitt in *The Dual Economy* (New York: Norton, 1968); and by Robert Seidman, "Contract Law, the Free Market, and State Intervention: A Jurisprudential Perspective," *Journal of Economic Issues*, 7 (December 1973): 553–575.

7. Seymour Martin Lipset, *The First New Nation* (New York: Basic Books, 1963), especially Chapters 1 and 2.

8. John Maynard Keynes, *General Theory of Employment, Interest, and Money* (New York: Harcourt Brace, 1936).

9. P. Teske, *Regulation in the States* (Washington, DC: Brookings Institution, 2004).

10. Stephen Labaton, "New View of Antitrust Law: See No Evil, Hear No Evil," *New York Times*, May 8, 2006.

11. G. W. Roster, Jr., *The Status of Class Action Litigation*, American Bar Foundation, Research Contribution No. 4 (Chicago, 1974), examines the development of class action litigation in the United States. See also Deborah R. Hensler, *Class Action Dilemmas: Pursuing Public Goals for Private Gain* (Santa Monica, CA: Rand, 2000).

12. *U.S. v. E. C. Knight*, 156 U.S. 1 (1895).

13. *Loewe v. Lawler*, 208 U.S. 274 (1908).

14. John A. Jenkins, "How to End the Endless Delay at the FTC," *Washington Monthly* (June 1976): 42–50.

15. John O. Haley, *Antitrust in Germany and Japan: The First Fifty Years, 1947–1998* (Seattle: University of Washington Press, 2001); Richard Lehne, *Industry and Politics.*

16. Deborah K. Belasich, *Enterprise Zones: Policy Perspectives of Economic Development* (New York: Garland, 1993); Peter Hall, "Enterprise Zones: A Justification," *Journal of Urban and Regional Research*, 6 (1982): 417–421.

17. William Fulton and Morris Newman, "The Strange Career of Enterprise Zones," *Governing*, 7, No. 6 (March 1994): 32–36; Welcome to the Community Renewal Initiative, U.S. Department of Housing and Urban Development, www.hud.gov/offices/cpd/economicdevelopment/programs/rc; Accessed June 23, 2010.

18. Conrad Weiler, "GATT, NAFTA and State and Local Powers," *Intergovernmental Perspective*, 20 (Fall 1993–Winter 1994): 38–41.

19. Marlon G. Boarnet and William T. Bogart, "Enterprise Zones and Employment: Evidence from New Jersey," *Journal of Urban Economics*, 40 (September 1996): 198–215; L. Papke, "Tax Policy and Urban Development: Evidence from the Indiana Enterprise Zone Program," *Journal of Public Economics*, 54 (1994): 37–49; and Ian Pulsipher, *Evaluating Enterprise Zones*. National Council of State Legislatures/Annie E. Casey Partnership on Family Economic Success, http://ncsl.org/IssuesResearch/EconomicDevelopmentTradeCulturalAffairs/EvaluatingEnterpriseZones/tabld/12806/Default/aspx; Accessed June 21, 2010.

20. J. A. Elvery, *The Impact of Enterprise Zones on Resident Employment: An Evaluation of the Enterprise Zone Programs of California and Florida* (College Park: University of Maryland Graduate School Dissertation, 2004), p. 103.

21. A. Peters and P. Fisher, "The Failures of Economic Development Incentives," *Journal of the American Planning Association*, 70, No. 1 (Winter 2004): 27–37.

22. W. P. M. M. Van De Ven, "Response: The Case for Risk-based Subsidies in Public Health," *Health Economics, Policy and Law*, 1 (2006): 195–199.

23. W. M. Capron and R. G. Noll, "Summary and Conclusion," in W. M. Capron, ed., *Technological Change in Regulated Industries* (Washington, DC: Brookings Institution, 1971), 221.

24. W. M. Crain, *The Impact of Regulatory Costs on Small Firms*, Office of Advocacy, U.S. Small Business Administration, 2005, www.sba.gov/advo/research/rs264tot.pdf;

U.S. Office of Management and Budget, Office of Information and Regulatory Affairs, *Draft Report to Congress on the Costs and Benefits of Federal Regulations*, www.whitehouse.gov/omb/inforeg/2007_cb/2007_draft_cb_report.pdf; Accessed September 19, 2007.

25. Gary Hull, ed., *The Abolition of Antitrust* (New Brunswick, NJ: Transaction Publishers, 2005); and Martin Fridson, *Unwarranted Intrusion: The Case Against Government Intervention in the Marketplace* (Hoboken, NJ: John Wiley & Sons, 2006).

26. Raymond J. Ahearn, *CRS Report for Congress: Globalization, Worker Insecurity, and Policy Approaches*, Congressional Research Service, www.fas.org/sgp/crs/misc/ RL34091; and Gary Clyde Hufbauer, *Answering the Critics: Why Large American Gains from Globalization are Plausible*, Peterson Institute for International Economics, http://iie.com/publications/papers/paper.cfm?ResearchID-929; Accessed June 23, 2010.

27. Raymond J. Ahearn, *CRS Report for Congress*; L. Josh Bivens, *The Gains from Trade: How Big and Who Gets Them?* Economic Policy Institute Working Paper (accessed 06-23-2010); James Petras and Henry Veltmeyer, *Globalization Unmasked: Imperialism in the 21st Century* (Halifax, Nova Scotia: Fernwood Publishing, Ltd., 2001); Ian Ramsay, Globalization, the Third Way and Consumer Law: The Case of the U.K, in Jane K. Winn, ed., *Consumer Protection in the Age of the "Information Economy"* (Burlington, VT: Ashgate Publishing Co., 2006), 59–80; and Dani Rodrik, *Has Globalization Gone Too Far?* (Washington, DC: Institute for International Economics, 1997).

RESOURCES

Books

Eisner, Marc Allen. *Regulatory Politics in Transition*, 2nd ed. Baltimore: Johns Hopkins University Press, 2000.

Evenett, Simon J., Lehman, Alexander, and Steil, Benn, eds. *Antitrust Goes Global: What Future for Transatlantic Cooperation?* Washington, DC: Brookings Institution, 2000.

Francis, John G. *The Politics of Regulation: A Comparative Perspective*. Cambridge, MA: Blackwell, 1993.

Fridson, Martin. *Unwarranted Intrusion: The Case Against Government Intervention in the Marketplace*. Hoboken, NJ: John Wiley & Sons, 2006.

Haley, John O. *Antitrust in Germany and Japan: The First Fifty Years, 1947–1998*. Seattle: University of Washington Press, 2000.

Hovenkamp, Herbert. *The Antitrust Enterprise: Principle and Execution*. Cambridge: Harvard University Press, 2008.

Hull, Gary, ed. *The Abolition of Antitrust*. New Brunswick, NJ: Transaction Publishers, 2005.

Irwin, Douglas A. *Free Trade Under Fire*, 3rd ed. Princeton, NJ: Princeton University Press, 2009.

Kerwin, Cornelius M. *Rulemaking: How Government Agencies Write Law and Make Policy*, 2nd ed. Washington, DC: CQ Press, 2003.

Schott, Jeffrey J., ed. *Free Trade Agreements: US Strategies and Priorities*. Washington, DC: Institute for International Economics, 2004.

Sherman, Roger. *Market Regulation*. Boston: Addison Wesley, 2008.

Sparrow, Malcolm K. *The Regulatory Craft: Controlling Risks, Solving Problems, and Managing Compliance*. Washington, DC: Brookings Institution, 2000.

Teske, Paul. *Regulation in the States*. Washington, DC: Brookings Institution, 2004.

Wallach, Lori, and Woodall, Patrick. *Whose Trade Organization? The Comprehensive Guide to the WTO*. New York: New Press, 2004.

Winn, Jane K. *Consumer Protection in the Age of the "Information Economy."* Burlington, VT: Ashgate Publishing Co., 2006.

Winston, Clifford. *Government Failure versus Market Failure*. Washington, DC: AEI-Brookings Joint Center for Regulatory Studies, 2006.

Websites

American Enterprise Institute–Brookings Joint Center for Regulatory Studies: **http://www.aei.org/**

Brookings Institution: **www.brookings.edu**

European Union: **www.eurunion.org**

Federal Communications Commission: **www.fcc.gov**

Federal Trade Commission: **www.ftc.gov**

Heritage Foundation: **www.heritage.org**

Securities and Exchange Commission: **www.sec.gov**

U.S. Department of Agriculture, Rural Development: **http://www.rurdev.usda.gov/Home.html**

U.S. Department of Housing and Development, Community Planning and Development: **http://portal.hud.gov/portal/page/portal/HUD/program_offices/comm_planning**

U.S. Department of Justice: **www.usdoj.gov**

Chapter 4

Economic Issues: Taxing, Spending, and Budgeting

Today, the federal government exercises a significantly greater role in economic policy than it did 100 years ago. This expanded federal role is now a source of intensified policy conflict that can be traced to both external and internal forces. External forces, such as World Wars I and II, created a need for government controls over wages, prices, and private-sector production levels in order to execute the war effort. Internal forces arising from the severe economic problems of the Great Depression in the 1930s contributed to public demands for an expanded governmental role in the American economy. The "New Deal" of President Roosevelt is an example of federal response to these internal forces. The economic recovery of the United States after the Great Depression demonstrated the effectiveness of governmental intervention to the American public and provided a foundation for continued economic intervention by the federal government.

These forces persist as the United States maintains a global diplomatic and military posture with a domestic economy increasingly dependent on global trade. Liberals/progressives and conservatives accept the legitimacy of governmental involvement in economic policy, a marked change from pre-Depression era America. These ideological groups, however, disagree on the nature of appropriate governmental economic intervention. Liberals/progressives tend to favor a managed economy, where conservatives tend to favor only limited governmental use of monetary and fiscal policies to promote private-sector initiative.

ISSUE BACKGROUND: CONCEPTS AND ISSUES

America has a mixed economy, with public expectations that government will take an active role to promote economic growth and maintain employment

(Chapter 3). At the same time, the social and political values that guide the nature of government's role are dynamic and involve significant conflict. Each value involves questions answerable only in the context of subjective policy preferences. These values establish the boundaries of government activity and provide policy direction for public officials.

One value relates to inflation and interest rates.[1] How much inflation is acceptable in order to sustain economic growth? Interest rates tend to mirror and climb with inflation. What is an acceptable and desirable interest rate that will promote economic growth yet control inflation? How extensive should the role of the federal government be in seeking to control inflation and interest rates?

A second value relates to employment and unemployment. Total employment may not be possible to achieve. What, then, is an acceptable unemployment rate? Economists and the two major political parties have historically accepted 4 to 5 percent unemployment as the appropriate definition of "full employment." Since 2009, the nation's unemployment level has hovered near 10 percent. What should the role of the federal government be in achieving a lower unemployment rate?

Employment, inflation, and interest rates are also linked. One effective tool to drive down inflation is to raise interest rates. This acts to cut demand (by increasing the cost of consumer borrowing) and exerts a downward pressure on prices. Unfortunately, a reduction in demand for goods also drives up unemployment as producers cut their workforce in response to reduced demand. What is an acceptable rate of inflation in order to maintain full employment? Which presents the greater threat to the economic system: inflation or unemployment?

A third value relates to economic growth.[2] The *gross domestic product* (*GDP*) represents the total value of all goods and services produced by the economy. What is the desired rate of growth of the GDP? What roles should the federal government play in promoting GDP expansion? What roles should state governments play in economic growth? What level of growth (as measured by GDP) should the federal government actively pursue?[3]

A fourth value relates to equality. What should the role of the federal government be in promoting economic equality? Is equality of economic opportunity sufficient, or should government actively pursue policies that seek redistribution of economic wealth and benefits in order to achieve some specified level of economic equality either for social groups or for geographic regions?

A fifth value relates to ideology.[4] What should the nature and level of government involvement be in economic policy? How much governmental involvement is consistent with the free-enterprise economic system? At what level of involvement does governmental action cease to be productive and become a counterproductive restriction on the economic system? This value involves significant social and political conflict over the appropriate role of government in a free-enterprise system.

In the absence of universal agreement concerning these values, economic policy becomes the product of either political compromises or the exercise of power by a political party.[5] Government creates and executes economic policy in an environment of political conflict. The use of compromise limits ideological consistency in economic policy. The exercise of power enhances ideological consistency but may create long-term conflict. Historically, economic policy in the United States has been neither completely liberal/progressive nor conservative, but has contained a contradictory combination of values.

Economic Policy Obstacles

Economic policy is created in a climate of conflict in a complex political environment. Consequently, a number of obstacles exist in developing an effective, consistent mix of economic policy options.

Fragmentation of governmental responsibility between the federal and state governments is a major obstacle in developing economic policy. In the American system of *federalism*, state governments share power and responsibilities with the national government, including economic policy options. Given the diversity of the fifty states, they often pursue divergent economic policies. The economic interests of agricultural states such as Iowa or Nebraska are not necessarily consistent with those of heavily industrialized states, such as New York. The federal system is an environment in which state governments and the federal government often pursue conflicting economic goals.

Fragmentation of responsibility for economic policy also exists within the national government. The president, representing a national constituency, shares responsibility with Congress for formulating economic policy options. This shared responsibility expands the number of actors legitimately participating in establishing economic policy. This means that every member of the U.S. Senate and the U.S. House of Representatives has the right to exercise a voice in economic policy. Members of Congress tend to represent the economic interests of their state or district with greater zeal than they do the economic interests of the nation as a whole. Conflict between the executive and legislative branches of government over economic policy is a legitimate characteristic of the American political system. The level of conflict between the president and Congress often becomes more intense when one party controls the White House, and the opposition party controls one or both chambers of Congress.

Fragmentation within the executive branch of government is another obstacle to developing economic policy. A number of cabinet-level departments share this responsibility, notably the Commerce Department, the Treasury Department, and the Labor Department. This fragmentation of responsibility within the executive branch is extensive. Various agencies below cabinet level also exercise economic policy responsibility. The *Office of Management and Budget (OMB)*, the *Council of Economic Advisers (CEA)*, and the independent *Federal Reserve Board (Fed)* are just three of a larger number of agencies that exercise an extensive economic policy role.

On the negative side, this extensive structural fragmentation reduces centralized control and coordination over American economic policy. Ineffective policy responses to economic problems may be the product of a lack of policy coordination. On the positive side, fragmentation allows significant private-sector freedom in economic policy, which is consistent with the values of the free-enterprise system.

A second obstacle involves linkages between economic policy options. This is an issue because of significant conflict between economic goals. For example, the pursuit of full employment tends to fuel inflation. Policies designed to reduce inflation often produce higher unemployment. Similarly, a decision to expand domestic spending may exert budgetary pressures for a reduction in military spending levels. This means that economic policies often conflict because they are the product of political compromise to resolve conflicting goals.

A third obstacle to effective economic policy involves uncertainty in predicting policy outcomes. Even when political consensus allows adoption of a specific economic strategy, no guarantee exists that the desired result will follow. For example, only after implementing a tax-rate change can analysts assess the actual impact of a tax-rate reduction on economic expansion and tax revenues. Economic forecasts rest on uncertain political and financial assumptions used to make predictions. The conflict generated by this debate in an environment of uncertainty becomes an obstacle to the development of economic policy.

A fourth obstacle involves the impact of *entitlement* programs such as Social Security, Medicare, and Medicaid on the federal budget and on the economy. Entitlement programs are redistributive in nature and involve the transfer of wealth from one group to another in order to provide some type of benefit. These programs are created by specific legislation that mandates spending that is independent of the normal budgetary appropriations process. By 2030, the costs for these programs will be more than double that of their level in 2000. Both political parties find it difficult to address the growth of entitlement programs because the American public now views these programs as a moral responsibility of government. The uncontrolled nature of entitlement programs remains a significant issue in formulating economic, taxing, and spending policy.

Macroeconomic Approaches

Traditionally, the free-market system was expected to be self-adjusting without sharp swings in the business cycle. However, as we have seen in Chapter 3, because the free-market system sometimes failed in self-regulation, government intervention was necessary to reduce the impact of downward economic cycles. With the passage of the Employment Act of 1946, Congress formally assigned responsibility for economic growth to the federal government. This legislation stated that the federal government should "use all practicable means (to achieve) maximum employment, production, and purchasing power." The act did not specify the exact means the federal government should use to achieve full employment. Congress was expected to formulate detailed strategies. The act also created the Council of Economic Advisors (CEA) within the Executive Office of the President to provide the president with economic policy advice.

The federal government uses two primary instruments, monetary policy and fiscal policy, to accomplish macroeconomic goals and achieve stabilization of the economy.

Monetary Policy.   *Monetary policy* refers to the efforts of government to control the flow of money in the economy. Money includes not only cash but also available credit and collateral used for credit or security. The major actor in monetary control is the Federal Reserve Board, commonly known as the Fed, which has powers that permit it to expand or contract the amount of money in circulation.

The Federal Reserve Act of 1913 created the Fed, which serves as the central bank of the United States. The Federal Reserve System sought to stabilize the banking industry through regulations developed and imposed by a seven-member board. The president, with Senate confirmation, appoints board members to fourteen-year terms. The chairperson of the Fed, also appointed by the president with Senate approval, serves a four-year term. Board members are removable only by impeachment resulting from the commission of a criminal act. They may *not* be removed over a disagreement about economic policy options with either the president or Congress. The Fed is therefore a stable, independent, and powerful force in economic policy.

As an independent agency, the Fed is free to pursue monetary policies that may conflict with those of either the president or Congress. In the past, the Fed has demonstrated a willingness to raise interest rates in order to cool the economy and reduce inflationary pressures even though the White House did not support this action.

A primary goal of the Fed is to regulate the economy through control over the *money supply*.[6] The currency in circulation today does not represent reserves of gold or silver held by the U.S. Treasury Department. The words "Federal Reserve Note" on paper currency reflect departure from a reliance on these metals, a change from the "Silver Certificate" of years past. The supply and value of money in circulation is independent of gold and silver.

What determines the value of American currency is the supply in circulation and the level of confidence in the American economy by both citizens and international bankers and investors. The Fed has both the power and the responsibility to control the supply of money in circulation. Increasing the supply of money stimulates demand and economic expansion (with the risk of inflation). Decreasing the supply of money reduces demand, and cools the economy down (with the risk of higher unemployment rates).

Thus, when the economy is in recession, monetary policy usually aims at encouraging people to spend money. Lower interest rates and increased availability of money are efforts to accomplish this goal. During inflationary periods, just the opposite is true: Government policy raises interest rates, making it less attractive for people to spend as it becomes more costly to borrow and encouraging savings by making it more profitable for people to save.

The Federal Reserve Board oversees the operation of banks participating in the Federal Reserve System and assists them by serving as a clearinghouse for banking transactions and by lending them money. Of particular impact on money supply is the power of the Federal Reserve Board to control the amount of money a bank must keep on reserve, the *reserve requirement*. As the amount required increases, banks have less to lend to customers; as the reserve decreases, banks have more to lend. Banks also borrow from the Federal Reserve System, and the rate of interest charged by the Fed on such loans, the *discount rate*, affects the costs to banks to lend money to others. Because the interest rates charged by the banks are directly affected by how much the money costs them, the Fed is able to exert control over interest rates charged by banks to consumers. Lower discount rates stimulate consumer borrowing, and higher discount rates discourage such borrowing. The discount rate is a powerful tool available to the Fed for stimulating or cooling off the economy.

The Federal Reserve Board also has the power to buy up government bonds held by investors. These are *open market operations*. Purchasing such bonds places money directly in the hands of potential spenders. Selling bonds, on the other hand, takes money out of circulation.

Monetary policy, though highly flexible, often proves difficult for the administration to control. Although the president may attempt to move in a particular direction, others, especially the Federal Reserve Board, are free to follow their own approaches.

Fiscal Policy.   *Fiscal policy*—which encompasses tax policy, government spending, and debt management—is the other major way in which government attempts to influence economic activity generally. Government can stimulate or discourage economic activity through its power to impose or reduce taxes. Tax reductions in the form of tax incentives, for example, can encourage corporations to invest in plant expansion. Plant expansion ordinarily increases employment and stimulates economic expansion, because more people have more money to spend on goods and services. The same is true of a general tax cut: The demand for goods and services usually rises if taxes take less money from people. However, some of the money freed through tax reductions may be saved, instead of spent. Thus, when government changes tax rates for reasons of fiscal planning, it pays attention to what the recipients of tax benefits are likely to do with their money. During times of inflation, there is some reason for increasing taxes to reduce the amount of money in circulation.

Managing the national debt is another fiscal policy activity often subject to controversy. A deficit occurs when the federal government spends more in a certain year than it collects in taxes. (A surplus is the opposite.) The *national debt* is the accumulation over time of annual deficits. *Deficit spending* stimulates demand in times of recession and unemployment. Nevertheless, it may also add to the money supply without adding to production; hence, many critics of the national government suggest that increases in the national debt contribute to inflation.[7] Deficit spending causes inflation if the government artificially expands the supply of money by printing ever–higher quantities of paper currency to pay for government spending. This type of expanded money supply decreases the value of the dollar with a resultant rise in inflation.

Government borrowing makes it possible to practice deficit spending without fueling inflation, at least in the short run. This approach has been used by all recent presidents (Ronald Reagan, George H. W. Bush, Bill Clinton, George W. Bush, and Barack Obama) to finance budget deficits with minimal inflationary pressure. The price for this approach in the 1980s, and again in the period since

2002, is a dramatic increase in the annual budget deficit and in the national debt. Interest payments on the debt consume a significant percentage of the federal budget. Currently, interest payments absorb about 7 percent of the federal budget.

These tools of monetary and fiscal policy are complex approaches to stabilizing the economy. There are those who think that government should act directly to increase the amount of money in the hands of consumers in hopes that they will spend it and thus stimulate economic activity. Others argue that government should make more money available to business in the hope that it will expand activities, increasing employment and putting more money in the hands of employees and therefore of consumers. The first approach, favored by liberals, is referred to as the percolate-up theory; the latter, championed by conservatives, is known as the trickle-down theory.

Other Measures.   Direct government action to set wage and price levels is also part of fiscal policy. Few economists now advocate wage and price controls (as were imposed in 1972–1973 during the Nixon administration). Beyond discouraging production, wage and price controls are difficult to maintain: Everyone has a justification for exemption, and government agencies become inundated with such requests. Additionally, when controls end, prices and wages surge upward—as happened in the mid-1970s.

In an another approach—known as *jawboning* in the past but today as *calling you out*—the administration attempts to persuade businesses, unions, or other groups to voluntarily comply with economic policy directives from the federal government. This kind of approach has a mixed record of success.

Wage and price control strategies are microeconomic techniques that are macroeconomic in purpose. These and other microeconomic policies (regulation, for example) have the potential for significant impact on the economy as a whole. Micro- and macroeconomic policies are not necessarily independent economic strategies.

CONTEMPORARY POLICY: APPROACHES TO MANAGING THE ECONOMY

Although there are controversies concerning exactly how government should approach economic problems, the reality of government intervention has become widely accepted. The following section examines approaches to managing the economy, including monetary, fiscal, deficit, and tax policies as part of current macroeconomic policy.

Traditional Economic Theory

With the exception of supply-side economics, fiscal and monetary policy tools reflect the *demand-side theory* of John Maynard Keynes. Keynesian economics holds that demand for goods and services drives the economy. A downward economic cycle occurs when business cuts production and downsizes its workforce in response to reduced demand. This, in turn, reduces demand further, which results in more downsizing. Unless some action interrupts this cycle, an economic recession or depression results. Accordingly, the federal government has an obligation to create demand by purchasing goods and services through increased spending. Keynes argued that government deficit spending (spending in excess of tax receipts) is appropriate in order to stimulate a sluggish economy and prevent recessions. During periods of prosperity, when inflation is a threat, government can reduce demand by increasing taxes, reducing spending, and balancing the budget. Keynesian economics is viable only if elected officials are willing to adopt politically unpopular measures, such as raising taxes.

Supply-Side Economics

An alternative economic approach to Keynesian economics is *supply-side economics.* Supply-siders believe that the best method to achieve economic growth is to allow the market system to operate with minimal governmental interference. One basic tenet of the supply-side theory is that the relative price of any good, service, or activity determines how people will act toward it. Consequently, if the market operates freely, private demand forces will be sufficient to sustain the economy. Government interference in stimulating demand disrupts the system and has, at best, only a temporary effect on economic growth. Supply-siders believe that government taxes, regulation, and spending only interfere with natural economic activity and that if government concentrates on stimulating production, demand will follow naturally because of the production process itself.

Supply-side economic policy favors low tax rates in order to stimulate production in the economy. The theory is that as tax rates rise above a certain level, they so discourage economic activity that total tax revenue falls. Most supply-side tax cuts focus on upper-income levels, especially corporate profits and capital gains, because they are the most likely sources of significant investment. Accordingly, lowering tax rates for businesses and individuals with higher income should lead to business investment. Investment leads to economic growth, with the bonus of higher levels of employment, a classic trickle-down argument. Supporters of supply-side economics believe that tax cuts pay for themselves through economic growth, because growth creates a greater number of prosperous taxpayers available to replace the tax money eliminated in the tax cut. Hence, a tax cut can actually raise tax revenue and reduce deficits by stimulating economic expansion. A fundamental tenet of supply-side economics is that the willingness to invest is a direct function of the tax rate on such risk-taking economic activity.

The American economy during the 1970s experienced high inflation with productivity below capacity. President Reagan, elected in 1980, pursued a policy of implementing tax cuts consistent with supply-side economic theory.[8] The tax cuts resulting from the Reagan administration's supply-side policies were a 5 percent cut in personal income taxes in 1982 and 10 percent cuts in 1983 and 1984. Also, corporations were allowed to depreciate equipment more easily. This depreciation reduced the overall corporate tax burden and was intended to encourage them to invest in business expansion.

Impact.   While tax reductions aimed at increasing the amount of money available for investment were important, other aspects of economic policy impact economic growth. For example, the Reagan administration viewed regulation as being burdensome to industry, so it accelerated the deregulation efforts of the Carter presidency. Conservatives and the business community consider regulations to be costly (see Chapter 3).[9] Reducing regulation means reducing expenses, which encourages investment.

Current advocates of supply-side economics argue that the economic expansion of the 1990s and the budget surplus created by the turn of the century were results of implementing supply-side tax cuts in the 1980s. This supply-side argument was the foundation for President George W. Bush's successful push for major tax cuts in 2001–2003. Supply-side economic theory remains an active force in economic policy today.

Budget Deficits

Budget deficits increased dramatically in the 1980s, as shown in Figure 4.1. The annual budget deficit grew to $80 billion in 1981, $212 billion by 1985, and $290 billion in 1992, before beginning to decrease during the Clinton years. These deficits were the result of a combination of factors: the large tax cuts in 1981–1983; increased levels of defense spending during the 1980s; the Persian Gulf War of 1991; a federally funded bailout of savings and loan institutions; continued growth in federal spending for Medicare, Social Security, and other *entitlement* programs; and the recessions of 1981–1982 and 1991–1992, which lowered

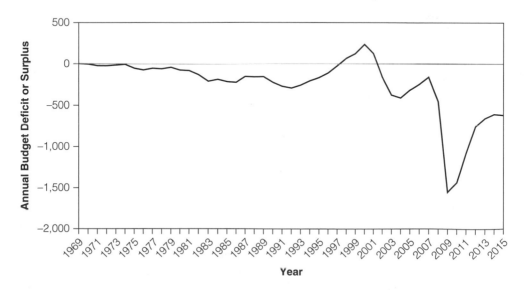

FIGURE 4.1 U.S. Total Budget Deficits and Surplus, 1969–2015

SOURCE: Congressional Budget Office, Historical Budget Data and *The Budget and Economic Outlook: Fiscal Years 2010 to 2020*, January 2010, http://www.cbo.gov/ftpdocs/108xx/doc10871/BudgetOutlook2010_Jan.cfm; Accessed April 2010.

tax receipts and increased federal expenditures for welfare and unemployment. The annual budget deficits serve as obstacles for federal spending on a variety of programs, such as crime, transportation, health care, education, and defense.

The data in Figure 4.1 indicate that the United States achieved a budget surplus in 1998 of almost $70 billion. The shift from budget deficits to budget surpluses was a function of several factors. First, the growth rate of government spending slowed after 1993 due to budget agreements between the president and Congress, particularly the Balanced Budget Act of 1997 (described in the Policy Evaluation section), which sealed an agreement between a Democratic president and a Republican Congress to set a realistic target for a balanced budget. The federal budget continued to grow, but at a slower rate than in the past. Second, the private sector experienced significant economic growth, which produced higher annual revenues than originally projected by either the Congressional Budget Office or the Office of Management and Budget. From 1992 to 1997, federal revenues increased at an average annual rate of 7.6 percent, while inflation remained under 3 percent, making the 1997 budget agreement possible. Moreover, a booming stock market in the 1990s meant higher state and federal revenues from capital gains. Third, the strengthened economy and low inflation rate reduced the rate of increase in spending for entitlement programs. Cost of living adjustments (COLA) for Social Security recipients were lower, and fewer individuals qualified for other entitlement programs due to low unemployment rates. (See Chapter 7 for a description of spending in Social Security and other income support programs.)

Budget deficits reappeared by 2002. The events of the September 11, 2001, terrorist attacks that destroyed the World Trade Center in New York contributed significantly to the return of the budget deficit. Following the terrorist attack, the American economy experienced a downturn. This resulted in lower levels of national tax revenue. At the same time, Congress and the president found it necessary to significantly increase spending for Homeland Security efforts. Under the broad umbrella of Homeland Security, federal spending increased, as dollars were transferred to state and local governments *earmarked* to increase security and reduce threats from terrorists. The creation of new federal agencies, such as the Transportation Safety Administration (TSA), also acted to increase spending and create a budget deficit.

The financial costs associated with Operation Iraqi Freedom, which followed the allied military action to replace the government of Saddam Hussein, also had a significant impact on the budget. Annual defense spending associated with the military efforts in Iraq and Afghanistan are projected to range between $121 and $148 billion by 2011 and add pressure on the budget.

Annual interest payments on the national debt exceed the annual cost of military operations in Iraq and Afghanistan combined, and consumed about 6 percent of the federal budget in 2009. Annual interest payments servicing a national debt of over $9 trillion will continue to increase from $187 billion in 2009 to an estimated $520 billion in 2015, when the national debt is projected to reach almost $15 trillion. (See Figure 4.2.) If the CBO projections are inaccurate because of a recession or increases in spending, this percentage will increase as the cumulative level of debt continues to increase. It is important to understand

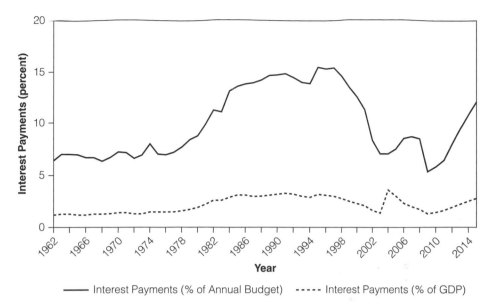

FIGURE 4.2 Interest Payments as Percentage of Annual Budget and Percentage of Gross Domestic Product, 1962–2015

SOURCE: Congressional Budget Office, *Current Budget Projections 2004;* Congressional Budget Office, *The Budget and Economic Outlook Fiscal Years, 2004–2014,* March 2004, Accessed March 2005; and Congressional Budget Office, Historical Budget Data: http://www.cbo.gov/budget/historical.shtml, Accessed September 2007; and Office of Management and Budget, Budget and Economic Outlook Fiscal Years, 2010–2020, January 2020.
http://www.cbo.gov/ftpdocs/108xx/doc10871/BudgetOutlook2010_Jan.cfm; Accessed May 2010.

that interest payments of $209 billion in 2010 did not pay for any new public services. This was simply a payment of interest on money borrowed in previous years to pay for public services provided during that time.

The impact of budget deficits on other parts of the economy is manifold. Budget deficits help contribute to higher interest rates because of the increased demand for available money as the federal government competes with private-sector borrowers. Higher interest rates and scarcity of capital may then discourage investment and weaken economic expansion. Higher interest rates also mean less spending by consumers, who find loans too expensive, which reduces domestic purchasing. Interest rates for home mortgages and consumer loans were in the 3 to 4 percent range during the 1960s, a period of balanced federal budgets. During the 1980s, when budget deficits were at their highest (as a percentage of GDP), home mortgage rates rose to the 12 to 14 percent range. The federal budget deficit was a major cause of these high interest rates.

Additionally, high interest rates usually encourage foreign interests to convert their currencies to U.S. dollars, thus driving the value of the dollar upward relative to that of other currencies. The rise in the value of the dollar makes it difficult for U.S. firms to compete in world markets, leading to a trade imbalance.[10] The strength of the dollar is a measure of the ability of the dollar to purchase (or be purchased by) foreign currency in international money. A strong dollar translates into greater purchasing power for the American dollar on the international market, since a strong dollar will buy more foreign goods than a weak dollar. At the same time, the strong dollar decreases foreign purchasing power in the American market, since it requires more of their currency to buy American goods. American firms then find it more difficult to sell goods abroad. A weak dollar increases the costs of imported goods to consumers but decreases the costs of American goods exported to other countries. One result is that a strong dollar benefits some sectors of the economy and may be harmful to others. Interest rates partially determine the strength of the dollar. Low interest rates tend to produce a lower consumer price index and add domestic stability to the strength of the dollar. Interest rates do have some impact on the strength of the dollar. Over the past ten years, the strength of the dollar has fluctuated, with recent trends indicating a general weakening of the dollar in comparison to other currencies such as the euro and the yen.

Tax Reform

Tax reform efforts are an integral component of the economic policy agenda.

Tax Reform Act of 1986. The Tax Reform Act of 1986 was an effort to establish a federal tax system that was fairer, simpler, and more efficient than the previous federal income tax structure.[11] Many of the act's provisions intended to create greater *fairness* in the federal tax system. The act retained most of the major deductions previously used in itemizing: home mortgage interest, charitable contributions, medical expenses, certain other taxes, and business expense deductions. By lowering the maximum tax rate for individuals from 50 percent to 39 percent, Congress sought to increase taxpayer confidence in the system and to reduce attempts to avoid tax liability. The act also sought to broaden the tax base of the federal government by eliminating certain deductions, such as interest on consumer loans, and by placing restrictions on the number of home mortgages that a person could claim. The act did provide some aid to low- and middle-income families by increasing the standard deduction, and it did provide limited tax relief to the elderly. After other tax code changes, five individual tax brackets remained (15, 28, 31, 36, and 39.6 percent).

Efficiency was a significant goal of the 1986 Tax Reform Act. Under past tax structures, unprofitable investments could reduce tax liability. Tax reformers argued that such a structure encouraged waste and inefficiency because taxpayers did not make investment decisions on their economic merits, but on their impact on tax liability. This tax reform sought to diminish the importance of tax laws in business decision making. Tax reform served as an economic policy instrument to expand the federal tax base and to change investment patterns.

Economic Growth and Tax Relief Reconciliation Act of 2001 (EGTRRA). This act followed the policy direction established by the 1986 act. EGTRRA cut income tax rates, created new tax incentives, and repealed the estate tax. *Fairness* was sought through implementation of lower tax rates. The legislation immediately implemented a new minimum tax rate of 10 percent. The federal tax rates were reduced to 10 percent, 15 percent, 25 percent, 28 percent, 33 percent, and 35 percent. Child tax credits increased and the marriage tax penalty (where married couples pay higher rates than do two single individuals filing separately) was decreased. Taxpayers with incomes under $130,000 could receive new education subsidies. The law gradually reduced the estate tax and targeted it for repeal in 2010. Over the ten-year life of the EGTRRA, tax reductions would total some $1.35 trillion.

An intriguing element of EGTRRA is the fact that all of the changes included in the bill sunset in 2010. This means that, unless Congress reapproves the legislation, all of the changes produced by the 2001 act will terminate, and tax policy will revert to pre-EGTRRA policy. The sunset provision was placed in the legislation to limit its effect of increasing the budget deficit.

The Jobs and Growth Tax Relief and Reconciliation Act of 2003 (JGTRRA). This act continued the supply-side economic approach to the economy favored by President George W. Bush. JGTRRA acted to provide tax cuts to individuals and businesses. Individual taxpayers were provided with an increase in the child tax credit to $1,000 from the previous $600 and with additional relief from the marriage penalty. Implementation of EGTRRA's changes in tax rates was accelerated. Businesses and corporations received tax cuts as well, including a reduction in capital gains tax rates and increases in depreciation rates.

The Bipartisan Tax Fairness and Simplification Act of 2010. This proposed legislation by Senators Wyden (D-OR) and Gregg (R-NH) remains on the policy agenda for congressional and presidential action. It would reduce the number of tax brackets for individuals from six to three (15 percent, 25 percent, and 35 percent) and it would eliminate the Alternative Minimum Tax (AMT). The AMT now requires individuals to compute their taxes twice and pay the highest amount to the federal government. It would help the middle class by tripling the standard deduction and retain deductions for such items as mortgage interest payments and charitable contributions. In order to help American companies compete in a global environment, the act would impose a single rate of 24 percent on corporations. Tax policy remains an active item on the policy agenda whether or not the Bipartisan Tax Fairness and Simplification Act of 2010 is enacted into law at some future date.

POLICY EVALUATION: SUCCESS OR FAILURE?

In any policy evaluation effort, the perspective of the analyst has an impact on the conclusions. Economist John K. Galbraith argued that the economic planning system, well-developed and representing the people with money, does not help those who need help the most.[12] Business and financial interests have captured monetary and fiscal policy; therefore, consumers, workers, and the poor do not receive sufficient consideration. In an alternative view, Milton Friedman suggested that government controls stifle economic activity because they make business too costly to operate profitably.[13] Regardless of perspective, many critics of economic policies agree that these solutions tend to distort economic development and lead to the maldistribution of resources in the society. How that maldistribution is explained depends on the critic's point of view.

Inflation and Growth

The Reagan administration emphasized inflation as a greater economic problem than unemployment. Inflation threatened the smooth operation of the market and eroded individual wealth. The decision to finance federal spending with a massive program of debt proved to be an effective strategy against inflation, though it helped to produce the high deficits of the 1980s and early 1990s. The inflation rate dropped from 13 percent in 1980 to a low of 1.9 percent during 1986 and remained in the 3 percent ranges from 2000 to 2008. The major recession of 2007–2010 produced high unemployment (10 percent), low economic growth, and a drop in the rate of inflation, as reflected in Figure 4.3.

Economic growth in the United States remained at about 5 percent of GDP until 2009, when the nation experienced negative economic growth, as reflected in Figure 4.4. The economic policies of the 1980s and 1990s are associated with this domestic economic growth. Some of the downturn in economic growth in 2001 has been attributed to the effects of the September 11, 2001, terrorist attacks on the World Trade Center in New York.

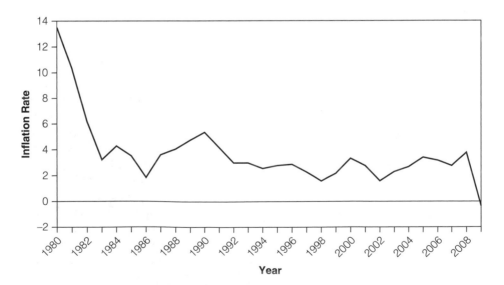

FIGURE 4.3 Inflation Rates, 1980–2009

SOURCE: U.S. Department of Labor, Bureau of Labor Statistics, *Consumer Price Index History Table, 1913–2009.*
ftp://ftp.bls.gov/pub/special.requests/cpi/cpiai.txt; Accessed May 2010.

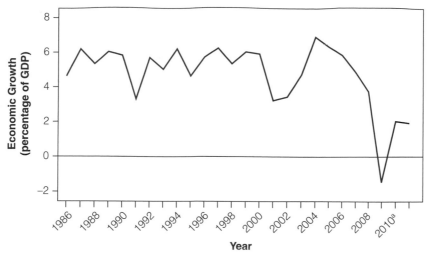

^aProjected

FIGURE 4.4 Economic Growth, 1986–2009

SOURCE: Congressional Budget Office, The Budget and Economic Outlook, 2010–2020, January 2010.
http://www.cbo.gov/ftpdocs/108xx/doc10871/BudgetOutlook2010_Jan.cfm; Accessed May 2010.

Fiscal Policy

The supply-side economists took pride in the fiscal and monetary policies that they claimed fueled the economic recovery of the 1980s, which persisted through 2001, longer than any other recent period of recovery and expansion. The tax reductions pumped more money into the economy, aiding in an industrial investment boom.

Critics of these fiscal policies focused on two issues. The first was the fairness issue related to the equity of tax and spending reductions. Some constant themes of opponents to tax cuts were that those policies favored the rich and hurt the poor, that the impact of domestic budget cuts would increase the real income of those in the highest income categories, and that the majority of taxpayers would experience either no increase in income or a decline. (Chapter 7 discusses the growth of economic inequality during the last two decades.)

The second issue raised by critics was that these policies expanded the national debt and the budget deficit, whose long-range consequences are severe. Figure 4.5 shows the growth of the national debt. The national debt peaked in 1997–1998 and then decreased only slightly with the advent of budget surpluses (see Figure 4.1). The upward trend of the national debt resumed from 2003–2004. The United States economy now carries over $9 trillion in debt, which continues to increase dramatically each year. The deficit spending creates two policy problems. First is a habit of annual deficit spending that is difficult to break. Second, and probably more severe, is the increasing size of the national debt.

The size of the debt presents long-term costs to the wealth of the nation. Even with the elimination of the annual deficit, interest payments will continue to consume a significant percentage of the federal budget. Stated another way,

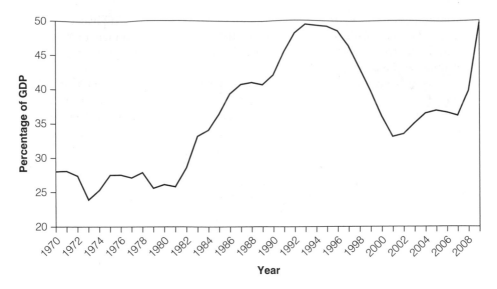

FIGURE 4.5 Cumulative National Debt, 1970–2009

SOURCE: Congressional Budget Office, The Budget and Economic Outlook Fiscal Years, 2010–2010, January 2010.
Table F-11 http://www.cbo.gov/ftpdocs/108xx/doc10871/frontmatter.shtml; Accessed May 2010.

interest payments in 2009 absorbed over $187 billion of federal spending. The CBO projects this will increase to $459 billion by 2015, spending that must be diverted from productive uses.

Budget Deficit Control Efforts.   In its attempt to reduce the deficit and stop growth of the national debt by imposing spending limitations, Congress passed the Balanced Budget and Emergency Deficit Control Act of 1985, otherwise known as the Gramm-Rudman Act. This act resulted in two significant changes in the federal budget process. First, the act specified target deficit levels for fiscal years 1986 through 1991 that both Congress and the president were required to follow. As originally enacted, the measure called for a maximum federal deficit of $72 billion for 1989 and $36 billion for 1990, and a balanced budget by 1991.

The second provision of the act required imposing automatic spending cuts across the board if spending exceeded the targeted budget deficit levels. This process of *sequestration* would come into play if Congress and the president were unable to agree on spending priorities that would reduce the deficit.

The Gramm-Rudman process was amended in 1987 to establish new budget deficit goals with deficit targets of $100 billion for 1990, $64 billion for 1991, $28 billion for 1992, and a balanced budget for 1993. In the event of sequestration, half of the spending cuts would come from defense spending, with the other half falling on domestic spending.

Impact of Gramm-Rudman.   Gramm-Rudman proved ineffective in reducing the federal budget deficit. In fact, the 1992 budget had a then-record deficit of $362 billion. One reason for its ineffectiveness was that Gramm-Rudman deficit targets had to be met at the beginning of a fiscal year based on revenue and spending projections. It was therefore possible to achieve compliance only on paper. The actual deficit at the end of the fiscal year continued to be higher than the target deficit level because of differences between projections and actual revenue receipts.

Congress and the president further weakened Gramm-Rudman in 1990. These changes were to remain in effect until 1995 with new budget rules that avoided sequestration if spending were the result of events "beyond the control" of the president and Congress. This allowed the deficit to exceed the Gramm-Rudman limits and avoid spending cuts associated with sequestration. The experience with Gramm-Rudman demonstrated that the strategy of imposing legal mandates on Congress and the president would be ultimately unsuccessful. Economic expansion would prove to be the factor that would temporarily eliminate annual federal deficits.

The National Commission on Fiscal Responsibility and Reform.   Created by President Obama by executive order in 2010, the commission consists of eighteen members charged with developing a deficit reduction strategy for submission to Congress. The Commission has reported that tax cuts and spending cuts are open for consideration. Membership consists of six Democratic and six Republican members of Congress with an additional six members drawn from industry, labor, and former civil servants. The requirement that fourteen of the eighteen members must agree before any recommendation can be forwarded to Congress serves as a potential obstacle for policy recommendations. The creation of the Commission does reflect the importance of annual budget deficits and the national debt and major economic issues.

Federal Revenues and Spending

In order to understand the possibilities and limits of fiscal policy, and the obstacles to deficit reduction faced by Congress and presidents, one must grasp the nature of federal income and expenditures. Figures 4.6a and 4.6b along with Figure 4.7 provide a visual display of spending and revenues in 2009. As

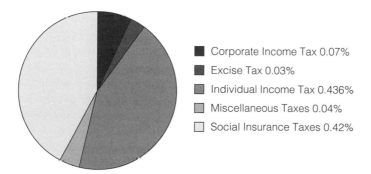

FIGURE 4.6a   Federal Revenue by Source 2009 (Percent) Excludes Deficit

SOURCE: Office of Management and Budget, Budget of the United States Government: Browse Fiscal Year 2010. Table S-4, http://www.gpoaccess.gov/usbudget/fy10/pdf/summary.pdf; Accessed May 2010.

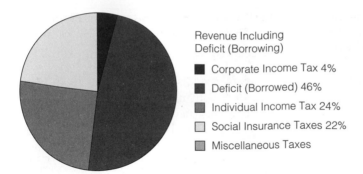

FIGURE 4.6b Federal Revenue by Source 2009 (Percent) Includes Deficit Borrowing

SOURCE: Office of Management and Budget, Budget of the United States Government: Browse Fiscal Year 2010. Table S-4, http://www.gpoaccess.gov/usbudget/fy10/pdf/summary.pdf; Accessed May 2010.

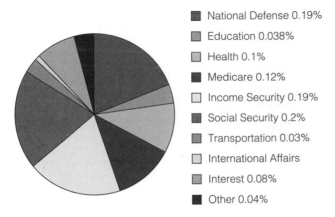

FIGURE 4.7 Federal Spending By Category, 2010 (percent)

SOURCE: Office of Management and Budget, The Budget for Fiscal Year 2011. Historical Tables, Table 3.1—Outlays by Superfunction and Function: 1940–2015, http://www.whitehouse.gov/omb/budget/Historicals/; Accessed May 2010.

indicated in Figure 4.6a, when deficit borrowing is excluded, individual income taxes and social insurance taxes account for 85 percent of federal revenues. Corporate income taxes cover about 7 percent of federal revenues. When deficit borrowing is included, as in Figure 4.6b, federal borrowing accounts for 46 percent of spending. The combined total for individual income taxes and social insurance drops from 85 percent to about 49 percent of federal income. A significant point is that federal borrowing dropped from over 12 percent of spending in 1995 to a minor level by 1997 as budget surpluses emerged. The level of federal borrowing has changed dramatically and borrowing is now the largest source of income for the federal government. With annual budget deficits increasing from $157 billion in 2002 to over $1.5 trillion in 2009, borrowing is a significant source of funding for federal spending.

Eliminating the budget deficit for the period 1998 to 2001 temporarily reduced the pressure of interest payments on the federal budget. During that

TABLE 4.1   **Defense Spending, 1996–2012 (in billions of dollars)**
Defense Spending, Selected Years, 1996–2010 (in billions of dollars)

	1996	1998	2000	2002	2004	2006	2008	2010	2012*
Dollars	244	268	295	325	452	521	616	719	681*
Percent of Budget	15.0	14.5	16.0	17.6	18.8	19.6	20.7	19.0	18.2

*Estimated.

SOURCE: Office of Management and Budget, *The Budget for Fiscal Year 2011*. Historical Tables, Table 3.1—Outlays by Superfunction and Function: 1940–2015, http://www.whitehouse.gov/omb/budget/Historicals/, Accessed May 17, 2010.

period, interest payments dropped from the third to the fifth highest spending category in the federal budget. They now consume almost 9 percent of federal spending and are projected to reach 18 percent of the federal budget by 2020. The associated costs of the war on terror following the September 11, 2001 terrorist attacks and military action in the Middle East have had a marginal impact on defense spending. Defense spending increased from 16 percent of federal spending in 2000 to 19 percent of federal spending in 2010 (see Table 4.1).

Fiscal Policy Evaluation

In 1992, the deficit was projected to rise to the $400 billion range by 1994 and to continue increasing through the decade. These projections were inaccurate, and the federal budget deficit disappeared by 1998 (only to reappear again 2002). What were the policy changes that produced this disappearance?

1990 and 1993 Budget Compromises.   First, the Omnibus Budget Reconciliation Act of 1990 (OBRA-90) contained tax increases and spending cuts designed to reduce the deficit by almost $500 billion by 1995. The tax increases generated $158 billion in new revenues, raised individual income tax rates for high-income taxpayers, and included a $.05 per gallon motor fuel tax. A variety of entitlement programs received cuts, including $57 billion from Medicare and other federal health programs.

OBRA-90 also imposed spending caps on discretionary categories and established spending ceilings for defense, domestic, and international categories. A companion Budget Enforcement Act (BEA) introduced a *pay-as-you-go (PAYGO)* provision. Existing programs could be maintained, but spending for any new program or increased spending for existing programs would have to be matched by a corresponding tax increase or cuts in other programs.

The provisions of OBRA-90 and the BEA did not reduce the deficit to the levels promised in 1990 but the spending caps held, and the PAYGO provisions acted to discourage both tax cuts and major spending increases in entitlement programs.

In 1993, Congress enacted OBRA-93, extending the provisions of the BEA, including spending caps and PAYGO, through 1998. OBRA-93 also included income tax increases and increased taxes on motor fuels. Medicare spending was targeted for a reduction of some $77 billion. OBRA-93 sought to generate an additional $240 billion in new revenues and a reduction in the growth of federal programs by some $200 billion.

The Balanced Budget Act of 1997.   Strong economic growth, producing higher tax revenues, facilitated the *Balanced Budget Act of 1997 (BBA)*. Through a combination of spending reductions and tax changes, the BBA projected a declining deficit and a modest budget surplus by fiscal year 2002. In 1998 a budget surplus was created. This set in motion political maneuvering over whether to use the surplus to (1) reduce the national debt; (2) finance new programs or expand old ones; or (3) finance tax cuts.

The healthy economy allowed Congress to support modest new spending programs. Economic growth reduced the annual federal budget deficit and ultimately eliminated it by 1998. In 1999 and 2000 Congress enacted legislation relaxing BBA reductions in health care spending (see Chapter 8) created numerous emergency-spending bills exempt from the provisions of BBA, and eliminated PAYGO provisions for fiscal years 2001 and 2002. The presence of significant budget surpluses began to erode congressional budget discipline.

Impact of EGTRRA (2001) and JGTRRA (2003).   These two supply side-oriented policies were designed to stimulate the economy by reducing taxes. The result of their enactment was a short-term effect on stimulating demand in the economy. The policies did have the impact of reducing federal revenues as more dollars were retained by taxpayers. In 2007 a Congressional Budget Office review found that EGTRRA and JGTRRA had resulted in a reduction of revenue totaling some $165 billion, which added an additional $46 billion in interest costs to the budget. In the event that Congress and the president extend these policies beyond 2010, the impact on the budget, the deficit, and interest payments will increase.

Level of Debt.   Some analysts argue that the deficit is a relatively minor economic issue. The annual budget deficit remains between 2 and 3 percent of GDP. They argue that this low percentage places only minor pressure on the nation's economy. Other analysts argue just the opposite. They emphasize the size of the total debt, not the annual deficit. The difference is that the total debt is approximately 50 percent of GDP and is projected to increase to 80 percent of GDP by 2020. The issue concerning how much debt the American economy can support remains unresolved.

Defense Spending

Defense spending places a somewhat consistent pressure on the budget. As indicated in Table 4.1, defense spending increased to $719 billion in 2010. Projected spending in future years includes special appropriations necessary to finance military operations in Iraq and Afghanistan. Likely defense spending levels reflect the impact of major American involvement in Iraq and Afghanistan and in other areas of the world for years to come in response to international terrorism. These threats do have the potential to increase defense spending in response to future attacks and significantly alter budgetary policy.

The new patterns of defense spending have potentially significant impacts on military preparedness. The 1990s witnessed a drop in conventional forces as a function of both the breakup of the Soviet Union and budget pressures from the annual deficit in the early to mid-1990s. Deployment of the American military now requires cooperation and extensive support from allies if any type of long-term, theater-wide action is anticipated. One result has been the significant pressure placed on the United States to secure the cooperation of allied nations. This cooperation is needed to effectively pursue the military and diplomatic goals in Iraq that began with Operation Iraqi Freedom. The Iraq and Afghanistan Wars have strained the military forces, requiring extensive and expensive mobilization of National Guard and Reserve units plus increased pay, benefits, and recruitment spending. Replacement of equipment destroyed in these conflicts will also be very expensive.

FUTURE ALTERNATIVES: SPENDING, TAXES, THE DEFICIT, AND ECONOMIC STIMULUS PROGRAMS

Conflict marks debate over economic policy. The issue of governmental involvement in the economy is complex and reflects basic ideological values. During the 1980s, a desire to reduce the role of government in the economy guided policy-making departments of the executive branch of government. Others outside the executive branch argued that more, not less, government intervention is necessary to stabilize the economy. The progressive wing of the Democratic Party, with its egalitarian values, is the most committed to this approach. Its proposals include such items as industrial policy, plant closure warnings, and an increase in the national minimum wage. Such policies would intensify centralization of economic policy. In fiscal and monetary policy, liberals favor attention to unemployment and other symptoms of economic stagnation. They prefer stimulus of the economy even at the cost of some inflation and increasing deficit spending. Traditionally, conservatives tend to be stronger advocates of balanced budgets and believe that inflation is more dangerous than rising unemployment.

The administration of a Democrat, Bill Clinton, saw the brief disappearance of the budget deficit. Indeed, with the election of a Republican president and a Republican Congress in 2000, fiscal discipline evaporated, ushering in both deficits and historic increases in pork barrel spending for legislators' pet projects in their districts. Although Republicans continued to speak the language of fiscal discipline, the more ideologically driven wing of the party became increasingly disturbed by its record in power. The Democratic takeover of Congress in 2006 put renewed vigor into Republican attempts to hold the line on spending, setting up major battles over the budget in following years. Tax policy and responses to the deficit and economic uncertainty will drive the agenda of future presidents and Congresses.

Troubled Asset Relief Program (TARP).   The Emergency Economic Stabilization Act of 2008 created the TARP program, which expanded the role of the federal government in regulating and controlling the American financial system.[14] Lending institutions had allowed individuals to borrow money for homes through the use of subprime mortgages well beyond their ability to repay. As individuals were unable to meet payments, the rate of mortgage defaults escalated and created a significant economic crisis.[15] TARP provided that the U.S. Treasury could spend up to $700 billion to purchase troubled assets, such as home mortgages, and to provide funds to car industry companies in risk of default, such as General Motors and Chrysler, to prevent their collapse. TARP also contained provisions that allowed the federal government to control some of the salaries paid to executives in institutions participating in the program. As of mid-2010, the U.S. Treasury had made commitments of almost $460 billion, lower than the original $700 billion estimate for the program.

The American Recovery and Reinvestment Act of 2009 (ARRA).   This act provides federal spending of some $787 billion and was signed into law by President Obama in 2009.[16] This expanded federal spending bill was created to stimulate the American economy and to create jobs in order to reduce unemployment from the 10 percent level. When Congress approved the bill, no Republicans voted for passage. This reflects the depth of policy disagreements over the role of the federal government in economic policy. Progressives and liberals tend to favor the Keynesian approach of engaging in significant deficit spending to stimulate economic growth. Conservatives tend to reject this philosophy and rely on market forces to provide economic growth.

As of 2010, the policy preferences of the Obama administration clearly favored an expanded federal role in the use of fiscal policy to regulate and stimulate the nation's economy.

Taxes

Legislators regularly propose tax reforms. Tax cuts are often confused with tax reform, though the two are not the same. *Tax reforms* change the basic type and incidence (who pays) of taxation; *tax cuts* merely reduce the rate of taxation. The tax reform achieved in 1986 acted to shift tax incidence. Critics of the tax reform (and of tax cuts in 2001 and 2003) claimed that deductions and exemptions favor high-income brackets and hurt middle-income people and the poor. Middle- and upper-income taxpayers bear the largest burden of national income taxes. State and local taxes, however, fall somewhat harder on lower-income groups. Pressure to alter and modify the 1986 tax reforms resulted in the tax increases for wealthier taxpayers in 1990 and again in 1993. In 2001 and again in 2003, Congress adopted Bush administration proposals to reduce tax rates for all income levels.

The issue of fairness for federal income tax policy is often linked to discussions about the impact of the tax structure on low-income individuals. Progressives argue that tax cuts for the "rich" impose additional tax burdens on the "poor." Conservatives have observed that in 2010, some 47 percent of Americans will not pay any federal income tax: Either their incomes are too low or they qualify for a range of tax credits (primarily deductions and exemptions) that remove their total tax liability. An additional factor is that the earned income tax credit (EITC) program enacted in 1975 has expanded over the past 35 years to the point that in 2009, some 24 million taxpayers received EITC, totaling about $50 billion.[17] EITC has resulted in the bottom 40 percent of taxpayers not only avoiding paying federal income taxes but receiving payments from the federal government. The EITC has become a negative income tax as its benefits have expanded over time. Nevertheless, all indications are that efforts to influence tax incidence continue as economic agenda items.

An item on the economic agenda for this decade centers on tax policy appropriate to an era of budget deficits. Conservatives continue to propose a reduction in capital gains taxes (somewhat achieved in 2001 and 2003), but progressive Democrats favor some combination of middle-income tax cuts and tax increases on the wealthy. Any form of tax cut will increase the deficit in the near-term unless accompanied by a corresponding cut in spending or by significant economic growth that produces higher tax revenues.

Alternative tax proposals include the flat-tax proposal. The flat-tax approach would eliminate many deductions and reduce the number of tax brackets.[18] Additionally, the proposals call for lowering the maximum rate that everyone would pay. Although a true flat tax is unlikely because of the many special interests supporting deductions, it is almost certain that this alternative, along with others, will continue to be debated. The major conflict is how and where to generate additional tax revenues.

Another tax reform proposal is a value-added tax (VAT) to supplement income taxes. The value-added tax is like a national sales tax on goods as they pass through each phase of the economic system. As economic activity adds value to each natural resource or good, a tax is paid on the increase in value. European nations frequently employ a VAT. Members of the Brookings Institution have proposed another approach, which is a cash-flow tax based on a household's gross income minus savings. Thus, all income would be included in figuring the tax. This proposal would encourage saving, as savings would be subtracted from total income for tax purposes. It would make a similar reform in corporate taxes. Again, this proposal is appealing in that it is simple and arguably fair. Moreover, higher rates of savings would stimulate economic investment and growth. Political reality, however, suggests that those with a stake in the current complex tax system would work hard to retain their special position.

Other Future Issues

Budget Deficit.   The passage of OBRA-90 and OBRA-93, along with the Balanced Budget Act of 1997, provided some restraint in the growth of spending. The economic expansion of the late 1990s gave the government new revenues that eliminated the annual budget deficit for a short period of time. Yet other social developments push toward higher government spending that will increase the deficit unless they are offset with higher taxes or sustained economic growth. As discussed earlier, EGTRRA and JGTRRA critics argued that these acts add to the annual budget deficit, while proponents argue that the tax cuts continue to stimulate the economy. Proponents hold that increased economic growth will increase tax revenues without the need to raise taxes. The policy debate surrounding extending all or part of these two policies will continue in the near-term.

Defense spending will follow the patterns discussed earlier. Although the American military presence in Europe and other areas is being reduced, peace-keeping missions in various areas of the world, the war on terror, and the wars in Iraq and Afghanistan will continue to exert budgetary pressures, as will spending for programs associated with promoting Homeland Security.

The aging of the population (Chapters 7 and 8), concern for crime and education (Chapters 6 and 9), environmental protection (Chapter 5), transportation needs, and many other priorities will press themselves upon policymakers and place strain on the budget from the spending side. These tend to be progressive/liberal priorities. Conservatives will place pressure on the budget from the revenue side by opposing tax increases and pressing for implementation of tax cuts. These twin pressures will make it difficult to eliminate budget deficits in the coming decade.

Monetary Policy.   A widely accepted view is that changes in monetary policy do not have long-term impacts on prices and interest rates. If the Fed restricts the supply of money, this will only defer demand, not eliminate it. When it lifts restrictions, demand will surge forward. Interest rates and economic activity tend to respond in only a short-term manner to changes in monetary policy. There is less agreement about the impact of long-term monetary policy changes on the GDP. The Congressional Budget Office (CBO) has used two econometric models, the Washington University macroeconomic model and the Data Resources, Inc. model, to predict the impact of monetary policy on GDP. The CBO found that a gradual increase in the supply of money is necessary to support economic growth in order to avoid deficits without adversely affecting the economy by reducing growth of the GDP. Accordingly, actions by the Fed to tighten the supply of money may be counterproductive.

Balanced Budget Amendment.   In the late 1980s and early 1990s a popular conservative proposal to address deficits involved amending the Constitution to mandate a balanced federal budget. A significant weakness with this approach is that the policy actions and enforcement mechanism necessary to balance the budget were not (and probably cannot) specified in the amendment. Experience with Gramm-Rudman demonstrated that even when enforcement mechanisms exist, political strategy can negate their effectiveness. The passage of the Balanced Budget Act in 1997 demonstrated that genuine deficit avoidance comes only when the president and Congress together have the political will to make difficult choices about specific spending and tax programs.

A balanced budget amendment also presents a number of problems. First, there is an absence of consensus concerning the composition of the federal budget. Defense spending, entitlement spending, spending for health care, and other programs compete for limited fiscal resources. This competition would encourage Congress and the president to achieve compliance on paper by using such budgetary gimmicks as overly optimistic economic forecasts, moving some agencies and programs to an off-budget status, and transferring financial responsibility for programs to state and local governments. Second, such an amendment restricts the ability of the government to deal with emergencies like military actions, economic recessions, and natural disasters that require an immediate federal response.

Line Item Veto. Most recent presidents have argued that they should have the line item veto, the power to veto specific budget items. Proponents of the line item veto claim that presidents would use it to eliminate unnecessary federal spending, known as pork barrel projects, due to their national perspective. Supporters note that forty-three of fifty governors possess the line item veto and that state governments operate with balanced budgets.

Critics of granting this power to the president argue that it represents a major shift in power among the three branches of government and concentrates too much power in the hands of the president. Others observe that the line item veto would probably not have a significant impact on the deficit because it applies only to discretionary and not mandatory federal spending. Discretionary spending accounts for only 25 percent of the federal budget. Presidents would be tempted to use the line item veto to support their spending programs rather than to reduce overall spending and reduce the deficit. Detractors also argue that this power will simply replace congressional budget priorities with those of the president, not reduce federal spending.

Congress granted this power to the president in 1996, and President Clinton used it for the first time on August 11, 1997. Some members of Congress, however, challenged the constitutionality of the line item veto as usurping powers given only to Congress. The U.S. Supreme Court ruled that the law was unconstitutional as written, and there have not been recent attempts to revive it.

Entitlement Programs. Outlays for mandatory spending, often called entitlements (for example, Social Security, Medicare, Medicaid), consume over half of the federal budget. Congress cannot easily impose caps on these programs. Social Security checks and medical benefits cannot legally be stopped when a budgetary spending ceiling limit is reached. In order to limit entitlement spending, Congress must adopt policy options that would modify the programs, restrict benefits, or transfer them to discretionary status. An inability to address the continuing growth of entitlement spending may produce a number of undesirable alternatives such as significant tax increases, a reduced rate of national economic growth, increased competition between entitlement (elderly and health) programs and other programs (defense, transportation, education) for funding, and a potential increase in generational conflict between the taxpaying young and the beneficiary recipient elderly population. Chapters 7 and 8 consider the difficulty of limiting spending in such programs.

Energy Costs.   The price of oil has fluctuated since 1973 (see Chapter 5) with significant economic consequences. A drop in oil prices has a direct economic impact by exerting a downward pressure on inflation. Oil prices remained relatively low (in the $13 to $20 per barrel range) until 2004. Oil prices increased dramatically in 2004, reaching $90 and higher per barrel in 2007. Increases in the market price for oil exert inflationary pressures on the American economy and affect economic growth.

Homeland Security.   Following the terrorist attacks of September 11, 2001, the United States began an extensive program to strengthen homeland security. Congress has approved over $17 billion in spending for homeland security, and that figure continues to increase. Given the open nature of American society, efforts to protect government institutions and the population from terrorist activities are expensive undertakings. There will be a continued emphasis on this type of spending. Its total impact on the nation's economy is uncertain.

ENDNOTES

1. See Timothy Cogley, "What Is the Optimal Rate of Inflation?" *Federal Reserve Bank of San Francisco Economic Letter,* No. 97–27 (September 19, 1997), for a discussion of the factors the Federal Reserve System can use to determine an optimal rate of inflation.

2. Herbert Stein, "Should Growth Be a Priority of National Policy?" *Challenge* (March/April 1986): 1–17. Late in 1991, the Commerce Department changed its economic measure from gross national product (GNP) to gross domestic product (GDP). Figures in this book are GDP unless otherwise indicated.

3. See Mary C. Daly, "Assessing the Benefits of Economic Growth," *Federal Reserve Bank of San Francisco Economic Letter,* No. 97–30 (October 17, 1997), for a discussion of various approaches to assess benefits of economic growth.

4. Anthony Solomon, "Economic Ideology and Public Policy," *Challenge* (July/August 1986): 11–17.

5. Edward R. Tufte, *Political Control of the Economy* (Princeton, NJ: Princeton University Press, 1978).

6. See Brian Motley, "Should Monetary Policy Focus on 'Core' Inflation?" *Federal Reserve Bank of San Francisco Economic Letter,* No. 97–11 (April 18, 1997), for a discussion of some of these issues.

7. Thomas J. Cunningham, "The Long-Run Outcome of a Permanent Deficit," *Economic Review* (May 1986): 25–33.

8. Arthur Laffer, "Supply Side Economics," *Financial Analysts Journal* (September/October 1981): 29–43.

9. Marc Levinson, "The Verdict on Deregulation," *Dun's Business Monthly* (November 1986): 30–34. See Christopher Douglass, Michael Orlando, and Melinda Warren, *Regulatory Changes and Trends: An Analysis of the 1998 Budget of the U.S. Government* (St. Louis: Center for the Study of American Business, August 1997).

10. C. Fred Bergsten, "The Second Debt Crisis Is Coming," *Challenge* (May/June 1985): 14–21.

11. "Tax Reform—At Last," *Business Week* (September 1, 1986): 54–58.

12. John K. Galbraith, *Economics and the Public Purpose* (Boston: Houghton Mifflin, 1978).

13. Rick Tilman, "Ideology and Utopia in the Political Economy of Milton Friedman," *Polity*, 8 (Spring 1976): 422–442.

14. See the U.S. Treasury Department website, www.financialstability.gov, for current information on TARP and the Emergency Economic Stabilization Act of 2008 (accessed June 8, 2010).

15. For a discussion of the origin and impact of subprime mortgages, see Dwight M. Jaffee, "The U.S. Subprime Mortgage Crisis: Issues Raised and Lessons Learned" in Annez, Patricia C., *Urbanization and Growth*, Washington, DC: The World Bank, 2009.

16. See **www.recovery.gov** for current information on the American Recovery and Reinvestment Act (accessed June 8, 2010).

17. See the U.S. Internal Revenue Service website, **www.eitc.irs.gov**, for detailed information on the Earned Income Tax Credit (accessed June 2010).

18. Robert Hall and Alvin Rabushka, *Low Tax, Simple Tax, Flat Tax* (New York: McGraw-Hill, 1984).

RESOURCES

Books

Andersson, Krister, Eberhartinger, Eva, and Oxelheim, Lars, eds. *National Tax Policy in Europe*. New York: Springer, 2007.

Brooks, Arthur C., *The Battle: How the Fight Between Free Enterprise and Big Government Will Shape America's Future*. New York: Basic Books, 2010.

Brunori, David. *Local Tax Policy: A Federalist Perspective*, 2nd ed. Washington, DC: Urban Institute Press, 2006.

Dobbs, Lou. *War on the Middle Class*. New York: Penguin Books, 2007.

Friedman, Milton. *Capitalism and Freedom*. Chicago: University of Chicago Press, 1981.

Greenspan, Alan. *The Age of Turbulence*. New York: Penguin Books, 2007.

Knoop, Todd A. *Recessions and Depressions: Understanding Business Cycles*. Westport, CT: Praeger, 2004.

Lehne, Richard. *Government and Business: American Political Economy in Comparative Perspective*, 2nd ed. Washington, DC: CQ Press, 2005.

Peet, Richard. *Geography of Power: Making Global Economic Policy*. New York: Palgrave Macmillan, 2007.

Ridderstrale, Jonas, and Nordstrom, Kjell. *Karaoke Capitalism: Daring to be Different in a Copycat World*. Westport, CT: Praeger, 2005.

Rivlin, Alice M., and Antos, Joseph R. *Restoring Fiscal Sanity 2007: The Health Spending Challenge*. Washington, DC: Brookings Institution, 2007.

Rubin, Irene. *The Politics of Public Budgeting: Getting and Spending, Borrowing and Balancing*. Washington, DC: CQ Press, 2005.

Schick, Allen. *The Federal Budget, Third Edition: Politics, Policies, Process.* Washington, DC: Brookings Institution, 2007.

Sobel, Andrew C. *Political Economy and Global Affairs.* Washington, DC: CQ Press, 2005.

Stabile, Donald R., and Cantor, Jeffrey A. *The Public Debt of the United States: An Historical Perspective, 1775–1990.* Westport, CT: Praeger, 1991.

Steuerle, C. Eugene. *Contemporary U.S. Tax Policy,* 2nd ed. Washington, DC: Urban Institute Press, 2008.

Thorndike, Joseph J., and Ventry, Dennis J., Jr. *Tax Justice: The Ongoing Debate.* Washington, DC: Urban Institute Press, 2002.

Thurow, Lester. *The Zero-Sum Society: Distribution and the Possibilities for Economic Change.* New York: Penguin, 1981.

Wildavsky, Aaron. *The New Politics of the Budgetary Process,* 2nd ed. New York: Harper-Collins, 1992.

Websites

American Enterprise Institute: **www.aei.org**

Brookings Institution: **www.brookings.edu**

Cato Institute: **www.cato.org**

Century Foundation: **www.tcf.org**

Congressional Budget Office: **www.cbo.gov**

The Kauffman Foundation: **www.kauffman.org**

Heritage Foundation: **www.heritage.org**

Homeland Security: **www.dhs.gov**

Homeland Security (Military): **www.defendamerica.mil**

National Commission on Fiscal Responsibility and Reform: **www.fiscalcommission.gov**

Office of Management and Budget: **www.whitehouse.gov/omb/**

Office of Tax Policy, United States Treasury: **www.ustreas.gov/offices/tax-policy/**

Organization for Economic Cooperation and Development (OECD): **www.oecd.org**

Urban Institute: **www.urban.org**

U.S. Federal Reserve System: **www.federalreserve.gov**

Chapter 5

Energy and Environmental Policies: Policy Instability

Complacency describes the attitude of the American public toward the development of a national energy policy and environmental protection strategies until the 1970s. Energy policy was not a public concern due to an abundant supply of cheap energy. The vast supply of natural resources contributed to the public policy value that regulatory and protective environmental policies were unnecessary. An absence of policies designed to protect the environment contributed to the development of cheap energy and the resulting economic prosperity of the United States.

ENERGY POLICY ISSUE BACKGROUND: COMPLACENCY AND CRISIS

The 1973 Arab oil embargo triggered a new era in U.S. energy policy. Energy policy in the United States falls into two periods: up to 1973 was the "traditional" period; the years following the embargo are marked by shifts from crisis to uncertainty to complacency and currently to renewed concern.

Traditional Energy Policy

Before 1973 the U.S. policy was guided by the belief that the private sector could provide the nation with an unlimited supply of inexpensive energy. America had an abundance of *fossil fuels*: coal, oil, and natural gas; all developed and provided by the private sector. The limited government regulations that did exist were primarily designed to protect the economic security of the energy producers by maintaining stable prices. Energy policy was a mix of state and federal actions designed to encourage consumption with little emphasis on conservation, efficiency, or national energy independence. Consequently, the U.S. was not prepared for the events of 1973 in the Middle East that threatened the nation's energy supply and moved energy policy onto the public agenda.

Policy Values.   The Mineral Leasing Act of 1920 allowed government leases that encouraged energy exploration and production on public lands. Energy producers paid royalties to both states and the federal government under this system. During the 1940s, conflict arose between coastal states and the federal government over leasing powers for offshore oil and gas exploration. This dispute was resolved in 1953, when the states obtained leasing responsibility for lands within their traditional boundaries (three to ten miles offshore) with the federal government retaining control over all other offshore lands. One result is that today the federal government exercises primary control over offshore drilling in the United States; it determines what offshore areas (such as the Gulf of Mexico) are open for drilling activities.

Taxation.   From World War I until 1973, the primary value guiding energy tax policy involved granting tax breaks to energy producers in order to encourage exploration and production. This resulted in both a significantly increased supply and overproduction, which led to calls for prorationing. *Prorationing* involves governmental regulations that impose production quotas on private companies in order to reduce supply. This strategy worked to achieve market stability by protecting producers from unlimited competition. Prorationing became accepted policy for both federal and state governments.

Antitrust Policy.   The federal energy policy of prorationing conflicted with antitrust policies. In 1911, the federal government abolished the Standard Oil Trust in order to increase competition. During World War II, the government dropped its limited antitrust efforts targeting the oil and gas industry in order to increase production. By the 1950s, antitrust actions targeting oil companies were viewed as counterproductive to meeting the increasing demand for oil.

Decentralization.   Traditional energy policy reflected a commitment to the private-sector and free-market operations. This fragmented and decentralized energy policy allowed the private sector the freedom to provide energy to the nation. No single level of government or regulatory body had responsibility for developing energy policy options. Decentralization and fragmentation of policy responsibility was consistent with an emphasis on private-sector market operations.

Coal.   Coal supplied almost 75 percent of the nation's energy consumption until the late 1920s. An abundant coal supply provided cheap energy but also acted to depress prices. This resulted in both low profits for companies and low wages for miners. The oversupply of coal became so extensive that by 1932, over 4,000 coal companies had failed and only 300 of the 1,864 companies in operation reported a profit.[1] The Bituminous Coal Acts of 1935 and 1937 were adopted with the support of both the United Mine Workers (UMW) and coal companies. These acts attempted to impose production quotas in order to stabilize profits and protect wages. The nation's shift to oil as the preferred energy source after World War II limited the impact of these acts on prices and miner's wages.

Oil.   The long history of oil policy has involved attempts by the states and the federal government to limit production and create a balance between supply and demand through prorationing. Since most American oil came from Texas, the policy decisions of the Texas Railroad Commission (which regulated oil production in Texas) tended to define national oil policy between the 1930s and 1950s. Production limits set by Texas influenced other oil-rich states to adopt similar policies regulating production and distribution of this valuable resource.

The *oil depletion allowance* adopted in 1926 by the federal government exemplified the protective nature of energy policies. At the end of World War I, the U.S. Geological Survey (USGS) predicted that the nation's oil reserves would be depleted within ten years. The oil industry used this prediction and argued that just as machinery wore out and buildings deteriorated, oil wells also lost their value over time as the underground reservoir emptied. Congress responded with legislation that allowed oil companies to deduct 27.5 percent of their gross income from taxable income, if the total amount deducted did not exceed 50 percent of the company's net income. The USGS prediction was inaccurate, as oil exploration efforts led to the addition of vast reserves in Oklahoma and East Texas by the 1930s. The oil depletion allowance was continued because it protected the producer's profit margin, which did encourage continued exploration across the United States and around the world as the tax savings and profits were used to fund new oil drilling expeditions.

Natural Gas.   *Natural gas* has a long history of regulation. Natural gas production requires very little refining before use and involves three major activities: production in the field, distribution through pipelines, and a specialized distribution network to consumers at the end of pipelines. The 1938 Natural Gas Act assigned federal regulatory authority to the Federal Power Commission (FPC). The FPC regulated pipeline construction and the price of natural gas in the interstate market.

The primary policy impact of these regulatory powers was to maintain a supply of low-cost natural gas. Interstate rates for natural gas were significantly less than the unregulated intrastate rates. Gas selling for $2.50 per thousand cubic feet in the intrastate market could be sold for only $1.00 in the interstate market. One consequence was waste, since the low-price structure did not encourage efficiency or conservation. Interstate price regulation encouraged increased demand for natural gas but it also reduced profits for suppliers. This discouraged exploration for new gas supplies, which then lowered production of natural gas.

Nuclear Power.   During the 1950s and 1960s nuclear power was viewed as a potential major source of energy for both the United States and Western

Europe. Congress established the Atomic Energy Commission (AEC) to promote and regulate the development of this new source of power. Construction
of nuclear reactors for commercial generation of electricity was assigned to the
private sector.

Western Vulnerability: OPEC and the Arab Oil Embargo

Americans benefited from an abundant supply of energy combined with the ability to control foreign energy resources. The most important of these were the oil
fields of the Middle East and North Africa. Before the 1973 Arab oil embargo,
those oil-producing countries did not control the oil industry within their own
borders. Major American and European oil companies exercised nearly complete
control over the production of oil, its market price, and the profit levels they
chose to share with producing countries.

The Power of Western Oil Companies.   As the oil industry developed in the
1930s, seven major companies dominated oil production and distribution: Standard
Oil of California (Chevron), the Texas Company (Texaco), Socony-Vacuum
(Mobil), Gulf Oil, Standard Oil of New Jersey (Exxon), Royal Dutch Shell, and
British Petroleum (BP). These companies found cooperative arrangements to be in
their best interests for international oil exploration. One result was a reduction in
competition in the international oil market. Competition eroded when the
Arabian American Oil Company (Aramco) was organized by four companies
(Standard Oil of New Jersey, Standard Oil of California, Socony-Vacuum, and
Texaco) in 1947 to develop the enormous oil reserves of Saudi Arabia. This and
other cooperative efforts were so successful that by 1952, the seven oil companies
controlled over 90 percent of the total crude oil production outside North
America and the communist nations.

 This control was so effective that when Iran attempted to nationalize the
Anglo-Iranian Oil Company between 1951 and 1953, the major companies boy-
cotted Iranian oil and increased production in the fields of other countries to
offset the shift from Iranian oil. A similar situation occurred when Iraq nationalized
its oil fields in 1961.[2]

The *Organization of Petroleum Exporting Countries* (OPEC).   The oil-producing
states sought to create an organization that would achieve control over price and
production levels. OPEC began in 1960 with the membership of seven Arab
nations—Algeria, Iraq, Kuwait, Libya, Qatar, Saudi Arabia, and the United
Arab Emirates—and six non-Arab nations—Ecuador, Gabon, Indonesia, Iran,
Nigeria, and Venezuela. Several factors acted to limit the strength of the new
organization. First, the United States was nearly self-sufficient in the production
of oil, with relatively little need for imports. Second, the cooperative agreements
among the major oil companies created an international oil cartel with near-
monopolistic powers. Third, the production of crude oil exceeded international
demand, which produced a buyer's market and limited the power of suppliers.
The low price of oil restricted oil tax revenues for producing nations.

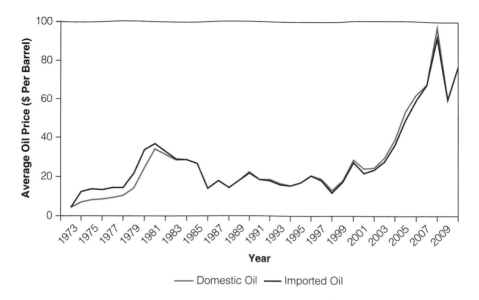

FIGURE 5.1 Average Price of Domestic and Imported Oils, 1973–2009

SOURCE: U.S. Energy Information Administration, Monthly Energy Review, April 2010, Table 9-1 Crude Oil Summary Prices, http://www.eia.doe.gov/emeu/mer/pdf/mer.pdf; Accessed May 2010.

The 1973 Arab Oil Embargo. October 6, 1973, marked the opening date of the Yom Kippur War between Israel and the Arab states. This event provided a catalyst for Arab unity and demonstrated the power of collective action to OPEC members.[3] On October 17, the Arab oil ministers met in Kuwait and resolved to use oil as a weapon in the struggle against Israel. Accordingly, they imposed a 5 percent monthly reduction in exports to nations supporting Israel. Nations supporting the Arab cause were exempted from the embargo. The embargo had limited impact on oil imports by the United States, as non–Arab sources—primarily Venezuela and Iran—were readily available. The Arab nations lifted the embargo against the United States in March 1974, following the Egyptian–Israeli cease-fire. The embargo did achieve some of its original political objectives, as support for Israel in Western Europe and Japan softened. The real value of the 1973 Arab oil embargo was the dramatic example of power through unified policy that it gave to OPEC nations. OPEC ministers realized that if action were taken in concert by all thirteen member states, their demands would be impossible to resist. This period marked the beginning of a rapid escalation in the price for OPEC oil and of systematic controls on production levels by producing nations. Figure 5.1 shows the price paid for oil between 1973 and 2009 for domestic and imported oil. The rapid increase in oil prices depicted in Figure 5.1 coincides with the 1973 embargo. Within its first three months, the price of Arabian oil had increased dramatically from $3.00 per barrel to $11.65 per barrel.

The increasing cost of oil exerted inflationary pressure on the economies of the oil-consuming West. These inflationary pressures and a desire by OPEC nations to generate revenues acted to fuel an upward spiral in oil prices. During the late 1970s, OPEC could not agree on a fixed price for oil, so a price increase by one nation stimulated similar increases by other producers as well.[4] The reality of oil selling at $50 or even $100 per barrel seemed imminent. By 1982–1984, a combination of forces, including a reduction in demand, discovery of reserves outside OPEC, overproduction, and OPEC disunity, brought about a drop in global crude oil prices, which stabilized in the $19-per-barrel range until late 1999 and early 2000. Oil prices again began to increase significantly to the $100-per-barrel range in late 2007 and early 2008 and hover near $80 to $85-per-barrel in 2010.

CONTEMPORARY POLICY: FROM COMPLACENCY TO CRISIS TO RENEWED CONCERN

Energy Problems Emerge

The Arab oil embargo coincided with the end of American energy self-sufficiency. In 1947, the nation began to import oil for domestic use. The amount was minimal, less than one-half of 1 percent of total oil consumption. By the mid-1950s, foreign imports accounted for 10 percent of America's oil consumption, in part because of the lower cost of imported oil, typically about half that of domestic oil. A refinery might pay $3.00 per barrel for American oil, but could obtain imported oil for $1.50 per barrel.[5]

In order to protect the domestic oil industry, President Eisenhower imposed an import quota equivalent to 12 percent of domestic production in 1959. By 1973, American oil consumption reached nearly seventeen million barrels per day, with domestic production levels slightly less than eleven million barrels per day. This gap between domestic supply and demand prompted President Nixon to remove all import quotas on oil in the spring of 1973, which allowed imported oil to reach the current figure of about 65 percent of total American oil consumption (see Figure 5.2).

Domestic natural gas production reached a peak of 24.7 trillion cubic feet in 1975 and then began a gradual decline to some 20.6 trillion cubic feet in 2010. Currently, annual consumption levels are at some 22.5 trillion cubic feet in 2009, making it necessary to import approximately 2.5 to 3 million cubic feet of natural gas per year. The U.S. Department of Energy projects this level of production, usage, and imports to remain relatively stable through 2020.[6] Nuclear power did not develop into a source of unlimited energy because of problems with the safety of the technology. A major accident in 1979 at the Three Mile Island nuclear plant in Pennsylvania and less serious incidents at other nuclear power facilities acted to shift American policy priorities away from this energy option in the 1980s. Coal furnishes a large percentage of energy consumption, but environmental problems exist with this energy source. Gases produced by the burning of coal contribute to acid rain and strip-mining activities degrade the environment. Other sources of renewable energy such as

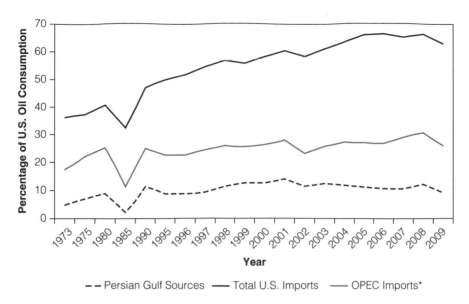

FIGURE 5.2 U.S. Dependence on Oil Imports, 1973–2009 Persian Gulf, OPEC, and Total U.S. Imports as Percent of Total U.S. Oil Consumption

*OPEC – Some Persian Gulf Suppliers Are Members of OPEC

SOURCE: Monthly Energy Review, U.S. Department of Energy, April 2010, Table 3.3a, "Petroleum Trade Overview" http://www.eia.doe.gov/emeu/mer/pdf/pages/sec3_7.pdf; Accessed May 2010.

solar power, wind power, and geothermal technologies have yet to develop sufficiently to offset any reduced dependence on oil and natural gas. The United States continues to depend on fossil fuels as the primary source of energy. This reality means continued reliance on oil imports.

Global Dependence on Fossil Fuels

Dependence on oil as a primary energy source continues to be a worldwide pattern. Figure 5.3 reflects the importance of oil and natural gas as primary energy sources. The proportion of energy provided by these two sources is now approximately 65 percent of total global energy consumption, an increase from some 36 percent in 1950. Coal has declined as a primary source of fuel in Western Europe from slightly over 85 percent to less than 19 percent of total energy consumption in 2006. The same pattern holds true for Japan, as its reliance on coal has dropped from over 86 percent to less than 19 percent of total energy consumption. Oil and natural gas are now the world's primary energy sources, except in communist Asia. There, coal remains a primary energy source, even though oil and natural gas are becoming increasingly important as fuels.

Dependence on imported oil is especially significant for the industrialized democracies of the free world.[7] The United States now imports over two-thirds of its oil. The figure is substantially higher for Europe and Japan,

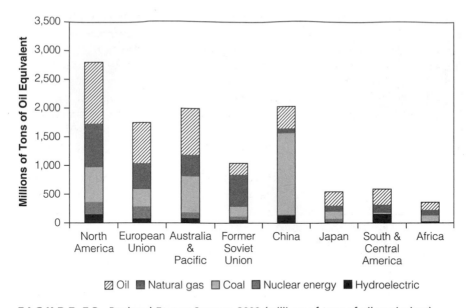

FIGURE 5.3 Regional Energy Sources, 2009 (millions of tons of oil equivalent)

SOURCE: British Petroleum, Statistical Review of World Energy, June 2009, Primary Energy, Consumption by Fuel
http://www.bp.com/liveassets/bp_internet/globalbp/globalbp_uk_english/reports_and_publications/statistical_energy_
review_2008/STAGING/local_assets/2009_downloads/statistical_review_of_world_energy_full_report_2009.pdf;
Accessed May 2010.

with oil imports accounting for 74 percent of European oil consumption and 99 percent of Japanese oil consumption. Important sources of oil for Western Europe and Japan are the Middle East and North Africa. Approximately 59 percent of the oil that Japan imports originates in the Islamic world. The United States has established a pattern since the mid-1970s of obtaining between 10 and 12 percent of its imports from Islamic nations. This means that the West's economic stability depends upon the uninterrupted flow of oil from the Islamic world and, therefore, upon political stability in the Middle East.

Energy Policy after 1973

The disruption of oil supply and the rapid increase in the cost of oil created by the 1973 oil embargo resulted in a dramatic expansion of the role of the federal government in energy policy.[8] President Nixon announced Project Independence in 1973 as a strategy to achieve energy self-sufficiency by 1980. The basic elements of the plan were: (1) imposition of a national speed limit, (2) adoption of daylight-saving time on a year-round basis, (3) increased federal funding for energy research and development, (4) standby authority for gasoline rationing, (5) relaxation of environmental standards to increase the use of coal, (6) deregulation of natural gas, (7) construction of the trans-Alaska pipeline, and (8) the creation of a Federal Department of Energy.

Political and technological constraints made self-sufficiency by 1980 an unrealistic goal. With the lifting of the Arab oil embargo in the summer of

1974, the crisis atmosphere surrounding energy evaporated. Energy policy drift-ing as agreement on a unified energy policy could not be achieved.

During this period, Congress acted to authorize construction of the trans-Alaska pipeline over objections of environmental groups. In 1974, it adopted a national fifty-five-mile-per-hour speed limit and created two new governmental agencies, the Federal Energy Administration (FEA) and the Energy Research and Development Administration (ERDA). These agencies had the responsibility to develop and coordinate new federal energy policies. The emphasis on an increased federal role led to the creation of the Department of Energy in 1977.

Legislation. The National Energy Act of 1978 sought to encourage increased energy efficiency, reduce consumption, and change energy use patterns. First, it deregulated natural gas by ending federal price controls in an effort to encourage increased exploration. Second, the Act contained provisions aimed at reducing consumption of oil and natural gas and encouraging conversion to coal as a major fuel source in generating electricity. Third, the Act mandated changes in utility rate structures to represent the true cost of supplying electric service to customers. Declining block rates, in which the unit cost of electricity decreased as the level of consumption increased, could be retained only if the reduced rate actually represented the costs of providing the electricity. These increases in the cost of electricity were designed to reduce oil and natural gas consumption by reducing the demand for electric power produced through the burning of both fuels.

The Act relied on a mixture of taxes and tax credits to encourage a reduc-tion in energy consumption and development of renewable, nonfossil energy sources. Homeowners received income tax credits for a percentage of the expenses spent on insulation or the installation of solar, wind, or geothermal energy equipment in homes. An important provision of the Act included a tax, paid by the manufacturer, on gas-guzzling cars. The tax initially ranged from $200 to $500 for the 1980 model year and gradually increased to a range of $500 to $3,850 by the 1986 model year. The *Corporate Average Fuel Economy* (*CAFE*) standard required that the automobile industry produce a mix of cars with an average fuel efficiency of 27.5 miles per gallon (mpg) by 1985. The tax and CAFE standard contributed to a change in the size and fuel efficiency of automobiles, which reduced oil consumption by American drivers. Chrysler Corporation achieved total compliance with the new standards. When faced with the prospect of imposing severe tax penalties on General Motors in 1986 (the fleet of GM cars did not meet the new standards), Congress balked and reduced the CAFE standard to 26.0 mpg for the 1986 model year. The auto manufacturer was given more time to achieve compliance in order to protect the jobs of GM workers. In October 1990, the Department of Transportation adjusted the CAFE standard to 27.5 mpg. In 2010, the CAFE standards were increased to 34.1 mpg for the 2016 model year. The popular sport utility vehi-cles, or SUVs, were classified as trucks and originally exempted from CAFE stan-dards. Under the new CAFE rules, modified mileage and emissions standards will apply to light trucks and SUVs.

The National Energy Act of 1978 encouraged increased efficiency and conservation but did not move the nation toward the long-range goal of U.S. energy independence. The Act did not contain provisions to develop major alternative energy sources. Therefore, American dependence on foreign oil supplies continued.

Decontrol and the Windfall Profits Tax.   Federal regulation of domestic oil prices began in 1971 as a mechanism to control inflation. Low prices encouraged American consumption of oil. Proponents of decontrol argued that the removal of price controls would reduce oil consumption by up to 100 million barrels of oil per year, because the increased cost would reduce consumer demand. A second impact would be the stimulation of domestic production as increased profits encouraged additional oil exploration efforts. Critics of decontrol argued that significant social and economic problems would emerge because the poor and elderly would face increased financial burdens during winter months and increased energy costs would add inflationary pressure to the economy.

Under the provisions of the Energy Policy and Conservation Act of 1975, all price controls on domestic oil were targeted for elimination by 1981. In order to reduce opposition to decontrol, Congress adopted the Crude Oil Windfall Profit Tax Act of 1980, which imposed a tax rate in the 30 percent range (with a host of exemptions) until $227 billion in revenues were reached, with the tax being phased out by 1993. These revenues were intended (among other things) to help the poor and elderly cope with energy costs.

Energy policy thus moved in two conflicting directions. Decontrol intended to provide economic incentives to spur domestic production and exploration. At the same time, taxes reduced the magnitude of the economic incentives provided by decontrol. Following decontrol there was a huge increase, followed by a decline, in the level of oil and gas exploration in the United States (see Figure 5.4). By 1995, exploration levels had dropped lower than in 1973. It was not until the election of President George W. Bush in 2000, and rising worldwide oil prices, that exploration efforts for natural gas and oil began to increase.

Energy Policy after 1980

Energy policy changed dramatically with the election of President Reagan in 1980 and was guided by values significantly different from the previous decade. First was a belief that the United States had an abundance of energy supplies.[9] This resulted in the rejection of energy conservation and regulation strategies based on the belief that the energy policy of the 1970s was counterproductive and had discouraged domestic exploration and production. Policy efforts focused on increasing both production and consumption. Second, clean energy was rejected as a dominant policy value. Accordingly, the environment was not to take precedence over energy policy, and environmental standards for clean air and water were subject to relaxation. The operation of the market economy would create optimal environmental standards with a balance between energy for growth and a clean environment. Third, market operation, not government action, could best secure an abundant energy supply for the United States.

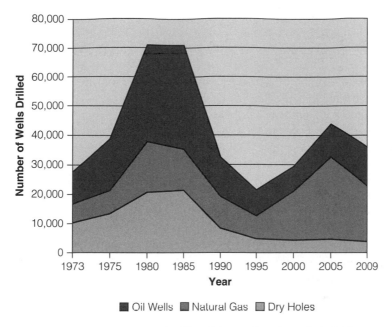

FIGURE 5.4 U.S. Domestic Oil and Gas Exploration, 1973–2009 (Thousands of Wells)

SOURCE: U.S. Energy Information Administration, Monthly Energy Review, April 2010, Petroleum Overview, Table 5-2 "Crude Oil and Natural Gas Exploratory and Development Wells, http://www.eia.doe.gov/emeu/mer/pdf/pages/sec5_4.pdf; Accessed May, 2010.

Import quotas, conservation measures, and prorationing were inappropriate and counterproductive. The private sector, not government action, would provide a secure energy supply for the future needs of the United States.

These policies were a significant change of direction and emphasized the decontrol of oil, opposed the windfall profits tax, encouraged offshore exploration for oil and gas, and favored opening federal lands to oil and gas exploration. Conservation programs were reduced on the assumption that market forces are the most appropriate means of regulating energy consumption. One link to the past was a continued interest in nuclear energy in the form of federal research and development funding. On the other hand, federal support for research and development of synthetic fuels was curtailed in favor of private investments (which were not forthcoming). Federal funding support for solar energy development declined by 70 percent by 1982.

Energy Policy after 2000

Since 1980, energy policy generally sought to rely on incentives to the private sector through the operation of market forces and to reduce the role of government. It should be noted that the United States has never followed a program of unrestricted competition in energy policy. The federal government and the state governments imposed regulations only after industry demanded protection from unlimited competition—that is, from threats to their profits. The movement

toward deregulation (Chapter 3) was motivated not only by an ideological commitment to the free-enterprise system but also by a desire to shift the costs to
consumers as a vehicle for maintaining industry profits.[10]

Bush Energy Policy Values.   The *Energy Policy Act of 2005* reflected the policy
preferences of the Bush administration. These include four primary goals: promotion of energy conservation and efficiency, increasing domestic energy production,
diversification of energy supply, and modernization of the energy infrastructure.
Policy options to achieve these goals included: (1) tax credits of between $1,700
and $4,000 for purchasers of electric or hybrid vehicles; (2) increased funding sup-
port for the development of hydrogen-fueled vehicles; (3) tax credits for individuals
of between $200 and $500 to offset the cost of installing high-efficiency home fur-
naces, air conditioners, solar water heating systems; (4) additional tax credits to support the use of alternative and renewal energy sources, such as wind, solar, and
biomass gases; and (5) funding support for an expanded role of nuclear power as
an energy source. The 2005 Energy Policy Act also served to maintain more traditional elements of energy policy. No changes were made in the CAFE standards for
automobile fuel efficiency, and there was an absence of any provision dealing with
global climate change. In many respects, the act maintained a traditional emphasis
on oil, gas, coal, and nuclear energy. Renewable energy sources such as wind, solar,
geothermal, and ocean power received only marginal support in this legislation.
This is further evidenced by President Bush's advocacy of policy options that
allow increased oil and gas exploration in the Arctic National Wildlife Refuge
(ANWR), where an estimated thirty billion barrels of oil may be recovered in
order to increase oil and gas production.

Obama Energy Policy Values.

> So we have a choice to make. We can remain one of the world's lead-
> ing importers of foreign oil, or we can make the investments that would
> allow us to become the world's leading exporter of renewable energy.
>
> *President Obama, 2009*

Obama's policy values have resulted in several initiatives. First, the implementation of increased CAFE standards for the automobile industry as discussed earlier in
this chapter is a change in American energy policy. A second policy change involves
expansion of offshore drilling for oil and natural gas. The devastating oil leak by a
British Petroleum drilling platform in the Gulf of Mexico in the spring of 2010 may
result in modifications to Obama's announced policy of expanding offshore drilling.
A third change involves a renewed emphasis on nuclear power as a source of electricity. This involves increased federal funding for research and development of nuclear
technologies for the future. A fourth initiative involves a number of actions to promote energy efficiency and conservation, including increased household appliance
efficiency, weatherization programs for homes and public buildings, and improvements in the power transmission grid for the nation. In a departure from the past,
the Obama administration is also seeking to create a link between environmental
issues (emissions, development of "green" industries, and "green" buildings) and
energy policy. A fifth policy value involves expanded federal leadership as opposed

to reliance on the private sector to deliver energy to the nation. The implementation of these values over the next few years has the potential to impact energy policy in the United States. Achieving "energy independence" appears to have evaporated as an energy policy goal in the U.S.

POLICY EVALUATION: CONTINUED
FOSSIL FUEL DEPENDENCE

Energy consumption patterns reflect a continued reliance on oil and natural gas combined with an increase in the importance of coal, nuclear, and hydroelectric power. Imposition of reduced speed limits, the automotive fuel economy standards, energy tax credits, and other programs have affected energy usage. Some analysts argue that changes in consumption patterns have been the result of economic conditions, not energy policy or technological changes in energy. Figure 5.5 indicates U.S. energy consumption patterns since 1973.

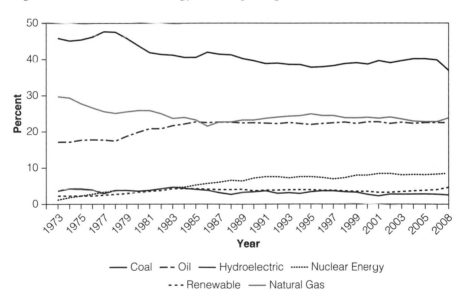

FIGURE 5.5 U.S. Energy Consumption by Source, 1973–2008 (Percentage)

(Oil and Natural Gas includes domestic and imported products; Renewable include solar, wind, biomas, coke and imported electricity)

SOURCE: Annual Energy Review, Energy Information Administration U.S. Department of Energy, June 2009, Table 1.3 "Primary Energy Consumption by Source," http://www.eia.doe.gov/emeu/aer/pdf/pages/sec1_9.pdf; Accessed May 2010.

Alternatives to Fossil Fuels

Research and Development.   The energy crisis of the 1970s increased interest in alternative sources of energy, such as solar, wind, and geothermal power. Before the rapid rise in the cost of fossil fuels, these alternatives were too expensive to utilize as major energy sources. With the drop in the price of oil to less than $17 per barrel by 1992, the economic incentives for continued research and development of alternative energy sources were again minimal. Federal funding for energy research and development activities was reduced as a national priority.

Solar Energy. An element of President Carter's energy program in the 1970s was the proposed national goal that by the year 2000, the United States should meet 20 percent of its energy need by solar power. Congress did not adopt this goal; solar power experienced relatively little development in the United States. The major piece of legislation so far has been the Solar Heating and Cooling Demonstration Act of 1975. This act created a limited solar demonstration program and clearinghouse. To date, the president, Congress, and private-sector energy companies have not established solar power as a major source of energy for the near future.

Coal Liquefaction. The liquefaction of coal into a crude-oil substitute provides the ability to convert coal into a relatively clean-burning fuel. The 1980 Energy Security Act, which created the Synthetic Fuels Corporation, provided authority for federal funding for research and development of this technology. The drop in the market price of crude oil that began in 1986, combined with an abundant global oil supply, limited the economic viability of coal liquefaction. This energy source remains undeveloped.

Geothermal Energy. Tapping the heat deep within the earth to convert water to steam for electricity generation is the goal of proponents of *geothermal* energy. Geothermal energy development would be most promising in scenic geologically active areas, such as Yellowstone National Park and Hawaii Volcanoes National Park. Concern over potential environmental damage led to congressional restrictions in 1994 on geothermal developments in the Yellowstone area. The Geysers, located in California, produce limited geothermal electricity. Expanding geothermal energy in the United States is no longer a policy priority.

Wind Energy. Harnessing wind to generate electricity is a green energy strategy. As of 2007, wind turbine facilities generated some thirty-one billion kilowatt-hours (kWh) of electricity, an amount sufficient to supply three million American homes. Wind technology has evolved in that the wind turbines in use in 2007 are capable of generating over twice the electrical power of turbines installed in 2000. Some estimates indicate that one turbine today can supply the electricity required for between 400 and 500 homes. The industry is now installing significantly larger projects than it did in 2000. One example is the 735 mega-watt Horse Hollow Wind Energy Center in West Texas. Wind energy has the advantage of being clean, renewable, and relatively inflation resistant. After initial construction, costs for wind energy farms remain stable and typically involve relatively low-cost maintenance. As the cost of oil and natural gas increases, wind becomes an attractive energy source. Issues involving expanding wind power include mechanisms to integrate electricity from wind farms into the current electrical grid, a grid that was not designed to incorporate long-distance transmission of wind-generated electricity. A second issue involves implementation of funding for continued research and development to produce ever more efficient wind turbines and tax credits to encourage private-sector investment in wind as a source of electricity. Wind power remains a potentially significant source of environmentally friendly energy.

Nuclear Power

Nuclear power is a nonfossil energy source receiving increased policy attention. The development of the nuclear energy industry and the emphasis on nuclear technology as a source of energy were products of the government's desire to use nuclear energy for peacetime purposes. There are two different nuclear processes, fission and fusion. Fission is splitting atoms; fusion produces energy by fusing atoms. To date, fusion technology is still in the research and development stage. Nuclear-fission technologies grew out of the nuclear submarine program of the U.S. Navy, in which light-water reactors (LWR) use Uranium 235, a relatively scarce substance, to produce heat for steam generation of electricity. Current fission technologies use the more abundant Uranium 238, converting it into Plutonium 239.

Although nuclear power plants do account for nearly 10 percent of America's energy consumption, expanding nuclear energy remains questionable because it has yet to overcome three problems: safety, waste disposal, and decommissioning strategies.[11] Initial research indicated that nuclear safety would not be a problem. The 1975 Rasmussen Report issued by the Nuclear Regulatory Commission (NRC) concluded that nuclear accidents would probably never occur and provided a foundation for expanding nuclear power. The March 1979 accident at Three Mile Island in Pennsylvania dramatically demonstrated the inaccuracy of the Rasmussen Report. Then, in 1981, investigators discovered that the earthquake protection system at the Diablo Canyon, California, nuclear power plant had been installed backwards.

Safety.   The issue of nuclear safety continues to have a significant impact on energy policy in the United States. Construction issues remain a challenge to the nuclear industry. Adequate training and supervision of plant personnel are still a major issue for the industry. Adequate planning in the event of a major accident has also been difficult to achieve. Nuclear plants may also be at risk from attacks by international terrorists.

The experience of the Department of Energy (DOE) with nuclear reactors utilized by the Department of Defense to produce material for the nation's atomic arsenal illustrates the potential problems with nuclear safety. Most of these facilities were constructed in the late 1940s and the 1950s and are now approaching the end of their useful life. Construction standards in place at the time were less stringent than today's. In late 1988, investigation revealed that some of these nuclear facilities created significant environmental contamination and had major safety defects. Inspection revealed cracks in reactor vessels, deficiencies in emergency cooling systems, defective fire-protection systems, obsolete and deteriorated equipment, and routine maintenance unperformed.

Waste.   Nuclear waste disposal has also proved to be a problem without a solution. Initially, experts assumed that spent nuclear fuel could be reprocessed into new fuel. This technology did not develop. Given the failure of the reprocessing option, the problem of long-term disposal of nuclear wastes remains unsolved. However, nuclear waste will not reach the high levels projected during the 1970s. This is primarily because utility companies have not ordered any new reactors for over ten years. While the volume of waste generated has not reached projected levels, the costs associated with nuclear waste management have skyrocketed dramatically. In 1983, DOE estimates for nuclear waste management were $23 billion. By 1988, this had almost doubled to $40 billion. These costs continue to escalate given the technological difficulties of managing nuclear waste.

Another difficulty with nuclear waste management involves the identification of old, inactive sites that pose a threat to health and the environment. Authorities have identified some 1,200 inactive waste sites, and DOE officials expect to identify over 1,700 sites as the process continues. The majority of these sites do not provide adequate containment of radioactive waste, and analysts cannot estimate accurately the costs associated with providing adequate storage until there has been a thorough and systematic evaluation of each site.

Nuclear Plant Age and Decommissioning.   The nation's nuclear generating plants operate under forty-year licenses issued by the NRC. These licenses began to expire in 2000 for the oldest plants; by 2020, the licenses of over half of the current 104 nuclear power plants will expire. The potential loss of these plants represents a serious energy problem since they generate 20 percent of the nation's electricity. One current strategy is to extend their operating license on a case-by-case basis by an additional ten to twenty years.

License extensions are a source of intense controversy. Opponents argue that it is unwise to extend to fifty or sixty years the operating life of nuclear plants designed and manufactured for a forty-year life cycle. Neither the NRC nor the nuclear industry has data on the structural integrity of materials continuously exposed to radiation in a nuclear reactor. Supporters argue that proper maintenance and repairs can easily extend the life cycle. In 1992, the NRC adopted procedures for extending the license of existing nuclear power plants on a case-by-case basis. One controversial component of the policy involves the decision to use the plant's current license requirements as a basis for extension. Critics argue that the more rigid safety standards based on today's knowledge should guide license extension, not the standards that were in place when a plant was first licensed some twenty to thirty years ago.

Decommissioning a nuclear power plant means shutting down and deactivating the plant to the extent that the site poses no environmental threat. To date, the NRC has not specified the guidelines and standards that will apply to future decommissioning activity. There are three options: dismantlement, mothballing, and entombment. Dismantlement presents problems of storage, because the fuel rods, containment buildings, and the reactor vessel will be radioactive for several thousand years. Some estimates indicate that up to 800 tons of radioactive material will require permanent storage from each nuclear unit dismantled. Mothballing simply means locking the facility behind a security perimeter and waiting several thousand years until the radioactive material decays on its own. This approach has been entitled SAFSTOR, or safe storage, by the NRC. Entombment takes mothballing a step further by constructing a large concrete structure around the facility. Both options present problems of protecting people and the environment from dangerous material for up to 80,000 years.

The actual costs for decommissioning a nuclear power plant are subject to debate. In 1978, the NRC estimated that costs would range between $43 million and $58 million, but the Rand Corporation published information that these costs might be in the $500 million range. The actual costs to achieve a partial decommission at Three Mile Island exceeded $1 billion. Actual costs vary significantly by the type of decommissioning selected: dismantlement is the most expensive, followed by SAFSTOR and the entombment strategy. As of 2007, there were fourteen nuclear facilities closed following the SAFSTOR strategy and ten facilities following a complete dismantlement strategy.

Costs associated with decommissioning may be transferred to utility customers over a protracted number of years. For example, its owners shut down the Maine Yankee nuclear facility in 1991, and customers of the utility have continued to pay for the decommissioning process through rate increases for electricity. State agencies and the Federal Energy Regulatory Commission (FERC) granted the utility rate increases to cover these costs. The costs of decommissioning a nuclear facility will fall on future customers over ten to twenty years after the plant has closed.

A national policy to apportion the costs of decommissioning a nuclear power plant has yet to be developed. Some plans call for the states to be involved and the federal government to assume all costs. The financial liability of the utility company that constructed and operated the plant has yet to be determined, and the impact on consumers served by utility companies operating nuclear power plants is unknown.

An unresolved policy issue is how to keep future generations informed (for 10,000 to 80,000 years) concerning the location and lethal nature of radioactive wastes. If such a mechanism had been in place since 1940, policymakers would know the location, nature, and the threat posed by nuclear wastes to the public and the environment today. No mechanism exists either for short-term (fifty to one hundred years) or long-term (thousands of years) transmittal of knowledge. Policy adopted by the Department of Energy in 1980 states, "Although this generation bears the responsibility for protecting future societies from the waste it creates, future societies must assume the responsibility for any risks, which arise from deliberate and informed acts, which they choose to perform."

The Future.   The United States has moved away from nuclear technology as an energy option. Power plant construction has ceased, projects have been

TABLE 5.1   Operating Nuclear Power Plants in the United States, 1960–2008

Year	Number of Operating Plants	Percent of U.S. Electricity
1960	3	0.1
1965	13	0.3
1970	20	1.4
1975	57	9.0
1980	71	11.0
1985	96	15.5
1990	112	19.0
1995	109	20.1
2000	104	19.8
2008	104	19.6

SOURCE: U.S. Department of Energy. *Annual Energy Review 2008*, Nuclear Energy, Table 9-2, Nuclear Power Plant Operations 1957–2008, June 26, 2009, http://www.eia.doe.gov/emeu/aer/nuclear.html; Accessed May 19, 2010.

canceled, and the licensing procedure has been stiffened. Since 1978, the utility industry has placed no new orders for nuclear power plant construction. Nuclear power plant construction was virtually complete by 1990 (see Table 5.1). President Obama advocates a significant policy change that would foster the construction of new nuclear power plants to replace aging nuclear facilities and increase utilization of this source of energy.

This pattern does not hold true for other nations. Currently there are 438 nuclear power plants in operation around the world, with 57 more facilities under construction and still more in the planning phase. Table 5.2 depicts the status of global nuclear power plants. On a global scale, nuclear power continues to be a major source of energy.

Global reliance on nuclear power traces to two factors. First, construction of nuclear power plants represents an investment of billions of dollars. The size of this investment exerts economic pressure to maintain the nuclear power plants in order to obtain a return on the massive construction expenditures. Second, many countries simply have no other currently available viable source of electricity. As of 1988, approximately 15 percent of global electricity was the product of nuclear power. By 1990, this figure had increased to over 20 percent. Even a major nuclear accident such as that at Chernobyl in the former Soviet Union has not deterred emphasis on nuclear power plants on the international scene. Figure 5.6 reflects the relative importance of nuclear power in the generation of electricity for countries with nuclear power plants.

Political Impact of Continued Oil Dependence

There are political consequences of the free world's dependence on oil imports. The first is the uncertainty of supply. Interruptions or threats to the supply of oil

TABLE 5.2   Operating Nuclear Power Plants by Country, 2010

Country	Reactors	Long-Term Shutdown	Under Construction
Argentina	2		1
Armenia	1		
Belgium	7		
Brazil	2		
Bulgaria	2		2
Canada	18	4	
China	11		23
Czech Republic	6		
Finland	4		1
France	58		1
Germany	17		
Hungary	4		
India	19		4
Iran			1
Japan	54	1	1
South Korea	20		6

Country	Reactors	Long-Term Shutdown	Under Construction
Lithuania		1	
Mexico	2		
Netherlands	1		
Pakistan	2		1
Romania	2		
Russian Federation	32		9
Slovak Republic	4		2
Slovenia	1		
South Africa	2		
Spain	8		
Sweden	10		
Switzerland	5		
Ukraine	15		2
United Kingdom	19		
United States	104		1*
Taiwan	6		2

SOURCE: *Tennessee Valley Authority in Tennessee (projected completion: 2012)
Total Reactors: 438
Long-Term Shutdown: 4
Permanent Shutdown: 1
Total Under Construction: 57
International Atomic Energy Agency (IAEA), http://www.iaea.cr.at/programmes/a2/; Accessed May 19, 2010.

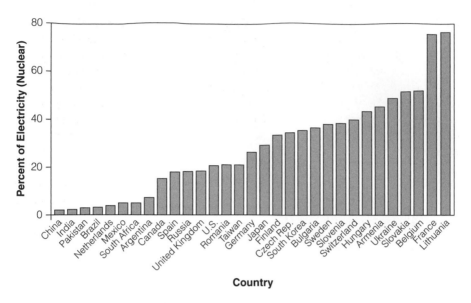

FIGURE 5.6 Percent Nuclear Electricity by Country (2009)

SOURCE: International Atomic Energy Agency, Power Reactor Information System (PRIS), 2009 http://www.iaea.or.at/programmes/a2/; Accessed May 2010.

can severely weaken the West's economic, political, and military power. The West's Achilles' heel is its dependence on imported oil. Interrupt the oil flow, and the West faces economic collapse. The oil reserves that the West must have to survive are located mainly in the highly volatile Middle East. Another consequence is that the Western world has been drawn into increased military and political involvement in the Persian Gulf region, with a primary goal of promoting internal stability in order to maintain an adequate oil supply (see Chapter 12).[12] Western involvement ranges from military sales and assistance to air and naval bases in the Middle East. Currently, the United States has either an established military presence or arrangements for military bases in Iraq, Oman, Egypt, and Saudi Arabia. The United States military presence in the Persian Gulf region has expanded dramatically since Operation Desert Storm (1990–1991) in response to the Iraqi invasion of Kuwait and again in 2003 with the military action in Iraq that removed Saddam Hussein from power.

The dissolution of the former Soviet Union is a source of concern for stability in the Middle East. Some of the now-independent republics have a predominantly Islamic population, and the known oil reserves in what was the Soviet Union are unevenly distributed among the new republics. The foreign policy values and orientations of these new nations remain unclear, and the political, military, and economic consequences for stability in the Middle East and Central Asia remain uncertain.

Hidden Costs. A consequence of dependence on imported oil is the impact on military and defense spending. In order to maintain economic stability within the United States, it is necessary to protect America's sources of oil from disruption. This involves a significant military commitment in the Persian Gulf region. The cost of this military presence is not included in the price of imported oil. Imported oil adds significantly to military spending of the United States.

American reliance on imported oil has the potential to contribute a structural element to the trade deficit. As oil imports rise, the trade deficit of the United States increases. Oil imports account for approximately 50 percent of the U.S. trade deficit. The cost of imported oil saddles the American economy with an international trade burden.

Organization of Petroleum Exporting Countries (OPEC). An additional element of Western dependence on imported oil has been an inability to control the price of oil. When OPEC acted from a position of strength, the oil-consuming West demonstrated a marked inability to limit price increases. This was a major problem in the late 1970s, when an upward spiral in oil prices placed increased inflationary pressure on Western economies. Erosion of OPEC unity was a major factor in the dramatic drop in global oil prices. OPEC disunity is a function of disagreement over oil prices, production levels, and political conflicts. Disagreement over production levels also reduced OPEC unity. As the West began to become more energy efficient, demand for oil also began to decrease slightly. The most appropriate strategy to maintain price when demand drops is to reduce supply. OPEC has not been able to establish an allocation formula for reducing production levels. Member states —in need of revenues—have produced at levels higher than global demand, which acted to keep oil prices under control until 2004. At this time, the global demand for oil began to increase, allowing the price to steadily increase.

Political disunity also is a factor. The prolonged war between Iraq and Iran during the 1980s contributed to higher production levels as each nation sought revenues to fund the war effort. In the aftermath of the Persian Gulf War of 1991, Iraqi production was at minimal levels and the oil fields in Kuwait were inoperable because the retreating Iraqi army had set a large number of oil wells on fire. These fires were extinguished beginning in late 1991. By 1993, production from the Kuwaiti fields had been restored. Today, military and political conflict in the Persian Gulf contribute to uncertainty over oil production levels as the security of oil fields across the region remains a question.

Conflict between Israel and the Arab nations has the potential to strengthen unity within OPEC. In 1973, the Arab members of OPEC found that oil was a common weapon to weaken support for Israel around the world. The possibility exists that any future Arab–Israeli conflict may provide a force to significantly strengthen OPEC unity again in the future.

Although the strength of OPEC has varied, it would be a mistake to minimize the potential impact that the organization can have on oil supply and costs. Internal events in the member nations can disrupt production, and external events can promote OPEC unity, as demonstrated during the mid- to late 1970s.

FUTURE ALTERNATIVES: ENERGY POLICY CONCERN

The energy crisis of the early 1970s evaporated, and the public concern that stimulated energy policy activity diminished. Lower energy prices and an adequate supply of oil mark the period until 2004–2006. The result was a return to an attitude of complacency toward energy policy.

One factor that contributed to the energy shortfall of the early 1970s was a product of faulty demand projections by the energy companies and governments. During the 1950s and 1960s, experts continually underestimated demand for oil. Ten-year projections were off by as much as 25 or 30 percent.[13] A gap of five to ten years exists between the decision to seek additional oil and gas reserves and actual production from new sources. Before the 1970s, the routine underestimation of demand failed to stimulate sufficient exploratory efforts to maintain a balance between supply and demand. By the early 1970s, energy consumption patterns, which were the cornerstone of forecasting, produced projections of dramatic increases in energy demand for the decade of the 1980s and beyond. The OPEC unity achieved in 1973, which provided a framework for price increases and limited production quotas, added credibility to the projections of a continuing future gap between supply and demand. Between 1973 and 1978, the growth in the demand for oil did exceed the growth in the oil supply, with several consequences. First, decisions were made to increase the oil supply by exploring the North Slope in Alaska, to increase exploration in the North Sea, and to intensify exploration efforts in other regions of the world as well as across the United States.

Second, the increase in the cost of energy produced slow but continuous changes in consumption patterns. Homeowners insulated their homes better. The efficiency of residential and commercial heating units increased. Fuel efficiency became an important value in the transportation industry as new trucks and aircraft were designed and manufactured. Changes in manufacturing techniques also provided increased energy efficiency. These changes acted to decrease the rate at which energy demand grew. A gradual change to more energy-efficient automobiles took place. However, during the late 1990s, consumer preference for less fuel-efficient vehicles began to increase with the popularity of trucks and sport utility vehicles (SUVs). This shift in consumer purchasing preferences is another indication of complacency toward energy supply.

Third, OPEC economies were becoming more dependent on the oil consumption patterns of the West. Modernization and development programs created an ever-increasing demand for oil revenues within OPEC nations. The need to market oil and maintain production became a driving force within OPEC nations. Between 1974 and 1988, non-OPEC oil production increased by over 80 percent, from seventeen million to over thirty-one million barrels per day. This increase in production, combined with the improvement in energy efficiency and other conservation measures, acted to create an imbalance in which supply exceeded demand by 1988. The availability of an adequate energy supply and lower prices had a major impact on the United States. Complacency replaced public concern, as oil remained a primary energy source.

RENEWED CONCERN

This complacency was not justified. Contrary to public perceptions, the energy system is considerably more volatile and dynamic now than in the past. Before 1973, the actions of the international oil companies largely controlled the supply and price of energy. During the 1970s, the OPEC oil cartel acted to control oil supply and prices. The power of these two systems of control has evaporated as oil supply, production, and cost respond to international market forces and competing international interests.

Global demand for oil continues to increase. One source of this significantly increased demand for oil is China. As China experiences significant industrial and economic growth, its appetite for oil increases. One result of this new source of demand for oil is an increase in the price for oil on the global market.

Another area of concern is the potential for political unrest in the Middle East to disrupt the flow of oil to the West. Military and sectarian conflict in Iraq and other areas has the potential to reduce oil exports from that region. Potential actions by international terrorists also reduce the certainty of oil from the Middle East and to force oil prices to ever-higher levels. Market uncertainty over the impact of political unrest also contributes significantly to increases in oil prices. In late 2007, the per-barrel price for oil had increased to the $100 range as a result of increased demand and market uncertainty over an uninterrupted supply of oil.

This has at least two policy implications for the United States. First, continued dependence on oil ties American economic strength to access to foreign energy sources. Any disruption in oil supply will have potentially profound economic consequences. One consequence of this dependence on imported oil is the requirement for what may be a prolonged military presence in the Persian Gulf to maintain the flow of oil to Europe, Japan, and the United States. Second, low international prices act to reduce domestic oil production in the United States and reduce investment in alternative energy sources. The dramatic increase in the price of oil provides the United States with an opportunity to invest in the development of wind, solar, geothermal, and ocean wave technologies that can potentially increase energy self-sufficiency and improve environmental quality though a reduced reliance on fossil fuels.

OPEC also faces challenges: In order to maintain high prices for its oil it must (1) maintain a balance between production levels and prices to discourage the development of alternative energy sources, (2) follow strategies that will minimize expansion of non–OPEC oil sources, (3) increase dependence on OPEC as a primary source of energy, and (4) develop strategies that will minimize the impact of political and military unrest on their ability to provide oil to the global marketplace.

Moreover, the insatiable American appetite for energy places energy companies in strong political positions. Concern about foreign imports, and about sufficiency of energy supply, impact the environment. The Bush administration pushed for opening the Arctic National Wildlife Refuge (ANWAR) to oil drilling. President Obama announced a policy of expanding offshore drilling to increase the nation's supply of domestic oil and gas. Natural disasters, such as Hurricane Katrina in 2005, also impact the supply of energy to the nation. As Katrina moved through the Gulf of Mexico, oil well platforms were forced to cease operation as crews were evacuated. Following the storm, it took time to repair the platforms in order to resume production. Hurricanes also present a significant danger to oil refineries located in Texas and Louisiana.

Drilling accidents impact offshore oil and gas exploration. Due to pressure from environmental groups, offshore drilling has moved into ever-deeper waters. British Petroleum's *Deepwater Horizon* drilling platform was producing oil from a well five-thousand feet below the surface when a major accident destroyed the platform and created an unprecedented oil spill in the Gulf of Mexico in 2010. Because of the Gulf oil spill, Obama reversed himself and ordered a six-month moratorium on deep-water drilling, but a federal judge invalidated the moratorium. The administration has promised to appeal the judge's decision.

An important policy issue involves whether to 1) allow drilling closer to shore where repairs are easier, 2) allow drilling on federal lands such as the Alaska National Wildlife Reserve, 3) restrict drilling offshore and on federal lands, or 4) continue the current policy of encouraging deep-water drilling. Offshore drilling is in the sphere of federal responsibility with policies flowing from the federal government not state governments.

ENVIRONMENTAL POLICY

Public concern over the environment was minimal until the end of the nineteenth century. Westward expansion of the United States reflected little concern for soil depletion, deforestation or the devastation from soil erosion. Minerals were mined and metals smelted with minimal concern for their effects on freshwater supplies; when contamination did result, it seemed a minor problem, because alternative sources of water seemed endless.

Following industrialization, and rapid population growth, the problem of environmental preservation and protection could no longer be easily avoided. From the 1870s through the 1930s, conservation was the dominant theme of environmental policy. Examples include the establishment of Yellowstone Park as the first national park in 1872 and the 1897 legislation that created an extensive national forest system. Although conservation provided a general policy focus, there was significant disagreement over specific strategies. To some, conservation meant resource management for effective utilization, such as scientific forestry; others viewed conservation primarily as wilderness preservation. This conflict over strategy remains present today as a major policy issue.

Despite a history of conservation policies, fundamental concerns with environmental protection were absent from the policy agenda as late as the 1950s. The publication of *Silent Spring* in 1962 drew attention to the dangers of pesticides, such as DDT, in the food chain.[14] This book was a major catalyst to mobilize a heightened environmental consciousness. The sense of social responsibility that emerged in the 1960s also moved environmental policy from the background to the forefront of the policy agenda.

ISSUE BACKGROUND: A LEGACY OF ENVIRONMENTAL ABUSE

Indifference and neglect left their mark on the physical environment of the United States. The environmental problems the nation now faces are the product of a historic lack of public concern with the unintended but harmful consequences of economic growth and development of an industrialized society. Air pollution, water pollution, solid-waste pollution, toxic- and hazardous-waste pollution, acid rain, and changing land-use patterns, as well as global climate change, all pose important problems.

Air Pollution

Air pollutants can be categorized in two groups: particles and gases. Particulate matter includes such material as ashes, soot, and lead (a noncombustible gasoline additive). Though particulate pollution is a problem, the dangers presented by the release of gases into the air are just as real but probably less well understood by the public. The major air pollutants sort into the following five categories.

1. **Carbon monoxide (CO).** Carbon monoxide is a colorless by-product of the incomplete combustion of carbon fuels. Gasoline engines are its primary source.
2. **Sulfur dioxide (SO2).** The combustion of fuels containing sulfur produces sulfur dioxide. When combined with water vapor, it can form sulfuric acid and fall as acid rain.
3. **Hydrocarbons (HC).** Hydrocarbons, consisting of various combinations of hydrogen and carbon, are the unburned fuel resulting from incomplete combustion. The compounds have a major impact in the production of photochemical smog in urban areas.
4. **Nitrogen oxide (NO).** Nitrogen oxide is a by-product of fossil fuel combustion at high temperature levels. It combines with hydrocarbons to produce smog.
5. **Particulate matter.** Particulates include liquids or solids released into the atmosphere.

In 1980, the Environmental Protection Agency (EPA) estimated substantial increases in air pollution by the year 2000, with total emissions of particulate matter projected to double by that year.[15] As indicated in Figure 5.7, the emission of these *greenhouse gases* has increased but at a lower rate than initially projected by the EPA. As indicated in the graph, there has been a slight reduction in greenhouse gas emissions in the U.S. since 2005.

A focus on measuring the raw amount of individual pollutants produced can be a deceptive approach to the problem, because serious health problems can result from either short-term exposure to high levels of these compounds or long-term exposure to relatively low levels. There is also evidence that these

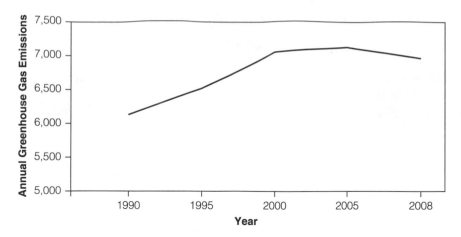

F I G U R E   5.7   Trends in U.S. Greenhouse Gas Emissions, 1990–2008

SOURCE: Environmental Protection Agency, 2010, U.S. Greenhouse Gas Inventory Report, April 2010, Table 2-1 "Recent Trends in Greenhouse Gas Emissions and Sinks," http://www.epa.gov/climatechange/emissions/usinventoryreport.html; Accessed May 2010. Data reflects units of teragrams of carbon dioxide equivalent (Tg CO_2 Eq.), which weigh each gas by its global warming potential (GWP).

pollutants act synergistically on animal and plant life. This means that exposure to the compounds together produces more harmful impacts than would result from exposure to them separately.

Not all emissions are easily categorized as either harmless or polluting. Such is the case with carbon dioxide (CO_2). (See Figure 5.8.) Scientists are increasingly concerned that high levels of CO_2 in the atmosphere may warm the earth and result in major climatic changes, which is known as the "greenhouse effect." Increased atmospheric levels of CO_2 trap the earth's heat by reducing the escape of infrared radiation from the surface into space. There is debate within the scientific community over the seriousness of the greenhouse effect. Debate also focuses on the origins of the rising levels of atmospheric CO_2. Some experts attribute high CO_2 levels to the use of fossil fuels; others believe that the rapid deforestation in Africa, South America, and Asia is the primary cause.[16]

Ozone Layer.   A thin layer of *ozone* some thirty miles above the surface protects the earth from excessive ultraviolet rays. The production and use of *chlorofluorocarbons* (CFCs) threatens the integrity of that protective layer. Scientists have documented a thinning of the ozone layer above North America and Europe. Depletion of the protective ozone layer could result in a higher incidence of skin cancer, cataracts, and other health problems. This is primarily due to the harmful nature of ultraviolet-B radiation from the sun.

Chlorofluorocarbons are viewed as the primary cause of ozone depletion. Air-conditioning and refrigeration units employed CFCs extensively. In 1987, the European Economic Community (EEC), the United States, and twenty-nine other nations initially approved the Montreal Protocol on Substances that Deplete the Ozone Layer, a group that represented 82 percent of the world's

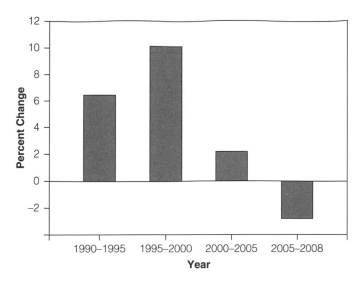

FIGURE 5.8 Trends in U.S. Carbon Dioxide Emissions, 1990–2008 (change in percents)

SOURCE: U.S. Environmental Protection Agency, 2010, U.S. Greenhouse Gas Inventory Report, April 2010, Table 2-1: Recent Trends in U.S. Greenhouse Gas Emissions and Sinks (Tg CO2 Eq.), http://www.epa.gov/climatechange/emissions/downloads10/US-GHG-Inventory-2010_Chapter2-Trends.pdf; Accessed May 2010.

consumption of CFCs. A number of other nations have since signed the protocol with the result that CFC emissions significantly declined during the 1990s.

Water and Solid-Waste Pollution

Water Pollution.   Neglect of the nation's waterways has been a major environmental problem. Perhaps the most dramatic incident illustrating the seriousness of water pollution occurred in the 1960s: the Cuyahoga River in Cleveland caught fire because of the extensive discharge of flammable wastes into the river. Although this was not a typical event, virtually all surface waterways have experienced some type of pollution.

Even though water pollution is a well-documented nationwide problem, its severity varies considerably among the different regions of the country. Waterways of the industrialized Northeast and Midwest have been especially abused. Even though sources of water pollution vary greatly, it is possible to classify most pollutants into four categories.[17]

Industrial wastes contain a wide range of organic and inorganic compounds, including heavy metals, such as mercury and zinc. A relatively new water-pollution phenomenon is thermal pollution; the cause is the discharge of heated water into rivers and lakes after cooling equipment used primarily in electric power plants. Thermal pollution heightens the toxicity of some other pollutants and, by accelerating the decomposition of organic matter, also lowers the oxygen level in surface waters.

Domestic and municipal wastes include human wastes and other compounds disposed off by people in their day-to-day lives.

Agricultural wastes include animal waste and other compounds that may pose health risks, such as fertilizers and pesticides that run off into waterways and enter the food chain. One of the greatest threats posed by agricultural wastes is the excess nutrients that enter lakes, rivers, and streams. These nutrients foster rapid growth of algae and other microorganisms that deplete the oxygen supply for fish and other organisms. One such organism, *Pfiesteria piscicida*, killed millions of fish in the late 1990s in the mid-Atlantic states of Maryland, Virginia, and North Carolina. The Centers for Disease Control and Prevention (CDC) notes that *Pfiesteria* outbreaks occur in watersheds that drain large concentrations of chicken, hog, and other livestock operations.

Miscellaneous pollutants may be natural and include silt and sedimentation entering surface waters following rains. Also included are more serious pollutants, such as those from accidental oil spills. While offshore oil spills from supertankers and drilling accidents receive publicity due to their magnitude, the hundreds of other smaller spills that occur each year receive relatively little attention. Mining activity also adds to water pollution. Strip mining exposes sulfur compounds in the soil, which react with rain to form sulfuric acid, which then runs off into surface waters. Already a major pollutant in Appalachian mining regions, it is now also a problem in Western states where coal mining has been on the increase.

One approach to reducing water pollution involves aggressive wastewater treatment by cities and industry to eliminate most of the contaminants before they enter surface waters. There are three levels of waste treatment. Primary treatment uses settling chambers to remove solid contaminants before the water returns to streams and rivers. Secondary treatment filters the remaining wastes through beds of rock and sand to remove organic contaminants, with the addition of chlorinates to kill bacteria. Tertiary systems use additional filtration (such as activated charcoal) to remove inorganic compounds and heavy metals.

There is no lack of waste-treatment technologies available to municipalities and industry to minimize the discharge of contaminants. The major obstacle to their use is cost. Construction and operation of a tri-level treatment system is beyond the financial means of many cities and industries. Such a system can cost three to four times as much as a bi-level treatment system. The reality of immediate economic costs has historically acted to shift policy options away from a completely aggressive waste-treatment strategy.

Solid-Waste Pollution.   Solid-waste pollution correlates directly to the level of economic activity. The United States produces a variety of *solid wastes* each year, including agricultural solid wastes, residential and commercial solid wastes, industrial solid wastes, and mineral solid wastes (primarily slag and mill tailings). The traditional approach has been simply to bury the waste in landfills, an option that is less than satisfactory given the projections of continued growth in annual solid-waste production. Despite this veritable landslide of solid waste, recycling is not a major priority in the United States with the majority of municipal solid waste sent to landfills.

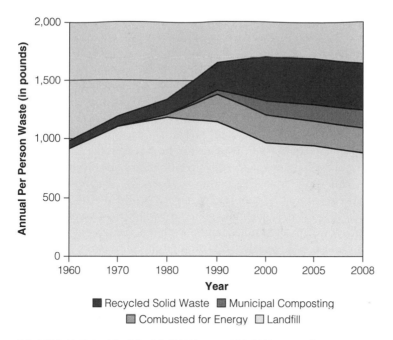

FIGURE 5.9 Municipal Solid Waste, 1960–2008, Annual Per Person Waste (in pounds)

SOURCE: U. S. Environmental Protection Agency, Municipal Solid Waste in the United States, 2008. Adapted from Table 4: Generation, Materials, Recover, Composting, Combustion With Energy Recovery and Discards of MSW, http://www.epa.gov/epawaste/nonhaz/municipal/msw99.htm; Accessed May 2010.

As indicated in Figure 5.9, recycling is now at approximately 25 percent of municipal waste generated. The slow growth in recycling can be attributed to the fact that it is economically expedient, in the short run, to discard processed materials and utilize new raw materials in the production process. For example, it is cheaper to use pulp timber than to recycle paper. Government action mandating recycling is already done in some localities, but remains unlikely at the national level within the next decade. The proportion of waste transported to landfills has decreased since 1990 as some components of municipal waste have been burned in the generation of electricity.

Toxic and Hazardous Waste

Hazardous wastes are those wastes that pose a significant threat to either health or the environment due to their "quantity, concentration, physical, chemical, or infectious characteristics."[18] Safe disposal of hazardous wastes remains an environmental issue. In fact, estimates indicate that only a relatively small amount of toxic wastes are disposed off safely.

The impact of improper toxic-waste disposal may emerge only decades later, as illustrated by the events at Love Canal in Niagara Falls, New York. The Hooker Chemical Company buried more than 20,000 tons of chemical wastes containing over 300 different chemicals at Love Canal in the 1950s. Two decades later, in the 1970s, residents in the Love Canal area experienced major health problems directly attributed to the buried toxic wastes. It took over $30 million to clean up the site and relocate residents.

One type of increasingly important hazardous waste is radioactive waste. The two main sources of radioactive waste are the nuclear weapons program and nuclear power plants used to generate electricity. Some of these high-level wastes are so toxic that they must be stored for 500,000 years. Low-level wastes also pose a major problem. The United States produces over three million cubic feet of this waste, which requires safe storage for hundreds of years. Nuclear waste-management policy is an area marked by controversy and uncertainty.

Safe disposal of radioactive wastes has continued to prove an elusive goal. As the United States developed nuclear technology during World War II, there was minimal concern for safe disposal techniques. Radioactive wastes were typically burned, buried in shallow pits, or simply dumped into the existing sewage system. The governing philosophy was that safe disposal involved simply the dilution of radioactive wastes, which facilitated dispersal of the wastes in the environment. During the late 1940s and the 1950s, the high volume of waste required developing a new disposal system: ocean dumping. This technology involved using containers (primarily fifty-five-gallon drums) to hold radioactive wastes. These containers were then filled with concrete and dumped off the coast of the United States.

Between 1945 and 1967, the United States dumped almost 100,000 of these containers into the waters off the Atlantic and Pacific coasts. This practice was terminated by 1970 because of the long-term threats posed to the environment. Gradually, the containers corrode and the wastes become exposed to ocean currents and enter the food chain. Currently, ocean dumping of radioactive waste is not a formal policy of any nation.

With the elimination of ocean dumping, land disposal is now the method of choice. The only problem is that a viable technology for long-term disposal does not yet exist. Current surface facilities are rapidly reaching or exceeding capacity. A safe, technologically feasible storage system is not in existence, and the level of radioactive waste continues to accumulate.

One policy obstacle to solving the problem of toxic-waste dumps, nuclear and otherwise, is that many sites are not yet identified. The EPA has located over 17,000 potentially dangerous sites, but possibly thousands more still await discovery. Virtually every state in the union contains at least one hazardous toxic waste dump. Congress has not provided the EPA with the budget and the personnel to complete this critical first step of identifying them.

Acid Rain

A persistent environmental problem is the phenomenon of acid rain. This is produced when sunlight chemically converts air pollutants, primarily sulfur dioxide, nitrogen oxides, and hydrocarbons, into sulfates, nitrates, and other acidic compounds, which are returned to earth by rain and snow, and gradually change the acidic balance in both water and soil.

Acidity is measured in pH units on a scale ranging from 0 to 14, with the pH value of 7 representing neutrality. Values greater than 7 represent alkalinity, and values less than 7 represent acidity. The logarithmic nature of the scale means that a pH level of 5 is ten times more acidic than pH 6 and that pH 4 is one hundred times more acidic than pH 6. For example, a lake that increases in acidity from pH 4.5 to pH 4.2 has doubled its level of acidity. A lack of understanding of pH levels has minimized public concern with the potential threat posed by acid rain.

When acidity in a body of water exceeds the level of pH 5, the water loses the ability to support fish and plant life. Given that over twenty million tons of sulfur dioxides and twenty million tons of nitrogen oxides enter the atmosphere each year, the United States faces a potential problem of enormous magnitude. Data from the EPA indicate that the acidic level for rain and snow is below the level of pH 5 for the entire eastern half of the nation. This means that increased levels of acidity threaten virtually all rivers and lakes in the affected region. There are geologic differences, however, that can reduce the impact on bodies of water in this region. For example, the limestone floors of some lakes in New England neutralize some of the acidity. The problem is that often more acidity enters a lake or stream than it can neutralize naturally.

The Environmental Legacy

The absence of an aggressive environmental-protection strategy produced potentially severe air, water, and toxic-waste problems. Land-use practices also pose problems for the nation. Both conventional and strip-mining activities continue to have significant impacts. Without extensive reclamation efforts after *strip mining*, the land is permanently unusable for productive or recreational purposes. The tailings from conventional mining activity also present problems as wind and rain transport contaminants into the ecosystem. This is a significant problem for uranium mining, because it leaves radioactive debris in the open in mammoth sand piles. Land-use patterns are also an issue of concern. Topsoil erosion, the loss of wetlands, and forestry practices remain areas of policy conflict. An area of increasing concern is indoor air pollution. The traditional view presumed that pollution was only an outdoor problem: People could escape the problem by remaining inside. However, such is not the case; studies have documented serious indoor health hazards, such as formaldehyde foam (used in building insulation), asbestos, and other toxic substances.

As with energy, the environmental policy legacy has been one of historical neglect of environmental protection, which allowed environmental abuse to develop into a significant public policy problem.

CONTEMPORARY ENVIRONMENTAL POLICY

Although there are significant environmental problems facing the United States, government has undertaken efforts to address them. This section will look at these major policy responses, including the historical background of some environmental legislation, and will outline the most important features and goals of the evolving public policies.

Water-Pollution Policy

The federal government gradually and partially assumed leadership in this policy area. The origins of the federal role go back to the Refuse Act of 1899, which sought to limit the blockage of navigable rivers by municipal and industrial debris. Although largely ignored, the Act did indicate the necessity for action by the federal government to respond to a problem that extends beyond state borders.

Congress gradually expanded this federal role. The Water Pollution Act of 1948 provided federal funds for sewage-plant construction, leaving standards and enforcement largely to the states. In 1956, Congress amended the Act to assign the Public Health Service (PHS) a permanent role in monitoring water quality standards in municipalities across the nation. The 1961 Water Pollution Control Act and the 1965 Water Quality Act continued to provide federal funds for sewage-plant construction and to assign primary responsibility for water standards and enforcement to the states.

The underlying assumption of the emphasis on state responsibility held that states would be vigilant in protecting their own water resources, but this was not typically the case. State governments proved unwilling to enact strict standards for fear of driving industry into other states with less stringent standards. Most adopted very weak water-quality standards.

The Clean Waters Restoration Act of 1966 signaled the beginning of the transfer of water-quality enforcement responsibility from the states to the federal government. The Water Pollution Control Act Amendments of 1972 continued this trend of increased federal responsibility. The unrealized goal of this Act was to end the discharge of pollutants into waterways by 1985 by mandating that industry and municipalities adopt the "best available" sewage-treatment technology. The 1974 Safe Drinking Water Act continued the emphasis on federal action by assigning to the EPA responsibility for establishing minimum standards for drinking water.

Air-Pollution Policy

Attempts to control and improve air quality in the United States followed a similar pattern of gradually expanding the federal role. The first action taken by Congress, the Air Pollution Control Act of 1955, did little more than fund research on air quality. The federal role was gradually increased as the Clean Air Act of 1963 provided funds for state air-quality programs, and the Motor Vehicle Air Pollution Control Act of 1965 empowered the former Department of Health, Education, and Welfare (HEW) to set automobile-emission standards. This was the first federal program to regulate emissions directly. The National Emissions Standards Act of 1967 expanded the program.

The 1970 Clean Air Act amendments signaled a major change in air pollution policy in the United States. This major piece of legislation sought to reduce, by 1975, all air pollutants that constituted a health threat. Congress delegated primary responsibility for establishing and enforcing standards to the EPA. Initially, these standards reflected a primary emphasis on protection of public health and welfare, with a secondary emphasis on economic issues. The 1977 Clean Air Act Amendments reflected an effort to respond to the energy crisis by relaxing emission standards. Emission standards for the automobile industry were delayed for four years but other efforts to relax standards had mixed results. An important addition to the 1977 Act was adoption of a nondegradation or clean growth component designed to protect air quality in regions with air cleaner than that required by federal standards.

Congress enacted another series of amendments to the Clean Air Act in November 1990. These amendments aimed to move air quality toward the standards originally targeted for 1975. One specific provision includes reducing SO_2 emissions in order to reduce the threat of acid rain. The amendments also allowed tailoring some air-quality standards to the degree of pollution in individual communities, as opposed to setting uniform nationwide standards for all emissions. Critics of these amendments argue that they do not contain sufficiently stringent nationwide air-quality standards. Supporters hold that these amendments did embody a move in the direction of the standards in the original Clean Air Act.

The National Environmental Policy Act (NEPA)

The National Environmental Policy Act (January 1, 1970) reflected a major change in environmental policy by the federal government.[19] The Act placed greater emphasis on federal leadership in formulating national environmental policy through the creation of the Council on Environmental Quality (CEQ), within the Executive Office of the President, to provide advice on environmental policy issues. Although the CEQ was largely an advisory body only, its existence within the Executive Office provided the framework for a strengthened federal role under the leadership of the president. The legislation also mandated that the president submit an annual environmental quality report to Congress and that federal agencies submit environmental impact statements to the CEQ on any action that would affect the environment. The Act sought to force public agencies to undertake a deliberate and thorough analysis of the potential environmental consequences of any projects under their control.

The Environmental Protection Agency was part of a reorganization of the federal bureaucracy. The EPA combined some fifteen offices and agencies into a single agency assigned responsibility for (1) water pollution, (2) air pollution, (3) solid-waste management, (4) radiation control, and (5) pesticide and toxic-substance control. The legislation intended that the new agency centralize federal power in environmental policy by eliminating the previous pattern of fragmentation and decentralization.

Unlike the advisory Council on Environmental Quality, the EPA is a regulatory agency with power to establish and enforce policy. The actual impact of the EPA on environmental issues is a function of the values and assumptions of the president and of the administrator that guides the agency in interpreting and enforcing environmental rules and statutes. Political values and arrangements influence the agency. Critics periodically charge the EPA with making sweetheart deals with major industrial polluters and with scheduling EPA cleanup projects based on political considerations instead of environmental concerns. Critics also charge that the White House has the ability to significantly edit EPA reports prior to their release. For example, in 2007 the Bush administration was charged with editing an EPA report on the health impact of various levels of air pollution and with editing reports dealing with global climate change in an effort to minimize the issue of global warming.

The Hazardous-Waste Superfund.   One program that continues to embody controversy is the Superfund, created during the Carter administration by the 1980 Comprehensive Environmental Response Compensation and Liability Act (CERCLA). The Superfund provided the EPA with the authority and the funds to assist in cleanup operations at toxic- and hazardous-waste sites across the country. The creation of the fund intended to allow an active role for the EPA in dealing with emergencies and with abandoned toxic-waste sites. By 1984, the EPA had identified over 17,000 disposal sites, with estimates that an additional 5,000 sites exist. EPA estimates indicated in 1984 that the cleanup operations at the 2,000 most dangerous sites would cost between $8 billion and $16 billion, roughly five to ten times the size of the original level of the Superfund.

The provisions of the Superfund act have generated a limited number of site cleanups. In fact, a number of the sites have been cleaned by simply transferring the wastes to another toxic-waste site. This transfer of wastes from one location to another does not indicate progress in a cleanup program. The Superfund program has been hindered by a lack of federal financial support.

POLICY EVALUATION: SEARCHING FOR DIRECTION

Current Policy Direction and Values

The 1960s and 1970s were decades in which extensive environmental legislation was enacted and regulatory policies and agencies created. The trend toward increased regulation and federal leadership changed, as new values became the source of environmental policy during the 1980s. The favored policy position during this period was to relax standards and to reduce federal regulatory activity.[20]

In addition, the bubble concept was developed. It applied clean-air standards to an industrial plant as a whole, rather than to the specific parts of the plant causing emissions. This meant that increased levels of pollution at one source within a plant were acceptable if the overall levels of contaminants for the particular plant remain within EPA guidelines. Although this concept makes emissions enforcement easier, it reduces pollution more slowly than shutting down specific pollution points. Proponents advocated cost–benefit analysis and market forces as the most appropriate mechanisms for guiding environmental policy. They valued economic growth over environmental protection. Advocates saw market values as an appropriate mechanism for determining environmental policy. Environmental protection policies were to be avoided if the associated costs to society were higher than the monetary benefits. This approach emphasized a stronger role for state governments, as opposed to federal government regulation, in environmental legislation.

Environmental activists greeted the election of Bill Clinton and Al Gore with enthusiasm in 1992. Al Gore's book *Earth in the Balance*[21] reflected a major concern with environmental problems and with the need for governmental action to remedy those problems. Clinton and Gore seemed to represent the opportunity for a more active and aggressive federal role in environmental protection. The new administration did not meet these expectations. Immediately after the election, President Clinton called for "peaceful coexistence" between environmentalists and the business community. His policy actions indicated an environmental policy that varied in style but not in substance from those of his predecessors. In 1995, he signed a logging exemption bill that expanded timber industry access to national forests. When signing the legislation President Clinton stated, "I've done more for logging than anyone else in the country."[22]

A significant shift in the federal role did not occur for two reasons. First, there was a growing concern that environmental policy had been based on popular opinion, not on scientific evidence. According to former EPA Administrator William Reilly, environmental policies have been "based on responding to the nightly news. What we have had in the United States is environmental agenda-setting by episodic panic."[23] Second, concern for reducing the federal deficit and achieving a balanced budget provided a basis for questioning the validity of environmental spending programs. Given the competition for increasingly scarce federal monies and strong reaction to unfunded mandates imposed by the federal government on state and local governments (see Chapter 2), environmental spending programs must increasingly provide more benefits than they cost.

The administration of George W. Bush continued to pursue this course. President Bush, unlike President Clinton, did not use executive orders to set aside wilderness areas to protect them from economic activity. He reduced a number of environmental standards, and his administration strongly favored energy exploration in environmentally sensitive areas, such as the Arctic National Wildlife Refuge. President Bush supported an amendment to the Clean Air Act in 2003, entitled the Clear Skies Act. The Act did not achieve congressional approval because critics charged that the initiative actually involved a reduction in the requirements of the Clean Air Act.

Public Environmental Concern

The beginning of the twenty-first century witnessed marked changes in the intensity of public opinion supporting aggressive environmental policies. Conflicting scientific reports concerning causal relationships in environmental policy created differing levels of public confidence in environmental research findings. Costs associated with environmental protection escalated. Lifestyle values were in conflict with pro-environmental policies as the popularity of large, gas-guzzling SUVs in urban areas indicated a willingness to sacrifice environmental concerns with energy conservation and emissions reductions for personal lifestyle preferences. The public continues to verbalize a concern for the environment, but since the 1980s, some public consumer behaviors became inconsistent with strict environmental policies and programs.

The Politics of Regulation

The regulatory process itself is subject to political pressures from competing interests, which can influence the formulation of an effective environmental policy. One political factor that affects regulation is the pressure on administrators and elected officials to emphasize short-term economic benefits as opposed to long-term consequences of environmental damage. A second factor involves emphasis on the primacy of economic growth as a basic value in the political system. Economic growth carries an environmental cost almost universally, and the American system has historically concentrated on the desirability of growth. A third factor that directly affects the regulatory process is the value placed on compromise in our political system. The Constitution itself is a product of compromise, and the American system places a great deal of importance on seeking the middle ground. Although compromise is a politically expedient technique for making policy, it is not necessarily the best approach in establishing an effective environmental policy. Compromise becomes a factor in the delay and weakening of environmental-protection policies.

Given the nature of the political system, regulatory policy tends to be a product of political pressures, a fact that hinders development of effective policy choices. Even if lawmakers could formulate policy without these factors, problems with enforcement would remain.

Enforcement Problems

Effective enforcement of environmental policy is difficult to achieve for a variety of reasons. A major obstacle is the climate in which the EPA must operate. The EPA has the mandate to provide scientific evidence to support the environmental standards established by Congress. The procedure of establishing a solid scientific base for its regulations required financial and personnel resources beyond what the EPA had available. Increasingly, the courts placed the burden of proof on the EPA to defend the standards it proposed to enforce. Gathering and documenting this evidence is a time- and resource-consuming activity. From the late

1980s onward, the EPA received less political and budgetary support. This decline in support eroded the ability of the agency to pursue aggressively a policy of strict enforcement.

FUTURE ALTERNATIVES: UNRESOLVED POLICY ISSUES

International Treaties

The role of international agreements and treaties remains unresolved concerning environmental policy in the United States. There has been increasing interest in the international arena concerning the need for a coordinated international approach concerning threats to the global climate. The United Nations has been active in this area through the activities of the Framework Convention on Climate Change (FCCC). One product of U.N. activity is the Kyoto Protocol of 1997. This protocol is the result of negotiations dating back to 1995. The basic provision of the Protocol involves a global reduction in the emission of greenhouse gases to a level 5 percent below 1990 levels. This reduction is to happen between 2008 and 2012. Under the protocol, the European Union would reduce emissions by 8 percent, the United States by 7 percent, and Japan by 6 percent.

The protocol was rejected by the United States Senate vote of 95–0 in 1997 during the Clinton administration. The protocol would have had the force of law if ratified, and it could have had a significant impact on both environmental policy and economic activity within the United States. Critics of the Kyoto Protocol observed that China was exempt from the emissions standards even though it produces a significant amount of CO_2 emissions (2,893 million metric tons per year as compared to 5,410 million tons from the United States). Requiring the United States to reduce emissions while exempting China, a major source of pollution, would have placed the nation at a significant economic disadvantage as compared to China.

An unanswered question involves the appropriate role of international agreements in defining American environmental policy. Opponents to these types of international agreements argue that such agreements restrict national sovereignty, will have a detrimental impact on the American economy, and rest on unverified scientific research.[24] President George W. Bush announced soon after assuming the presidency that the United States would remain consistent and not agree to ratify the Kyoto Protocol, thus signaling a continuing commitment for the United States to forge its own environmental policy path.

Self-Regulation of the Market

Should government take an active role in planning and regulating activities that affect the environment? Alternatively, can this issue best be solved by a minimal governmental role, with the primary responsibility shifted to the operation of the free-market system?[25]

Conservatives, advocating reduced environmental regulation and increased reliance on the market, point to the negative consequences of environmental regulations. Regulations mean higher costs to business and so contribute to inflationary pressures on the economy.[26] These critics also contend that regulations interfere with national business planning, are difficult to comply with, are often arbitrary, and lack a scientific consensus. They point to the once-stringent clean-air standards, which they contend are a good example of arbitrary and unrealistic standards forced to bend to more practical needs.[27]

Market-oriented individuals argue that the market economy would not produce rampant environmental spoilage. Rather, the free market would produce conditions that make it profitable for the private sector to recycle waste products and to develop technologies to reduce pollution at the source. The level of pollution that did exist would be a product of the relationship between the costs and benefits to society.

Liberals, however, strenuously disagree.[28] They point out that consumers tend to purchase the least expensive item when quality is similar. Industry would never voluntarily install pollution-control equipment that would drive up the prices of its goods and put them at a competitive disadvantage. Thus, the market could not provide a basis for making intelligent environmental policy choices. Therefore, liberals argue, without governmental regulation, the environment will continue to deteriorate. Pollution is an externality, an indirect impact of market activity, which will continue to have costly social and economic effects without the policy hand of government to minimize them.

Taxes and Legal Action

There are several alternatives to the current administrative enforcement mechanisms for achieving environmental goals and compliance with environmental regulation.[29] First, taxes or fees for the discharge of pollutants might replace the system of rules, regulations, guidelines, and air and water-quality standards. Such a system represents a modified market approach popular with many neoconservatives. It would, they argue, reduce the administrative costs associated with regulation and allow industries to calculate the costs and benefits of environmental damage themselves. Critics of this alternative point out that some level of government would have to monitor discharges precisely in order to compute the tax; taxes would have to be set and adjusted continuously for particular pollutants; and companies in noncompetitive sectors of the economy could simply continue to pollute and pass the cost of the tax to consumers.

A second alternative, employed in some situations today, is the use of injunctions to halt pollution. This means obtaining a court order requiring that pollution be eliminated or reduced by a specified time or the polluter will be forced to cease operation. This strategy has the advantages of clarity and finality, but it is available only on a case-by-case basis.

A third alternative rewards enterprises that reduce pollution by awarding them tax subsidies or underwriting the cost of pollution-control equipment. This approach provides economic incentives to cease pollution activities and has a parallel in the tax credits already given to industries that install energy-conservation equipment. Yet, tax subsidies ultimately transfer the cost of environmental protection from the polluter to the public.

Stiff fines and jail sentences are a fourth approach to the problem. They would impose a strong negative incentive to cease pollution. Nevertheless, enforcement problems remain. Even when prosecutors obtain a conviction, perpetrators almost never receive jail terms in these types of white-collar crimes, and fines—considering the resources of big industry—may be absorbed as routine business expenses.

Other alternatives to enforcing environmental compliance have been debated and sometimes used, but, like those discussed here, they have met with limited success, and no consensus has been reached. An effective strategy to achieve compliance with pollution standards remains elusive.

The Role of State Governments

The issue of state responsibility for environmental enforcement remains unresolved. Early regulatory efforts concentrated authority in the hands of state government, with limited success. There is evidence that a reduction of the role of the federal government and transfer of responsibility for environmental policy to the states will result in a general weakening of standards.

One reason is that the governing coalitions within state governments have a relatively narrow political base. In other words, compared with the national level, the proportion of the population concerned with political events at the state level is relatively small. Public-opinion polls indicate that less than 30 percent of the electorate regularly follows state government actively. Consequently, it is relatively easy for a special-interest group to gain considerable power in state government.

State governments also face severe staffing problems. Job vacancies reach levels as high as 20 percent in the regulatory agencies of some states, and the turnover of trained, qualified personnel is a problem. Limited fiscal resources are a primary source of this problem.

A third problem emerges when federal agencies, primarily the EPA, fail to issue regulations in a timely manner. The result is a negative impact on state enforcement procedures. Inconsistency, confusion, and delay follow as states operate without federal leadership.

A fourth problem grows from a perception that federal regulations fail to appreciate the states' unique needs, producing inflexible program requirements. The states view the inflexibility as a barrier to state initiative, as states must implement rigid programs that may not meet their needs.

A fifth problem stems from the perception that federal EPA officials may not be interested in establishing meaningful communication with the states. A lack of responsiveness by the EPA builds perceptions at the state level that the feds do not understand and do not care about the problems and issues faced by state officials.

A sixth problem is conflicting interests among the states themselves. The same environmental pollutants do not threaten all states to the same degree. Acid rain is unevenly distributed across the nation and is not an issue in certain areas of the country. States vary with respect to their economic base. Strict environmental policies have differing levels of economic impact across the nation. Given the differences among the states, dissatisfaction with environmental policies adopted at the federal level will occur at the state level, and interstate conflict may lead to policy deadlocks in Congress and the EPA.

These six problems relate to the issue of dividing leadership responsibility between the federal government and the fifty states. Leadership requires the expenditure of financial resources. The states have not been overly eager to assume the leadership role in enforcement policy.

Public Attitudes

Attitudes within the American public have changed somewhat since 2000.[30] There has been a drop in the proportion of individuals who believe that the environmental movement has done more good than harm, from some 75 percent in 2000 to about 60 percent in 2009. This may reflect a slightly less sympathetic attitude toward aggressive environmental policies, as the nation's economy has weakened. Public opinion data does seem to suggest that politicians can lose votes by appearing uncaring about the environment, even though they cannot gain many votes by taking dramatic steps.

Energy and the Environment

Global Climate Change.   Global climate change, commonly referred to as global warming, is an issue on the policy agenda. Economic growth seems to produce energy consumption patterns that threaten the environment. Reliance on fossil fuels results in massive emissions of carbon dioxide that may generate a greenhouse effect, in which the earth's atmosphere warms excessively. Global warming is reflected in warmer winters, not necessarily hotter summers. Critics argue that there is an absence of direct, undisputed scientific evidence linking human activity to global climate changes and that the changes may be natural and cyclical in nature. Proponents argue that an undisputable linkage exists between human activity, the continued production of greenhouse gas emissions, and the phenomenon of a global warming.

The debate over the issue of global warming intensified in 2009 and 2010 with reports that publications and reports from the Intergovernmental Climate Change Panel (IPCC) of the United Nations were factually inaccurate and that IPCC reports contained a number of flaws and inaccuracies. One IPCC report stated that glaciers in the Himalayas would melt by the middle of this century and result in severe water problems for India. Critics discovered that the report was not based on scientific evidence but a statement in a graduate student's dissertation and nonscientific articles in mountaineering magazines.

Former Vice President Al Gore narrated the film *An Inconvenient Truth* in 2006. His narration of the film heightened public awareness of the global warming as a policy issue. He shared the Nobel Prize with the IPCC in 2007, which provided the film with additional legitimacy. At the same time, debate concerning some of the assumptions and conclusions relative to global climate change remain questionable. The Copenhagen Climate Conference in December 2009 did not produce an agreement on climate change policy, nor an agreement to pursue a global strategy in 2010. Opposition to such an agreement was broad-based, with significant opposition from the European Union stemming from the negative economic impacts resulting from a strong environmental policy. Public opinion polls in the United States and Europe now seem to indicate that concern over the economy has significantly reduced public support for strict environmental policies.

The debate over the nature, extent, and causes associated with changes in the global climate will continue as an item on the policy agenda.

Other Issues.   Environmental regulatory policies often conflict with efforts to increase the supply of energy available to the nation. The onset of the energy crisis and the need for economic growth created pressures to postpone compliance deadlines and to relax environmental standards and rules. This linkage between energy policy, economic expansion, and environmental policy is a source of conflict, as was graphically demonstrated in March 1989, when the *Exxon Valdez* ran aground in Prince William Sound and spilled between 10 and 12.5 million barrels of oil in the coastal waters of Alaska. In April 2010, a British Petroleum drilling platform, *Deepwater Horizon*, in the Gulf of Mexico caught fire and collapsed, with the loss of the lives of eleven workers. The resulting oil spill is the largest in American history and eclipsed that of the *Exxon Valdez*. The extensive contamination of the gulf, coastline, and damage to wildlife illustrates a basic public policy conflict: the desire for a pristine environment and a commitment to produce energy to maintain economic stability. This event followed an announcement in April 2010 by President Obama that the federal government was expanding offshore drilling for oil and natural gas, a moratorium now on hold because of a court decision invalidating it. Currently, there are over 3,500 offshore drilling platforms of various types in the Gulf of Mexico. Offshore drilling is an essential element in providing oil to the nation and remains a source of environmental risk. It will remain on the policy agenda for the foreseeable future.

Emphasis on development of coal as a major fuel source intensifies several environmental problems. Increased utilization of coal generates higher levels of CO_2 because coal contains higher levels of carbon than either oil or natural gas. This strategy would also result in higher emissions of sulfur dioxides, a major factor in the acid-rain phenomenon.

The process of energy resource development also poses significant environmental threats. Strip mining for coal denigrates the environment, because it removes the ground surface to reach the underlying coal beds. Shaft-mining techniques for coal and uranium present problems because an effective policy for handling the tailings from the mines has yet to be developed and implemented. Offshore oil drilling efforts present significant environmental threats as well. Oil spills, leaks, and seepage threaten both water quality and wildlife.

The process of developing synthetic fuels from nontraditional fossil fuel sources (obtaining crude oil from oil shale or from the process of coal liquefaction) also presents significant environmental risks. These include surface and subsurface water contamination, air pollution, and disposal of the tailings and other solid waste from the associated mining activities.

Nuclear energy exploitation also presents significant environmental threats. Miners are exposed to carcinogenic radon gas, and the mine tailings contain low-level radioactive materials that are scattered beyond the immediate mining area by the process of wind and water erosion. The wastes from nuclear plants present an environmental risk apart from the potential damage from a nuclear accident, such as the disaster at the Chernobyl facility in the former Soviet Union.

Given the close relationship between energy-use patterns and the environment, basic values within society come into conflict. The American public has a long history of valuing nature, and the history of environmental legislation reflects this. One example is the creation and expansion of the national park system. At the same time, the American public has come to expect continued economic growth and personal prosperity. The result is a willingness to accept potential risks to the environment to guarantee a ready supply of energy. Given its traditional confidence in science and technology, the American public finds it plausible to believe in an optimal scientific mix for energy and environmental issues.

The integral bonds between energy and environmental policies are the political, social, and economic issues and the conflicts they produce. The task for political institutions and actors is to resolve or minimize the conflicts and develop policies that promote growth in the energy supply and the economy while protecting the environment.

ENDNOTES

1. For a discussion of the coal industry, see Duane Lockard, *Coal: A Memoir and Critique* (Charlottesville, VA: University of Virginia Press, 1998).

2. Raymond Vernon, ed., *The Oil Crisis* (New York: Norton, 1976).

3. Melvin A. Conant and Fern R. Gold, *The Geopolitics of Energy* (Boulder, CO: Westview Press, 1978).

4. David Davis, *Energy Politics*, 2nd ed. (New York: St. Martin's Press, 1978).

5. See Seymour Warkov, *Energy Policy in the United States* (New York: Macmillan, 1978).

6. U.S. Department of Energy, Energy Information Administration, *Annual Energy Outlook 2010*, http://www.eia.doe.gov/oiaf/aeo/index.html.

7. Douglas Evans, *Western Energy Policy* (New York: Macmillan, 1978).

8. Marc H. Ross and Robert Williams, *Our Energy Future: Regaining Control* (New York: McGraw-Hill, 1981).

9. Don Kash and Robert Rycroft, *U.S. Energy Policy* (Norman: University of Oklahoma Press, 1984).

10. For a complete discussion of cost allocation, see Lester Thurow, *The Zero-Sum Society* (New York: Penguin, 1980).

11. See Raymond L. Murray, *Nuclear Energy: An Introduction*, 6th ed. (New York: Elsevier, 2009) for a discussion of issues related to nuclear energy.

12. Hanns Maull, *Europe and World Energy* (London: Butterworth, 1980).

13. Peter Schwartz, "What Happened to the Energy Crisis? The Dilemma of an Energy Decision Maker in a Dynamic World," in Jack M. Hollander, Harvey Brooks, and David Sternlight, eds., *Annual Review of Energy* (Palo Alto, CA: Annual Reviews, 1987).

14. Rachel Carson, *Silent Spring* (Boston: Houghton Mifflin, 1962).

15. *Environmental Outlook*, 1980 (Washington, DC: U.S. Environmental Protection Agency, 1980).

16. See Shawna Vogel, "Has Global Warming Begun?" *Earth* (December 1995): 24–35; and Mark Dowie, "A Sky Full of Holes," *The Nation*, July 8, 1996, pp. 11–12, for a discussion of this issue in greater depth. For a skeptical look at claims of global warming and other environmental disasters, see Bjorn Lomborg, *The Skeptical Environmentalist: Measuring the Real State of the World* (New York: Cambridge University Press, 2001).

17. For example, see Environmental Protection Agency, *Quality Criteria for Water* (Washington, DC: Government Printing Office, 1976); and "Water Pollutants," *Environmental Outlook*, 1980, Chapter 6.

18. The Resource Conservation and Recovery Act, PL 94-580, Section 4001 (1976).

19. National Environmental Policy Act, PL 91-190, January 1, 1970.

20. George C. Eads and Michael Fix, eds., *The Reagan Regulatory Strategy: An Assessment* (Washington, DC: Urban Institute Press, 1984).

21. Al Gore, *Earth in the Balance* (New York: Houghton Mifflin, 1992).

22. Alexander Cockburn and Jeffrey St. Clair, "Slime Green," *The Progressive*, May 18, 1996, pp. 18–21.

23. Keith Schneider, "New View Calls Environmental Policy Misguided," *New York Times*, March 21, 1993, p. 1.

24. See Frederick H. Rueter, *Framing a Coherent Climate Change Policy* (St. Louis: Washington University, Center for the Study of American Business, October, 1997); and William H. Lash, *Green Showdown at the WTO* (Washington University, Center for the Study of American Business: St. Louis, March 1997), for a discussion of some of these issues.

25. See Guy Benveniste, *Regulation and Planning* (San Francisco: Boyd & Fraser, 1981); and Thurow, *Zero-Sum Society*.

26. Murray Weidenbaum, Christopher Douglas, and Michael Orlando, *Toward a Healthier Environment and a Stronger Economy: How to Achieve Common Ground* (St. Louis: Washington University, Center for the Study of American Business, 1997).

27. Stephen Huebner and Kenneth Chilton, *EPA's Case for Ozone and Particulate Standards: Would Americans Get Their Money's Worth?* (St. Louis: Washington University, Center for the Study of American Business, 1997).

28. See Benveniste, *Regulation and Planning*, Chapter 9.

29. Stuart S. Nagel, "Incentives for Compliance with Environmental Law," in Lester W. Milbrath and Frederick R. Inscho, eds., *The Politics of Environmental Policy* (Beverly Hills, CA: Sage, 1975).

30. Riley E. Dunlap, *The State of the Environment in the U.S.* (Princeton, NJ: Gallup Organization, 2007).

RESOURCES

Books

Aswathanarayna, U. and Divi, Rao S. *Energy Portfolios*. New York: Taylor and Francis (CRC Press), 2009.

Barry, John, Dobson, Andres, and Stephens, Piers, eds. *Contemporary Environmental Politics: From Margins to Mainstream*. Oxford: Routledge, 2006.

Chastko, Paul. *Globalization and the World Oil Industry*. New York: CRC Press, 2011.

Gore, Al. *Earth in the Balance*. Boston: Houghton Mifflin, 1992.

Gore, Al. *An Inconvenient Truth. (DVD)* Los Angeles: Paramount Home Entertainment, 2006.

Kraft, Michael. *Business and Environmental Policy*. Cambridge: MIT Press, 2007.

Lomborg, Bjorn. *The Skeptical Environmentalist: Measuring the Real State of the World*. New York: Cambridge University Press, 2001.

Loulou, Richard, Zaccour, Georges, and Waaub, Jean Philippe. *Energy and Environment*. New York: Springer, 2005.

Mallon, Karl, ed. *Renewable Energy Policy and Politics: A Handbook for Decision-making*. London: Earthscan Publications, Ltd., 2006.

Michaels, Patrick J. and Balling, Robert C. Jr., *Climate of Extremes: Global Warming Science They Don't Want You to Know*. Washington, DC: Cato Institute, 2010.

McIntyre, Kevin J., Kirkwood, Martın V., and Leif, Jason F. *Energy Policy Act of 2005: Summary and Analysis*. New York: LexisNexis, January 2006.

Miller, Norman. *Environmental Politics*, 2nd ed. New York: Taylor and Francis (Routledge), 2009.

Morgenstern, Richard D., and Portney, Paul R. *New Approaches on Energy and the Environment*. New York: Resources for the Future, 2005.

Morris, Paul M., ed. *National Energy Policy: Major Federal Energy Programs and Status*. New York: Nova Science Publishers, Inc., 2005.

Nersesian, Roy L. *Energy for the 21st Century: A Comprehensive Guide to Conventional and Alternative Sources*, 2nd Edition. New York: ME Sharp, 2010.

Rosenbaum, Walter A. *Environmental Politics and Policy*, 7th ed. Washington, DC: CQ Press, 2007.

Smith, Zachary A. *The Environmental Policy Paradox*. Saddle River, NJ: Pearson Prentice Hall, 2009.

Sovacoo, Benjamin K., and Brown, Marilyn A., eds. *Energy and American Society: Thirteen Myths*. New York: Springer Verlag, 2007.

Spellman, Frank R. and Bieber, Revonna. *The Science of Renewable Energy*. New York: CRC Press, 2011.

Tulkens, Henry. *Public Goods, Environmental Externalities and Fiscal Competition*. New York: Springer, 2006.

Vig, Norman J., and Kraft, Michael E. *Environmental Policy: New Directions for the 21st Century*, 7th ed. Washington, DC: CQ Press, 2009.

Websites

Energy Policy–Related Websites

American Petroleum Institute: **http://api-ec.api.org/**

Intergovernmental Renewable Energy Organization: **http://www.ireoigo.org/**

International Atomic Energy Agency: **www.iaea.org/**

Listing of Professional Energy Associations Nuclear Regulatory Commission: **www.nrc.gov**

Organization of Petroleum Exporting Countries (OPEC): **www.opec.org/opec_web/en/**

Solar Energy Association Listing: **http://www.energybible.com/solar_energy/Organizations.html**

U.S. Department of Energy: **www.energy.gov/**

White House Energy Policy: **www.whitehouse.gov/issues/enrgy-and-environemtn/**

Environmental Policy–Related Websites

Audubon Society: **www.audubon.org**

CATO Institute: **www.cato.org**

European Topic Centre on Air and Climate Change: **http://etc-acc.eionet.europa.eu/**

Institute for European Environmental Policy: **www.ieep.eu/**

Pew Center on Global Climate Change: **www.pewclimate.org/**

U.S. Department of Energy, Environmental Policy: **www.energy.gov/environment/index.htm**

U.S. Environmental Protection Agency: **www.epa.gov**

U.S. EPA Climate Change Website: **www.epa.gov/climatechange/**

Chapter 6

Crime and Criminal Justice: Dilemmas of Social Control

The public, throughout the late twentieth century, perceived crime as having reached intolerable levels, especially in America's major cities, not only with respect to the incidence of criminal acts but also with respect to the exponentially rising monetary costs to society. Each of the first five editions of this book reported the gloomy consensus that crime appeared to be out of control. That perception created a widespread demand that government do something to attack the problem. In the 1992 presidential campaign, the eventual winner, Bill Clinton, promised major legislation to attack the crime problem in America. The result of this pledge, the 1994 Crime Bill, will be discussed below. The 1990s saw a dramatic reversal of the crime trend. Violent crime, the kinds of crime that Americans fear the most and that most affect Americans' life style, declined throughout the 1990s into the twenty-first century. Crime levels continued to decline throughout much of the first decade of the twenty-first century, as indicated by the *Uniform Crime Report*, issued yearly by the Federal Bureau of Investigation (FBI), although the rates of decline in crime were not nearly as large as in the late 1990s. Still, crime rates are much lower today than they were 20 years ago. What accounts for these changes in the crime rate, and can public policy reduce the rate of crime?

The estimated number of persons murdered in the United States in 2008 was 16,272, down significantly from 23,040 murders in 1980, and on par with number of murders not seen since 1970. This drop in crime is significant, even when compared to 1970, as there are a lot more people living in the U.S. today than in 1970. The rate of violent crime is down sharply from the 1980s. Two decades ago, in 1986, the violent *crime rate* was 620.1 per 100,000 population; this decreased to 454.5 by 2008, a reduction of 27 percent. The homicide rate, at 5.4 murders per 100,000 population in 2008, is down about 50 percent from the 1993 figure of 9.3 per 100,000. It should be noted, however, that even this lower homicide rate still places the United States significantly higher in this category than any other Western democracy, although significantly lower than some less–modern systems, as Table 6.18 will show. Actually, it is the homicide rate that makes America appear to many as a crime-plagued nation. The United States does not rank particularly higher than other nations in other crime categories. For example, it was recently reported in one British newspaper that the United Kingdom had a higher rate of violent crime than even the U.S.[1]

In general, the trends displayed in Figures 6.1 and 6.2 show violent crime and property crime rates decreasing slightly over the first decade of the twenty-first century.

Overall, violent crime has dropped slightly over the decade of the 2000s; however, that decline is not nearly as large as the decline in crime seen in the 1990s. Property crimes, far more pervasive than the more feared violent crime (an estimated 9.7 million offenses in 2008), declined significantly in the 1990s, and continued to decline, although more gradually, in the first eight years of the twenty-first century. In 2008, there were 3,212.5 reported property crimes per 100,000 people. This figure is 37 percent lower than the 5,107.1 property crimes per 100,000 people as reported in 1989.[2] Thus, while this chapter in the first five editions primarily focused on explaining the burgeoning crime rates of postwar America, the last several editions have tried to explain the clear and significant reversal of that trend. This edition will try to explain why the dramatic reductions in crime rates in the 1990s seem to have tapered off somewhat. Thus, the five-year span from 1995 to 2000 witnessed an 18.7 percent drop in the rate

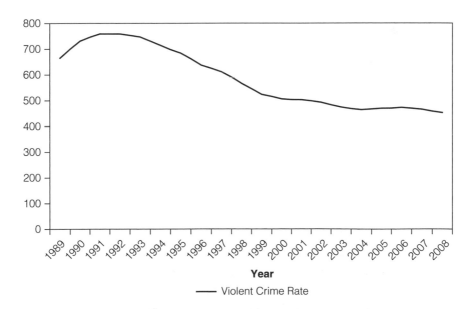

FIGURE 6.1 Violent Crime Rates Per 100,000 People since 1989

SOURCE: www.fbi.gov, Federal, Bureau of Investigation: Uniform Crime Reports. 2008 Online at http://www.fbi.gov/ucr/cius2008/data/table_01.html

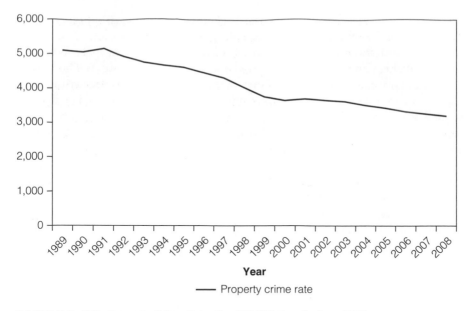

FIGURE 6.2 Property Crime Rates Per 100,000 People since 1989

SOURCE: www.fbi.gov, Federal Bureau of Investigation: Uniform Crime Reports. 2008 Online at http://www.fbi.gov/ucr/cius2008/data/table_01.html

of property crimes as opposed to the 11.2 percent drop of the next eight years. Can the good news of declining crime rates be attributed to public policies that are at last "working," or is the trend due to impersonal forces beyond the control of government? And why have these dramatic reductions been followed by a much more gradual decrease over the last several years?

This chapter will describe policies developed to deal with crime, analyze the impact of these policies, and suggest alternatives presently available. The chapter will focus on one widely assumed strategy for the prevention of crime: *deterrence*. Deterrence refers to the discouragement of criminal acts by imposing prohibitive costs on criminals. In general, this means severe punishment. Research shows, however, that a high probability of punishment and the swift execution of the punishment are more conducive to deterrence than is increasing the severity of the punishment. The chapter will examine the factors that may impede such punishment and those that keep the perpetrators of crime out of jail. In addition, this chapter will investigate those factors that allow criminals to escape with punishments less severe than those allowed by law or demanded by a widespread sense of justice.

Evaluating the impact of public policy on crime depends on knowing the nature and extent of crime. It is therefore necessary to assess the extent to which the incidence of crime has actually changed one way or the other in recent years. It is important to note that crime is not an undifferentiated phenomenon. There are different types of crime with different rates of occurrence and different causes, and they require different policies to reduce their incidence. Policies designed to reduce one kind of crime may have no effect on, or may even increase, other types of crime. The unintended consequences, or spillover effects, of public policy are crucial to the evaluation of crime policies.

Too often, politicians generalize about one type of crime, for example, "crime in the streets," as if that type of crime encompasses the universe of the crime problem. Actually, crime is any behavior that some duly constituted legislative body has chosen to make illegal. These behaviors include crimes against property (robbery and auto theft), crimes against persons (assault, murder, and rape), *white-collar crimes* (stock fraud and price-fixing), "victimless" crimes against a dominant moral code (public intoxication, vagrancy, sodomy, and the sale of pornography), and political crimes (illegal campaign contributions and bribery). These are distinct types of activities, the causes and prevention of which differ. Even within these categories, many distinctions may be discerned. Carefully planned murders, spontaneous killing in anger or in a fight, and violent rape born out of a general hatred for women—all crimes against persons—will not respond to the same remedies. Because the concept of crime covers too diverse a category of actions to be analytically useful, this chapter will distinguish various types of illegal activities with respect to their causes and means of prevention.

ISSUE BACKGROUND: THE GROWTH AND DECLINE OF CRIME

The Extent of Crime

It is not difficult to find factual support for the perception that crime increased at an alarming rate in the first four decades after World War II. The crime rate, as defined by the Federal Bureau of Investigation's *Uniform Crime Report,* rose dramatically for the two decades after the current method of tabulating the FBI index went into effect, until 1981. This crime index refers to the number of crimes per 100,000 population for seven categories of crime: (1) murder and manslaughter, (2) forcible rape, (3) robbery, (4) aggravated assault, (5) burglary, (6) larceny, and (7) auto theft. Burglary is defined by the FBI Uniform Crime Reporting Program as "the unlawful entry of a structure to commit a felony or theft." Larceny is defined as "the unlawful taking, carrying, leading, or riding away of property from the possession or constructive possession of another," and examples of larceny include theft of bicycles, shoplifting, pocket-picking, etc.

The rise in index crimes of violence from 1967 to 1978 was 192 percent, and the rise in index crimes against property was 168 percent.[3] Clearly, these statistics represent significant increases, whatever the definitional problems. Significant increases also were recorded in the four years from 1988 to 1992 in those categories that generate the most fear among the population: violent crime, murder, aggravated assault, and forcible rape, with increases of 19 percent, 11 percent, 19 percent, and 14 percent, respectively. These are the kind of figures that caused a public perception of a public safety crisis.

However, beginning in 1992, the crime rate reversed in a downward trend in all categories. Moreover, this downward trend was especially strong in those categories that generate the greatest fear among the population. Thus, the drop in homicide rates in the decade from 1994 to 2003 was 33.4 percent compared to a 23 percent drop in property crimes for the same period. However, in the eight years from 2001 to 2008, the homicide rate remained somewhat constant (only a small drop from 5.6 to 5.4 murders per 100,000 has occurred), while in that same period the rate of property crimes declined. The total number of murders in the U.S. over the years is listed in Table 6.1. As is apparent, the total number of murders in 2008 is fairly close to the total number of murders in 1970, despite the relatively large increase in the population since then. Rates of crime over the last decade listed by the type of offense appear in Table 6.2.

From 1960 to 1990, with respect to violent crimes per capita (the kind of crimes that generate the most fear and have a consequently severe impact on urban life), the crime rate grew a spectacular 355 percent. This included a rise in violent crime against random victims (unrelated to the identity or behavior of the victim), thus exacerbating a widespread fear of crime. This fear and the perception of victimization are illustrated by the fact that, according to the February 9, 1992, edition of the *New York Times*, sales of home alarm systems increased by 80 percent from 1986 to 1992.

As we have shown, crime then took a sharp downward direction; this was especially pronounced in those categories that generate fear of crime. The violent crime rate decreased 7.4 percent in the one year from 1995 to 1996, while the clearance rate for such crime increased from 45 to 47 percent in that same year.[4] As noted earlier, the homicide rate has stabilized in the past five years (Table 6.2). After a brief lag, public perceptions of the threat of crime are beginning to catch up to the data. The change in these perceptions is shown in Table 6.3.

There is varied speculation but no consensus among social scientists trying to explain the drop in crime in the 1990s. Many refer to the demographic factor of the aging of the baby boom generation. Crime is most prevalent among males

T A B L E   6.1   Homicides by Year in the United States

1970	16,000	2001	16,037
1975	20,510	2002	16,229
1980	23,040	2003	16,528
1985	18,980	2004	16,148
1990	23,440	2005	16,740
1993	24,540	2006	17,034
1995	21,606	2007	16,929
2000	15,586	2008	16,272

SOURCE: U.S. Department of Justice, Bureau of Justice Statistics, www.ojp.usdoj.gov/bjs/.

TABLE 6.2 Crime Rates, 2001–2008 (per 100,000 population)

	Violent Crime	Murder	Forcible Rape	Robbery	Aggravated Assault
2001	504.5	5.6	31.8	148.5	318.6
2002	494.4	5.6	33.1	146.1	309.5
2003	475.8	5.7	32.3	142.5	295.4
2004	463.2	5.5	32.4	136.7	288.6
2005	469.0	5.6	31.8	140.8	290.8
2006	473.5	5.7	31.0	149.4	287.5
2007	466.9	5.6	30.0	147.6	283.8
2008	454.5	5.4	29.3	145.3	274.6

	Property Crime	Burglary	Larceny-Theft	Motor Vehicle Theft
2001	3658.1	741.8	2485.7	430.5
2002	3630.6	747.0	2450.7	432.9
2003	3591.2	741.0	2416.5	433.7
2004	3514.1	730.3	2362.3	421.5
2005	3431.5	726.9	2287.8	416.8
2006	3334.5	729.4	2206.8	398.4
2007	3263.5	722.5	2177.8	363.9
2008	3212.5	730.8	2167.0	314.7

SOURCE: Federal Bureau of Investigation, *Uniform Crime Report*, "2008, Crime in the United States," http://www.fbi.gov/ucr/cius2008/data/table_01.html.

TABLE 6.3 Public Attitudes toward Crime: Percentage of Sample Naming Crime and Violence as "Most Important Problem"

1984	1994	1998	2000	2002	2007
4	37	20	13	1	3

SOURCE: *Sourcebook of Criminal Justice Statistics*, 2008, http://www.albany.edu/sourcebook/tost_2.html#2_o.

from the early teens to the mid–twenties. Accordingly, when large numbers of baby boomers were in that age category, crime rates went up. As they have aged beyond that category, the rates went down. Certainly, the "graying of America," the gradual increase in the average age of Americans continues; yet, crime is essentially a young person's activity. Other scholars refer to aggressive police tactics and longer prison sentences instituted in the 1980s. These are discussed below.

White-Collar Crime.   Problems of the definition and interpretation of crime statistics abound, however. The crime index does not exhaust the universe of illegal activities. For example, the index does not include most white-collar crimes, which cost the American public more in lost dollar value than does the total of all the index crimes.[5] The scandals associated with the collapse of energy giant Enron Corporation in early 2001 cost employees and investors billions of dollars including, in many cases with employees, their entire life savings and retirement plans. The alleged fraud involved the upper management and their accountants covering up the financial state of the company, partly by hiding company losses in numerous covert "partnerships," and encouraging employees and investors to tie up their money in company stock, thereby inflating the price of that stock, just prior to management unloading their own stock at billions of dollars in profits. Enron chairman Ken Lay reaped $37,683,887 in stock sales between May 2000 and August 2001. In the previous four years, Lay made $205 million in stock option profits.[6] Other Enron executives made similar profits while their employees lost everything. Meanwhile, at one point, management actually "locked down" the 401(k) retirement packages, preventing employees from selling them. Shortly thereafter, the company's bankruptcy rendered the stock virtually worthless, as it plunged from $90 a share to 26 cents. While one of Enron's chief financial officers, Andrew Fastow, served time for his role in the scandal, Ken Lay remained unpunished and died of a heart attack in July 2006 just before he could be brought to trial. The harm to American society from such "insider trading" and stock fraud cases is indirect. It may contribute to a loss of confidence in the integrity of the market, which would make it more difficult to accumulate capital from the growing source of millions of small investors thereby slowing economic growth. Hence, such white-collar criminals do not appear threatening to the average American, enabling them to retain a level of popularity and public acceptance unavailable to a convicted mugger, pedophile, murderer, or rapist.

FBI figures estimate that for 1988, the total loss to victims of street crime was $16.6 billion, if one adds in less direct costs, such as pain, suffering, and the risk of death. The U.S. Chamber of Commerce estimated that embezzlement, fraud, commercial theft, and "business-related arson" cost the public over $40 billion per year in the late 1970s, ten times the value of the property lost through street crime. Anti-trust violations may cost another $160 billion per year. The financial meltdown and mortgage crisis of the banking system in late 2007, which some financial experts blamed on the creation of credit-default swaps, cost American taxpayers hundreds of billions of dollars in the government-funded bailouts of banks and Wall Street brokerage firms. Congress, the state of New York, and the Justice Department of the Obama Administration each launched their own investigations into the dealings of a number of Wall Street firms and large U.S.

banks to determine whether wrongdoing had occurred. In 2010, for example, the Obama Justice Department opened an investigation into Goldman Sachs to figure out whether the firm had engaged in fraud or other federal crimes in the time leading up to and during the financial crisis.[7] Former Bush administration Treasury Secretary Hank Paulson, who orchestrated the 2007 bailout of banks and pressed Congress to pass the legislation, had also previously served as CEO of Goldman Sachs, which, as it turns out, was an indirect beneficiary of the taxpayer bailout money (government bailout money paid to the insurance company AIG was then promptly used by AIG to pay off financial obligations to Goldman Sachs). While Paulson was not accused of breaking any laws, such cozy connections between those running the private sector market and those in government erode the perception that market competition is "fair" and thus erode the legitimacy of unequal market-based outcomes.

Another high profile example of potential white-collar crime involved the scandal surrounding President Bill Clinton's involvement in the Whitewater resort investment scheme when he was governor of Arkansas. The scandal involved allegations that then–Governor Clinton used his position to ease state regulation of a savings and loan association that was financing property in which the Clintons were heavily invested. While the president and his wife were never prosecuted, the matter undermined trust, and illustrates accusations of "political crime." The convictions of lobbyist Jack Abramoff and Republican Congressman Duke Cunningham for bribery constitute another such "political crime." The public officials elected to uphold and implement the law can prove to be among the more flagrant white-collar criminals and add to the atmosphere of disrespect for the law. Public officials may betray their trust in various other ways. President Clinton's lack of candor about his sexual relationship with his intern, and the apparent similar lack of candor in late 2001 by Democratic Congressman Gary Condit with regard to a similar relationship with one of his interns (who subsequently disappeared and was discovered murdered) illustrate a casual disregard for the rules on the part of people who may act as role models for many young Americans.

The acquittal of former football player and movie star O. J. Simpson of the murder of his wife and her friend in the early 1990s, despite a mountain of circumstantial evidence, exacerbated the perception that the rich and powerful can break the rules of society with impunity, rules that constrain ordinary Americans. Examples of malfeasance in high places further erode the declining trust that Americans have in their political system, a trend that was substantially exacerbated by the Watergate scandal of the Nixon presidency. Watergate refers to a series of acts to abuse powerful but supposedly neutral administrative institutions and powers of government in order to punish and suppress political opposition. Such political malfeasance came into focus in 1997 with widespread charges of illegal solicitation of campaign funds by President Clinton and Vice President Gore. The charges included solicitations of donations from within government offices located in the White House itself in violation of the Pendleton and Hatch Acts designed to prevent government officials from using their power to coerce money from their clientele. Also, it was charged that such contributions came from foreign sources, which are proscribed in order to protect the integrity of our electoral process from foreign governments. Clinton's defense was that both parties engaged in such practices.

"Victimless" Crimes.   Acts among willing adults that violate some moral principle supported by the dominant forces in society constitute a substantial fraction of crimes. Although some such acts may in fact inflict genuine harm—for example, drug use that leads to crimes to pay for the habit, or prostitution that spreads disease—they are called "*victimless crimes*," because participation in such activity is presumed to be voluntary. Obviously, reasonable people differ with respect to the identification of victims. Thus, pro-life forces would regard an aborted fetus as a victim, while pro-choice forces regard abortion as a "victimless" activity. Estimates vary with the definition of the term and the range of activities proscribed, but in many estimates, arrests for victimless crimes account for over half the total number of arrests. Such laws often attempt to ban conduct that is widely practiced. Consequently, they are often ineffective in altering the actual behavior of people strongly disposed to engage in the proscribed conduct. Thus, the impact of these laws is not to prevent the conduct in question, but rather to criminalize large segments of the American population.

Many Americans at some time in their lives violate some of the laws regulating sexual behavior. These laws once included bans on sodomy, fornication, and adultery. Sodomy refers to unnatural or abnormal sex. Because what is natural or normal in sexual behavior is a subjective judgment over which reasonable people disagree, many respectable citizens violate vaguely drawn sodomy statutes. Such statutes often prohibited any form of oral sex, even among married partners, with prison penalties of up to thirty years. Yet not only has the existence of moral legislation failed to prevent the conduct being banned; there are indications that with the growing secularization of our society and with the "sexual revolution," the rate of such conduct actually increased. Despite all efforts to punish prostitution, it continues unabated. Because the behaviors or services (such as drugs) proscribed by such legislation are strongly demanded by certain segments of the population, an illegal network has been created to take the risks of supplying them. Thus, the development and maintenance of organized crime is a spillover effect of banning strongly desired behaviors for moral purposes.

Street Crime.   Although white-collar crime may cost American society in the aggregate more money than street crime does, James Q. Wilson persuasively argued that what is called crime in the streets has a more negative impact on America's sense of community.[8] Even for those who are not actually victims of crime, the fear of street crime alters one's lifestyle and patterns of interaction. People may no longer feel free to walk the streets and in effect become prisoners in their own homes. In many cities, downtown businesses have failed to prosper because people no longer feel safe in those areas: such failures can be considered to be an indirect cost or spillover effect of street crime, a cost that does not enter into the crime statistics themselves. The perception that there is a relationship between street crime and violence adds to fear and makes even the prospect of such crime more traumatic than that of white-collar crime, regardless of the dollar value lost. Furthermore, the perception that there is a relationship between potentially violent street crime and race or ethnicity exacerbates the problem of prejudice against and distrust of America's minorities.

The Rising Costs of Crime.   The dollar value lost to society because of crime has risen so sharply in the past three decades that it cannot be ignored. According to estimates by the Justice Department, insurance companies, and academic researchers, the overall costs to society of street crime by the mid-1990s were in the neighborhood of $163 billion, up from $43 billion (adjusted for inflation) in 1965—an almost fourfold increase. The value of stolen property alone for all reported index crimes in 2000 was $16.4 billion. Other factors contributed to the remaining costs of crime. The following example serves to illustrate the expense incurred by each crime. When on June 7, 1994, eighteen-year-old James Hunter was murdered in Washington, DC, police officers, detectives, and forensic experts came to the scene, costing the city $4,626. An emergency vehicle rushed Hunter to the hospital, costing another $1,310. The autopsy cost $1,046. Thus, even while police pursue his killer, the murder of one person has cost that city about $7,000. The costs of the prosecutorial resources must be added if a suspect is apprehended, plus over $22,000 per year to keep someone in the district prison in the event of a conviction. This not-atypical crime was just one of more than 200 that occurred in the first three quarters of 1994 in the DC area alone.

Reported Crime.   The FBI index includes only reported crimes. Sample surveys, on the other hand, report that two to three times more crimes are committed than are reported. This rate of underreporting, such "victimization surveys" indicate, varies according to geographical area. The crime rate as indicated by the official index, therefore, depends on what proportion of actual crimes is reported and becomes a statistic. A greater proportion of crimes being reported would lead to an increase in the crime rate even if the actual crime rate did not increase. Such a reporting increase occurred in the 1970s and 1980s.

There are two reasons for this. First, the development of computers and other data-processing equipment has facilitated the accuracy and completeness of collecting and tabulating crime data. Second, more stolen property is now insured, and in order for the benefits of a policy to be claimed, a police report must normally be filed. In past years, the likelihood that the perpetrator of a crime would be apprehended or that stolen property would be recovered was always low; therefore, there was little incentive outside insurance considerations to report crimes. This generates a rise in the crime index even if the number of actual crimes committed remains constant. Some types of crime (murder) are more likely to be reported than others (robbery). Rape was once seriously underreported, in part because of the kind of treatment rape victims received in court. With court reforms easing the potential embarrassment of victims who press charges, the rate of reporting rape may be going up significantly, in turn affecting the statistics for that crime. (The category of forcible rape, which has held steady in the twenty-first century, involves violence or the threat of violence against the victim, as opposed to statutory rape, which refers to an adult having sex with an underage partner. Forcible rape constitutes 89.5 percent of all rapes.)

Reasons for Crime

It is important to keep in mind that a "crime" is an activity that some legislative body has chosen to make illegal. This activity may be one that harms persons or property; it may be an activity that offends some ethical principle adhered to by the segment of society that dominates the lawmaking process; or it may be some silly or innocent activity, the illegal status of which is inexplicable. Old laws are seldom repealed, whereas new ones are continually being passed as each generation seeks to ban something that it finds odious. The number of proscribed activities has expanded over time. Clearly, the more things that are declared illegal, the greater the crime rate will be, even if behavior patterns remain constant. A statistical increase in crime does not necessarily reflect changes in behavior patterns.

Drugs.   Drug abuse may constitute a special category among victimless crimes. When a nonaddicted youth is seduced into drug use by a "pusher," the concept of voluntary, or victimless, behavior is stretched quite thin. Because many mind-altering drugs are physically or psychologically addicting—or both—the demand for them by the addicted is largely unaffected by costs, including potential punishments for their use. Consequently, the disposition to use such drugs is unlikely to be deterred by the threat of punishment. The legislative control of drug use in the United States is far from a recent phenomenon; however, this legislation has failed to stem a rise in the use of mind-altering drugs in recent decades. As the national surveys in Tables 6.4 and 6.5 indicate, a significant minority of students in high school and college have used drugs in the last year.

Drug users in search of money to finance their expensive habits have brought higher rates of property crime along with the drug epidemic. In the

T A B L E 6.4 Use of Drugs by High School Seniors in 2006 and 2008

Drug	2006 Within 12 months	2006 Within 30 days	2008 Within 12 months	2008 Within 30 days
Marijuana	31.5%	18.3%	32.4%	19.4%
Cocaine	5.7%	2.5%	4.4%	1.9%
Alcohol	66.5%	45.3%	65.5%	43.1%
Heroin	0.8%	0.4%	0.7%	0.4%

SOURCE: U.S. Department of Justice, Office of Justice Programs, Bureau of Justice Statistics, http://bjs.ojp.usdoj.gov/content/dcf/du.cfm.

T A B L E 6.5 Drug Usage by College Students

	1995	2000	2005	2008
Marijuana				
Within last month	18.6%	20.0%	17.1%	17%
Within last year	31.2%	34.0%	33.3%	32.3%
Cocaine				
Within last month	0.7%	1.4%	1.8%	1.2%
Within last year	3.6%	4.8%	5.7%	4.4%

SOURCE: U.S. Department of Health and Human Services: National Institutes of Health, *Monitoring the Future: National Survey Results on Drug Use, 1975–2008.* Vol. II, 2009, http://www.monitoringthefuture.org/pubs/monographs/vol2_2008. pdf.

mid-1970s, the Drug Enforcement Administration estimated that an average heroin habit cost $57.50 per day, or $21,000 annually to support.[9] This cost is beyond the financial capability of typical upper-middle-class people, not to mention addicts who have a diminished capacity to pursue middle-class careers. Consequently, addicts have little choice but to turn to crime to support their habit. Given the rigid demand, the successful interception of the drug supply would only make the drugs scarcer and more expensive. This would produce the spillover effect of increasing the crime rate even further.

The high rate of drug addiction in the post-Vietnam period would therefore account for the high rate of street crime in that era. Heroin was relatively inexpensive and easy to obtain in the so-called "Golden Triangle" of Southeast Asia in an era characterized by widespread rebellion against "the establishment" and its taboos. The war involved a mixing of the conscripted middle class and the drug-using underclass in a situation of great stress. Hence, many middle-class veterans brought a drug addiction home from Vietnam. Table 6.6 shows a sharp upswing in drug-related arrests from the 1980s into the 90s. Since the 1990s, reported marijuana use within the last 30 days among high school seniors has increased from 12 percent in 1992 to 19 percent in 2008, but that is still much lower than the high point of 37 percent of high school seniors in 1978 who reported using marijuana within the last 30 days.[10] That figure of 19 percent is even lower than in the mid 1980s.

T A B L E 6.6 Arrests for Drug Use in the 1990s

Arrests for all drugs from 1991 to 2000	up 49.4%
Arrests for all drugs from 1995 to 1996	up 35.5%
Arrests for all drugs from 1980 to 1995	up 153.5%
Arrests for heroin-cocaine 1990 to 1996	up 5.7%
Arrests for heroin-cocaine 1980 to 1995	up 741.5%

SOURCE: U.S. Department of Justice, Federal Bureau of Investigation, *Uniform Crime Report,* 1996, p. 280; and 2000, p. 19.

While a fair percentage of Americans had experimented with cocaine at least once in their lifetimes (14.5 percent tried cocaine), a much smaller number (1.5 percent) tried heroin, according to a national survey on drug use and health taken in 2007.[11] Currently, about 114 million Americans ages twelve or older (46 percent of the population) have reported using illegal drugs at least once in their lifetime. However, the overall percentage of regular drug users (i.e., used within the past 30 days) among persons aged twelve or older in the United States in 2008 was about 8 percent, and that rate has remained stable since 2002, when it was 8.3 percent.[12]

More people are arrested by U.S. law enforcement for drug abuse than for any other type of crime, according to the FBI's 2008 *Uniform Crime Report* (1,702,537 persons arrested in 2008, accounting for 12.2 percent of all arrests). Total arrests for drug abuse are up slightly from the 1990s in comparison to arrests for other types of crimes. In 1997, drug abuse arrests (1,583,600 persons) accounted for 10.3 percent of all arrests, a slightly smaller percentage than in 2008.[13]

While law enforcement may be arresting more people for drug abuse, the percentage of those arrests involving heroin or cocaine, or their derivatives, has fallen since the 1990s (see Table 6.7). For example, in 1995, possession of heroin or cocaine accounted for 27.8 percent of all drug arrests; but in 2008, arrests for possession of heroin or cocaine represented only 20.1 percent of all drug arrests. Heroin and cocaine are most frequently associated with street crime, and thus such a drop can account for much of the decline in street crime in cities like New York. This decline contributed significantly to the reputation of urban leaders, such as former New York City Mayor Rudy Giuliani, as the increase in drug usage during the 1970s and 1980s accounted for the apparent wave of street crime in that period. One can only speculate about the reasons for the decline in drug usage in the early twenty-first century. Certainly, aging and rising economic status of the baby boom generation may be one factor. The aggressive education campaign against drug usage, especially among middle-class youth, may finally be showing a measure of success.

Table 6.6 shows how drug usage might account for much of the high rate of street crime increase before 1995. The arrests for the sale of the two most addictive drugs went up over seven times in that period while arrests for possession increased slightly less than that. Clearly, increases of this magnitude must necessarily lead to significant increases in the rate of crime committed to sustain such addictions. Moreover, the spread of crack cocaine in America's inner cities was

T A B L E 6.7 Percentage of All Drug Arrests Involving Heroin or Cocaine or Their Derivatives

Arrest offense	1995	1997	2001	2005	2008
Sale or Manufacture	14.7%	10.3%	9.7%	8%	7.7%
Possession	27.8%	25%	23.1%	22.2%	20.1%

SOURCE: FBI Uniform Crime Reports, http://www.fbi.gov/ucr/ucr.htm.

accompanied by the formation of rival youth gangs seeking to control the inner city for the sale of crack. These gangs engaged in an armed struggle of unprecedented violence among themselves for control of that turf. This violence claimed the lives not only of rival gang members but of innocent bystanders as well, frequently children, who were caught in the crossfire. However, while the percentage of drug arrests compared to total arrests for other types of crimes has not changed much over the last decade, Table 6.7 indicates that arrests for the most addictive drugs (heroin or cocaine or their derivatives) have gone down as a percentage of total drug arrests.

Demographic Change.   Other categories in the crime statistics increase with the influence of demographic trends, such as the urbanization of America. Cities offer a greater crime potential than do smaller towns and rural areas. The high concentrations of people in America's urban population centers mean more interaction among people, more opportunities for crime, and less chance of being apprehended. There is normally a greater selection of valuable, concealable, and transportable goods in cities than in rural areas. Furthermore, the anonymity of a city makes it easier for the perpetrator of a crime to escape detection or capture. Until recently, crime was a distinctly urban phenomenon, and the fact that a greater proportion of the population lived in urban areas meant more crime. In recent years, however, crime in small-town and suburban settings has been increasing faster than has crime in urban areas, and the gap between the two types of settings has not only disappeared, but has in fact overtaken crime in large cities (see Table 6.8). Thus, in 2008, cities outside metropolitan areas had a crime rate for violent crime and property crime of 4,138 offenses per 100,000 population (for offenses known to the police), while metropolitan areas (large cities) had a rate of only 3,841. The reasons for this may be that with urban sprawl, previously isolated smaller towns are being absorbed as suburban parts of a metropolis. The rate of crime for rural areas is still relatively low, at 1,886 in 2008. The data in Table 6.8 also bolsters other evidence presented in this chapter showing that crime has continued to decrease somewhat since 2001.

**T A B L E 6.8 Urban-Rural Crime, 2000, 2002, and 2008:
Offenses Known to Police**

Crime Area	2001 Offenses (per 100,000)	2002 Offenses (per 100,000)	2008 Offenses (per 100,000)
Metropolitan Statistical Area*	4,428	4,409	3,841
Other Cities	4,485	4,524	4,138
Rural areas	1,864	1,908	1,886

*Central city or urbanized area of at least 50,000 people.

SOURCE: *Sourcebook of Criminal Justice Statistics,* 2008, http://www.albany.edu/sourcebook/tost_3.html#3_v.
(These figures include only offenses involving violent crime and property crime; other types of offenses, such as drug abuse, are not included.)

Another demographic trend that contributed to the increased incidence of crime in the past several decades is that those categories of people statistically more likely to commit crimes grew as a proportion of the total population. Youth is an important crime indicator, with 55.8 percent of offenders in 2001 between fifteen and twenty-five years of age and only 13.2 percent between forty and fifty years old. Until recently, there was a growing proportion of the population under twenty-five, due in part to the postwar baby boom. However, this trend has ended with the aging of the "baby boom" generation, and with increasing longevity, the proportion of the older population is beginning to rise. This fact could also partially account for the recent downturn in crime rates.

The fact that crime is very much a young person's activity—especially with respect to "street crimes"—further weakens the argument that the deterrence measures of the criminal justice system prevents crime. Much of the most vicious crime is committed by juveniles, and the most active part of a career criminal's life is over by around the age of twenty-five or thirty. By one set of data, slightly over 35 percent of those arrested in one year for index crimes were juveniles. Marvin Wolfgang and his associates, however, find that a small number of delinquents—juveniles who have had five or more recorded contacts with police—are responsible for a majority of all crimes and two-thirds of all violent crimes.[14]

Yet the criminal justice system does not fully accept the responsibility of minors for their actions, a fact exacerbated by the *Roper* case (discussed on page 189) in which the Supreme Court ruled the execution of anyone for a crime committed when younger than eighteen violates the Eighth Amendment's ban on cruel and unusual punishment. The perpetrator in the case bragged how he could escape serious punishment because of his status as a minor. Sentences usually are lighter; alternatives to actual incarceration are preferred; the police records of minors are erased; and in many cases they are released from the custody of the juvenile detention system when they become twenty-one years old. For example, a Rhode Island civil rights officer filed a brief in that state's supreme court in July 1994 for the unconditional release of one Craig Price on his twenty-first birthday, despite his having stabbed a thirty-nine-year-old widow and her ten-year-old daughter to death (the latter was stabbed sixty-two times), and stabbed another twenty-seven-year-old women some fifty-eight times, all before his fifteenth birthday. Long-term imprisonment is generally not a likely possibility until an adult record is well-established, and, as we have seen, this is usually after the most active part of the criminal career is over. Hence, despite sharp increases in the prison population, an increasing number of inmates are older persons who do not present the greatest current and future danger to society. However, in recent years more juveniles are being tried as adults.

For many juveniles in lower-class neighborhoods, a brush with the law is not the mark of shame among one's peers that it would be to middle-class youths. Rather, it is often a source of pride and status for having stood up to the system. The kinds of light punishments at stake in the juvenile justice system do not present credible deterrents to teenage *recidivist* criminals who grow to understand that they can flout the law with impunity as long as they are minors.

Recent downturns in crime could also be due to the changes in demographics resulting from the legalization of abortion in the Supreme Court case of *Roe v. Wade* (1973). University of Chicago Economics Professor Steven Levitt has suggested in his bestselling, co-authored book *Freakonomics* (2005) that the legalization of abortion in the 1970s cut down on crime in the 1990s. As Professor Levitt described on his blog at the *New York Times*, "The logic is simple: unwanted children have an increased risk of growing up to be criminals, and legalized abortion reduces the number of unwanted children. Consequently, legalized abortion lowers crime in the future."[15] Recently, however, rates of abortion have been declining, raising the question of whether crime will once again rise in the future due to the lack of abortions. But as Levitt has pointed out, it is unclear whether the most recent decline in abortion will cause a future rise in crime because researchers are still unclear as to why abortion rates are falling. There are a number of possible explanations for the decline, "and none of these have dire crime implications."[16]

Family Structure.   The divorce rate has climbed dramatically in the latter part of the twentieth century, to the point where half of the marriages in this country end up in the divorce court. Hence, a majority of America's children are not raised in a traditional two-parent household. While many single parents successfully raise children with good results, the data show that in general, children raised in traditional two-parent households tend to be more successful in their academic, professional, and personal lives. Therefore, the products of America's increasingly unstable family structure may be more likely to experience problems in their lives; problems that may involve perpetrating crime.

Socioeconomic Causes.   Certain types of crime are clearly related to poverty and unemployment, a fact that accounts for much of the apparent correlation between crime and race or ethnicity. The philosophical question is to what extent persons, regardless of their individual circumstances, remain free to choose between criminal and law-abiding behavior and hence are responsible for their actions. To the extent that criminality is a choice made under conditions of free will, one cannot posit socioeconomic conditions as a cause of certain types of criminality. Conservatives tend to emphasize free will and individual responsibility for criminal behavior; whereas liberals are more likely to attribute such behavior to sociological circumstances, such as poverty and racism, which they argue cause the individual to act in aberrant ways. Of course, sociological conditions are more amenable to public policy solutions than are defects in individual character, and liberals tend to be more optimistic than conservatives are about the prospect of reducing crime by improving the environment in which people live.

Whatever conclusions one draws about this question, the fact remains that people in certain socioeconomic circumstances are statistically more likely to engage in criminal behavior. Accordingly, whether such circumstances are a cause of crime or a rationalization for it, a reduction in such circumstances may subsequently reduce the rate of certain types of crime. It may not be a coincidence that the slowing in the decline in crime (i.e., crime is still decreasing, but at a more gradual rate as compared with the 1990s) occurred at approximately the same time as the 2001 recession.

ISSUES IN EQUAL PROTECTION AND GOVERNMENT RESPONSE TO CRIME

The Supreme Court has interpreted the Equal Protection Clause of the Constitution's Fourteenth Amendment as prohibiting selective enforcement of the law based on race (see *United States v. Armstrong*, 1996).[17] Notwithstanding the Supreme Court's constitutional pronouncements, measures enacted by government to respond to crime do not always impact all racial, religious, and cultural groups equally. In fact, there is a strong sense among the African American population that they experience a particular injustice at the hands of the government's criminal justice system. The lower level of trust in the criminal justice system on the part of African Americans as compared to whites is summarized in Table 6.9, and this is a fact that threatens the overall legitimacy of the system. These differences in perceptions have narrowed recently, perhaps due in part to the election of our first African American president. But, even in 2009, there are more African Americans who have very little or no confidence in the justice system (35 percent), as compared to 26 percent of whites with little or no confidence.

This gap in perceptions is not surprising given the huge differences in arrests in America between African Americans and other races. In 2008, African Americans made up approximately 12.8 percent of the national population; however, 28.3 percent of the persons arrested for serious crime were African Americans, a figure down from 33.8 percent in 1978, but virtually unchanged from 28.9 percent in 1996. The data for homicide in 2008 show a disproportionate percentage of African Americans arrested. In that year, 50.1 percent of those arrested for homicide were black, up from 39 percent in 2000. Of course, a disproportionate number of murder victims in 2008 (over 40 percent of all murder victims) were also African Americans (separate data for Hispanics were not provided). The rates of arrest are summarized in Table 6.10. Some civil rights groups argue

T A B L E 6.9 Confidence in the Criminal Justice System, 2005 and 2009

		A great deal	Some	Very little	None
2005	White	36	41	21	1
	African American	25	40	32	3
2009	White	28	45	24	2
	African American	30	35	31	4

SOURCE: U.S. Department of Justice, Federal Bureau of Investigation, *Sourcebook of Criminal Justice Statistics*, 2005, p. 113; and *Sourcebook of Criminal Justice Statistics*, 2009, http://www.albany.edu/sourcebook/csv/t2112009.csv.

T A B L E 6.10 Arrests by Race, 2008 in Percentages
(Hispanics were classified with whites)

Crime Category	White	Black	Native American	Asian-Pacific Islander
Murder-manslaughter	47.9	50.1	1.0	1.1
Forcible rape	65.2	32.2	1.2	1.4
Robbery	41.7	56.7	0.7	0.9
Aggravated Assault	63.3	34.2	1.4	1.2
Burglary	66.8	31.4	0.9	0.9
Larceny-Theft	68.1	29.3	1.3	1.4
Motor Vehicle Theft	59.7	38.1	1.1	1.2
Arson	75.8	21.7	1.2	1.2
All Violent Crime*	58.3	39.4	1.2	1.1
Total All Crimes	69.2	28.3	1.3	1.1

*Includes murder and manslaughter, forcible rape, robbery, and aggravated assault.

SOURCE: U.S. Department of Justice, Federal Bureau of Investigation, *Uniform Crime Report, 2008,* http://www.fbi.gov/ucr/cius2008/data/table_43.html.

that these numbers are simply a reflection of a higher propensity on the part of the police to arrest African Americans for crimes that might otherwise go overlooked among whites. They argue that the evidence of arrests support suspicions that there is some racial bias in the dispensing of justice. Prominent scholars, such as Professor Charles Ogletree of Harvard Law School, charge that many of the young African American males in prison are in fact innocents caught up in a racist system.[18] However, whether the disparity is entirely due to racial bias is a much more complicated issue to statistically examine and understand. Certainly, differences in socioeconomics among African Americans and whites may also contribute to higher rates of criminal arrest among African Americans. Undoubtedly, the explanations could be a combination of both socioeconomic factors and racial bias by individuals in government.

Not only are African Americans disproportionately arrested, but they also disproportionately populate America's jails. In 2008, African Americans constituted 39.2 percent of the prison population, despite representing less than 13 percent of the population.[19] The fact is that African Americans who are arrested are much more likely than whites to end up incarcerated in prison.[20] Imprisonment rates for both whites and African Americans have risen since 1975, but the rate of African American imprisonment has risen much more rapidly.[21] But, of course, rates of imprisonment (as opposed to rates of arrests) are more likely to represent political decisions of the community rather than a reflection of rates of crime. Sociologist Pamela Oliver of the University of Wisconsin–Madison notes in one study that "[i]t appears that blacks are more likely to be imprisoned [in states and communities] where they are a smaller, politically weaker, and economically marginalized population."[22]

A related issue with regard to race and crime and the disproportionate percentage of incarcerated African Americans is racial profiling. This refers to the disposition on the part of numerous law enforcement personnel to regard the fact of being African American, in and of itself, as grounds for suspicion of past or prospective criminal activity. African Americans, without showing any other indications of criminality, are more likely than comparable whites to be stopped by police, interrogated, searched, and arrested for minor infractions. This issue undercuts perceptions by African Americans that the system is fair. Furthermore, the Civil Rights Division of the U.S. Justice Department argues that racial profiling is not only morally wrong, but also ineffective in terms of the public policy goal of reducing crime.[23]

The issue of racial profiling has also affected other minority groups. The issue has become a cause of concern for Muslims of Middle Eastern descent in America. The Justice Department's Civil Rights Division has issued guidelines that prohibit law enforcement in the federal government from outwardly profiling Muslims (in airports, for example) simply because of their ethnicity or religion. However, a notable exception to this guideline is made for the realm of national security. Those same Justice Department guidelines state that "Federal law enforcement officers who are protecting national security or preventing catastrophic events (as well as airport security screeners) may consider race, ethnicity, and other relevant factors to the extent permitted by our laws and the Constitution"[24]

The issue of racial profiling of Hispanics became a political concern in Arizona in 2010 after the state passed a law to combat illegal immigration. Arizona has become a popular point of crossing for illegal immigrants, and a rise in crime in human trafficking and drug trafficking has resulted from this influx. In an effort to stem the tide of illegal immigrants and the resulting crime, the state passed a law, which allows law enforcement, when detaining an individual during the investigation of a crime or during a traffic stop, to inquire into the detained individual's immigrant status. Even though the law specifically prohibits authorities from engaging in racial profiling, some civil liberties groups and advocates for Hispanic rights are concerned that the law could nevertheless be used to unconstitutionally racially profile Hispanics. The passage of the Arizona law spurred a hail of protests and boycotts and even precipitated criticism of the law from President Obama. The U.S. Justice Department filed a lawsuit to block the state of Arizona from implementing the law. In July 2010, a Federal district judge sided with the Obama administration and issued a preliminary injunction to stop key provisions of the law from going into effect. As this book goes to print, a three-judge panel at the United States Court of Appeals for the Ninth Circuit is considering Arizona's request to lift the injunction and allow implementation of the state law.

The perception of justice denied is periodically renewed and exacerbated when the violent treatment of African Americans is apparently not prosecuted and punished with the same vigor as would be the comparable treatment of whites. Events that generate a perception of injustice include the 1980 acquittal of three Miami policemen after they had beaten an African American suspect to death; the acquittal of several Nazi party members and Ku Klux Klansmen of killing some North Carolina radicals pressing for African American advancement; and the 1991 videotaped beating by Los Angeles policemen of an African American, Rodney King.

Perceptions of an unfair and unjust system give rise to the phenomenon of "jury nullification," where a jury renders a verdict of "not guilty" even in the face of an overwhelming body of evidence to the contrary. For example, a young African American, Lemrick Nelson, who was in possession of the knife (stained with the victim's blood) used to stab Yankel Rosenbaum to death in the Crown Heights riots in New York in 1991 and who bragged about committing the deed, was nevertheless acquitted because African Americans on the jury said they could never vote to convict a fellow African American in such a racially biased system. The racial divide over the verdict in the case of O. J. Simpson, cited earlier, illustrates the black distrust of our criminal justice system. The practice of jury nullification was a technique formerly used by Southern white juries to protect whites who had killed or assaulted African Americans. Paul Butler, a professor at George Washington University Law School argued in a *Yale Law Review* article that "it is the moral responsibility of black jurors to emancipate some guilty black outlaws."[25]

CONTEMPORARY POLICY: CONSTITUTIONAL RIGHTS AND THE DETERRENCE OF CRIME

Common sense tells us that criminal behavior can be prevented by confronting the prospective perpetrator with the threat of punishment. Accordingly, the conventional idea is that severe treatment of criminals will deter subsequent criminality and that lenient treatment will encourage it. This conventional outlook, voiced principally by conservatives, attributes the problem of rising crime in large part to a significant expansion in the rights of persons accused of crime, an expansion that was associated with the Supreme Court under the chief justiceship of Earl Warren (1953–1969). This expansion, however, was largely halted with the appointment of several Supreme Court justices under the Reagan and first Bush administrations, justices thought to be politically conservative and less sympathetic to an expansive view of individual rights implicitly protected by the Constitution. This Court, now headed by Chief Justice Roberts and buttressed by the addition of Justices Alito, Scalia, Kennedy, and Thomas, now has a more conservative profile. (See Chapter 13 for a list of current members of the Court and their judicial orientations.) President Obama did recently place two new justices on the court (Sotomayor and Kagan) who are liberal in orientation, but they simply replaced existing liberal justices on the court (Souter and Stevens). Thus, the George W. Bush appointments of Roberts and Alito give the Court a narrow conservative majority, despite some surprising liberal votes from Kennedy. (His opinion in the *Roper* case is discussed later in the chapter.) This apparent balance makes it unlikely that procedural rights will be significantly expanded in the near future. However, the respect that legal scholars in the Anglo-American common law system have for the force of precedent probably limits the extent to which the Court can undo the revolution in procedural rights.

Because in our system the accused is presumed innocent until proven otherwise, the rights of the accused are the rights of the innocent. These rights require the judicial system to proceed according to the rules of evidence, rules that prevent people from being punished on the basis of hearsay, rumor, emotional prejudice, or other factors that do not objectively establish guilt. Given the choice of punishing all of the guilty, even if some innocent are also caught in the net, or taking care not to punish the innocent, even if some guilty people thereby escape punishment, Western society has opted for the latter alternative. It must be remembered that each of these procedural rights came into being in response to a particular abuse of government power. As Justice Felix Frankfurter once said, "The history of liberty has largely been the history of procedural safeguards."

This expansion of rights has come about in two ways. First, it has involved an expanded meaning of the U.S. Constitution's Fourteenth Amendment to incorporate the federal Bill of Rights, making them applicable to state governments. The Bill of Rights (the first ten amendments to the Constitution) was originally written by the Founding Fathers only for the purpose of limiting the national government's criminal law and trial procedures in federal courts. In other words, until the Fourteenth Amendment was passed after the Civil War, state governments did not have to follow the Bill of Rights because it initially only applied to the federal government. Most crimes, however, are violations of state law. Consequently, most criminal trials happen in state court, not federal court. It is only through the Fourteenth Amendment's provision that "no State shall deny any person life, liberty or property without due process of law…" that the U.S. Constitution imposes any restriction on state criminal procedure. Legal scholars disagree as to what process is due to the accused—for example, does the entire Bill of Rights apply or only some portions of it? That question is actually answered by the Fourteenth Amendment itself, because an earlier clause in the Amendment affirms that "no state shall make or enforce any law, which shall abridge the privileges or immunities of citizens of the United States." Since citizens of the U.S. enjoy all the privileges and immunities of the Bill of Rights, one would naturally assume that states now have to follow the entire Bill of Rights. But the U.S. Supreme Court decided, for its own political purposes, to make the Privileges and Immunities Clause of the Fourteenth Amendment meaningless in the *Slaughterhouse Cases* of 1873. The legal community, for whatever reason, has acquiesced to this decision to render the clause meaningless. When the Court began using the Fourteenth Amendment's Due Process Clause in the twentieth century to force states to comply with the Bill of Rights, it decided to pick and choose which of the Bill of Rights applied to the states in a case-by-case basis rather than revisiting the wisdom of the *Slaughterhouse Cases*. Not all justices have agreed to this selective incorporation of the Bill of Rights (see, for example, the writings of Justice Hugo Black).

As of now, most of the Bill of Rights applies to state governments, but some notable exceptions include the right of an accused to require that an indictment be handed down by a grand jury instead of a prosecutor. While the right to a grand jury is available in federal court, state courts are not required by the Constitution to use a grand jury to indict someone and begin criminal proceedings against them. Rather, many states simply allow for a prosecutor to make that decision. There are drawbacks for allowing states to use a prosecutor instead of a grand jury (an impartial panel of citizens) to decide whether there is sufficient evidence to prosecute a suspect. Overzealous prosecutors or state governments may use this discretion to prosecute people for political reasons or other unscrupulous reasons, and so the right is part of the checks and balances used to ensure a fair criminal process.

The second mode of expansion of the rights of the accused has been through a broadened interpretation of existing rights. With each of these rights, the question was not whether it existed, but rather what it meant or implied. The question of the implications and meaning of the rights of persons accused of a crime has come into sharper focus since the beginning of the "war on terror" and the United States Patriot Act, passed in the wake of the September 11, 2001 attacks, and the subsequent indefinite incarceration of citizens and noncitizens believed to be associated with terrorism. The act significantly expanded the ability of law enforcement agencies to search telephone and e-mail communications along with medical and financial records, and enhanced the discretion of law enforcement agencies to detain and deport illegal aliens. The ability to indefinitely detain illegal immigrants has been criticized by civil libertarians and in September, 2007, the American Civil Liberties Union filed a lawsuit challenging the ability of government agencies to monitor phone conversations. The act was due to sunset at the end of 2005, but it was reauthorized and signed into law by President Bush on March 9, 2006.

The expansion of the rights of the accused has generated the most controversy in three areas:

1. The right to counsel and the admissibility of confessions
2. The exclusionary rule and the admissibility of illegally obtained evidence
3. Constraints on the use of capital punishment

Confessions and the Right to Counsel

It was decided quite early that the right to counsel applied to state criminal proceedings. What this right entails, however, has changed over the years. To the founders, it was understood by its common-law meaning: the right to hire an attorney. The concept that the state had any obligation to pay for one's attorney is a modern extrapolation from this earlier concept. The practice of providing defense counsel in federal criminal trials had long been standard procedure but not a constitutional requirement. The first expansion of the right to counsel occurred in 1932, when the Supreme Court held in the infamous Scottsboro case that the accused had in capital cases (cases in which the death penalty is a legal possibility) the right to be provided with effective counsel in state court.[26] The Scottsboro opinion noted that even intelligent laypersons lack "skill in the science of the law." Clearly, the prosecution is legally trained and, in an adversary proceeding, has a distinct advantage in knowing how to manipulate the rules of evidence and procedure. The logic of this argument prevailed as the Court extended the right to counsel at state expense to all indigent defendants facing felony trials in state courts in the 1963 case of *Gideon v. Wainwright*.[27] Finally, the courts have extended the right further to include "effective assistance of counsel." Thus, a federal appeals court in 2001 threw out a death sentence issued in a Texas state court after the defendant's court-appointed attorney slept through most of the capital murder trial. The federal appeals court stated that a sleeping attorney is like having no attorney at all.

Even this expansion of the meaning of the due process clause did not satisfy all the needs of defendants for counsel in state criminal processes. Most convictions in fact have been obtained from confessions, often through plea bargaining, before the cases ever come to trial. *Plea bargaining* is a frequently used process involving an agreement between the prosecution and the defendant by which the latter is allowed to plead guilty to a lesser crime than he or she is charged with. In return, the prosecution drops the more serious charge. The prosecution in this way avoids the necessity of satisfying the burden of proof for the more serious charge; the crowded court docket is relieved of another time-consuming case; the state thus saves money; and the defendant is freed from the threat of the more serious punishment.[28] This "bargain" is generally offered to a defendant with either the implicit or explicit threat that if the deal is rejected, successful prosecution under a more serious charge will be the outcome. Even innocent people may in such circumstances be persuaded to "cop a plea" in order to escape the threat of dire punishment. Furthermore, prosecutors sometimes overcharge in order to allow themselves room to bargain. At the same time, plea bargainers who have committed serious crimes may get by with more lenient punishment and early release from detention. The pressure from overcrowded court dockets on harried, overworked prosecutors to dispose of cases in this shortcut fashion can thus frustrate the goal of physically removing dangerous criminals from society for long periods of time and can detract from whatever deterrent effect serious punishment may exercise.[29] Potential criminals thus have good reason to assume that they can obtain leniency by plea bargaining.

Thus, for a period of time, many cases were being settled in the pretrial stage, when defendants did not have a guaranteed recourse to counsel. The *Escobedo*[30] and *Miranda*[31] cases extended the right of counsel provided by the state effectively to the point of arrest. Culminating in the famous "*Miranda* rule," this right now includes: (1) the right to remain silent, (2) the right to know that anything said could and would be used against the accused in court, and (3) the right to be represented at that time by counsel, at state expense if necessary. Before any confession or damaging statement can be entered as evidence, all of the above rights must be consciously waived by the accused. Of course, the first thing that an attorney is likely to do is advise his or her client to say nothing, thereby placing the burden of proof on the police or prosecution to prove their case. This would seem on the surface likely to reduce the rate of convictions, because so many are obtained by confession. Furthermore, the decision seemed to mean freeing, on a legal technicality, a person who had voluntarily confessed to a heinous crime before being read her rights. For many, it epitomized a dangerous precedent for freeing other criminals on similar technicalities. The *Miranda* decision was widely perceived as symbolic of a trend toward an obsessive concern for the rights of the accused at the expense of the swift and severe punishment of criminals, and it was therefore roundly criticized by many as an excellent example of misguided liberalism interfering with the maintenance of law and order. At any rate, the concept of *Miranda* warnings offered up by the Supreme Court in 1966 were not unique to America. Scotland already barred the used of confessions obtained through police interrogation, and in India, confessions to police without a magistrate present were excluded from evidence at trial since 1872, while England also had some provision (pre-*Miranda*) for police to caution suspects, before questioning, that they were not obligated to talk.[32]

The Exclusionary Rule and Search and Seizure

The *exclusionary rule* is the principle that evidence obtained in an illegal search and/or seizure may not be admitted in a court of law. The Fourth Amendment proscribes "unreasonable searches and seizures." A legal search and seizure requires one of two conditions. In the case of someone's home, police need to obtain a search warrant, issued by a judge, which authorizes the police to search private property without the consent of the property owner and specifies what is being sought. A judge can only issue the warrant on the showing by the police of probable cause that illegal activity may be occurring. In all other instances that occur outside the home or off private property, the police usually only need to prove to a court they had probable cause to make a search.

What happens when police conduct a search without a search warrant or without a showing of probable cause that a crime is being committed, and they then find evidence of a crime? The Constitution is altogether silent about what happens to evidence that is found during an unconstitutional search, and whether that illegal evidence can be used at trial. Some law-and-order conservatives argue that the Fourth Amendment ought not to be construed as excluding illegally obtained evidence, because such a principle would protect only the guilty, whereas constitutional rights are designed to protect the innocent. Furthermore, they say that if one is not guilty of a crime, an unreasonable search and seizure will not yield any incriminating evidence. The secondary argument against the exclusionary rule is that other remedies are available to deter police from illegal searches; namely, police can be sued or arrested for such behavior. Despite these arguments, the Supreme Court held in the famous *Mapp* decision that the Constitution requires the exclusion from court of illegally obtained evidence.[33] In *Mapp v. Ohio* (1961), the Court rejected the argument that the exclusionary rule protects only the guilty. The Court found that other remedies were ineffective; hence, the exclusionary rule was a necessary means to enforce the admittedly fundamental right to be free from such illegal searches. The rule protects more than the guilty, because if illegally obtained evidence is inadmissible, there is no motive for police to make illegal searches of the guilty or the innocent. Police are less likely to undertake illegal searches if they know that they cannot use any incriminating evidence they find through such searches.

The Court in *Mapp* cited evidence that alternative procedures to deter illegal searches have been ineffective; therefore, the exclusionary rule is a necessary deterrent to illegal searches.

There are a number of exceptions to the exclusionary rule that allow police to search places without probable cause or a search warrant. For example, police do not need to have a search warrant or show probable cause that a crime is being committed in cases of exigent circumstances (such as when police believe a person may be dying in a home or suspect a bomb in a house). Nor are these rules necessary to search people at border checkpoints. The exceptions are too varied and complex to name all of them here, but many of these exceptions also revolve around the concept of protecting the safety of officers. Thus, in a lawful arrest in which a warrant has not first been obtained, the following forms of search may be made: (1) the person and pockets of the arrestee and (2) the arrestee's car or the room in which he or she was arrested ("the area under his possession"), but not the entire house.[34] A person merely stopped for questioning may be subjected to a pat down or frisk for weapons in the name of officer safety, even if that person is not suspected of engaging in any crime.[35] The very complexity of these rules illustrates the difficulty that the courts have in trying to balance two important conflicting values: the right of individuals to be free from governmental oppression or harassment and the control of crime and punishment of criminals. Wiretapping someone's phone (even a public payphone enclosed in a booth) typically requires a warrant issued by a judge.[36] But in the "war on terror," the Bush administration argued for an exception to the rule of needing a warrant for wiretaps in cases of national security, where a suspected terrorist is calling someone overseas.

The two biggest exceptions to the exclusionary rule occurred in the 1980s. The Supreme Court in 1984, driven by then Chief Justice Burger's avowed hostility to the exclusionary rule, chipped away at the rule without specifically overturning it. The Court announced a decision in the case of *Nix v. Williams* (1984) that held that illegally obtained evidence would now be admissible if the Court found that the police would have discovered the evidence sooner or later by legal means. This "inevitable discovery" rule pleased conservatives, who argued that it would render clearly guilty people less likely to be released on a mere "technicality." But liberals fear that this dampening effect on the disposition of the police to engage in illegal searches may be seriously weakened by this case. Subsequently, the Court made another inroad on the exclusionary rule in the case of *U.S. v. Leon* (1984), in which it held that if the police acted in "good faith" that the search was legal (for example, if a magistrate issued a search warrant, but it turns out the magistrate made an error because there wasn't sufficient probable cause), the fact that the search turned out to be technically illegal would not be grounds for suppressing any evidence found.[37]

Capital Punishment

The third area in which the expansion of the rights of the accused has provoked the most controversy is capital punishment. The relevant constitutional provision is the Eighth Amendment protection against "cruel and unusual punishment," which opponents of the death penalty have variously held either prohibits the imposition of capital punishment itself or, failing that, at least limits the mode and circumstances of its imposition. Given the ambiguity of the words "cruel and unusual punishment," their implications for the practice of capital punishment are something on which reasonable and informed legal scholars can and do disagree. The controversy is exacerbated by serious disagreement over the importance of capital punishment as a deterrent to capital crime.

The Supreme Court has affirmed that there are two legitimate social purposes that may be served by the death penalty: deterrence and *retribution*. Most of the published arguments supporting retention and use of capital punishment have focused on its putative value as a deterrent to future crime; the essentially normative, retributive argument is apparently distasteful to many scholars. Yet for the person in the street, retribution is also a real consideration. There are some crimes for which mere imprisonment seems an inadequate punishment. Many people's intuitive sense of justice is deeply offended when a brutal mass murderer, such as Jeffrey Dahmer, convicted in 1992 not only of killing but also of cannibalizing his victims, is allowed to live on in prison. (Dahmer was murdered in prison in 1994.) The issue of retributive justice was raised in 1997 in the case of the perpetrators of the bombing of the federal building in Oklahoma City that killed 168 people. For this act of terrorism, the worst in U.S. history prior to September 11, perpetrator Timothy McVeigh was sentenced to death, but co-conspirator Terry Nichols was spared the death penalty by a jury. As an ethical argument, the issue of retributive justice cannot be resolved; yet, it may more easily withstand scrutiny than the more frequently relied-upon deterrence argument.[38] The retributive argument regards capital punishment as an end in itself, while the deterrent argument regards capital punishment as a means to the end of preventing serious crimes. Accordingly, the question of whether capital punishment serves as a deterrent is in principle an empirical question, a question resolvable by observable data.

Deterrence?   If, on the basis of common sense, it seems clear that punishment deters proscribed acts, it follows that death should deter such acts more effectively than less severe punishment will. As the British Royal Commission on capital punishment stated in 1953, "*Prima facie*, the penalty of death is likely to have a stronger effect as a deterrent to normal human beings than any other form of punishment...." There is in fact evidence that punishment in general does deter crime. However, another body of research indicates that it is the swiftness and certainty of punishment, rather than its severity, that most effectively operates as a crime deterrent. Yet, the death penalty, in the American context, can neither be swift nor certain. It is hedged by automatic appeals and the right of almost any judge personally to stay an execution based on any question about the manner of arrest or conviction. It is limited also by the reluctance of judges and juries to impose the death sentence and the even greater reluctance of states to carry it out. Sociologist Thorsten Sellin has reported that, historically, the risk of suffering the death penalty in the United States if caught and convicted of capital murder *during a period of widespread executions* (1933–1950) was only 3.67 percent.[39] In 2008, there were 16,272 homicides; yet, in that same year there were only 3,207 inmates on death row and thirty-seven executions. A person sentenced to die can usually find a judge to stay the execution on some grounds, delaying the implementation of the death penalty for lengthy periods. There is a less than 1 percent probability that a convicted murderer will be executed; however, more important in terms of the deterrent effect of "swift and certain" punishment, there is virtually no chance that a murderer will be executed within two years of conviction. The relative frequency of people sentenced to death and the frequency of people actually being executed in recent years are indicated in Table 6.11. At the rate of the current high-water mark of ninety-eight executions per year, it would take more than thirty-three years to dispatch everyone currently under sentence of death, assuming no one else is so sentenced in that period.

There is very little doubt that if every person convicted of murder were to be immediately dispatched, other murders would be deterred. However, the foregoing data suggest that there is very little likelihood of such a policy being implemented. First, the system seeks through appeals and rehearings to resolve all uncertainty before carrying out an execution. Second, America's more secularized society is uncertain about judging who deserves to live and die. Finally, there appears to be a cultural strengthening of the sanctity of life itself under way in the nation. Consequently, to execute promptly all or even most people convicted of murder is politically unthinkable. Failing that extreme approach of quick execution, it is hard to see how capital punishment can have a greater deterrent effect than do other forms of punishment. Despite these reservations about the deterrent effect of capital punishment, belief in that deterrent effect continues to be a widespread, although by 2000 a minority, opinion. Specifically, 42 percent of a national sample believed that the death penalty deters crime, and 52 percent said it does not, with 7 percent unsure.[40] Thus, supporters of the death penalty may be playing to public opinion rather than social scientific knowledge.

T A B L E   6.11   Death Sentences and Executions

Year	Under Sentence of Death	Executed
1996	3,219	45
1997	3,335	74
1998	3,465	68
1999	3,540	98
2002	3,562	71
2004	3,320	59
2008	3,207	37
2009	3,263	52

SOURCE: U.S. Department of Justice, Federal Bureau of Investigation,
Sourcebook of Criminal Justice Statistics, 2000, p. 549; and
http://www.deathpenaltyinfo.org/article.php?scid+8&did=839; Accessed October 15, 2007.

There are some data on the actual deterrent effect of the death penalty, but they are inconclusive.[41] For example, studies have compared homicide rates of states that administer the death penalty with states that have abolished it. If the administration of executions were in fact a deterrent to capital crime, the murder rates in death penalty states should be significantly lower than those in the abolitionist states. It is worth noting that Texas, which far and away has the highest number of executions of all states, had a homicide rate in 2008 (at 5.6 per 100,000 inhabitants) that is not much different from the national average (of 5.4). Louisiana, which also has the death penalty (although it does not execute as many people per capita as Texas), had an incredibly high murder rate in 2008 at 11.9 per 100,000. Meanwhile, Massachusetts, which has outlawed the death penalty, had a murder rate in 2008 of 2.6. If the death penalty were working as an effective deterrent, one should think that the Texas murder rate would at least be lower than the national average. In 2008, almost half the executions in the U.S. occurred in Texas (18 executions, which was an atypically low number for Texas that year). Since capital punishment was reinstated in the United States in 1976, Texas has put over 450 people to death. In 2000, there were 85 executions in the United States, and Texas racked up 40 of them, its highest total of executions in recent years. Most executions in the United States occur in the South, yet it has a disproportionate share of the murders, given its population size, when compared to other regions of the country (see Table 6.12). According to Amnesty International, there are 59 countries that still retain the death penalty as a form of punishment, and of those, the countries with the most number of executions in 2008 included China (at least 1,718 executions), followed by Iran (at least 346), Saudi Arabia (at least 102), and the United States (at least 37), then Pakistan (at least 36), Iraq (at least 34), Vietnam (at least 19), Afghanistan (at least 17), North Korea (at least 15), Japan (15).[42] Out of the entire list of all countries worldwide who executed anyone in 2008, the only democratic industrialized country other than the United States to carry out executions was Japan.

Currently, 35 states, plus the U.S. government and the U.S. military, continue to provide for the death penalty by law. The death penalty has been abolished in the remaining states. Table 6.13 compares murder rates in death penalty states to those in nondeath penalty states. Contrary to expectations, the death

TABLE 6.12 Percentage of Homicide Rates by Region, 2008

	Percentage of U.S. Population	Percentage of Murders in the U.S.
Northeast	18.1%	14.1%
Midwest	21.9%	19.7%
West	23.3%	21.1%
South	36.7%	45.2%

SOURCE: U.S. Department of Justice, Federal Bureau of Investigation, *Crime in the United States*, 2008.

TABLE 6.13 Murder Rates in Death Penalty and Nondeath Penalty States Compared

Year	Death Penalty States Rates	Nondeath Penalty States Rates	(%) Difference
1990	9.5	9.16	4
1992	9.51	8.63	10
1994	9.23	7.88	17
1996	7.72	5.37	44
1998	6.51	4.61	41
2000	5.70	4.25	35
2002	5.82	4.27	36
2003	5.91	4.10	44
2004	5.71	4.02	42
2005	5.87	4.03	46
2006	5.9	4.22	40
2007	5.83	4.10	42

SOURCE: http://www.deathpenaltyinfo.org/article.php?scid=12&did=168; Accessed October 15, 2007.

penalty states in fact had slightly higher mean homicide rates than did the abolitionist states. Not only are the homicide rates greater in the death penalty states, but the percentage difference between these two categories has continually grown over the years to a significant 42 percent in 2007. Overall, death penalty states have had a higher homicide rate than abolitionist states, data that clearly do not support the claim that the availability or exercise of capital punishment acts as a deterrent to the perpetration of murder.

This failure to find a significant impact of the death penalty on capital crime may be attributable in part to the fact that murder, the major capital offense, is, relative to property crimes, one of intense passion. Whether much rational calculation goes on in the mind of a murderer about the probable costs (punishment) of the act is doubtful. It seems fair to conclude, then, that the death penalty as it may conceivably be practiced in the United States would not have a significant deterrent effect on the crime of murder. Therefore, the justification of capital punishment would have to rely on the retributive argument (an issue discussed shortly).

Capital Punishment and the Law.   The legal status of capital punishment itself has always been accepted by a majority of the Supreme Court. The Eighth Amendment prohibition of cruel and unusual punishment, however, does constrain the *manner of execution*. Reasonable people differ on what forms constitute cruelty. It is safe to presume that practices of medieval torture, such as the use of the rack or the screw, burning victims alive at the stake, drawing and quartering people, or crucifixion, would violate the amendment; however, beyond such obvious cases, states have been given wide latitude. Recent years have witnessed a trend in favor of adopting the method of lethal injection as the presumptively least painful execution method over other forms. All states have lethal injection as their primary method, but back-up methods or alternatives exist in some states. Table 6.14 lists the number of states that provide for either alternative methods of execution (allowing the prisoner to choose), or back-up methods for execution in case lethal injections were declared unconstitutional. In the 2008 case of *Baze v. Rees*, the Supreme Court decided in a 7–2 vote that lethal injections (or at least, the three-drug cocktail employed in Kentucky) did not violate the Eighth Amendment's Cruel and Unusual Punishment. Other types of methods are still used in some other states if the condemned prisoner chooses the alternative method. For example, among the nine states listed in Table 6.14 that have the electric chair as an alternative to lethal injection, four of them (Alabama, Florida, South Carolina, and Virginia) currently allow prisoners the choice of opting for the electric chair. In Utah, prisoners had the option (until 2004) to choose execution by a five-man firing squad. Ronnie Lee Gardner, who chose that method before the deadline, was executed by firing squad in June 2010. Although a few inmates have been grandfathered into the option in Utah and will be shot by firing squad, that state no longer allows the practice for any future death row inmates. Currently, only Oklahoma has execution by firing squad, and this is only available as a back-up method if lethal injection and electrocution were both declared unconstitutional.

Although practice and precedent in our common-law system support the legality of the death penalty itself, such common-law principles should also reflect "evolving community standards," a favorite phrase for those justices who argue for banning all or some portion of executions in the face of a long established legality of that punishment. Legal principles responsive to community standards have become more restrictive on the manner and circumstances of imposing the death penalty and categories of people to whom it should not be assigned, and it is in these areas that constitutional challenges to the death penalty have been based.

The weak deterrent effect of capital punishment is caused in large part by the improbability of it being assigned for any given homicide. As noted, only a minority of those prosecuted for murder are even charged with capital murder. Capital murder is homicide for which the death penalty may be assessed. It is

T A B L E 6.14 Methods of Execution in the United States, 2000–2010; Number of States Using That Method at That Time

Year	Lethal Injection	Electrocution	Gas	Hanging	Firing Squad
2000	35	10	5	3	3
2010	35*	9	5	2	1

*All states that have the death penalty use lethal injection as their primary method of execution. Other methods that still exist are either offered as an alternative to the condemned prisoner or serve as a back-up method should lethal injection ever be judged as unconstitutional.

SOURCE: U.S. Department of Justice, Federal Bureau of Investigation, *Sourcebook of Criminal Justice Statistics Online*, Table 6.87, http://www.albany.edu.sourcebook/pdf/t6872008.pdf; Accessed May 15, 2010.

limited to premeditated murder and, since *Gregg v. Georgia* (1976), limited to certain types of premeditated murder, such as multiple killings, homicide committed in the course of another felony, or killing a police officer in the line of duty. Moreover, even conviction for capital murder in a death penalty jurisdiction far from guarantees that the death penalty will actually be assigned. In California, from 1950 to 1975, only 104 of the 2,111 persons convicted of capital murder were sentenced to die.[43] This raises the question of whether there are consistent criteria for determining why one murderer is sentenced to die and another is not, criteria based on the nature of the act itself.

Research shows that rather than the nature of the act, factors such as the defendant's race, socioeconomic status, or gender have proved to be better predictors of whether the death penalty will be assigned. African Americans have been executed in disproportionate numbers in American history, especially in Southern states. For instance, a study of executions in North Carolina from 1933 to 1937 showed eighty-one African Americans being executed, but only forty-five whites. A study of capital cases in Texas from 1924 to 1968 produced a higher percentage of convicted African Americans being executed than convicted whites, and the difference was statistically significant.[44] From 1930 to 1997, while African Americans made up only 12.5 percent of the population, they comprised 52 percent of those executed. In 2009, 22 African Americans were executed out of a total of 52 executions or 42 percent. These figures should be viewed in the context of the fact that African Americans are even more disproportionately likely to be convicted of murder. Furthermore, socioeconomic status has been an important determinant of suffering or avoiding the death penalty, because such status is related to the ability of one's lawyer. The disproportionate tendency for African Americans to suffer executions is shown in Table 6.15.

Such data on the impact of race constituted the bases of several challenges to the constitutionality of the death penalty. The Supreme Court under Chief Justice Rehnquist, however, did not appear to be receptive to such challenges, and the current Roberts court appears to be even less receptive. Most notably, in 1987, in *McCleskey v. Kemp*, the Court rejected the argument that the Georgia death penalty statute should be invalidated because the death penalty was more likely to be assigned when the victims of capital murder were white than when

T A B L E 6.15 Executions by Race in the United States

Year	Total	White	African American
1930–1997	4,291	2,016	2,228
1995	56	33	22
2004	59	36	19
2009	52	23	22

SOURCE: U.S. Department of Justice, Bureau of Justice Statistics, *Sourcebook of Criminal Justice Statistics*, 2001 (Albany, NY: SUNY, Hindelang Criminal Justice Research Center), p. 560, updated via http://deathpenaltyinfo.org/executions-united-states-2009; Accessed May 15, 2010.

the victims were African American, as well as more likely when the perpetrators were African American than when they were white. Julian Epstein, an aide to Michigan Representative John Conyers, reported a study of thirty-two states that revealed that killers of whites have an 11.1 percent chance of reaching death row, whereas the killers of African Americans have only a 4.5 percent chance. In some states, the discrepancy is even greater. For example, in Maryland, the killer of a white person is eight times more likely to receive the death penalty than the killer of an African American.[45] In another study, Professor Jack Boger and Dr. Isaac Unah of the University of North Carolina found that defendants whose victims are white are 3.5 times more likely to be sentenced to death than if the victims were black.[46] The racial discrepancy in who gets executed generated one of the major issues of the 1994 Omnibus Crime Bill. The Congressional Black Caucus insisted that a provision be inserted in the bill providing that such statistical disproportionality be grounds for a legal challenge that the execution of any particular African American is based upon racial bias, what was called "the racial justice amendment"; however, the bill passed without the amendment.

Gender, though not widely discussed in this context, is perhaps an even better predictor than race. Women are far less likely to be assigned the death penalty than are men. From 1930 to 1967, of the 3,334 persons executed for murder in the United States, only 30, or 0.8 percent, were women. Of course, such data should be seen in relation to a comparison of capital crime convictions of men with those of women. Unfortunately, such convictions are not broken down by gender in the available data. However, statistics do provide clues: in 1978, there were 12,736 arrests of men for murder and nonnegligent manslaughter (the index category that includes capital murder) and 2,234 such arrests of women. Because women, who accounted for about 17.5 percent of capital murder arrests, also accounted for less than 1 percent of the executions in earlier years, the conclusion that women are significantly less likely than men to be assigned the death penalty appears to be reasonable. Of the 3,122 prisoners under sentence of death in 1966, only 1.6 percent were women. In 1998, Texas—which has accounted for a third of the nation's executions since 1977—executed a woman, Karla Faye Tucker, for the first time in 135 years. Karla Faye Tucker had once claimed that she derived sexual pleasure with each blow of an ax to her two victims. She later claimed that she found God, and some religious groups sought to intervene on her behalf to stop the execution, but Governor George W. Bush declined that request. This reprises the issue raised two years earlier by Guinevere Garcia in Illinois, who implored the review board considering whether to commute her death sentence, "Do not consider this petition on the basis that I am a woman."

Furman v. Georgia.   It was the importance of such determinants on who receives the death penalty—rather than the nature of the criminal act—that the Court found objectionable in the landmark case of *Furman v. Georgia* (1972), in which the Court laid down the first major explicit constitutional restraint on the practice of capital punishment in the United States.[47] Although a majority clearly rejected the notion that capital punishment is inherently cruel and unusual, five justices agreed that it was cruel and unusual as it was then practiced in this country. There is no single pattern of reasoning to be discerned in these five diverse opinions, but one concept is that the imposition of capital punishment shall not be arbitrary. That is, its imposition must be on consistent criteria grounded in the nature of the criminal act.

POLICY EVALUATION: FLAWS IN THE CRIMINAL JUSTICE SYSTEM

In the preceding section, the evolution of contemporary policy in the area of constitutional rights and the deterrence of crime were studied with an emphasis on the two reasons for the expansion of such rights: (1) the expanded meaning of the U.S. Constitution's Fourteenth Amendment to incorporate more of the federal Bill of Rights guarantees, and (2) the broadened interpretation of existing rights. It is this second category that has generated the most controversy in three areas:

Confessions and the Right to Counsel

As already seen, *Miranda v. Arizona* pointed up the legal ramifications of not informing a suspect of his or her rights before entering any confession or damaging statement as evidence. Many feared that the rights of the accused would be excessively protected at the expense of obtaining otherwise valid confession and swift punishment.

Some argue that the fears by conservatives (or hopes by liberals, for that matter) of Miranda having a significant impact on law enforcement appear unfounded.[48] According to judicial scholar and political scientist Gerald Rosenberg, the empirical evidence suggests that "While warnings appear to be given routinely, and counsel is provided, '*Miranda's* effect on law enforcement has been negligible'"[49] According to Rosenberg, some suspects continue to talk to police even after being informed of their rights, and to some extent, some of the worst practices of police brutality to force confessions were already disappearing from police forces even before *Miranda* had been decided. Yet even after *Miranda*, Rosenberg notes that police brutality still occurs and argues that the "evidence strongly suggests that the confession rate did not change because the *Miranda* warnings were unable to alter [the] imbalance" of power between police and suspect.[50] To illustrate Rosenberg's point, one study found that a third of eighty-five defendants processed did not choose even to avail themselves of the services of a lawyer on hand in the police station for that purpose; 75 percent of the defendants did not exercise their option for counsel other than the station house counsel; and 40 percent chose to make incriminating statements after having waived their *Miranda* rights.[51] These somewhat startling data become explicable in the light of the findings in the same study that 15 percent of the eighty-five defendants failed to understand their right to remain silent, 18 percent did not understand their right to the presence of counsel at that time, and 24 percent failed to understand that the state would appoint counsel at its expense.

Not everyone agrees with all of Rosenberg's conclusions. Others have found that *Miranda* may have lowered the rate at which confessions are obtained in the first place. One study found that in Pittsburgh, in 1964, the police obtained confessions in 54.5 percent of the cases before *Miranda* procedures were implemented and in only 37.5 percent of the cases after the procedure was implemented.[52] Moreover, studies of the frequency of suppressing confessions on *Miranda* grounds do not take into account cases dismissed in preliminary stages or arrests not made because of the requirements of the *Miranda rule*.[53]

A related question is the extent to which confessions are necessary to dispose of cases. The *Miranda* case illustrates this point. The victim's bloodstained effects were found in Miranda's car; Miranda could not account for his whereabouts at the time the crime occurred; and he was identified by the victim. Hence, Miranda confessed when confronted with an overwhelming case against him. When the Supreme Court quashed the conviction on the admissibility of the confession, it did not acquit Miranda. Rather, when the Court nullifies conviction on constitutional grounds, it is saying that there is a problem with the manner in which the conviction was obtained, but the Court is not determining guilt or innocence. The case is remanded back to the prosecution, which may then choose to retry the accused in a manner consistent with the Supreme Court ruling. Miranda was in fact convicted on other evidence.

The point is that if the only ground for conviction is a confession obtained from an uninformed suspect under the psychological stress of an intense interrogation, the possibility exists that the suspect may in fact be innocent. If the accused is guilty, there should be a good chance that physical evidence or witnesses can be found to implicate him or her in the crime without a pressured confession. Moreover, when it is easy to pressure a confession from any plausible suspect, police may be tempted to use that technique to avoid the difficulty of seeking evidence to find out who really committed the crime.

The Exclusionary Rule and Search and Seizure

We have already discussed the immediate importance of *Mapp v. Ohio*; that is, that the due process clause of the Fourteenth Amendment requires the exclusion from court of *illegally* obtained evidence. In effect, the Court rejected the argument that the exclusionary rule only protects the guilty; instead, it felt that if illegally obtained evidence is inadmissible, there is no motive for police to make illegal searches of the guilty or the innocent. However, Chief Justice Burger, who came onto the Court after the *Mapp* decision, disagreed with such conclusions about *Mapp*'s effects. In his attack on the exclusionary rule, he made two claims: that it has a negative effect on successful prosecutions and that there is no evidence that it has a countervailing effect of deterring illegal police behavior.

But the empirical story is much more complicated. The reality is that it is difficult to prove statistically how and in what way *Mapp* has affected police practices: studies offer conflicting accounts of its effects. According to data cited by judicial politics scholar Stephen Wasby, Burger was wrong on both counts. With regard to Burger's fears that *Mapp* will allow guilty people to "get away with it," Wasby did note a substantial decrease of some 41 percent in the number of suspects actually reaching trial in New York in 1961, immediately following *Mapp*. However, he found that the rate of successful prosecutions rose again the following year, suggesting that police were becoming adjusted to the new constraints on their behavior. Political scientist Stuart Nagel also found increased police adherence to the rules on legal searches and seizures.[54]

Political scientist and judicial scholar Bradley Canon looked at the rate of arrests for search and seizure offenses that occurred for several years before and after the *Mapp* case in nineteen cities. He found that about one-third of cities showed a decline in arrests for these types of offenses, leading him to conclude that the exclusionary rule "works sometimes."[55] But, as public law scholar Donald Horowitz has pointed out, Canon's findings do not say what proportion of those arrests after *Mapp* were illegal, and so cannot tell us whether illegal arrests declined. Horowitz also notes that, "Canon's findings could also be consistent with a continuing pattern of unlawful searches accompanied by greater discrimination in the making of arrests."[56] As Horowitz sees it, *Mapp* does not control police harassment of suspects, when police engage in illegal searches that do not result in an arrest. Furthermore, the case has encouraged some police to engage in false testimony or perjury in order to justify their search under the Fourth Amendment. Thus, *Mapp* has had consequences rather unintended by the Supreme Court majority, which authored the case. Still, Horowitz believes that the Canon study does indicate that police behavior did change to some extent after *Mapp*, but the effects are difficult to measure because states and locales have varied in the strictness with which they have applied the *Mapp* ruling. Police training also varies widely, and some police may not be aware of the rules of *Mapp*. Moreover, in many departments, there are no sanctions for engaging in illegal searches and seizures. In terms of Burger's assertions that many guilty would go free, Horowitz and others do not see much evidence that this happened. The dictates of the Supreme Court are not self-enforcing; the mere handing down of a ruling does not automatically alter behavior. That is why there is a growing body of research on the compliance with and the impact of such rulings.

Capital Punishment

After *Furman* outlawed capital punishment as practiced, but invited new statutes to conform to the standard of not being arbitrary, many states passed new laws that listed specific mitigating and aggravating circumstances as guides to be considered in deciding whether to assign the death penalty in a particular case, rather than making the imposition of the penalty mandatory for an entire category of crimes.[57] The legality of capital punishment applied in this way was explicitly reaffirmed by the Court. Liberals expressed the fear that this would bring about a flood of executions. The rate did increase, especially in the southern states (Texas and Louisiana alone accounted for 224 of the 598 executions carried out between 1977 and 1999), but the increase has slowed in recent years because of fears of the execution of innocent persons, mentally retarded persons, and minors.

Debating Capital Punishment.   The capital punishment issue epitomizes widespread confusion with regard to the purposes of punishment. Although capital punishment is usually defended in terms of its deterrent effect, it is clear from the discussion earlier that capital punishment, as it can conceivably be practiced in the United States, is unlikely to have any significant deterrent effect on crime. It is possible, however, that many of those who defend capital punishment on deterrence grounds are really concerned about maintaining its role in retribution. The Court has explicitly said that retribution is a constitutionally valid purpose of punishment, stating in *Gregg v. Georgia* (1976) that

> ... capital punishment is an expression of the society's moral outrage at particularly offensive conduct. This function may be unappealing to many, but it is essential in an ordered society that asks its citizens to rely on legal processes rather than self-help to vindicate their wrongs.... Retribution is no longer the dominant objective of the criminal law but neither is it a forbidden objective.

Many claim that the Eighth Amendment ought to be interpreted as banning capital punishment *per se*, but much of this argument is framed in ethical terms. Justices Brennan and Marshall, in making this argument, repeatedly evoked "the evolving standards of decency that mark the progress of a maturing society" to argue that a penalty that was permissible at one point in our history is no longer permissible today.[58] The precise content, however, of such "evolving standards of decency" is a subjective judgment on which reasonable people may disagree. The issue of whether the Eighth Amendment does or should prohibit capital punishment becomes instead the defining issue of how morally abhorrent capital punishment has become.

Execution of Minors.   The constitutionality of applying the death penalty to capital crimes committed while the perpetrator was a minor has been a hotly debated issue since the 1980s. Opponents characterized the practice as "killing our children" and pointed out that the United States was virtually the only remaining Western nation that executes teenagers. By 2005, 30 states prohibited the execution of minors. The presumption of these opponents was that minors are not fully aware of the nature and consequences of their actions; therefore, they should not be held as fully responsible for their actions as are adults. Justice Kennedy's opinion in the *Roper* case stresses that a worldwide consensus against the execution of minors had evolved; hence, Kennedy argued that we ought to interpret our constitution in the light of that consensus. In that case, *Roper v. Simmons* (2005), Kennedy, speaking for the Court, found that evolving standards of decency and world opinion entail the conclusion that the execution of a person for a crime committed before the age of eighteen violates the Eighth Amendment ban on "cruel and unusual punishment." Kennedy's opinion reversed *Stanford v. Connecticut* (1989), which held that the execution of sixteen- and seventeen-year-olds was not constitutionally barred. His "evolving standards of decency" argument cited *Atkins v. Virginia* (2002), which reversed *Perry v. Lynaugh* (1989) by arguing that "evolving standards of decency" categorically exempt the mentally retarded from execution.[59]

Those who support the application of the death penalty in such cases argue that violent and even vicious crimes increasingly are committed by teenagers. The problem of gang warfare in our large urban centers, a phenomenon discussed elsewhere in this chapter, only highlights the violence and mayhem that can be committed by teens. As noted earlier in this chapter, crime is to a large extent a young person's phenomenon; therefore, the policy of protecting the very sector of the population most likely to commit serious crimes from serious punishment weakens whatever deterrent effect that punishment might have. Indeed, Simmons boasted that he would get away with premeditated murder because he was a minor. (He abducted a woman, bound her hands and feet, and threw her from a bridge into a river where she drowned.)

Limits on the Death Penalty.   Although there remains significant public support for the retention of the death penalty, the Court has established a general trend of circumscribing its application without invalidating the penalty itself. In *Sumner v. Shuman* (1987), the Court struck down the Nevada statute that made the death sentence mandatory for murder perpetrated by a prisoner who was serving a life sentence without the possibility of parole at the time of the crime.[60] Justice Blackmun, writing for the Court, argued that the mandatory nature of the sentence did not allow consideration of mitigating circumstances or factors and therefore did not allow the punishment to be clearly related to the individual or unique nature of the crime.[61] In *Maynard v. Cartwright* (1988),[62] the Court struck down an Oklahoma death-penalty statute on the grounds that the state's phrasing of aggravating circumstances as crimes that are "especially heinous, atrocious or cruel" was unconstitutionally vague.

This trend of circumscribing the death penalty has been balanced by the tendency of the more conservative Court beginning with the 1990s to pull back from its previous defendant's rights emphasis, perhaps informed by the public's demand for a greater stress on victim's rights. This pullback began with *McCleskey v. Zant* (1991), which overruled the 1987 case of *Booth v. Maryland* and allowed victims' impact statements to be read with regard to sentencing decisions.[63] The *McCleskey* decision permitted statements read by the families of a murder victim testifying as to the devastating impact of their loss on their lives, statements that were followed by a death sentence to McCleskey. The liberal defense position continued to be that such statements constitute an emotional appeal that is extraneous to the hard facts of the case and therefore ought not to be salient in the assignment of appropriate punishment. However, information about difficulties and deprivations in the background of the convicted perpetrator have long been admissible in sentencing decisions. The expansion of the range of crimes subject to the death penalty under federal law by the Death Penalty Act passed by Congress in 1994 was challenged in 1999. The Supreme Court upheld that statute.

Reservations about the death penalty have been reinforced in recent years with the introduction of DNA evidence into the criminal trial process. This genetic material often enables one to resolve questions of guilt or innocence definitively. DNA evidence has overturned several long-standing and seemingly solid death penalty convictions by proving that the condemned persons were innocent of the crime for which they were convicted. Renewed awareness of the reality of mistakes in the criminal process causes a reluctance to impose so final a punishment as death. On the other hand, supporters of the death penalty argue that DNA evidence actually makes such mistakes less likely.

Conclusion: Crime and Criminal Procedure

These issues surrounding capital punishment apply in large part to the broader question of the impact of expanded rights of defendants on the crime rate. Any rights that affect only the severity of punishment are unlikely to have an adverse impact. Rather, it is the rights that actually diminish the likelihood or swiftness of punishment that could lessen the deterrent effect and thus "encourage" more crime. The principal question in deterrence, therefore, is the perceived probability that the person who commits a crime will in the foreseeable future have to face some serious punishment.

Have expanded defendants' rights indeed served to hobble the deterrent effects of punishment? Before answering such a question, it is important to keep in mind that the theoretical route from criminal act to punishment is marked by numerous exit points, only one of which is an overturned conviction due to the expansion of defendants' rights (see Figure 6.3).

First, the rights of the accused can only come into play *after* a suspect is arrested. In fact, however, it is unlikely that any given criminal act will ever lead to an arrest. Even before the rise in crime rates in the 1960s and 1970s, one scholar estimated about twelve arrests for every one hundred crimes in the United States.[64] James Q. Wilson claims that the odds are fourteen to one that the

FIGURE 6.3 Exit Points in the Criminal Justice System

perpetrator of any given felony will not be caught.[65] In any event, the chances that a given criminal act will never lead to an encounter with the criminal justice process are extremely high, probably over 90 percent; therefore, the nature and content of that process remain largely irrelevant to crime deterrence. (See Table 6.16.) Recall that there are *at least* twice as many crimes as are reported. In 2008, as reported in Table 6.16, about 20 percent of crimes for larceny-theft were cleared, according to the FBI's *2008 Uniform Crime Report.* Clearance rates tabulated by the FBI's report refer to instances where law enforcement solves the crime and the case is closed out. A cleared case does not mean the accused was put in jail, it basically only means that the case was solved by police and presumably the file was turned over to the prosecutor's office for further action. Let's assume that in the mythical city of X in state Y, there were 200 larcenies that year, and as previously noted, studies indicate that only about half of crimes are actually reported to the police (thus only 100 larcenies are reported to police in mythical City X). If only 20 percent of reported larcenies are cleared by law enforcement, that would mean that only 10 percent of all larcenies (i.e., 20 cases out of 200 in City X) get resolved by the police. That suggests that few crimes are ever really resolved. Even after law enforcement "clears" the crime, the accused criminal may still avoid punishment through any number of escape hatches listed in Figure 6.3, either through a plea deal, dismissal by the judge, acquittal at trial, or early parole, etc.

A second factor detracting from the deterrent effect of punishment is the bail system together with the delay of trial. In those cases coming to trial, everyone except those accused of the most heinous capital crimes is accorded the option of posting bail and remaining free until the trial. For a large percentage of the accused who can afford the cost of bail, punishment is postponed until after the trial—and sometimes until after a series of appeals. Given the slowness with

T A B L E 6.16 Crimes Cleared by Arrest, 2008*

Type of Crime	Percentage Cleared
Murder	63.6
Aggravated assault	54.9
Forcible rape	40.4
Robbery	26.8
Total violent crimes	45.1
Larceny-theft	19.0
Motor vehicle theft	12.0
Burglary	12.5
Total property crimes	17.4

*Index crimes only; does not include unreported crimes.

SOURCE: U.S. Dept. Justice, Federal Bureau of Investigation, *Crime in the United States,* 2008, http://www.fbi.gov/ucr/cius2008/offenses/clearances/index.html.

which our overburdened judicial system operates, punishment could and often does take years. Yet it is the swiftness and certainty of punishment that most deter crime. Studies show that from 30 percent to 70 percent of robbery suspects out on bail are rearrested for the commission of other crimes.[66]

As the clearance rates shown in Table 6.16 indicate, the overwhelming preponderance of crimes are not cleared. However, violent crimes showed a significantly higher clearance rate for 2008 (45.1 percent, including 63.6 percent for murder) compared to the clearance rate for property crimes (17.4 percent). The possible explanation for this discrepancy is violent crimes are investigated more vigorously and such crimes often leave a victim who can identify the perpetrator; however, less than half of even violent crimes are cleared.

Finally, because of the overcrowded nature of the judicial system, 95 percent of convictions within one year of arrest are obtained through plea bargaining; about 80 percent of these convictions involve a felony. This fact also gives potential criminals reason to believe that they can escape serious punishment even if they are caught.

Thus, the expansion of defendants' rights has played a very small role in impeding or postponing the punishment of those who commit serious crimes. In other words, even if we returned to a pre-expansion of rights period before the rulings of *Miranda* or *Mapp*, there's no reason to believe justice would be swift and operate as a useful deterrence against crime. On the other hand, these rights do help protect the innocent and enhance the perception of the system as a just one, thereby contributing to the legitimacy of the system. It can be concluded that the restriction of defendants' rights does not offer a cost-efficient method for controlling crime. However, alternative policy options do exist, and these will be explored in the following section.

FUTURE ALTERNATIVES: POLICY OPTIONS FOR REDUCING CRIME

One obvious goal of public policy aimed at reducing crime is to increase the cost of illegal activity to the criminal, a result that a classic economic model predicts should reduce the quantity of crime.[67] These costs include material costs, time costs, and psychic costs as well as the familiar costs of expected punishment.

For example, encouraging, or even requiring, increased security devices in homes and businesses can add both to the time and the materials needed to commit a crime. Logically, it may be surmised that if the perceived opportunities for earning a better return by noncriminal means exceeding the opportunities for the return from crime (breaking into the now electronically secure business has become too much trouble), assuming an equal expenditure of time and effort, the potential criminal would find it rational to opt for noncriminal pursuits and crime would be reduced. (This kind of analysis points to an oft-cited conclusion: programs to reduce unemployment and to provide jobs for the most crime-prone segments of the population would cut crime.)

The logic of this argument presumes that criminals are rational, economically motivated beings. This assumption is only imperfectly valid. It would most likely apply to property crimes, but crimes against persons are frequently acts of passion or anger that have nothing to do with the rational pursuit of economic rewards. Even in the case of some property crimes the economic assumption remains imperfectly valid, most notably in crimes to support drug addiction.

Drug-Related Crimes

Estimates vary on what proportion of street crime (for example, mugging, robbery, and auto theft) is committed to support an addiction to illegal drugs; however, such estimates uniformly place the figure at over half and sometimes as high as three-quarters. As explained earlier, the high cost of addictive drugs on the illegal market combined with an inflexible and economically inelastic demand for such drugs almost requires the addict to commit crimes to support the addiction. Clearly, a reduction in the extent of drug addiction should lead to a reduction in crimes against property. Moreover, since intravenous drug users are a primary source of new AIDS cases, reducing drug addiction would affect the spread of that disease.

Attacking Supply.   The first strategy to reduce drug addiction—and perhaps the most popular to the public—is to try to intercept the supply, usually referred to as a "war on drugs." President Nixon, for example, initiated the much-heralded "Project Intercept." This strategy was reemphasized in the Reagan and first Bush administrations. Though the heroic efforts of federal agents to catch drug smugglers, punish them, and confiscate their wares make sensational newspaper headlines, such efforts do not have a positive impact on the extent of drug addiction. The supply may be temporarily diminished, an unintended consequence of which raises the price of the remaining available drugs. The demand for drugs, however, is not sensitive to price, at least among chronic users. Therefore, the higher price probably has the effect of driving addicts to commit more crime in order to afford the higher prices.

Efforts to intercept the drug supply can never be completely successful. The nation's borders are too extensive, and the many ways of concealing smuggled illegal drugs make thorough searches impractical. For example, smugglers now swallow balloons full of pure cocaine and retrieve them after clearing customs, when the balloons have passed through their alimentary canal. Because most drugs, such as cocaine and heroin, are highly diluted for street sale, a valuable quantity of pure, uncut white powder occupies very little space. Furthermore, the stakes are so high and the potential profits so great that there will always be someone willing to take virtually any risk or go to any lengths to supply the drugs.

Indeed, with the amount of money at stake, law enforcement officials can frequently be bought off. This is the case just across the border in Mexico, over which a large portion of illegal drugs enter. The high stakes have given rise to an escalating degree of violence among rival drug gangs, even challenging American Border Patrol officials. According to one 2010 *El Paso Times* article, the violence across the border has been so high that there were more homicides in

Juarez (4,992) between 2008 and April 2010 than there have been U.S. military deaths in Iraq since 2003.[68] There is, indeed, increasing skepticism about relying heavily on "drug war" tactics; both here and in other nations, there is a growing sentiment to approach drugs as a physical and mental health matter and to find different strategies to stem the demand for illegal substances.

Attacking Demand.   A second strategy in dealing with the drug problem is to attempt to prevent addiction in the first place and to rehabilitate addicts when prevention fails. This means assigning criminal addicts to a hospital-type facility rather than a prison. Here, addicts receive psychological counseling in conjunction with medically supervised withdrawal. Yet early studies placed the failure rate of such programs to be well over 90 percent.[69] Smaller community rehabilitation efforts have had a somewhat better record, but they process too few addicts to resolve the drug problem. Moreover, addicts frequently return to heroin use even years after withdrawal. Apparently, the anxieties that produce the heroin hungers still exist for such people, even though the physical addiction may be over.

A third strategy is maintaining the addict on a heroin substitute, usually methadone (a synthetic narcotic developed by the Germans in World War II). Methadone maintenance programs have achieved some success in stabilizing known addicts and removing them from the drug subculture, which leads to a life of crime and other anti-social behavior. One study of 1,000 patients in such a program reported a 92 percent reduction in arrest records over a four-year period. This study also reported a substantial increase in the rate of employment, from 26 to 61 percent at the end of one year.[70] Methadone is, however, an addictive drug itself, and a black market has grown up around the legal dispensing of methadone. Moreover, methadone has proved to be less than a totally satisfactory substitute for heroin from the addict's point of view, in that methadone can only relieve the agonies of heroin withdrawal—it cannot duplicate the euphoric "highs" that heroin offers to new addicts. Therefore, a market for expensive heroin continues to exist, and pushers still have the economic incentive to find new addicts.

The drug epidemic in the United States was exacerbated in the late 1980s with the introduction of crack, which is apparently more highly addictive than ordinary cocaine and even more so than heroin. Moreover, its misuse can easily result in death. Crack has replaced heroin as the drug of choice in the inner-city slums. Methamphetamines seem now to be the drug of choice in rural, small town, or even suburban areas.

Violence against Women

The crime of rape and other forms of violence against women have come into increasing focus in recent years, due in part to the rising prominence of the feminist movement and to a couple of high-profile incidents of such violence (those involving O. J. Simpson and Scott Peterson, for example; the latter was convicted of the brutal murder of his wife and their unborn child).

TABLE 6.17 Percent Change in Rates of Forcible Rape, 2007–2008

Total	−2.4%
Northeast	+1.0%
Midwest	−1.3%
South	−4.2%
West	−2.2%

SOURCE: U.S. Department of Justice, Bureau of Federal Investigation, *Preliminary Uniform Crime Reports,* December 2005, Table 2, http://www.fbi.gov/ucr/ucr.htm.

Technically, rape consists of using force or the threat of force to obtain sexual interaction with a woman against her will. Rape has come to be widely perceived not merely as a means of obtaining sexual gratification but rather as an extreme manner of expressing hostility to women (misogyny). This broader definition of the term is related to the heightened awareness that far more often than not sexual aggression occurs within the context of courtship or friendship relationships (called "acquaintance rape" or "date rape") or even that of marriage. Although serious discussion of acquaintance rape has arisen only recently, Laurie Bechofer and Andrea Parrot trace it back to the biblical book of Samuel.[71] Susan Brownmiller, in *Against Our Will,* calls rape "nothing more than a conscious process of intimidation by which all men keep all women in a state of fear."[72]

Traditionally defined rape is an ongoing problem in American society, but along with other types of crime, it has seen a slight decrease in the last decade (see Figure 6.4). While rape is 6.4 percent lower when compared to 2004 levels, the crime is only 0.5 percent below 1999 levels. There were noticeable regional variations in rape, with the Midwest in 2008 showing the highest levels of rape at 34 per 100,000 people (follow by the South at 30.4, the West at 30.2, and the Northeast, which had a rate of only 20 per 100,000 people, far fewer than any other region). The number of rapes was down from 2007 to 2008 in all regions of the country except the Northeast (see Table 6.17). While the Northeast has lower rates of rape when compared to other regions of the country, it was the only region that saw a slight increase in rape between 2007 and 2008.

There can be no disagreement that men, who are typically stronger than women, all too frequently beat their wives and girlfriends. The sexual violence issue revolves around the question of the actual extent of violence perpetrated against women by husbands and boyfriends. At the high end of the estimates, some have publicly alleged that as many as 4 million women are regularly beaten by their male partners. Others, including some feminists, dispute that estimate. Two sociologists who specialize in domestic violence, Murray Strauss and Richard Gelles, conducted a survey in which they found that fewer than 5 percent of the families surveyed experience what they call "extreme violence," which would include punching and kicking.[73] While some allege as many as 4,000 women are killed by spousal abuse each year, Justice Department figures

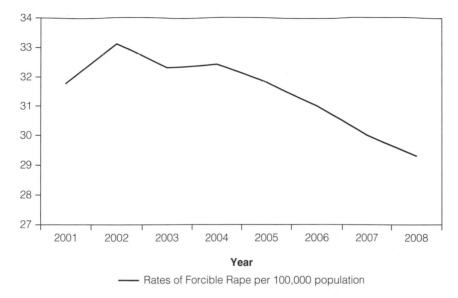

FIGURE 6.4 Rates of Forcible Rape in U.S. per 100,000 population between 2001–2008

SOURCE: http://www.fbi.gov/ucr/cius2008/index.html

show that in the high-risk category of eighteen to thirty-four years of age there were 702 fatalities in a year. Moreover, some data suggest that domestic violence is not all one way. Justice Department data show that in 1992 some 38 percent of white spousal murder victims were men and 47 percent of black spousal murder victims were men. However, in the longer run, it is 2.4 times more likely that a husband will kill his wife than she will kill him. Still, in St. Paul, Minnesota, one can find the only shelter in America for battered men. In fact, Strauss and Gelles claim that in domestic violence, men and women are equally likely to be the aggressor. However, it is likely that many women who murder their spouses do so in response to being abused. Whatever the truth behind these conflicting claims, the public is now more aware that domestic violence is a serious public issue and not the private family matter that police all too frequently regarded in the past as none of its business.

Despite its vicious and exploitive nature, the crime of rape presents unique problems for the criminal justice system, which is, after all, dedicated to providing due process for those accused of even the most heinous acts. With an expanded definition of rape, it confounds a *sine qua non* of criminal law: that the behavior being proscribed is precisely defined. For sexual activity to be rape, it must occur against the will of the victim. Prosecutions for rape have always been weakened by problems of evidence and especially by the ages-old myth of implied consent, that is, the assumption or the assertion that although the woman said no, she must really have meant yes. Moreover, even expressed consent is frequently held by some to be implicitly coerced by the asymmetrical power relationship between men and women, a position reported by law professor

Susan Estrich, who indicates, "Many feminists would argue that so long as women are powerless relative to men, viewing yes as a sign of true consent is misguided."[74] This presumption that women are necessarily "powerless relative to men" and that they are incapable of rejecting the sexual advances of a man regards women as victims and thus conflicts with the equality wing of the feminist movement discussed in Chapter 10.

Clearly, there is heightened sensitivity to the problems of rape. Reflecting this heightened sensitivity is the $1.6 billion in the 1994 Crime Bill to fund the Violence Against Women Act (VAWA). The challenge is to fight rape in all its forms while protecting the rights of women and men. Rape is typically a state matter, and Congress's authority in this area is constrained, since the Constitution says little about the federal government's authority in this area. Portions of VAWA were struck down by the Supreme Court in 2000, as the Court stated that Congress had exceeded its authority under the commerce clause of the Constitution.

Crimes of Violence and Gun Control

Drug-related crimes are primarily crimes against property, that is, theft in order to support expensive addictions. Of course, violence is frequently involved in such crimes as a means of obtaining the economic benefit. When the violence becomes the end in itself, the causes and the means of combating such crime are quite different from those in the case of crimes against property.

When the goal of the crime is material gain, a certain amount of rational calculation—cost–benefit analysis—may indeed go into the decision to commit the crime. Even drug-related crimes, with the addict's inelastic demand, can be curbed by removing the pusher's economic incentive and the addict's economic need. When the goal of the criminal act is violence to another person, however, the element of rational calculation diminishes. Although there may be certain psychic benefits that accrue to the perpetrator of a crime of violence, it is doubtful whether much rational calculation is involved. Rape, for instance, is now thought by most psychologists to be an act of woman hating or misogyny rather than an act motivated by sexual passion or need. For example, rapists have been known to commit their crime within hours of experiencing consensual sexual relations.

A 2007 Small Arms Survey shows that the U.S., with less than 5 percent of the world's population, accounts for 35 to 50 percent of the world's civilian-owned guns. U.S. civilians are estimated to own 270 million firearms as of 2007, about eighty-nine guns per 100 people. Contrast this to the Netherlands, which has about four guns per 100 people or Scotland, which has about five guns per 100 people.[75] Such data have been used to infer a relationship between the pervasiveness of gun ownership in the U.S. and the much higher than average homicide rate in this country (see Table 6.18 for a sampling of homicide rates around the world). Perhaps it's not surprising that the Netherlands, with one of the lowest gun ownership rates, also has one of the lowest homicide rates in the world at 1 person killed per 100,000 people. Note that the homicide rate in the U.S. is more than four times higher than Germany or Japan. Even

TABLE 6.18 **International Murder Rates per 100,000 Population in 2008**

Iceland	0.0	Romania	2.2
Japan	0.5	United States	5.2
Switzerland	0.7	Lithuania	8.6
Germany	0.8	Mexico	11.6
Spain	0.9	Russia	14.2
Netherlands	1.0	South Africa	36.5
France	1.4	Venezuela	52.0
United Kingdom	1.49*	Jamaica	59.5
Canada	1.7	Honduras	60.9

*The data from the United Kingdom represents a three-year average, from 2005–2007.
SOURCE: United Nations Office on Drugs and Crime,
http://www.unodc.org/unodc/en/data-and-analysis/homicide.html.

less-developed Romania, for example, has a considerably lower homicide rate than the U.S. With the exceptions of Estonia and Lithuania (with rates of 6.3 and 8.6 respectively), the U.S. homicide rate is exceeded only by third-world countries.

But it would be misleading and overly simplistic to claim that the large volume of guns in the U.S. is primarily responsible for America's higher murder rates. Iceland, for example, is the fifteenth highest country in gun ownership in the world (at 30.3 guns per 100 people), yet its homicide rate in 2008 was 0! Germany is also tied with Iceland in rates of gun ownership, and its murder rate is quite low. Switzerland, which has the third highest rate of gun ownership in the world, at 45.7 guns per 100 people, also has one of the lowest murder rates in the world at 0.7 murders per 100,000 people. France ranks twelfth in gun ownership (31.2 guns per 100 people), but its murder rate is also very low. Honduras, on the other hand, was ranked eighty-eighth among countries in rates of gun ownership, with only 6.2 guns per 100 people, yet it had the highest homicide rate in the world in 2008. Venezuela and Jamaica also have very low rates of gun ownership (rates of 10.7 and 8.1 per 100 people, respectively), but these two countries also have staggeringly high murder rates. Thus, the amount of guns in a society cannot be much of an explanation for high murder rates. If you live in Jamaica, one of the murder capitals of the world in 2008, the cliché "Guns don't kill people, people kill people" must appear rather true, given the fact that most people in that society don't own guns. On the other hand, one cannot ignore the role of guns in crime in the United States, since firearms represent the most frequently used weapon to kill.

Guns and Violence.   Firearms are used to shoot over 200,000 people per year, some 29,573 of whom died in 2001. In that year, the U.S. homicide rate per 100,000 population was 5.5. In 2008, there were 16,272 murders known to police, of which 66.9 percent were committed by firearms (see Table 6.19).

T A B L E 6.19 Murders in the United States by Weapon (percent)

	1995	2000	2003	2008
Guns (all)	68.2	65.6	66.9	66.9
Handguns (only)	55.8	53.4	53.4	47.6
Knives, etc.	12.8	13.5	12.6	13.4
Blunt objects (clubs, etc.)	4.5	4.7	4.5	4.3
Hands, feet, etc.	5.9	7.0	6.5	6.1
Strangulation	1.9	1.3	1.3	0.6
Fire	0.8	1.0	1.1	0.6
Poison	0.9	0.1	0.1	0.1
Explosion	0.1	0.1	0.1	0.1
Asphyxiation	0.6	0.7	0.9	0.6
Other	6.1	5.9	5.6	7.1

SOURCE: *Statistical Abstract of the United States*, 1997, p. 204; U.S. Department of Justice, Federal Bureau of Investigation, *Uniform Crime Report*, 2000, 2003 and 2008.

Firearm violence extends beyond criminal activity to suicide and accidents. As for types of firearms, estimates indicate that some 20,000 to 22,000 people are killed by handguns each year, if approximately 11,000 annual suicides using these weapons are included. Experts estimate that only one person in ten who attempts suicide really intends to die. Many stage the attempt to draw sympathy or get attention. However, the presence of a gun renders many of these suicides successful, whereas someone swallowing pills or standing on a window ledge may be saved (see Table 6.20). Clearly, while there are numerous ways to kill, guns constitute the easiest and surest way, which is why guns are used in such a high proportion of homicides and suicides. The suicide rate in the United States

T A B L E 6.20 Suicides by Method in the United States, 2006

Method	Number	Rate per 100,000	Pct. of suicides
Firearms	16,883	5.6	50.6%
Suffocation, Hanging	7,491	2.5	22.5%
Poisoning	6,109	2.0	18.3%
Fall	725	0.2	2.1%
Cut, pierce	598	0.2	1.8%
Drowning	402	0.1	1.2%
Other	1,092	0.3	3.2%
Total Suicides	33,300	11.1	

SOURCE: Centers for Disease Control, "National Vital Statistics Reports," Vol. 57, No. 14, April 17, 2009, pp. 89–90, http://www.cdc.gov/nchs/data/nvsr/nvsr57/nvsr57_14.pdf.

in 2006 was 11.1 per 100,000 people, nearly twice as high as the murder rate. Men are much more likely to commit suicide than women.

Moreover, the proliferation of guns in society has meant that career criminals have easy access to them, particularly guns of the more high-powered variety. We have already alluded to the growth of gang warfare associated with drugs. Gangs frequently possess sophisticated weapons, especially semiautomatic assault rifles, such as the Israeli-made Uzi and the Chinese-made AK-47. Eruptions of gang violence often involve drive-by shootings in which innocent bystanders are killed. This caused geometric increases in the murder rates in some areas. A public outcry to control the widespread ownership of these weapons, stimulated by the random shootings of schoolchildren, motivated the previously anti–gun control president George H. W. Bush to impose a ban on the importation of assault rifles. This did not address the sale or manufacture of these weapons domestically. President Clinton's crime bill, passed with modifications in August 1994, included a ban on stipulated models of assault weapons. Despite vigorous lobbying efforts by the National Rifle Association (NRA), this provision was left in the final bill. However, the ban expired in 2004, and Congress declined to renew it.

Guns also often fall into the hands of children, who are less likely to use them responsibly. In 1987, an average of one child under the age of fifteen died in the United States each day from a handgun accident, and ten others were injured, according to the Center to Prevent Handgun Violence. Many of these tragedies occur because gun owners leave their weapons where children can find them. Accordingly, a number of state and local governments have either adopted or considered legislation holding gun owners responsible under both civil and criminal laws for any harm caused by leaving weapons accessible to children. Not surprisingly, the National Rifle Association (NRA) opposes such legislation insofar as it covers young people fourteen years of age or older, claiming that fourteen-year-olds are capable of making their own decisions about guns. The NRA legislative counsel further opposes legislation that mandates criteria for storing weapons. As we shall see again below, this lobbying group for gun owners has consistently opposed any effort to regulate firearms possession and use, and its power and influence as an interest group is drawn largely from the fact that most Americans support the right to own guns.

Regulation of Guns.   Given the amount of gun violence in America, government has tried to respond by placing further regulations on the ownership and prevalence of guns. Since the vast majority of murders result from the use of handguns (more than any other type of firearm), state governments and the national government have focused regulations directed at this type of firearm. Thus, the Brady Bill, passed by Congress in 1994, required that prospective purchasers of handguns undergo background checks. The bill was named after presidential aide James Brady, who was critically wounded in John Hinckley's attempt to kill President Reagan in 1981, and after Sarah Brady, his wife, who has become one of the leading activists for handgun control. The bill mandates background checks for prospective purchasers of handguns to determine if they are part of a high-risk group (a convicted felon, a former mental patient, and such). These checks take a day or two, and purchasers have to wait five days before taking possession of guns, a period of time that also serves as a "cooling-off period." Opponents of this bill, led by the NRA, argue that criminals will get their guns by illegal means anyhow. Meanwhile, they argue, this bill creates unnecessary regulations adding to the costs of doing business for purveyors of guns and making for unnecessary inconvenience for prospective purchasers of guns. Supporters of the Brady Bill note that in the four years after its passage, over 100,000 applications to buy guns were denied under the Brady Bill because the applicants were in the proscribed high-risk categories: having a record of felony convictions or mental illness. If just 1 percent of these people were prevented from killing someone (assuming they didn't buy a gun on the black market), that would be 1,000 lives saved. Obviously, supporters of the bill argued, the denial of so many applications constitutes evidence that some people who might misuse firearms do try to purchase them legally and may lack the resources to obtain them by other means.

The Supreme Court in 1997 struck down the part of the Brady Bill that requires state officials to do the background checks on prospective purchasers of guns on federalism grounds. In other words, the Supreme Court ruled that the Constitution did not give the federal government the authority to pass laws and then force states to implement their laws without compensating them. Many people believed that this takes the heart out of the Brady Bill by removing the means of implementation. However, some states still do the checks, and the federal government is now in the business of doing background checks. A major loophole in Brady is that it only applies to licensed gun dealers; hence, one could purchase firearms at a gun show without either the waiting period or the background check. Gun control advocates have concentrated efforts in recent years to close that loophole. These efforts have thus far been unsuccessful–they were not a high priority for the Democratic Congress of 2009-2010. Meanwhile, the Republican Party is strongly opposed to increasing regulations on gun shows. With Republicans regaining control of the House of Representatives in the 2010 elections, it is unlikely this issue will be addressed in the near future.

Semiautomatic Weapons and the Crime Bill of 1994.   The debate on the control of semiautomatic weapons, which hold many rounds of ammunition and allow many more rounds to be fired in less time, was activated by several mass killings, one having been the murder of five children and the wounding of some thirty others in a Stockton, California, elementary school in 1989 by a deranged man with a semiautomatic assault rifle. In the wake of that killing, the Bush administration banned the import of assault rifles, such as the Israeli-made Uzi, but refused to extend the ban to the domestic manufacture of such weapons, even though three-fourths of the country's weapons are produced domestically. This debate continued when a Glock 17 was used by another deranged gunman, George Hennard, to kill twenty-two people and wound many others in a Killeen, Texas, cafeteria in October 1991. The Glock has the advantage of being semiautomatic, with a large seventeen-round magazine like an assault rifle, which renders it efficient in killing large numbers of people. It is a 7.4-inch-long, 21.8-ounce pistol that, unlike an assault rifle, is concealable. The significance of large ammunition magazines was highlighted in a random mass shooting in 1993 on the Long Island Railway, a commuter train into New York City, by an African American man angry at whites in general. It was only after the assailant had emptied his magazine and was reloading that he was subdued by bystanders. A provision in the Omnibus Crime Bill of 1994 bans the domestic manufacture and sale of nineteen types of these semiautomatic weapons and limits the size of ammunition magazines. Although this provision would not have outlawed the Glock, it would have prevented the legal sale of the seventeen-round magazine that can kill so many so quickly. In addition to banning some weapons by name, the bill stipulates certain attributes of other weapons that would render them illegal. The opposition to the Crime Bill of 1994 was eventually overcome in the face of widespread public perception that crime was one of the nation's most important problems. However, the passage of the bill spawned an industry of producing "copycat" weapons that were not specifically named or that lacked one or more of the stipulated criteria. For instance, if a gun lacked a folding stock or a special muzzle, it could still be a legal clone of an AK-47 or Uzi, grenade launcher and all. Although the Colt AR-15 assault rifle was banned by the bill, Olympic Arms Company began manufacturing a nearly identical weapon, the PCR-1 (initials stand for "politically correct rifle"). The only difference between the PCR-1 and the AR-15 is that the former lacked a flash suppressor and a bayonet mount. Other provisions in the bill provided federal money to hire more policemen and to build more prisons. Since the local governments would have to match these federal grants, it was not clear that as many new policemen would be hired as promised by the bill's supporters. Moreover, it appears that the bill assumed that after three years the local community would pick up the tab for the new policemen, and many communities would be financially unable to do so. Hence, some of these policemen would be temporary. It also appeared that many of the communities getting grants for additional policemen were very small towns with little or no crime problem. The bill also provided funds for programs for inner-city youths in the name of crime prevention, programs, such as midnight basketball leagues, to keep potential gang members off the streets. Conservatives in Congress strongly objected to the idea of fighting crime with spending on social programs. These conservatives also provided key opposition to the Crime Bill of 1994 and forced a reallocation of funds from such programs to funding more jail space. The bill expired in 2004 as the second Bush Administration, with political ties to the NRA and gun enthusiasts, did not support its renewal.

Debate Over Gun Control.   The question remains, however, whether these gun control laws had any significant effect on crime. The debate over gun control and whether it affects crime continues to be argued both among liberal and conservative ideologues and social scientists. Supporters of gun control frequently point to the fact that most murders in the United States result from being at the other end of the barrel of a gun. As Table 6.19 illustrates, most murders are committed using a gun. Furthermore, supporters of gun control point out, quite logically, that it is both physically and psychologically easier to kill someone with a gun than with a blunt instrument or with a knife. It takes a greater degree of strength, passion, commitment, and insensitivity to bash in a head with an andiron or to plunge a knife between someone's ribs than it does to stand across a room and pull a trigger. The possibilities of resistance are much greater in a knife or club attack, and requires physical proximity, rather than when one is shot from a distance. The proliferation of firearms makes the act of murder easier to carry out. The ease of taking lives with firearms as opposed to alternative methods is clearly shown in the figures for suicides by firearms in Table 6.20. It should be noted that despite the availability of numerous other means to commit suicide, firearms were used in over half the cases in the 1970s and since then, through the 1990s, account for almost two-thirds of all suicides. Taking one's own life is frequently an essentially irrational or impulsive act, and one that might not have taken place had the victim been forced to cool off in the light of day or to use some other, possibly unsuccessful, means.

Supporters of gun rights first point to two individual concerns that warrant allowing people to own guns. First, a number of people in America hunt game for recreation. Severe restrictions on guns or the banning of guns could adversely affect an activity that is seen by many, particularly in rural America, as an American tradition. A second, even more important individual concern arises from people who genuinely need a gun for protection. This would include those who work in high-crime neighborhoods, those who must travel late at night, and those whose safety has been threatened. The needs of these people constitute another important argument against gun control legislation. The argument is that law enforcement institutions and the justice process are unable to protect citizens from being victims of serious crime; therefore, such people have the right and the obligation to seek protection for themselves and their families. The argument states that if potential criminals believed that most people kept guns in their homes and knew how to use them, the number of break-ins would decrease dramatically. The death toll in cases of random violence would be lessened, it is argued, if armed citizens are able to defend themselves and others against the assailant.

Consistent with the logic of this argument, most states have now passed laws giving most persons the right, subject to a permit, to carry concealed weapons. To qualify for such a permit, the applicant has to have a record free from any felony conviction or mental illness and must take a course on firearm use and safety. In Texas, between January 1, 1996, when the law went into effect, and January 1, 1998, the state had issued 163,096 licenses to carry weapons. Supporters of this law argue that it will lead to a decrease in street crime because potential perpetrators will be aware that their potential victim may be hiding the means to blow them away. Opponents of the law, especially groups and individuals actively working for firearms control in general, argue that many of the holders of these permits use their guns to commit crimes.

Supporters of greater gun control also point out that the majority of homicides are not premeditated, but are crimes of passion committed on the spur of the moment. The argument that would end with a punch when a gun is not available may end with someone dead if a gun is available. Many shootings occur in domestic quarrels or in drunken arguments in bars. If the combatants had to go out the following day and seek a firearm from illegal sources, surely some of their passion would have decreased in the sober light of day.

Advocates of gun control also may make comparisons to different states with varying gun control laws. For example, in 2008, Rhode Island, with strict gun control laws, had 2.8 total murders per 100,000 population, whereas Texas, with a high incidence of gun ownership, had 5.6 murders per 100,000 population. But such comparisons are not particularly meaningful, since there are a number of explanations for the difference in crime in these two states. For one, Rhode Island has a much different culture and is essentially devoid of large metropolitan areas that breed crime (such as Houston, Dallas, or San Antonio in Texas). Furthermore, this argument falls flat when one also sees that the District of Columbia, which has some of the strictest gun control laws in the country, also has murder rates (at 31.4 per 100,000 residents in 2008) that are higher than many third-world countries.

Given these data, many gun rights advocates argue that gun control would not correct the crime problem. Opponents of gun control point out that guns are not the only available deadly weapon. Knives and blunt instruments can and do serve as instruments of violence, yet no one seriously advocates restricting the private ownership of such items. Opponents of gun control hold that if guns were not available, potential perpetrators of crime would simply resort to other means. It is further argued that persons determined to commit crimes would find illegal ways of acquiring firearms even if laws banned them. Prohibition did not prevent the use of alcoholic beverages, nor do laws eliminate prostitution, pornography, or illegal drugs. Therefore, gun control would by definition take guns away from law-abiding citizens, while leaving them in the hands of criminals.

In fact, it is hard to draw definitive conclusions from the empirical research as to how guns relate to violence and murder. There's a battle over data and statistics among social scientists using a lot of sophisticated statistical analyses, but no definitive answers in the debate have evolved. Economist John Lott, in his book *More Guns, Less Crime* (1998), finds that rates of violent crime and murder *fell a lot faster in states that adopted laws allowing for the carrying of concealed weapons* when compared to states that didn't adopt such laws. Lott analyzed crime data from more than 3,000 counties in the United States over twenty-five years.[76] A number of other social scientists have confirmed Lott's more general findings that more guns contribute to fewer murders and less violent crime.[77]

But not all social scientists agree with the findings or the analysis of the data in Lott's work and other studies. A 2001 study by a University of Chicago economist found that in the United States, "increases in gun ownership lead to substantial increases in the overall homicide rate," although there appear to be little relationship between gun ownership and other types of crime.[78] Coming at the issue from a public-health approach, Harvard professor David Hemenway finds that more guns cause more gun violence, that the deterrent effect of guns does not exist, and that all the available data show that arming people where they live, work or go to school will only increase violence.[79] But even some skeptics of the notion that more guns reduce crime have had a difficult time explaining away Lott's findings. Hashem Dezhbakhsh and Paul H. Rubin reanalyzed Lott's data and questioned the statistical methods he employed to reach his findings. In the end, they grudgingly concluded that the effects of concealed weapons laws in reducing crime were real, but that the effects were much smaller than Lott claimed.[80] As two supporters of gun control conceded in the *Stanford Law Review*, "We conclude that Lott and Mustard have made an important scholarly contribution in establishing that these laws have not led to the massive bloodbath of death and injury that some of their opponents feared."[81] Still, these scholars think that the evidence that these laws reduced crime is weak. As noted earlier, an alternative explanation for drops in crime in the U.S. in the 1990s comes from economist Steven Levitt, who argues that the legalization of abortion in the 1970s contributed to that decline.[82]

In a 2007 article in the *Harvard Journal of Law and Public Policy*, criminologists Don B. Kates and Gary Mauser take a more cautious perspective on the current debate over the effects of gun policy. By drawing on evidence across a multitude of countries, they examine whether a total ban on guns would reduce homicide or suicide rates. They do not find a pattern of more guns equaling more homicide or suicide. For example, they point out that Greece has nearly three times as much gun ownership as the Czech Republic, and a somewhat higher rate of gun suicide, yet overall suicide rates among Czechs are 175 percent higher than among Greeks. And in Luxembourg, where handguns are banned and ownership of guns is severely restricted, the murder rate in 2002 was nine times higher than neighboring Germany, which has a fairly high rate of gun ownership. According to these criminologists, "whether causative or not, the consistent international pattern is that more guns equal *less* murder and other violent crime."[83] In other words, they point out that for the most part, there tends to be a relationship between having more guns and less violence in a society, but caution that this correlation does not necessarily imply that guns are the reason for less violence (i.e., the old social scientist adage, correlation does not imply causation). Thus, these two researchers do not necessarily subscribe to the view that having more guns actually causes crime levels to go down. They suggest that there may be no causal link at all between either guns and lower violence/murder or guns and higher violence/murder. Instead, these two criminologists reiterate a very traditional view that "the determinants of murder and suicide are basic social, economic, and cultural factors, not the prevalence of some form of deadly mechanism."[84] In fact, an alternative explanation for the relationship of more guns and less violence could simply be because countries that are safer and have lower rates of crime are less troubled by the concept of allowing people to own guns and thus these countries choose to allow for more gun ownership.

As it seems, however, it is unlikely that extremely strict gun control laws or bans on all guns could ever be adopted in the United States, based both on public support for gun rights in America as well as the Supreme Court's interpretation of people's Second Amendment rights to own guns. First, while divided on some aspects of this issue, public support is fairly united in other aspects. In an

October 2007 Gallup Poll, participants were asked, "In general, do you feel that the laws covering the sale of firearms should be made more strict, less strict, or kept as they are now?" About half (51 percent) said they supported stricter gun control laws, while 8 percent wanted less strict laws, 39 percent said the laws should be kept the same as they currently exist, and 2 percent had no opinion.[85]

The trend in recent years has been toward a public that is more divided over the issue and less supportive of additional gun control laws. These numbers are down from the near 60 percent support for more gun control in polls in the 1990s. But the American public is less divided over whether severe gun control laws should be enacted. In this same 2007 Gallup Poll, a large majority of respondents polled (68 percent) stated that they were opposed to a ban on handguns. In terms of trend lines, sizeable majorities of Americans have opposed the idea of banning handguns. In essence, Americans like their right to own a gun, and thus the idea that legislatures or Congress would attempt to ban, outlaw, or confiscate all handguns (as was the case in the United Kingdom in 1997) seems very unlikely in the near future.

Furthermore, even if Congress attempted to enact a ban, such legislation would be declared unconstitutional under the Second Amendment right to bear arms. In the 2008 Supreme Court case *D.C. v. Heller*, the High Court struck down the District of Columbia's onerous regulations on firearms as a violation of the Second Amendment.[86] The 1976 District of Columbia law under scrutiny in the case banned private ownership of handguns, and stated that shotguns and rifles could only be owned if they were registered, kept unloaded, and either disassembled or disabled by trigger locks. Some legal scholars have read the Second Amendment as only conferring a collective right to own guns because of its phrase, "A well-regulated militia, being necessary to the security of a free state...." However, the second part of the Second Amendment seemingly confers an individual right because it reads, "the right of the people to keep and bear arms, shall not be infringed." To be sure, most constitutional law scholars agree that the Second Amendment is poorly worded. But the Court had never really directly answered whether an individual had a right to a gun until the *Heller* case. The Court rejected the notion that the amendment only conferred a collective right to bear arms, asserting that while the federal government could place some regulations on guns (that a person's right is not "unlimited"), the Second Amendment protects an individual's right to bear arms. Incidentally, an overwhelming majority of Americans agreed with the *Heller* decision that the Second Amendment protects an individual's right to bear arms (73 percent agreed with the Court decision in one 2008 Gallup Poll). While the *Heller* case, which occurred in Washington, D.C., resolved the issue as to whether the right to own a gun was an individual right recognized by the federal government, questions remained as to whether this right also applied to state governments and state laws regulating or banning guns. Recall the discussion earlier in the chapter that not all of the Bill of Rights apply to the states. In the 2010 case of *McDonald v. Chicago*, the Supreme Court answered this question by ruling that the Fourteenth Amendment also required states to recognize the individual right to bear arms.[87]

Decriminalization and Deterrence

Recall that the swiftness and certainty of punishment are thought to be the major ingredients in deterring crime. There are two factors at work in the criminal justice system that greatly slow down the meting out of that punishment. One is the long period of time that criminals spend free between arraignment and trial, and the other is the enormous case load of "victimless crime" defendants.

A substantial portion of the total justice system case load is processing so-called victimless crimes. Arrests for such things as prostitution, public intoxication, or drug abuse take up a large portion of the court time in any large city, time that might otherwise be used to prosecute more swiftly the perpetrators of crimes against persons or property. Prosecutorial forces, court-appointed defense attorneys, and police efforts take up more time. Police are pressured to apprehend people who engage in victimless crime (i.e., prostitutes, addicts, and gamblers), not because of any threat they pose to public safety, but solely because they offend the dominant morality. These laws are also selectively enforced against social undesirables. Police arrest streetwalkers but rarely arrest expensive call girls. Lower-class people are arrested for public intoxication on the street, but middle-class people are rarely bothered for intoxication except when driving. These laws against prostitution, gambling, or drugs also encourage organized crime, which provides criminalized services. Finally, these laws fail to prevent the conduct they proscribe; they may not even substantially reduce such conduct. *Decriminalization*, the legalization of such conduct or the substantial reduction of penalties associated with it, is a policy option that would permit a reallocation of criminal justice resources to crimes against persons and property.

It is protested, however, that the legalization of such "immoral" conduct would in effect constitute a legitimization of it, an official stamp of approval that would result in its expansion. Laws against murder do not prevent the crime from occurring, but they reduce its incidence and place society squarely in the position of saying that murder is not tolerable. It is argued that there are principles of ethical conduct that define the essence of society as a community. Others argue that there is a basic difference between laws proscribing crimes against persons and property and laws proscribing conduct that a dominant group finds immoral. With the former case, there is a widespread consensus on the wrongful nature of acts, such as murder, robbery, and rape. With the latter, there is no such consensus on the immorality of such conduct as getting intoxicated, gambling, or smoking marijuana. The legislation of morality is thus an attempt to impose a moral unity in a society in which ethical pluralism is a fact of life.

Strengthening the Police

Providing for more police or enhancing their technical law enforcement capabilities would seem to be an effective means of deterring crime. It is not clear, however, what effective actions specifically can be taken to secure this end. Some of the most obvious innovations have been shown not to be effective as indicated above in the discussion of the addition of police personnel as a result of the 1994 Crime Bill.

For instance, an experiment was conducted on the effect of increasing the number of police in a given geographical area. Political scientist Robert Lineberry reported on an experiment in Kansas City that reduced the police presence in one section of the city, greatly increased the police presence in a second section, and left a third section unchanged. The experiment failed to reveal significant differences in crime rates among the three neighborhoods.[88] The report did not deal with arrest rates, however, and the experiment was in place for only a short period of time. Obviously, one study is inconclusive, and increasing the police in one area may simply displace crime to other areas. These data caution us from expecting great reductions in crime from the provisions in the Crime Bill of 1994 to fund the placing of thousands of additional police on the streets even if the doubts, discussed above, about how many new policemen will actually be hired are resolved. It is not clear that police forces use the personnel they have in the most effective way for battling crime. For example, a large portion of police personnel's time is devoted to the enforcement of minor traffic violations, although a 1994 study shows that writing significantly fewer tickets had no effect on traffic safety. However, placing more patrol officers on the beat in a neighborhood, one tactic instituted by former New York Mayor Rudy Giuliani, has been credited with having some impact on the sharply reduced crime rates in that city in recent years.

Increased physical paraphernalia, such as riot control vehicles, or higher police salaries and sophisticated recruitment practices have also not been shown to have a significant impact on police effectiveness. Although increasing the resources allocated to police may give the psychological satisfaction of supporting the forces of law and order, it does not hold out much promise of contributing to the goal of deterring crime.

Penal Reform, Sentencing, and Recidivism

Criticisms of the disposition of our criminal justice system to impose insufficiently harsh penalties are frequently directed at the discretion available to judges to impose sentences. The issue over whether the maximization of jail time served will in fact reduce the crime rate involves assumptions about the impact that prison time served has on the criminal. It is widely assumed that discretionary sentencing has resulted in excessive leniency for serious criminals, as well as resulting in unjustly harsh sentences that depended on which judge was presiding in a given case. It is assumed, in other words, that society cannot trust judges to mete out punishments suitable to the circumstances and nature of each particular crime. These assumptions have led to a demand for standardization in sentencing.

Mandatory sentencing at the state level may mean limiting the alternatives to jail time served, or it may mean imposing a minimum of time served before parole eligibility. However, the impact of such laws would be undercut by plea bargaining and the greater disposition to enter such bargains in the face of a mandatory sentencing law. At the federal level, an elaborate and comprehensive set of guidelines for the standardization of sentencing was enacted into law in 1987. Of course, such federal laws have no impact on the vast preponderance of crime that involves state law, except insofar as the federal policy serves as a model for the criminal justice systems of several states. The Supreme Court struck down parts of the federal sentencing guidelines in *U.S. v. Booker* (2005) and limited how states could employ mandatory sentencing guidelines in *Blakely v. Washington* (2004).[89] In essence, the Court stated that one's Sixth Amendment right to a jury trial prohibited judges from enhancing a defendant's criminal sentence if the enhancement was not based on facts either admitted by the defendant or found by a jury. The Supreme Court declared that federal sentencing guidelines would only be advisory for judges instead of mandatory.

The fact that most career criminals will serve prison time at some point in their lives renders the recidivism rate one of the more important facts about criminality. *Recidivism* is the rate at which crime is committed by people who have been convicted of previous crimes. A high recidivism rate indicates that people who have been punished for committing at least one crime have a higher probability of committing subsequent crimes than do people who have never been so punished. One authority has estimated that as many as 80 percent of all felonies are committed by people previously convicted of other felonies; others place the rate as low as one-third.[90] Widely accepted estimates suggest that recidivists account for around 60 percent of all felonies. One study of 18,000 people arrested in 1963 found that within three years, 55 percent had been arrested again, and another study of persons arrested for robbery found that 38 percent went back to jail within two years. Problems of definition and data gathering account for the wide variation among these statistics. The serious implication of the high recidivism rate is that rather than deterring individuals from committing additional crimes, punishment and incarceration appear to make it more likely that they will engage in criminal behavior again. The recidivism rate attests to the failure of our prison system. Its importance becomes even more obvious in light of the more than 1 million people incarcerated in American prisons, and the desire to curb this relentless relapse into criminality has inspired concern for the reform of the prison system.

By midyear of 2008, state and federal prisons had in custody 1,610,446 inmates; local jails held another 785,556. Between 1995 and 2003, the incarcerated population grew at the rate of 3.4 percent annually. In 2008, 3.2 percent of the adult residents of the U.S. or one in thirty-one adults were in the criminal justice system: on probation, on parole, or in jail.[91]

Many charge that the prison system increases inmates' tendency toward criminality. First, the system is seriously overcrowded. This fact in turn results in the bitterness and dehumanization that occur when people must spend years in substandard conditions. The 1994 Crime Bill allocated billions of new dollars for prison space. The new space, however, was immediately filled by new inmates, as are similar spaces built-in state prisons. Second, prisons are understaffed with respect to trained personnel who could help rehabilitate inmates. Third, improper supervision by staff and a lack of standards for choosing them result in such brutalizing experiences as beatings by guards, rape, and interracial violence. Yet it is dangerous to characterize the prison system as if it were an undifferentiated whole. Although clearly some prisons have been notoriously brutalizing places—city jails, such as the Cook County Jail in Chicago and the Tombs in

New York City, are frequently cited in this regard—other places are well-staffed, modern facilities that resemble college campuses as much as institutions for punishment, complete with gyms and cable TV.

Another characteristic of the prison system alluded to by its critics is a failure to prepare inmates to lead productive lives upon their release. Little is done to impart the skills needed to make the inmates more employable than when they turned to crime. Drugs are easily available within many prisons, and some prisoners become addicts under the pressures of prison life. This addiction, of course, almost guarantees the subsequent criminal activity of such inmates.

Among the suggested strategies in prison reform are better vocational training and improved psychological counseling, rehabilitative services aimed at changing the circumstances in which the individual became a criminal. (This argument assumes, however, that "environment" breeds criminality, an assumption not universally accepted.) Overcrowded conditions can be addressed by building more facilities, by shorter sentences, by probated or suspended sentences, by work release programs, and by early paroles. Work release programs offer the added benefit of additional vocational training. But some reform proposals are controversial, and that is due in large part to confusion and ambivalence over the goals of the prison system. Liberals and many social scientists assume that the main purpose of the prison system is rehabilitative and correctional. Prisons are in fact frequently called "correctional facilities." Others stress the deterrent effect of punishment. Still others see prisons as places to house and isolate crime-prone individuals from society, sociopaths who have no hope of rehabilitation, thus physically preventing them from inflicting any further harm.

The kind of malevolent conditions that would seem best to fulfill the function of punishment are different from the more benevolent prison conditions frequently held to encourage rehabilitation. Therefore, those who seek to use the prisons for punishment charge that they are "schools of crime" because convicts are treated too kindly.[92] Yet many believe that by making prisons more brutal in order to punish criminals effectively, we make prisons less able to rehabilitate criminals into law-abiding citizens. The recidivism estimates cited above are used as evidence for this interpretation. The main impediment to serious prison reform is financial. As it stands, the nation already spends over $24 billion per year on its prison system. Prison reform would almost certainly require substantial tax increases, and that is not much of a winning election issue for politicians.

Zero Tolerance for Petty Street Crime

A number of policies instituted by former New York Mayor Rudy Giuliani have been given partial credit for the sharply reduced crime rate in that city during his administration that ended in 2001. One of these was a policy on cracking down on vandals and graffiti artists who deface a neighborhood. Once a neighborhood becomes so defaced, its demographic character may change and people may take less pride in the neighborhood. Moreover, the perpetrators of such petty crimes perceive that they can get away with flouting the laws and standards of society. New York believes this zero-tolerance policy has been a success.

Limiting the Alternatives to Punishment

The deterrent effect of prospective punishment is further reduced by the various mechanisms for circumventing the full weight of the law even when a person is convicted. The widespread availability of such mechanisms gives criminals reason to believe that the chances are remote that they will ever suffer the maximum punishment provided by law. These mechanisms include the defense of insanity, indeterminate sentencing with the widespread use of parole, probated or suspended sentences, and the separation of juvenile offenders from the regular criminal justice system. All of these mechanisms (except the insanity defense) reflect the problem of our overcrowded criminal justice system. They promote the release of inmates short of the maximum penalty provided by law, thereby freeing prison facilities for the continued influx of new inmates. Indeterminate sentencing means that the judge specifies a range of time for incarceration, say, two to ten years. The inmate then becomes eligible for parole any time after the minimum period is served. Parole is a process by which a convicted inmate is released from prison before serving the full extent of the sentence; a parole board decides whether an inmate can and probably will lead a socially constructive existence. Such a parolee must report for the duration of his or her sentence to a supervisory official known as a parole or probation officer. There is a movement to specify mandatory sentences of determinate length for certain types of crimes but it has not been widely adopted. Indeterminate sentencing is still the norm, however, because penologists feel that it offers the needed flexibility to fit the punishment to the unique circumstances of each case.

When a defendant is convicted of a crime, a judge or jury may, at their discretion, suspend the sentence, in effect waiving all incarceration for the convicted criminal. The only thing the convicted criminal suffers is the onus of having the conviction on his or her record. A probated sentence means that incarceration is not imposed, but the judge imposes a requirement that the convicted criminal must report to a probation officer at specified intervals. Judges and juries have the discretion to hand down suspended or probated sentences for a wide range of crimes. Although this discretion clearly lowers the deterrent impact of legally possible punishment, the mandatory incarceration of all convicted felons, especially for the length of their maximum sentences, would necessitate a substantial increase in available jail space. Neo-conservatives tend to favor reducing these alternatives in favor of more determinate but shorter sentences. Their motive is both for the deterrent effect (every conviction means jail) and for the retributive effect (determinate sentencing as punishment).

The question of the insanity defense came into prominence anew in 1998 when "Unabomber" suspect Ted Kaczynski was put on trial for killing and maiming numerous people with mail bombs over a seventeen-year period in protest of the perceived evils of modern technology. Kaczynski, a brilliant former mathematics professor, had dropped out and was living in the Montana wilderness in a wooden shack without plumbing. He objected to his lawyers claiming that he was innocent by reason of insanity. The legal definition is the McNaughten Rule, that the accused could not tell that the act was wrong. It was argued by some that anyone living like an animal and sending lethal bombs to strangers through the mail should be considered insane. On the other hand, others argued that he must have known his acts were "wrong" because he had to work to evade capture for seventeen years. The case showed that the finding of insanity (a legal concept) or of psychosis (a medical concept) is a subjective enterprise; equally eminent psychologists can disagree with respect to a given case. Conservative scholars like criminal justice expert James Q. Wilson argue that too often perpetrators perceive that they can escape responsibility for their acts by claiming that they were victims of some imprecisely conceptualized pathology, especially legal insanity.[93]

Earlier we alluded to the fact that juveniles commit much of the violent crime in this country. Yet because we do not hold juveniles fully responsible for their actions, they are immune from the regular punishments of the criminal justice system. Moreover, their juvenile record does not carry over beyond their minority; they begin adulthood with a clean slate, regardless of the number or nature of their criminal acts as minors. Whatever deterrent effect the punishments of the criminal justice system may provide, it does not apply to teenagers, the age group most likely to commit crimes against persons and property. The idea that children cannot be held responsible for their actions in the same ways as adults can appeals to our sense of fairness. After all, little children cannot be expected to possess the powers of judgment to discern right from wrong. But it is not clear that this inability to discern right from wrong also applies to people in their middle to late teens, the time of greatest criminality. Therefore, there are those who suggest that for violent and serious crimes, the laws of the regular criminal process ought to apply at a younger age. Obviously, we would not want to imprison a five-year-old, regardless of what act was perpetrated. But few would have problems with incarcerating a seventeen-year-old murderer, rapist, or mugger. It is this gray area in between where the lack of consensus exists. At what age do we draw the line? Alternatively, it has been suggested that juvenile records be carried into adulthood to establish recidivist patterns immediately upon coming of age.

Among conservatives, the preferred strategy toward the crime problem is to lock up those individuals who are a threat to society and to keep them locked up. Specifically, this would involve preventive detention and selective incapacitation. The former strategy would authorize judges to deny bail to accused persons whom they consider likely to commit additional crimes. The latter would target chronic offenders for long-term incarceration. Related to this is the proposal to notify communities when former sex offenders are released in their midst. Similarly, the 1994 Crime Bill contains provisions for life imprisonment for persons convicted of three federal felonies—the so-called "three strikes and you're out" principle. Versions of this principle have also been enacted in various states. Critics argue that it floods the prisons with aged inmates and persons convicted of nonviolent felonies. Samuel Walker argues that such strategies would fail significantly to reduce crime because of two factors: the prediction problem and the costs of incarceration.[94] The prediction problem means that we cannot really identify who is dangerous and likely to commit more crimes, and we cannot predict which criminals would likely commit violent crimes. Therefore, we would not incarcerate those who would actually commit the crimes we are trying to prevent, while we would incarcerate many people who are not really dangerous. The cost problem is that these policies would significantly increase the population of our already overcrowded prison facilities. The estimated cost for new facilities is between $45,000 and $70,000 per inmate. Costs of keeping an inmate in prison vary from $8,000 to $50,000 per inmate. Using the lower estimates, Walker calculates that the cost of implementing preventive detention and selective incapacitation over the next five years would be around $120 billion, an astronomical sum in an era of budget deficits.

ENDNOTES

1. The "UK 'has worst violent crime rate in Europe,'" *The London Evening Standard*, February 7, 2009, http://www.thisislondon.co.uk/standard/article-23714675-uk-has-worst-violent-crime-rate-in-europe.do; Accessed May 10, 2010.

2. Federal Bureau of Investigation, *Uniform Crime Reports*, 2008, http://www.fbi.gov/ucr/cius2008/index.html; Accessed June 20, 2010.

3. U.S. Census Bureau, *Statistical Abstract of the United States*, 100th ed. (Washington, DC: U.S. Government Printing Office, 1978), p. 177.

4. Federal Bureau of Investigation, *Uniform Crime Reports, 1996* (Washington, DC: U.S. Government Printing Office), p. 204.

5. Mark Green, Beverly Moore, and Bruce Wasserstein, "Criminal Law and Corporate Disorder," in Jerome Skolnick and Elliot Currie, eds., *Crisis in American Institutions*, 4th ed. (Boston: Little Brown, 1979), pp. 527–547.

6. The figures for the Enron scandal are drawn from *Newsweek*, January 21, 2002, pp. 19–25.

7. Zachary A. Goldfarb and Jerry Markon, "Justice Probe of Goldman Goes Beyond Deals Cited by SEC," *Washington Post*, May 1, 2010, p. A1.

8. James Q. Wilson, *Thinking about Crime*, rev.ed. (New York: Basic Books, 1983), especially Chapter 2.

9. David Hellman, *The Economics of Crime* (New York: St. Martin's Press, 1980), p. 147.

10. U.S. Department of Health and Human Services, National Institutes of Health, http://monitoringthefuture.org/pubs/monographs/overview2008.pdf; Accessed October 20, 2010.

11. National Survey on Drug Use & Health, 2007, http://www.oas.samhsa.gov/NSDUH/2k7NSDUH/tabs/Sect1peTabs1to46.htm#Tab1.1A.

12. National Survey on Drug Use & Health, 2008, http://www.oas.samhsa.gov/NSDUH/2k8NSDUH/2k8results.cfm#Fig2-2.

13. FBI's *Uniform Crime Report*, 1997, http://www.fbi.gov/ucr/97cius.htm.

14. Cited in Samuel Walker, *Sense and Nonsense about Crime*, 2nd ed. (Pacific Grove, CA: Brooks/Cole, 1989), p. 38, p. 55.

15. Steven D. Levitt, "What Do Declining Abortion Rates Mean for Crime in the Future?" *New York Times* blog, "Freakonomics," January 22, 2008, http://freakonomics.blogs.nytimes.com/2008/01/22/what-do-declining-abortion-rates-mean-for-crime-in-the-future/.

16. Steven D. Levitt, "What Do Declining Abortion Rates Mean for Crime in the Future?"

17. 517 U.S. 456 (1996).

18. Cited in Stephan Thernstrom and Abigail Thernstrom, *America in Black and White: One Nation, Indivisible* (New York: Touchstone, 1997), p. 268.

19. *Sourcebook of Criminal Justice Statistics*, 2008, http://www.albany.edu/sourcebook/tost_6.html#6_ao.

20. Pamela E. Oliver, "Racial Disparities in Imprisonment: Some Basic Information," *Focus*, Vol. 21, No. 3 (Spring 2001): pp. 28–31.

21. Oliver, "Racial Disparities in Imprisonment: Some Basic Information."

22. Oliver, "Racial Disparities in Imprisonment: Some Basic Information," 31.

23. "Guidance Regarding the Use of Race by Federal Law Enforcement Agencies," Civil Rights Division, U.S. Department of Justice, June 2003, http://www.justice.gov/crt/split/documents/guidance_on_race.php.

24. "Guidance Regarding the Use of Race by Federal Law Enforcement Agencies," Civil Rights Division, U.S. Department of Justice, June 2003, http://www.justice.gov/crt/split/documents/guidance_on_race.php.

25. Paul Butler, "Racially Based Jury Nullification: Black Power in the Criminal Justice System," *Yale Law Journal*, 105 (December 1995): 677.

26. *Powell* v. *Alabama*, 287 U.S. 45 (1932).

27. *Gideon* v. *Wainwright*, 372 U.S. 335 (1963). This case was made even more famous by the nonfiction book *Gideon's Trumpet* (New York: Vintage Books, 1964) written by *New York Times* reporter Anthony Lewis.

28. The Court has ruled that once a guilty plea has been entered under such a plea bargain, the prosecution's side of the bargain must be kept. Failure by the prosecution to keep its bargain will cause the conviction to be vacated. *Santobello* v. *New York*, 404 U.S. 257 (1971).

29. For a more detailed discussion of the public policy issues involved in plea bargaining, see Lawrence Baum (2008) *American Courts: Process and Policy*, 6th ed., New York: Houghton Mifflin Company. For an inside look behind the machinations of the plea bargaining process, see Milton Heumann, *Plea Bargaining* (Chicago: University of Chicago Press, 1978).

30. *Escobedo* v. *Illinois*, 378 U.S. 478 (1964).

31. *Miranda* v. *Arizona*, 384 U.S. 436 (1966).

32. Lee Epstein, and Thomas G. Walker, *Constitutional Law for a Changing America: Rights, Liberties, and Justice* (Washington, DC: CQ Press, 2010).

33. *Mapp* v. *Ohio*, 367 U.S. 643 (1961).

34. *Chimel* v. *California*, 394 U.S. 752 (1969).

35. *Terry* v. *Ohio*, 392 U.S. 1 (1968); *Sibron* v. *New York*, 392 U.S. 40 (1968).

36. *Katz* v. *United States*, 389 U.S. 347 (1967).

37. *Nix* v. *Williams*, 467 U.S. 431 (1984); *U.S.* v. *Leon*, 468 U.S. 897 (1984).

38. See the argument that the criminal justice system must be perceived as "just" in James Q. Wilson and Richard Hernnstein, *Crime and Human Nature* (New York: Simon & Schuster, 1985), pp. 506–507.

39. Thorsten Sellin, *The Penalty of Death* (Beverly Hills, CA: Sage, 1980), pp. 80–81.

40. U.S. Department of Justice, Federal Bureau of Investigation, *Sourcebook on Criminal Justice Statistics 2000*, p. 147.

41. Isaac Ehrlich, "The Deterrent Effect of Capital Punishment: A Question of Life and Death," *American Economic Review*, 65 (June 1975): 398; Peter Passell and John Taylor, "The Deterrence Controversy: A Reconsideration of the Time Series Evidence," in Chester Pierce and Hugo Bedau, eds., *Capital Punishment in the United States* (New York: AMS Press, 1976), 359; Sellin, *Penalty of Death*, Chapter 10.

42. Amnesty International, *Death Sentences and Executions in 2008*, http://www.amnesty.org/en/library/asset/ACT50/003/2009/en/0b789cb1-baa8-4c1b-bc35-58b606309836/act500032009en.pdf.

43. These data are from Sellin, *Penalty of Death*, 52.

44. Guy Johnson, "The Negro and Crime," *The Annals of the American Academy of Political and Social Science*, 217 (1941): 100. Cited in *Furman v. Georgia*, 408 U.S. 32 (1972).

45. Cited in *Dallas Time Herald*, November 17, 1985; *McClesky v. Kemp*, 481 U.S. 279 (1987).

46. http://www.deathpenaltyinfo.org/article.php?scid=19&did=246; Accessed October 15, 2007.

47. 408 U.S. 32 (1972).

48. James Ridella, "Miranda: One Year Later—The Effects," *Public Management*, 49 (July 1967): 183–190. This author found that in data drawn from St. Louis, less than 1 percent of those arrested had been freed on *Miranda* grounds.

49. Gerald N. Rosenberg, *The Hollow Hope: Can Courts Bring About Social Change?* (Chicago: The University of Chicago Press, 1991), p. 324, quoting in part, Welsh S. White. 1986. "Defending *Miranda*: A Reply to Professor Caplan," *Vanderbilt Law Review* Volume 39: 20.

50. Rosenberg, *The Hollow Hope*, p. 329.

51. Richard Medalie, Leonard Zeits, and Paul Alexander, "Custodial Police Interrogation in Our Nation's Capital: The Attempt to Implement *Miranda*," *Michigan Law Review*, 66 (May 1968): pp. 1347–1422.

52. Richard Seeburger and Stanley Wetlick, "*Miranda* in Pittsburgh: A Statistical Study," in Theodore Becker and Malcolm Freely, eds., *The Impact of Supreme Court Decisions*, 2nd ed. (New York: Oxford University Press, 1973), p. 154.

53. Stephen Wasby, *The Impact of the United States Supreme Court: Some Perspectives* (Homewood, IL: Dorsey Press, 1970), p. 156.

54. Wasby, *Impact*, 162; Stuart Nagel, *The Legal Process from a Behavioral Perspective* (Homewood, IL: Dorsey Press, 1969), p. 314.

55. Canon, Bradley. 1977. "Testing the Effectiveness of Civil Liberties Policies at the State and Federal Levels: The Case of the Exclusionary Rule." *American Politics Quarterly*, Volume 5, p. 75.

56. Donald L. Horowitz, *The Courts and Social Policy* (Washington, DC: The Brookings Institution, 1977), p. 232.

57. *Proffitt v. Florida*, 428 U.S. 242 (1976); *Gregg v. Georgia*, 428 U.S. 153 (1976); *Jurek v. Texas*, 428 U.S. 262 (1976).

58. Marshall in *Furman*, 408 U.S. 238, at p. 329; Brennan at p. 269.

59. *Stanford v. Connecticut*, 492 U.S. 361 (1989); *Atkins v. Virginia*, 536 U.S. 304 (2002); *Perry v. Lynaugh*, 492 U.S. 302 (1989); and *Roper v. Simmons*, 543 U.S. 551 (2005).

60. 483 U.S. 66 (1987).

61. See also *Booth v. Maryland*, 482 U.S. 496 (1987); *Payne v. Tennessee*, 501 U.S. 808 (1991).

62. 486 U.S. 356 (1988).

63. *McClesky v. Zant*, 499 U.S. 467 (1991); *Coleman v. Thompson*, 501 U.S. 722 (1991); *Yost v. Nunnemaker*, 501 U.S. 797 (1991).

64. Attributed to Norval Morris as reported in Norton Long, "The City as Reservation," *Public Interest*, 25 (Fall 1971): 31.

65. Wilson, *Thinking about Crime*, p. 118.

66. Wayne H. Thomas, *Bail Reform in America* (Berkeley: University of California Press, 1976).

67. Hellman, *Economics of Crime*, p. 49.

68. Daniel Borunda, "Juarez Nears 5,000 Killings," *El Paso Times*, April 26, 2010, http://www.elpasotimes.com/ci_14959082?source=most_emailed; Accessed June 20, 2010.

69. Alexander Smith and Harriet Pollach, *Some Sins Are Not Crimes* (New York: New Viewpoints, 1975), p. 100.

70. Cited in Smith and Pollach, *Some Sins*, p. 104.

71. Andrea Parrot and Laurie Bechofer, *Acquaintance Rape: The Hidden Crime* (New York: Wiley, 1991), p. 15.

72. Susan Brownmiller, *Against Our Will: Men, Women, and Rape* (New York: Simon & Schuster, 1975), p. 15.

73. Murray Strauss and Richard Gelles, *Intimate Violence: The Causes and Consequences of Abuse in the U.S. Family* (New York: Simon & Schuster, 1989).

74. Susan Estrich, *Real Rape: How the Legal System Victimizes Women Who Say No* (Cambridge, MA: Harvard University Press, 1987), p. 102.

75. http://www.smallarmssurvey.org/files/sas/publications/yearb2007.html

76. John Lott, *More Guns, Less Crime* (Chicago: The University of Chicago Press, 1998). See also the third edition; published in 2010. Lott's book is based on research collected by Lott and his colleague David Mustard. "Crime, Deterrence, and Right-to-Carry Concealed Handguns," *Journal of Legal Studies*, Vol. 26, pp. 1–68.

77. See, for example, Bruce L. Benson and Brent Mast, "Privately Produced General Deterrence," *Journal of Law & Economics*, Vol. 44 (2001): 1; Stephen G. Bronars and John R. Lott, Jr., "Criminal Deterrence, Geographic Spillovers, and the Right to Carry Concealed Handguns," *American Economic Review*, Vol. 88 (1998): p. 475; Carlisle E. Moody, "Testing for the Effects of Concealed Weapons Laws: Specification Errors and Robustness" *Journal of Law & Economics*, Vol. 44 (2001): p. 799; David B. Mustard, "The Impact of Gun Laws on Police Deaths," *Journal of Law & Economics*, Vol. 44 (2001): p. 635; Florenz Plassman and John Whitley, "Confirming More Guns, Less Crime." *Stanford Law Review*, Vol. 55 (2003): p. 1313.

78. Mark Duggan, "More Guns, More Crime," *Journal of Political Economy* Vol. 109 (2001): p. 1112.

79. David Hemenway, *Private Guns Public Health* (Ann Arbor, MI: University of Michigan Press, 2004).

80. Hashem Dezhbakhsh and Paul H. Rubin, "Lives Saved or Lives Lost? The Effects of Concealed-Handgun Laws on Crime," *American Economic Review* Vol. 88 (1998): p. 468.

81. Ian Ayres and John J. Donohue, III, "Shooting Down the 'More Guns, Less Crime' Hypothesis," *Stanford Law Review*, Vol. 55 (2003): p. 1201.

82. See John J. Donohue, III and Steven D. Levitt, "The Impact of Legalized Abortion on Crime" *Quarterly Journal of Economics*, Vol. 116 (2001): p. 379. See also John Donahue, III and Steven Levitt, "Further Evidence That Legalized Abortion Lowered Crime: A Reply to Joyce," *Journal of Human Resources*, 39, No. 1 (2004): pp. 29–49; and Steven Levitt, "Understanding Why Crime Fell in the Nineties: Four Factors That Explain the Decline and Six That Do Not," *Journal of Economic Perspectives*, 18, No. 1 (2004).

83. Don B. Kates and Gary Mauser, "Would Banning Firearms Reduce Murder and Suicide? A Review of International and Some Domestic Evidence." *Harvard Journal of Law and Public Policy*, Vol. 30, No. 2 (2007): p. 673.

84. Kates and Mauser, 2007, p. 663.

85. Gallup Poll, October 4–7, 2007, http://www.gallup.com/poll/101731/Shrunken-Majority-Now-Favors-Stricter-Gun-Laws.aspx.

86. *D.C. v. Heller*, 128 S. Ct. 2783 (2008)

87. Gallup Poll, February 8–10, 2008, http://www.gallup.com/poll/108394/Americans-Agreement-Supreme-Court-Gun-Rights.aspx.

88. Robert Lineberry, *American Public Policy* (New York: Harper & Row, 1977), p. 189.

89. *United States v. Booker*, 543 U.S. 220 (2005); *Blakely v. Washington*, 542 U.S. 296 (2004).

90. Daniel Glaser, "The Effectiveness of a Prison Parole System," in Vergil Williams, *Dictionary of American Penology* (Westport, CT: Greenwood Press, 1979), pp. 217–219.

91. Bureau of Justice Correction Statistics, http://bjs.ojp.usdoj.gov/index.cfm?ty=tp&tid=11.

92. For example, Ramsey Clark, *Crime in America* (New York: Simon & Schuster, 1970), Chapter 13; Duane Lockard, *Perverted Priorities of American Politics*, 2nd ed. (Prentice Hall, 1976), p. 306.

93. James Q. Wilson, *Moral Judgment: Does the Abuse Excuse Threaten Our Legal System?* (New York: Basic Books, 1997). See also Charles Sykes, *A Nation of Victims* (New York: St. Martin's Press, 1992).

94. Walker, *Sense and Nonsense*, p. 79.

RESOURCES

Books

Banner, Stuart. *The Death Penalty: An American History*. Cambridge, MA: Harvard University Press, 2002.

Baumgartner, Frank R., De Boef, Suzanna, and Boydstun, Amber E. *The Decline of the Death Penalty and the Discovery of Innocence*. New York: Cambridge University Press, 2008.

Berns, Walter. *For Capital Punishment: Crime and Morality of the Death Penalty*. New York: Basic Books, 1979.

Cole, George, and Smith, Christopher. *The American System of Criminal Justice*, 10th ed. Belmont, CA: Wadsworth, 2004.

Gelles, Murray, and Strauss, Richard. *Intimate Violence: The Causes and Consequences of Abuse in the American Family*. New York: Simon & Schuster, 1989.

Gould, Jon B. *The Innocence Commission: Preventing Wrongful Convictions and Restoring the Criminal Justice System*. New York: New York University Press, 2008.

Hellman, David. *The Economics of Crime*. New York: St. Martin's Press, 1980.

Haney, Craig. *Death by Design: Capital Punishment as a Social Psychological System*. New York: Oxford University Press, 2005.

Jenkins, Phillip. *Crime and Justice, Issues and Ideas*. Pacific Grove, CA: Brooks/Cole, 1984.

Kleck, Gary. *Targeting Guns: Firearms and Their Control*. New York: Aldine de Gruyter, 1997.

Lott, John. *More Guns, Less Crime*, 3rd ed. Chicago: The University of Chicago Press. 2010.

Schur, Edwin. *Crime without Victims*. Englewood Cliffs, NJ: Prentice Hall, 1965.

Sellin, Thorsten. *The Penalty of Death*. Beverly Hills, CA: Sage, 1980.

Sykes, Charles. *A Nation of Victims*. New York: St. Martin's Press, 1992.

Van Den Haag, Ernest, and Conrad, John B. *The Death Penalty: A Debate*. New York: Plenum, 1984.

Walker, Samuel. *Sense and Nonsense about Crime*, 2nd ed. Pacific Grove, CA: Brooks/Cole, 1989.

White, Welsh S. *Litigating in the Shadow of Death: Defense Attorneys in Capital Cases*. Ann Arbor: The University of Michigan Press, 2006.

Wilson, James Q. *Thinking about Crime*, 2nd ed. New York: Basic Books, 1984.

Wilson, James Q. *Moral Judgment: Does the Abuse Excuse Threaten Our Legal System?* New York: Basic Books, 1997.

Websites

American Civil Liberties Union: **http://www.aclu.org**

Brady Campaign to Prevent Gun Violence: **http://www.bradycampaign.org**

Federal Bureau of Investigation Uniform Crime Report: **http://www.fbi.gov/ucr/ucr.htm#cius**

Moratorium Campaign (Death Penalty): **http://www.moratoriumcampaign.org**

National Rifle Association: **http://www.nra.org**

Pro-Death Penalty.com: **http://www.prodeathpenalty.com**

Public Agenda: **http://www.publicagenda.org**

Restorative Justice Online: **http://www.restorativejustice.org**

Chapter 7

Poverty and Social Welfare Policy

In response to problems associated with poverty and income insecurity, social welfare programs in the U.S. cover Social Security, public assistance, job training, public health, unemployment compensation, and education. This chapter discusses the following: *social insurance programs*, which are generally linked to individuals' past contributions and provide for those separated from the labor market due to age, injury, disability or unemployment; and *social assistance programs*, which are means-tested and aim to minimize economic hardship and alleviate poverty for those not covered by social insurance. Chapters 7 and 8 cover social programs in health care and education. The policies discussed here comprise what most people consider to be the U.S. welfare state, charged with ameliorating the causes and consequences of poverty.

ISSUE BACKGROUND: POVERTY

The answer to the question "What is poverty?" is to some degree technical, but it also tends to be mired in political and policymaking controversy. Is poverty defined by income? By inequality? Or by hardship? It is important to know *what* the problem is before trying to solve it. After discussing issues that surround the definition of poverty, this section reviews historical responses to poverty and then describes the general characteristics of the U.S. welfare state.

Defining Poverty

Most societies have a view of poverty that is based on a combination of two views: economic need and behavioral malfunction. In terms of economic need, some people are simply unusually needy (orphans, the disabled, widows, widowers), and a minimum level of income is needed to support them. Their situation is not self-created; rather, they are victims of unfortunate circumstance. In contrast, considering the behavioral dimension of poverty's definition, vagrants, for example, cannot function within society, so they are outcast, but considered victims by their own choice and actions. This is where the politically charged question of deservingness arises. Controversy surrounds our understanding of poverty because of attempts to suppress one or the other of these elements of its definition.

Whether one considers the economic or behavioral dimension to be primary, the general concept of poverty is that one's resources are insufficient to meet basic needs. In the U.S., poverty is defined by an absolute measure; in much of the rest of the developed world, poverty is measured relatively. In addition to these absolute and relative measures, some scholarship also considers hardship-based, psychological, and social exclusion dimensions of poverty.

Absolute Definitions.   The federal definition of poverty in the U.S. is economic only. In 1964, Mollie Orshansky in the Social Security Administration developed a guideline, an income threshold below which one is considered to be poor. Orshansky studied the consumption patterns evident in a 1955 data set and found that one-third of spending among lower-income families was on food. As a result, three times what the USDA called the "thrifty food plan budget" was identified as the *poverty line*. The amount varies by family size and is adjusted year to year for inflation by using the consumer price index. Each March, the *Current Population Survey* (CPS) documents people's previous year's earnings and derives the national poverty rate for that year by comparing their incomes to the absolute poverty line. In 2009, the official poverty line for a family of four was $22,050; it ranged from $10,830 for a one-person family to $40,750 for a family of nine or more.

Orshansky never intended this absolute measure to persist, but it has; and in recent decades, researchers have been examining the implications of changing the definition of poverty. Some problems with the U.S. poverty definition that have compelled this research *underestimate income and therefore overestimate the proportion of people living in poverty*. For instance, the official poverty rate is calculated by 1955 consumption patterns; however, the share of a family's budget now spent on food is less (some say a fifth or sixth rather than a third), primarily because of changes in technology and consumption patterns. Next, the official poverty threshold counts only cash income and not in-kind benefits. Since the 1960s, the value of in-kind benefits has increased substantially. In addition, people tend to underreport their income on surveys such as the CPS. Another problem is that assets are not considered, meaning that a family may have no income from work in a given year but may have a house and substantial savings—minimizing any hardship they may face—and these are not considered by the official U.S. definition of poverty. These criticisms suggest that the measure may be too high.

Conversely, some problems with the official definition serve to *overstate income and therefore understate the proportion of the population in poverty*. Taxes (income, withholding) are excluded from the computation. A family near the poverty line before paying taxes may fall below the poverty line after paying taxes. The regressive nature of payroll taxes in particular disproportionately affects low-income workers. Moreover, expenses associated with work are ignored. This means that working people might not be considered poor by the official definition, but after considering their work expenses, their incomes may fall below the poverty line. Another criticism is that in the definition there is no regional variation. It is more expensive to live in New York City, for example, than in Mississippi, but the poverty line is the same in both places.

In the early 1990s, the National Research Council (NRC) proposed changing the poverty measurement by doing the following: (1) Define poverty using current consumption patterns. It would look at the budget for basic necessities and then use a percentage of that to identify the poverty line (that percent would be a political decision). The result would be to raise the amount of measured poverty. (2) Include in-kind benefits that are close to cash, such as housing and energy assistance and food assistance. This would raise measured incomes and therefore reduce the rate of poverty. (3) Consider only disposable income (after taxes and work expenses). The net effect of these changes, according to NRC, would be to raise the measured poverty rate by about four percentage points. It would change the shape of the income distribution, toward more working poor and less welfare-receiving poor.

Since then, debate and research on restructuring the poverty measure has been active, and for many years now the U.S. Census Bureau has produced a set of what it calls "experimental poverty measures," which incorporate and refine many of the NRC suggestions and allow us to understand the implications of varying poverty measures on the composition of the poor population. Most recently, the Obama administration has committed to creating an alternate poverty measure and determining how best to phase it in, and for what purposes. It is doubtful that the official definition will go away. But having other measures of poverty for comparison can help us to understand, by varying definitions, the extent to which the official rate is an inadequate representation of the proportion of poor people in the U.S.

The World Bank is the other main institution that uses an absolute poverty line globally, which previously calculated it at $1 per person per day in developing countries. Beginning in 2005, it raised this threshold to $1.25–$2 per day, depending on the country. Clearly, this absolute measure is even less nuanced than the U.S. official poverty line. An important implication of using an absolute poverty line is that one can imagine raising the incomes of all of those below the line so that they might no longer be considered poor. In the U.S., researchers sometimes use a "poverty gap" measure to identify the amount of money that would be needed in order to raise all those below poverty up to the poverty line. From some perspectives, using an absolute poverty measure represents an optimistic view since it suggests a possible cure.

Relative Definitions.   The kind of poverty measure in use in most of the rest of the developed world is a relative one, which compels a focus on inequality. Most commonly, a relative poverty measure is defined as being below one-half of a nation's median income. That is, a family is poor if its income is insufficient to bring it to the current median standard of living in society. By this measure, in the last forty years, a constant one-fifth of the population has been in poverty; that is, about 20 percent of families earn less than half the median income. In comparative perspective, the U.S. has very high poverty, as Figure 7.1 shows. The most recent figures show that 17.3 percent of the U.S. population (21.2 percent of children) falls below 50 percent of the median income; whereas, 4.9 percent of the population in the Netherlands (and 6.3 percent of their children) fall below this measure of poverty. In nine of the nations listed, child poverty rates are actually lower than the overall poverty rate. Finland, for example, has an overall poverty rate of 6.5 percent, while the child poverty rate is just 3.7 percent, the lowest of these developed nations.

The gap between those at the bottom and the richest Americans is widening. In 1970, the poorest quintile's share of income was 5.4 percent and the top quintile's share was 40.9 percent; by 2008, inequality had increased so that the poorest quintile's share of income had decreased to 4.0 percent and the top quintile's share had increased to 47.8 percent. The United States has the largest

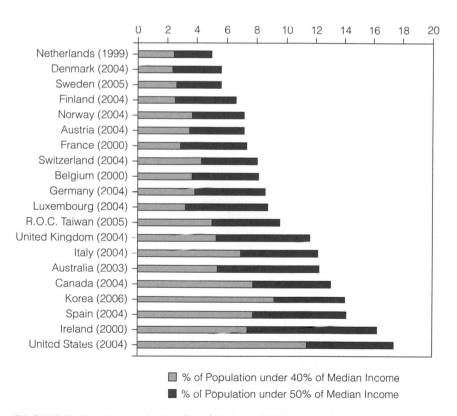

FIGURE 7.1 Poverty in Developed Nations, 2004

SOURCE: Computed from Luxembourg Income Study (LIS) Key Figures, http://www.lisproject.org/key-figures.htm; Accessed June 8, 2010.

gap between rich and poor of any modern democracy (see Table 7.1 and Figure 7.2).[1]

In addition to the absolute and relative definitions of poverty, some lines of debate center on defining material hardship, the psychological dimensions of poverty or social inclusion and exclusion. For the sake of simplicity, we will focus our next two questions—how many people are poor, and who are they?—by using only the official, absolute measure of poverty, since it is the most common perspective used in the U.S.

TABLE 7.1   Share of Aggregate Family Income Received, by Population Quintile, 1960–2008

Year	Poorest Quintile	Second Quintile	Third Quintile	Fourth Quintile	Richest Quintile	Richest 5 Percent
1960	4.8	12.2	17.8	24.0	41.3	15.9
1970	5.4	12.2	17.6	23.8	40.9	15.6
1980	5.3	11.6	17.6	24.4	41.1	14.6
1990	4.6	10.8	16.6	23.8	44.3	17.4
2000	4.3	9.8	15.4	22.7	47.7	21.1
2008	4.0	9.6	15.5	23.1	47.8	20.5

SOURCE: Table F-2, Share of Aggregate Income Received by Each Fifth and Top 5 Percent of Families, All Races: 1947 to 2008, http://www.census.gov/hhes/www/income/histinc/incfamdet.html; Accessed June 3, 2010.

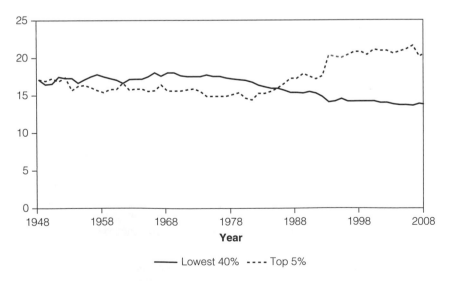

— Lowest 40% ···· Top 5%

FIGURE 7.2 Share of Aggregate Family Income Received by Bottom 40 percent and Top 50 percent, 1948–2008

SOURCE: Computed from Table F-2, Share of Aggregate Income Received by Each Fifth and Top 5 Percent of Families, All Races: 1947 to 2008 http://www.census.gov/hhes/www/income/histinc/incfamdet.html; Accessed June 3, 2010.

How Many Poor?

Debates over the definition of "poverty" link with disagreements about the cause of poverty and the number of poor persons in America. As can be seen in Figure 7.3, poverty as measured by the official poverty measure declined sharply between 1959 and 1970, from 40 million poor (22 percent of the population) to 25 million poor (13 percent); since that time, however, the poverty rate remained relatively constant at roughly 12 to 14 percent. In 2009, 43.6 million persons, or 14.3 percent of the population, fell below the poverty threshold. The most recent recession has seen an uptick in the poverty rate, from 12.3 in 2006 to 13.2 percent in 2008 to 14.3 by 2009.[2]

The Census Bureau data used in Figure 7.3 disguise a basic reality generally accepted by both conservative and liberal economists and elaborated in the section on the official federal poverty measure. These data reflect pretax cash income, including government transfer payments. That is, social insurance and public assistance cash benefits are counted as family income. Thus, if by "poverty" one refers to income earned without government help, removing cash payments from the measure reveals that 21.4 percent of the population is poor, even at the very low official definition of poverty. That is, more than one-fifth of the entire American population is unable to avoid poverty without government help. On the other hand, the official poverty figures do not take account of the income value of in-kind benefits, such as medical care and food assistance, or employer-provided health care or other benefits, nor are they adjusted for the tendency of people to under-report income. Adjusting for these factors leaves about 10 percent poor, a figure cited in support of the enormous success of

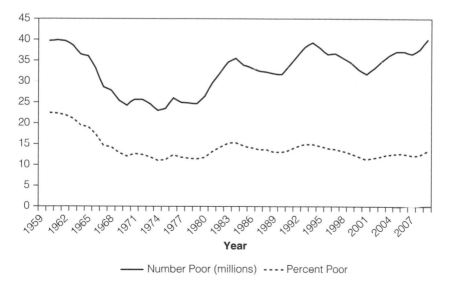

Year

— Number Poor (millions)   - - - - Percent Poor

FIGURE 7.3 Poverty Trends

SOURCE: http://www.census.gov/hhes/www/poverty/histpov/perindex.html for 1959–2006, accessed June 3, 2010; http://www.census.gov/hhes/www/poverty/detailedpovtabs.html for 2006–2008, Accessed June 7, 2010.

income maintenance and job programs. Although official statistics disguise the number of persons highly dependent on government aid, they also hide the success of federal programs in reducing poverty. Data on the effect of different ways of counting appear in Table 7.2.

Who Are the Poor?

The incidence of poverty does not fall evenly across the nation. Particular areas, groups, and classes bear a far higher incidence of poverty than others. Specifically, having or being a single mother, being young, being nonwhite, not working, and having a limited education are correlates of poverty, as is the location where one lives. Although a majority of the poor is white (they make up about 68 percent of those in poverty; see Table 7.4), the incidence of poverty is higher among racial minorities, reflecting racial prejudice, low job skills, and poor education. As Table 7.3 shows, although only 8.6 percent of non–Hispanic whites are poor, 23.2 percent of Hispanics and 24.7 percent of blacks are poor. Poverty among Native Americans is even higher. Over time, however, the story of African Americans reflects success: in 1960 over half (55.1 percent) of blacks were poor, and that has been cut in half, at least in part to the successes of the civil rights movement.

Among children, almost one-quarter live in a single female–headed household, and more than half of these households are poor. Over time, change in the composition of who is poor has been referred to the "feminization of poverty,"[3] reflecting demographic trends discussed in Chapter 2. In 1960, less than one in ten children lived with a lone mother. While that rate has more than doubled (to 23.9 percent in 2008), so too has the rate of poverty among these household types (from 23.7 percent in 1960 to 56.2 percent in 2008). High rates of divorce and unwed childbearing place a disproportionate share of women with small children in poverty. Lacking adequate child care and thus unable to work full-time and care for their children, they are much more likely to fall below the

TABLE 7.2   Effects of Taxes and Government Transfers on Poverty, 2008

The Census Bureau's various "Experimental Poverty Measures"	Persons in Poverty (millions)	Percentage of Persons in Poverty
1. Official poverty definition	39.8	13.2
2. Definition 1 − government transfers	64.4	21.4
3. Definition 2 + EITC and payroll taxes	61.6	20.5
4. Definition 3 + means-tested cash transfers	34.5	12.5
5. Definition 4 + means-tested in- kind transfers	30.7	9.8

Note: EITC refers to the earned income tax credit (see later discussion in text).
SOURCE: http://www.census.gov/hhes/www/cpstables/032009/rdcall/2_001.htm; Accessed June 4, 2010.

poverty line than are two-parent households. Sometimes these women do work full-time, but at jobs that do not pay enough to support their families.[4]

Employment in general is, not surprisingly, correlated with poverty. Among those who work full-time and full-year, poverty rates are extremely low (2.6 percent). Working only part-time or not all clearly increases one's risk of poverty, and factors that complicate one's ability to work have implications for well-being. Nevertheless, as Table 7.4 reveals, among those who are poor, 10.1 percent still worked full-time in 2008, and 37.1 percent worked part-time, suggesting that work alone is not sufficient to prevent poverty or solve income insecurity.

Age is also associated both with poverty and with the government efforts to minimize poverty. Although the overall poverty rate was 13.2 percent in 2008, for those greater than age sixty-five, it was 9.7 percent. Poverty among the elderly has dropped sharply due to government assistance. As Table 7.3 shows, more than one-third (35.2 percent) of the elderly were poor in 1960 before substantial expansion of pension and health assistance, which has been touted as an enormous success for bringing elderly poverty as low as it is. In contrast, poverty among children is substantially higher, with about one in five children being poor. Benefits to the elderly, principally Social Security, are generally indexed to keep pace with inflation. Benefits for others are not indexed and therefore decline over time in terms of real purchasing power. Subsequently, they have less potential to reduce poverty.

Poverty also correlates with education and residence. People lacking a high school diploma are disproportionately poor: they make up 14.9 percent of the overall population, but 23.5 percent of the poor. In contrast, only 12.6 percent of those with a high school degree are poor. In 1960, the distinctions in poverty by geographic location were much greater than they are today. Then, rural residents were poor at the rate of 33.2 percent: this has been cut by more than half to 15.1 percent by 2008. The rural poor tend to be more chronically poor than the urban poor, more dispersed, and less likely to use public assistance. While poverty rates in metropolitan areas in general are about the same as the national average, this masks that urban cores tend to have higher poverty rates, with suburban areas having lower rates. Over time, these geographic trends have converged, making geographic variation less distinct. Further, those who live in the southern U.S. experience poverty at higher rates than in other regions of the country, a trend that has persisted but also become less distinct over time.

Although some characteristics are associated with greater or lesser poverty, as these tables and the corresponding discussion show, correlation does not infer causation. Substantial debate surrounds what actually causes poverty, and it is this topic we consider next.

What Causes Poverty?

What one considers the primary cause of poverty mirrors the general concept of poverty having economic and behavioral dimensions. Is poverty caused by external, economic forces or is it the result of one's own behavior and choices? Before 1973, poverty was much more directly responsive to changes in the macro economy than

TABLE 7.3   **Percent of the U.S. Population that is Poor, by Characteristic, 1960–2008**

Characteristic	1960	1970	1980	1990	2000	2008
All people	22.2	12.6	13.0	13.5	11.3	13.2
All families	20.7	10.9	11.5	12.0	9.6	11.5
Families with lone female head	48.9	38.1	36.7	37.2	28.5	31.4
Age						
Children (<18 years)	26.5	14.9	17.9	19.9	15.6	18.5
children in lone-mother households	23.7	45.8	52.8	57.9	57.2	56.2
(…in nonpoor lone-mother households)	9.2	11.6	18.6	21.6	22.3	23.9
Elderly (65+ years)	35.2[1]	24.6	15.7	12.2	9.9	9.7
Sex						
Male		11.1	11.2	11.7	9.9	12.0
Female		14.0	14.7	15.2	12.6	14.4
Race & Ethnicity						
White	17.8	9.9	10.2	10.7	9.5	11.2
Black	55.1[1]	33.5	32.5	31.9	22.5	24.7[2]
Hispanic		22.8[3]	25.7	28.1	21.5	23.2
Geographic Location[1,4]						
Metropolitan area	15.3	10.2	11.9	12.7	10.8	12.9
Central City	18.3	14.2	17.2	19.0	16.3	17.7
Suburban	12.2	7.1	8.2	8.7	7.8	9.8
Rural	33.2	16.9	15.4	16.3	13.4	15.1
Region[5]						
Northeast		8.6	11.1	11.4	10.3	11.6
Midwest		9.6	11.4	12.4	9.3	12.4
South		17.9	16.5	15.8	12.8	14.3
West		10.4	11.4	13.0	11.8	13.5
Employment Status						
Worked full-time full-year				2.6	2.4	2.6
Worked less than FT-FY				12.6	12.1	13.5
Did not work at all				22.1	19.8	22.0

SOURCE: Tables 2, 3, 6, 7, 9, 10, 25, http://www.census.gov/hhes/www/poverty/histpov/perindex.html; Accessed June 7, 2010.
Notes:
[1] Year reported is 1959 rather than 1960.
[2] In 2008, black is measured as black-alone (not multiracial); whereas prior years include those of multiple races.
[3] Year reported is 1972 rather than 1970.
[4] 1960–2000 categories are metropolitan, central city, noncentral city (suburban), nonmetropolitan (rural); 2008 categories are: inside MSA (urban), inside principal cities (central city), outside principal cities (suburban), outside MSA (rural).
[5] Year reported is 1969 rather than 1970.

TABLE 7.4   **Selected Characteristics of the Poor, 1966–2008**

Characteristic	1966	1970	1980	1990	2000	2008
Age						
Children (<18 years)	43.5	41.1	39.4	40.0	36.7	35.7[1]
People 18–64 years	38.6	40.1	47.3	49.1	52.8	54.7[1]
Elderly (65+ years)	17.9	18.9	13.2	10.9	10.5	9.5[1]
Race & Ethnicity						
White	67.7	68.8	67.3	66.5	68.5	67.8[2]
Black	31.1	29.7	29.3	29.3	25.3	23.5[2]
Hispanic			11.9	17.9	24.5	27.6
Employment Status						
Worked at all			40.6	41.0	40.4	37.1
Worked full-time, full-year		8.7	9.8	11.6	10.1	

SOURCE: Tables 14, 15, 18, http://www.census.gov/hhes/www/poverty/histpov/perindex.html; Accessed June 7, 2010.
Notes: Some figures do not add to 100 percent due to rounding, or, in the case of ethnicity, of excluded or nonmutually exclusive categories.
[1] Year reported is 2007 rather than 2008.
[2] In 2008, white and black are measured as White-alone and Black-alone (not multiracial); whereas prior years may include those of multiple races.

it has been since then. Generally, the liberal view is that the various characteristics of the economy are to blame for poverty; the conservative view is that the poor themselves are to blame for their own condition; and the radical view is that the fundamental nature of our capitalism system keeps poverty thriving. Historical moment determines the extent to which more evidence exists for one view or the other. Over time, collectively we have changed our view of who is deserving of assistance or not, related at least in part to the state of the economy. Each of these positions is summarized briefly next.

Liberal Views—External Locus.   Liberals and progressives dispute the notion that individual behavior compels poverty but claim instead that external forces in our economy are the main cause of poverty. The poor are no different from the nonpoor; they simply lack the opportunities for education, employment, and job training. Specifically, jobs are not available in the right place, at the right time or with the right skill set. If employment opportunities were available, then the poor would take advantage of them. There is no firm evidence, the liberal perspective asserts, that government programs decrease work effort, increase illegitimacy, or promote family breakup.

Liberals emphasize that the opportunities offered to the poor must be real. Job-training programs must provide salable skills, not temporary, menial work with no future. Entry-level jobs must connect to higher rungs in the labor market, providing supportive career advancement. With lack of genuine opportunity as the root cause of poverty, the poor lack chances for success in a society and economy structured against them. Poverty is a result of the harmful side effects, the indirect costs, of a capitalist, free-enterprise economy where the pay for less-skilled jobs falls so low that even some full-time workers do not make a wage high enough to keep their families out of poverty. Changing that structure of the economy could break the cycle of poverty.

According to liberal theory, racial discrimination against blacks, Hispanics, and other minority groups and sex discrimination against women are important causes of poverty among these groups. Discrimination affects progress in school, employment choices, job advancement, wages, and housing conditions. Racial minorities and women have high poverty rates because of the pervasive discrimination they still suffer.

Conservative Views—Internal Locus.   Conservatives argue that the economy provides plenty of opportunities, is not at all as inhospitable as liberals would have us believe, and so consequently little involuntary poverty exists in the U.S. Those who wish to work and to achieve a decent standard of living can do so by taking advantage of the free enterprise system's opportunities. For those unable to work because of age, physical handicap, or other disability, sufficient resources exist from social insurance programs and private philanthropy. Healthy adults who are poor, in this view, are poor because they lack the self-discipline to work hard, save, and to delay immediate pleasures for a better future—that is, the poor must choose not to pursue the educational and employment opportunities available to everyone. Conservatives also attribute these supposed qualities of the poor to a culture of poverty. Poor people learn attitudes and behaviors from the culture around them, which teaches immediate gratification, irresponsibility, and satisfaction with a life of casual social relationships. The religious right points to the decline of moral standards leading to family breakup, drug use, unwed pregnancy, and other social disorders as key causes of poverty.

Conservatives and neo-conservatives argue that traditional government welfare programs cannot prevent or cure poverty because they do nothing to change the basic attitudinal causes of poverty. In fact, they contend, government programs have the unintended consequence of encouraging people to remain poor by guaranteeing support for this way of life. These programs encourage families to break up or not to form, by increasing benefits for additional, often illegitimate, children, and make only very weak work demands on recipients. Cheating and fraud are rampant in public assistance programs in the view of many conservatives. Policy, in turn, must be paternalistic in its delivery, forcing individuals to abide by a social contract to behave by a certain code.[5]

Radical Views—Capitalism.   Radicals on the left agree with much of the liberal analysis of the causes of poverty, but they see the roots of its family strife, unemployment, and discrimination lying deep within the American socioeconomic system itself. From a classically Marxist perspective, such radicals argue that capitalism necessitates poverty because it exists to create wealth for a small group of property owners. Poverty is necessary in a capitalist society because it provides a large pool of surplus labor to do menial and dirty tasks and to keep general wages low. Fear of the hardship and shame of poverty keeps the middle class hardworking and subservient to the attitudes and desires of the upper class. The culture of poverty is also useful to the middle and upper classes, as it offers them such outlets as gambling, prostitution, and charity work. Moreover, the violence, crime, and immorality of the poor provide a convenient focus for moral indignation, neatly deflecting attention from the corruption, injustice, and crass materialism of capitalist culture.

Welfare is publicly distributed in ways that keep it demeaning and despised, whereas handouts for the rich are dignified in hidden tax loopholes, investment credits, loans and loan guarantees, and government grants and contracts. Further, government support for the poor must remain low, but not too low as to incite revolution. Radicals scoff at the potential of government programs to create jobs and economic expansion. Such tactics will not work because poverty is built into the structure of the economy itself; only radical economic change that transforms the capitalist system can attack poverty.

Each of the liberal, conservative and radical perspectives has been dominant at some point in the history of poverty and responses to it as discussed next.

History. Discussion of social welfare has ancient roots.[6] The Greeks and Romans viewed love and charity as the highest of virtues. Ancient Judaic law called for caring for the needy: the old Testament taught that giving was a duty, and the Talmud states, "Each and everyone should be supplied with what he needs." Central to Christianity are many of the same ideas, with emphasis on good deeds and loving the less fortunate; similarly, the central Islamic text, the Koran, exhorts believers to show charity to the unfortunate. Starting in the sixth century, monasteries were the basis of social provision. By the eleventh century, the system of governance known as feudalism prevailed; although it sharply curtailed individual rights, it had a built-in system of providing for workers and their families. Medieval hospitals served as social service agencies and were often governed by monasteries and then by municipalities as they appeared in cities. From this tradition came the civic-religious link in providing for the poor. The breakdown of feudalism saw the growth of urbanization and incipient industrialization, and with them new needs.

In England, the 1601 Poor Law codified several prior statutes into one coherent law. By our standards, it allowed for harsh treatment of the able-bodied poor if they refused to work, but it provided care for the dependent poor, and situated responsibility with local authorities. The Poor Law combined both "indoor" and "outdoor" relief. It was judged to be successful at helping many needy by putting the able-bodied to work and setting children up with apprenticeships. Underlying the law were two ideas. First, some poor people were deserving and others were not; the able-bodied poor were treated punitively if they did not work, and those less able were taken care of. Second, poverty is rooted in economic problems, not individual failings. The English Poor Law firmly established *civic* responsibility in dealing with poverty because it was in the state's economic best interest to do so.

The Poor Law also provided the basis for treating poverty in the American colonies. The American colonies imported the Poor Law, locating care for the poor in local administration. The early colonies set up systems of local social welfare provision for the poor, the aged, the disabled, the blind, and so on, by adopting laws quite similar to the 1601 Poor Law. During this period, the most common procedure was to place those who could not support themselves into private homes; others were given tax relief and some grants. As in England, "sturdy beggars" were treated harshly in the New World. As Cotton Mather proclaimed, "For those who indulge themselves in idleness, the express command of God unto us is, that we should let them starve."[7] Those deemed lazy faced compulsory labor, and children were sent to families to care for them and teach them a trade. In general, caring for the poor was commonplace in the colonies, where they tended not to blame or punish the poor, at least the white poor. They provided good treatment as a civic responsibility, inspired by moral and spiritual duty.

In the latter part of the eighteenth century, during the period of the American Revolution, there was an increase in spending on poverty to deal with the rise in poverty that came from a variety of sources, including immigration; military skirmishes or men lost at sea, both of which created widows and orphans as well as disabled soldiers and refugees of war; the seasonal nature of jobs; the rise in illegitimacy, through which children became the responsibility of the state; economic hardship and depression; illness and plagues; and growing overcrowding in cities.

The Enlightenment revered reason, and the ideas embodied in the Declaration of Independence emphasized individual equality, and these pointed to the need to improve the common person's lot. Living in the New World, with its abundant resources, instilled an *obligation* to eliminate poverty—as a condition, and not just to help the poor be relatively less destitute—so that all citizens could engage in democracy. As a result, the *state* became an "instrument for advancing the welfare of the entire population."[8] Before the revolution, local civic and religious authorities dealt with poverty. After the revolution, public poor relief became entirely a secular matter at the county level.

The federal system emphasized states' rights and did not explicitly provide for centralized poor relief. As a result, states had control, and there was therefore great variability in their codes as well as flexibility to meet local needs. Without any specific state action, counties and families continued to assume much of the responsibility in caring for the poor.

The nineteenth century saw the rise of individualism and a retreat from caring for the poor. At first, independence brought little change in the social welfare system, but the rise of market-based economics and of laissez-faire philosophy in England reached America, and Americans took it even further. Also growing was the Darwinian idea that the fittest will survive, and the idea that poverty was caused by individual weakness became increasingly widespread.

There was the desire to abolish support for the poor, and to make public aid less easy to receive. Emphasis shifted to caring for the poor in institutions, almshouses, and workhouses, and those not institutionalized might receive moral assistance, but not material aid. When the Civil War broke out, care was nearly all local, mostly institutional, and there was a strong sense that poverty had individual roots and that widespread public care for the poor was not good or necessary.

The first federal effort to provide relief from poverty came in 1865, when Congress established the Bureau of Refugees, Freedmen, and Abandoned Lands, also called simply the Freedmen's Bureau. At first it was authorized to administer temporary relief during the war. Later, it aided blacks in making the transition from slavery to freedom through its wide range of functions: providing relief or employment; assisting settlement; offering educational, welfare and health services; and providing legal aid. Although the Bureau closed in 1872, it provided a crucial demonstration that the federal government could provide welfare when local care broke down; reformers pointed to it when they called for further federal involvement.

After this, some states began coordinating otherwise incoherent efforts to serve the needy, but this was still less common than private charity efforts, which also followed a similar trend toward coordination across a variety of organizations. The federal withdrawal of involvement in social welfare in the 1870s came with the initiation and growth of the "Charity Movement," which created a new set of civic organizations, the Charity Organization Society (COS). These charity groups were highly organized, they had state-level associations aimed to consolidate diverse efforts to reduce duplication of services, and they kept detailed records, marking important beginnings of public administration research. The COS workers embraced the philosophy that material aid was harmful and should not be provided. Deprivation, they believed, was a crucial incentive. Nevertheless, they thought that poverty could be alleviated via changing individual morals and behaviors. That is, the poor needed individual guidance and exposure to middle and upper class values and behavior.

The depression of the 1890s gave fresh rise to the view that the economy and not personal deficiencies was to blame for poverty. In this context and as part of the Progressive movement arose the settlement house movement, which criticized the COSs for not providing enough and stressed that government must intervene. Four settlement houses existed by 1890, 100 by 1900, and 400 by 1910, among the most famous of which are Hull House in Chicago and the Henry Street Settlement in New York City. Settlements were residences of highly educated social reformers, many of them women, who combined social service work with social reform. Their goal was to improve city life with less of a focus on the individual and more on social institutions and neighborhoods. Out of this movement came the founding of the NAACP (1909), the National Urban League, and an array of services, including day care, health care, education, public parks, and legislation that would influence housing and work conditions. Settlement Houses declined after World War I but ongoing professionalization of social work continued.

A significant event in the growth of a federal role in addressing poverty was the White House Conference (1909), which raised social work into prominence and reopened the question of a federal role in poverty alleviation. It emphasized the need for family preservation, challenging the prohibition of outdoor aid. The conference led to legislation in 1912 that established the U.S. Children's Bureau, primarily a research agency, which focused on the study of children's conditions and the protection of children. Based on her research on infant and maternal mortality, Julia Lathrop, the head of the Children's Bureau, introduced what became the *Sheppard-Towner Act* in 1918. This act established grants in aid from the federal government to the states in support of a range of child health–related programs. This was really the first modern federal effort to deal with poverty-related issues. Although the program ceased in 1929 because of physicians' opposition to government's takeover of medicine, the Act set the stage for the future relationship between the federal government and states in the provision of social welfare policy.

Between 1911 and 1919, thirty-nine states passed *mother's pension laws*. By 1935, all but two states provided legislatively-based pensions to widows with children. The establishment of mother's pensions is recognized as a crucial turning point in social policy development. Between 1909 and 1920, forty-three states adopted workers' compensation laws. With the economic crisis of the Great Depression, one-fourth of the population was unemployed, and possibly as much as half to two-thirds were considered needy. This context and the policy activity earlier in the century poised the federal government to take an increasing role in combating poverty, which it did in several robust ways. From 1933–1935 the Federal Emergency Relief Administration (FERA) gave financial relief to people in need: in 1934, 20 percent of people received relief, and over the entire decade of the 1930s, 35 percent of the public received relief assistance. Even then assistance was unpopular. President Roosevelt recognized that cash assistance could be considered "a narcotic, a subtle destroyer of the human spirit," and so *work relief* substituted for simple cash assistance. From 1935 through World War II, the Works Progress Administration, the Civilian Conservation Corps, and the Civil Works Administration created jobs at public expense.

Most notably in our social welfare policy history is the passage in 1935 of the *Social Security Act*, which combined welfare and pension programs to provide assistance to those disconnected from the labor market due to age, unemployment or disability. Despite the build-up of the welfare state during the 1930s, there was little entitlement expectation among the public. In the decades that followed, the welfare state evolved and expanded in new directions. In particular the *Great Society* (1961 to 1978) included the "*War on Poverty*," which was associated with anti-poverty programs and was most active between 1964 and 1972. New civil legislation and court rulings provided important new protections for minority Americans. Confidence in macroeconomic policy saw executives using tax cuts to stimulate the economy to higher levels of production, growth, and employment.

While the Great Society initiated no major new social insurance programs, the old ones were massively expanded through both higher benefits and larger caseloads. For example, the Social Security rolls grew sharply due to aging population. Repeated benefits increases were followed in 1972 by the indexing of benefits to keep pace with inflation. This resulted in huge wealth transfer to the elderly, substantially reducing their poverty. Similarly, unemployment insurance rolls grew sharply in the 1970s due to recessions, extended benefits voted by Congress, and more lenient administration.

On the social assistance side, cash public assistance—then referred to as Aid to Families with Dependent Children (AFDC)—liberalized and grew sharply, and important in-kind (health, food) benefits were added. The Food Stamp Program was established in 1964. The program afforded poor families the opportunity to buy food, and subsequently was reformed and liberalized in 1971 and 1977. The *Supplemental Security Income* (SSI) was established in 1972, providing income security to the aged, blind, and disabled. Welfare reforms in 1962 and 1967 allowed welfare recipients to keep more of their earnings if they work. And some important court cases liberalized public assistance receipt. During this welfare boom from 1965–1975, the AFDC rolls grew from about 4.4 to 11.4 million people due to higher benefits and liberalized procedures at the local level and driven by Community Action and the welfare rights movement.

In addition to these expansions of the welfare state, the federal role in education, training, and social services saw substantial growth. For the first time, the federal government undertook a broad range of subsidies for both public and higher education, with most of the benefits aimed at the disadvantaged. For example, the Head Start program began in 1965; and in the same year, particularly under Title 1 of the Elementary and Secondary Education Act (ESEA), new funding came about to support better education in public schools, especially for minorities and the disadvantaged. A wide variety of federally sponsored training programs developed, mostly voluntary, aimed at the low-skilled, including manpower training, youth job corps and public service employment. New social services amendments were added to the Social Security Act, including federal funding for child care among many other services. Attention to place-based initiatives grew as well, with federal programs for rural area and urban development, including community development block grants and subsidized housing assistance.

Following the Great Society's expansion of a wide variety of social supports, criticism that the welfare state compelled dependency and illegitimacy resulted in a new wave of welfare reforms that restricted assistance and tightened oversight. Conservatives had three arguments for cutting programs. First, the Federalist argument suggests that the national government should not tempt states and localities to run programs if they do not want to. This view asserts that states should initiate and design policy rather than respond to the availability of federal funds. Second, conservatives argued that social programs were failing, seizing on the modest impacts and lack of effects of employment and training and workfare programs, as documented by evaluations. To take this argument further, some noted authors—particularly George Gilder (*Wealth and Poverty*) and Charles Murray (*Losing Ground*)—argued that programs are not merely unsuccessful, but they make problems worse. In the 1980s, people began to listen to this line of reasoning. The third type of justification for cutting social programs was general opposition to *entitlement*; conservatives used moral arguments against the permissiveness encouraged by entitling individuals to receive social supports.

Conservative opposition to big government and concern for the permissiveness of welfare compelled a trend of enforcing work, and states began to experiment with reforms. By 1987, as many as forty states had developed *workfare* programs; research, however, presented a fairly negative picture of the results. In turn, a major piece of legislation was passed in 1988, the Family Support Act (FSA), which was one of the first expressions of "*civic conservatism*," that is, the idea that social rights should be secured by meeting some social obligation, such as working.[9] The FSA established the Job Opportunities and Basic Skills (JOBS) program, which required the states to set up workfare programs; required states to meet enrollment quotas and enroll welfare recipients in education or training programs; stiffened child support enforcement; and added transitional child care and health assistance for people moving off of welfare into work.

By 1994, welfare rolls covered 14.1 million people, representing 5 million families, an all-time high that represented about 5 percent of the U.S. population (see Figure 7.4). Public disdain for welfare resulted in a renewed effort to reform. Although presented as a radical shift in policy, President Clinton's vow to "end welfare as we know it" can be viewed simply as a continuation of prior policy evolution. Basing some decisions about work and time-limited assistance on academic research, the Clinton policy (which became known as the Personal Responsibility and Work Opportunity Reconciliation Act [PRWORA]) contained four conservative themes: it cut the budget by $54 billion, further devolved cash public assistance to the state level, limited the assistance teen mothers could receive, and imposed tougher work requirements. Most notably, it placed a time limit on how long one can receive assistance (at least supported by federal dollars), ending what had been an entitlement since 1935. The act, with minor

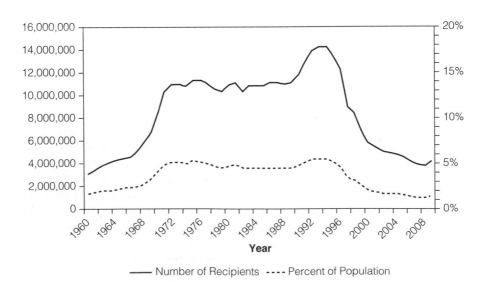

FIGURE 7.4 AFDC (1960–1996) and TANF (1997–2009) Recipients and Percent of Population, 1960–2009

changes, was reauthorized in the Deficit Reduction Act of 2005; at this writing it is awaiting reauthorization.

The Welfare State

As this brief history of social policy history reveals, dozens of federal programs provide social insurance and social assistance to Americans. They range from huge programs such as *Old Age, Survivors, and Disability Insurance* (OASDI) and Social Security, to relatively small programs such as the *Women, Infants, and Children* (WIC) nutrition program. Federal expenditures were roughly $1,140 billion in 2008 with an additional $192 billion contributed by states.[10] Administration varies by program. Many programs are joint federal–state ventures, requiring fifty different sets of rules; this state variation has implications for policy delivery and the experience of claimants contingent on state of residence. At the federal level alone, jurisdiction is divided among numerous committees in the House of Representatives and the Senate and among various executive departments and agencies. The majority of federal aid recipients benefit from two or more programs, with most receiving aid from three. The package of supports that families receive at the state level has them interacting with many different agencies and receiving assistance through varied means.

The U.S. in Comparative Perspective

Despite the extensive income support programs just summarized, the United States is not a welfare state in the way that term is normally understood. It is important to understand the difference in approach to social welfare between the United States and Western Europe. The essential feature of the European welfare state is that it aims to guarantee a generous minimum standard of life through social services, education, public assistance, social insurance, and employment programs to all citizens as a political right, not as charity.[11] In Western Europe, subsidized housing, health services, child care, employment, and other benefits are available not only to the poor, as in the United States, but to all or most citizens. They are provided largely through public programs funded by taxes. With the exception of public education, government social services in the United States, including cash public assistance, social insurance, nutrition, health care, and housing, focus on the concept of the deserving poor and therefore are based on minimum-income criteria (*means tests*) or on the recipient's previous self-contributions (as in social insurance programs). Although the means test exists in Great Britain, Sweden, France, the Netherlands, and other welfare states, it plays a far smaller role than in the United States.

The basic programs of social insurance—retirement, disability, and unemployment compensation—are similar across nations. Public assistance to the aged, blind, disabled, and children is universal, as are job training and retraining and job creation programs.[12] However, significant divergence exists between American policy and policy in other countries. Nations such as Sweden and

Germany, among others, have more extensive programs of sick leave and maternity benefits, and all have programs of family or children's allowances, which, in effect, provide assistance to poor families without the stigma of public assistance. Subsidized housing and child care for extensive segments of the population are available in Europe, providing decent low-cost housing for the poor and freeing mothers to work. Pressures in the European welfare system are building, however. Housing shortages are increasingly common, and there is a constant demand for expansion of child care facilities as more women enter the labor force. Chronic high unemployment, rising income support expenditures, and budget crises have forced many European countries to look toward reduction of welfare state spending or reorganization of programs.

What is characteristic of United States programs of income support is the mixture of public and private provision: Public health care programs *plus* employment-based insurance; Social Security *plus* private pensions. In addition, instead of directly funding support programs, American policy often works through tax subsidies, loan guarantees, and regulation of private benefit programs. Rates of participation among those eligible for public assistance are higher in Europe than in the United States. In Europe, case workers actively seek to enroll eligible people, but in the United States there is a widespread attitude that public assistance should be difficult to obtain, even for those who qualify. The United States may be more properly described as an "opportunity-insurance state,"[13] in which the focus is on making opportunities for success available to the vast majority of citizens and on rewarding those who succeed. Minimal public assistance programs partially cushion those who fail. Moreover, the United States provides assistance through a complex web of direct (Social Security, for example) and indirect (tax breaks, for example) benefits and through government partnerships with not-for-profit service agencies unique among developed nations.

This difference in approaches to public programs to assist the poor, combined with lower wage rates for full-time workers in the United States, produce higher levels of poverty than most other economically prosperous nations. As Figure 7.1 demonstrates, although cross-national comparisons of absolute and relative poverty are difficult, it appears that despite greater economic prosperity than the nations of Europe, Japan, and Australia, poverty in the United States is from 50 percent to nearly 100 percent higher than the average in such nations, depending on the measure used.[14]

Income support in both the United States and Europe extends far beyond the "needy poor" definition of programs discussed in this chapter. The modern state supports the income and the standard of living of the wealthy and the middle class to an even greater extent than it does the poor. Government grants, loans, loan guarantees, and subsidies to farmers, transportation companies, small businesses, large corporations, trade associations, and thousands of other interests help prop up the incomes of workers, managers, and owners. Income support is a way of life throughout modern nations, accounting for a good deal of the political support and legitimacy of modern governments. The policies considered in this chapter are only part of these endeavors.

In brief, the U.S. welfare state is bifurcated, with social insurance policies and programs being contributory and valued, and with social assistance programs being means-tested and generally stigmatized. The ways in which programs within each of these two tracks of social welfare policy are administered mirrors the extent to which they have political and public support. The top tier of programs tends to be federally administered, universal and respected, while the lower tier tends to involve much state discretion, is categorical and devalued. Whether separations from the labor market are compelled by internal or external forces, policy responses to dealing with poverty and income insecurity have four main purposes: to replace lost earnings, provide minimum income security, offset unavoidable expenses, and motivate work. The programs discussed in the next section do one or more of these things in responding to poverty.

CONTEMPORARY POLICY: SOCIAL INSURANCE AND SOCIAL ASSISTANCE PROGRAMS

This section describes the main social insurance and social assistance programs and policies that make up the U.S. welfare state. Generally, the social insurance programs are contributory in their funding, universal in their coverage, effective in reducing poverty, and popular among the public and politicians. In comparison, the programs that provide social assistance are categorical and means-tested in their eligibility, limited in their coverage, stigmatized in their receipt, and subsequently not well-regarded publicly or politically. Nevertheless, these are the programs that exist to provide a minimum level of well-being among those dislocated from work for a variety of reasons, and together they form a package of assistance from government.

Social Insurance

Social Security.   Originally a retirement program only, Social Security added survivors' benefits in 1939 and disability insurance in 1956. Health insurance (Medicare, covered in Chapter 8) was added in 1965. Today, Social Security and National Defense roughly tie as the two largest items of federal spending. In 2008, of the $2,983 billion in federal outlays (Table 7.5), $617 billion was Social Security and $616.1 billion was Defense (2009 estimates have Social Security at $680.5 billion and Defense at $690.3 billion). Together, these programs account for half of federal spending. Social Security covers over 95 percent of the working population, including the self-employed. Over 16 percent of the population (about 50 million persons) currently receives benefits; Social Security accounts for almost one-quarter of federal expenditures and revenues. In addition to the Social Security program covering most workers, the federal government also administers special retirement programs for federal workers, railroad employees, and veterans. These programs constitute the vast bulk of government *entitlement* spending; that is, benefits to which persons have a legal right because they meet program criteria.

240   CHAPTER 7

T A B L E 7.5   **Federal Outlays Overall and On Social Insurance and Assistance, 2008–2009, Estimated (in billions)**

	2008	2009 (estimated)
All federal outlays	2,982.9	3,997.8
Income security	431.3	519.3
General retirement and disability insurance (excluding social security)	8.9	8.0
Federal employee retirement and disability	109.0	115.9
Unemployment compensation	45.3	106.5
Housing assistance	40.6	53.3
Food and nutrition assistance	60.7	80.1
Social Security	617.0	680.5
Education, training, employment, social services	91.4	90.8

SOURCE: Computed from Table 461, U.S. Census Bureau, *2010 Statistical Abstract*, http://www.census.gov/compendia/statab; Accessed June 3, 2010. The education, training, employment, social services category includes the value of charitable contributions and education tax credits, among other items.

The program is administered by the Social Security Administration, an independent federal agency, headed by a commissioner and deputy commissioner, advised by a seven-member, bipartisan advisory board. This status and independence signify political support for Social Security and the political power of its growing number of aged recipients.

Social Security is financed by a payroll tax, in theory paid in equal shares by employer and employee. Most economists, however, believe that the burden of the employer's share is nearly always passed on to the employee in the form of lower wages. The bulk of the tax goes to two trust funds, Old Age and Survivors' Insurance, and Disability Insurance, which finance the benefits paid out of these programs. Originally set quite low, both the payroll tax rate and the wage base on which it is applied have steadily risen, from the original 1 percent each for employer and employee on the first $3,000 of wages to 6.20 percent each (for a total tax of 12.4 percent) on a wage base of $106,000 in 2010. (In addition, Medicare imposes a tax of 1.45 percent on *all* wages, without an upper limit. This portion goes to a Hospital Insurance Trust Fund, discussed in Chapter 8.) The most rapid increases have come in the last three decades.

Benefits under OASDI follow a complicated formula using the worker's previous average monthly earnings and a schedule that pays higher percentages of average earnings for lower income brackets. Thus, the highest-paid workers receive higher benefit amounts up to the maximum amount, but lower-paid workers receive higher percentages of their average wages in monthly benefits. In 2008, the average benefit for a retired worker was $1,105 per month. The maximum depends on the age of retirement; for a worker retiring at age sixty-six, the maximum was $2,346 per month. Disability benefits are calculated in a similar way. A divorced spouse (male or female) can receive benefits on a former husband's or wife's Social Security record if the marriage lasted at least ten years. The divorced spouse must be at least sixty-two and unmarried and must wait until two years after the divorce to receive benefits for the first time. Benefits and expenditures have risen rapidly with growth in the number of aged recipients, their longer life span, and liberalized definitions of disability.

Inflation is also an important factor, because benefit levels have been indexed since 1972 to increases in the cost of living through Cost of Living Adjustments (COLAs). The 2009 COLA, for example, was 5.8 percent, but given recent slow rates of economic growth, this adjustment may overcompensate for inflation and has been a topic of contention. Total OASDI expenditures were about $576 billion in 2007. It is important to note that Social Security benefits are not the only source of income for retired workers and their dependents, particularly those who have earned high wages. Private retirement plans have proliferated in recent decades, and Congress acted in 1974 to ensure retirees' rights to benefits and the financial integrity of such plans.

Unemployment Compensation. Unemployment Insurance and Workers Compensation are the other two main programs that provide social insurance. Unemployment insurance benefits and wage replacement rates vary across the states, but are generally sufficient to support the temporary unemployment they were designed for, particularly when combined with the benefits available from some unions and from other forms of public assistance. Long-term unemployment is a more serious problem, but the unemployment insurance system was never intended to handle it. In 2008, about 36 percent of the unemployed received unemployment insurance. This rate is as low as it is because of eligibility restrictions and limited benefit periods. Unemployment insurance is of most help to those with stable work histories and good prospects for finding a new position rapidly. Those with weak job skills and erratic work experience frequently find themselves ineligible for benefits. Low benefit levels and complex eligibility requirements also discourage many low-income workers from applying when they become unemployed. Although federally mandated, unemployment insurance is funded through state systems that collect funds from employers, usually via complex state-specific formulas that often preference employers with little experience laying off employees that would then collect from the system. The most recent recession has changed this, with the federal government requiring that states extend the period of eligibility, from twenty-six to ninety-nine weeks; and federal funds have been made available to the states to cover the increase in unemployment insurance payments both due to this eligibility extension and to overall greater demand.

Unemployment insurance and workers' compensation provide the supports that workers need in situations where labor market disconnections occur, be they from employment terminations or injury. Together with Social Security, these programs benefit from public and political popularity. Their contributory funding structures and generally streamlined administrative processes minimize stigma associated with claiming these benefits; nevertheless, the universal programs have meaningful redistributive properties that make them effective anti-poverty policies, despite not being viewed by the public explicitly as such. Between 2008 and 2009 federal outlays in unemployment insurance—despite it being a predominantly state-funded program—doubled in direct response to extreme need caused by recession and high and persistent unemployment.

Social Assistance.   Among social assistance programs, cash public assistance is generally thought of as "welfare." This assistance intends to help certain categories of persons whose circumstances place them in poverty. Its goal is to assist families who are temporarily unable to support themselves and to help persons who are ineligible for social insurance but need help because of age or disability. Historically, we have assumed that cash public assistance should go only to people who deserve it, that is, those not responsible for their own poverty; therefore, cash public assistance has traditionally been available to children and to adults who are aged, blind, disabled, or guardians of small children. Adults who are none of these are assumed to be undeserving and are seldom eligible for assistance.

As identified in the history section, these federal programs to assist the poor have their origins in the Social Security Act of 1935. General tax revenues pay for public assistance programs, and any person within an eligibility category may qualify to receive benefits, making these programs categorical in their eligibility. In addition, benefits are related not to previous earnings, but to present need. They are means-tested. Examples of these social assistance programs are *Temporary Assistance to Needy Families* (TANF), Supplemental Security Income (SSI), and the *Supplemental Nutrition Assistance Program* (SNAP).

Public assistance programs come in two forms: cash assistance and in-kind assistance. Cash assistance is simply a transfer of money from a government agency to an individual. In-kind assistance refers to programs in which a tangible benefit, but not cash, is given to the recipient. SNAP benefits, for example, are convertible into food but not into money, and subsidized child care pays providers part of the fee associated with day care, thereby reducing parents' out of pocket costs. Assistance to the poor also comes in the form of services. Examples are literacy training, job training, family planning, and foster care.

Cash Transfer Programs

Temporary Assistance to Needy Families.   Most people are familiar with the phrase "welfare reform," but welfare programs have been in a state of reform almost since their inception. The most recent incarnation of these reforms was the 1996 welfare reform legislation—the Personal Responsibility and Work Opportunity Reconciliation Act (PRWORA)—which accelerated devolution of cash assistance provision for families and children to the states. Under a new system of block grants to states, PRWORA ended the federal entitlement to assistance and imposed new work requirements and time limits on recipients.[15] The goals of PRWORA were: (1) to assist needy families so that children can be cared for in their own, or a relative's, home; (2) to end welfare dependency by promoting work and marriage; (3) to reduce unwed pregnancy; and (4) to promote two-parent families.

TANF replaced the former Aid to Families with Dependent Children (AFDC) program. Instead of reimbursing the states for expenditures linked to eligible individuals (as in AFDC), TANF is a block grant to the states of approximately $16 billion per year, distributed based on states' previous welfare spending. States have wide discretion in determining who is eligible for assistance under TANF and in setting various requirements for recipients. In the earlier years of PRWORA, incentive grants helped states encourage marriage, deal with fast-growing populations or high unemployment, and move welfare recipients to work.

States have a constellation of federal rules to choose from and modify to meet their own needs and interests. For example, states may deny federal TANF funds to adults who have received welfare for more than a cumulative total of five years in their lifetime or for adults who do not work after two years of assistance. States may impose shorter time limits and may exempt some of their caseload from the five-year time limit, reflecting the reality that many adults are so limited in their abilities as to be nearly unemployable. States also may deny assistance to unwed mothers under eighteen and to children born to TANF recipients. States vary substantially in their eligibility criteria, administrative practices, and choice of other rules that recipients must abide by. States are free under TANF to divert some funds from income support to pregnancy prevention, job training, or other services. There is also no guarantee that devolution of responsibility must stop at the state level. States can transfer financial responsibility to county or city governments. Some states have contracted with private businesses to perform eligibility and other functions formerly done by state employees. Recognizing that child care assistance is vital for public assistance recipients seeking to find and keep employment, PRWORA folds all major federal child care programs into the existing Child Care and Development block grant. By 2009, federal funding rose to $7 billion, which included $2 billion provided by the American Recovery and Reinvestment Act (ARRA); states must use at least 70 percent of the funds to help welfare recipients seeking work or those at risk of needing welfare.

Supplemental Security Income.   Some states have created explicit "diversion" programs as part of TANF, where they may offer families a lump sum of, say, three-months' worth of cash assistance, in lieu of not enrolling in the program for the longer term. Related to this, some states have taken their much-harder-to-serve population, those with severe problems who are unlikely to be employable in the short term, and diverted them to the Supplemental Security Income (SSI) program, which provides a cash transfer to those with disabilities. Established in 1974, the SSI program replaced the jumble of state and federal programs for the aged, blind, and disabled with a single, centrally administered program. It is the only guaranteed minimum-income program in the United States funded from general revenues. The Social Security Administration sets benefit levels, adjusting them annually for cost-of-living increases. In 2010, a couple with no other income received a maximum of $1,011 per month. An individual without other income received $674 per month maximum.

Although initial SSI recipients were predominantly aged, higher Social Security benefits and rising rates of Social Security disability reduced the aged proportion of SSI recipients to about one-third. Slightly over half of all beneficiaries are disabled adults between eighteen and sixty-four years of age. Despite the expectation of one simplified, consolidated program, SSI has turned out to be quite complicated. First, the benefits have been insufficient, with benefit levels low enough that most states supplement SSI with their own funds. Second, the federal government is not the only administrator; some states administer their supplemental programs directly. Third, SSI supplements OASDI when its payments are below SSI standards. In fact, about 60 percent of all aged recipients and nearly 30 percent of all blind and disabled recipients use SSI to supplement Social Security. Federal and state SSI expenditures totaled $41.2 billion in 2007 for 7.4 million recipients.

Earned Income Tax Credit.   First established in 1975, the *earned income tax credit* (EITC) for low-income working families has been an increasingly important form of social assistance. It was substantially expanded in 1986, and again in 1990, 1993, and 2001, and most recently under the American Recovery and Reinvestment Act. The EITC is now the largest federal, means-tested cash benefit program, and, as of 2010, twenty-two states have adopted state earned income credits as well. The federal EITC gives taxpayers a credit from the government for each dollar earned up to a certain point; the credits gradually phase out as income rises. This credit is refunded to eligible taxpayers who claim it on income tax forms. The EITC provides a benefit of anywhere from a few hundred dollars to a maximum of $5,657 in 2010 for a family with three qualifying children. This program is a very important part of anti-poverty efforts, because it rewards workers, a strong emphasis for both Democrats and Republicans. In 2010, for families with two children, a couple's earnings up to $45,373 generated a very small credit, with the largest credits going to those earning between about $10,000 and about $22,000. In 2008, over 24 million tax filers received credits amounting to $50 billion dollars.

In-Kind Benefits

Public assistance in the form of in-kind benefits now constitutes a higher proportion of public assistance than cash benefits. Medicaid (described in Chapter 8) is the largest in-kind public assistance program and in most states its eligibility is administered jointly with cash and food assistance. The in-kind programs discussed here include food and housing assistance.

Food Assistance.   The Supplemental Nutrition Assistance Program (SNAP) was established as the Food Stamp Program in 1974. Families below certain income levels receive a near-cash benefit (now in the form of a loaded debit card) that can be used in grocery stores specifically for food items. The fact that cash does not go directly to recipients reveals basic assumptions about welfare and poverty in America, rooted in the desire to see the poor adequately fed but also in a distrust of their spending habits.

The program is administered by the Department of Agriculture, which pays the entire cost of the food and almost two-thirds of each state's administrative costs. Benefits follow the price of food, the cost of a decent diet, family size, and income. Most recipients between the ages of sixteen and sixty now must be either seeking work, working an average of twenty hours per week, or in work training in order to receive SNAP benefits. PRWORA requires states to terminate food stamp benefits after three months in any thirty-six-month period for recipients not working or participating in employment programs, although states may exempt 15 percent of such recipients. States also have the discretion to align SNAP with TANF and other parts of public assistance, creating a uniform set of eligibility and work requirements.

Because eligibility guidelines differ from the income levels in cash assistance programs, many persons ineligible for the latter are eligible for SNAP. Because TANF and SSI income are counted in determining eligibility, persons in states with high TANF and SSI benefits receive fewer food stamps, and vice versa. This feature of the program tends to narrow the interstate disparities of cash assistance. SNAP is very sensitive to changes in the economy; in times of recession and unemployment the program expands.

Federal expenditures for SNAP totaled approximately $34 billion in 2008 for 28.4 million recipients. The federal government operates other nutrition programs, such as the Women, Infants, and Children (WIC) program and the school breakfast and lunch programs. WIC expenditures of $4.5 billion in 2008 covered 8.7 million recipients; the school breakfast program expended $2.4 billion for 10.6 million recipients; and the school lunch program expended $8.3 billion for 31 million recipients. Combined, these programs make major efforts to ensure the food security of our population, with SNAP being considered an essential part of our social safety net and the other programs serving children and other vulnerable, nutritionally needy populations.

Housing Assistance.   In 2008, 1.59 million people were homeless in the U.S., with six in ten of them being in shelters and the remaining four in ten living on the street.[16] The U.S. Department of Housing and Urban Development (HUD) aims not only to tackle this problem of homelessness, but also aims to help the millions of Americans who live in substandard, dilapidated, and overcrowded dwellings or who are paying too much for shelter. In 2008, 13.6 million renter households spent more than 35 percent of their incomes on housing, and 8.7 million renter households paid more than half.[17] Programs to meet housing needs include public housing, rural farm labor housing, housing for the homeless, service-supported housing, homeownership assistance, rent and mortgage subsidies, the Community Development Program, and neighborhood rehabilitation. All attempt, in one way or another, to restore urban and rural housing and to provide decent shelter for low-income persons.[18] Yet federal housing aid makes only a small contribution toward this goal.

Among the many HUD programs is public housing, which involves the federal government funding local housing authorities to build and maintain subsidized public housing units for qualified low-income individuals and families. Public housing accounts for about $7 billion dollars, covering 1.2 million housing units and 2.3 million low-income Americans.[19] Far larger are the Section 8 tenant-based rental assistance program and housing vouchers (about $17 billion), which assist about 5.5 million very low-income renters with rental certificates, rental vouchers, and moderate rehabilitation assistance.[20,21] This level of assistance means that only one in four eligible households can receive any form of housing assistance.[22]

In addition, federal policy, through the deductibility of mortgage interest payments and home loan guarantee programs, provides more housing assistance to middle- and upper-income than to poor families. Indeed, federal tax expenditures provide a wide array of benefits for the nonpoor and are much larger in magnitude.[23]

In addition to assistance with affording housing itself, the federal government also administers the Low-Income Home Energy Assistance Program (LIHEAP) to help people afford the energy costs associated with heating and cooling their residence or to weatherize for improved efficiency and lowered costs. Federal LIHEAP dollars are allocated to states in the form of a block grant, which was $4.5 billion in 2009.

Work Supports—Subsidized Child Care, Health Assistance, Employment Programs, and Other Services.   Through cash transfers, made either directly or through the tax system, and through in-kind assistance, intended to offset important costs, usually associated with work, the federal government, in partnership with the state, provides substantial work support to otherwise vulnerable households. The most important of these are health assistance (Medicaid; Chapter 8) and child care subsidies. As noted in the section on PRWORA, the Child Care and Development Fund (CCDF) provided $7 billion to states in 2009 to assist low-income families in obtaining child care in support of work, training, and education. Some of these funds must go toward improving the quality of child care and coordinating resources to serve families through an integrated child care subsidy program.

In addition to the in-kind work supports that low-income households can access, the federal government and states also provide assistance in the form of services, including, importantly, remedial and vocational job training. The primary purpose of job-training programs is to help nonworkers attain marketable skills or to retrain dislocated workers for better jobs. These programs provide funds for training welfare recipients and others in job skills. They offer grants to state and local governments for skills training, counseling, remedial education, subsidized employment, and job creation in areas with high unemployment. They also fund the Job Corps, summer youth employment, and the Young Adult Conservation Corps. Since the mid-1980s, job training has been redirected toward the private sector. The Job Training Partnership Act (JTPA) placed most job-training programs in the hands of local Private Industry Councils, constituted by business persons, educators, labor officials, and other community representatives. This has since been replaced by the Workforce Investment Act (WIA) programs, which provide training services. PRWORA directed major attention to job readiness and job training for public assistance recipients.

What's Missing

Although here we describe the welfare state as being bifurcated into the social insurance and social assistance sets of policy responses to poverty, some have made the argument that the state is actually trifurcated. What we have ignored is the substantial assistance that goes to middle- and upper-income households through either employers or the government. For example, many jobs carry with them employer-provided health insurance and benefits; and major tax benefits come to homeowners in the form of the home mortgage interest tax deduction. These are very costly benefits that raise the well-being of those who are already in a relatively favorable position in society. The amount expended in this third tier of assistance is even more substantial than what we spend to minimize poverty and provide a safety net for those more vulnerable members of society. For example, the tax revenue forgone by having the home mortgage interest tax deduction amounted to $108 billion in 2008, which is almost seven times the size of the federal TANF block grant to states.

POLICY EVALUATION: DO SOCIAL WELFARE POLICIES REDUCE POVERTY?

Growth in public assistance caseloads and associated spending during the 1970s and 1980s, as well as the media's "welfare queen" images, contributed to the unpopularity of these assistance programs among the American public.[24] One reason for that growth was demographic: as divorce and unwed childbearing rates climbed, so did public assistance expenditures. These programs grew also because of high unemployment generally characteristic until the mid-1990s. Programs designed for the working poor and the unemployed grow rapidly in such periods. This led ultimately to PRWORA's passage in 1996. Since then, public views have softened, first in response to rapidly declining caseloads and later in response to greater sympathy among the public compelled by real hardships caused by the most recent recession. In terms of their impact on the total budget, social insurance programs, which account for 70 percent of income support expenditures, dwarf public assistance. Moreover, all federal expenditures for public assistance, other than medical care and education, amounted to $322 billion in 2008, which represents 10.8 percent of the federal budget and about 2 percent of GDP. Even within public assistance itself, the relatively popular EITC and food stamps are the two largest programs. Widespread dislike of, and dissatisfaction with, public assistance in the 1990s had shifted by the turn of the twenty-first century, when caseloads appeared to have eliminated anyone perceived to be undeserving, retaining only the hardest to serve. Since the 2008 shift in the economy, the view that the economy, not personal failings, cause poverty is once again more dominant; this has resulted in broader public support for a strong safety net, since a greater number and diversity of people are now forced to access it. This section summarizes the accomplishments and criticisms of these two tiers, the social insurance and social assistance programs.

Accomplishments and Criticisms of Social Insurance

Although social insurance spending greatly exceeds spending for public assistance programs, until the late 1970s it generated comparatively little controversy. First, these programs, particularly OASDI, have a good record of accomplishing their goals. Their direct impact on the target populations of retirees, survivors, and disabled workers has been favorable. In terms of intended consequences, Social Security has achieved its goals. Moreover, because benefits are related to the self-contribution mechanism under the insurance aspect of OASDI and unemployment compensation, they are compatible with American values. Most see benefits as a return on an investment, albeit a mandatory one, rather than as a handout.[25]

OASDI and unemployment insurance have done a good job of keeping recipients out of poverty, particularly when combined with tax breaks, private pensions, and other benefits, such as SSI, Medicare, Medicaid, and food assistance, for which beneficiaries may also be eligible. Social Security helps keep the elderly poverty rate lower than the national average, making it America's most successful anti-poverty program. Social Security gives retirees, survivors, and the disabled a fair return on their investment, as most can expect to receive more in benefits than their taxes. Current retirees, especially those with lower incomes, will likely recoup their payroll tax contributions, but middle- and higher-income workers will find their contributions and benefits closer to equivalence.[26]

Despite the fears of many younger workers that the Social Security system will be bankrupt by the time they retire, Congress regularly acts to ensure its financial stability. In 1983, for example, Congress raised the tax rate and the wage base for Social Security contributions and mandated a gradual increase in the retirement age from sixty-five to sixty-six by 2009 and to sixty-seven by 2027. At the same time, it subjected to federal taxation half of the Social Security benefits of approximately one-third of retirees with the highest incomes. These provisions will keep the program solvent until the late 2030s. In the next decade, Social Security will require further adjustments to maintain solvency.

Accomplishments and Criticisms of Social Assistance

The strong economy of the late 1990s made it possible for many former welfare recipients to find work. The economy plus restrictive TANF provisions produced a dramatic decline in public assistance enrollment, and, along with it, the public's disdain for welfare and those who rely on it softened. The recession of 2001 made it more difficult for persons to find work, but strict TANF restrictions still kept enrollment falling. With the renewal of TANF in 2005, Congress kept

TANF's basic structure, but strengthened work requirements and state account-ability for job placement, made it more difficult for recipients to attend college while on TANF, and reduced treatment length for substance addictions and mental illness. The renewal also appropriated $150 million for healthy marriage and responsible fatherhood initiatives. The most recent recession has carried with it many budget crises across the states, and public assistance has been less able to minimize hardship among those affected by the poor economy than in the prior recession. But, TANF is just one of the many programs that form the social safety net in the U.S. Because there are so many social assistance programs and policies and because all aim at the general problem of poverty and its manifesta-tions in poor health, nutrition, and housing, each program cannot be evaluated separately. Rather, this section considers both particular programs and the suc-cesses and failures of public assistance as a whole.

Because of the radical differences in their perspectives on poverty and its causes, critics of various ideological stripes have different evaluations of income support, with little agreement on their impacts or outcomes, direct or indirect. Conservatives, given their belief that poverty is the fault of the poor and of mis-guided welfare spending, generally evaluate public programs negatively, though they tend to believe that PRWORA has been a success. Liberals, believing that poverty is involuntary and related to lack of opportunity, have a generally favor-able attitude toward welfare and income support programs, but find PRWORA restrictions counterproductive. Radicals see poverty programs only as bandages on a wound, neither intended to nor able to accomplish prevention or cure. It is the economic system itself, not government programs, that causes persistent poverty.

Americans are highly ambivalent about public assistance programs. Most believe that government programs are ineffective in relieving poverty and that most recipients do not deserve help. Yet a majority also are highly compassionate, believing that government should spend more money, not less, on helping poor persons with food, housing, medical care, and income.[27]

Despite these highly critical public attitudes, the welfare system has accom-plished many intended goals. First, social assistance, through its combination of cash and in-kind aid, moves many Americans out of poverty. For many unfortu-nate enough to suffer from poverty, it will be a transitory experience ending in economic health. The public assistance programs, examined in isolation, have important shortcomings and inequities, but taken together, they provide a basic minimum living standard for many of the poor. This combination effect is the reason that many liberals oppose cutting what, to some, may appear to be exces-sive spending in particular programs.

The EITC has been the most effective mover of persons out of poverty. In 2009, 6.6 million people, including 3.3 million children, were lifted out of pov-erty.[28] One estimate suggests that the poverty rate for children would be a full one-third higher than it is if it were not for the EITC.[29] It is highly effective also in reaching its target: people who work hard but on earned income alone cannot support a family. The EITC encourages single parents to enter the work force and to work more hours. At the same time, it enables some married couples to have one parent spend more time at home with the children or rewards two-parent households who work but still have low earnings. Moreover, the EITC is efficient and affordable to administer, as it uses the existing tax structure. On the other hand, the EITC has very high error rates, as it is difficult for many persons to determine whether their family situation qualifies them for EITC. On the whole, however, the EITC retains strong liberal, conservative, and popular support.

Food assistance programs contribute to improved nutrition among the poor. More than half of all recipients are children, who would have severe nutrition problems in the program's absence. Moreover, the near-poor can maintain decent living standards when economic hard times place severe restrictions on income. SNAP in particular is more than an anti-hunger program; it is now an essential part of the network of supports that provide a safety net. Housing assistance, subsidized child care and other in-kind programs also supply many basic needs while supporting work. America's great wealth makes its residual poverty shocking; even more shocking would be the extent of poverty if no public assistance programs were available. Without government programs 64.4 million Americans would be poor; with them, the number drops to 30.7 million (see Table 7.3). Public assistance is more successful than usually acknowledged in alleviating poverty, hunger, ill health, and inadequate housing. But the fact remains that, even with these programs in place, 30.7 million of our population are poor; and living under such resource constrained conditions has long-term and important consequences, especially for children.

The use of public assistance by most American families conforms to the policy's intention, to provide temporary help until jobs are found, health is regained, or the divorced or widowed are remarried. Accessing welfare is primarily an economic decision influenced by the unavailability of jobs and by prevailing wage rates. Despite widely held opinion, fraud and corruption are no more or less of a problem than in most other government programs or in private business, for that matter. Moreover, social science research consistently shows that public assistance does not produce an increase in illegitimacy or additional children as a means of receiving more money.[30]

Liberal critics obscured these successes by shifting the issue from poverty to income inequality. During the 1960s, liberal action focused on remedying absolute poverty. During the 1970s, the focus implicitly changed to an attack on inequality. Although public assistance made strides in minimizing the former, it did little about the latter.[31] Loyalty to government's responsibility to support low-income persons remains strong among progressives. However, liberals tend to confuse their strong sense of justice and compassion for the poor with the ability of public assistance to solve the poverty problem. Conservatives, on the other hand, are ideologically predisposed to oppose public assistance programs. Yet public assistance has protected American private enterprise from its own shortcomings. The very success of social assistance (and social insurance) programs in reducing poverty smothers demands for a more radical reform of the American political and economic system, as radicals lament.

Did the policy change that created TANF, in particular, improve the performance of the system of social assistance? The liberal, conservative, and radical differences in perspective on public assistance and on poverty and its causes suggest highly divergent responses to this question.

Cost and Administration.   Conservatives are generally pleased that TANF has kept low the cost of cash public assistance to mothers and children. The program's block grant feature ensures this result. SSI, EITC, and SNAP expenditures, however, continue to grow, which displeases conservatives. Yet, the total cost of all federal nonhealth social assistance is only about 10 percent of the federal budget and is dwarfed by other public expenditures in areas that are much less publicly and politically contentious. However, the total amount spent is not inconsequential, administrative expenses are high, and the multitude of overlapping programs creates inefficiency in getting funds to the target populations and numerous unintended consequences. Moreover, social assistance, especially in times of economic slowdown, just when people most need this assistance, puts a severe financial strain on some state and local governments.

The problem of administrative complexity is a serious dilemma for public assistance programs of all modern nations and an important cause of high administrative costs. Confusion and complexity are inherent in categorical and means-tested programs because hundreds of questions, forms, and regulations are needed to define categories and levels of need and to establish whether particular persons are needy and fit the defined categories. Multiply this by the determination process for other programs, add periodic rechecking of eligibility to reduce fraud and waste, and the administrative burden of these programs becomes staggering. On top of all this is the complexity of having separate rules and regulations at each level of administration: federal, state, and local.

Paradoxically, anti-fraud regulations unintentionally contribute to high error rates. As regulations to close loopholes pile up, program complexity increases. As this happens, program employees are more prone to mistakes; caseworker turnover increases, and new workers—having had less time on the job—are even more prone to mistakes. A double bind operates. Public assistance can be either lower in administrative costs and higher in fraud and mistakes, or higher in administrative costs and lower in fraud and mistakes. Low overhead and low error rates cannot be achieved simultaneously. PRWORA did not change this equation.

Adequacy of Benefits and Reduction of Poverty.   Traditionally, liberals and progressives have evaluated public assistance programs by their ability to support individuals and families in dignity (adequacy) and in their ability to reduce the number of poor persons. Poverty rates in the United States remain much higher than in comparable nations. TANF, SNAP, SSI, and other benefits barely provide any kind of decent living standard. Moreover, there are substantial gaps in public assistance coverage, particularly for single individuals and childless couples under sixty-five. Pegged as they are to the "deserving" poor, social assistance programs contribute little to relieving the poverty of these people. Few programs provide assistance solely on the basis of need; most exclude certain categories of people. The prosperous economy of TANF's first five years reduced poverty rates and masked the seriousness of the adequacy problem. The economic slowdown beginning in 2001 threw many out of work, pushed poverty rates higher, and highlighted the inadequacy of benefit levels from the liberal perspective. The more recent recession, beginning in 2008, is both deeper and lengthier, and these assistance programs have been more intensely accessed, though at a time when state governments' budgets have been in crisis, thereby limiting assistance just when it is needed most. With evident hardships extending further up the income distribution, the programs that make up the social safety net have gained somewhat wider popularity. Because of the lack of entitlement and time-limit placed on cash assistance receipt, the change to TANF likely makes the adequacy problem worse for many families, particularly during recessionary economic times.

Work.   Whatever their disagreements on cost, administration, and adequacy of benefits, conservatives and liberals, Republicans and Democrats, agree in preferring an economy and a system of public assistance that encourage work, equip persons to work, and reward work. Commentators often frame this issue in terms of dependency: the extent to which citizens depend on government programs for their basic needs, rather than being able and willing to find work to provide for these needs. In this regard, PRWORA presents a decidedly mixed picture, one that conservatives tend to interpret favorably and liberals unfavorably.

The most universally recognized problem of public assistance prior to 1996 was that, despite work requirements, there were discouragements to work (and thus encouragements to dependency) built into program structures, particularly given the effect of multiple programs and the lack of time limits. Little empirical evidence shows large effects, but some were real. Work disincentives keep recipients dependent even when work is available to them, obviously an unintended and undesirable effect. These disincentives come into play because in many programs benefits are phased out as earned income increases. Yet, in too many cases, for every dollar earned, the recipient lost a dollar or more in benefits. In addition, there were points in the benefit scale (notches) at which an additional dollar of earnings did not simply reduce benefits, but made a family totally ineligible for benefits. The loss of Medicaid for families with health problems was a particularly strong work disincentive. The work requirements, transitional health assistance, and child care support built into TANF were designed to create work incentives.

Now more than a dozen years after PRWORA, it is possible to evaluate its strengths and weaknesses in terms of work and poverty rates among former recipients.[32] TANF caseloads dropped precipitously so that fewer people rely upon government cash assistance. Evidence shows that 60 to 70 percent of adults leaving TANF worked at least some time, and the percentage of income derived from work among low-income, female-headed families rose from 30 percent of all income to nearly 60 percent. At the same time, liberal predictions of rising poverty among adults and children were not fulfilled. Poverty rates either remained the same or declined, until the economy turned again in 2008.

These good results are not all attributable to TANF. The economy of the 1990s was exceptionally strong, helping provide jobs and reduce poverty. The EITC expanded in these years as well, as did health care benefits and the child tax credit, helping to make low-income families better off. Moreover, poverty remains persistently high, and nearly 40 percent of those leaving public assistance because of exhausting their limits do not work consistently. Most have the kinds of handicapping conditions of low education, poor mental or physical health, and lack of job skills that make it unlikely that they and their children will ever escape poverty. PRWORA has made their living conditions worse.

Finally, job training and job advancement are critical if former public assistance recipients are to remain off the rolls and out of poverty. Progressives contend that too much of PRWORA's efforts have been on having recipients land in a job. After that, they are on their own. Moreover, the simple truth is that work plus the EITC often is not enough to support a family in dignity, if its wage earners have little education or job skills, and particularly if their jobs do not include health insurance and other benefits, as many low wage jobs do not. The poverty rate among working single-mother families (after government benefits and taxes) remains stubbornly high. Local food pantries continue to report an increase in long-term need for food assistance, especially among working families. As many as 12 million American families currently report not having enough food or fear of going hungry. Many more must weekly decide whether to pay medical bills or buy gas for the car to get to work, whether to buy food or clothes for the children.[33]

Equity. Inequity, in two senses, is a problem in social assistance. Horizontal inequity refers to the fact that poor persons with the same degree of need frequently do not receive the same degree of aid. Vertical inequity refers to a two-fold imbalance: the neediest often do not receive aid, and the system sometimes offers high benefits to some of the poor, while providing none for the near poor. These inequities have two main sources: benefit level variation from state to state and the categorical nature of the programs. Because each state sets eligibility and benefit levels for TANF, a poor family receives different income depending on where it lives. A family with an income of $10,000 in California receives higher benefits (even adjusting for differences in cost of living) than a family in similar circumstances with the same income in Alabama.

Additionally, families with an earned income slightly above guidelines receive no support, where others without such income are eligible for a variety of programs, the combined benefit of which makes them better off than the working family. SNAP, the EITC and other programs available to the working poor reduce some of these inequities, but substantial ones remain. Because many in-kind programs are funded at a low level, their benefits are not available to all those technically eligible. Only a fraction of those who could qualify receive housing assistance, for example.

Family and Marriage. The family and marriage goals of PRWORA have been the least enthusiastically pursued by state governments, as most bureaucrats and most Americans remain ambivalent about government responsibility to intervene in private choices about marriage and family. Liberals support this reluctance and wish to minimize attention to these aspects of welfare reform; conservatives advocate strongly for attention to these.

The goals of child care and child support are central to welfare reform. When work is required of adult guardians of children, where will good quality child care be found? Conservatives argue that existing child care funding is adequate and that strong efforts at requiring absent fathers to pay child support are needed. Liberals argue for increased child care funding, contending that good quality, affordable child care remains difficult to find. The fact of the matter is that it is cheaper to pay welfare recipients to stay at home and take care of their children than it is to pay for job training and placement and to pay for the child care of persons in low-skill jobs with minimum wages. Unless the child care available to now-working, former TANF mothers is relatively high quality, then PRWORA may produce higher rates of crime, poor education, and addiction as unintended consequences of child neglect and lack of quality supervision.

Summary of Accomplishments and Criticisms.   It is now abundantly clear that the poor are not an undifferentiated group. First, there are the elderly and disabled, for whom direct income assistance is considered to be the most appropriate form of aid. Indeed, it is this group that has been most assisted out of poverty, particularly by Social Security. A second group of the poor is single mothers with young children. To move out of poverty, they need flexible, quality child care, child support from absent fathers, health insurance, and assistance in finding jobs along with secure jobs that pay enough to support a family and offer advancement opportunities. Another group is the working poor, who are underemployed or employed only part-time or at minimum wage. Their primary need is a solid EITC, remedial education and job training for higher-wage skills, a labor market that includes good jobs with advancement opportunities, and health insurance; and they need unemployment insurance for protection when jobs run out. This complexity is the deepest challenge for the future of social insurance and social assistance programs.

FUTURE ALTERNATIVES: SOCIAL WELFARE POLICY CHANGE

While social insurance programs enjoy broad popularity and are relatively efficient and effective in meeting their goals, social assistance policies remain charged with addressing two primary intractable dilemmas: (1) the large number of children spending all or part of their childhood in poverty, and (2) the availability of jobs that lift people out of poverty. (The discussions of family demographics in Chapter 2 and family policy in Chapter 13 are particularly pertinent in this regard.)

Children and Poverty

The number of children spending years in poverty, living in squalid conditions, dependent on public assistance, and learning few job skills became one of the most striking indictments of public assistance before 1996. Public assistance had been designed many years ago as a temporary support for children and their mothers. For many, it served that purpose. For others, poverty became a way of life linked to many social problems—drug abuse, crime, poor housing, chronic unemployment—and their consequences.

One important goal of welfare reform has been to reduce nonmarital child-bearing and to strengthen family life, by extension reducing the high proportion of children growing up in poverty. By any standard, to have one-fifth of children in poverty is too much. In part for the favorable increase in mothers' labor force participation, more children are in child care and after-school programs. Child support enforcement on absent fathers has raised the percentage of support judgments and collections, though these rates remain stubbornly low. PRWORA was one marker for a reorientation of public assistance away from entitlements toward an idea of reciprocity in American social policy.[34] In return for cash assistance, child care support, increased EITC, and other supports, adults should exercise responsible parenthood—take care of their children, work to support their families, seek out job training when needed, and so forth. Families that fail in their responsibilities can expect to be sanctioned.

It is difficult, however, to say that this new reciprocity—or paternalism, as some call it[35]—has been fully developed in public policy. In fact, many states have devoted very little attention to implementing the child and family provisions of TANF, instead focusing on increasing employment and reducing welfare rolls. The states vary widely in their efforts and success in reducing child poverty.[36] Some evidence shows that low-income young children are doing better in school, but adolescents may be faring worse in terms of their criminal activity.[37] Finally, welfare rolls declined far more rapidly than the child poverty rate.

As reported in the first section of this chapter, children are disproportionately poor. One of almost every five lives below the official poverty line at any given time, and many more live in poverty for at least part of their childhood. Moreover, children are increasingly living in single-parent families, most of which are headed by lone mothers. Twenty-five percent of all children under eighteen live in such households, and about half of all children will do so at some time. Many go for years without seeing their fathers, even for short visits. A growing proportion of TANF benefits are directed to "child only" cases, meaning that the children receive aid while parents do not, either because the parents have exceeded their time on TANF, or because the child lives with grandparents or other relatives, or because the parents are ineligible for benefits because of their immigration status.

The consequences of child poverty and family breakup are severe, including poor education, teenage pregnancy, child abuse, suicide, drug addiction, and high crime rates. Moreover, poorly educated, addicted, abused, or imprisoned children have a difficult time growing up to be productive citizens. Government spending on children is not very effective, especially when compared with spending on the elderly. In 1965, government spending on the elderly was 21 percent of all income maintenance and other social welfare spending, while 37 percent went to children. By the late 1980s, spending on children was

24 percent, and spending for the elderly reached 33 percent. These expenditures lifted out of poverty 82 percent of the elderly who would have been poor without government programs. Only 32 percent of children were lifted out of poverty.[38]

Other wealthy, democratic nations have far more generous programs for children, without slighting the elderly. Most, for example, have a universal children's allowance, amounting to from 5 to 10 percent of the median wage. They also provide cash benefits to parents at the time of childbirth, as well as allowances that support a parent for taking time away from work in the first months (and in some cases years) of the child's life. Other nations generously support preschool and child care programs.

Children's advocates advance many proposals to attack the problem of child poverty and associated social problems. Reducing the tax burden on families with children finds support among both liberals and conservatives; recent tax legislation went some distance in this direction by creating a per child tax credit, providing tax credits and deductions for college expenses, and reducing the tax burden on married families. But these will do little for *poor* children unless their parents find and keep jobs with reasonable income and benefits. Cash public assistance, TANF, itself can not have a large effect on child well-being since it is merely one part of a whole constellation of policies and programs that share poverty alleviation as a goal. Given the lessons from the success of social insurance programs—their nearly universal coverage and wide popularity—policies to address the causes and consequences of poverty for children would be most effective if universal, maximizing coverage and minimizing stigma.

Employment Issues

In responding to PRWORA, many state public assistance programs focused first on those recipients most job-ready because of their education, former employment history, and motivation. These were easiest to place and to take credit for under the new PRWORA rules and expectations. Recipients who are more difficult to place because of long-term dependency, low education, drug or alcohol abuse, criminal record, or histories of being sexually abused are far more difficult (and far more costly) to work with.[39] This is doubly so because, under current federal law, all persons required to work must receive a minimum wage and be covered by employment rights, such as health and safety regulations. Moreover, the children of public assistance recipients are more likely than average to have health or behavioral problems that make it difficult for their mothers to obtain and hold full-time work, especially considering related day care needs and supply. Expenditures for training, educating, and placing such people, when it is done well, are more costly than traditional welfare.

Job training alone is insufficient to ensure work for all, as is made particularly evident in the current economic climate, where even skilled workers are being laid-off or seeing their wages cut. In poor neighborhoods, there are multiple applicants for the few jobs that open up. All the training in the world will not produce a job when no jobs are available. Job creation strategies must accompany work requirements for welfare reform to be effective. Yet there is little consensus and less experience in making more employment available in areas suffering high rates of poverty and economic decline, as well as high rates of addiction and other challenges.

Progressive and conservative welfare reformers agree that work is the best and most permanent path out of poverty. It is not clear, however, how to make that path available. Proposals run from the most extreme, cold-turkey approach on the libertarian side (abolition of all public assistance with each individual responsible for finding work in the private sector) to proposals to imitate the German system of apprenticeship, in which schools and businesses combine for three-year education and job training programs. In the middle of these extremes is reform of the current system to expand on work expectations and opportunities while also considering the role of education in reducing poverty. At this writing, the broader state of the economy is taking policy priority over additional tinkering with a policy, as re-authorized under PRWORA, that elected officials find generally acceptable.

In addition to considering employment for welfare recipients in particular, it is important to consider more broadly the hard-core unemployed and the challenges they face. Often with long-standing substance abuse problems, criminal histories, or mental instability, this small part of our population finds employment difficult. Work requirements or job training requirements that are part of TANF do not tackle these problems and therefore are unlikely to be successful. Addressing these problems is very difficult and costly.

Next, the jobs available to the those with low skills, whether they receive public assistance or not, are likely to be low paying, without such benefits as health care, and without decent possibilities of advancement. Even successful workfare programs have only marginally improved the lives of participants, in large part due to the inhospitability of the lower rung of the labor market. Even if those leaving welfare for work secure jobs paying $6 to $7 per hour, these jobs are very likely to carry with them little or no benefits, meaning that these workers must still access housing assistance, health assistance, and possibly food assistance in order to support a family. In times of economic stress, both government and charitable services are burdened not only with the long-term chronically poor but also with an influx of those with short-term needs. Neither those who escape welfare for work nor those who are working but remain poor can fully escape some dependence on government help. What happens when they lose their jobs, become sick or injured, or grow old? If perceptions of public assistance lead Americans to think that work and dependence are mutually exclusive alternatives, they will be sadly surprised.

Conclusions

Current social insurance and social assistance programs in the U.S. combine features in tension with each other. Sympathy for the plight of the elderly, widows, widowers, and children drives policy in a progressive direction; that is, toward the notion that all members of society deserve an income and sufficient economic dignity to support a decent life in a prosperous, democratic society. On the other hand, commitment to the free market and suspicion that government programs encourage dependency drive policy in a conservative direction. It may well be that recent changes, particularly in public assistance, signal not so much liberal–conservative tension as movement toward a more communitarian political ideology. Here, the focus is on opportunity and responsibility, where government programs should provide opportunities and support to persons so that they can succeed if possible on their own; at the same time, every person has a responsibility to use his or her talents to make the most of the opportunities furnished by government and the market.[40] The primary challenge is to discover what combination of public policies best enacts opportunity and responsibility with respect to income support and with respect to health care, the topic of the following chapter.

ENDNOTES

1. Lawrence R. Jacobs and Theda Skocpol, eds., *Inequality and American Democracy: What We Know and What We Need to Know* (New York: Russell Sage Foundation, 2005).
2. U.S. Census Bureau, *Income, Poverty, and Health Insurance Coverage in the United States: 2009*, Table 4 http://www.census.gov/prod/2010pubs/p60-238.pdf; Accessed November 10, 2010.
3. Diane Pearce, "The Feminization of Poverty: Women, Work and Welfare," *Urban and Social Change Review*, 11 (1978): 128–36.
4. Research by Kathryn Edin and Laura Lein shows that because cash public assistance benefit levels are well below poverty standards in most states, virtually all women receiving welfare benefits supplement their income with off-the-books work and sporadic contributions from friends and relatives. Kathryn Edin and Laura Lein, *Making Ends Meet: How Single Mothers Survive Welfare and Low-Wage Work* (New York: Russell Sage Foundation, 1997).
5. Lawrence M. Mead, *Beyond Entitlement: The Social Obligations of Citizenship* (New York: The Free Press, 1985).
6. This section uses the Trattner and Patterson histories as main sources: Walter I. Trattner, *From Poor Law to Welfare State: A History of Social Welfare in America*, 6th ed. (New York: The Free Press, 1999); James T. Patterson, *America's Struggle against Poverty in the Twentieth Century* (Cambridge, MA: Harvard University Press, 2000).
7. Walter I. Trattner, *From Poor Law to Welfare State*, 22.
8. Walter I. Trattner, *From Poor Law to Welfare State*, 39.
9. Lawrence M. Mead, *Beyond Entitlement*.
10. U.S. Census Bureau, *2010 Statistical Abstract*, Table 461, http://www.census.gov/compendia/statab; Accessed June 3, 2010.
11. See Norman Furniss and Timothy Tilton, *The Case for the Welfare State* (Bloomington: Indiana University Press, 1977); and Alfred J. Kahn and Sheila B. Kamerman, *Not for the Poor Alone: European Social Services* (New York: Harper

Colophon Books, 1977). Recent comparisons between the United States "welfare regime" and European "welfare states" are Jacob S. Hacker, *The Divided Welfare State: The Battle over Public and Private Social Benefits in the United States* (New York: Cambridge University Press, 2002); and Christopher Howard, *The Welfare State Nobody Knows: Debunking Myths about U.S. Social Policy* (Princeton: Princeton University Press, 2007).

12. This section draws on Arnold J. Heidenheimer et al., *Comparative Public Policy*, 3rd ed. (New York: St. Martin's Press, 1990), chapter 7; Richard L. Siegel and Leonard B. Weinberg, *Comparing Public Policies* (Homewood, IL: Dorsey Press, 1977), Chapter 6; and Kahn and Kamerman, *Not for the Poor Alone*.

13. Theodore R. Marmor et al., *America's Misunderstood Welfare State: Persistent Myths, Enduring Realities* (New York, NY: Basic Books, 1990), 31ff.

14. Timothy Smeeding, Lee Rainwater, and Gary Burtless, "United States Poverty in a Cross-national Context," *Focus*, 21 (Spring 2001): 50–54.

15. Two accounts of the history of welfare reform are Anne Marie Cammisa, *From Rhetoric to Reform* (Boulder, CO: Westview Press, 1998); and R. Kent Weaver, *Ending Welfare as We Know It* (Washington, DC: Brookings Institution, 2000).

16. U.S. Department of Housing and Urban Development, *HUD Strategic Plan: 2010–2015*, http://portal.hud.gov/portal/page/portal/HUD/program_offices/cfo/stratplan/ HUD_Strategic_Plan_FULL.pdf; Accessed June 10, 2010.

17. Rob Collinson and Ben Winter, "U.S. Rental Housing Characteristics: Supply, Vacancy, and Affordability," HUD PD&R working paper 10-01, January 2010, http://www.huduser.org/Publications/PDF/FinalReport_Rental_Housing_Conditions_Working_Paper.pdf; Accessed June 10, 2010.

18. For a brief but comprehensive review of U.S. housing policies, see Richard K. Green and Stephen Malpezzi, *A Primer on U.S. Housing Markets and Housing Policy* (Washington, DC: Urban Institute Press, 2003); and Sar A. Levitan, Garth L. Magnum, Stephen L. Magnum, and Andrew M. Sum, *Programs in Aid of the Poor*, 8th ed. (Baltimore: Johns Hopkins University Press, 2003), pp.102–114.

19. Center for Budget and Policy Priorities, "Policy Basics: An Introduction to Public Housing," December 2008, http://www.cbpp.org/files/policybasics-housing.pdf; Accessed June 11, 2010.

20. National Low-Income Housing Coalition, "FY11 Budget Chart for Selected HUD Programs," February 2010, http://www.nlihc.org/doc/FY11-Budget-Chart-HUD-Programs.pdf; Accessed June 11, 2010.

21. Rob Collinson and Ben Winter, 18.

22. Center for Budget and Policy Priorities, "Policy Basics: An Introduction to Public Housing," December 2008, http://www.cbpp.org/files/policybasics-housing.pdf; Accessed June 11, 2010.

23. See *Statistical Abstract*, 2007, Table 468.

24. Martin Gilens, *Why Americans Hate Welfare: Race, Media and the Politics of Antipoverty Policy* (Chicago: University of Chicago Press, 2000).

25. A thorough orientation to Social Security is the *Online Social Security Handbook*, www.ssa.gov/OP_Home/handbook/; Accessed August 20, 2007.

26. Congressional Budget Office, *The Outlook for Social Security*, June 2004, Chapter 2.

27. See Richard Morin, "A Welfare Tug of War," *Washington Post National Weekly Edition*, March 14–20, 2001, p. 34.

28. Center for Budget and Policy Priorities, "Policy Basics: The Earned Income Tax Credit," December 2009, p. 2, http://www.cbpp.org/files/policybasics-eitc.pdf; Accessed June 9, 2010.

29. Center for Budget and Policy Priorities, "Policy Basics: The Earned Income Tax Credit," 2009, p. 2, http://www.cbpp.org/files/policybasics-eitc.pdf; Accessed June 9, 2010.

30. See Ellen K. Coughlin, "Experts Add Their Voices to Welfare-Reform Debate," *Chronicle of Higher Education* (August 3, 1994): A6–A7.

31. Government tax and transfer payments have little effect on redistributing income among groups or in reducing inequality. See Patricia Ruggles, "The Impact of Government Tax and Expenditure Programs on the Distribution of Income in the United States," in Lars Osberg, ed., *Economic Inequality and Poverty* (Armonk, NY: M. E. Sharpe, 1991), 220–245.

32. These paragraphs draw upon Ron Haskins, "Welfare Reform, 10 Years Later," *Poverty Research Insights* (Fall 2006): 1–7. See also Ron Haskins, *Work over Welfare: The Inside Story of the 1996 Welfare Reform Law* (Washington: Brookings Institution Press, 2006), especially Chapter 10.

33. Griff Witte, "Off Welfare, but Back in Poverty," *Washington Post National Weekly Edition*, October 4–10, 2004, pp. 29–30; Griff Witte, "The Vanishing Middle Class," *Washington Post National Weekly Edition*, September 27–October 3, 2004, pp. 6–9; Associated Press, "More Than 12 Million Families Went Hungry," *Lubbock Avalanche-Journal*, November 20, 2004, p. D11; and Stephanie Armour, "What Recovery? Working Poor Struggle to Pay Bills," *USA Today*, June 9, 2004, pp. B1–B2.

34. Christopher Beem, "Work, Parenthood, and the Idea of Reciprocity in American Social Policy," *Focus*, 24 (Spring-Summer, 2006): 18–23.

35. Lawrence M. Mead, *The New Paternalism: Supervisory Approaches to Poverty* (Washington, DC: Brookings Institution Press, 1997).

36. Harrell R. Rodgers, Jr., and Lee Payne, "Child Poverty in the American States: The Impact of Welfare Reform, Economics, and Demographics," *Policy Studies Journal*, 35 (February 2007): 1–21.

37. Jeffrey R. Kling, Jens Ludwig and Lawrence F. Katz, "Neighborhood Effects on Crime for Female and Male Youth: Evidence from a Randomized Housing Voucher Experiment," *Quarterly Journal of Economics* (2005): 87–130.

38. Paul Taylor, "Like Taking Money from a Baby," *Washington Post National Weekly Edition*, March 4–10, 1991, p. 31.

39. Kristin S. Seefeldt, "After PRWORA: Barriers to Employment, Work, and Well-Being among Current and Former Welfare Recipients," *Poverty Research Insights* (Fall 2004): 1–7.

40. See Mark Rom, "From Welfare State to Opportunity and Responsibility (OAR) Inc.," *Policy Currents*, 11 (Summer 2001): 2–7.

RESOURCES

Books

Blank, Rebecca M., Danziger, Sheldon H., and Schoeni, Robert F., eds. *Working and Poor: How Economic and Policy Changes are Affecting Low-Wage Workers*. New York: Russell Sage Foundation, 2006.

Hacker, Jacob S. *The Divided Welfare State: The Battle over Public and Private Social Benefits in the United States*. New York: Cambridge University Press, 2002.

Haskins, Ron. *Work over Welfare: The Inside Story of the 1996 Welfare Reform Law*. Washington, DC: Brookings Institution Press, 2006.

Howard, Christopher. *The Welfare State Nobody Knows: Debunking Myths about U.S. Social Policy*. Princeton: Princeton University Press, 2007.

Levitan, Sar A., Mangum, Garth L., Mangum, Stephen L., and Sum, Andrew M. *Programs in Aid of the Poor*, 8th ed. Baltimore: Johns Hopkins University Press, 2003.

Mangum, Garth L., Mangum, Stephen L., and Sum, Andrew M. *The Persistence of Poverty in the United States*. Baltimore: Johns Hopkins University Press, 2003.

Mead, Lawrence M., and Beem, Christopher. *Welfare Reform and Political Theory*. New York: Russell Sage Foundation, 2005.

Rainwater, Lee, and Smeeding, Timothy M. *Poor Kids in a Rich Country: America's Children in Comparative Perspective*. New York: Russell Sage Foundation, 2003.

Weaver, R. Kent. *Ending Welfare as We Know It*. Washington, DC: Brookings Institution, 2000.

White, Joseph. *False Alarm: Why the Greatest Threat to Social Security and Medicare Is the Campaign to "Save" Them*. Baltimore: Johns Hopkins University Press, 2001.

Websites

AARP: **www.aarp.org/issues**

Brookings Institution: **www.brookings.edu**

Cato Institute: **www.cato.org**

Center on Budget and Policy Priorities: **www.cbpp.org**

Heritage Foundation: **www.heritage.org**

Institute for Research on Poverty: **www.ssc.wisc.edu/irp**

Manhattan Institute: **www.manhattan-institute.org/**

Research Forum on Children, Families, and the New Federalism: **www.researchforum.org**

Social Security Administration: **www.ssa.gov/SSA_Home.html**

Social Security Network: **www.socsec.org**

U.S. Department of Health and Human Services: **www.hhs.gov**

Urban Institute: **www.urban.org**

Chapter 8

Health Care: Historic Change?

Spring 2010 witnessed historic change in Washington. After nearly a century of struggle, debate, false starts, and incremental change, major health care reform legislation passed both houses of Congress and was signed by President Obama. President Obama and the Democratic House and Senate achieved what presidents Franklin Roosevelt, Harry Truman, Richard Nixon, and Bill Clinton (and their respective congresses) had failed to accomplish: significant movement toward universal health insurance coverage and the promise of substantial change in the way health care is delivered and financed.

Yet the victory occurred by the narrowest of margins in an extraordinarily rancorous political climate, following an ideological and political battle of epic scale and complexity. That the passage of the *Patient Protection and Affordable Care Act* (*PPACA*) was historic cannot be doubted. What is, however, very much in doubt at this writing (a few months after the signing) is whether the legislation will produce its intended effects. Indeed, the *survival* of PPACA remains in doubt. The national Republican Party pledged to make repeal of the new bill a major campaign issue in the 2010 elections. With the overwhelming Republican victory in the 2010 mid-term elections, it is possible (though doubtful) that by the time you are reading this chapter, PPACA will not have *made* history, but will *be* history! It is no exaggeration to say that the Obama presidency will be judged by the ultimate effect and final fate of health care reform.

The same perplexing logic and inherent goal conflicts that characterize the income support policies described in Chapter 7 plague health care policy. Indeed, an intimate connection between the two areas makes it essential to consider them together. First, high medical bills plunge many Americans into poverty. Second, the poor and the aged are more likely than the rest of the population to suffer illness and to struggle with gaining access to health care. Goals and priorities, moreover, are in conflict—pursuit of one goal (greater access to medical care for the uninsured, for example) seems to preclude pursuit of others equally desirable (long-term care insurance for the elderly, for example).

More profoundly perplexing is the fact that potential need for health care is unlimited; yet individual and social resources are finite. Health care reform will either continue and exacerbate these contradictions, or it will begin to alleviate the fundamental distress at the heart of one of our largest social systems.

ISSUE BACKGROUND: THE HEALTH CARE SYSTEM AND ITS DISCONTENTS

The Structure of American Health Care

The traditional American health care system combines public and private institutions without central planning or coordination. At the highest level of the health care profession—among physicians, dentists, psychiatrists, and psychologists—solo, *fee-for-service (FFS)* practice was the rule until recent decades. That is, the professional provider of health services established his or her own office, with perhaps one or two others sharing the same specialty, saw only his or her own patients, and charged a separate fee for each individual service performed; for example, a bill would have separate charges for injections, blood work, urinalysis, an office visit, and so forth. Institutions such as hospitals, clinics, and laboratories operated primarily on the same FFS basis. This traditional system changed in fundamental ways during the last two decades, moving away from FFS toward *managed care* systems (see below). Nevertheless, a substantial part of the system is still FFS (especially Medicare) or discounted FFS reimbursement systems. In a discounted system, FFS continues, but insurance companies negotiate reductions from typical fees with hospitals, physicians, and other providers in exchange for directing their subscribers to these providers. Medical care in this kind of environment is fragmented, difficult to coordinate for persons with multiple or serious medical conditions, and very expensive. In FFS, the economic incentives are clearly to provide more services to patients, even if they are of questionable or limited value.

Despite radical changes under way in American health care delivery, the same fragmented and expensive care continues as a legacy of the system's origins. "Managed care" emerged as a force in American health care in the 1980s as a method to hold down the increasing cost of health care. Through managed care, the federal government, employers, and private insurers attempt to hold down costs by using selective contracting; that is, requiring patients to see only certain providers, either through a health maintenance organization (HMO), a preferred provider organization (PPO), or an independent practice association (IPA).[1] Incentives to control costs are built into HMOs. Because the premiums are prepaid and providers are salaried or working for reduced fees, unnecessary or questionable services produce no additional income, only additional costs. Hospital care is not used unless clearly necessary. Physicians, who may be given bonuses if costs are kept low, have an incentive to offer preventive care and early diagnosis and treatment.

In addition to these elements, managed care introduced other novel delivery structures. One feature is the gatekeeper, a primary care physician who must see patients first and whose permission is needed for patients to see specialists, whose care is generally more costly. Utilization review is another key managed care practice; this requires some combination of second opinions before surgery or hospitalization, prior approval before a major procedure, and case management teams to coordinate all aspects of major and lengthy treatments. Along the same line are drug formularies, treatment protocols, and disease management programs (sometimes summarized under the heading of "evidence-based medicine") requiring physicians to prescribe only certain lower-cost drugs or to use proven low-cost treatments before attempting more expensive and newer treatments. These constraints generated a backlash, primarily orchestrated by physicians, against managed care. The term now has strongly negative connotations with the general public.

Although by 1999, more than 90 percent of all insured employees were enrolled in one form or another of managed care, there was scant evidence of improved quality or cost-reductions. Moreover, physicians, hospitals, and other providers have learned their way around the most restrictive elements of managed care, adding other institutional transformations that have made medical care, if anything, more fragmented, more complex, and more costly.

During the last ten to fifteen years, many states enacted restrictions on some of the most controversial managed care practices. At the same time, developments in the insurance industry following public, employer, physician, and government resistance to limiting health care choices produced substantial weakening of gatekeeping, utilization review, and other restrictive features of managed care. By the early years of the twenty-first century, the health care system seemed to be moving back toward fee-for-service and toward greater freedom for both patients and physicians, with managed care companies loosening a variety of restrictions and becoming less concerned with controlling expenditures.[2]

Delivering and Paying for Health Care

These changes have produced effects not yet well understood. As advances in medicine reduce admissions and length of stay, hospitals are closing or redirecting their missions. Outpatient surgeries and freestanding surgical units, or specialty hospitals, as well as minor care clinics (some in grocery stores or drug stores), direct care away from traditional hospital in-patient care. Thirty years ago, hospital employment accounted for two-thirds of all health care employment; now it is less than half. A more competitive hospital environment generated a wave of hospital mergers and the emergence of major hospital systems, many organized by for-profit corporations, instead of the charitable institutions that operate most hospitals. Hospitals are also developing partnerships with (in some cases even ownership of) physician practices that use their facilities. Physicians, who formerly practiced principally in small groups or solo practices, are now joining larger group practices or opting for employment at hospitals, as well as investing in specialty hospitals in order to better control their incomes and working conditions. The result is a disjointed and wasteful system of medical care that proponents of health care reform hope will be rationalized and streamlined by the new legislation.

Medical bills are paid through complicated arrangements among government agencies, individuals, and private insurers. Federal, state, and local governments provide a number of health-related services directly, for example, inoculations, health inspections, vector control, veterans' care, and epidemic control. They also operate some hospitals and other facilities and reimburse private medical providers through direct payments for services. Individuals pay for a variety of services directly, but they also pay indirectly by purchasing health insurance from private insurance companies and Blue Cross Blue Shield plans. These companies then reimburse providers for covered services, which vary widely according to the terms of particular policies. Most private insurance is purchased through employers, with the employers passing their share of premiums to employees in the form of lower wages.

The U.S. health care system absorbs a massive share of national resources. Health care expenditures, and the health care premiums paid by employers and employees, far outstrip the growth in wages or in the economy generally. Total spending from all sources was $2.4 trillion in 2008 (the last year for which we have data), a sum that amounted to 16.2 percent of the GDP for that year, an average of $7,681 for every man, woman, and child in the nation. That share of the GDP has been growing; fifty years ago, medical expenditures were less than 6 percent of GDP. Public sources now pay 47 percent of the total bill, individuals pay 12 percent directly, and private insurance picks up 33 percent of the tab.[3] These percentages, however, vary greatly with the type of service. For example, direct out-of-pocket payment by individuals for hospitalization represents less than 10 percent of the total, but direct payment for dental care represents over half.

Other Nations

The United States is unique among industrial nations in its mix of private insurance, public financing, and direct patient spending.[4] In other nations, compensation of physicians by salary or by capitation is more common. Where FFS practices do exist, fee schedules established in negotiations between the government and providers restrain the size of private fees.

There are two main types of health care systems: The central government either (1) operates a national health service, as in Great Britain; or (2) mandates universal insurance coverage through employer or other private policies plus government insurance for the population unable to obtain private insurance, as in Canada, Germany, Sweden, France, and Italy. England's National Health Service is the only health care system in the developed world that may properly be called *socialized medicine*, for in it health care institutions are government owned and operated. Specialist physicians and many other providers work for the government; only general practitioners have private practices. *National health insurance* systems, on the other hand, vary widely in the amount of government control and are not socialized medicine. For example, in Sweden, the central and local governments do not actually operate all health care programs, but they do exercise considerable influence over them; compare this with Germany, where government control is minimal.

The health care systems of developed democracies (excluding the United States) have other important features in common (notwithstanding wide differences in organization). In these nations, virtually the entire population is covered by mandatory insurance for all, or the major part, of its health needs. The only exceptions in some nations are higher income persons, who may opt out of the mandatory system and seek private health care. In the United States, however, prior to PPACA, government-guaranteed insurance covers only the military, veterans, the elderly, and some of the poor, although tax subsidies encourage it for others. Thus, gaps in U.S. health care coverage are far more substantial than elsewhere, with millions of persons lacking appropriate access to needed health care.

Insurance in other nations is generally broader than coverage by public or private insurance in the United States. Coverage for nursing home care, medicines, eyeglasses, and dental services is the norm rather than the exception. These systems often cover home health care, as in England, where health workers regularly visit new mothers and children. In Sweden and the Netherlands, social service agencies visit the elderly regularly to care for their health and other needs. In the case of children, these visits provide low-cost preventive services; in the case of the aged, they limit the need for expensive nursing home care.

Although some systems, such as those in France, New Zealand, and Sweden, employ relatively high deductible and coinsurance requirements, generally third-party payments cover a higher percentage of medical bills than in the United States. Patients have fewer out-of-pocket expenses than Americans do, and none of these nations allows medical bills to place a catastrophic financial burden on families.

Yet there are problems in these systems as well. Virtually all are facing cost escalation. Even in systems that serve all, regardless of financial status, there are inequities in access to care and in the health of different classes. Rural areas have less access to good medical care than urban locations. Most nations have introduced some elements of cost control and limitation on services. Despite more extensive coverage than the United States, costs in other nations are lower (see Table 8.1). All nations seek ways to hold down health care spending and most succeed better than the United States. There seems to be no correlation between the type of health care system and the amount of money, public and private, spent on health care. Nor is there any correlation with general levels of citizen health; indeed the population of most of these nations enjoys a health quality higher than American citizens.

Because other nations stress physicians in general practice, strict controls on hospital utilization, and comprehensive coverage, they avoid most of America's major problems. The numbers of specialists and primary care physicians are in rough balance, financial burdens from medical care are absent, and, because programs are comprehensive, access is universal. Its proponents hope that the 2010 health care reform legislation will allow the United States to reap some of the benefits of more universal systems.

T A B L E 8.1   Total Health Expenditures as Percentage of GDP (selected years)

	1970	1980	1990	2000	2007
Australia	n/a	6.3	6.9	8.3	8.9
Belgium	3.9	6.3	7.2	8.6	10.2
Canada	6.9	7.0	8.9	8.8	10.1
Denmark	n/a	8.9	8.3	8.3	9.8
France	5.4	7.0	8.4	10.1	11.0
Germany	6.0	8.4	8.3	10.3	10.4
Japan	4.6	6.5	6.0	7.7	8.1*
Netherlands	n/a	7.4	8.0	8.0	9.8
Sweden	6.8	8.9	8.2	8.2	11.1
United Kingdom	4.5	5.6	5.9	7.0	8.4
United States	7.1	9.0	12.2	13.6	16.0

*2006 data.

SOURCE: http://www.oecd.org/document/16/0,3343,en_2649_34631_2085200_1_1_1,00.html; Accessed May 25, 2010.

How Healthy Is America?

Expenditures for medical care cannot be translated directly into better health or longer life. Genetic endowment, the physical environment, social class, and behavioral choices have a larger effect on health status and longevity than does medical care. Medical technology, however, certainly keeps many persons alive and in good physical condition. Intensive care units, coronary bypass surgery, and hemodialysis, as well as immunizations, fillings of dental cavities, and antibiotics, lessen pain and prolong life for millions.

The most widely used statistics on health are encouraging. By 2006, life expectancy at birth in the United States averaged just under 78 years, and the death rate for infants during the first year of life had fallen to 6.7 per 1,000 live births, the lowest rate ever. These figures represent considerable improvement over previous decades, but they are more than matched by other nations (see Table 8.2). Even though American medical technology is the most advanced in the world, the United States ranks equal to or behind such countries as Sweden, Japan, the Netherlands, Denmark, Canada, France, England, and others in life expectancy and infant mortality. Life expectancy for the very aged in the U.S., however, is slightly above the median, reflecting an emphasis on the elderly in American health care policy. Although the United States and Canada started from the same point in the late 1960s, universal coverage in Canada seems to have produced better outcomes on most measures and at lower cost. These figures indicate that there is substantial room for improvement in American health.[5] Other phenomena point to major problems in the U.S. health care system.

TABLE 8.2   Comparisons of Infant Mortality and Life Expectancy, 2007 or Nearest Year

	Infant Mortality (deaths per 1000 live births)	Life Expectancy at Birth (males)	Life Expectancy at Birth (females)	Life Expectancy at Age 65 (males)	Life Expectancy at Age 65 (females)
Australia	4.2	79.0	83.7	18.5	21.6
Belgium	4.0	77.1	82.6	17.3	21.0
Canada	5.0	78.4	83.0	18.2	21.4
Denmark	4.0	76.2	80.6	16.5	19.2
France	3.8	77.5	84.1	18.0	22.2
Germany	3.9	77.4	82.7	17.4	20.7
Japan	2.6	79.2	86.0	18.6	23.6
Netherlands	4.1	78.0	82.3	17.0	20.5
Sweden	2.5	78.9	83.0	17.8	20.7
United Kingdom	4.8	77.3	81.7	17.4	20.1
United States	6.7	75.4	80.7	17.4	20.3

SOURCE: http://www.oecd.org/document/16/0,3343,en_2649_34631_2085200_1_1_1_1,00.html; Accessed May 25, 2010.

The perception is widespread among professionals and the public alike that, despite improvements in health statistics and advances in medical knowledge and technology, Americans are only marginally healthier now than in previous decades. Despite massive increases in health care expenditures, it is not clear that the additional benefits have outweighed the additional costs. Most Americans, although satisfied with their individual care, believe that there is a crisis in the system as a whole.[6]

If the basic ills of the American health care system are looked at generally, an overall pattern is clear: the health care system emphasizes some kinds of care at the expense of others. In particular, cure of acute medical conditions, those lasting less than three months and requiring medical attention or restricted activity, takes priority over care for chronic conditions, those debilitating illnesses lasting over three months. Expensive, high-technology, curative hospital care receives more attention than disease prevention, health education, rehabilitation services, chronic care, primary care, or public health measures.

The main problems of U.S. health care can be grouped into three categories: access, cost, and quality—problems connected in their roots and in their solution. The following paragraphs describe the three problems. The Contemporary Policy and Evaluation sections describe and evaluate federal policies designed to affect them. The Future Alternatives section describes the 2010 legislative reforms intended to fulfill the seemingly contradictory goals of broadened access, cost reduction, and high quality of care. That section also discusses emerging ethical questions in medical policy and the problem of providing long-term care, especially for the elderly.

Inequities in Access to Health Care

The Uninsured.   The percentage of the population having health insurance coverage has declined since 1980. For 2009 (the most recent data), the U.S. Census Bureau counts more than 50 million persons (nearly 20 percent of the population under age sixty-five) lacking public or private health insurance coverage and thus with serious difficulty obtaining health care services. The Great Recession of the late 2000s caused these numbers to increase rapidly. Even those living close to health care facilities, if they lack insurance, are likely to experience great difficulty in getting needed medical care. Uninsurance is a dynamic condition, with people moving into and out of insured status constantly. For some, uninsured spells are brief, with over 60 million persons going without insurance at least one month each year. However, for about 26 million persons, being uninsured lasts more than a year.[7] About 25 percent of working age adults making less than $25,000 per year are uninsured and an additional 10–20 percent have experienced a spell of uninsurance during the preceding two years. Medicaid, the federal health care program for the poor, covers only about half of the poor and near-poverty population, leaving millions of such persons without insurance. Three-quarters of those without insurance work full-time or live in families with at least one full-time worker, but whose employer does not provide insurance or who cannot afford the premiums.

Of course, health insurance is not health care, and health care is not health itself. Health *practices*, such as fitness, adequate rest, avoidance of smoking, and so forth, contribute more to life and well-being than health *care*. Yet, if illness or injury strike, medical care becomes vital to a person's health. Health *insurance* is the ticket to medical care in the United States.

Many Americans believe that persons without insurance do not go without health care, because they can receive treatment in a hospital emergency depart ment if they are truly sick. Although this is true, the care received is often too little and too late. Emergency care received when a condition has progressed beyond the initial stages is far more expensive than the basic care that could have alleviated the condition earlier. Moreover, persons treated in this fashion remain ill longer, have more disability, and experience more obstacles to productive work. In addition, uninsured persons, even when admitted to hospitals, receive less care, fewer tests and other procedures, and are dismissed earlier than insured persons with the same conditions; their death rates are substantially higher. The quality of care received by the uninsured, even when they can see medical professionals, is significantly inferior to that received by those with insurance. Moreover, the "safety net" of public hospitals, clinics, and charity care has become decidedly frayed. Competition, mergers, and financial belt-tightening have reduced the number of beds in safety net hospitals for the poor and have made it more difficult for clinics providing free or reduced cost care to remain open. Physicians and other health professionals have reduced their levels of charity care.

Lack of access has a number of dimensions not apparent from the bare statistics above. Since health insurance is so closely tied to employment, many persons experience "job lock"; that is, they are tied to jobs that they may wish to change but fear changing because a new employer may not provide insurance. Similarly, unemployed persons with health problems find difficulty securing employment, because prospective employers cannot afford to carry them on their health insurance policies. These problems are now beginning substantially to affect the middle class, and they are growing worse. Rates of uninsurance escalate in periods of economic slow-down, such as the recession that began in late 2007, when employers, particularly small businesses, lay off workers or drop insurance to save money. Employment is falling in the traditionally well-insured manufacturing sector, and growing in the service and part-time sectors, which have high rates of uninsurance.[8] These factors have other indirect effects, placing more of a burden on taxpayers, public hospitals, and employers who continue to offer insurance benefits. The direct costs of being without insurance are felt by individuals and families. The indirect costs are experienced by businesses in the form of greater absenteeism and lower productivity. They are experienced by government and taxpayers in the form of higher taxes needed to cover charity care and bad debt in public hospitals, and by health insurance policy holders in the form of higher premiums.

Disparities.   Medical care is maldistributed; that is, the areas and persons with the greatest needs for health care are not the areas and persons with the greatest access to care. Hospitals, clinics, doctors, dentists, and other health care professionals are disproportionately located in well-to-do urban and suburban areas. The residents of these areas have better access to care than do the poor and residents of rural areas. This phenomenon is particularly true for access to specialized institutions and personnel, but it is also true, to a lesser extent, for general practitioners and basic care institutions. Ability to pay rather than need determines who receives medical care.

Health care researchers in recent years have documented significant disparities. *Disparities* refer to unjustified inequalities in the receipt of health care and differences in health outcomes according to race and ethnicity, income, education, and occupation. The limited-access pattern described above contributes to the poor health and shorter life expectancy of those who are poor or live in rural communities. African American infant and maternal mortality rates are nearly twice those of whites and comparable to many countries in the Third World. The average life expectancy for African Americans is seven years lower than for whites. Nearly one-third of Hispanics and one-fifth of African Americans are uninsured, compared to about 11 percent of whites. Sixteen percent of African Americans and 10 percent of Hispanics rely on emergency rooms for their primary care, compared to 5 percent of whites. Poor children tend to be inadequately immunized and to suffer more than other children do from chronic and acute conditions, such as vision problems, low hemoglobin, upper respiratory ailments, and elevated blood lead levels; a quarter have severe dental problems. Substantial racial gaps exist in incidences of heart attack and stroke, kidney disease, meningitis, and pneumonia. African Americans are less likely than whites (even at the same income levels) to receive coronary bypass and kidney transplant surgery. The poor suffer as well from significantly higher rates of mental illness, and they have many more days of restricted activity, bed disability, and lost work than those who are not poor.[9] Thousands of rural communities have no health care professionals or hospitals. The number of medical doctors per 100,000 persons is half the metropolitan rate. Life expectancy is lower, infant mortality higher, and the incidence of accidents and chronic illness greater in rural areas than in metropolitan areas.

High Cost

Cost escalation in the medical field has been constant. Table 8.3 and Figure 8.1 illustrate this trend. Although the rate of health care inflation slowed in the mid-1990s, it resumed at a high rate by 2000 and remained well above the general rate of inflation in the economy, slowing down only when the recession struck all economic sectors in the late 2000s. However, health care spending growth remains higher than GDP growth; therefore, it will consume ever higher percentages of GDP and of federal, state, and private budgets. By the mid-2000s, nearly one-third of uninsured Americans had major financial burdens from health care costs. There is no universal agreement among students of the problem on all the reasons for cost increases or on their order of priority. Some factors, however, are commonly accepted as important.[10]

Third-Party Payments.   Third-party payers are not health care providers (hospitals, doctors, and the like) or patients, but are those who pay the charges to providers on behalf of the patients. The primary third-party payers are government (Medicare and Medicaid) and private health insurance companies. Formerly,

TABLE 8.3   Aggregate & Per Capita National Health Expenditures, Selected Years

	Aggregate ($ billions)	$ per Capita	Percentage of GDP (GNP before 1965)
1960	27.5	148	5.2
1970	74.9	356	7.2
1980	253.4	1,100	9.1
1990	714.2	2,814	12.3
2000	1,352.9	4,789	13.6
2005	1,982.5	6,701	15.7
2008	2,338.7	7,681	16.2

SOURCE: http://www.cms.hhs.gov/NationalHealthExpendData/downloads/tables.pdf, Table 1; Accessed May 25, 2010.

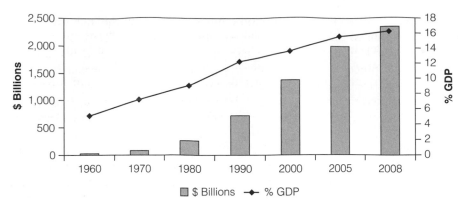

FIGURE 8.1 Health Expenditures, 1960–2008
SOURCE: Data from Table 8-3.

patients paid most health costs directly from their own resources. Now, most are paid indirectly, through privately purchased or employer-provided health insurance or through public programs. Patients, not seeing the direct cost, ask for the best in service. In general, public and private insurers do little to hold down costs, preferring the easier route of passing them on to consumers in the form of higher insurance premiums and taxes. In general, third-party payment does *not* currently contribute to health care cost increases, because the percentage of such payments has not climbed much in recent years. Moreover, the percentage of third-party payers is higher in other nations; yet they have considerably *lower* costs than the U.S.

Technology. Continuing advances in medical technology, including new prescription drugs, are the most important cause of rapidly growing spending. Diagnostic and treatment procedures—such as magnetic resonance imaging (MRI) (for exact images of internal tissues and organs), neonatal intensive care units, chemotherapy, coronary bypass surgery, and fiber-optic surgery—are tremendously expensive, because of the equipment and materials themselves and the specialized personnel needed to operate them. Yet there has been little scientific assessment of the effectiveness of most new treatments in extending life or improving well-being.[11] Some argue that they have not contributed importantly to an increased life expectancy and that they carry their own dangers of harm to the patient from risky diagnostic procedures, unnecessary surgery, and drug side effects. Others contend that such criticisms are exaggerated, and that many persons have benefited from the new procedures through longer life and freedom from pain and disability.[12]

Some new technologies do reduce costs. New drugs can treat conditions formerly requiring surgery. MRI scanners can look inside the body to make diagnoses that formerly required exploratory surgery. Such cost reductions apply, however, to the cost of individual procedures. Because they are noninvasive, doctors now perform such procedures more often than the old ones they replaced, adding to the total cost of the health care system. This is an example of technological change producing increased *service intensity*. Patients tend to receive more procedures today than they did before. New procedures do not necessarily replace old ones. Of course, the system of payment for procedures is also an incentive to service intensity. FFS rewards volume, not quality. Service intensity may, indeed, be the most important cause of higher health care costs, because it interacts with all of the other cost increase factors.[13]

Serious cost problems associated with medical technology flow from status competition among hospitals and doctors. Helicopter ambulances, open-heart surgery units, and chemotherapy units have become items of high prestige, and often hospitals in the same area duplicate technology, irrespective of actual need. The result is high acquisition costs, underutilization of equipment and staff, and the danger that medical skills will become rusty. Each patient entering the hospital helps subsidize the equipment.

Prescription Drugs. Prescription drugs claim an increasing share of the national health budget. Drug costs increased by 18 percent in 1999 and 14 percent in 2000, helping to fuel the latest round of health care cost inflation. Four factors drive prescription cost inflation: third-party payers now provide more generous drug coverage; physicians write more prescriptions per patient; new and expensive drugs entered the market in great numbers in the late 1990s; and drug companies raise the price of existing drugs. Aggressive marketing of new drugs to the public and to doctors reinforces these tendencies. Drug cost inflation highlighted Medicare's lack of prescription coverage and stimulated passage of the Medicare Modernization Act in 2003 (see "Medicare Modernization Act of 2003" section on page 279). With medicines in the research and development pipeline and with no slowing of physician or public interest in the latest "miracle drugs," pharmaceuticals will remain a major contributor to cost increases, although their rate of increase has slowed in the most recent period.

Labor Costs. Medical care remains a highly labor-intensive field, despite its high technology. The fact that medicine is the only major industry that is both labor and technology intensive is a primary contributor to its high costs. In 1972, American hospitals employed 221 persons for every 100 patients. By 1992, the number employed had more than doubled to 525 per 100 patients. American hospitals employ a higher ratio of staff to patients than any other nation. Because it has become more difficult to find registered nurses and some other medical professionals, salaries and bonuses are rising rapidly, an additional cost pressure. Interestingly enough, although there has been a dramatic rise in the number of workers per patient, there has also been a sharp increase in complaints from patients about lack of attention and care. Job responsibilities become fragmented among various levels of nurses, aides, and therapists so that effective supervision is difficult to achieve.

In addition, U.S. health care costs far more than other nations because health care professionals in the US are paid considerably more than their international counterparts.[14]

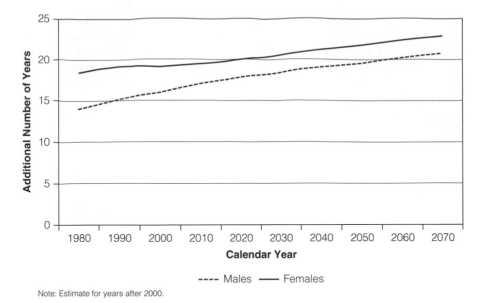

Males - - - -   **Females** ———

Note: Estimate for years after 2000.

FIGURE 8.2 Additional Years of Life at Age 65

Note: Estimates for years after 2000.

SOURCE: *www.cms.hhs.gov/DataCompendium/15_2009_Data_Compendium.asp*, Table IV.11; Accessed May 25, 2010.

Age. The aging of the population also drives health cost increases, though it is not as significant a factor as often imagined. Life expectancies at ages sixty and eighty-five began to increase significantly in 1950. By 2008, male life expectancy at age sixty-five had increased to an additional 17.4 years; for females, an additional 20.3 years. This means that the average sixty-five-year-old female will live to age eighty-five (see Table 8.2 and Figure 8.2). Presently, there are about 15 million Americans over age seventy-five; in thirty years, there will be twenty-five million. The aged have more severe health care problems than working adults or children. They also have more instances of disability and of inability to perform the ordinary activities of daily living. The elderly require substantially more acute care, more chronic care, and more assisted living care than persons of other ages. On the other hand, rates of disability among the elderly have declined, and most persons over sixty-five are in good health compared to their counterparts four decades ago.

Public Expectations. The public's exaggerated expectations of medical science, coupled with its unprecedented fear of illness, old age, and death, also contribute to the cost problems. Americans treat these as abnormal conditions, rather than as part of human life. Thus, the sick and aged increasingly use medical specialists, hospitals, and nursing homes. As the population ages, the demand for these services increases dramatically. Medical science discovers more and more "risk factors" for disease and at earlier ages, thus placing more and more people under medical care.

The public's exaggerated expectations of the health care system also account for the rise in costs, when they spend billions of dollars each year on visits to the doctor for colds, flu, and other self-limiting illnesses and for undifferentiated pains and anxieties. As a result, primary care physicians and many specialists spend most of their time providing psychological reassurance, rather than physical "curing." The increasing tendency of public and private insurance to cover treatment for mental illness, drug addiction, and other addictions means that more persons use the health care system for such conditions, also adding to the total cost.

Other. Contributions from employers to employee health insurance are non-taxable. Moreover, individuals may deduct some medical expenses from income taxes. Thus, the federal tax system encourages employees to take additional income in the form of insurance benefits and to use deductible medical services. These tax policies cost the treasury approximately $168 billion in 2009. Most of these benefits go to middle- and upper-class persons. When health care insurance was made tax deductible in the early 1950s, it was to ensure that Americans obtained health insurance; now it has the unintended consequence of driving up health care costs.

A small proportion of health cost increases is owed to medical malpractice suits filed by injured or disgruntled patients. Malpractice insurance companies raise their premiums to providers, who in turn raise their fees to consumers to cover the additional costs. Moreover, doctors practice "defensive medicine" by ordering more extensive tests and procedures than strictly necessary, in order to guard themselves against possible lawsuits. Malpractice, however, has been exaggerated as a reason for the high cost of health care, contributing recently to less than 10 percent of health care inflation. Physicians and the public often attribute to "defensive medicine" tests and procedures that would have been performed anyway because of the desire for absolute certainty in diagnosis and because of "service intensity." However, malpractice insurance increases in certain regions have driven some specialist physicians to relocate or to abandon the practice of medicine altogether, a contributor to access and quality problems.

Although there is a widespread assumption that immigrants, legal and illegal, are a major cause of the rising cost of health care, such is not the case. The cost of providing care to immigrants is significantly lower than to U.S. natives, although immigrants are more likely to have health care visits that are uncompensated.[15]

Quality of Health Care

Health statistics are improving, and most Americans are satisfied with their personal health care. American medical technology and health care innovation are the best in the world. Yet, fear of high health costs, possible loss of insurance, and increased complexity of health care leave Americans feeling uneasy. Formerly convinced that the *quality* of health care was uniformly high, Americans are discovering a different reality.[16]

First, the focus of American medicine on developing and applying new technologies in drugs, diagnostic tests, and surgical procedures produces a service intensity that not only increases cost, but also produces a greater likelihood of medical errors that harm patients. Even though the *percentage* of errors is low, the large number of procedures per patient produces a high *number* of errors. In 1999, the Institute of Medicine shocked the nation with an estimate of up to 100,000 hospital deaths per year resulting from medical errors. The Institute followed up in 2001 with another report recommending substantial changes in American medicine to reduce unacceptable quality problems. Even if, as some experts allege, the number and magnitude of medical errors have been exaggerated, such indicators point to serious concerns. Moreover, there is no single federal agency responsible for monitoring the quality of American health care. Responsibility is divided among a wide variety of federal, state, and private actors.

Second is the severe problem of uninsured Americans and unequal access to care, discussed above. It is difficult for Americans to claim to possess the highest quality of care in the world when such a high proportion of the population lacks access to it and suffers unnecessary disability, pain, and death.

Third is the focus of the American system on sickness, not health. Although we do very well in curing life-threatening conditions and treating trauma, we do not do well in providing basic prevention and wellness services. These failures produce lower quality of life and health.

A fourth quality problem, linked to the first three, is overspecialization among physicians. Primary care physicians, that is, family doctors and general practitioners, now constitute a small proportion of American physicians. Cardiologists, neurosurgeons, urologists, and other specialists dominate the medical profession. In 1950, two-thirds of all physicians were general practitioners; today, less than one-fourth practice primary care. In other nations, the percentages are significantly higher.

Serious consequences flow from the predominance of specialists.[17] Lack of primary care physicians may help account for the rather poor performance on measures of infant mortality and life expectancy relative to those of other developed nations. Such measures are more sensitive to high-quality routine care than to sophisticated, exceptional procedures. Overspecialization also contributes to the high cost of medical care, because specialists charge more and use hospitals more than do general practitioners. It leads to poor coordination of care and confusion about prescriptions. Areas with a large number of specialist physicians per capita often have poorer health outcomes than less well-endowed areas. American physicians are by far the most well compensated in the world, particularly among specialists.

An additional problem, especially for the quality of hospital care, is the looming shortage of nurses. Many nurses retire early because of the stress of the job and for other reasons. Other nurses leave hospital-based practice for the less stressful and more predictable hours of physician offices or home health or private duty nursing. U.S. nursing schools are not able to keep up with the demand for new nurses, principally because of the shortage and low pay rates for nursing instructors. During the 1990s, one solution was to import nurses from Africa, India, and the Philippines. Since September 11, 2001, however, visas for international nurses have been far more difficult to obtain, and these areas have become a less reliable source of recruitment.

CONTEMPORARY POLICY: HEALTH CARE
FOR THE POOR AND AGED

The federal government has long provided direct medical care to active duty military personnel and veterans. Beginning with the establishment of the National Institutes of Health (NIH) in 1937, the federal government has supported biomedical research. In addition to NIH, the National Science Foundation, the Department of Health and Human Services, and the Department of Agriculture also fund research. Between 1950 and 2008, federal expenditures for health research and development increased dramatically from $160 million to nearly $34 billion, accounting for over half of the nation's health research spending.

In the mid-1960s, the volume and complexity of federal health legislation increased dramatically, and expenditures exploded. Medicare and Medicaid, the most important programs, were enacted in 1965 after years of debate. The degree of government involvement with the nation's health care system has risen since then in an attempt to address the issues of access, cost, and quality of health care. The prevailing assumption, frequently challenged by conservative health policy advocates, is that the free market cannot efficiently or fairly allocate medical resources. The conditions for an effectively operating market (see Chapter 3) are not sufficiently present, a concept known as "*market failure*." In the case of health care, market failure derives from barriers to entry of competing providers (principally through medical licensure requirements), inequality of information between buyers (patients) and sellers (health care providers), the large presence of not-for-profit hospitals, nursing homes, and other institutions, the high degree of uncertainty and fear that surround medical decisions, and other factors related to the presence of insurance.

Medicare

Congress designed *Medicare* as a supplement to Social Security for elderly persons, who have more extensive medical needs and expenses than the general population.[18] Medicare aims to protect this population against the risks of medical disaster. Approximately 46 million persons benefit from Medicare coverage, which consists of four parts: hospital insurance (Part A), medical insurance (Part B), Medicare Advantage (Part C), and prescription drug coverage (Part D). Part A, hospital insurance, covers a broad range of hospital and post-hospital services, subject to some deductibles and coinsurance. (A deductible is a set dollar amount that a patient must pay directly before insurance benefits begin. Coinsurance is a percentage of the bill that a patient must pay directly after meeting the deductible.) For a given benefit period, beneficiaries pay a deductible for hospital care set at the approximate cost of one day of hospital care, $1,100 in 2008, after which Medicare pays the cost of the first sixty days in the hospital. Patients pay coinsurance of $275 per day for days sixty-one to ninety, and $550 per day for stays beyond ninety days. To encourage early discharge from expensive hospital care, Medicare covers certain types of post-hospital care, such as skilled nursing facilities and home health service. Beneficiaries pay $138 per day from twenty-one to one hundred days in a skilled nursing facility. Thereafter benefits cease. Medicare does not pay for ordinary nursing home or routine home care, but it does cover hospice care for terminally ill patients.

A special payroll tax finances Part A of Medicare. Both employer and employee pay a tax of 1.45 percent of the employee's total wage. In addition to the aged, hospital insurance since 1974 has covered persons with end-stage renal (kidney) disease and disabled persons, if they have been entitled to Social Security disability payments for at least two consecutive years.

Medical insurance, (Part B), is a voluntary insurance program for persons age sixty-five and older. Monthly premiums were $110.50 in 2010. (Recipients with taxable incomes over $85,000 single or $170,000 joint return pay higher premiums, up to $354 per month for the highest income groups.) These premiums cover 25 percent of the total cost of Part B; general tax revenues pay for the remaining 75 percent of expenditures. The premium is so low that over 90 percent of the elderly elect to buy coverage. Part B covers physicians' services, outpatient hospital services, some home health, and other medical services. After a yearly deductible of $155, Medicare pays 80 percent of allowed charges (the maximum fees that the government specifies) for most covered services. Physicians who accept Medicare fees and bill the program directly receive more rapid payment, and patients are responsible only for the 20 percent coinsurance. Physicians not accepting assignment may charge higher fees, but no more than 115 percent of the Medicare-approved fees, and they must collect directly from patients, who then claim Medicare reimbursement themselves. Medicare Advantage, (Part C), is a managed care option that combines both Parts A and B (and sometimes Part D) into one contract with an insurance company for all covered services, plus other services that such plans may offer. Recipients may choose to enroll in a Medicare Advantage Plan instead of the traditional Parts A and B, and premiums vary by plan design. Part D, the prescription drug plan created by the Medicare Modernization Act (MMA) of 2003, allows coverage of outpatient prescriptions. Its base monthly premium was $31.94 in 2010, and it contains a complex set of co-payments.

Many of the elderly in traditional Medicare (those not in Part C) retain private insurance coverage from their previous employers or choose to purchase private health insurance to cover those parts of their care not covered by Medicare Part A or B. These private choices are referred to as *medigap* policies. Federal law regulates coverage and rules for such policies. Elderly persons whose low income makes them eligible for Medicaid are automatically covered by Medicare in most states, which have elected to "buy in" to the program by paying the recipient's premiums, deductibles, and coinsurance. Persons with both Medicare and Medicaid are "*dual eligibles.*"

Medicare Modernization Act of 2003.   Forty years ago at Medicare's creation, prescriptions were an inexpensive and relatively minor part of medical care. Now they are expensive, front-line medicine. Medicare's lack of drug coverage became a heavier burden each year, especially for those without coverage from a previous employer and unable to afford medigap plans that include prescriptions. Originally, Medicare paid for drugs only as part of in-patient care. Many of the aged, especially those with major prescription needs, had high and increasing out-of-pocket expenditures because of deductibles and coinsurance, averaging $2,200 per year, an enormous burden for low-income seniors. Numerous seniors failed to take all the drugs prescribed for them, because they could not afford to fill the prescriptions.

In late 2003, Congress passed and President Bush signed the *Medicare Modernization Act*. The Act's centerpiece is an out-patient prescription drug benefit. Risk-bearing private insurance plans offer voluntary drug coverage, either as stand-alone plans or as part of Medicare Advantage. Medicare beneficiaries select among the competing plans annually. The standard benefit plan in 2010 has 25 percent co-insurance up to $2,830 paid by beneficiary and plan. However, coverage then ceases (a coverage gap or "*doughnut hole*") until co-payments have reached $4,550, after which drug coverage kicks in; this time with 5 percent co-insurance. All the figures are indexed to medical spending growth. Moreover, each Medicare Advantage plan and each pharmacy benefit provider has multiple variations of coverage and premiums, making enrollment choices very difficult. Low-income recipients receive a special subsidy to help with premiums, deductibles, and co-payments. The coverage gap does not apply to them.

Although the new prescription coverage is technically voluntary, various provisions make it difficult for seniors to turn down, even those who already have adequate coverage. Medigap policies, for example, may no longer provide drug benefits. Still, the complexity of the new arrangement, not to mention the expense of premiums, co-pays, and coverage limits, is likely to frustrate many. At the same time, co-pays and gaps in coverage mean that many middle- and upper-income retirees receive little or no advantage over their prior coverage.

Medicare Costs.   The costs of Medicare have been prime contributors to health cost inflation. Medicare costs rose from $224 billion in 2000 to $500 billion in 2009. Figure 8.3 shows the increases in costs since the program's beginning. The reasons for this growth are clear. Growth in hospital costs, physician's fees, drug prices, and technology discussed above are the prime causes. Moreover, because the proportion of the elderly is growing and they are living longer, the increases in beneficiaries and years covered contribute substantially to cost escalation. In the most recent period, care of recipients with chronic conditions such as diabetes, hypertension, and arthritis, has accounted for more of Medicare's growth than hospital-based treatment of acute illnesses such as heart attacks.[19]

Congress took action in the 1980s to change the way Medicare pays hospitals and physicians. These policy changes slowed Medicare's rate of growth, but not its overall tendency. Medicare first replaced its system of reimbursements to hospitals with a system of prospective payments. Instead of reimbursing hospitals

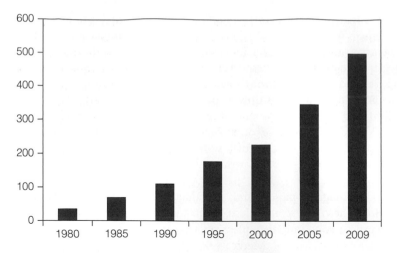

FIGURE 8.3   Medicare Benefit Growth ($ Billions)

SOURCE: Katherine R. Levit, *et al.*, "National Health Expenditures," *Health Care Financing Review*, 13 (Fall 1991), Table 3, and http://www.cms.gov/DataCompendium/15_2009_Data_Compendium.asp; Tables I.1 and II.10; Accessed May 27, 2010.

for their claimed "reasonable costs" for patient care, as in the past, the *prospective payment system* (PPS) utilizes a fixed scale for treating nearly 500 different conditions (Diagnosis-Related Groups, or DRGs). The hospitals have incentives for cutting costs and making sure that only necessary services are given to patients, for if their costs are higher than the set fee for their treatments, they must still accept the DRG-established fee as payment in full and may not charge the patient the difference. On the other hand, if their costs are below the PPS payment, they keep the difference as profit.

Hospitals responded to these changes by moving many procedures from an in-patient to an out-patient basis and developing satellite clinics, skilled nursing facilities, and home health agencies to perform many procedures formerly covered in the hospital. This change is partly a reflection of new technology, but also a response to the fact that out-patient procedures were not subject to PPS. When spending for these forms of care grew in the 1990s, Congress responded by directing the federal agency responsible for administering Medicare (and Medicaid), the *Centers for Medicare and Medicaid Services (CMS)*, to develop and implement prospective payment systems for outpatient, skilled nursing, rehabilitative, and home health treatments.

Medicaid and private insurers also have implemented prospective payment systems. Yet these systems have important limits. Hospitals faced with declining revenues place subtle and not-so-subtle pressures on physicians to discharge patients more quickly. Additionally, the expansion of DRGs forced some hospitals to close unprofitable departments. Private insurers now work increasingly hard to cut their costs and have clamped down on hospitals' ability to "cost shift" Medicare losses to private patients. In turn, this forced hospitals into rapid restructuring and, in some cases, into severe financial difficulty. Some failed, leaving communities without local hospitals.

Congress also reformed the way in which Medicare reimburses physicians. There is an annual cap on Medicare physician payment increases, the so-called "sustainable growth rate (SGR)," and a new scale of reimbursement called the "resource-based relative value scale" (RBRVS) is in effect. Over time, the primary care specialties, such as family practice and internal medicine, saw reimbursement rates increase, while surgeons, anesthesiologists, ophthalmologists, and other specialists saw their rates rise more slowly or, in some cases, even decrease. The intended effect was to encourage more use of lower-cost primary care and less of high-cost specialists, as well as to provide incentives for physicians to enter the primary care fields.

Universally acknowledged flaws in the sustainable growth rate formula have produced chaos in physician payment schedules and widespread physician dissatisfaction with Medicare. Over the last decade the formula, if it had been applied, would have *reduced* Medicare payments to doctors (a 21 percent reduction in FY2010, for example). Because of physician resistance to reductions and fears that doctors would cease accepting Medicare patients, Congress has suspended the formula each year, but not changed it. Therefore, by the time of the health care reform debate in 2010, fixing the SGR was estimated to have cost over $200 billion (for ten years). Since that much money would have forced PPACA over the limit of $1 trillion (ten years), Congress did not include a SGR fix in the legislation, leaving physician payments in limbo at the time of this writing.

Medicaid

Medicaid is a public assistance program funded out of general revenues. Like TANF (reviewed in Chapter 7), it is a federal–state program with benefits varying among the states. States must cover SSI beneficiaries, those who would have been qualified for AFDC under pre-TANF rules, and certain other poor persons, particularly young children and pregnant women. The states must cover all children in families with incomes below the poverty line. In addition, they may choose to cover children in families with incomes up to 185 percent of poverty and other "medically needy" persons as defined by state law. Because of state variations in definitions of eligibility and difficulties in enrolling eligible persons, the proportion of the poor actually enrolled varies by state. Nationally, fewer than half of the poor and near-poor receive Medicaid coverage. By 2014, however, under PPACA, these Medicaid coverage rules will change considerably.

To receive Medicaid funds, states must offer certain basic medical services without cost to the patient. Depending on the state's per capita income, the federal government reimburses 50 to 80 percent of the costs for these services, which include inpatient and outpatient hospital services; physician's services; prenatal care; laboratory and X-ray services; home health services; skilled nursing; nursing home care; treatment of physical and mental defects in those under twenty-one; and family-planning services and supplies. Additionally, states may include other services for which the federal government will reimburse a proportion of costs. Optional services include clinical services, dental care, physical therapy, drugs, dentures, and eyeglasses. All states offer some optional services.

The states can "buy in" to Medicare for elderly Medicaid recipients by paying Part B premiums. The reverse is also true, as many poor Medicare recipients also are eligible for Medicaid, particularly for nursing home care and other services not covered by Medicare. About one-fourth of all Medicaid recipients are supplementing Medicare, and Medicaid costs reflect this, with over 40 percent going for nursing home and intermediate care. Medicaid supplies nearly half of all nursing home revenues. Although the aged, blind, and disabled are only 25 percent of Medicaid recipients, their care accounts for 70 percent of the program's cost. Less than one-third is expended on children, their mothers, and other nonaged, nondisabled recipients.

Just as with Medicare, the costs of Medicaid exploded far beyond original estimates, growing 200 percent between 1980 and 1993, accounting for two-thirds of all public assistance spending by the mid-1990s. This explosive growth severely strained state budgets. Combined federal and state expenditures were about $400 billion in 2009 for over 55 million recipients. Figure 8.4 shows the program's growth in federal and state costs. Medical inflation and the high costs of nursing home care for the impoverished elderly and disabled account for most increases. In recent years, the large number of persons without medical insurance strained local public hospital budgets, for state law often mandates that they provide indigent health care on an emergency basis. Local governments faced with these bills pressured state governments to make more persons eligible for Medicaid, thus passing part of the costs on to the federal government. The recession of the late 2000s also made increasing numbers of persons eligible for Medicaid.

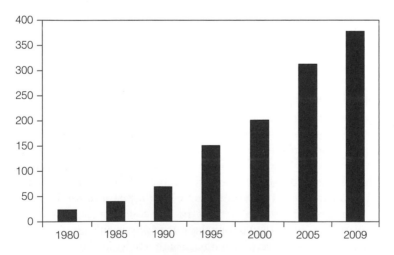

FIGURE 8.4 Medicaid Benefit Growth ($ Billions)

Note: Combined federal and state expenditures for years indicated.

SOURCE: Katherine R. Levit, *et al.*, "National Health Expenditures," *Health Care Financing Review*, 13 (Fall 1991), Table 3; Aaron Catlin, *et al.*, "National Health Spending in 2005: The Slowdown Continues," *Health Affairs*, 26 (January/February 2007), Exhibit 4, and Christopher J. Truffer, *et al.*, "Health Spending Projections Through 2019: The Recession's Impact Continues," *Health Affairs*, 29 (March 2010), Exhibit 4.

State Children's Health Insurance Program (SCHIP)

Children are the one group of uninsured for which it is easiest for legislators of both parties and all ideological stances to show sympathy. The Balanced Budget Act of 1997 (BBA) established a federal block grant to the states, which could use funds to expand Medicaid to children not presently eligible, or they could use it to establish a separate child health insurance program. States plans must meet minimum federal standards and receive approval from the Department of Health and Human Services. (See Chapter 2 for discussion of block grants and their conditions.)

This law intended to cover as many as half of the estimated 10 million children who were without insurance in 1997. By 2009, about 8 million children were enrolled. States created seamless application forms for Medicaid and SCHIP and began extensive programs of outreach through schools, churches, health fairs, shopping centers, and the mass media. These efforts intend to help parents to know about the availability of these federal programs for their children and to make it easier and less bureaucratic to enroll them. Late 2007 saw a major political battle over SCHIP renewal between the Democratic-controlled Congress and President Bush and many congressional Republicans. Congress wished to renew the program, expand its eligibility to children in families up to 300 percent of the poverty level and double the spending. President Bush vetoed the renewal as too expensive and too generous in eligibility. With the election of Barak Obama and a Democratic Congress in 2008, SCHIP was renewed and expanded in February 2009, now spending approximately $14 billion annually.

Other Federal Programs

Though Medicare, Medicaid, and SCHIP account for most public health expenditures and for nearly one-fifth of the entire federal budget, there are other important federal health programs designed to attack the problem of access.

Thousands of Federally Qualified Health Centers and other federally funded systems of rural, urban, and migrant clinics serve 17 million persons annually, primarily low-income and uninsured. Approximately 1,200 Community Health Centers are a major part of this effort, receiving special appropriations from Congress worth about $2.0 billion per year. Both the 2009 economic stimulus bill and the 2010 health care reform legislation appropriated significant funds for expanding the number and capability of Community Health Centers.[20] In addition to the system of local public hospitals, they are the central "safety net" health care institutions for the uninsured. The federal government also funds three health-related block grants to the states: Maternal and Child Health Services; Alcohol, Drug Abuse, and Mental Health; and Preventive Health Services. Through its spending on medical research and education, the federal government helps to support the medical and allied health schools that train physicians, nurses, and other medical care providers. Medicare and Medicaid pay teaching hospitals nearly $10 billion per year in Direct Medical Education and Indirect Medical Education funds to help train new resident physicians and other health personnel. In addition, there are special programs aimed at training providers for rural and other underserved areas, particularly the National Health Service Corps, the Disadvantaged Minority Health Improvement Act of 1990, and the Health Careers Opportunity Training Program.

POLICY EVALUATION: HEALTH CARE AT THE CROSSROADS

When policy analysts evaluate health care policy in terms of its intended goals, a mixed picture emerges. Federal programs have helped to train thousands of health care providers and to fund path-breaking research. U.S. health care, for acute life-threatening conditions and injuries, is superb. Medicare and Medicaid have reduced the financial burden of health care for the elderly and poor and addressed inequitable distribution of care by lowering financial barriers to medical care. Yet burdens remain for much of the population, and serious problems of access persist. The cost escalation in health care continues unabated. Quality of care is good, but not as good as it should be.

Health statistics have improved continually, and government support of medical research, federal training programs for health workers, and public financing of medical care for the aged and poor have assisted this advance. Infant mortality, for example, has declined more than 50 percent in the last twenty-five years. Deaths from heart attack, high blood pressure, and stroke are down substantially, and deaths from most major diseases are decreasing in the forty-five to sixty-four age group, meaning longer and healthier life. Medical research has developed chemotherapies for cancer treatment, artificial joints, computer-aided imaging, and electronic fetal monitoring. Medical professionals and the public know far more today about the hazards of smoking, environmental pollution, and poor diet. Yet the American health care system is far more successful in delaying the onset of death from acute illness than it is in relieving the effects of chronic conditions, such as diabetes and arthritis, or in providing preventive services. The United States lags far behind the rest of the developed world on most health status measures.

Medicare and Medicaid

Successes.   Medicare and Medicaid are responsible for some of the most dramatic gains in health.[21] Most people see physicians regularly, though gaps between poor and nonpoor still persist. More than 45 million persons each month benefit from Medicaid and a similar number from Medicare. These two programs pay for about 18 million hospital stays per year, and about 42 million persons receive physician services annually. Over four million receive home health services.

Measures of health also show improvement for the poor and aged. Data are not available on death rates by social class, but data by race show that age-adjusted rates fell 10 percent for whites and 13 percent for African Americans and others between 1965 and 1974, the years immediately following the implementation of Medicare and Medicaid. Infant mortality declined in this period by 38 percent for nonwhites and 31 percent for whites. The 1980s and 1990s continued declines in death rates from diseases particularly afflicting the elderly. Medicare and Medicaid achieve these results with extremely low administrative costs, less than 2 percent of benefits paid for Medicare and less than 5 percent of expenditures for Medicaid, a result far better than private health insurance carriers.

Problems. Medicare and Medicaid, however, have failed to do all that their sponsors hoped and have led to increasingly high costs. Both programs have, moreover, some structural flaws that inhibit their ability to deal most effectively with the major problems in health care. Access to health care remains a problem, along geographical, racial, and income lines. Large differences in death rates, life expectancy, and infant mortality persist. Because of state variations in eligibility definitions, half of the poor are not covered by Medicaid. Burdensome qualification procedures keep millions of persons from receiving benefits for which they are otherwise qualified. Some states, because of cost increases in Medicaid, have placed limits on coverage or have reduced eligibility.

Gaps in coverage exist within the Medicare program. It has no dedicated long-term care component; therefore, it is highly restrictive on nursing home and home care. Elderly persons who need this care indefinitely, unless they are well-to-do, must "spend down" their financial resources until they are poor enough to qualify for Medicaid. Medicare pays only about 45 percent of the health costs of the aged. The rest must come from Medicaid, out-of-pocket spending, or privately purchased "medigap" insurance.

Structural problems also inhibit the effectiveness of Medicare and Medicaid, preventing them from accomplishing all their goals. They contribute to cost escalation in health care by underwriting the most expensive forms of care. Medicare regulations allow its most generous payments for acute hospitalization; Medicaid pays nearly half of all nursing home costs and has largely financed the expansion of that industry. Medicare costs remain very high, placing severe pressure on both the Hospital Insurance Trust Fund and the federal budget. Its financial problems parallel those of Social Security (described in the previous chapter), but are more imminent and more severe. The Trust Fund is projected to be safe only for the next ten years, and the retirement of the "baby boom" generation beginning in 2011 will put extreme pressure on Part A. Finally, Medicare's structure largely reflects the practice of medicine and methods of insurance coverage prevalent in the 1960s when the program was created. FFS predominates, and acute care is more richly rewarded than preventive or chronic care.

State governments have been reeling under the burden of the rapidly increasing Medicaid costs. These costs and problems in state health care for the indigent led many states to work toward reform of their Medicaid programs.

Federal government spending for health care concentrates on the elderly, to the neglect of children and others. To some extent this concentration is necessary. The elderly need more health care. Yet the consequences of poor pre-natal and postnatal care for mothers and their children are serious and long term. They produce weakened general health, decreased learning ability and poor per-formance in school, and decreased motor skills, resulting in poorer employability.

An additional structural problem in Medicaid is that many physicians and dentists refuse to accept Medicaid patients because they must then legally accept the Medicaid fee schedule as full payment. The Medicaid fee structure varies by state, but is about two-thirds of Medicare (which itself is significantly lower than private insurance fee levels) for the same procedures. The result is a barrier to care even for those low-income persons with Medicaid.

Questioning the Health Care System

Beyond the challenges facing particular government health care programs, the American medical system faces challenges to its very direction. From the political left come charges that the health care system discriminates against rural residents, low-income persons, and racial minorities. According to this view, persons in these groups are less healthy than others because they are powerless, unable to control or to gain equal access to quality health care. Medicare, Medicaid, and other programs have alleviated conditions only marginally. They point out that one of the most important trends of the last decade has been the entry of for-profit corporations into the health care industry, especially managed care orga-nizations, outpatient treatment centers, and specialty hospitals. The growth of for-profit health care, the decline of public hospitals, and the new emphasis on cost cutting have the potential to reverse the gains made in health care for low-income persons. Hospitals and specialty outpatient facilities compete for paying patients through advertising and special services. The medically indigent patient, even when covered by Medicaid, is not a source of profit, and such patients may be turned away to overcrowded, declining public clinics or hospitals, or to nowhere at all, if public facilities are not locally available. These trends produce severe financial pressure on the "safety net" of public and nonprofit hospitals and clinics, placing their survival in doubt. For these reasons adherents of the political left believe that the primary impact of public programs has been to aid the wealthy providers of health care. Liberals, therefore, stress greater federal regulation of the health care industry and removal of financial barriers to access by enacting comprehensive national health insurance.

Conservatives and neo-conservatives find no hope in regulation. The medi-cal market, they argue, is not truly competitive. Making it more competitive would produce efficiencies that will lower the rate of cost increase and serve patients better. The political right charges that the regulated system penalizes both professionals and the productive public. Excessive government intervention leads to lower medical standards and higher costs. Medical decisions should be left in the hands of the professionals qualified to make them. If government were to cease regulating the medical market and subsidizing third-party payments, they believe that consumers' freedom of choice, coupled with the availability of alter-native types of health insurance, would make the market more competitive and less costly. Let the current market-driven changes have a chance to work, they argue. They favor the growth of health savings accounts and "consumer-driven health plans" and strongly oppose government-mandated health insurance coverage.

Another group of critics contends that the principal problems of health are the fault of an overemphasis on medical care. More funding, they argue, should go toward the environmental causes of ill health. The great advances in health and life expectancy made early in the last century came through immunizations, inoculations, and public health measures, creating a more sanitary environment. Comparable gains likely will not come through cancer and heart research and treatment, through preventive medicine, or through increased spending on doctor, hospital, and nursing home care. Rather, progress will come from attending to cancer- and other disease-causing agents in the workplace, air, and water. Society knows what many of these are and should devote its resources to removing them and preventing their entry into the environment. Environmentally induced cancers, lung diseases, kidney diseases, and other ailments are already costing billions of dollars for health care and lost work time. Expenditures to reduce their causes would be prudent investments in health and economic productivity.

Accompanying environmental concerns is the notion of preventive self-measures for personal health. The greatest determinants of premature death, apart from individual genetic makeup, are behavioral, followed by socioeconomic status, and environmental conditions. Inadequate medical care is responsible for only 10 percent of premature deaths.[22] The greatest potential for improving health and extending life may lie within the personal control of the individual, which can add years to life through basic health habits, such as regular exercise, moderate alcohol consumption, not smoking, and regular sleeping and eating patterns. The obesity and diabetes "epidemics" that receive so much attention beginning in the mid-2000s are a perfect example of structural problems in health care. The medical system of physicians and hospitals generally treat only the *results* of adult and childhood obesity—diabetes, hypertension, heart disease, and so forth. It is the family system, education, the media, transportation, electronic gadgets and many other social phenomena that will have to take the lead in addressing such problems, according to this perspective. Therefore, greater public investment in social prevention strategies is more likely to have a benefit than investment in medicine's treatment of preventable diseases.

Individual control also appeals to those who distrust the medical establishment and turn to "alternative medicine" practices, such as herbal remedies, acupuncture, and massage therapy. Patients often find in these practices the individual, holistic concern that often seems missing in conventional medicine.

Progressives who emphasize these ideas also strongly support government programs of occupational safety and health, strict controls on disease causing chemicals, efforts to clean up the environment, and anti-obesity campaigns. Government's responsibility for public health cannot be avoided, as the H1N1 (or "swine flu") outbreak of 2009 demonstrated. Without strong public health measures and good individual health practices, the cost of health care based on acute, curative medicine will be unaffordable in the future.[23] Moreover, worries about bird flu mutating into the next worldwide influenza pandemic, and the potential of terrorists to use biological weapons, strongly support a far greater investment in public health infrastructure, according to these advocates.[24]

Conservatives, on the other hand, point to individual responsibility, arguing that the choice of whether to practice good health habits is essentially outside government influence and that personal risk-taking is not an appropriate area for strong government action. But society even now ends up paying for individual decisions adversely affecting health through Medicare, Medicaid, public hospitals, and increased health insurance premiums. Surprisingly, however, preventive medicine itself does not seem clearly to lead to reduced medical costs, and preventive measures can have serious externalities. Lifestyle factors may be used to deny insurance or raise premiums; health screening may be used to deny or terminate employment or promotions.[25]

FUTURE ALTERNATIVES: RESHAPING A COMPLEX SYSTEM

In late March 2010, President Obama signed historic legislation that will (unless modified or repealed in the next few years) create major changes in response to the problems outlined above. The politics surrounding the writing and final passage of the Patient Protection and Affordable Care Act and the accompanying budget reconciliation bill, the *Health Care & Education Reconciliation Act*, were the most intense in recent memory. (The pages to follow will refer to these pieces of legislation as "Reform.") The political polarization was profound, and the Reform debate contributed in no small measure to the rise of the Tea Party Movement. Reform evoked intense political, philosophical, religious, and moral beliefs. The entire episode proved the wisdom of the assessment by political scientists David Blumenthal and James A. Morone:

> Major health care reform is virtually impossible: difficult to understand, swarming with interests, powered by money and resonating with popular anxiety. The first key to success is a president who cares about it deeply. Only a president with real commitment will invest in such a dangerous and risky venture. It costs time, energy, and political capital. This is no arena for half-hearted efforts.[26]

As Reform unfolded, there were indeed no half-hearted efforts by supporters or opponents in Congress, interest groups, or the public.

Summary of the legislation will consider Medicare Reform; widened access to insurance, including Medicaid; quality improvement; controlling spiraling cost increases; ethical controversies, such as abortion and embryonic stem cell research; and financing long-term care for an increasingly aging population. See Box 8.1 for an implementation timeline of major Reform provisions.

Box 8.1   Timeline of Health Care Reform Provisions

Between 2010 and 2013, a series of interim changes go into effect to prepare for the major adjustments in health care policy that will take place between 2014 and 2020. The descriptions of these provisions are much abbreviated here. For full descriptions, see the sources cited in note 26.

2010
- High-risk insurance pools to provide affordable coverage for uninsured persons with significant medical problems.
- Health insurance plans must cover dependent children up to age 26. Such plans cannot deny coverage for children with preexisting medical conditions.
- Temporary reinsurance program to help companies continue coverage for early retirees (age 55–64).
- Insurance companies barred from placing lifetime or annual limits on coverage.
- Phase-out of Medicare prescription coverage "doughnut hole" provides a $250 rebate to seniors who fall into the gap. The refund increases each year until 2020, when the "hole" is fully closed.

2011
- Annual fee imposed on pharmaceutical companies.
- Chain restaurants and vending machines must disclose nutritional content of their food.
- Medicare makes 10 percent bonus payments to primary care physicians.
- Medicare Advantage payments frozen at 2010 levels.
- Voluntary long-term care insurance program begins.
- Funding increases for community health centers.

2012
- Payment rates for Medicare Advantage plans decline.
- CMS tracks hospital readmission rates and enacts financial incentives to reduce preventable readmissions.
- CMS enacts payment reforms by encouraging creation of Accountable Care Organizations and other pilot programs that encourage higher quality, more efficient care.
- Nonprofit health insurance co-ops compete with commercial insurance.
- Special fees imposed on various parts of health care industry.

2013
- Medical expenses deduction limit on income taxes increase from 7.5 percent of taxable income to 10 percent.
- A 2.9 percent excise tax is levied on sale of medical devices.
- Medicare payroll tax increased for high-income earners (individuals above $200,000 and married couples above $250,000). Medicare tax also imposed on investment income.
- Insurance company paperwork to be standardized.
- Medicaid payment rates for primary care physicians increased to same level as Medicare payments.

(continued)

B o x 8.1   *(Continued)*

2014
- State-based insurance exchanges open.
- Premium credits and cost-sharing subsidies available to help persons afford insurance.
- Health plans cannot exclude adults with preexisting conditions or charge such persons higher premiums.
- Individual mandate requires most citizens and legal residents to buy insurance or pay a fine.
- Employers with 50 or more employees who do not offer coverage and who have employees buying insurance on the exchange with government subsidies, pay a fine.
- Insurance companies begin paying a fee based on market share.
- Medicaid expands to all individuals under age 65 with incomes below 133 percent of federal poverty level.
- Medicare and Medicaid Disproportionate Share (DSH) payments to hospitals decreased.

2015
- Medicare creates a physician payment plan rewarding quality of care rather than volume of services.

2018–2020
- Excise tax imposed on employer-provided insurance plans that cost more than $10,200 per individual or $27,500 for a family (2018).
- Medicare prescription coverage "doughnut hole" is completely eliminated (2020).

Reform and Medicare

As described in the Evaluation section, the Medicare program in 2010 faced significant challenges, especially how to finance the program when the baby boom generation begins reaching age sixty-five in 2011.[27] Reform was not designed primarily to address Medicare's problems. However, since Medicare is such a large program and because its policies affect all parts of the health care system, policymakers could not leave Medicare out of the new law.

Congress had three alternatives to make Medicare solvent as part of the new health care system. First, Medicare could preserve its present structure, but continue to squeeze payments to physicians, hospitals, and other providers. This approach by itself it would not generate savings sufficient to restore solvency. Second, Medicare could keep its present structure, but payroll taxes could be raised on present workers to fund the Hospital Insurance Trust Fund. In addition, Part B premiums could be increased, especially on higher-income Medicare recipients. In principle, such tax and premium increases could fund Medicare indefinitely if they were set high enough. Third, the age for becoming eligible for Medicare could be increased from sixty-five to seventy-seven (or even higher). This would parallel increases in Social Security eligibility. Such a measure makes a good deal of sense for that reason; yet, without guaranteed health insurance coverage for all Americans, an age increase would produce a higher number and percentage of uninsured persons than present unacceptable levels.

In the Reform, Congress, against strong Republican resistance, adopted a combination of strategies one and two plus other measures designed to restrain the growth of Medicare spending. It did not act to raise the age for eligibility. (Medicare strategies that rely primarily on delivery system reform and quality improvement, although they have important financial implications, will be discussed below.) Other changes were not focused on costs or quality, but on reforming aspects of the 2003 MMA that weighed heavily on seniors. In particular, Reform sets in motion a ten-year process gradually to close the MMA's "doughnut hole." By 2020, Medicare prescription coverage will be much simplified. Seniors will pay 25 percent of all prescription costs until they reach a "catastrophic" threshold; after that, the co-pay will be 5 percent of prescription costs.

Major changes are in store for Medicare Advantage. Democrats believe that its payment structure results in overpayment to insurance companies offering this product, with these companies receiving more than they would under traditional, fee-for-service Medicare. Therefore, in 2011, changes will begin in the payment structure, such that spending per beneficiary under Medicare Advantage will come more into line with traditional Medicare spending per beneficiary. This change is estimated to decrease payments by 12 percent and produce $132 billion in Medicare savings over ten years. Insurance companies will respond by increasing Advantage premiums to enrollees, and the growth of these plans will slow or even cease, favoring the traditional Medicare model.

Savings in Medicare will be achieved in other ways as well. As more people come to be insured under the Reform provisions described below, hospitals, clinics, physicians, and other providers will see fewer uninsured persons and will absorb fewer financial losses associated with the uninsured. Therefore, Medicare will gradually decrease its inflation updates to their fee schedules. This is a continuation of the traditional strategy of funding Medicare by squeezing providers. These adjustments, however, are quite modest in historical terms and will likely be offset by higher revenues from other insurers.

Medicare will see additional revenues from changes in premiums. First, high income individuals (incomes over $200,000 per year) and married couples (over $250,000 per year) will see their Medicare Part A premiums rise during their working years from 1.45 percent of income to 2.35 percent. Also, an estimated one million Medicare beneficiaries (individuals with incomes over $85,000; and couples with incomes over $170,000) will see their Part B and Part D premiums increase.

In addition, beginning in 2011, Medicare recipients will not have to pay any out of pocket costs for a variety of preventive services (annual exams, screening tests, assistance with smoking cessation, and the like).

Reform and Access to Insurance

Deep ethical and political disagreements surround the question of universal access to health care. At its most basic, the question is whether there is or should be a right to health care. Closely tied to a right to health care is the question of whether the right, if it exists, is an equal right. Those who argue that there is a right to health care and that it is an equal right (primarily persons on the left of the political spectrum) support expansion of health insurance to cover all citizens fully.

Such advocates base the right to health care on the principle that health is a requirement for a decent life, equally as important as food, clothing, shelter, and political and civil freedom. Because law and policy guard these aspects of life, they should guard health. Those who need health care because of injury or illness deserve to get it. Government has the responsibility to see that all persons, insofar as humanly possible, have access to the care needed to preserve health. Justice demands that government act to secure the right to health care for all citizens. This position largely prevailed in the 2010 Reform. Those who oppose this position contend that the Anglo-American constitutional tradition recognizes political and civil rights (such as freedom of speech and the right to a trial by jury), but it has never recognized rights to the public distribution of economic goods, such as food, health care, and shelter. Government may, indeed, provide these for citizens, but not as rights to which all have a claim. They are given as charity or as services. They also argue that this form of charity is already available to uninsured persons, because they have the right, under federal law from the 1980s, to receive treatment in a hospital emergency department for injuries or illnesses.

Proposals for major reform of American health care to create universal access have emerged approximately every twenty years starting in the early 1920s. Since the passage of Medicare and Medicaid in 1965, major legislative debate focused on the issue of whether the United States should follow the European lead and develop a comprehensive federal insurance scheme covering the major health needs of the entire population. The decline of employer-based coverage since the 1980s; the growth of managed care; the increased cost of premiums and of medical treatment, and the fragmentation of health care interest groups opened a window of opportunity for reform toward universal coverage in the early 1990s.[28] President Clinton's reform proposal, the *American Health Security Act*, aimed to guarantee health care insurance to all citizens. The ultimate failure of the Clinton Plan and all other health care reform in 1994 doomed comprehensive health care reform for the rest of the 1990s. The political ascendance of conservative Republicans in the early 2000s blocked major public insurance expansion.

By the election of 2008, the issue of expanding access to insurance was once again prominent on the political agenda. During the primaries and the general election, Democratic and Republican presidential candidates advanced significant proposals. With the election of Barak Obama and a Congress with a very strong Democratic majority, the stage was set for the Reform ultimately produced in 2010.

In general, Congress had only three options to reach universal or near-universal insurance coverage: a "single-payer" system, universal employment-based insurance, and individual purchase of health insurance. Each of the three options must include a mandatory feature if health care access is truly to become universal. Absent mandated coverage, lower-income workers, relatively healthy young workers, and some higher-income workers will opt out of coverage.

Failure to cover all would continue the pressures that have created a situation of one in seven uninsured in 2010.

Single-Payer.   In light of the complexities of the current system of public and private insurance, some policy advocates favored a complete restructuring of American health insurance. This restructuring, known as the *single-payer plan*, would provide public health insurance to every person as a right of citizenship. Health providers would still be private; government would not take over private hospitals or physicians' practices. But such a program would eliminate all private insurance, as well as Medicaid, in favor of a national or state-administered single health insurance program. This program would be financed by a system of payroll taxes, supplemented by other government revenues. It would vastly simplify administration. Patients would have complete freedom of choice among physicians and other providers, and the public system would reimburse such providers for all covered care at the same rate.

Because such a plan would be so highly public and because it would work such fundamental change in the entire system, it had little support in 2010, although opponents of Reform continually characterized any government mandate to purchase insurance as a "government takeover" of health care, equivalent to a single-payer system.

Universal Employment-Based Insurance.   This approach would have required the least change from the current system, in which over 60 percent of workers and their families already obtain health insurance through their employers. Legislation to modify the current system to create universal coverage would require that all employers offer health insurance to their employees, both full-time and part-time, with some choice of insurance plans. Employees would have to accept one of the offered plans. Both employer and employee would have to make a percentage contribution to the cost of the insurance, usually specified as an 80 percent to 20 percent ratio. Because many employers and employees would have great difficulty affording the coverage, the federal government would create subsidies for low-income workers and for businesses with low-wage scales.

In most variations of this scheme, Medicare and Medicaid would be retained in order to provide coverage for those who do not work because of age, disability, or inability to find work. Alternatively, Congress could create a new public program for such persons or for workers who might be exempt from the mandate. This idea came to be called the "public option" during the 2010 debates. Such a combination of public and private insurance would ensure that all Americans have health insurance. There were many variations of this approach in 2010, and many Democrats supported them strongly.

Mandatory Individual Insurance Purchase.   Ironically, the third approach, usually associated with conservatives and Republicans, evolved during the 2009–2010 debates into the "Obamacare" reform that congressional Republicans in both houses unanimously opposed! Reliance on markets has been the reform of choice for conservatives for many years. They are skeptical of group health insurance, whether provided by government or employers. One analogy could be automobile insurance. All states have laws requiring drivers to purchase a minimum insurance policy in order to protect themselves and the general population, but the states allow wide latitude for citizens individually to purchase policies above the minimum from whatever private companies meet legal qualifications. In the same way, health insurance could be divorced from employment and left to individuals to determine their own needs, as long as everyone purchased a basic minimum policy for themselves and their families. Proposals along these lines formed the main Republican alternative to President Clinton's 1993 health care reform proposal, as well as forming the heart of the 2006 Massachusetts health care reform signed into law by then-Governor Mitt Romney, a Republican candidate for president in 2008, who disavowed that very approach during his run for the Republican presidential nomination!

Although these principles appeal to conservatives, they did not in 2010 favor a government mandate to buy health insurance. Instead, they advanced incremental proposals that, they believed, would expand coverage and reduce the number of uninsured by using principles of freedom of choice without requiring health insurance purchase. A prominent proposal on their agenda was expansion of *health savings accounts* (HSA). Health savings accounts are individual tax-free savings plans used to cover medical expenses. They can be set up by employers or purchased on the individual insurance market. Customers purchase a high-deductible insurance policy at relatively low cost for coverage of very expensive illnesses or accidents. Ordinary medical care is paid for out of tax-favored saving accounts. Republicans argue that this encourages people to conserve on medical care, using it only when necessary, thus slowing the rising cost of health care and making it more affordable.

Republican proposals also included using the income tax system to provide health insurance vouchers in the form of refundable tax credits or tax deductions to assist low-income persons to purchase individual health insurance policies or HSAs (a feature of the eventual Reform). Persons without insurance would receive government subsidies of a few thousand dollars per family per year to purchase insurance. The system of private health insurance companies would remain in place. Employers would not be required to provide or purchase insurance for workers, but small businesses would be encouraged to band together into voluntary "association health plans" to obtain better rates from insurance companies. Consumers would make choices of insurance among the most cost-effective plans. Republicans also favored malpractice reform to hold down cost increases. The 2010 Reform made a small nod in this direction, funding a variety of state-based malpractice reform demonstration projects.

The States and Health Care Reform.   During the debates, many congressional Republicans argued that states should be the foundation of health care reform. Prior to 2010, some states enacted insurance market reforms to help small employers pool their risks in order to obtain insurance and to create risk pools for the hard-to-insure. Some states, most notably New York, moved to a more radical insurance reform, replacement of experience rating of insurance premiums with community rating.[29] Experience rating, used by most commercial insurance companies, sets higher premiums (or even denial of coverage) for groups with older or sicker members, thus making it more likely that they will lose coverage from inability to pay. Community rating charges the same (or nearly the same) premium for all groups, spreading the costs of older and sicker members among all the insured. Community rating would make it possible for some of the uninsured to afford coverage, but would raise rates for all groups, thereby driving others out of the market, as has been the experience in New York. Modified community rating, along with an individual mandate that would prevent younger and healthier persons from dropping out of the pool, is a basic feature of the Reform of 2010.

It is difficult, however, for states to carry the burden of health care reform without federal guidelines and requirements, such as those in the Reform. ERISA (the federal Employee Retirement Income Security Act of 1974) forbids states from regulating self-insured health care programs and from mandating a standard benefit package. Courts have interpreted ERISA to forbid states to enact employer mandates on self-insured firms. In a desire to escape regulation, more and more employers (especially large companies) have turned to self-insurance. Therefore, states find it difficult to enact comprehensive reform. Despite these obstacles a few states, Massachusetts most notably, enacted reforms in recent years to expand coverage to all their citizens. The Massachusetts plan, fully implemented at the end of 2007, combines employer and individual mandates, plus state regulation, to guarantee coverage to nearly every state resident. The federal Reform legislation eventually enacted adopted this framework.

The harsh reality is that the states lack the financial flexibility to lead the drive to cover the uninsured. The recessions of 2001 and 2008 underscored this truth, as one state after another imposed either enrollment limits or sliced provider reimbursements in Medicaid and SCHIP in order to restrain accelerating health care spending.

Access under 2010 Reform.   Congress designed the Reform legislation with multiple strategies unfolding over nearly ten years. There were a couple of reasons for this complicated approach. American health care itself is complex, touching every person, thousands of different interests, and 16 percent of the economy. There was no way, apart from a single-payer system, to make change simple, and even single-payer would be more complex than it appeared. Such complexity requires long lead time to design new programs, create the regulations and hire the personnel to implement them, and to roll them out in such a way as not to disrupt suddenly the insurance that people are used to relying on. Finally, a long phase-in smoothes the budgetary impact, especially by postponing major financial implications to later years (and other presidents and congresses!).

Reform is intended to expand access to 32 million persons, which will be achieved by three fundamental requirements: First, an individual mandate will require most citizens and legal residents to purchase an insurance policy with "minimum credible coverage." Federal subsidies will be available for persons with incomes up to 400 percent of the federal poverty level (approximately $90,000 for a family of four). Those not required to purchase are individuals for whom the insurance premium (even with the subsidy) is still too expensive (more than 8 percent of their income, or whose income is below the federal income tax filing threshold of $9,350 for an individual). Medicaid will be expanded to cover more low-income individuals. These changes take place primarily in 2014. It is estimated that nearly half of the 32 million newly insured will be covered by mandated commercial insurance and somewhat more than half by the expansion of Medicaid eligibility. A penalty will encourage individuals to buy insurance. The penalty begins in 2014 at $95 or one percent of income (whichever is larger) and rises in 2016 to $695 or 2.5 percent of income. (There are no criminal penalties for refusal to purchase insurance.) Whether the size of these penalties will be enough to encourage persons to buy insurance is a major item of speculation. However, the vast majority of persons currently without insurance wants to buy coverage, but cannot afford it without the kinds of subsidies available under the Reform.

Persons in the United States illegally are not allowed to purchase insurance on the state exchanges or to receive subsidies; therefore, the vast majority will not be covered. They will constitute most of the estimated twelve to fifteen million persons still without insurance when the Reform is fully implemented.

The second prong of the three-prong approach is a mandate on some employers to provide insurance under certain circumstances, or to pay a fine if they do not. Thus, the Reform combines elements of the employer and individual mandate described above. Small businesses will be eligible for subsidies to assist them in providing insurance for their employees, and employers with fewer than 100 employees will be eligible to access the individual market insurance exchanges as a source of affordable employment-based insurance. Beginning in 2017, the states have the option of opening the exchanges to firms with more than 100 employees.

The employer mandate works this way. Firms with fifty or more employees will have to pay a penalty of $2,000 per employee if they do not offer insurance and if some of their employees enter the exchanges to receive government subsidies. Firms that do offer insurance will have to pay a fine of $3,000 for any employee who refuses to take the firm's insurance, but instead uses a federal subsidy to purchase individual insurance on the exchange. Firms with fewer than fifty employees do not have a mandate, but they are eligible for a complex set of federal subsidies if they do offer insurance.

The third prong of the three-prong approach is insurance market reform. This includes state-based health insurance exchanges that will allow individuals and small businesses to shop for a qualifying insurance product that allows them to fulfill the mandate at reasonable cost. The exchanges are to be up and running by 2014. These will be designed to offer a limited number of plans that have different co-pays and coverage. Buyers will use information available in the exchanges to compare insurance companies, including quality of care and price. The exchanges will also make available "catastrophic" plans to individuals under thirty and those exempt from the mandate. Such plans would be less expensive and cover only major medical costs.

Other insurance market reforms are to begin in 2010 and be implemented by 2014. These include high-risk insurance pools to provide affordable coverage for uninsured persons with significant medical problems; required dependent coverage up to age twenty-six; prohibition on insurance plans with annual or life-time coverage limits; prohibitions on denials of coverage for pre-existing conditions (children by 2010; adults by 2014); and limits on the ability of insurance companies to charge different rates for different persons (modified community rating).

In addition to these measures, the Reform law requires state Medicaid programs to cover all individuals, adults and children under 133 percent of the federal poverty line by 2014.[30] The federal government will pick up most of the cost of states to cover the newly eligible: 100 percent from 2014 to 2016, declining to 90 percent by 2020 and subsequent years. Some states already have more generous limits than 133 percent of poverty, and persons would continue to be eligible under the rules in effect in those states. Medicaid payments to primary care physicians are to rise to the level of Medicare rates by 2013. The federal government will also more heavily subsidize SCHIP, and states must maintain SCHIP eligibility levels until 2019.

Paying for Expanded Access.   Official government estimates at the time of Reform's passage were that the expansion of coverage would cost nearly $1 trillion over the first ten years, but that cost savings in Medicare plus additional revenues would fully pay for the program during that period and would more than pay for it in the second ten years. Many who believe that program expenses are underestimated and expenditure decreases overestimated doubt those figures. They either opposed the legislation or worried that it would in fact add to the already massively growing federal debt.

New Revenues. For the most part, Reform is paid for by taxes and fees on upper income earners. Individuals with taxable income of $200,000 per year (and couples with $250,000) will pay a Medicare tax of 2.35 percent (instead of 1.45 percent) on income over those amounts. They will also pay a 3.8 percent "contribution" to Medicare on unearned income (such as dividends, interest, and capital gains). In addition, beginning in 2018 there will be a tax on expensive "Cadillac" health plans provided by employers (plans costing more than $10,200 per year for individuals and more than $27,500 per year for family coverage). Revenues will also be raised from the penalties described above on individuals and employers for not obtaining or not providing insurance. Also, the threshold for claiming an income tax deduction for medical expenses will be raised from 7.5 percent of adjusted income to 10 percent, and there will be limits on contributions to tax-favored flexible spending accounts set up by employers. Finally, the health insurance industry, in return for getting so many millions of additional subscribers, will pay new fees, as will pharmaceutical companies and medical device makers.

Spending Reductions. Medicare Advantage payments, already discussed, will be reduced by nearly $140 billion over ten years. In addition, hospitals and other providers of patient care agreed to Medicare fee schedule reductions of nearly

$200 billion over the same period, as a trade-off for a major decrease in their charity care and bad debt costs, since so many more patients will have insurance. Finally, there will be a Medicare Independent Payment Advisory Board authorized (beginning in 2014) to submit recommendations for fee schedule reductions if Medicare spending targets are not hit. The Reform law projects as well that medical cost increases will be reduced by the delivery system reforms described below. These reforms are designed principally to improve the quality of health care; however, the experience of the health care industry is that improved quality makes a major contribution to more efficient and therefore less costly care.

Delivery System Reform and the Quality of Health Care

As difficult as it will be to reform health care to increase access to care and to reduce cost escalation, improving the quality of care renders the challenge even more complex. The difficulty is not from lack of trying. Over the last decade, numerous private and government organizations, as well as health care providers, have undertaken major initiatives. Major corporate employers such as General Motors and General Electric formed the Leapfrog group to jump start quality improvements that would benefit employers and save health care dollars. Health industry trade associations such as the National Quality Forum, the Institute for Health Care Improvement, and the Joint Commission on Accreditation of Health Organizations have either mandated or supported significant quality improvement measures.

Improving health care quality is difficult because there is no definitive location of responsibility, no national system for error-tracking or for tracking unqualified providers, and no adequate information technology.[31] Payment mechanisms are not aligned. Those who potentially reap the benefit of improved quality—patients, CMS, and insurance companies—are unlikely to increase reimbursement levels to pay the cost of quality improvements undertaken by hospitals and physicians.

On the governmental side, the Centers for Medicare and Medicaid Services years ago instituted a major *pay for performance (P4P)* program. The idea was to give financial incentives (bonuses) or financial disincentives (payment reductions) to hospitals and physicians that employ (or fail to employ) proven, evidence-based medicine to improve the quality of care delivered to patients. Initially, incentives were given for publicly documenting use of such measures, but gradually the incentives (and disincentives) will be based on use rather than documentation. Additionally, since 2008, CMS no longer reimburses hospitals or physicians for treatment costs necessitated by errors due to hospital-acquired injuries such as falls, objects left behind in surgery, and surgical-site infections.[32]

The 2010 Reform included numerous measures, mainly pilot programs, to address quality and to build upon these early efforts. Most of these measures aim at hospitals and specialist physicians in an effort to reduce the use of high-cost care focused on episodes of illness. The goal is to reduce the number of such episodes by better coordinating care for chronic illnesses before, during, and after a hospital stay. One goal is to decrease admissions and re-admissions; another is to shift as much care to primary physicians as possible.

The new law creates pilot programs based on "bundled payments" to hospitals and physicians who cooperate on measures to coordinate care and to reduce the number of unneeded physician consults and testing. Reform also creates a demonstration project to encourage providers to care for high-need Medicare and Medicaid patients at home, instead of in the hospital. The most talked-about pilot project involves cooperation between doctors and hospitals and other providers to establish "accountable care organizations" (ACO) and "patient-centered medical homes." Such pilots would remove some current legal barriers to physician-hospital sharing of revenues that result from higher quality, lower cost care. Medicare would save dollars if such experiments are successful, and the ACOs would be allowed to distribute bonus payments to members if the savings are realized.[33]

Quality and cost savings are also the aim of various penalties created by Reform. Starting in 2012, Medicare payments will be reduced for hospitals with high rates of preventable readmissions and hospital-acquired infections. In the same year, CMS will establish a value-based purchasing program in which hospitals will be paid more based on whether they achieve higher quality care, as evidenced by their hitting certain performance measures.[34] This is the latest evolution of pay for performance.

Although it appears that most of the quality-improvement (and cost containment) mechanisms are focused on Medicare, it is expected that state Medicaid agencies and private insurance companies will follow suit by creating their own policies based on successful pilots. Quality and payment mechanisms have followed this pattern over recent decades. Using its Medicare leverage, CMS implements quality and cost measures that, if successful, are imitated by the states and private industry.

Improving the ability of health care professionals, hospitals, and clinics to deliver quality medicine is only part of what is needed to improve the over-all quality of American medicine. Primary care physicians, nurses, radiology technicians, surgical technicians, and other auxiliary health care providers are in short supply—leading to understaffing, long hours, low morale, and difficult working conditions that endanger quality. Recruitment of students to go into these fields (and the faculty to teach them) will take considerable funding and federal–state initiatives difficult to establish in tight budgetary times with many other priorities facing legislative bodies. Both ACOs and medical homes, along with millions of newly-insured patients, will depend upon the availability of primary care physicians to take the lead in their evaluation and care. Reform includes a variety of measures to increase payments for the evaluation and management services that such physicians employ, as well as loan forgiveness and increased residency slots to make careers in primary care more attractive to medical students. In addition, Reform appropriates additional funding to train nurses, nurse practitioners, and physician assistants to staff the new care models contemplated by the new legislation.[35]

A major contributor to the quality improvement (and cost reduction) model is enhanced focus on electronic health records. The 2009 American Recovery and Reinvestment Act already provided incentives for doctors to install such records in their practices. Expensive electronic medical records, computerized physician order entry, and other information technology in the long run promise to improve quality and reduce cost. The United States lags European nations in such systems that automatically check for adverse drug interactions, right dosage, and previous medical history, thus helping to reduce both errors and unneeded and duplicative tests and procedures. Federal initiatives in this area have focused on developing national standards so that systems can talk to each other; but funding has lagged to pay for computers, software, and training, especially for financially strapped small physician practices. With the 2009 legislation and with Reform, additional money will be available; hospitals and physicians will be allowed to cooperate to create such records; and (as an incentive) they will receive additional Medicare payments if they meet "meaningful use" targets in 2012. By 2015, their reimbursements from CMS will be reduced if they do not use electronic medical records.

Finally, quality would be improved by effective methods of disease prevention and modification of unhealthy behaviors that lead to high risk for cancer, diabetes, and other diseases. Currently, attention focuses on what has become an alarming rate of childhood and adult obesity. There is, however, no consensus on the best way either to prevent obesity or to pay for prevention.[36] Reform contains numerous provisions to research the best means of enhancing prevention, to make such preventive measures more affordable in public and private insurance plans, to create incentives for individual behavior modification toward better health, and to allow certain benefits for employers who adopt qualified wellness plans for employees.[37]

Cost Control Beyond Reform

As indicated in the immediately preceding sections, most of the quality improvement provisions of Reform assume that higher quality care will in the long run save money by reducing duplicative tests and procedures, using primary care rather than specialists, and avoiding preventive hospitalizations. In addition, two new organizations will be created within CMS to kick-start better quality care and explore expenditure reduction proposals. The first is the Center for Medicare and Medicaid Innovation. It will test innovative payment and service delivery models to reduce program expenditures. The second is the Independent Payment Advisory Board, which will recommend changes in Medicare to hold down projected costs, especially after 2018. These will use *comparative-effectiveness research* to establish the highest quality, low-cost care paths for the treatment of certain illnesses.

Comparative–effectiveness research studies the relative success of medical treatments, tests, and pharmaceuticals in curing or alleviating various medical conditions. Sometimes this research includes comparisons of the cost of different treatments in conjunction with their effectiveness. Those treatments found to be most effective and least costly should be promoted and covered by public and private insurance. This approach contrasts with the treatment of disease based on the experience of particular physicians. Comparative–effectiveness research uses experiments and the experiences of numerous physicians to establish "best practices." Such practices have the potential to improve the quality of medical care and to reduce cost growth. Skeptics, however, worry that comparative–effectiveness research could produce "cookie cutter" medicine or even be used to "ration" care.

Yet, no matter how the Reform experiments turn out, it is unlikely that they will "bend the cost curve" enough to keep health care expenses from rising at the current unsustainable rates. Health policy must confront the question of how to allocate limited resources to different kinds of need. The health needs of the young and old differ substantially. Is it more just to invest enormous sums under Medicare and Medicaid in high-cost acute care technologies for seriously ill old persons or in expensive long-term nursing home care, or should these sums go to support the basic medical, dental, and psychological care needed by the young, whose lives are just beginning? Similarly, policy advocates debate whether research and treatment should focus on the major fatal diseases, such as heart disease and cancer, as they do now, or on long-term, chronic, crippling diseases, such as mental disorders, arthritis, and senility. These are moral, rather than medical or scientific, questions because they involve the values that determine how society should allocate scarce resources among its different segments.

The truth is that all health systems ration care. Many deny that rationing exists in the United States and worry that Reform will lead to rationing. Yet Reform will only alter the *type*, not the *fact* of rationing. At present, American health care is rationed by insurance status, place of employment, income, insurance policy coverage limitations, willingness to wait in line, and other factors. These will continue, though perhaps in less severe form, under Reform. Extending coverage to more persons would change the dimensions of some factors, but it would neither create nor eliminate rationing. Similarly, measures to control costs raise issues of whether it is ethical to ration care according to the age of patients, according to the imminence of their death, according to the quality of their life, or other considerations. These kinds of questions are forbidden in American policy debate up to this point. Indeed, one of the most emotionally powerful arguments in Congress and the public during the 2009 and 2010 debate over Reform was that it would lead to "European-style rationing." So powerful was this fear that CMS cannot use results of its comparative-effectiveness research to "ration" care. Such arguments ignore, of course, the current American-style rationing built into our medical care.

These are serious questions that raise significant ethical debates. Refusal to address them will not keep rationing from happening; it will merely permit present structures to remain and allow others to emerge without conscious decision. Ultimately, the rising cost of health care may focus the rationing question on how aggressively to pursue life-saving, technological innovation when other desirable goods become unaffordable. Because the principal driver of medical cost inflation is the development of new technologies, there is no way to rein in the cost of health care without either slowing technological innovation (an idea rejected by most Americans and by both political parties) or by limiting insurance coverage of expensive new technology (also a politically unpopular idea). The difficulty of directly confronting the need for health care rationing suggests pessimism about the possibility of limiting unsustainable increases in future health care spending.

Reform and the Beginning and End of Life

The subjects of birth and death raise major policy questions. Abortion, discussed in Chapter 13 in a different context, is such a question. In the realm of health care, the debate centered on whether Reform would preserve the Hyde amendment abortion restrictions in any new insurance products created by the new law. The Hyde Amendment, upheld by the Supreme Court in 1980, bans federal Medicaid funding for most abortions. Some argue that this denial discriminates against the poor; others, that it saves the lives of thousands of unborn infants. The abortion debate nearly killed Reform at different times in the House and Senate. Ultimately, a complex compromise was achieved; one that supporters of Reform argue preserves current prohibitions against federal funding of abortion. Insurance plans on the exchanges are forbidden to use federal subsidy funds for abortion coverage. Instead, persons who wish to purchase insurance with abortion coverage must use their own funds to pay the difference between a plan with that coverage and a plan without it. Insurance companies must keep federal funding and monies to cover abortions strictly segregated. Opponents, however, argued that these provisions are not strong enough, thereby substantially weakening Hyde prohibitions and allowing federal dollars to fund abortions for the first time.[38]

At the other end of life, debate includes whether society should fund or encourage the use of sophisticated medical technology to keep alive those, particularly the aged, with terminal illnesses. One question is whether certain expensive procedures should be available to all persons or whether they should be denied to persons beyond a certain age, since at that point they are unlikely to prolong the quality or length of life significantly.[39] Examples of such procedures are kidney dialysis, heart transplants, and chemotherapy for the very old. Should government discontinue funding such treatments in order to use the resources elsewhere? The myth of "death panels" in the legislation crystallized this concern during the 2009 phase of Reform debate.[40]

State "living will" laws allow persons to refuse extraordinary technologies should they become terminally ill. Federal law requires hospitals to give patients the opportunity to complete living wills or durable powers of attorney on admission, even for minor surgery. Some ethicists go farther, arguing in favor of active euthanasia, that is, allowing terminally ill persons to request and receive an injection or other means to end their lives. Dramatic examples of physician-assisted suicide raised the issue to national prominence during the 1990s, and Oregon voters approved a measure making it legal for physicians to assist terminally ill persons to commit suicide. Physicians have assisted dozens of persons to die under this law. The state of Washington followed suit with a similar law enacted in the mid-2000s. Many oppose these measures on the ground that they cheapen life, making it a matter of economic calculation. They also believe that such policies diminish the religious value of suffering for the human spirit and that they "play God" by allowing the state, physicians, or individuals to determine the time and manner of death.

Moral Dilemmas of Research and Technological Development.   As medicine moves into the realm of genetics, new moral dilemmas emerge. As difficult as these will be, however, their inherent difficulty will merge with the already-existing cost dilemma to create significant challenges for policymakers in the next decade.

American medicine is high-tech medicine, depending fundamentally on research and development of new drugs and medical techniques. The new research frontier is the human genome itself. To unlock its secrets, it seems, is to unlock the secret to curing many devastating diseases. The debate over federal funding for research on human embryonic stem cells illustrates the moral dilemmas. Within the human embryo in its first weeks of development are stem cells that during the course of growth toward birth differentiate into all the cells of the human body. Many scientists believe that such cells could be used to cure conditions in adults; for example, stem cells could be grown to form heart tissue to repair heart damage or to form kidney cells to repair those damaged by diabetes. Yet harvesting embryonic stem cells destroys the embryo itself; that is, it ends nascent human life. Current policy allows this promise of healing to be assisted by federal funding through the National Institutes of Health, even justifying destruction of the embryo. And what about creating embryos specifically for research purposes? Scientists, religious groups, and ordinary citizens divide on these questions. The issue of whether it is permissible to clone human beings for therapeutic or reproductive purposes presents similar moral and political issues. Therapeutic cloning involves the same embryo destruction as above, and reproductive cloning (creating a genetic double of a child or adult) raises substantial questions of the meaning of human identity. Even farther down the road, as the secrets of the human genome become known, is the prospect of genetic engineering; that is, operating directly on the cellular make up of a person to cure a disease (Parkinson's, for example) or to enhance performance (increase height or intelligence, for example). Germ-line engineering would apply these techniques in such a way as to reproduce them in all of a person's descendents. Many citizens believe that such techniques not only are morally permissible, but hold great promise of curing disease, reducing suffering, and extending life. Others equally strongly believe that permitting such things tampers with human life itself, setting the present generation as the arbiter of the lives of all future generations. Such techniques would, in their view, lead to genetic discrimination, eugenics programs, and swollen human pride.

Yet government must decide. In general, it has four options for any new medical research or technique (really the same options as for any controversial social development). First, it may *encourage* the technique by funding it. Second, it may *permit*, but not fund the technique. This is equivalent to leaving it to the free market to develop or not develop the research. Third, government may permit the technique, but *regulate* its development or implementation through laws that restrict what the market may do. Fourth, government may *forbid* the activity, as the House of Representatives voted to do with human cloning in summer 2001. Congress as a whole, however, has not been able to arrive at a consensus on therapeutic and reproductive cloning.[41] In the absence of federal legislation, some states have enacted bans or regulations on cloning.

The issues raised by human cloning, embryo research, and genetic engineering are not limited to those above. Medical treatments resulting from them most likely will accelerate the rising cost of health care. Remember that technology is the principal driver of health care inflation already. These techniques, at least initially and perhaps indefinitely, will be very expensive. Covering them through public or private insurance will help to keep American medicine the most costly in the world. Not to cover them will leave them to the wealthy, exacerbating already existing health care injustices. These are some of the policy issues that legislators must face in coming decades.

Reform and Long-Term Care

A major issue for the future is how to finance long-term care for the elderly. Expenditures on long-term care have risen dramatically in recent decades, along with the increase in the number of aged persons (see Figure 8.5). When the baby boom generation begins to retire, the problem will intensify. Medicare, as previously mentioned, does not pay for ordinary nursing home care, although Medicaid does. Therefore, Medicare recipients who need such care must first exhaust all of their personal resources so that they become poor enough to be eligible for Medicaid. On any given day, about 5 percent of those over sixty-five and 20 percent of those over eighty-five are in nursing homes. Moreover, about 20 percent of the elderly have some disabling condition, and nearly one-third of all American health care expenditures benefit the aged.[42]

Policymakers must pay attention to finding ways to fund less-expensive care provided at home and to develop continuity of care for the many different health-related needs of the aged. The current set of programs is highly fragmented, with responsibility for establishing a continuum of care falling largely to the elderly themselves or their children, who often lack the ability to navigate complex regulations and agencies to put together a coherent system of care. Nevertheless, any solution will be costly, and little alternative exists to Medicare and Medicaid. The coordination of care experiments in Reform nudge medicine in this direction. Congress created tax incentives in 1996 to encourage individuals to purchase their own long-term care insurance policies. However, private insurance is prohibitively expensive if purchased after sixty-five, and the young hesitate to invest scarce dollars in policies designed to cover possible nursing home care many years in the future.

To address this dilemma, Reform legislation includes the Community Living Assistance Services and Supports (CLASS) Act. By 2012, citizens will be able to purchase special long-term care insurance. Premiums will be tiered to the age of the enrollee. Employers will be encouraged to offer CLASS insurance as a

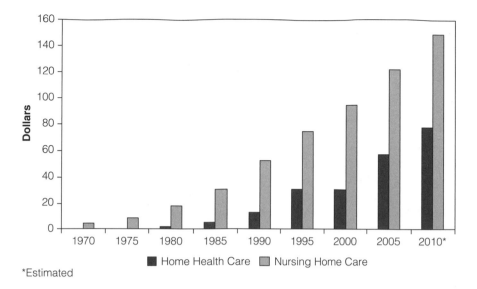

*Estimated

FIGURE 8.5 Growth in Long-Term Care Spending (in $billions)

SOURCE: http://www.cms.hhs.gov/statistics/nhe/default.asp#download; accessed 1-21-05; and Aaron Catlin, *et al.*, "National Health Spending in 2005: The Slowdown Continues," *Health Affairs*, 26 (January/February 2007), Exhibit 1, and Christopher J. Truffer, *et al.*, "Health Spending Projections Through 2019: The Recession's Impact Continues," *Health Affairs*, 29 (March 2010), Exhibit 1.

benefit. Cost of premiums will rise with age, so there will be incentives for younger persons to enroll. Premiums are designed to keep the program solvent for seventy-five years, but should average less than $100 per month. The average benefit will be $50 per day once a person becomes disabled and needs the assistance. The benefit will be paid in cash, thereby helping recipients to fund nonmedical assistance required to facilitate staying in their own home, thus avoiding expensive nursing home care. Existing private, long-term care policies will continue to be available as supplements to or competitors to CLASS policies.

Health Care Politics in the Future

The cost, access, long-term care, and ethical dilemmas make health care politics highly contentious, involving the politics of distribution, redistribution, and regulation (Chapter 1). The 2010 PPACA Reform has far-reaching consequences for all citizens, for employers, and for one-seventh of the entire national economy. Substantial structural changes in the health care system affect everyone as a consumer of health care, but also affect powerful interests that have conflicting purposes. Building a political coalition for such change was extraordinarily difficult and a major achievement of President Obama and Congress. However, serious questions remain about the long-term viability of Reform.

First, the legislative framework must be implemented, an extraordinarily complex matter involving both federal and state governments cooperating to create new programs, modify existing policies, and cooperate to design others, such as the exchanges. This will mean devising thousands of particular regulations, negotiating with health care interest groups, and hiring new or retraining existing administrative personnel. As Chapter 1 described, passing laws is (relatively) easy. Implementation makes or breaks a policy. Congress did authorize additional resources for CMS to implement Reform; however, it is not clear whether those resources will be sufficient.[43]

Second, the success or failure of PPACA depends substantially on the delicate balance of subsidies and penalties on individuals and businesses to encourage purchase of insurance. If the subsidies or penalties are too low, many individuals will simply pay the penalty instead of buying insurance, thus defeating the law's purpose. A similar calculus exists for businesses trying to decide whether to maintain existing insurance offerings or to establish new ones under Reform. Congress toyed with higher penalties, but could not get sufficient support for them. It considered more generous subsidies too, but these would have raised the total cost of Reform above agreed-upon levels.

Third, most unclear is whether the cost controls projected in the law will be sufficient to contain future increases in health care spending. If they are not, and particularly if the economy is slow to recover from the downturn that began in 2008, then Reform will have to be substantially modified.

Finally, substantial modification or even repeal of the new law is part of the Republican political agenda. Public opinion support for Reform was quite shaky immediately after passage, and there was a substantial proportion of the population strongly opposed to the legislation. Yet, substantial majorities supported the essential components of PPACA, and public opinion on the legislation often depended on survey question wording.[44] One line of attack on Reform began almost immediately when legal challenges to the constitutionality of PPACA were filed by attorneys general in more than a dozen states. They argued that (1) new Medicaid requirements on the states were an unconstitutional imposition and (2) there is no warrant in the Constitution for a legal mandate to purchase insurance.

The second line of attack was an appeal to the unpopularity of the legislation with many voters and to the anti-incumbent sentiment in the electorate. These factors did not bode well for congressional Democrats going into the 2010 midterm elections in November. Democrats were counting on two factors: (1) that the public would gradually grow more supportive of Reform as its provisions became better know and its benefits more available; (2) that Republican gains would not be sufficient to provide a winning margin in Congress for repeal or substantial modification in the face of a certain veto from President Obama. Moreover, by 2011, many citizens will have begun to feel the benefits of the early provisions of Reform, making Republicans loath to repeal benefits already in place.

None of these factors is close to certainty at the time of this writing, and the early years of the decade from 2011 to 2020 will see health care policy continue near the top of the political agenda. What is clear is that either the repeal of PPACA or the failure of Reform to achieve its ambitious goals could mean a return to the pre-Reform health care system and its ever-deepening crises.[45] The price of failure is extraordinarily high.

ENDNOTES

1. For a summary of changes toward managed care and an explanation of managed care terminology, see Jonathan P. Weiner and Gregory de Lissovoy, "Razing a Tower of Babel: A Taxonomy for Managed Care and Health Insurance Plans," *Journal of Health Politics, Policy, and Law*, 18 (Spring 1993): 75–103; also R. A. Dudley and H. S. Luft, "Managed Care in Transition," *New England Journal of Medicine*, 334 (April 5, 2001): 1087–1092.

2. James C. Robinson, "The End of Managed Care," *Journal of the American Medical Association* (May 23/30, 2001): 2622–2628.

3. Other private funds account for 8 percent of the total. See Christopher J. Truffer, et al, "Health Spending Projections Through 2019: The Recession's Impact Continues," *Health Affairs*, 29 (March 2010): 522–529.

4. The comparative material in this section is based on Robert H. Blank and Viola Burau, *Comparative Health Policy* (New York: Palgrave Macmillan, 2004); and Joseph White, *Competing Solutions: American Health Care Proposals and International Experience* (Washington, DC: Brookings Institution, 1995), Chapter 2. See also Lynn Payer, *Medicine and Culture: Varieties of Treatment in the United States, England, West Germany, and France* (New York: Penguin Books, 1988) and Jacob S. Hacker, *The Divided Welfare State: The Battle over Public and Private Social Benefits in the United States.* (New York: Cambridge University Press, 2002).

5. Barbara Starfield, "Is US Health Really the Best in the World?" *Journal of the American Medical Association*, 284 (July 26, 2000): 483–485; and Barbara Starfield, "Reinventing Primary Care: Lessons from Canada for the United States," *Health Affairs*, 29 (May 2010): 1030–1036.

6. Cathy Schoen et al., "Comparison of Health Care System Views and Experiences in Five Nations, 2001," in Charlene Harrington and Carroll L. Estes, eds., *Health Policy: Crisis and Reform in the U.S. Health Care Delivery System* (Sudbury, MA: Jones & Bartlett, 2004), 366–371.

7. Katherine Swartz, *Reinsuring Health: Why More Middle-Class People Are Uninsured and What Government Can Do* (New York: Russell Sage Foundation, 2006). For later data see Kaiser Family Foundation, www.kff.org/uninsured/profile.cfm.

8. Swartz, *Reinsuring Health.*

9. See, for example, David McBride, "Black America: From Community Health Care to Crisis Medicine," *Journal of Health Politics, Policy, and Law*, 18 (Summer 1993): 319–337; and Gregory Pappas et al., "The Increasing Disparity in Mortality between Socioeconomic Groups in the United States, 1960 and 1986," *New England Journal of Medicine*, 392 (July 8, 1993): 103–109.

10. J. A. Poisal, et al., "Health Spending Projections Through 2016: Modest Changes Obscure Part D's Impact," *Health Affairs*, Web Exclusive (February 21, 2007); J. S. Skinner, et al., "Is Technological Change in Medicine Always Worth It? The Case of Acute Myocardial Infarction," *Health Affairs*, Web Exclusive (February 7, 2006); Ernst R. Berndt, "The U.S. Pharmaceutical Industry: Why Major Growth in Times

of Cost Containment?" *Health Affairs*, 20 (March/April 2001): 100–114; and Peter J. Cunningham, "The Growing Financial Burden of Health Care: National and State Trends. 2001-2006," *Health Affairs*, 29 (May 2010): 1037–1044.

11. H. David Banta, "Technology Assessment in Health Care," in Anthony R. Kovner, ed., *Health Care Delivery in the United States*, 4th ed. (New York: Springer, 1990), chapter 15; and Kant Patel and Mark E. Rushefsky, eds., *Health Care Politics and Policy in America*, 3rd ed. (Armonk, NY: Sharpe, 2006), Chapter 8.

12. D. M. Cutler, et al., "The Value of Medical Spending in the United States, 1960–2000," *New England Journal of Medicine*, 355 (August 31, 2006): 920–927.

13. See Kenneth E. Thorpe, "Health Care Cost Containment," in Kovner, ed., *Health Care Delivery*, chapter 11; and Henry J. Aaron, *Serious and Unstable Condition: Financing America's Health Care* (Washington, DC: Brookings Institution, 1993), Chapter 3.

14. Gerard F. Anderson, et al., "It's the Prices, Stupid: Why the United States Is So Different from Other Countries," *Health Affairs*, 22 (May/June 2003): 89–105.

15. Jim P. Stimpson, et al., "Trends in Health Care Spending for Immigrants in the United States," *Health Affairs*, 29 (March 2010): 544–550.

16. Starfield, "Is US Health Really the Best in the World?" See also John M. Eisenberg and Elaine J. Power, "Transforming Insurance Coverage into Quality Health Care," *Journal of the American Medical Association*, 284 (October 25, 2000): 2100–2107; and Agency for Healthcare Research and Quality, *National Healthcare Quality Report: 2007*, www.ahrq.gov/qual/nhqr07/nhqr07.pdf; Accessed May 25, 2010.

17. Rosemary A. Stevens, "Specialization, Specialty Organizations, and the Quality of Health Care," in *Policy Challenges in Modern Health Care*, ed. David Mechanic et al., (New Brunswick, NJ: Rutgers University Press, 2005): 206–220.

18. Marilyn Moon, *Medicare: A Policy Primer*. Washington, DC: Urban Institute Press, 2006.

19. Kenneth E. Thorpe, "Chronic Conditions Account for Rise in Medicare Spending from 1987 to 2006," *Health Affairs*, 29 (April 2010): 718–724.

20. Anthony T. Lo Sasso and Gayle R. Byck, "Funding Growth Drives Community Health Center Services," *Health Affairs*, 29 (February 2010): 289–296; and John K. Iglehart, "Health Centers Fill Critical Gap, Enjoy Support," *Health Affairs*, 29 (March 2010): 343–345.

21. Information on these gains comes primarily from Karen Davis and Cathy Schoen, *Health and the War on Poverty: A Ten Year Assessment* (Washington, DC: Brookings Institution, 1978), chapters 2–4; and Stephen M. Davidson and Theodore R. Marmor, *The Cost of Living Longer: National Health Insurance and the Elderly* (Lexington, MA: Heath, 1980). Utilization figures come from www.cms.hhs.gov/researchers/pubs/datacompendium (accessed 05-25-10).

22. Steven A. Schroeder, "We Can Do Better—Improving the Health of the American People," *New England Journal of Medicine*, 357 (September 20, 2007): 1221–1228.

23. Daniel Callahan, *False Hopes: Overcoming the Obstacles to a Sustainable, Affordable Medicine* (New Brunswick, NJ: Rutgers University Press, 1998).

24. Lawrence O. Gostin, "Influenza Pandemic Preparedness: Legal and Ethical Dimensions," *Hastings Center Report*, 34 (September–October 2004): 10–11.

25. Louise B. Russell, *Is Prevention Better Than Cure?* (Washington, DC: Brookings Institution, 1986); Jack A. Meyer and Marion Ein Lewin, eds., *Charting the Future of*

Health Care (Washington, DC: American Enterprise Institute, 1987), part III; Deborah A. Stone, "The Resistible Rise of Preventive Medicine," in Lawrence D. Brown, ed., *Health Policy in Transition* (Durham, NC: Duke University Press, 1987), 103–128.

26. Quoted in The Staff of *The Washington Post, Landmark: The Inside Story of America's New Health-Care Law and What It Means for Us All* (New York: Public Affairs Report, 2010), 3. The summary of the 2010 Reform law draws extensively upon this book, as well as on Rob Lazerow's presentation to Covenant Health System, "The Reform Paradox" (Health Care Advisory Board, 2010), and the excellent and extensive analysis on the Kaiser Family Foundation website, http://healthreform.kff.org/.

27. For a review of challenges and policy options, see Moon, *Medicare*.

28. Accounts of the events of 1993–1994 include: Henry J. Aaron, ed., *The Problem that Won't Go Away: Reforming U.S. Health Care Financing* (Washington, DC: Brookings Institution, 1996); and Theda Skocpol, *Boomerang: Clinton's Health Security Effort and the Turn Against Government in U.S. Politics* (New York: Norton, 1996).

29. For an outstanding discussion of the meaning of these terms, the complexity of insurance rating, and the ethical issues involved, see Deborah A. Stone, "The Struggle for the Soul of Health Insurance," *Journal of Health Politics, Policy, and Law*, 18 (Summer 1993): 287–317.

30. Sara Rosenbaum, "A 'Customary and Necessary' Program—Medicaid and Health Care Reform," *New England Journal of Medicine*, 362 (May 27, 2010): 1952–1955.

31. Elizabeth A. McGlynn and Robert H. Brook, "Keeping Quality on the Policy Agenda," in *The Social Medicine Reader, Volume 3: Health Policy, Markets, and Medicine*, 2nd edition, ed. Jonathan Oberlander (Durham, NC: Duke University Press, 2005): 230–239.

32. See Karen Milgate and Sharon Bee Cheng, "Pay-for-Performance: The MedPAC Perspective," *Health Affairs*, 25 (March/April 2006): 413–419; also Arnold Epstein, "Paying for Performance in the United States and Abroad," *New England Journal of Medicine*, 355 (July 27, 2006): 406–408.

33. Mark McClellan, et al., "A National Strategy to Put Accountable Care into Practice," *Health Affairs*, 29 (May 2010): 982–990.

34. Michael G. Chernow, et al., "Evidence that Value-Based Insurance Can Be Effective," *Health Affairs*, 29 (March 2010): 530–536.

35. See the theme issue on "Reinventing Primary Care," *Health Affairs*, Volume 29 (May 2010).

36. Michelle M. Mello, et al., "Obesity: The New Frontier of Public Health Law," *New England Journal of Medicine*, 354 (June 15, 2006): 2601–2610.

37. See *Landmark*, Chapter 10, for details.

38. See the discussion of the political arguments and the provisions of the compromise language in *Landmark*, pp. 31–38 and 179–182; and George J. Annas, "The Real Pro-Life Stance—Health Care Reform and Abortion Funding," *New England Journal of Medicine*, online publication #10.1056/NEJMp1003944, published April 7, 2010 at NEJM.org (accessed 04-25-10).

39. For introduction to the debate, see Daniel Callahan, *Setting Limits: Medical Goals in an Aging Society* (New York: Simon & Schuster, 1987); and Timothy M. Smeeding, ed., *Should Medical Care Be Rationed by Age?* (Totowa, NJ: Rowman & Littlefield, 1987).

40. *Landmark*, pp. 3, 26, 132–133.

41. See Andrea L. Bonnicksen, *Crafting a Cloning Policy: From Dolly to Stem Cells* (Washington, DC: Georgetown University Press, 2002).

42. See William P. Brandon and Dana Burr Bradley, "The Elderly and Health Politics: The 'Coming of Age' of Aging," in Theodore J. Litman and Leonard S. Robins, eds., *Health Politics and Policy*, 3rd ed. (Albany, NY: Delmar Publishers, 1997), 323–351; and Judith Feder, Harriet L. Komisar, and Marlene Niefeld, "Long-Term Care in the United States: An Overview," *Health Affairs*, 19 (May/June 2000): 40–56.

43. Henry J. Aaron and Robert D. Reischauer, "The War Isn't Over," *New England Journal of Medicine*, online publication #10.1056/NEJMp1003394, published March 24, 2010 at NEJM.org, and Christopher C. Jennings, "Implementation and the Legacy of Health Care Reform," *New England Journal of Medicine*, online publication #10.1056/NEJMp1003709, published March 31, 2010 at NEJM.org; Accessed April 8, 2010.

44. Robert J. Blendon and John M. Benson, "Public Opinion at the Time of the Vote on Health Care Reform," *New England Journal of Medicine*, online publication #10.1056/NEJMp1003844, published April 7, 2010 at NEJM.org; Accessed April 25, 2010.

45. Bowen Garrett, et al., "The Cost of Failure to Enact Health Care Reform: 2010–2020" (Washington: Urban Institute, March 2010.

RESOURCES

Books

Callahan, Daniel. *False Hopes: Overcoming the Obstacles to a Sustainable, Affordable Medicine.* New Brunswick, NJ: Rutgers University Press, 1998.

Hackey, Robert B., and Rochefort, David A., eds. *The New Politics of State Health Policy.* Lawrence: University Press of Kansas, 2001.

Howell, Joseph H., and Sale, William Frederick, eds. *Life Choices: A Hastings Center Introduction to Bioethics*, 2nd ed. Washington, DC: Georgetown University Press, 2000.

Jacobs, Lawrence R., and Skocpol, Theda. *Health Care Reform and American Politics: What Everyone Needs to Know.* New York: Oxford University Press, 2010.

Mann, Thomas E., and Ornstein, Norman J., eds. *Intensive Care: How Congress Shapes Health Policy.* Washington, DC: American Enterprise Institute and Brookings Institution, 1995.

Marmor, Theodore R. *The Politics of Medicare*, 2nd ed. New York: Aldine de Gruyter, 2000.

Mechanic, David, Rogut, Lynn B., Colby, David C., and Knickman, James R., eds. *Policy Challenges in Modern Health Care.* New Brunswick, NJ: Rutgers University Press, 2005.

Morone, James A., and Jacobs, Lawrence R., eds. *Healthy, Wealthy, & Fair: Health Care and the Good Society.* New York: Oxford University Press, 2005.

Rivlin, Alice M., and Antos, Joseph R., eds. *Restoring Fiscal Sanity 2007: The Health Spending Challenge.* Washington: Brookings Institution Press, 2007.

Rovner, Julie. *Health Care Policy and Politics A to Z*, 2nd ed. Washington, DC: CQ Press, 2003.

Staff of *The Washington Post. Landmark: The Inside Story of America's New Health-Care Law and What It Means for Us All.* New York: Public Affairs, 2010.

Weissert, Carol S., and Weissert, William G. *Governing Health: The Politics of Health Policy*, 3rd ed. Baltimore: Johns Hopkins University Press, 2006.

White, Joseph. *Competing Solutions: America's Health Care Proposals and International Experience.* Washington, DC: Brookings Institution, 1995.

Websites

Centers for Medicare & Medicaid Services: **http://www.cms.gov**

Consumers for Health Care Choices at the Heartland Institute: **http://www.heartland.org/healthpolicy-news.org**

The Hastings Center: **http://www.thehastingscenter.org**

Health Affairs: **http://www.healthaffairs.org**

The Henry Kaiser Family Foundation: **http://healthreform.kff.org/**

Robert Wood Johnson Foundation: **http://www.healthreformgps.org/**

U.S. Health Policy Gateway: **http://ushealthpolicygateway.wordpress.com**

Chapter 9

Education: Conflict in
Policy Direction

Conflict over education policy exists because education policy decisions reach deep into the daily lives of American families. The depth of this impact virtually guarantees that conflict will be an integral part of policymaking. The pluralistic nature of American society produces disagreement over establishing the basic values that should guide education policy. Consequently, controversy and conflict tend to accompany the education policy debate. Much of this conflict can be traced to two opposing traditions within education theory: conservative and liberal/progressive thought.

Conservative thought links personal development to individual initiative and responsibility. Conservatives tend to view differences in initiative and ability between people as natural. Responsibility for educational achievement rests with the individual. Most resulting economic and social inequalities should be attributed to differences in personal initiative and ability. This emphasis on the individual places traditional conservative thought in general opposition to an expansion of federal involvement in education policy. Conservatives emphasize the responsibility of the family, state government, local school boards, and private institutions, such as the church, as the appropriate structures for determining education policy. Societal rewards are accumulated through competition not intrusion by the federal government.

Liberal/progressive thought reflects a conviction that government has an obligation to compensate for social inequities resulting from individual differences. Liberals emphasize programs designed to eliminate the effects of privilege, discrimination, and individual differences in ability. Liberalism favors the creation of an educational system that promotes equality of opportunity. This concern with equality leads progressives to advocate an expanded role for the federal government in education policy. The achievements of the federal government in promoting equality in areas such as civil rights provided a framework for advocating an expanding federal role in education policy as a means to remedy past state and local policies that produced unequal educational opportunity. One example of these state and local policies was the enforcement of school segregation, which was eliminated by federal court actions.

These two traditions generated cross-pressures and conflicting goals in American education policy. Schools are assigned multiple and sometimes conflicting tasks of teaching students basic skills (reading, writing, arithmetic, science), creating high self-esteem, defining a lifelong value system for students, laying the groundwork for an integrated society through contacts with individuals from different racial and ethnic backgrounds, providing the nation with an adequate supply of highly trained citizens for scientific and technical enterprise, and creating a sense of loyalty to American values.

ISSUE BACKGROUND: HISTORICAL PERSPECTIVES AND THE ONSET OF FEDERAL INVOLVEMENT IN EDUCATION

Two principles direct education policy in the United States: first, education should be free and universal, and second, control over education should be centered on the local level.

The Tradition of Free Public Education

Thomas Jefferson believed that a system of free public education was a basic requirement for democracy. He wrote in 1816, "If a nation expects to be ignorant and free, in a state of civilization, it expects what never was and never will be."[1] Jeffersonian thought embodied three educational goals: first, to provide literacy training to children; second, to expand access to education without regard to social background in order to open positions of leadership to those with high levels of educational achievement; and third, to provide an educational system in which leaders could be trained in the United States rather than in Europe. The free public education system of the United States reflects these values. Education was viewed as the means to enable the public to make choices consistent with democratic values and maintain stability of the republic. Free education was a strong force for maintaining the existing social order.[2]

Education served as a tool for political socialization in the melting pot approach to nation building. Immigrants to America brought to the new nation a variety of religions, languages, customs, and political values. Immigrants arriving from countries without democratic institutions needed to develop an understanding of democracy and establish a new identity as Americans. A free public education system promoted this integration into the American social and political system. Education was an instrument for promoting national

---

B o x 9.1   Federal Education Programs

1787 Northwest Ordinance: Required one section of land in each township of the Northwest Territory to be reserved for the support of education.

1862 Morrill Land Grant Act: Provided public land for colleges that would specialize in agricultural and mechanical arts.

1867 Office of Education Act: Created the U.S. Office of Education.

1917 Smith-Hughes Act: Provided limited federal funds for vocational education.

1920 Smith-Bankhead Act: Provided for vocational rehabilitation grants to the states.

1935 Social Security Act: Provided for vocational rehabilitation of the handicapped.

1941 Amendment of the 1940 Lanham Act: Provided federal funding for construction of schools in areas with extensive federal tax-exempt property.

1944 Servicemen's Readjustment Act (GI Bill): Provided financial assistance to veterans in education programs; these benefits were extended to Korean conflict-era veterans in 1952 and to Vietnam-era veterans in 1966.

1946 National School Lunch Act: Provided students nutrition subsidies through school lunch programs.

1950 Federal Impacted Areas Aid Program: Authorized federal funds for aid to school districts in which large numbers of federal employees and tax-exempt federal property contributed to high school enrollment and a reduced local tax base, such as school districts serving military institutions.

1950 National Science Foundation (NSF): Created with the goal of promoting scientific research and improving the quality of teaching in the areas of science, mathematics, and engineering.

1958 National Defense Education Act: Provided federal financial support to strengthen the areas of science, mathematics, and foreign language instruction, and to establish a system of direct loans to college students.

---

unity, and the tradition of free public education became entrenched in American thought.

The Tradition of Local Control

The U.S. Constitution does not specifically provide for federal involvement in, or control over, the educational system. The American educational system grew out of an English heritage in which the church and home were responsible for education. This heritage evolved into the district school in America. Residents of each independent district decided policy issues relating to education such as tax rate, appointment and removal of teachers, school calendar, and selection of classroom materials. Community control remains a basic tenet of American education as demonstrated in the local school district of today. Federal control over education was viewed as an inappropriate exercise of national power in the early years of the nation.

B o x   9.1   (Continued)

1964 Economic Opportunity Act: Provided federal work-study grants to students from low-income families.

1965 Elementary and Secondary Education Act (ESEA): Provided limited financial assistance to local schools for textbooks, libraries, and other instructional materials.

1968 Elementary and Secondary Education Act Amendments: Provided financial assistance for educating handicapped children.

1974 Educational Amendments: Consolidated some federal programs and established the National Center for Educational Statistics.

1978 Career Educational Incentive Act: Provided for the creation of career education programs in elementary and secondary schools.

1979 Department of Education Organization Act: Created the cabinet-level Department of Education by consolidating education programs from other federal departments.

1985 Montgomery GI Bill: Provided education benefits to veterans entering active duty after 1985 (extended in 1991).

1994 Goals 2000: Educate America Act: Created the National Education Standards and Improvement Council to develop voluntary national skills standards for local districts.

1997 Taxpayer Relief Act of 1997: Created the Hope Scholarship Program for college students.

1998 Charter School Expansion Act: Provided for expansion of charter schools.

2002 No Child Left Behind Act (NCLB): Reauthorized the Elementary and Secondary Education Act and contains the policy initiatives of President George W. Bush, which include testing and accountability measures and school choice provisions for parents of children attending low-performing schools. NCLB remains in effect but was not reauthorized in 2007 and remains on the policy agenda in 2010.

An Emerging Role for State and Federal Governments

State governments gradually assumed an expanded role in education policy. State government creates local school districts, which can exercise only those powers specifically granted to them by the state. As state funding for local schools increased, states exercised greater control over education policy. State education departments now determine education policy guidelines for local districts, specify curriculum models and teacher certification standards, and establish guidelines for education programs.

State governments also establish the framework for financing education. Local districts are free to tax and spend only within guidelines established by the state. State governments have primary responsibility for establishing minimum expenditure levels for local districts. The increasing power and influence exercised by state governments conflicts with the tradition of local control.

In the last half of the twentieth century, the role of the federal government in education policy emerged as a major issue. Yet the federal government played some role in education from the earliest years of the republic. A partial history of major federal education programs appears in Box 9.1.

The various programs described here do not represent a major federal financial role in education. Federal aid to education today remains limited in scope. Supporters justified these programs on the grounds that they represent limited solutions to specific problems. Given this orientation, most Americans accept a limited federal role in education.

The Elementary and Secondary Education Act of 1965: Expanding the Federal Policy Role

The baby boom at the end of World War II produced a dramatic increase in school enrollment beginning in the 1950s. During the Great Depression and WWII, capital expenditures for education had been reduced, and in some states they were almost completely suspended. Thus, after the war, the nation's schools faced a challenge to accommodate dramatically increased enrollments.

Even though public opinion supported expanded federal financial aid to education, federal aid legislation failed to pass because it had become entangled in two broad areas of social conflict: public education versus private sectarian education (the problem of separation of church and state) and integrated versus segregated schools (the problem of racial discrimination).

Interest groups also divided along national versus local control lines. Liberals/progressives tended to support increased federal aid and viewed federal funding as a means of improving education quality and as a solution to the problem of inequality in educational spending. An increase in federal dollars would help equalize per-pupil spending across geographical regions and eliminate this source of inequality. Groups opposing federal aid tended to be conservative. Given the tradition of local control, many conservatives felt that federal funding would allow expanded federal control over education policy, an event to be resisted. Federal control over education policy was in basic conflict with their commitment to limited government.

Even more controversial than the issue of federal control were the issues of race and religion. Minority groups, such as the National Association for the Advancement of Colored People (NAACP), and many liberal groups opposed federal aid to segregated schools. For this reason many liberals wished to prevent the enactment of such legislation until segregation had been abolished, as mandated by the Supreme Court in its landmark decision *Brown v. Board of Education* (1954), which outlawed "separate but equal" educational facilities.

In 1964, President Johnson abandoned the strategy of enacting a general program of federal aid and instead adopted an approach that emphasized a broad range of categorical assistance programs designed to remedy specific problems, especially the educational needs of disadvantaged children. The *Elementary and Secondary Education Act (ESEA) of 1965* provided federal funding to local public schools. Under the concept that ESEA gave aid to children but not to schools, the law authorized funds to parochial schools for the purchase of nonreligious textbooks and library materials, but excluded teachers' salaries.

Intergovernmental Conflict on ESEA.   Despite the passage of ESEA, the role of the federal government in providing financial aid remains relatively minor, although federal regulations increased in number and scope. Figure 9.1 indicates that the federal government today still accounts for only 9 percent of funding for public schools, with about 91 percent of education revenue provided by state and local sources. ESEA had the long-term effect of significantly expanding the federal regulatory role in education policy without a corresponding requirement for an increase in federal dollars, involving the issue of unfunded mandates. Congressional reauthorizations of ESEA in 1994 and again in 2002 contain provisions that require states to comply with additional federal regulations without providing a significant increase in federal funding dollars.

State government revenues increased in importance as a source of revenue for local districts. State governments now supply nearly 50 percent of the revenues to local districts, a far higher proportion than a few decades ago. This increase in state funding has translated into increased power over education policy. For example, curriculum content and structure as well as minimum competency standards for students and teachers are now the domain of state governments. The tradition of local control is weakened as the role of state government in financing schools expands.

Problems also have surfaced with the federal government's expanding role. Federal officials continue to impose policies and mandates on state and local authorities, often without the funding necessary for implementation, an issue

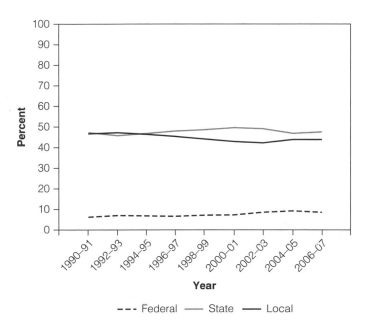

F I G U R E 9.1 US Education Expenditures by Source (1990–2007)

SOURCE: U.S. Department of Education, National Center for Education Statistics, Digest of Education Statistics, table 172, *Revenues for public elementary and secondary schools by source of funds: selected years 1919–20 through 2006–07.* http://nces.ed.gov/programs/digest/d09/tables/dt09_172.asp; Accessed April 2010.

discussed in Chapter 2. State and local officials lament this federal policy intrusion, especially the accompanying financial burden. Many state and local officials fear that the federal government will increasingly control policy through a strategy of withholding financial aid without adequately considering the values of local residents.

The Federal Role in Higher Education

Tax-supported public institutions dominate higher education in the United States today. Before the 1940s, private colleges and universities were dominant. The southern states began the tradition of establishing public colleges. The enactment of the Morrill Act in 1862 resulted in the rapid and extensive development of public higher education. The agricultural and mechanical colleges resulting from the Morrill Act had a practical orientation that increased public support for universities. Today, almost 80 percent of the nation's college students attend public institutions of higher education. Increasing numbers of people have decided to attend college. In the words of a former Department of Education official, "In a democratic society there is really no choice but to accommodate the educational demands of the people."[3] This demand for access to higher education presents the problem of maintaining a quality education while allowing almost unrestrained public access to higher education.

State institutions of higher learning rely primarily on state funds and tuition payments for operation, but a variety of federal funding programs exist. Work-study programs, loan programs, and the GI Bill provide financial assistance to university students. Federal aid in the form of grants for research also subsidizes higher education (see Figure 9.2). Universities have utilized this additional money to underwrite costs through support of research activities and the funding of faculty positions. These federal research dollars have increased the ability of the federal government to exercise influence over the educational policies of recipient institutions. Universities now find it necessary to comply with federally mandated policies in order to receive research grants and contracts.

CONTEMPORARY POLICY: REMEDYING SOCIAL INEQUALITY THROUGH EDUCATION

Disagreement on the objectives of education remains a source of policy conflict. Education can serve as an equalizing and leveling institution, or it can be a mechanism that maintains an existing stratification system. The concept that education is to function as an equalizer was not widely accepted at the time of Washington and Jefferson. Attempts to use education for such purposes only served, in the opinion of many, to "pull down what is above, never raise what is below." This conservative orientation conflicts with the liberal concern for the creation of an egalitarian education system.

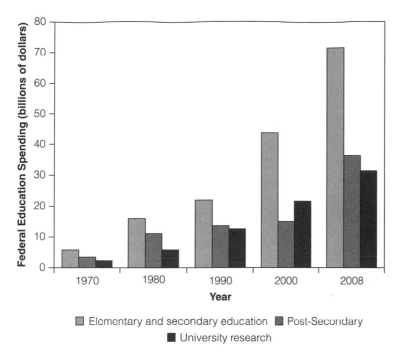

FIGURE 9.2   Federal Education Spending 1970–2008 (in billions of dollars)

SOURCE: U.S. Department of Education, National Center for Education Statistics, Digest of Education Statistics: Table 373 *Federal support and estimated federal tax expenditures for education, by category: Selected Fiscal years 1965 through 2009.* http://nces.ed.gov/programs/digest/d09/tables/dt09_373.asp; Accessed April 2010.

Leveling is central to the socioeconomic goals of education directly related to educational equality. Equalization of educational opportunity provides students with the potential for social and economic advancement. Yet, *Plessy v. Ferguson* (1896) legitimized inequality for much of American education. In this ruling, the U.S. Supreme Court established the doctrine of "separate but equal" regarding race in American life. One result was the establishment of a dual education system in the South based on race. This segregated system was unequal, both in physical facilities and in the quality of education provided. Even though the Supreme Court recognized the effects of separate educational systems and rejected the "separate but equal" doctrine in 1954, it was not until the administration of President Johnson (1963–1968) that equalizing educational opportunities became a national education policy priority.

The Issue of Unequal Financial Resources

Because of the uniquely American tradition of local control, local tax sources, primarily the property tax, generate over 40 percent of elementary and secondary school revenues. The result is a system in which local school district funds are limited by the value of taxable property, which varies widely from district to district within a state. This unequal distribution of resources works to the disadvantage of residents of poor districts. Revenue is a product of the tax rate multiplied by the value of taxable property (the tax base).

Districts with extensive property wealth can generate a large amount of revenue with a relatively low tax rate. A less wealthy district must tax at a higher rate to generate the same amount of revenue. The result is a disparity in per-pupil expenditures. In many cases the districts with low levels of spending are taxing at a relatively high rate, yet they lack the financial base to support spending at higher levels. This situation exists at the state and regional levels as well.

The national per-pupil spending average for 2007 was $10,209, ranging from $6,060 in Utah to $15,940 in Vermont.[4] Education spending per pupil is a function of wealth (tax base), the willingness to tax (tax rate), and the number of students to be educated. Another significant, yet difficult, factor involves the relative cost of living. In states with a lower cost of living, per-pupil spending tends to be less than in those states with higher costs of living.

One policy option to equalize per-pupil spending across the nation would be a massive infusion of federal dollars. This approach is not feasible for two reasons. First, state governments and local districts desire to retain primary responsibility for education policy. This would be threatened by significantly increased federal funding. Second, and probably most important, competing demands on the federal budget and the significant federal deficit prevent such action. The federal government has not played a leadership role in encouraging financial reform, nor has it attempted to provide assistance to states that are wrestling with the problem. The result is an emphasis on state assistance to local districts, with the result of uneven spending across the nation and within individual states.

There are often high levels of financial inequality among districts within a given state. Per-pupil financial disparities within a state can be profound as illustrated in per-pupil spending between districts in the 5th and 95th percentiles in states such as: Texas, $8,298 to $24,220; Illinois, $7,600 to $16,797; Utah, $6,589 to $15,930; New York, $13,561 to $36,045.[5] State court challenges to finance formulas have cited such significant gaps.[6] Financial inequality remains a policy issue in many states, with a ratio of unequal spending of two or even three or four to one being common. Urban school districts in large cities tend to face the problem of low fiscal resources to a greater extent than suburban and rural districts. Federal aid has not been a factor as a remedy for fiscal inequities between districts within a state.

Efforts to Reform Financial Disparities.   Attempts were made at the state level to force school finance reform to foster greater equality. The California Supreme Court ruled in *Serrano v. Priest* (1971) that under the provisions of the California constitution, education is a fundamental right that cannot be a condition of the wealth of a child's parents or neighbors.[7] This doctrine of fiscal neutrality found that reliance on the property tax resulted in excessive financial disparities among school districts. Following the *Serrano* decision, lawsuits were filed in about thirty states in an attempt to spread the California reform to other states.

The U.S. Supreme Court, in 1973, declared the issue of school finance reform off-limits to lower federal courts. In the case of *San Antonio Independent School District v. Rodriguez*, the Court refused to equate inequities in property values and the resultant differences in educational expenditures with violation of the equal protection clause of the Fourteenth Amendment.[8] The Court reasoned that the United States Constitution did not explicitly or implicitly guarantee the "right" to an education. Furthermore, differences in spending levels could not be equated with "interference with fundamental rights." The Court supported the continued use of the property tax in Texas by stating that there was no evidence that the arrangement deprived Texans of "an adequate minimum educational offering." Because many state constitutions do guarantee the right to an education, litigation concerning school finance reform was restricted to state court systems.

Since the 1990s, various state supreme courts heard some twenty-one cases concerning school finance reform. About half of these cases required the affected state to engage in some type of funding change. Lawsuits attempting to change the existing approach to funding education have met with some success, as supreme courts in states, such as Montana, Kentucky, and Tennessee, ruled that school funding practices violated provisions of their state constitutions. The record is one of mixed success in developing and implementing funding formulas that achieve a degree of equality in per-pupil spending. Although the state court system acts as a lever to stimulate change, state legislators demonstrate a hesitancy to redistribute money from wealthy districts to poor districts.

Conflict over School Finance Reform.   The reform movement embodies significant policy conflict.[9] Conservatives often see finance reform as one more attempt to solve a problem by simply spending more money. Accordingly, they argue that reform efforts should focus on education philosophy, not spending and finance. Education finance has been traditionally distributive in nature, with little emphasis placed on a redistribution of financial resources within a state. The redistributive nature of school finance reform is in conflict with conservative thought. Redistributive policies are often liberal in inspiration. The politics of redistribution involve far more conflict than distributive policy. Increased power and control over education exercised by state governments also concerns proponents of local control. This type of financial reform is therefore viewed as a threat to a basic tradition in the American educational system.

The controversy over financial equalization reflects the conviction that expenditures affect quality of education.[10] The relationship between expenditures and educational achievement, however, is less than clear. Conventional wisdom holds that the future opportunities of students attending poor districts are restricted when compared with the future opportunities of others. Consequently, it is assumed that deprived students will achieve less in life, have lower incomes, find it more difficult to advance economically and socially, and contribute less to making America economically competitive than will students from wealthier schools. Studies in this area have not resolved the question because of conflicting results and differing interpretations.[11]

There is little doubt, however, that expenditures do affect the educational environment provided to students. Wealthy districts do spend differently than poor districts.[12] Poor districts tend to: (1) have a higher student–teacher ratio, (2) spend more on core instructional programming and less on college preparatory electives, (3) spend less on capital projects (building construction and maintenance), and (4) have lower teacher salaries than wealthier districts.

Because the research is ambiguous, it is not unequivocally clear that students attending districts with high expenditure levels will have higher levels of achievement than will those attending districts with lower expenditure levels. On the other hand, it is clear that the educational options available to students in poor districts are less extensive than to those attending wealthier schools. Part of the problem with building a strong case for school finance reform is the lack of clear evidence that dollars make a difference in educational achievement. If such data existed, the reform movement would be strengthened.[13] What we do not know relative to school district spending for specific education purposes complicates the issue of financial equity. First, it is possible to assess total per-pupil spending between districts, yet information relative to the costs of elementary education as compared to secondary education within a district are less easily understood. Understanding the relationship between cost of providing instruction across subjects (for example, high school chemistry as compared to high school social studies or English) and student achievement is also less than clear. Related issues involve the issue of per-pupil spending within a district. "Should per-pupil spending be the same for all schools, for all grade levels, and for all subject areas within a district?" remains an unanswered question in the debate surrounding financial equity.

A second factor involves differences surrounding cost-of-living issues for various regions within a state. Schools in higher cost-of-living areas face higher costs (teacher salaries, land acquisition costs, student transportation costs, labor costs for support staff) in the delivery of equivalent education programs than do other schools within the same state. A mechanism for adjusting these differences remains elusive.

A third factor involves establishing accountability measures for school districts in student achievement when a program of financial reform provides additional funding. With the contention that increased spending will result in higher student achievement, what specific student outcomes should be expected to be produced (higher graduation rates, reduced absenteeism and truancy, higher standardized test scores) in districts benefiting from additional state dollars?

State court cases now tend to focus more on disparities in student achievement than on disparities in per-pupil spending when dealing with finance reform cases. Debate increasingly centers on defining adequate spending and the appropriate mix of state and local funding necessary to achieve that spending level.[14] This emphasis on adequacy is a significant shift in thinking about school finance reform, since it does not require equal per-pupil spending.

Adequacy implies a sufficient minimum level of funding that will promote student achievement, an outcome of the education system. Reform efforts focusing on equality of spending reflect a concern with inputs in the education system. Historically, adequacy was simply assumed and defined in terms of available tax revenues raised by a local district. This approach was modified over time as states adopted foundation formulas that provided a mechanism for distribution of additional state dollars to local districts designed to guarantee a minimum spending level across the state. These spending levels were never equal, and the school finance reform movement challenged them.

Increasingly, adequacy is now defined in terms of goals related to student achievement. This means that the school finance reform movement may increasingly emphasize student performance gaps as the foundation for changing funding patterns, rather than claims based solely on differences in per-pupil spending.

Equality in Education

All, regardless of race or class or economic status, are entitled to a fair chance and to the tools for developing their individual powers of mind and spirit to the utmost. This promise means that all children by virtue of their own efforts, competently guided, can hope to attain the mature and informed judgment needed to secure gainful employment, and to manage their own lives, thereby serving not only their own interests, but also the progress of society itself.[15]

The concept of equality is a central tenet of American ideology. Yet, when asked to define equality, most Americans find it difficult to provide an explanation free of contradictions. The definition of equality in education has slowly changed over time.[16] Initially, conflict centered on the appropriate role of government in guaranteeing equal opportunity. Gradually, the more liberal position prevailed, and education as a means of achieving equal life chances became public policy.

The notion of *equality of opportunity* implies that the rules for success and failure are fair. The concept of educational equality varies along a liberal–conservative continuum. The conservative orientation holds that individuals possess differing levels of ability. Accordingly, efforts to guarantee an equal education are an exercise in futility. Intelligence and motivation rather than equal opportunity determines the individual's life chances. This conflicts with the liberal/progressive orientation, which emphasizes equality of opportunity. All external barriers should be removed to allow complete development of individual potential. Social and background characteristics should not determine individual opportunity. Government should use its power to assure each child an equal education. The emphasis lies on the inputs of education, that is, on the expansion of special programs designed to give graduates equal standing for competition in a free-enterprise system.

This concern for equality of opportunity gradually gave way to a concern for *proportional equality* as reflected in affirmative action policies. The focus shifted from the inputs to the outputs of education policy, that is, to the occupational outcomes of education. Increasingly, education policy is assessed by the degree to which employment patterns reflect population demographics. (In the perfect model, for example, the same percentage of blacks as in the total U.S. population would be found employed in, say, engineering careers.) Effectiveness then would depend on the advancement experienced by previously disadvantaged groups. This shift of concern from the inputs to the outputs of education policy has widened the gaps between conservatism and liberalism.

Educational Inequality Outside the United States

Equality as an issue in education is not limited to the United States. There has been concern in Western Europe with the relationship between educational opportunity and life chances available to citizens. Various surveys and studies indicate the existence of a general lack of equality of educational opportunity. Although the GI Bill greatly expanded education opportunities in America after World War II, only 2 to 5 percent of the same age group in Western Europe enrolled in higher education.

In Europe, education tends to select individuals based on test scores and early tracking of students, devices that tend to reflect society's class structure. In postwar Sweden, over 60 percent of university students came from the upper and upper-middle classes. Only 6 to 7 percent had origins in the lower socioeconomic strata (which made up about 55 percent of the population). The same was true for all of Western Europe. Studies in Germany, England, and France revealed similar patterns: only a small percentage of university students were drawn from the lower and lower-middle classes. European reform efforts in recent decades have moved to change these patterns.

Equality of educational opportunity is also restricted in the former communist countries. Although the data are not so readily available, some pertinent observations exist. The vast majority of students attending universities come from the upper socioeconomic levels. Even though the United States is not alone in the struggle to increase educational equality, it has made greater efforts than has Western Europe to achieve equality of opportunity.

POLICY EVALUATION: EDUCATIONAL QUALITY IN THE UNITED STATES

Concern with the educational system in the United States has led to a variety of efforts to evaluate the quality of education provided to students. A variety of measures of quality have been employed, and there remains considerable debate about how best to measure educational quality. In the following section, attention will be given to some of the common measures of the various dimensions of quality: SAT scores, minimum competency tests (MCTs), teacher competency, master teachers, bilingual education, and multiculturalism.

Concern over Poor Student Achievement

During the 1960s and 1970s, many school districts adopted innovative programs that reduced the emphasis on the traditional three Rs and instead focused on students' emotional growth, self-direction, and individualism. Because these changes coincided with a decline in student achievement, the public came to believe that these curriculum reforms were not academically adequate. Performance levels of students on such standardized tests as the SAT declined since 1967, as indicated in Table 9.1.

In 1996, this pattern of declining SAT scores artificially appeared to be reversed because the test was re-centered to provide an average score of 500 for both the verbal and math scales. In the words of the College Board, "Setting the average verbal and math scores at 500 means that most students' scores will be higher."[17] On the new re-centered scale, a verbal score of 500 would have been a score of 422 on the original scale, and a math score of 500 would have been a score of 474 on the original SAT scale. Re-centering means that interpreting SAT scores must now be based on a contemporary rather than a historical reference group. Critics of education policy and curriculum are in a position to argue that re-centering SAT scores to a higher level is indicative of a loss of overall rigor and quality in the nation's schools.[18]

Although there is little debate on the fact that the average performance on standardized tests declined over an extended number of years, there remains disagreement concerning the causes of the decline. Many analysts cite parental attitudes and societal changes as the major factors contributing to low levels of performance. On the other hand, many parents and taxpayer groups believe that the departure from education basics—reading, writing, and arithmetic—fostered the decline in student achievement.

Investigators of the decline in the SAT mean scores have attributed it to several factors.[19] More students are taking the test now than in any previous period. Specifically, there has been a marked increase in the number of students from families that have not traditionally attended college. Low scores by this group tend to lower the mean score on the test as a whole (see Figure 9.3). Accordingly, the SAT average scores may not be an accurate barometer of student

T A B L E   9.1   SAT Scores (average), 1967–2009

	1967	1975	1980	1984	1988	1992	1996[*]	1996[**]	2000[***]	2004[***]	2009[***]
Verbal	466	434	424	426	428	423	427	505	505	508	501
Math	492	472	466	471	476	476	484	508	514	518	515

*1996 scores on original scale.

**1996 re-centered scale scores.

***2000 and later scores based on re-centered scale.

SOURCE: College Board http://professionals.collegeboard.com/data-reports-research/sat/equivalence-tables (discusses re-centering) (accessed 04-16-10); http://nces.ed.gov/programs/digest/d09/tables/dt09_143.asp (for SAT scores) (accessed 04-16-10); http://nces.ed.gov/programs/digest/d95/dtab124.asp (historic SAT scores); Accessed April, 15, 2010.

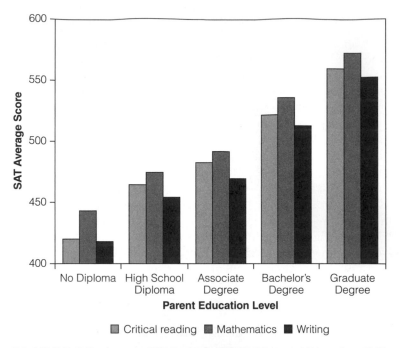

FIGURE 9.3 Average SAT Scores by Level of Parental Education, 2009

SOURCE: http://professionals.collegeboard.com/profdownload/cbs-2009-national-TOTAL-GROUP.pdf; Table 11: Student Background Information and Characteristics; Accessed April, 2010.

achievement in the society as a whole. Television viewing and family instability have lowered the motivation of students to excel. The findings of these studies have not been conclusive, and research into factors that might explain the decline has remained problematic.[20] Figure 9.4 indicates the variation in average scores between demographic groups on the SAT. White students had higher average verbal and mathematical scores than did all other demographic groups, with one exception, the Asian American math score. This pattern has persisted over time and has contributed to the question of cultural bias in standardized tests.

If high school curricula decline in rigor, a pattern of declining SAT scores could result. The College Board, which administers the SAT, has indicated that the decline in SAT scores indicates a "disturbing pattern of educational disparity" in the nation's schools. There is concern that the nation's schools may be producing two categories of students: a small group of well-educated students and a larger group of ill-educated students.

Family background characteristics clearly affect student SAT performance, as indicated in Figure 9.3. The higher the level of parental education, the higher the average SAT score earned by the child. Children of parents with a graduate degree had average reading and math scores of 559 and 572, respectively. Children of parents without a high school diploma had average reading and math scores of 420 and 443, a difference of 139 points on the reading scale and 129 points on the math scale! Since level of education is one indicator of

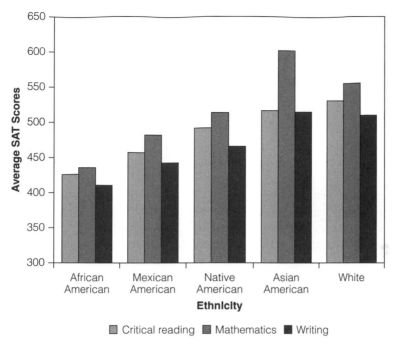

FIGURE 9.4   SAT Average Scores by Selected Ethnicity, 2009

*Ethnicity as reported by College Board

SOURCE: College Board, *Total Group Profile Report 2009,* Total Mean Scores by Ethnicity. http://professionals.college-board.com/profdownload/cbs-2009-national-TOTAL-GROUP.pdf; Accessed April 2010.

socioeconomic status, a positive relationship between socioeconomic status and student performance appears to exist.

Student performance on the ACT has remained stable over time. The ACT is a different type of test than the SAT. ACT scores range from 1 to 36, and questions on the test are designed to reflect high school curriculum, with scores reported in English, mathematics, reading, and science. ACT scores would not necessarily reflect a decline in the rigor of high school curriculum. Since 1970, the national average on the ACT, about 20, has remained very stable, varying less than a half-point.

Minimum Competency Tests.   Concern over low student achievement levels led to the adoption of *minimum competency tests (MCTs)* in over forty states by 1990. The tests were developed to serve a variety of purposes: criteria for student promotion, diagnostic tools to determine the need for remedial training, or assessments of the quality of local instruction. A passing grade on the MCT became a requirement for receiving a high school diploma in over twenty states. Most of the MCT exams required performance on an eighth- or ninth-grade level.[21] Minimum competency testing was advocated as a way to force schools to stress the basics of education, to add value to the high school diploma by confirming the graduate had mastered specified levels of knowledge, and as a method to combat what the public perceived as a trend toward lower academic standards.

Critics of *MCTs* charged that the examinations were biased, statistically unreliable, and a simplistic solution to a complex problem. Representatives of minority groups charged that cultural differences and vestiges of segregation are the primary cause of their problems with the exam. Given their disproportionate impact on minority students, it was argued that MCTs measured the impact of racial discrimination in education, not student achievement.[22]

Research indicated that between 60 and 80 percent of students pass these types of exams on their first attempt and that the vast majority of high school students (some 99 percent) eventually passed the test by the end of their senior year.[23] Critics argued that MCTs did not measure essential skills or even skills that applicable to life outside the classroom. MCT programs emphasized a narrow range of academic abilities as a means of determining the quality of the education system. Several negative impacts for education resulting from an emphasis on student testing can readily be identified. These include emphasizing the teaching of test content materials and excluding nontested curriculum materials, which narrows the curriculum; devoting time to teaching test taking techniques rather than developing critical thinking skills; contributing to the dropout rate of high school students; and, finally, reducing emphasis on teaching and student creativity due to the increasingly more mechanical nature of teaching. The proliferation of MCT examinations reflected a belief that testing was the appropriate mechanism to measure student academic performance. Following the adoption of the *No Child Left Behind Act* (NCLB) in 2001, testing analogous to that of MCTs became national education policy. Under NCLB, terminology was changed to place an emphasis on proficiency rather than minimum. In reality, the proficiency levels of NCLB testing have become the new minimum levels for both students and schools.[24] Due to the emphasis on assessing student achievement through testing, conflict concerning their use continues as high stakes testing under the requirements of NCLB have become a fixture on the educational landscape.

Questioning Teacher Competency

Accompanying the concern for student performance has been a concern for the level of teacher competency in the nation's schools. Today, every state uses some form of competency testing for initial certification of classroom teachers. The National Teacher Examination (NTE) developed by the Educational Testing Service (ETS) has been replaced by a series of exams known as Praxis I (measuring basic academic skills), Praxis II (measuring general and subject specific knowledge) and Praxis III (Teacher Performance Assessment). Most states require either passing selected Praxis examinations or a test developed and approved by that specific state.

The validity of the competency tests, however, remains under serious question. There is an absence of data to support the assertion that the tests actually measure competency. There are two components to effective teaching: mastery of knowledge and mastery of teaching strategies. Even if competency tests do validly measure mastery of academic material, their power to assess mastery of teaching skills remains unconfirmed. Despite the problems with determining teacher competency, the use of such testing will continue in this decade.

Another related problem centers on the starting salaries of teachers. Average starting salaries for teachers range from $5,000 to $15,000 less per year than for other career fields, such as business administration, engineering, sales and marketing, and liberal arts. This salary gap does not disappear as teachers gain experience and earn master's degrees. Many experts argue that, given the lack of financial rewards after graduation, teacher education programs have a disadvantage in recruiting students. The policy implications arising from this situation present issues in any attempt to improve the quality of education. First, in order to enhance the appeal of teaching as a career, salary levels may have to increase. A counterargument to the need to dramatically increase teacher salaries involves job security and retirement. This view holds that teachers benefit from greater job security and from generous defined retirement pay plans more than do other career fields.

Second, projections indicate that the demand for teachers exceed the supply in a number of disciplines. This is currently a problem in the areas of math and science. The challenge is to produce an adequate supply of high-quality teachers in an environment that has made it difficult to recruit and retain teachers. The issue of teacher competency is bound up in the policy of teacher compensation as reflected in the issues of merit pay and master teachers.[25]

Merit Pay and Master Teachers

Merit Pay.   The emphasis on quality education led to an advocacy of merit pay as one appropriate way to attract and retain quality teachers. The Report of the National Commission on Excellence in Education (*A Nation at Risk*) recommended that merit pay plans be adopted across the nation. State governments experimented with various types of merit pay provisions for teachers. In a majority of states, individual districts have developed some variant of teacher incentive pay plans.

Although merit pay does appeal to the public, there are problems in implementing the concept. First, because the merit pay concept intends to attract and retain exceptional teachers, it is best implemented after teachers' salaries are elevated to levels competitive with those of the private sector. Merit pay is not a substitute for an adequate salary scale.

A second problem with the concept is the validity of merit pay as a motivating force in teacher behavior. Because many of the nation's quality teachers remain in the profession despite low salary scales, salary may not be the main factor in recruiting and retaining the highest-caliber teaching force.

A third problem is establishing an unbiased operational definition of merit as applied to teachers. No group, whether teacher organizations, school boards, state education commissions, or federal agencies, has been able to determine exactly what constitutes merit or effective teaching. For example, student test performance is not an acceptable measure, because such performance is primarily related to parental education and economic status; therefore, teachers are very much captives of the students assigned to their classrooms. Because the students taught by individual teachers change every year, the ability to measure teacher performance becomes complex. Does student performance in a fifth grade class change over several years because of teacher performance or is the change the result of a different group of students taught by that teacher? Answering this question is a problem for advocates of merit pay.

A fourth problem with merit pay is associated with impact on teacher behavior arising from development of unambiguous terms and standards defining merit. In order to qualify for merit pay, teachers may abandon their own creativity in order to comply with a rigid set of standards. Merit pay may become a threat to teachers' experimentation and creativity if teachers follow established guidelines to meet merit standards.

A fifth problem with merit pay is cost. A genuine merit plan would increase costs to local districts. The federal government does not plan to expand its role in financing teacher salaries. Given the climate of opposition to local property taxes, school boards will find it more difficult to pass tax increases necessary to fund a merit pay system. This means that state governments are the only viable source of revenues to pay for a merit plan. At the same time, because of fiscal limitations, state legislatures resist demands to assume greater responsibilities in financing programs.

A sixth problem with merit pay is that job status, not the contribution of the job to the organization, historically governs compensation.[26] Historically, salary reflects rank within both public- and private-sector organizations in the United States. Principals and assistant principals always will receive higher pay than teachers, just as executives are paid more than other employees are in companies. Merit pay advocates seem to ignore this historical pattern.[27]

Some policy advocates support merit pay as a remedy for the nation's education system. However, during the 1920s, the concept of merit pay was widely supported in the United States[28] and the rhetoric of that period closely resembled that of today. Nevertheless, merit pay plans failed to be adopted then because of the problems of defining merit and evaluating teachers. The impact of merit pay plans for teachers on teacher performance, student learning, and educational outcomes is unresolved and is a topic for continued investigation.[29]

Master Teachers.   The concept of classifying master teachers closely relates to the concept of merit pay. This system may include merit pay components as well as career ladders for teachers as they progress. Master teachers are to provide a variety of services and fill a range of roles, depending on the educational climate and needs of each school district. Typically, a master teacher plan includes the identification of exceptional teachers, a system of merit-based financial rewards, and the use of master teachers as resource personnel in a supervisory capacity over other teachers to encourage higher levels of teaching effectiveness.

The master teacher movement remains a factor in education across the nation as teacher organizations, universities and colleges, states, and local school districts develop this designation for teachers. Selection criteria, the role of teacher organizations in the process, and financial compensation procedures vary from state to state.

Bilingual Education

Bilingual education programs grew out of Title VI of the Civil Rights Act of 1964 and the Equal Educational Opportunities Act (EEOA) of 1974. The U.S. Supreme Court interpreted these acts to mandate that states and local school districts create programs to rectify language deficiencies of students from non–English speaking families. Program development and implementation remained in the hands of state and local education officials. The *Bilingual Education Act* of 1974 provided federal funds to meet the language needs of non–English speaking students. Throughout the 1970s, bilingual education was favored as the appropriate method to remediate language difficulties. Over 70 percent of these programs were created in the Southwest and Pacific coast areas where districts had high concentrations of non–English speaking families.

There are two primary types of bilingual programs. In two–way bilingual programs (TWBE), students receive instruction in both English and their native languages throughout their elementary education. In transitional bilingual programs (TBE), instruction is in English only after students achieve a specified level of proficiency in English. Evaluation of the effectiveness of bilingual education programs remains inconclusive.[30] Bilingual education is gradually coming to be simply one among a variety of suitable programs to remedy language deficiencies. Bilingual programs are increasingly not a right or entitlement, but simply an available policy option. In the absence of federal mandates to provide bilingual programs, any reduction in federal funds for these programs would place their future entirely in the hands of the state governments. Given the costs of the programs, the lack of positive evaluations, and the financial pressures on state governments, the future of bilingual education programs remains uncertain. One indication of this uncertainty is the 1998 passage of Proposition 227 in California, which mandated that limited English proficiency students receive instruction in sheltered English programs, rather than bilingual education, unless their parents personally request bilingual education. Arizona enacted similar legislation two years later.

Multiculturalism

In order to establish a greater appreciation for the contributions of the various ethnic groups in the United States, the multicultural movement emerged and is having a direct impact on education policy. One objective is to change public perceptions by reexamining traditional views of the Western European impact on the Americas. The resulting emphasis on redefining the diverse and disparate ethnic elements in American society and revising the history books accordingly will have significant consequences for curricula.[31] In fact, multicultural education has been defined, in social reconstructionist terms,[32] as a program designed to create social changes beyond increasing tolerance and understanding. In 1973, the American Association of Colleges for Teacher Education (AACTE) defined multiculturalism as a rejection of "the view that schools should seek to melt away cultural differences or the view that schools should merely tolerate cultural pluralism."[33] The AACTE defined multiculturalism in terms of embracing such concepts as multilingualism, multidialectism, empowerment, equity, and cultural and individual uniqueness. The political dimensions of multicultural education are extensive, and any attempt to depoliticize it is inconsistent with its very nature.[34]

Redefinition of the African American contribution, for instance, requires that African culture and values be identified and taught. Such curriculum revisions have the effect of expanding students' knowledge of cultures often ignored in traditional curricula. The emphasis on Afrocentrism arises from a conviction that African American students' educational performance improves with a heightened sense of cultural pride.

The curriculum changes that accompany the multicultural movement generated considerable conflict. The emphasis on self-definition by various ethnic groups requires revision of both their contributions and the Western heritage. The result can be a significant alteration of traditional views. Some critics argue that basic American values brought from Europe—democratic principles, the Anglo-Saxon legal system, the importance accorded the individual, science and technology—will not receive sufficient attention in a revised curriculum. The 2010 Arizona legislature went so far as to ban public schools from offering ethnic studies classes because of these fears.

Multiculturalism is also at odds with the view of America as a melting pot, wherein an undeniable measure of political and social integration was synthesized from innumerable ethnic elements. The multicultural curriculum may be better characterized as a salad bowl view of America, stressing and encouraging diversity rather than homogeneity. Advocates of multicultural curriculum reject the concept of mainstream America as being nothing more than an attempt to foster an emphasis on Eurocentrism in education.

Opponents of the multiculturalist current note the ethnic conflicts accompanying the dissolution of the Soviet Union and the civil wars in Bosnia, Serbia, and Croatia following the disintegration of Yugoslavia. They fear that an emphasis on cultural diversity could lead to serious conflict, fragmentation, and weakness. Some critics argue that multiculturalism is a "poor substitute for the real inclusion" of all groups into the economic, social, and political system.[35] Multiculturalism has also emerged as an issue facing higher education with the concern for diversity.[36]

Minority Teachers.   Currently, minority teachers make up slightly more than 10 percent of the teaching profession. Some analysts argue that the salary structure for teachers causes many minority college students to reject teaching as a profession. Projections continue to indicate that minority Americans continue to be underrepresented in the teaching profession. This occurs at a time when minority children attending public schools comprise about 33 percent of the school-age population.

FUTURE ALTERNATIVES: COMMUNITY CONTROL, PRIVATE SCHOOLS, A CHANGING FEDERAL ROLE, AND CONFLICTING PRIORITIES

The questions regarding equality and education, the ability of schools to educate minority students, and the competence of both students and teachers produced calls for alternatives to the traditional public school system. Two frameworks dominate current discussion of educational reform. Liberals or progressives tend to emphasize federal leadership in establishing education policies and programs. Such leadership is necessary if schools are to achieve their social purposes. An acceptance of a strong role for education professionals as policy experts also marks this perspective. Liberals tend to combine an emphasis on public schools with a somewhat skeptical view of private and church schools. Conservative thought generally emphasizes local governance through community control of schools. This orientation is skeptical of using schools to advance the social agenda of education professionals, which may conflict with local values. Yet a conservative president, George W. Bush, made national education standards the signature of his education policy in the No Child Left Behind Act. The New Religious Right also is willing to de-emphasize public schools through measures to strengthen church schools and home schooling.

Community Control and Decentralization

Cutting across ideological lines, members of minority groups advocate effective local participation in school decision making in order to exercise power over the institutions that directly affect their lives. Other groups resisting federal and state intervention in local schools have made this same demand. Examples include controversies over textbooks, school prayer, and student drug abuse. Today, citizens expect education to be both technically advanced and responsive to the public. Often communities, angered by what they perceive as the failure of their schools to educate well, balk at paying any more in taxes for a system that is outside their control.

The Role of Professional Educators.   Professional education associations resist the movement toward decentralization and community control. One reason they present is the public's alleged lack of expertise, which prevents the effective evaluation of educational alternatives. However, the public often has strong opinions about education and usually agrees on general criteria for judging a school: qualified teachers, classroom discipline, and physical equipment.

Historically, professional educators tended to dominate state and local education bureaucracies and to mold education policy. A professional education establishment is inclined to resist giving power to groups it perceives as less well informed and qualified. Yet, community participation in education also serves to move minority Americans into wider-ranging positions of power and responsibility. Other conservative Americans have become more interested in local control as a way of challenging the educational bureaucrats who control the public education system.

District Consolidation and Decreased Local Power.   The issue of community control is linked to the evolution of the education power structure. The structures adopted during the twentieth century reduced the role of parents and the public while expanding that of professional educators and governmental institutions at the state and federal level. The move to consolidate school districts weakened the power of the community. Nationally, the number of school districts fell from over 100,000 at the turn of the twentieth century to fewer than 16,000 today.

The emphasis of the consolidation movement was on operating efficiency and economy of scale. Larger districts offer services at a lower unit cost than smaller districts. However, consolidation also has curtailed interaction between the public and school boards. Consolidation reduced the number of school boards, thereby dramatically increasing constituency size. These constituencies now number in the thousands and in large urban areas can include several hundred thousand. Consolidation also acted to diminish the ability of parents to influence education policy. The resultant sense of powerlessness led some parents to turn to private schools, or even to home schooling, which they feel may be more responsive to their needs. While economic issues have historically driven the consolidation movement, an unintended and unanticipated consequence was the increase of power of state government over local education policies.

The Issue of Private Schools

Since the 1970s, there has been some shifting of students from urban and suburban public schools to private schools. Most parents justify the shift to private schools as a concern for quality education. Parents also objected to mainstreaming, whereby students with disabilities (mental or physical) are integrated into regular public school classrooms. This practice has led to charges that teachers have to spend excessive time with the special students and neglect the needs of others. Parents then claim that their children are simply warehoused through the twelve grades.

Parental concern over religious beliefs and values has added to the enrollment support of private schools. Approximately 80 percent of private schools have religious ties. Today over ten million children attend private schools of various types. A major factor now appears to be a desire for an educational system that follows traditional curriculum and is committed to teaching moral values.

As reflected in Figure 9.5, the percentage of students attending private schools of all types has remained somewhat stable, varying by less than 1 percent since 1970. This indicates that public schools have not lost ground; nevertheless, they will continue to face competition from private schools throughout this decade, especially under any voucher system. Competition from charter schools may also increase significantly in the near future. Parents may choose to send

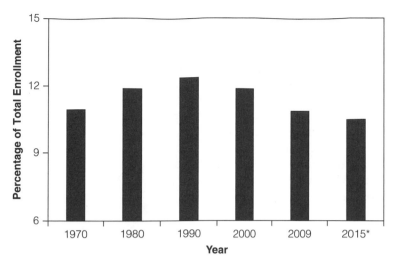

*2015 reflects estimated data

F I G U R E 9.5 Private School Enrollment (as a percentage of total enrollment), 1970–2015

SOURCE: U.S. Department of Education, National Center for Education Statistics, Digest of Education Statistics (2009) Chapter 1, Table 3. Enrollment in educational institutions, by level and control of institution: Selected years, 1869–70 through fall 2018; http://nces.ed.gov/programs/digest/d09/tables/dt09_003.asp; Accessed April 2010.

their children to specialized charter schools instead of public schools. Under the current provisions of No Child Left Behind, parents may send their children to another school if their public school fails to meet prescribed standards. Charter schools may benefit from this provision. This competition will involve not only enrollment numbers but also curriculum content, student achievement levels, social values, and financial support.

Education Vouchers and Tax Credits. One proposed reform of education financing is a system of *education vouchers* or tax credits that would allow parents to select the school best suited to the needs of their children. This reform has strong conservative support as well as support from private schools. Vouchers allow public tax dollars to be redeemed at private schools for education services. A voucher system allows parents to use them as tuition payment at either public or private schools. The origin of the voucher concept can be traced to economist Milton Friedman's contention that the education system would be strengthened by free market competition between public and private schools;[37] public and private schools would either develop quality programs or cease to exist as their enrollments evaporated. Others have long supported vouchers or tax credits as a way of facilitating parental control over their children's education.

Proponents of the voucher plan argue that it is necessary to overcome the inflexibility of the existing local public school districts. This view holds that public schools, dominated by rigid professional education bureaucracies, are incapable of developing the programs and incentives necessary for an effective teaching and learning environment.

The concept of school vouchers enjoys significant public support. By 1999, some 60 percent of public school parents indicated support for the voucher system with elected officials (both Republican and Democrat) evenly split on the issue.[38]

School choice plans vary significantly. Some concern public schools only and allow parents to send their children to any public school regardless of district of residence. Other plans encourage the option of attending private schools (including religious schools) through vouchers, tax credits, or tax deductions. Tax credits would allow parents to deduct educational expenses from their actual federal or state income tax bill. In effect, parents would use money for private education expenses instead of paying it as income tax and would therefore be free from the burden of paying both tuition costs for a private education and contributing to the upkeep of public schools that their children do not attend.

The adoption of a system of vouchers or tax credits might spur an enrollment shift toward private schools, which progressives and public educators oppose on egalitarian grounds. Professional educators also have an interest in maintaining their control over local schools. Before desegregation, a duality existed in the education system based on race. If middle-class students are removed from the public system, a new duality could arise based on socioeconomic status, and a two-tiered educational system would be the final result. Private schools, funded with public tax monies, would constitute the upper tier, with public schools relegated to the bottom. Supporters of vouchers and credits counter that students from all economic classes would use the financial aids and that suburban/urban schools are already two-tiered, as well as socially and economically segregated.

The use of a voucher system might create nationwide social problems, according to opponents. The educational system acts as a major vehicle for political socialization through which the young achieve a common set of values and level of knowledge concerning the political and social system. A common curriculum and the opportunity to interact with students from diverse backgrounds achieve this result. A voucher system would segregate students in accordance with parental preferences, and the diversity of experiences available to public school students would disappear.

Private religious schools provide students with an educational environment in which religion is an integral part of the curriculum. Financial aid from government for religious education instantly evokes the doctrine of separation of church and state. Here, it is sufficient to say that the Court has struck down as unconstitutional state programs of general aid to religious schools. However, at the same time, the Court has allowed public funding to support a variety of services to private religious schools, as well as limited voucher programs. Proposals for assisting private and religious schools continue to face a serious constitutional challenge; this issue will remain on the education policy agenda.[39]

Crisis in Education

If an unfriendly foreign power had attempted to impose on America the mediocre educational performance that exists today, we might have viewed it as an act of war. As it stands we have allowed this to happen to ourselves.[40]

Thus stated the 1983 report of the National Commission on Excellence in Education. The report was critical of the current state of the nation's education system and concerned about the implications for the future. The ability of the United States to maintain a preeminent position in commerce, industry, science, and technology was, in the words of the Commission, "at risk." Competition from Japan, South Korea, and Western Europe places a burden on our education system to produce skilled, creative individuals in order to ensure economic strength.

The Commission's concerns extended beyond economic matters to the role of education in strengthening the foundations of a free and open democratic society. The Commission shared Jefferson's conviction that an educated public is necessary to supply intellectual and moral strength to the Union. Education also offers an appreciation for a pluralistic society and fosters a common political culture. According to the Commission, the problems in education quality was the functional illiteracy of twenty-three million Americans, American students' lower performance than students from other industrialized nations on nineteen academic tests, the continued decline in achievement test scores, and the proliferation of remedial courses at the college level. In addition, for the first time in American history, the educational skills of the current student generation will be lower than those of their parents.

The Commission's report was significant because it reflected the concern of elected officials, education professionals, and the general public about the perceived decline in the quality of education. The commission's recommendations focused on curriculum reform, with a renewed emphasis on the basics of education (English, science, math, and social studies) and on a longer school day and year (seven-hour day, 220-day academic year). The commission also endorsed the concepts of merit pay, competency testing for students and teachers, and the implementation of a master teacher program. It gave the primary responsibility for financing education to the local school districts and the states, limiting the federal government's fiscal role.

The failure of the United States to make significant progress toward overall educational excellence was documented in October 1991 and again in 2001, with the release of reports of the National Assessment of Educational Progress, prepared by the National Education Goals Panel, a group of governors and federal officials, and the Third International Mathematics and Science Study. These reports depicted a challenging overall picture of nationwide academic achievement. First, the average performance of American students has remained stable over the past twenty years and has not increased relative to other industrialized nations. In a competitive global economy, stability may be equated with stagnation and translated into a competitive disadvantage.

Second, wide disparities remain between high-achieving and low-achieving students in the areas of science and mathematics, with significant numbers of students lacking what may be defined as basic literacy in those two areas of learning. Data also suggest that the disparity between high- and low-achieving students in reading and language arts is now increasing in the United States. And third, in the area of science and mathematics, the average performance scores of American students are below those of Western Europe, the industrialized Pacific Rim nations, and Russia. Historically, the lack of rigor in the curriculum of American schools has been viewed as the source of much of these differences.[41]

The high school dropout rate remains a continuing problem, the magnitude of which appears in Figure 9.6. The national dropout rate of almost 9 percent is high, but the Hispanic rate is 22 percent. The failure of a significant proportion of the population to earn a high school diploma encourages the development of an undereducated minority class.

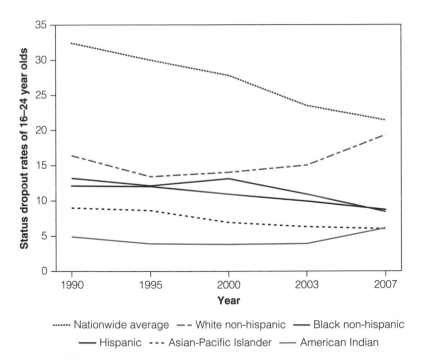

.... Nationwide average   – – White non-hispanic   —— Black non-hispanic
—— Hispanic   - - - Asian-Pacific Islander   —— American Indian

F I G U R E 9.6 Dropout Rates of 16–24 Year Olds: 1990 through 2007 by Race/Ethnicity*

*Race/Ethnicity used in the *Condition of Education, 2009* ". . . are in accordance with the 1997 Office of Management and Budget (OMB) standard classification scheme. . . . The 1997 standards emphasize self-reporting and self-identification as the preferred method for collecting data on race and ethnicity."

(Supplemental Note 1) Due to the small sample sizes for Asian-Pacific Islander and American Indian data for these two groups should be interpreted with caution.

SOURCE: U.S. Department of Education, National Center for Education Statistics, *The Condition of Education, 2009* Appendix A, Table A-20-2, pg. 183. http://nces.ed.gov/programs/coe/2009/section3/indicator20.asp; Accessed April 2010.

Changing Priorities in Federal Education Policy

The changing priorities of education policy are reflected in the changes of policy preferences at the federal level. The domestic policies of President Johnson (1963–1968), as embodied in his Great Society programs, encouraged new and innovative programs aimed at the educational needs of disadvantaged groups. Although the level of federal education spending did not increase dramatically, there was a general expectation that the proportion of federal aid would continue to increase. President Nixon (1969–1974) sought to shift the direction of federal education policy by placing greater emphasis on the role of state and local governments. The Carter administration (1977–1980) shifted slightly toward federal leadership in education policy. It created the Department of Education and renewed emphasis on governmental involvement in fostering equal educational opportunity.

President Reagan (1981–1988) led another shift in education policy, with attempts to transfer responsibility for education policy back to the state level. The 1980s also saw debate over curriculum content and reform. The Education Department developed two model curricula. *James Madison High School* (1987) and *James Madison Elementary School* (1988), published by the Department of Education, that embodied an emphasis on classical education with a college-preparatory focus. For example, the English requirement consisted of a four-year literature sequence: introduction to literature, American literature, British literature, and world literature. Three full years of mathematics included an emphasis on algebra, geometry, trigonometry, statistics, and calculus.

Although the approach pleased conservatives, because of its emphasis on traditional values, others were critical. Liberals, although commending the model's rigor, felt that it was overly narrow. While students were to read Homer, Shakespeare, the Bible, and other great literature, they would not be exposed to the works of contemporary women, minority, or ethnic authors.

Education Policy Priorities in the Twenty-First Century

The centerpiece of our National Education Strategy is not a program; it's not a test. It's a new challenge: to reinvent American education—to design new American schools for the year 2000 and beyond.
(*America 2000*, 1991)

In mid-1991, President George H. W. Bush released *America 2000: An Education Strategy*. Although *America 2000* presented very broad goals for the United States, some very specific policy preferences were included: adoption of a nationwide achievement test, publication of annual national and state report cards by the U.S. Department of Education to document student achievement levels, differential teacher pay for teachers in "dangerous and challenging environments," expansion of school choice options through the use of vouchers, and maintaining a limited federal financial role in funding education initiatives.

Implementation of *America 2000* was not achieved, primarily because the absence of federal funding made the plan unattractive. Figure 9.7 illustrates that

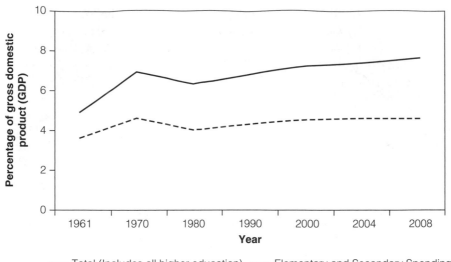

FIGURE 9.7 U.S. Education Spending as a Percentage of GDP, 1961–2008

SOURCE: U.S. Department of Education, National Center for Education Statistics, Digest of Education Statistics (2009), Table 26, Expenditures of educational institutions related to the gross domestic product, by level of institution: Selected years, 1929–30 through 2008–09; http://nces.ed.gov/programs/digest/d09/tables/dt09_026.asp?referrer=list; Accessed April 2010.

total spending on education, when measured as a percentage of GDP, rose in the 1960s and then declined from 1970 to 1980, rising only slightly in the most recent years. This increase is primarily from state, not federal, funds.

President Clinton proposed *Goals 2000* as the centerpiece of his education policy agenda. This program contained the same basic goals as those announced by President George H. W. Bush in his *America 2000* initiative. The importance of Clinton's education policy was to give the states participating in the program the option of either adopting the national standards developed by the National Education Standards and Improvement Council (NESIC) or developing their own standards, which must be of "equal or higher quality" than NESIC standards.

Goals 2000 involved a strategy of federal policy leadership in the areas of curriculum and education outcomes, but with minimal federal funding. This policy initiative involved a greater role for the federal government using mandated policy guidelines. These goals generated considerable debate between conservatives and liberals. Conservatives supported many of the individual goals, such as school choice and technological literacy, but they opposed the creation of national standards developed by a federal education bureaucracy. Conservatives were concerned about the impact of mandatory national testing programs and of the cultural values that might be mandated for inclusion in the school curriculum. Progressives tended to support these initiatives, but had reservations about some components, such as school choice and the creation of charter schools. Liberals tended to be less concerned about national standards and the values that education professionals would include in curriculum.

President George W. Bush developed an education policy initiative of his own when the *No Child Left Behind Act of 2002 (NCLB)* was signed into law in January 2002 as a reauthorization of the Elementary and Secondary Education Act. NCLB is best understood as a continuation and expansion of the education policy initiatives of President George H. W. Bush and President Clinton. Box 9.2 presents the significant provisions of this education initiative.

NCLB as a Source of Policy Conflict. The debate surrounding potential reauthorization of NCLB continues. The act remains in force but was not reauthorized in 2007 and remained on the agenda in 2010. First, federal funding levels to public schools have not increased significantly as a result of the Act. The primary funding source for education programs continues to be from state governments and the local school district. Liberals' criticism of NCLB is linked to this lack of federal funding for implementation across the fifty states. They argue that this federal program initiative should be accompanied by sufficient federal

---

B o x 9.2   The No Child Left Behind Act of 2001 (Re-Authorization of ESEA in 2002)

Accountability and Assessment: Annual assessment of student achievement in reading and math in grades three to eight, accompanied by school and state report cards. Districts required to demonstrate "proficiency" for all groups of students enrolled.

State and Local Flexibility: Reduces the number of ESEA programs from fifty-five to forty-five and allows states to transfer up to 50 percent of non–Title I funds into other ESEA areas without advance federal approval. Local districts may participate in "flexibility demonstration projects" to consolidate all federal funds in exchange for agreements to produce higher student achievement.

Expansion of Parental Choice: Parents of children in "failing schools" are allowed to transfer their child to a higher performing public school or charter school and to obtain supplemental education services from either public- or private-sector providers.

Emphasis on Reading: Provides federal funding assistance to local districts in order to achieve the goal that every child can read by the end of third grade.

Improvement of Teacher Quality: Provides federal grant funding to states to improve teacher recruitment and retention in exchange for agreements to improve student achievement.

Promoting English Proficiency: Consolidate bilingual and immigrant education programs with emphasis on improved teaching methods and testing of student achievement after a student has been in the school system for three consecutive years.

Safe Schools: Districts must use federal funding to implement drug and violence prevention programs with provisions that students in "persistently dangerous schools" be allowed to transfer to another public or charter school.

SOURCE: *A Guide to Education and* No Child Left Behind (Washington, DC: U.S. Department of Education, 2004), www2.ed.gov/nclb/overview/intro/guide/index.html; Accessed October 10, 2010.

dollars if the local districts are to successfully comply with the requirements. Conservatives are opposed to increased federal funding for NCLB, holding that implementation funding should rest with states and local districts in order to retain a degree of local autonomy in education policy. At the same time, conservatives tend to oppose NCLB because component parts of the Act control and direct curricular decisions that historically are the domain of local districts. Liberals find reason to support NCLB precisely because it seeks to establish national standards and is therefore a potential mechanism to promote equality of educational opportunity. NCLB is a source of conflict both within and between conservatives and liberals.

Critics of NCLB hold that the Act is a mechanism that imposes an unfunded mandate on local school districts and the states. In order to continue to receive existing limited federal funding, the states will be required to absorb the costs associated with implementation of the Act. Critics hold that any federal policy mandate should be accompanied by sufficient federal funding associated with that policy. Proponents of NCLB hold that the requirements accommodate significant latitude for states to establish their own goals, and therefore the states should assume primary responsibility for program costs.

NCLB generates conflict relating to the issue of national versus local control of education policy. A central component of the Act is the concept of *Adequate Yearly Progress*, or AYP. The NCLB requires that adequate yearly progress be achieved such that 100 percent of students in each class and each school are rated as proficient by 2014. Education professionals find that these requirements apply to all students regardless of their individual level of intelligence, motivation, learning disability, and family background. Each state is required to establish standards that measure the AYP of students as a mechanism to hold local districts and schools accountable for their educational performance. Each state is also required to establish clearly defined goals for student and school performance. Students in school that fail to meet their AYP goals become eligible to transfer to other schools. Proponents of the program argue that states have significant flexibility to define their own performance goals. Advocates of local control argue that NCLB will ultimately evolve into a mechanism for the imposition of national standards and national goals on local districts. Advocates of a more centralized education policy are concerned that the provisions allowing states to develop their own standards will not strengthen the curriculum and improve performance, but will foster continued decentralization.

An integral component of NCLB involves reliance on a program of regular testing of student performance to assess AYP. These tests have been identified as high-stakes testing for schools. Student performance on the tests will be used to assess school performance and will be reported to the general public. Schools not meeting their AYP goals may qualify for corrective action and students attending those schools may be allowed to transfer to other, higher performing schools. One result of this provision is a linkage between NCLB and the school choice movement. Proponents of school choice argue that students should have the freedom to move to higher performing schools if their own school is performing at a low level. Some proponents also see this provision for school choice as a potential mechanism for students to transfer to higher performing private schools. Critics of this provision argue that such high-stakes testing acts to weaken the commitment of the public to the public school system as parents may be given the ability to shop for higher performing schools. One potential result could be a renewed emphasis on charter schools that target students from low-performing schools.

Classroom teachers and school principals find themselves under intense pressure to demonstrate that the students under their care achieve proficient test scores. In order to adapt to the requirement for ever-increasing student performance on tests two strategies have developed. One involves a narrowing of the curriculum to teach primarily material on the standardized tests. The second involves beginning the school year in early August in order to provide more time to prepare students to take the tests that are typically administered in early fall. Professional educators and other critics have argued that NCLB guarantees that virtually all of the nation's schools will receive a failing grade by 2014.

Finally, to return to the writings of Thomas Jefferson, education in a democracy was intended to focus on such values as judgment, critical thinking, justice, civic responsibility, and independent thinking. The emphasis of NCLB on achieving proficiency on standardized test scores seems to be in conflict with this view of education.

Education Policy Initiatives of President Obama

My Administration's blueprint for reauthorization of the Elementary and Secondary Education Act is not only a plan to renovate a flawed law, but also an outline for a reenvisioned federal role in education. (President Obama, *A Blueprint for Reform* 2010)

The education policy preferences announced by President Obama reflect an expanding emphasis on federal education policy leadership with only a marginal increase in federal funding. As of mid-2010, President Obama's policy initiatives remained under discussion and were subject to modification in Congress. One element involves reauthorization of the NCLB legislation with an emphasis on requiring students to demonstrate progress in their test scores rather than achieving a specified level of proficiency as measured by testing. States receiving federal funding would also be required to strengthen teacher and administrator evaluation systems in order to improve school performance and enhance teaching effectiveness.

Under his plan, Charter Schools continue to be encouraged and would receive support as a mechanism to give parents more choice in the education of their children. Federal education funding to states would require states and local school districts to encourage the growth and development of charter schools.

President Obama also seeks to increase the emphasis on science, technology, engineering and mathematics (STEM) in local school districts. This initiative involves cooperation with the National Science Foundation (NSF) and other agencies in the development of education strategies in this area. Federal policy leadership would also be expanded though a range of initiatives targeting education such as Race to the Top, Promise Neighborhoods, Early Childhood Education programs, 21st Century Community Learning Centers, and a variety of other program initiatives that remain in the development stage.

Critics of the initiatives advocated by President Obama argue that the programs serve to expand federal control with an absence of federal funding. For example, Race to the Top provided minimal levels of new federal dollars ($100 to $700 million) to states *if* the developed programs were consistent with federal policy guidelines. As of mid–2010, four states had decided against applying for the first two rounds of Race to the Top funding (Texas, Vermont, North Dakota and Virginia). Critics also cite the fact that expansion of federal funding for elementary and secondary education was only in the $3 billion dollar range for FY 2011. Under the Race to the Top, program federal influence would continue to increase, but federal funding would not change from historic levels in the 8 to 10 percent range (see Figure 9.1). Given the significant federal budget deficit, federal aid to education will not be expanded in the foreseeable future.

The education policy initiatives of President Obama remained fluid in mid–2010 without Congressional action. Debate over the federal role in education will continue as federal policy initiatives continue to mandate policy direction without an increase in federal funding.

Unresolved Education Issues: Teachers and Curriculum

A number of unresolved issues remain on the education policy agenda. Drug abuse remains a serious problem for schools today. Violence and crime emerged as major issues in the 1990s and present significant challenges to the education system arising from the incidence of student violence and homicide at a number of schools. One response has been the development of zero tolerance codes for weapons, fighting, drugs, and other student behaviors in an effort to promote student safety.

National Teacher Certification. The qualifications of teachers remain an important issue. Professional educators created the nongovernmental National Board for Professional Teaching Standards in 1987 in response to the publication of a report by the Carnegie Forum on Education and the Economy titled *A Nation Prepared* (1986). The primary focus of this report was the establishment of *national* standards to assess and certify teachers, as opposed to the decentralized process used by the fifty states today. Proponents argue that teacher certification has too much of an impact on education quality to continue reliance on the states with their decentralized uncoordinated standards.[42] Before 2000, there were only some 9,500 nationally certified teachers; by 2010, this number had increased to over 87,000.

Workforce Preparation. Historically, the American public education system produced two types of graduates. One group was students on a college track, who would later become managers, decision makers, and scientific or technical experts. The second group consisted of students who would enter the workforce after graduation and assume nontechnical positions in the nation's factories.

Today's economy requires workers who are capable of rapid and continuous learning to improve productivity and enhance the global competitiveness of the nation.[43] Some federal programs provide limited financial assistance for partnerships among school districts, businesses, labor unions, and community groups, that provide high school students with work experience and insights into the education requirements for specific careers.

Proponents of these programs argue that students should be exposed to the relationship between education and careers while in high school, rather than after graduation. Such exposure will translate into increased student motivation in the classroom and an appreciation of the need for lifelong learning. Critics argue that the program simply provides academic credit for low-level, part-time jobs that have little relevance to a genuine career.

Moral Education. Conservatives argue that the schools have an obligation to provide a moral foundation for the nation's children through an emphasis on traditional values. The Northwest Ordinance in 1787 clearly linked "religion, morality, and knowledge" to good government. Federal legislation in the twentieth century did not emphasize moral foundations, but stressed values, such as national security, equality, and separation of church and state. Both liberals and conservatives are increasingly concerned that moral foundations be linked to the education process.[44] However, differences over substance are divisive. Conservatives emphasize values that stress the importance of the individual as shaped by institutions, such as the church, the family, and traditional political values. These values then shape collective societal values. Liberals, however, place greater emphasis on social values that shape institutions such as the church, the family, and the political culture. These collective values then shape the values of the individual.

A related movement, back to the basics, advocated an increased emphasis on basic skills, such as reading, writing, and arithmetic, but also traditional values of respect, obedience, and moral content.[45] The movement first emerged in the late 1950s after the Soviet Union launched Sputnik, the first space satellite. During this early period, the emphasis was on basic education as a foundation for national security. Basic skills of the 1950s did not focus on individual and personal goal attainment, but rather on the individual's responsibility to use basic skills to contribute to the national good. Current debates over curriculum can be traced directly to the back-to-the-basics movement.

Intelligent Design and Evolution. A significant policy issue involves conflict over inclusion of intelligent design in the curriculum as either a balance or opposing position to evolution. The issue is complex and involves two elements. The first element involves discussion relevant to the presence or absence of conflict between religions and generally accepted scientific precepts. When conflict is present (such as between theistic creationism and evolution), does the education system have the obligation to present materials advocating both positions? The conflict between evolution and intelligent design will continue in the next several years.

The second factor involves the issue of the establishment clause in the U.S. Constitution as related to separation of church and state. In 1968, the U.S. Supreme Court in *Epperson v. Arkansas*[46] ruled that states could not ban the teaching of evolution due to a conflict with religious beliefs. In 1987, the U.S. Supreme Court in *Edwards v. Aguillard*[47] ruled that states could not mandate that teachers include a discussion of creation science when discussing evolution. The federal courts tend to hold that teaching of either creation science or intelligent design involves establishment of religion and is therefore in violation of the Constitution. This topic remains a hot button issue on the policy agenda and will continue as a source of conflict.

Unresolved Education Issues: Structural Questions

Charter Schools.   The concept of the *charter school* was introduced in the mid-1980s and is designed to allow the creation of an independent legal entity with responsibility for delivery of education programs.[48] Under this concept, state boards of education grant a charter to either a public or private group to organize and operate a school. A charter school is a tuition-free entity that receives funding from the state and provides educational choice to students and parents. Charter schools blur the distinction between public and private school systems since they can be considered as either quasi-public or quasi-private entities. The charter school movement began with two schools in 1991 in Minnesota and has experienced significant growth. The number of charter schools is somewhat difficult to estimate because some schools cease to operate during any given year and because some schools receive charters but may not be in operation. Charter schools are in operation in over thirty states and have a total enrollment of over 550,000 students.

Local school boards have minimal responsibility for the operation of a charter school within their jurisdiction. Some states eliminated their responsibility. Proponents of charter schools argue that they present a unique opportunity for education reform. Critics of charter schools see the movement as simply a modification of a voucher system for private schools.

Charter schools may serve as a new approach to create autonomous schools that can respond to specific educational needs and develop creative strategies to improve student performance that are unattainable by current school systems.[49] For example, some charter schools build their entire program around the arts; others emphasize the sciences; still others focus on multicultural education; and so forth.

Privatization.   Another educational reform movement involves the creation of privately managed public schools. Education Alternatives, Inc. (EAI), in what is now known as the Edison Project, promoted this idea as a mechanism to improve the performance and quality of local schools.[50] Under this concept, the operation of either a single school or an entire district may be contracted out to a private firm. Proponents argue that initiative provided by the private sector provides a mechanism to improve the performance of schools by reinventing the curriculum and teaching techniques. Proponents also believe that privatization is consistent with the charter school movement. Critics argue that there is no evidence that privately operated public schools actually perform at a higher level than their public managed counterparts do and that concern for profitability of the enterprise will require that student needs become a secondary priority.

In 1995, four school districts (Baltimore City Public School District, Maryland; Dade County Public Schools, Florida; Hartford School District, Connecticut; and Minneapolis School District, Minnesota) had contracts with private companies for school management. In 1996, five other districts (Boston–Massachusetts, Mt. Clemens–Michigan, Sherman–Texas, Wichita–Kansas, and Wilkinsburg–Pennsylvania) entered into management contracts with private companies. This process continued with the City of Philadelphia assigning the management of forty-two schools to the private sector in 2002; other cities such as Detroit and Chicago followed suit in 2009. Often, privatization emerges as a last-ditch effort to salvage failing urban schools.

The authority granted to the private contractor varies from district to district. Mixed evaluation results produce significant conflict. Benefits included an increase in student attendance rates, a drop in suspension rates, increased access to computers in classrooms, and improved building maintenance. Privatization varies in scope, from contracting for limited services, such as cafeteria, maintenance, and transportation, to managing an entire school. Because privatization experiments are so diverse, it remains an unsettled issue on the education policy agenda.

Home Schooling.   Perhaps the ultimate form of privatization in education is the development of home schooling. Under this model, parents assume primary responsibility for the education of their children. Some parents undertake this effort because of dissatisfaction with their local public schools; others wish to provide a religious education specifically in keeping with their beliefs. Still other parents wish to allow their children to develop their learning more naturally, instead of through the perceived artificial organization of standardized public school curricula.

Estimates are that almost two million students participated in home schooling in 2010. Based on the limited evidence available, children participating in home schooling perform at a level higher than their public school contemporaries do. Parents involved in home schooling have organized at the state and national level to defend their right to educate their children at home with considerable success. Virtually all states now recognize the rights of parents to supervise their children's education in this setting; colleges increasingly accept home-schooled students, despite the lack of conventional transcripts and recommendations.

Single–Gender Schools.   Public education in the United States evolved from single-gender (boys only) to coeducational schools by the mid- to late 1800s. During the colonial period, formal education tended to be limited to boys, with girls receiving informal education at home. By 1890, coeducation was the norm across the nation. In 1972, Title IX of the Education Amendments prohibited discrimination against students based on sex and imposed limits on single-gender institutions. The Citadel and the Virginia Military Institute are two public universities forced to abandon their single-gender status and to admit women students. Some educators now advocate single-gender elementary and secondary schools as a viable alternative to increase student achievement. Proponents argue that single-gender schools for girls reduce distractions, provide greater self-confidence, enhance the development of leadership skills, and reduce the risk of educational failure. In 2006, the U.S. Department of Education's Office of Civil Rights (OCR) issued new policy guidelines that allowed waivers to Title IX and other statutes. Flexibility was provided to schools to provide single-sex schools, classes, and extracurricular activities.

Issues in Higher Education

Diversity and Affirmative Action.   Justice Powell introduced the concept of diversity as a rationale for group preferences in the *Bakke* decision dealing with the issue of reverse discrimination. (See Chapter 10 for discussion of this term and of affirmative action in general.) Diversity became a value embraced by colleges and universities across the nation. Higher education flourishes when varieties of racial, economic, ethnic, and social groups interact on the same campus. Moreover, graduation from college increasingly is necessary for economic and social advancement in American society. Minority groups and women see pursuit of diversity in higher education as a way to remedy the effects of historical discrimination. Diversity thus served as the primary legal justification in the admissions process for over fifteen years. It continues to be a significant value in higher education.

Affirmative action in admissions has been one of the primary means to achieve diversity in higher education (see Chapter 10). However, the future role of affirmative action admissions programs for colleges and universities is unclear. California's passage of Proposition 209 in November 1996 (an amendment to the state constitution that prohibits the use of race-based and gender-based preferences in hiring, contracting, and education) signaled a significant education policy shift. The amendment survived a challenge in the federal courts and affected 1997–1998 admissions policies. As Chapter 10 shows, the U.S. Supreme Court has interpreted the Constitution to permit limited forms of affirmative action in higher education, in which race and ethnicity are among a variety of factors that admissions officers may take into account.

Affirmative action programs have their greatest impact primarily in highly selective colleges and universities where there is considerable competition in the admissions process. At other colleges, the impact of affirmative action in terms of granting an advantage based on race or gender is actually relatively minor. This means that the elimination of affirmative action programs in university admission standards will not have a uniform effect on all university campuses. It does mean that some of the most selective public institutions may no longer be as accessible to some groups in society. Figure 9.8 indicates that Hispanics particularly continue to be underrepresented in higher education. An additional factor is that Hispanics and

African Americans tend to be overrepresented in two-year institutions and under-represented in four-year colleges and universities. Indications remain that voter in-itiatives will continue in an effort to limit affirmative action standards in state university admission processes. This will remain an area of policy conflict.

Cost of Higher Education.   One issue on the policy agenda involves the ever-increasing cost of higher education. Tuition increased dramatically for both public and private four-year colleges between 1975 and 2008 (see Figure 9.9), a rate sig-nificantly greater than the median household income increase for the same period.

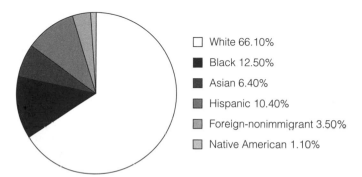

F I G U R E 9.8   Higher Education Enrollment, 2007 (as a percentage of total enrollment)

SOURCE: U.S. Department of Education, National Center for Education Statistics, Fast Facts, 2009. Pg. 344, Table 9.8. Percentage distribution of students enrolled in degree-granting institutions by race/ethnicity. http://nces.ed.gov/fact-facts/display.asp?id=98; Accessed March 2010.

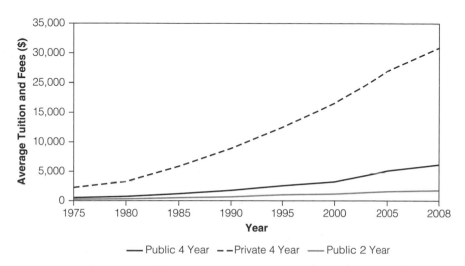

F I G U R E 9.9   Average Undergraduate Tuition, 1975–2008 (excluding room and board)

SOURCE: U.S. Census Bureau, *Statistical Abstract of the United States, 2010.* Table 278. Average Total Price of Atten-dance of Undergraduate Education; http://www.census.gov/compendia/statab/cats/education.html; Accessed April 2010.

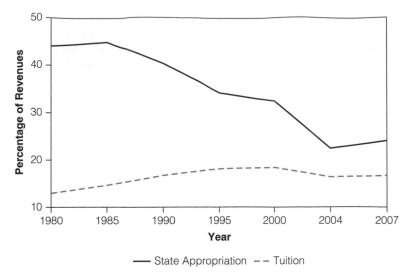

FIGURE 9.10 Tuition Dollars and State Appropriations for Four-Year Public Colleges 1980–2007

SOURCE: U.S. Department of Education, National Center for Education Statistics (2006), Digest of Education Statistics, 2007, Tables 337 and 338, http://nces.ed.gov/programs/digest/d06/tables_3asp#Ch3aSub7, Accessed July 2007 and U.S. Department of Education, National Center for Education Statistics (2009), The Condition of Education P. 345. http://nces.ed.gov/programs/coe/2009/section5/indicator46.asp; Accessed April 2010.

Two factors contribute most to the increase in tuition: spending increases by colleges and a greater dependency on tuition and a reduction in state funding as a source of revenue. Public universities are increasingly state-assisted rather than state-funded institutions. Figure 9.10 shows that state funding has decreased as a source of revenue. The decrease in public funding must be offset by an accompanying increase in tuition. Universities have been able to use research funding, gifts, and endowments only as a small buffer for tuition charge increases.

If the goal of higher education for most Americans is to be attained state legislators will have to make difficult choices about raising taxes to fund higher education or cutting other programs to free up funds.

ENDNOTES

1. Quoted in S. E. Frost, Jr., and Kenneth P. Bailey, *Historical and Philosophical Foundations of Western Education*, 2nd ed. (Columbus, OH: Merrill, 1973), 340.

2. William M. French, *America's Educational Tradition* (Lexington, MA: Heath, 1964), 54–60.

3. Robert L. Church, *Education in the United States* (New York: Free Press, 1976), 420.

4. U.S. Bureau of the Census, *Statistical Abstract of the United States, 2010*, Table 253, www.census.gov/compendia/statab/2010/tables/10s0253.pdf; Accessed April 25, 2010.

5. U.S. Department of Education, National Center for Education Statistics, *Revenues and Expenditures for Public Elementary and Secondary Schools Districts (Fiscal Year 2007)*, Table 1. Total revenues per pupil at the 5th percentile, median, and 95th percentile, federal range ratio, number of districts, and number of students, by state: School year 2006-07, fiscal year 2007, http://nces.ed.gov/pubs2009/revexpdist07/tables/table_01.asp; Accessed April 25, 2010.

6. See Mary E. Moran, "Standards and Assessments: The New Measure of Adequacy in School Finance Litigation," *Journal of Education Finance*, 25 (Summer 1999): 33–80, for an expanded discussion of court cases addressing financial disparities.

7. Serrano v. Priest, 5 Cal. 3d 584 (1971).

8. *San Antonio Independent School District v. Rodriguez*, 411 U.S. 1 (1973).

9. See Katharine L. Bradbury, "School District Spending and State Aid: Why Disparities Persist," *New England Economic Review* (January/February 1994), for a discussion of some of the factors that affect local district spending.

10. See Debora A. Berstege and Richard A. King, "The Relationship between School Spending and Student Achievement: A Review and Analysis of 35 Years of Production Function Research," *Journal of Education Finance*, 2 (Fall 1998): 243–262, for a review of the literature relating to school spending and student achievement.

11. See Mary E. Moran, "Standards and Assessments," for a discussion of student performance in the education funding debate.

12. See National Center for Educational Statistics, "Do Rich and Poor Districts Spend Alike?" (Washington, DC: National Center for Educational Statistics, December 1996); and "Disparities in Public School District Spending" (Washington, DC: National Center for Educational Statistics, February 1995).

13. See Anne T. Lockwood, *The Future of School Finance* (Madison, WI: National Center for Effective Schools, 1994).

14. See D. Van Slyke, School Finance Litigation: A Review of Key Cases (ERIC Document Reproduction Service, No: ED 394-195, 1995).

15. The National Commission on Excellence in Education, *A Nation at Risk: The Imperative for Educational Reform* (Washington, DC: U.S. Government Printing Office, 1983), 4.

16. N. F. Ashline, T. R. Pezzulo, and C. I. Norris, eds., *Education, Inequality and National Policy* (Lexington, MA: Heath, 1976), 49.

17. The College Board, *Balancing the SAT Scales* (Princeton, NJ: The College Board, 1994).

18. See Lawrence C. Stedman, "The Achievement Crisis Is Real," *Education Policy Analysis Archives*, 4, No. 1 (January 1996).

19. See, for example, Donald Rock et al., *Factors Associated with Decline of Test Scores of High School Seniors, 1972–1980* (Washington, DC: Center for Statistics, Department of Education, 1985).

20. See David C. Berliner and Bruce J. Biddle, *The Manufactured Crisis* (Reading, MA: Addison Wesley, 1995).

21. See Norman Frederikson, *The Influence of Minimum Competency Tests on Teaching and Learning* (Princeton, NJ: Educational Testing Service, 1994).

22. Diana Pullin, "Minimum Competency Testing: The Denied Diploma and the Pursuit of Educational Opportunity and Educational Adequacy" (ERIC Document Reproduction Service No. ED 228–279, 1982).

23. J. S. Catterall, "Standards and School Dropouts: A National Study of Tests Required for High School Graduation," *American Journal of Education*, 98 (November 1989): 1–34.

24. Danielle B. Kuper, "Reconsidering The Minimum Competency Test Strategy in No Child Left Behind: An Agenda for Reform," *Practical Assessment Research and Evaluation,* 11, No. 1 (January 2006), http://pareonline.net/getvn.asp?v=11&n=1.

25. See Dan Goldhabe and M. Hansen "Race, Gender, and Teacher Testing: How Informative a Tool Is Teacher Licensure Testing?" *American Educational Research Journal.* 47, No. 1 (March 1, 2010): 218–251.

26. See Rosabeth M. Kanter, "Attack on Pay," *Harvard Business Review*, 65 (1987): 60–67, for a complete discussion of the impact of position status on compensation.

27. A. I. Ramirez, "How Merit Pay Undermines Education," *Educational Leadership*, 58, No. 5 (February 2001): 16–20.

28. See Susan M. Johnson, "Merit Pay for Teachers: A Poor Prescription for Reform," *Harvard Educational Review*, 54 (May 1984): 175–188.

29. See Clive R. Belfield and John Heywood, "Performance Pay for Teachers: Determinants and Consequences," *Economics of Education Review,* 27, No. 3 (June 2008): 243–252.

30. See Elvia M. Hernandez, "The Effects of Proper Implementation of Bilingual Programs in Elementary Schools in the United States," in M.S. Plakotnik, S. M. Nielson, and D. M. Pane, eds., *Proceedings of the Eighth Annual College of Education Research Conference* (2009), pp. 62–68, http://coeweb.fiu.edu/Research_Conference/Proceedings.html; Accessed April 20, 2010.

31. See "Infusing Multicultural Education into Today's Schools, an Annotated Bibliography" (ERIC Document Reproduction Services, No. ED 369-703, 1993), for an extensive bibliography on multicultural education.

32. Nancy P. Greenman and Ellen B. Kimmel, "The Road to Multicultural Education: Potholes of Resistance," *Journal of Teacher Education*, 45, No. 5 (November–December 1995): 360–368.

33. American Association of Colleges for Teacher Education Commission on Multicultural Education, "No One Model American," *Journal of Teacher Education*, 24, No. 4 (September–October, 1973): 264–265.

34. Jesus. Garcia and Sharon L. Pugh, "Multicultural Education in Teacher Preparation Programs: A Political or an Educational Concept?" *Phi Delta Kappan*, 74, No. 4: 214–219. (Nov 1992).

35. Louis Goldman, "Misconceptions of Culture and Perversions of Multiculturalism," *Interchange*, 24, No. 4 (1993).

36. See Sonia Nieto, "Multiculturalism in Higher Education: Emerging Literature," *Equity and Excellence in Education*, 26, No. 3 (1993); and Lynne Goldstein, "Achieving a Multicultural Curriculum: Conceptual, Pedagogical, and Structural Issues," *The Journal of General Education*, 43, No. 2 (1994), for a discussion of some of the issues facing higher education.

37. Margaret Hadderman, "Educational Vouchers" (ERIC Digest, Number 137, May 2000, ERIC Clearinghouse on Educational Management, Eugene, OR).

38. "Annual Phi Delta Kappa/Gallup Poll of the Public's Attitudes toward Public Schools," *Phi Delta Kappan*, 81, No. 1 (September 1999): 41–55.

39. See Amy S. Wells and Stuart Biegel, "Public Funds for Private Schools: Political and First Amendment Considerations," *American Journal of Education*, 101 (May 1993): 209–233, for a discussion of the legal issues in the voucher debate.

40. The National Commission on Excellence in Education, *A Nation at Risk*, 5.

41. See Alan Vanneman, Linda Hamilton, Janet Anderson, Janet Baldwin, and Taslima Rahman, "Achievement Gaps: How Black and White Students in Public Schools Perform in Mathematics and Reading on the National Assessment of Educational Progress. Statistical Analysis Report," National Center for Education Statistics, 2009, for a discussion of educational achievement gaps in the United States.

42. Lee Shulman and Gary Sykes, *A National Board for Teaching? In Search of a Bold Standard* (Palo Alto, CA: Stanford University School of Education, 1986).

43. Benjamin Duke, *Japanese Schools: Lessons for Industrial America* (New York: Praeger, 1986).

44. Carl Kaestle, "Moral Education and Common Schools in America: A Historian's View," *Journal of Moral Education* (May 1984): 101–111.

45. Ellen V. Leininger, "Back to the Basics: Underlying Concepts and Controversy," *Elementary School Journal*, 79, No. 3 (1979): 167–173.

46. *Epperson v. Arkansas*, 393 U.S. 97 (1968).

47. *Edwards v. Aguillard*, 42 U.S. 578 (1987). Additional information for both positions is readily available on the World Wide Web. See the following intelligent design–related websites: Center for Scientific Creation, www.creationscience.com/online-book/; Intelligent Design Network, www.intelligentdesignnetwork.org/.

48. Louann A. Bierlein and Lori A. Mulholland, "The Promise of Charter Schools," *Educational Leadership*, 52 (September 1994): 34–40.

49. General Accounting Office, Charter Schools: New Model for Public Schools Provides Opportunities and Challenges (Washington, DC: U.S. Government Printing Office, 1995).

50. Benno C. Schmidt, Jr., "The Edison Project's Plan to Redefine Public Education," *Educational Leadership*, 52 (September 1994): 61–64.

RESOURCES

Books

Banks, James A., and McGee-Banks, Cherry A. *Multicultural Education: Issues and Perspectives*. 7th edition. Hoboken, NJ: John Wiley & Sons, 2010.

Bennett, William J. *James Madison High School: A Curriculum for American Students*. Washington, DC: U.S. Department of Education, December 1987.

Betts, Julian. *Taking Measure of Charter Schools*. New York: Rowman & Littlefield, 2010.

Cooper, Bruce, James Cibulka, and Lance Fusarelli, eds. *Handbook of Education Politics and Policy*. New York: Routledge, 2008.

Education Week. *The Obama Education Plan: An Education Week Guide*. San Francisco: Wiley, 2009.

Greenhaven Press. *Are School Zero-Tolerance Policies Effective?* Farmington Hills, MI: Greenhaven Press (Cengage), 2010.

Howell, William, ed. *Besieged: School Boards and the Future of Education Policies*. Washington, DC: Brookings Institution, 2005.

Jencks, Christopher et al. *Inequality*. New York: Basic Books, 1972.

Kozol, Jonathan. *Savage Inequalities*. New York: Crown, 1991.

Loveless, Tom, and Hess, Frederick, eds. *Brookings Papers on Education Policy: 2006–2007*. Washington, DC: Brookings Institution, 2007.

McQuinn, Patrick J. *No Child Left Behind and the Transformation of Federal Education Policy*. Lawrence, KS: University of Kansas Press, 2006.

National Commission on Excellence in Education. *A Nation at Risk: The Imperative for Educational Reform*. Washington, DC: U.S. Government Printing Office, 1983.

Odden, Allan R., and Picus, Lawrence O. *School Finance: A Policy Perspective*. New York: McGraw-Hill, 2007.

Ravitch, Diane. *The Death and Life of the Great American School System: How Testing and Choice Are Undermining Education*. New York: Basic Books, 2010.

Salisbury, David, and Tooley, James, eds. *What America Can Learn from School Choice in Other Countries*. Washington, DC: Cato Institute, 2005.

Shober, Arnold F. *Splintered Accountability: State Governance and Education Reform*. Albany: SUNY Press, 2010.

Walberg, Herbert J. *School Choice: The Findings*. Washington, DC: Cato Institute, 2007.

Websites

American Association of University Professors: **www.aaup.org**

American Federation of Teachers: **www.aft.org**

Annenberg Institute for School Reform: **www.annenberginstitute.org**

Center for Education Reform: **www.edreform.com/**

Charter Schools: **www.uscharterschools.org**

Edison Project: **www.edisonlearning.com**

Education Resources Information Center (ERIC): **www.eric.ed.gov/**

Homeschooling website: **www.home-school.com**

National Board for Professional Teaching Standards: **www.nbpts.org**

National Catholic Educational Association: **www.ncea.org**

National Center for Education Statistics: **www.nces.ed.gov**

National Center for the Study of Privatization in Education: **www.ncspe.org/**
National Education Association: **www.nea.org**
National School Boards Association: **www.nsba.org**
Regional Education Laboratory Program: **http://ies.ed.gov/ncee/edlabs/**
School Choices: **www.schoolchoices.org**
United States Department of Education: **www.ed.gov**

Chapter 10

Legal and Social Equality: The Struggle Against Oppression and Bigotry

Few concepts in the context of either domestic or international politics are capable of generating as much symbolic and emotional appeal as equality. Traceable in some form as far back as the concept of justice, its roots precede Plato. The term *equality* is certainly a familiar and recurring one in the history of Western thought.

Yet despite its strong symbolism and cultural familiarity, the substantive content of the term has remained imprecise, inconsistent, or both. A central theme of this chapter is that three distinguishable conceptualizations of equality have existed: equality under law, equality of opportunity, and equality of material well-being. Each conceptualization implies different goals for public policy, and the dominant reading of the term has changed over time. Indeed, definitional quarrels in the matter of race have become so pervasive that Stephen and Abigail Thernstrom contend that "today we argue without a common language" in this area.[1] A generation ago a widespread conception of racism involved judging the qualities of people by the racial group to which they belong and treating them accordingly. We will see later that a current conceptualization of symbolic racism includes a demand that race be used as a factor in selecting people for employment or admission to selective universities. Terms in this area are used as much for their emotional and symbolic content as for their precise meaning.

Not only has the meaning of the concept of racism evolved but the dominant attitudes about questions of race and equality have undergone tremendous changes in the past generation. Not long ago, when prominent African Americans such as Jesse Jackson or Al Sharpton put themselves up as candidates for the presidency, these candidacies were widely regarded as symbolic gestures. No serious political commentator argued that an African American could garner enough white votes to actually get the nomination, let alone actually win the presidency. However, the decisive electoral victory of Barack Obama in 2008 when he carried 52.9 percent of the national vote[2] suggested to many that the racism that would prevent a white person from voting for an African American simply because of his/her race has become the exception rather than the rule. While there is undoubtedly lingering racial bigotry in the United States, Obama's election suggests that race is no longer the absolute impediment for racial minorities to attain any high office to which they might aspire.

However, other scholars, such as Michael Lewis Beck, Charles Tien, and Richard Nadeau, argue that substantial racism continues to exist in the United States and that racism prevented Barack Obama from winning by a greater margin given the circumstances working against the Republicans.

This chapter will demonstrate that an expanding sense of equality of material well-being has come to dominate the policy process. Meanwhile, the roster of groups identified by the policy process and the media as official victims of discrimination has been expanding. To the evils of racism (referring to discrimination against African Americans, Hispanics, and Native Americans) and sexism (referring to discrimination against women) have been added ageism (discrimination against the elderly), ableism (discrimination against the handicapped), homophobia (discrimination against homosexuals), and nativism (discrimination against foreign born or immigrants). The law has further developed the concept of the rights of children independent of their families. Children have acquired the right to sue their parents and even to "divorce" their parents. The status and rights of foreign-born citizens and legal immigrants to this country is the ongoing controversy over the question of whether illegal immigrants have rights and whether these persons should be granted citizenship (see Chapter 11). This issue came to national attention with the 1994 passage of a referendum in California of Proposition 187, a vote that amended the California Constitution to deny public benefits, including welfare, access to public health facilities, and even the right to attend public school, to illegal aliens and their children. Spokespersons for Hispanic immigrants challenged the constitutionality of that proposition in federal court. A federal district court declared the proposition unconstitutional in 1998. Possible appeals are pending. Meanwhile, the issue of illegal entry into the United States, largely over our Southern border with Mexico, exploded in 2010 as one of the most divisive and passionately felt issues in the country. Many business and farming interests want to protect the flow of illegal immigrants, especially those coming across the Mexican border, as they provide a supply of cheap labor. Others, however, are concerned with security considerations and the costs to public facilities (e.g. schools, hospitals, and welfare programs), as well as the high crime rate among the illegal immigrants. They want to stem the flow and secure the border before addressing the question of the status of those already here. Some states have issued driver's licenses to undocumented persons, which have been used to obtain other documents; a policy which some argue could be used by potential terrorists. In the spring of 2010, the state of Arizona, one such border state that has borne a disproportionate share of the costs of illegal immigration, passed a highly controversial state law to control the flood of illegal immigrants across its southern border. The law states that if someone is detained for other legitimate reasons, such as a traffic violation, the police may demand that the detainee produce documentation of immigration status if "reasonable suspicion exists" that the person is in the U.S. illegally. A strong wave of criticism of the Arizona law, led by President Obama, argued that the law encourages law enforcement officials to detain and harass individuals just because they look Hispanic, an example of the widely denounced policy of *racial profiling.*

Racial profiling refers to the practice of selecting people of a given race or ethnicity for examinations to which others are not subjected merely because the selected group is believed to be disproportionately responsible for crime, violence, or terrorism. Black individuals are more likely to be stopped for questioning than whites. In recent years, a group of Arab men, behaving in a suspicious manner, were ushered off an airliner; subsequently, these so-called "flying Imams" sued the airline. The Israelis, especially their airline El Al, unabashedly profile individuals. They argue that given finite resources for heading off terror or violence, they must use those scarce resources against the more likely perpetrators of such acts. Thus, it makes sense to them to screen young Arab males rather than Swedish grandmothers. However, racial profiling has been used in the United States to disproportionately harass and embarrass racial and ethnic minorities.

Despite a widespread charge to the contrary, the Arizona law does not authorize detaining and checking the identifications of people based on how they look. In fact, the law expressly forbids racial profiling thusly defined. Nevertheless, criticism of the law remained strong because the law provides no criteria for what "reasonable suspicion" is as it refers to being in the country illegally. Several states and cities across the country have chosen to boycott Arizona products and boycott travel to Arizona as a result of the legislation. Some groups have filed law suits to overturn the legislation, and the national government is posed to do so as well, claiming that it is an infringement on the national government's authority over immigration.

The experience of the Israelis may also be relevant for controlling the flood of illegals. They constructed a wall separating Israel proper from the West Bank, from which most of the bombings and other terrorist incidents came (see Chapter 12). After construction of the wall, such attacks were reduced by over 95 percent. Experts disagree whether a wall completely across our southern border would have similar success.

The questions here, discussed at even greater length in the following chapter, are whether the treatment of illegal aliens is a civil rights issue or a matter of national security and the need for any sovereign nation to gain control of its own borders.

ISSUE BACKGROUND: THE IDEA OF EQUALITY

Equality under Law

The first conceptualization, *equality under law,* may be thought of as the minimum position, in that if the term means anything, it means at least this much. The concept of equality under law implies that government should treat people as individuals rather than as members of social groups, and that when those categorizations are used, they impose a heavy burden of proof on government to show that there is a valid and widely accepted public purpose behind them. This concept clearly implies that government should not allocate rewards and punishments to people on the basis of the racial, ethnic, or religious groups to which they belong. Clearly, the law does make many categorizations of people. It distinguishes criminals from noncriminals, the psychotic from the sane, children from adults, and so forth. The reason why law permits these categories is that there is widespread consensus that these categories are based on behavioral distinctions. Thus, we assume that criminals behave differently from noncriminals, psychotics from those defined as sane, and children from adults. However, insofar as the law has now completely rejected the belief that there are behavior patterns or dispositions that are intrinsic to members of a given race, at the very least, classification by race is inconsistent with the concept of equality under law.

Categorization of people on the basis of the group into which they are born, such as race and ethnicity, is generally presumed unconstitutional unless government can satisfy the burden of proof to demonstrate that they satisfy a *"compelling public interest."* Therefore, such categorizations are not always unconstitutional. Government conceivably could satisfy the required burden of proof. In recent years, the compelling public interest used to justify race-based selection has been given as diversity in the racial makeup of the workforce or student body. We will see that the current Supreme Court has recently questioned whether such diversity is a sufficiently compelling interest.

Some categorizations, such as sex, may be constitutional for some purposes but not for others. The law has come to reject the assumption that men are intrinsically more intelligent than women; therefore, laws banning women from occupations in which intelligence is the main qualifying criterion violate equality under law. However, the law may protect some residual assumptions that women are intrinsically less aggressive than men by excluding them from combat roles in the military. Even this assumption has been substantially eroded in the law by the recent acceptance of women for many combat roles in today's military, including that of combat pilot. It will become apparent from our discussion of sex discrimination that society's assumptions about the intrinsic properties of women are undergoing a process of evolution and that this process is affecting law and policy. Legal principles distinguishing the sexes that went unchallenged a generation ago are now being found to be in violation of the right to equal protection of the law or are now banned by statute, and women are increasingly appearing in roles previously assumed to be beyond the competence of the typical woman. A similar flexibility of roles is beginning to emerge for men. Thus, one can now find women working as doctors, lawyers, or judges, and men working as nurses, flight attendants, or grade-school teachers. Despite the breakdown of the exclusive domination of certain roles by one sex or the other, many roles remain dominated by the sex conventionally associated with that role. Most lawyers, doctors, and professors are men despite the inroads of the feminist movement, and most housekeepers, raisers of children, secretaries, receptionists, and grade-school teachers are women (see Figure 10.1). The former Speaker of

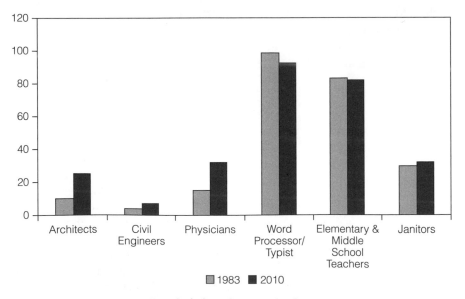

FIGURE 10.1   Percent Female (selected occupations)

SOURCE: Bureau of Labor Statistics, Current Population Survey, Table 11, http://www.bls.gov/cps/cpsaat11.pdf, Accessed 10-09-07 and Bureau of Labor Statistics, Current Population Survey, Table 11, http://www.bls.gov/cps/cpsaat11.pdf; Accessed July 4, 2010.

the U.S. House of Representatives, Newt Gingrich, made a controversial speech in early 1995 in which he asserted that women were physically unfit for combat roles in which they would have to "roll around in the dirt and get infections," while the naturally more aggressive men are disposed to go out and "hunt giraffes," indicating that sex-role stereotyping runs deep in high places.

Equality under Law in U.S. History.   The concept of equality under law historically has had a liberal implication. For many years in Western history, it was directed against legally mandated privileges of the various aristocracies or other dominant groups. These privileges included weighted voting and laws stipulating who could or could not own land, enter prestigious occupations, and so forth. Even in the United States, dominant groups were legally able to have laws—or rules supported by laws—that restricted the accessibility of social values to subordinate groups. It is well known that before the historic Supreme Court decision in *Brown v. Board of Education of Topeka, Kansas,* which struck down legally required racial segregation in public schools, state-mandated racial segregation existed to reserve the best public schools and facilities for whites. Furthermore, laws sanctioned discrimination in facilities licensed by the state to serve the public.[3] Inns and restaurants across the country freely and openly, with the blessing of the Supreme Court, restricted their clientele to the dominant groups. Although African Americans, women, Hispanics, and Jews were the most commonly excluded groups in most of the country, Asians and Native Americans also suffered severe discrimination, especially in the Western states. Until a decade or so after World War II, many major law schools and graduate schools overtly or covertly maintained quotas restricting the admission of Jews—who, it was feared, constituted a disproportionate share of such professions—regardless of the credentials of the individual applicants. In the 1920s, Harvard University, under the direction of the president, A. Lawrence Lowell, attempted to reduce the number of Jewish students by various means: limiting the amount of scholarship aid available to them, devising disguised quotas, requiring photographs on admissions applications, and making "character" a qualification for admission and then defining the term in such a way as to exclude negative attributes that Jews were considered to possess. Also tried was a system of geographical balance whereby applicants from New York City, with its large Jewish population, were passed over in favor of candidates from the South and West, regions with sparse Jewish populations. No method worked satisfactorily. In 1926, admissions officers began to reject candidates known or presumed to be Jewish without any stated reason. The number of Jewish students did in fact drop from 25 percent to 15 percent.[4]

It was alleged in 1988 that the University of California was using such an unofficial quota to restrict the proportion of high-achieving Asians among the students accepted to its several campuses. Although the university denied the charge, it is a fact that the percentage of Asians admitted was substantially lower than that of successful applicants whose objective qualifications (grade point averages and SAT scores) were inferior to those of the Asian students. According to Ernest Koenigsberg, a Berkeley professor who served on several admissions committees,

African American and Hispanic applicants are twenty times, or 2,000 percent, more likely to be admitted than are Asians with the identical academic records. In 1989, Berkeley rejected more than 2,500 Asian and white students with a straight A average. Asians as a group suffer from this more than whites because a higher percentage of them attain such credentials.[5]

In mid-nineteenth-century California, Chinese victims of crime were unable to obtain justice because the courts would not allow the Chinese to testify against a white person. Special taxes were levied against their laundries. In the first half of this century, laws prohibited intermarriage with Asians and segregated Asian schoolchildren. Asians were virtually excluded from immigration to the United States in the 1920s, and those who were already here were denied citizenship and were prohibited from owning agricultural land. Although legal discrimination against Asians is not as widely known to this generation of Americans as is discrimination against African Americans and Hispanics, "the intensity of discrimination against Japanese Americans in the first half of the twentieth century greatly exceeded that encountered by Mexican Americans."[6] This anti-Asian discrimination in official policy culminated in one of the most blatant examples of inequality under American law in this century, the compulsory internment during World War II of Americans of Japanese ancestry in what critics called concentration camps. The government euphemistically called them relocation centers. In 1988, the U.S. Congress did belatedly pay reparations to survivors of the Japanese internment, a move that generated pockets of vociferous opposition. This payment reflected a consensus among opinion leaders in the United States that the internment was a gross, racially motivated denial of basic due process of law.

For much of American history there was an explicit legal denial to Native Americans of equal access to the values of our society, a fact manifested in their being herded off their land and confined to residual pieces of unwanted territory called reservations.

Of course, the denial of equality under law to African Americans has been a well-known and widespread phenomenon. The Black Codes were one of the more blatant examples of this. These were a series of laws passed in many parts of the Old South after Reconstruction in attempt to nullify the reality of the Thirteenth Amendment's prohibition of overt slavery. The effect of these laws was to restore the almost complete black dependence on, and subservience to, the former slaveholders. African Americans were forbidden to hold jobs, receive an education, or even to walk the streets of cities and towns without permission from whites. General Colin Powell, chairman of the Joint Chiefs of Staff during the first Gulf War and secretary of state under President George W. Bush, recalls that in 1962, as he was driving through Virginia and about to leave for Vietnam, he and his wife were unable to find a bathroom they were allowed to use.[7] Until the impact of the *Brown* school desegregation case was finally established in the late 1960s, blacks continued to be singled out by law for specified disadvantages. They were routinely excluded from public facilities in the Old South.

Women have also been denied equality under law. Until the passage of the Nineteenth Amendment, only a few states allowed them to vote in state or national elections. Political wisdom was apparently held to correlate with gender.

Many vestiges of the notion of female inferiority continued until recent decades. In seven of the eight states with community property laws, the community property was under the control of the husband. Five states limited a woman's freedom to venture into business. Most states denied a woman the same rights as her husband to establish a separate domicile.[8]

It is argued that although the United States has never had a formal aristocracy to unseat and despite the commitment in American ideology to the idea of equality under law, there has been a more or less identifiable dominant group in this country, a group definable by gender and race or ethnicity, which directly or indirectly has used the law in addition to social discrimination to maintain other groups in a subordinate status. This dominant group has been white, male, and largely Protestant, especially the older, nonevangelical denominations, such as Episcopal, Congregational, or Methodist—as opposed to Baptist, Church of Christ, and Pentecostal.

Inequality in the Western World.   Dominant groups throughout the Western world create institutional arrangements to perpetuate their status and to minimize social mobility. The educational system has often functioned as this kind of selective institution in Western nations. In Great Britain and France, for example, rigorous competitive examinations determined who goes on to a university. England had its "eleven plus" exams until the early 1970s, and France still uses the baccalaureate; what these exams really test are those skills and attributes passed from parent to child in middle- and upper-class families. In England there are private and expensive secondary private boarding schools, paradoxically called public schools, the most prestigious of which (Eton, Harrow, Marlborough, Rutgers, and Winchester) have been the major avenue to Oxford and Cambridge, which educate most of Britain's elite. There is a similar system of preparatory schools in the United States (e.g., Groton, Exeter, Choate) that improves the chance of admission to prestigious higher education for the children of the affluent. The children who go to these selective prep schools are overwhelmingly children of parents who attended these schools, almost rendering the elites of these countries a semi-closed caste.

The culture defines dominant groups along ethnic, racial, or religious lines in situations where there is diversity of such attributes. In nations where there is more ethnic or racial homogeneity, stratification is mainly along the lines of social class. Nations with distinct subcultures, such as Belgium, the Netherlands, Canada, and Austria, usually contain one such subculture that is perceived as dominant and others as subordinate. Frequently, these divisions are along religious or linguistic lines. In general, whenever cultural, religious, racial, ethnic, or linguistic attributes are congruent with socioeconomic divisions, the political conflict between dominant and subordinate groups is intensified.

Equality of Opportunity

Laws that treat each individual equally do not necessarily have an equal impact on each individual. The impact of a law on an individual is a function not only of the substance of the law itself but also of the circumstances and attributes of the individual. Equality under law does not necessarily create genuine equality of opportunity. *Equality of opportunity* refers to the right of all individuals to realize their human potential to become whatever their wishes and personal abilities allow them to become, free from barriers imposed by society and its institutions. When government reserves certain roles or rewards in society for particular groups or classes of individuals, irrespective of performance or behavior, this in effect impedes the goal achievement of others. This would constitute a violation of equality of opportunity as well as of equality under law.

It is clear, however, that social and economic barriers exist, even though neither law nor public policy assigns privileges or disabilities to specified groups or individuals. The unequal distribution of such resources as wealth, abilities, and health will bestow advantages or disadvantages on individuals in competition for social or material values even when law and policies are neutral. People acquire things they value through the successful investment of resources they already possess. Those who lack such resources cannot use them for self-improvement even when permitted to do so by law. This is especially true in a capitalist system in which capital (resources deferred from consumption to investment) is used to generate more resources. One may need to be clever to succeed in the stock market, but one first needs capital to invest. Even such things as leisure time, transportation, and good health are resources that can be invested for self-improvement, but they are not evenly distributed throughout the population. Furthermore, people and institutions may make goal achievement more difficult for some than for others through mechanisms, such as prejudice.

Thus, it may be argued that governmental or legal neutrality perpetuates the existing inequalities of opportunity by permitting those who have superior resources to use them to maintain or increase their status relative to the have-nots. Without governmental regulation of the market, the gap between those who have more and those who have less tends to increase. This fact has been thought to epitomize the attitude of the Obama administration—as implied in Obama's comments during the 2008 presidential campaign—that substantial inequality in the distribution of material well being constitutes a denial of "social justice." As Vice President Biden put it, it is good to "spread the wealth around." Thus, the fact that many American families could not qualify for a mortgage loan was regarded as such a denial of social justice. The elevation of home-ownership to an "entitlement" (something a society owes everyone regardless of their competitive success) precipitated the "subprime mortgage crisis" (in which major lending institutions succumbed to pressure to issue mortgages to people whose financial status would not ordinarily have qualified them to receive the mortgage). The fact that all Americans do not have access to the level of health care available to our most affluent families was regarded by the Obama administration as another denial of social justice resulting in the massive health care reform act of 2010. (See the discussion of this law in Chapter 8.)

It is clearly unrealistic to assert that a child born to and raised by a poor, semi-literate, African American, single teenager in one of America's urban ghettos has the same chance of achieving high socioeconomic status as does the child of upper-middle-class, well-educated parents in an affluent suburb, even assuming that all legally imposed distinctions between these groups have been eliminated. The latter set of parents will impart skills, values, and resources to their offspring that the former parent cannot offer. The best single predictor of academic achievement is the educational level of one's parents. Although it is true that some individuals with superior talents and motivations may rise in Horatio Alger fashion from rags to riches, when genetically acquired properties are about equal, the child of affluence has a much higher probability of reaching his or her potential.

The principle in operation here is that *equal laws have unequal impacts on equal persons.* The French socialist Anatole France put it eloquently when he said, "The law, in its majestic impartiality, forbids the rich as well as the poor to beg in the streets, sleep under the bridges, and steal bread." Obviously, such laws do not prevent the rich from doing anything they are likely to do.

Consequently, the discrimination that makes a group of people socially and economically unequal will tend to cause the offspring of that group to continue to be socially and economically unequal after the original discrimination is discontinued and the current rules of the game apply equally to all. Thus, unequal opportunity may be generated from previous, legally imposed inequalities. A somewhat different unequal opportunity stems from differences in the talents and values that one is either born with or acquires early in life that do not stem from any socially or legally imposed discrimination.

A major controversy emerged in this regard with the publication of a book, *The Bell Curve,* written by the late Harvard psychologist Richard Hernnstein and Charles Murray,[9] which argues that there is a greater genetic component to IQ than society has been willing to admit. Since they further argue that IQ is a major determinant of wealth and social status, they offer the pessimistic conclusion that poverty and inequality are largely beyond the power of social policy to remedy, a conclusion that deeply offends many Americans. It should be clear, however, that their conclusions and the implications of them are vehemently challenged by a broad spectrum of scholars, writers, and policy analysts.

The idea of meritocracy, essentially a conception of what is meant by social justice, holds that the allocation of social values and status should be on the basis of performance standards in part derived from perceived contributions to the public good. Meritocracy entails the following assumptions: (1) some social roles contribute more to the good of the community than others do, and so rewards should be proportionate to such contributions; (2) the fulfillment of such roles frequently requires long and difficult training or rare talents; (3) special inducements are required to persuade people to fill these important and difficult roles; and (4) both justice and public need require that the occupants of some roles be rewarded a disproportionate share of social values. It is important to note that the concept of meritocracy entails the principle that people are rewarded on the basis of what they do rather than who they are.

It is also important to keep in mind that the assumption that performance is a function of material reward is one that has not been conclusively or even, to some, convincingly demonstrated. People contribute to the social order for many reasons, and it is unclear the extent to which such behavior is caused by the prospect of material reward.

It might be said that a consensus exists in America that people ought to be differently rewarded on the basis of performance standards, based in turn on talent, effort, and contribution to the social good; there is, however, a lack of consensus on how performance or social contribution should be measured. There is the question, for instance, as to whether the standards for admission to higher socioeconomic status in the United States, such as success in the educational system, reflect talent and potential social contribution or merely the cultural experiences of the dominant middle-class group. Does a higher grade point average, a standard on which certain groups consistently fall short, indicate a probability of being a superior physician, lawyer, or scientist? For example, Linda Wightman argues that race-based selection to America's law schools has been successful because the graduation rates of blacks admitted on race-based selection are not significantly different from those of whites. Stephen Thernstrom retorts, however, that since 89 percent of the whole sample graduates, this was a deceiving measure of black performance. A more accurate figure, he claims, is that whites were six times more likely to pass the bar examination on their first attempt.[10] To answer such a question of who is better in certain roles, one would have to be able to precisely measure performance in such roles. Because such measurement cannot now be made to the satisfaction of everyone regardless of their values, it remains impossible either to demonstrate or justify the social relevance of the performance standards on which a meritocracy is based.

Equality of Material Well-Being

Because of the aforementioned difficulties in using the principle of meritocracy to legitimate the material inequalities that exist in all societies, spokespersons for relatively disadvantaged groups and individuals have been arguing that government has a moral obligation to engineer a more equal distribution of material values, irrespective of traditional performance standards. Furthermore, because actual opportunities for upward social mobility depend on the resources with which one starts life, it is argued that equality of opportunity requires equality of material well-being. In short, equality of opportunity is held to be inseparable from equality of result. Thus, the list of entitlements continues to grow.

Proportional Equality.   The concept of *equality of material well-being* (sometimes called equality of result) would have to be precisely defined in order to be applied to actual social policy. This policy goal has been formulated in terms of the proportional equality of designated social groups. Proportional equality refers to the idea that a social group's percentage in the overall population should be equaled by its share of certain benefits, such as income and wealth, or the holding of desired social roles, such as membership in the professions, high socioeconomic status, and admission to professional schools. For example, if African Americans make up 12 percent of the population, they should make up approximately 12 percent of doctors, lawyers, and executives. It is inferred that if a group has less than its share of social values—for example, the 12 percent of African Americans comprises less than 6 percent of the nation's physicians—this is evidence that institutional factors, such as systematic discrimination or its pervasive effects, are operating to bring about underrepresentation. It is therefore implicitly assumed that if discrimination were not present, each group would acquire its proportionate share of society's goods. The distance between proportional equality and the actual inequality of the races is illustrated in Figures 10.2 and 10.3.

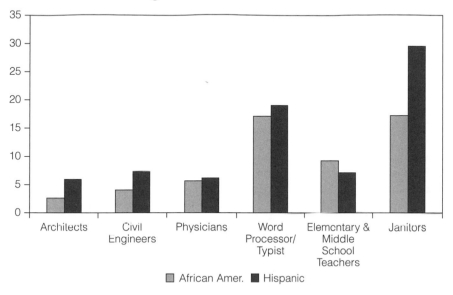

F I G U R E 10.2 Percent of Selected Occupations by Race, 2010

SOURCE: Bureau of Labor Statistics, Current Population Survey, Table 11, http://www.bls.gov/cps/cpsaat11.pdf; Accessed July 4, 2010.

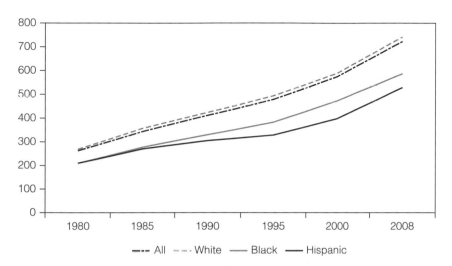

F I G U R E 10.3 Median Family Weekly Income by Race and Hispanic Origin

SOURCE: U.S. Census Bureau, *Statistical Abstract of the United States, 2007, Table 677,* www.census.gov/compndia/ statab/labor_force_employment_earnings, accessed 10-09-07 and Bureau of Labor Statistics, *Labor Force Statistics from Current Population Survey,* Table 14, http://www.bls.gov/cps/race_ethnicity_2008_14.htm; Accessed July 4, 2010.

The concept of proportional equality is important because it ultimately became the key goal of the social reforms championed by the American civil rights movement. That movement, however, came to this consensus only after a lengthy period of trial and error with other political tactics.

The Civil Rights Movement and Equality

The civil rights movement appears to have gone through three distinct stages in its political evolution. The first stage, dating from the early years of this century and the establishment of the National Association for the Advancement of Colored People (NAACP) and other organizations, was to attack denials of equality under law. Early cases addressed particular denials in law school admissions and public school facilities, culminating in the great school desegregation cases of the 1950s and 1960s. Goals were formulated for the elimination of Jim Crow laws that segregated African Americans and imposed legal disabilities on them.

Although this first stage was mostly successful, expectations for a more profound change in the lifestyle of the typical African American individual were not realized, leading to disappointment and dissatisfaction among civil rights leaders. With the goals of legal equality largely realized, the second stage of the movement, from the mid-1960s into the 1970s, concentrated on other goals, particularly equality of opportunity: (1) legislation to secure access to jobs and to public facilities, such as restaurants and places of accommodation (the *1964 Civil Rights Act*); (2) legislation to secure the right to vote (the *1965 Civil Rights Act*); and (3) legislation to end discrimination in the sale and rental of housing (the *1968 Civil Rights Act*). In other words, the second stage largely had to do with access to values and facilities privately owned but ostensibly available to the general public. Finally, the movement began to press for proportional equality, the third stage of the movement.

CONTEMPORARY POLICY: STRENGTHENING
CONSTITUTIONAL GUARANTEES OF EQUALITY

The Erosion of the Fourteenth Amendment

After the Thirteenth Amendment (1865) ended outright slavery in the United States, laws continued to exist that singled out African Americans and other racial and ethnic groups for discriminatory treatment. The Fourteenth Amendment (1868) was intended to end such discriminatory legislation by state governments, but two important decisions by the Supreme Court, *The Civil Rights Cases* (1883) and *Plessy v. Ferguson* (1896), greatly weakened the amendment's role and in fact legitimized existing forms of discrimination, specifically in education and access to public facilities. It is important to understand this weak interpretation of the intent of the Fourteenth Amendment because, in varying ways, each of the policy areas to be discussed in this section—school desegregation and integration, equal opportunity in employment and higher education, and equal rights for women—was an attempt to circumvent this eroded interpretation.

Restrictions on the Concept of State Action. A key portion of the Fourteenth Amendment has been the subject of much litigation concerning the struggle for equality over the years. It reads ". . . nor shall any state deprive any person of life, liberty or property without due process of law; nor deny to any person within its jurisdiction the equal protection of the laws." Among the important points to note about this passage are (1) that the language does not prohibit purely individual discrimination; and (2) that the language is passive—it tells what the state cannot do, but it does not explicitly command the state to do something actively.

After the Civil War and the enactment of the Fourteenth Amendment, it was assumed by many that the scope of the amendment was intended to encourage state governments to take action per se and also to extend such actions to businesses licensed by the state to serve the public. Because it is assumed by established common law principles that such businesses perform a public function under state aegis, they have customarily been considered state agents. In other words, because they derive their income from the public, they have an obligation to the public. Such an interpretation would have brought this form of discrimination, the most pervasive in our society, within the purview of the Fourteenth Amendment.

The Supreme Court rejected this traditional interpretation of the amendment in The *Civil Rights Cases* (1883) when it ruled that businesses licensed by the state to serve the public did not come under the concept of state action, an interpretation that still is in effect.[11] This ruling emasculated the amendment's effectiveness in dealing with this form of discrimination.

Ending Segregation

The emasculation of the Fourteenth Amendment as an effective instrument against segregation soon went even further than it had under *The Civil Rights Cases*. The Court ruled in 1896 to legalize active state intervention to segregate public facilities, including public schools. In *Plessy v. Ferguson,* the Court held that the equal protection clause of the amendment did not forbid laws requiring separation of the races.[12] Separation, the Court held, did not necessarily mean inequality. The opinion of the Court argued that any implication of African American inferiority derived from such Jim Crow laws was solely a function of the perceptions of African Americans themselves. Hence, in enunciating the so-called separate-but-equal doctrine, the Court officially legitimated such segregation laws. Moreover, in asserting that separation was legal, neither the Court nor society paid much heed to the equality portion of that doctrine. It was an accepted fact that the public facilities available to African Americans in localities where segregation was officially practiced, the states of the Old South, were not equal to facilities for whites.

The *Plessy* separate-but-equal principle remained in effect until 1954. After a series of cases that made inroads on its logic, *Plessy* was formally overruled in the 1954 landmark case of *Brown v. Board of Education of Topeka, Kansas,* which held that any state-mandated segregation in the field of education inherently violates the equal protection clause of the Fourteenth Amendment.[13] That 1954 decision is now known as *Brown I*. Chief Justice Warren, speaking for a unanimous court, held that the fact of segregation was widely understood as a badge of nonwhite inferiority and that this perception was likely to have a permanent destructive impact on the psychological development of African American children, irrespective of the physical equality of the facilities in question. In fact, Topeka, Kansas, was deliberately selected because the physical inequality of African American schools was not a serious issue there; therefore, the issue of the inherent inequality of segregated schools was brought to the fore. The unconstitutionality of Jim Crow laws was eventually applied to all other public facilities, such as parks, cemeteries, and hospitals.

It was one thing to hand down a principle of law; it is quite another to see that it is carried out. The response of the Southern state governments was by and large to resist the integration of their school systems as forcefully and as long as possible. Recognizing that the immediate dismantling of the dual school system would be disruptive and expensive, the Court had, in a separate opinion (known as *Brown II*), ordered the implementation of its *Brown I* decision "with all deliberate speed."[14] There was sufficient ambiguity in that standard to permit those Southern politicians who wished to do so to interpret the phrase as referring to the indefinite future. The South moved slowly toward the termination of its dual school systems. By 1964, only about 2 percent of the African American school children in eleven Old South states were attending integrated schools. As late as 1969, the Court was forced in *Alexander v. Holmes County* to inform a Mississippi school board that the time for "all deliberate speed" had run out and that further delays could not be granted.[15]

Meanwhile, under the Civil Rights Act of 1964, pressure was placed on local school districts to comply with the intent of *Brown I* by the threat of withholding federal funds from districts that did not satisfactorily respond. Under such pressures, desegregation in the Old South finally proceeded rapidly in the late 1960s. By 1970, a greater percentage of African Americans were attending schools with whites in that region than in the North. Thus, the first major goal of the civil rights movement, the elimination of Jim Crow laws, had succeeded. The movement had already turned its attention to the reality that the demise of such state-mandated segregation had failed to provide integration.

Enforcing Integration

Persisting discrimination against African Americans and Hispanics in the sale and rental of housing has exacerbated a widespread tendency in urban America toward racial and ethnic homogeneity in housing and residential patterns. Although each group of immigrants, Italian, Irish, Greek, Polish, and so forth, had displayed some tendency to seek out and live in neighborhoods peopled by those of its own derivation, housing discrimination against African Americans and Hispanics has added to the racial homogeneity of the neighborhoods of these latter two groups. Because assignment to public schools has traditionally been on the basis of sending children to their neighborhood schools, the traditional policy perpetuated racially homogeneous public schools. This racial separation of students due to the effects of discriminatory housing patterns is a form of *de facto* segregation. (De facto segregation is that not caused by law or public policy. *De jure* segregation is that so caused.)

Dissatisfaction with merely ending de jure (state-mandated) school segregation was given impetus by the Coleman Report of 1966, a study of the causes of educational achievement involving over a half-million students. This report found that among educational attributes, the one factor that had a significant effect on scholastic achievement was an intermingling of higher achievers and lower achievers. Peer group influence tended to upgrade the performance of the lower achievers without harming that of higher achievers. Moreover, the U.S. Civil Rights Commission found specifically that African Americans attending predominantly white schools had significantly higher levels of scholastic achievement than did African Americans attending predominantly African American schools when family background was held constant.[16] These results were interpreted to mean that actual intermingling of and interaction among black and white students would be an effective technique for upgrading the educational performance of black students.

This interpretation, of course, assumes a correlation between race and educational performance, a correlation that is statistically significant but far from perfect. To a large extent, the apparent correlation between race and educational performance and other behaviors or attributes, such as crime rates and unemployment, actually reflects a correlation between race and social class. African Americans and Hispanics are more likely to be among the lower socioeconomic class than are whites, and lower-class individuals are more likely to be academic underachievers than are those from the middle and upper classes. Therefore, it is inaccurate to assume that white students are always scholastic high achievers, whereas African Americans and Hispanics are always lower achievers. Coleman's study was concerned with school achievement levels, and the racial implications were largely read into it by others. It may be that simply mixing high- and low-achieving students, regardless of race, is what Coleman's data suggest, a policy contradicted by the widespread practice of tracking, or grouping students by ability.

In any event, the goals of the civil rights movement with respect to education came to be redefined in terms of the racial balance of the student body and faculty of each school, a goal first stipulated by the Supreme Court in *Green et al. v. County School Board of New Kent County* (1968).[17] Once this standard is accepted as the imperative of the Fourteenth Amendment, an active governmental role in assigning students to schools on a racial basis is inescapable. The explicit judicial mandate for compulsory integration, achieved by busing, came in *Swann v. Charlotte-Mecklenburg Board of Education* (1971).[18] The Court specifically stated that the lower courts may require busing as one means of achieving the racial balance goal, a goal that was expressed in terms of specific percentages (71 percent white to 29 percent nonwhite), but it held this up as a norm to be striven for rather than a rigid quota. The courts could not require busing to remedy racial imbalance that was purely de facto, that is, had occurred wholly independently of government action; however, any governmental activity, such as the opening or closing of schools, which contributed to such imbalance would justify a court-ordered busing remedy. Although the Court preserved a legal distinction between

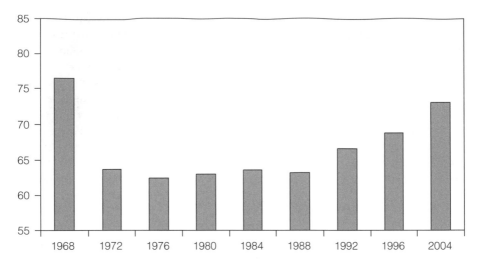

F I G U R E 10.4 School Integration
(percentage of African American students in schools with more than half minority students)

SOURCE: Harold W. Stanley and Richard G. Niemi, *Vital Statistics on American Politics, 1999–2000*, CD-ROM edition (Washington: CQ Press, 2000), Table 10-14; and U.S. Department of Education, National Center for Education Statistics, *Status and Trends in the Education of Racial and Ethnic Minorities*, Table 7.5, Percentage Distribution of Public Elementary and Secondary School Students of Each Racial/Ethnic Group, by Percent Minority Enrollment in School: 2004, http://nces.ed.gov/pubs2007/minoritytrends/tables/table_7_5.asp?referrer=report; Accessed October 9, 2007.

de facto and de jure segregation, in practice the broad range of governmental actions that have been held to justify busing orders, irrespective of any showing of governmental intent, weakened the distinction.[19]

Based on *Swann v. Charlotte-Mecklenburg,* many court-ordered busing programs were instituted in cities and smaller communities around the country, but the policy was very unpopular. In recent years, courts have begun to remove requirements for busing. Busing was ended in Oklahoma City in 1991; DeKalb County, Georgia, in 1992; and in Buffalo, Boston, and Little Rock soon thereafter. Due in large part to the intense dislike of busing among much of the white population, busing programs have become increasingly rare. Many school districts have come to rely on magnet school programs to effect greater racial balance among student bodies of given schools. In such programs, schools in target group neighborhoods offer special attractive programs to induce students from middle-class neighborhoods to voluntarily enroll in the school in the target group neighborhood. Progress in school integration is shown in Figure 10.4. Reasons for such limited progress are discussed next.

The Struggle for Racial Balance in Employment
and Higher Education

Civil Rights Act of 1964. Busing dealt with the integration of the public schools. This left the underrepresentation of the designated disadvantaged groups—usually African Americans and Hispanics, but occasionally including all nonwhites and women—untouched in various sectors of the American economy and in higher education. The *Civil Rights Act of 1964*, in its Title VII provisions, set up the *Equal Employment Opportunity Commission (EEOC)* to implement policy toward ending discrimination by any employer or labor union with twenty-five or more persons engaging in interstate commerce. Title VI of the same act requires that it shall be the responsibility of each federal agency to require an end to discrimination in any program or institution to which it allocates federal funds. The Office of Federal Contract Compliance is responsible for implementing this policy. As discussed earlier, the goal of ending discrimination has been interpreted as the achievement of proportional representation for designated groups in various valued social roles. Although the EEOC cannot require either quotas or preferential treatment from the mere fact of racial imbalance, it can use such imbalance as evidence of discrimination. The assumption again is that if discrimination were not at work, these groups would be present in various sectors in rough proportion to their numbers in society as a whole. This assumption overlooks cultural factors that may cause people from one community to pursue different goals than pursued by other communities. Academic achievement, for example, may get a higher priority in some sub-cultures than in others.

Expanding the Constitution's Commerce Clause.   Because *The Civil Rights Cases* weakened the Fourteenth Amendment, review of the constitutionality of the Civil Rights Act of 1964's provisions guaranteeing all citizens access to restaurants, motels, and other places of public accommodation required drawing on an expanded meaning of the Constitution's commerce clause. Federal power to regulate interstate commerce was used to forbid discrimination by businesses directly or indirectly involved in such commerce. This was upheld in the *Heart of Atlanta Motel* case in 1964. Another case that year, *Katzenbach v. McClung,* permitted the extension of the law's application to businesses whose only connections to interstate commerce were purchases from a national market.[20]

Equality of Result in Education and Employment.   The adoption of proportionality as a criterion of discrimination came into being largely because much discrimination is covert rather than overt and is thus hard to prove. For example, a school wishing to keep African Americans out may deliberately adopt entrance requirements that it knows African Americans will disproportionately fail; similarly, it is frequently difficult to establish why a particular job applicant was not hired for a job.

The remedies to imbalance in employment, in the composition of professions, or in admissions to higher education consist of some form of preferential treatment for members of the underrepresented groups or of an attack on the standards by which people are selected. Accordingly, the Office of Federal Contract Compliance and the EEOC laid down guidelines to the effect that any test for employment, promotion, or membership that is disproportionately failed by members of the designated groups constitutes evidence of illegal discrimination unless the job relevance of that test can be shown. In other words, it must be shown that those who score higher on the test or selection criteria actually perform better in the roles for which they are being selected.

Beginning with the case of *Washington v. Davis* (1976),[21] the Court tended to shift the burden of proof to the plaintiff to demonstrate the test was instituted with the intent to discriminate. Subsequent decisions in the appellate courts applied the latter standard of placing the burden of proof on the plaintiff alleging discrimination. It is this new rule of law that the controversial 1991 Civil Rights Act (described later) sought to overturn.

Another approach to proportionate equality is the idea of *preferential treatment*. Preferential treatment plans vary from using membership in one of the designated groups as one positive factor to be taken into account in employment or admission decisions to rigid quotas that require a set proportion of those selected to be members of such groups. But strict quotas generate considerable emotional hostility among some groups, for example, among Jews, because quotas were once used against them to exclude them from prestigious schools and professions. Often preferential treatment finds support in federal *affirmative action* policies. These require businesses and educational institutions guilty of past discrimination or in receipt of federal funding to demonstrate by positive action that they attempt to hire and admit minorities and women.

The Challenge to Race–Based Selection.   The opposition to selection on the basis of race, although frequently emanating from perceived self-interest, has been argued in terms of an interpretation of the equal protection clause of the Fourteenth Amendment. It is contended that preferential treatment for non–whites unconstitutionally discriminates against whites.

In the Alan Bakke case in 1978, the constitutional issue was addressed with great expectation that the Court would resolve it. This case involved the admissions procedure for the University of California Medical School at Davis, which had rejected Bakke's application for admission. This school had set aside a fixed number, sixteen places out of one hundred, for nonwhites. Because scores were compiled for each applicant on grade point averages (GPA), the Medical College Aptitude Test (MCAT), and a personal interview, the procedure created two separate applicant pools.

Although the applicants for the sixteen minority seats had to meet minimum standards on the given criteria and in that sense were qualified, the records of those selected from the minority pool on the two objective scores (GPA and MCAT) were significantly inferior to those selected from the regular pool and, perhaps more significantly, well below the record of some of those, like Bakke, who were rejected under the regular admission process. In fact, the average percentile ranking on MCAT scores of those admitted under the special program were from 36 to 52 percentile points below those selected from the general applicant pool in the years studied.[22] The GPA of regular admittees averaged 3.5 and 3.4 for those years, where the special admittees averaged 2.6 and 2.4.

The Court found itself as divided on the legality of such a program as society is divided over the issue. Four justices (Burger, Rehnquist, Stevens, and Stewart) held that the use of racial criteria violated Title VII of the Civil Rights Act of 1964. Therefore, these judges held that Bakke should be ordered admitted without considering whether such admissions policies violated the equal protection clause. By deciding the case on statutory rather than constitutional grounds, these justices gave Congress the opportunity of overriding the decision by ordinary legislation rather than constitutional amendment.

Four other justices (Blackmun, Brennan, Marshall, and White) argued that neither the Constitution's equal protection clause nor Title VII prevented the use of racial categories to remedy the effects of past discrimination.

Four-to-four stalemates do not make for constitutional decisions on a nine-person Court. It was left to Justice Powell to cast the swing vote to dispose of the case. His opinion constituted the official Opinion of the Court, although none concurred with it, thereby reducing its force as legal precedent. Agreeing that racial categorizations are suspect categories that place a severe burden of proof on the state to show a compelling public purpose, Powell held that this burden was satisfied by the need to secure "a diverse student body." However, Powell saw fit to distinguish a fixed quota of student slots assigned on the basis of race—a policy he found incompatible with the equal protection clause—from the use of race as one among several factors in selecting from an open applicant pool—a policy known as *racial preference plans* that he approvingly endorsed. Powell found the Davis program invalid on equal protection grounds, whereas the Burger group invalidated it on Title VII grounds, making a motley majority of five to order Bakke admitted.

Conclusion. Today, government and educational institutions continue to strive to ameliorate the underrepresentation of targeted groups in the economy and in higher education. However, programs to do so inevitably displace non-targeted people who are increasingly challenging such programs.

The Court dealt affirmative action a serious blow in 1995 when it ruled unconstitutional a University of Maryland scholarship, the Banneker Scholarship, that was set aside for African Americans only. This is consistent with *Bakke* and other cases in that the scholarship went beyond racial preference by restricting competition to African Americans only. The Court's 1997 decision in upholding the California Civil Rights Initiative, discussed later, struck another blow against affirmative action.

Equality and the Women's Movement

With the rise of the feminist movement in the United States, women have become identified as a target group in many social policies designed to bar and redress the repression of women and their consequent underrepresentation in valued social roles. In *Craig v. Boren* (1976), the Court set standards for when gender may be used to classify people: The government must convince the Court that its purpose is an important one and that the sex classification is "substantially related" to achieving that purpose.[23] This case invalidated a law that set a higher legal drinking age for boys than for girls. The Court was called upon to apply this standard in *Rostker v. Goldberg* (1981) when it upheld the right of Congress to exempt women from selective service.[24] However, some have said that the standard was poorly applied here, if not completely abandoned; the defenders of the selective service law made no real effort to show that the exclusion of women is substantially related to the goal of raising an army. This case appears to leave the legality of classification by gender with an uncertain status. Many affirmative action programs and laws, such as Titles VI and VII of the Civil Rights Act of 1964, identify women as one of the beneficiary groups.

In the sense of proportional equality, women have been and remain under-represented in higher-status positions (for example, doctors, lawyers, business executives, and professors) and overrepresented in lower-status positions (for example, elementary school teachers, secretaries, and nurses). (See Figure 10.1.) Even the minimal goal of equal pay for equal work has been difficult to obtain. The median income for women was only 60 percent that of men only two decades ago. By 1993, this gap had narrowed to the point where the median income for women was 77 percent that of men, progress attributed more to the increased entry of women into occupations formerly dominated by men than to any increase in the pay for those occupational roles traditionally held by women. This gap had not been significantly lowered by 2009 according to Bureau of Labor statistics, which showed that women were earning just 80.2 percent the earnings of men. Although the limited progress was hailed by supporters of the feminist movement, they took pains to point out that the gap remains unjustifiably large. Part of this large differential reflects the tendency for women still to be channeled into lower-status and thus lower-paying roles. Nevertheless, part of so large a difference probably also reflects the tendency to pay women less for some of the same jobs that men have. Pink-collar jobs, those traditionally held by women, often pay less than do those jobs tradition-ally held by men when the levels of skill or training demanded by the respective sets of jobs are comparable. One school district was starting its elementary school teachers at a slightly lower wage than it was paying the gardeners. Although men are increasingly occupying pink-collar jobs and women are increasingly moving into traditionally male jobs, most people still occupy roles conforming to gender-based expectations. Therefore, the movement for sexual equality concentrates on requiring equal pay for jobs of *comparable worth* (equal pay for different jobs requiring equal levels of skill, training, or responsibility). There is no reason, it is argued, why secretaries should be paid less than plum-bers, when comparable levels of training and responsibility are involved. The concept of comparable worth, however, has not made progress at the federal legislative level. It was feared that the concept would unleash a flood of liti-gation without providing precise standards for measuring comparable worth and thereby resolving such lawsuits.

Unemployment rates are higher for women than for men. This further reflects the overall economic discrimination against women that remains an on-going reality in American society. But the inferior status of women, as with other disadvantaged groups, is not entirely a function of public policy. Widely held stereotypes regarding the appropriate roles of each gender see prestigious tasks demanding intelligence, creativity, courage, or other admirable traits as being by definition man's work, while a woman's natural role is seen as housekeeper and mother. By comparison, women in the Western world still fare far better than women in parts of the Islamic world, where it is illegal to educate women, women must keep their entire body covered except for eye holes, and women may not choose their mate.

Overcoming these sex-role stereotypes is one of the most difficult tasks for the women's movement because they appear to retain a greater persistence in the public mind even than racial stereotypes. The creation of a more favorable public perception of efforts to alter the status of women is perhaps impeded by the fact that the National Organization for Women (NOW) is regarded by many as being outside the American mainstream and dominated by extremists. In general, the major women's organizations do not take a negative stance against men, but rather concern themselves with the maximization of social and economic choices available to women and focus intently on marketplace equity and reproductive freedom.

Part of the denial of marketplace equity to women may be traced to the fact that access to business opportunities was long restricted to male-dominated bastions. The effort of feminists to penetrate traditional male domains received a boost when the Supreme Court upheld a New York City ordinance that banned discrimination by private clubs on the basis of race, gender, creed, or national origin in *New York State Club Association v. City of New York* (1988).[25] The clubs in question were those membership associations in which business deals were actually concluded, employment decisions made, and professional contacts established, thereby preserving an old boy network in the upper echelons of American business. Such clubs have not only been restricted to whites but have also generally excluded women. The law defined the clubs covered in terms of the size of membership and the fact that they offered regular meal service and regularly received dues or fees from nonmembers for the use of space and services. Such clubs were considered not "distinctly private." Given the state's compelling interest in ensuring equality of opportunity in business and professional life, the First and Fourteenth Amendment values that might conflict with that interest were overridden.

The issue of the right of clubs to selectively determine their own membership was addressed in June 2010, when the Court ruled by a 5–4 margin in *Christian Legal Society v. Martinez* that a public university is not required to subsidize student groups that it considers discriminatory. The Christian Legal Society, defined by a commitment to conservative Christian values, did not admit homosexuals and non-Christians. This case follows the precedent of the *Dale* case discussed later in this chapter

Although sex-role stereotypes have had much to do with the formation of discriminatory laws against women, it is helpful to distinguish between their subtler effects and the blatant use of law to define the female role. The legal disabilities that women have faced should not be minimized. They did not obtain the right to vote, for example, until 1920, fifty years after African American men were accorded the right. Women also were once denied the right to serve on juries, work in bars, and pursue various other callings. Some laws with the ostensible purpose of protecting women—such as limiting the amount of weight they could be required to lift on the job or the maximum hours they could be required to work—had the negative effect of keeping women out of many jobs. Some critics have argued that this was deliberate. Such laws assume an inexorable connection between sex and physical strength, a relationship that is far from perfect. Nevertheless, most of the discrimination against women has been the product of social attitudes and sex-role stereotypes rather than the law per se.

It is not unusual, for instance, for men in hiring positions to avoid considering women for jobs in the belief that they will soon quit to get married or have babies. Prospective employers can continue to apply such sexist standards surreptitiously as long as they do not have to justify not hiring any particular applicant. Furthermore, for years, colleges and universities spent many times as much on men's athletics as on women's, principally for two discriminatory reasons. First, society in general regards athletic prowess as a male prerogative; that is, male athletes are admired, whereas their female counterparts were chided for being unfeminine. Second, given such attitudes toward women athletes, their sports have not been good collegiate revenue producers because, until recently, they did not attract large paying audiences. However, Title VII of the Civil Rights Act of 1964 bans discrimination on the basis of sex as well as race, and *Title IX of the Educational Amendment Acts of 1972* forbids any institution from receiving federal funds to engage in gender discrimination. Accordingly, the government now requires colleges and universities to equalize the amount spent on interscholastic athletics. This caused vociferous opposition from supporters of expensive but profitable football programs, and so the cost of these programs was exempted from the cost equation. The requirement has also resulted in the cancellation of a number of men's minor sports programs, such as swimming.

Issues central to the concerns of the leaders of the women's movement include the control of one's childbearing, which entails both access to information and support of effective contraception as well as freedom to receive legal abortions and the achievement of equity in job status and indices of material well-being. These are issues of symbolic and emotional as well as of substantive content. Control of one's fecundity is of crucial importance because becoming a parent is perhaps the most all-encompassing commitment that one can experience, one that will inevitably constrain one's life choices. The complex issue of access to abortion is discussed in detail in Chapter 13. Feminists are also concerned with the issues of rape and sexual harassment. The former offense is discussed in detail in Chapter 6; the latter in this section.

As was seen in the expanded conceptualization of rape in Chapter 6, the asymmetrical relationship between the sexes defined by the putative dominant power position of men over women in our society has given rise to an effort by feminists to utilize law and policy to protect women from *sexual harassment.* Here again we encounter a fundamental shift in the meaning of terms, the lack of a common language. While traditionally sexual harassment referred to a situation in which a man who holds a position of dominance over a woman repeatedly attempts to establish a form of sexual relationship (broadly defined) with her, a quid pro quo arrangement in which the dominant male offers professional or educational benefits in return for sexual cooperation, now sexual harassment refers to or includes actions that merely offend the victim or render her uncomfortable, producing what is perceived as a hostile environment. People have found themselves assigned real punishment because a woman has felt offended or uncomfortable when the alleged perpetrator may have had no intention to offend. For example, a sexual harassment suit was filed at the University of Nebraska because the plaintiff took offense at a photograph on a man's desk of his wife clad in a swimming suit. The most famous such suit is the one filed by Paula Jones against former President Clinton. Assuming Ms. Jones's account of the facts is 100 percent accurate, as Jeffery Rosen wrote in *The New Republic,* the President "made a pass at her, took no for an answer and reassured her that he meant no harm." His putative behavior, while clearly boorish, placed no pressure on or implied any threats to Ms. Jones. The case was eventually settled out of court for an undisclosed sum of money to be paid to Jones. In another such case, in 1994, a jury slapped a $500,000 judgment on a radio station because, as one juror put it, the station managers "seemed to feel it was partly okay to make jokes about women."[26]

New meaning of the term has been expanded to cover the creation of a "hostile workplace environment." Such a standard is vague in the extreme; what is actionable is a function of the perceptions and sensitivities of the observer. Not knowing what will bring a lawsuit makes people bend over backwards to avoid anything that could be offensive to the most sensitive person. Crude or boorish behavior has now become actionable. Clearly, the law cannot, consistent with a meaningful First Amendment, guarantee a right against being offended. Is there, therefore, a responsibility in a free society to be somewhat thick-skinned?

There have recently been a rash of countersuits alleging frivolous or unfounded lawsuits that have been won by men charged with such harassment, such as a suit won by political scientist C. Harmon Zeigler against his university. It is unclear whether this will discourage the more frivolous litigation in this area. The Jones case against Clinton was not reassuring in this regard.

Female critics of the goals and policies of the feminist movement include not only traditionally oriented women who aspire to domestic and child rearing roles but also women who consider themselves feminists and are very active in professional roles. Women, such as Camille Paglia and Katie Roithe, argued that the feminist portrayal of women as a victimized group demeans them. Roithe argues that the concept of sexual harassment as an "actionable offense" (one over which one can file a lawsuit) implies that women, unlike men, are incapable of warding off unwanted sexual advances.[27] The legal protection of women against the broadened conceptualization of sexual harassment demeans the strength and independence of women. Thus, the feminist movement remains divided between equality feminists—those who wish to abolish sex-based classification in law and policy so that women can be treated equally with men—and difference feminists, who wish to emphasize the distinct status and needs of women as a victimized group in need of special protection and treatment.

The difference between these two positions was illustrated by the controversy surrounding January 2005 remarks by then-president Lawrence Summers of Harvard at a conference concerning the underrepresentation of women in the fields of engineering and science. Summers speculated that, rather than this underrepresentation solely being the product of gender bias, women might be genetically less attracted to those fields than men. Biology Professor Nancy Hopkins was so upset at this opinion that she exited the meeting complaining that his remarks put her on the verge of vomiting. Whatever the merits of Summers's opinion, Hopkins' reaction typified the image of women as victim rather than an image of strength. Meanwhile, Summers's suggestion was so politically incorrect that he was forced to resign over this and other politically incorrect positions (especially his criticism of African American Studies professor Cornell West's scholarship, who subsequently left Harvard for Princeton).

The question remains, to what extent are there essential or natural differences between men and women, or are all differences socially conditioned? Though they would disagree with Summers's particular example, difference feminists would accept the assertion of some inherent differences between the sexes, while equality feminists would minimize such differences.

Bias against Homosexuals, the Handicapped, and Native Americans

Homosexuals are another group who have suffered discrimination in American society and who have increasingly asserted legal and constitutional rights to combat such discrimination. As awareness of the discrimination suffered by America's gays becomes more widespread, demand for protection of gay rights intensifies. Incidents such as the beating and brutal murder of gay student Matthew Shepard in Wyoming in 1998 underscores the scope and intensity of the problem of anti-gay feeling. Out of this increased awareness has come the increased visibility of the presence of gays. As of 2000, there were 579,241 known same-sex couples in the United States, ranging from over 92,000 in California to 703 in North Dakota. Americans remain uneasy about the expansion of gay rights. As of 2007, a plurality of Americans agreed that "gay rights have gone too far." This is related to the perception that homosexuals differ from the other targeted groups in that they are defined on the basis of implied behavior, not attributes.

One of the primary concerns of opponents of homosexual rights is the fear that homosexuals will somehow influence or recruit heterosexual but impressionable children to join their ranks. This fear conflicts with the prevailing psychological opinion that homosexuality is more an involuntary than a conscious choice, by either school-age children or adults. A study done in 1991, moreover, concluded that there are measurable genetic differences between the brains of homosexual men and those of heterosexual men. The implication of this study is that one is born with one's sexual orientation and that orientation will be unaffected by any system of rewards and punishments. Therefore, it does not make sense to regard homosexuality as something that can be deterred through criminal law. The study also suggests that the danger of heterosexual minors being recruited into the homosexual community is overstated and virtually nonexistent.

An Oklahoma law typified the widespread efforts to bar or remove homosexuals from teaching positions. The law criminalized "advocating, soliciting, or promoting public or private homosexual activity in such a manner that creates a substantial risk that such conduct will come to the attention of school children. . . ." Note that the law criminalized the advocacy of homosexuality, not the attributes of being a homosexual. However, a United States Court of Appeals struck down the law on the grounds that advocacy cannot be criminalized (especially when it is not carried out in a context of incitement). The Supreme Court upheld this ruling in 1985.

However, efforts continued to bar homosexuals from leadership or role model positions relative to young people with respect to the Boy Scouts of America instituting a ban on avowed homosexuals from scout leadership positions. Gay rights advocates challenged this ban, but the Court upheld the ban in *Boy Scouts of America v. Dale*.[28] Dale was a gay activist who sought a position as assistant Scout master. He had an outstanding record as a former Scout, reaching the rank of Eagle Scout, and was therefore otherwise well qualified for the post. The Court treated the Boy Scouts as a private organization and the issue as one of freedom of association as in the New York Club and the Christian scholars case discussed above.

President Bill Clinton sought to defuse the issue of gays in the military with a "don't ask, don't tell" plan. The plan was that the military would no longer inquire into the sexual orientation of their personnel or recruits; hence, gay recruits could serve in the military as long as they do not make that orientation public. However, gays are still subject to dismissal if they reveal their sexuality or are caught in homosexual acts. In the course of the debate, it was revealed that many gay people had served with valor and distinction in this nation's wars; however, many feared that the presence of gays in such close, and often intimate, quarters would detract from the central mission of the military. Moreover, reports on the implementation of the policy indicate that some military officers have been circumventing the intent of the policy by putting pressure on suspected homosexuals to reveal their orientation and then proceeding to discharge them on a less than honorable basis. In the year 2000, 1,231 gays were discharged from the military under the "don't ask, don't tell" policy. President Obama pledged to end the "don't ask, don't tell" policy and to admit recruits to the military regardless of sexual orientation. As of June 2010, Obama had asked Congress to repeal "don't ask, don't tell," but also said that it would not be done until the Defense Department completed a study on implementation of the repeal. Polls indicate that about 60 percent of the public support repeal. In October 2010, a federal district court judge ruled the policy unconstitutional but at this writing the decision is being appealed.

In the 1986 case of *Bowers v. Hardwick,* the Court upheld the Georgia sodomy statute with reference to its ban on homosexual behavior, a statute that criminalizes sex "against the laws of nature." However, the Court reversed this decision in 2003 in *Lawrence v. Texas,* a decision that banned the criminalization of consensual homosexual acts on privacy grounds.[29] (See Chapter 13 for a discussion of the inferred constitutional right of privacy.) The movement toward greater social tolerance of homosexuals and toward reducing the discrimination they suffer in law and social policy received a setback in the 1980s because of the spread of acquired immune deficiency syndrome (AIDS), a contagious and deadly disease. Homosexual men have constituted one of the high-risk groups in the United States for the disease and have widely been perceived as one of its major sources of contagion. Although there is a lack of certainty in this regard, the consensus among medical experts is that the disease is spread in the United States primarily through a kind of sexual activity especially prevalent among male homosexuals and through sharing of contaminated needles among intravenous drug users. In 2007, it was estimated that 46 percent of new AIDS cases were caused by homosexual sex, 25 percent from IV drug use and dirty needles, and 11 percent from heterosexual sex (usually involving a bisexual individual). Casual contact (drinking fountains, public toilet seats, etc.) does not transmit the disease. However, because of perceived uncertainty about the transmission and often fatal nature of the disease, there is still public pressure to identify and isolate homosexuals, costing them their jobs and right to function in society. The question is whether the AIDS issue is perceived as a civil rights issue or a public health issue. It is widely believed that the transmission of AIDS through transfusions of blood and blood products (a phenomenon that has made hemophiliacs a high-risk group) is still attributed largely to homosexual and bisexual males.

The specific policy issues related to AIDS and homosexuality involve the delicate balance of the right of homosexuals and of persons with AIDS to live out their lives free from harassment, with the public right to be given all possible protection against a usually fatal affliction. Yet some people lack confidence in the thoroughness and reliability of such screening. Public identification of carriers of the virus and identification of their sexual partners would help people who are sexually active to protect themselves from contracting the infection, but it would subject such carriers to public harassment and social ostracism. Proposals for mandatory testing of some sectors of the population carry the same potential benefits and risks. Such proposals also raise the questions of who shall be tested and at what cost. Another problem with proposals for mandatory testing is the fact that the tests are imperfect. Not only would the test fail to detect some people carrying the virus, it would incorrectly turn out positive for some noninfected people. These noninfected false positives would be subject to the same mental anguish and social ostracism as those who actually carry the virus. These issues involve the balancing of the right of persons with AIDS and of homosexuals to confidentiality regarding their sexual activity and the right of the public to be protected as much as possible.

The agenda of the leadership of the gay community has evolved from merely seeking tolerance from the rest of society to a goal of legitimating homosexuality as a morally equivalent alternative lifestyle. It was this goal that caused gays to demand a specifically gay contingent marching with their fellow Irish Americans in New York's annual St. Patrick's Day Parade. It was not an issue of whether gays could participate in one of the other units in the parade without declaring their sexual orientation; gays demanded recognition as gays.

The issue of same-sex marriage has come into prominence in recent years as another means of gaining the legitimation of moral equivalency that gays seek. Part of the issue involves the question of whether normal spousal rights—inheritance, visiting rights to an ill partner in hospital, custodial rights of adopted children—apply to the long-term partners of gays. Many of these concerns can be addressed in a formal legal arrangement called civil union, an arrangement that grants all the aforementioned legal rights without calling it marriage. Such an arrangement was adopted under state court order in Vermont in 2000 and has since been adopted in Washington, California, New Mexico, and New York. Nine states, not including those states already named which sanction gay marriage, allow some form of spousal benefits for gays. The resistance of straight social conservatives to allowing the term *marriage* to define gay relationships stems from their unwillingness to grant moral equivalence to the gay lifestyle. Thus, the action of an Iowa county judge in August 2007 to strike down that state's ban on gay marriage drew an immediate strong reaction from opponents of such marriage. While several gay couples immediately went to Polk County, Iowa, to take advantage of that locale's tentative allowance of gay marriage, higher courts reversed the ruling. The Defense of Marriage Act of 1996 forbids Congress from recognizing gay marriage; hence, supporters of gay marriage have concentrated their efforts on state law.

The courts of three states (Massachusetts, Hawaii, and California), declared that gays had a civil right to marriage under the constitutions of those states. The Hawaii case originated with the December 1990 application of six gay couples for marriage licenses. Hawaii set up a gay marriage bureau and invited gay couples to take advantage of the legal status of gay marriage there. However, in 1998, the voters of Hawaii voted to amend their state constitution to ban gay marriage. In 2004, by a 4–3 vote, the Massachusetts Supreme Court ruled that same-sex couples had an equal right to marriage. California voters approved a plebiscite reversing the legalization of gay marriage five months after its court approved it in 2008. Thus far, as of mid-2010, five states have legalized gay marriage under state law: Connecticut, Iowa, Massachusetts, New Hampshire, and Vermont. Washington, DC, New York, Rhode Island, and Maryland recognize gay marriages performed in other states but will not issue licenses for gays to marry in those states.

The legality of gay marriage in these states alarms social conservatives in the rest of the nation because "the Full Faith and Credit clause" of the U.S. Constitution requires each state to recognize the rights and credentials of citizens, possibly including marriage, of all the other states. Hence, the availability of same-sex marriage in one state could lead to its prevalence throughout the country.

To counter this threat, eleven states in the 2004 election adopted constitutional amendments to their respective state constitutions defining marriage as a heterosexual union: Arkansas, Georgia, Kentucky, Michigan, Mississippi, Montana, North Dakota, Oklahoma, Ohio, Utah, and Oregon. Many other states and the federal government have Defense of Marriage" acts that advance the same goal. Comparatively, ten Western countries sanction gay marriage: Belgium, Canada, the Netherlands, Norway, Portugal, South Africa, Spain, and Sweden. Israel recognizes gay marriage, but will not perform it. This battle over the legitimacy of the gay lifestyle reflects the cleavage between religious conservatives and secularized Americans, a cleavage that will not disappear any time soon.

Defining New Victims: The Handicapped and the New Disability.   Handicapped people have also recently become a visible minority with an agenda of
demands. The nature of their demands, however, differs considerably from those
of the aforementioned groups. The demands of the handicapped concentrate on
access to public places and various public benefits—for example, demands for ramps
where only stairs had been present, the availability of material in Braille for the
blind, closed-captioned television for the hearing impaired, and the like—with
much less concern for proportional equality, the placement of set or targeted proportions of handicapped people in valued roles. The concern of the leaders of the
handicapped appears to fit the idea of equalizing opportunity and competition
rather than the idea of equality of results. The goals are the amelioration of the
present effects of their disabilities rather than any compensation for the effects of
past discrimination, and so their claims have generated less controversy than have
those of the other groups previously discussed.

The most important legislation protecting the rights of persons with disabilities
is the *Americans with Disabilities Act* (ADA) of 1990. Its primary provisions extend to
handicapped persons the kinds of protection granted to minorities and women in
the 1964 Civil Rights Act. This legislation prohibits discrimination on the basis of
disability in employment, public services, and public accommodations. In employment, a qualified disabled person is one who, with or without reasonable accommodations, can perform the essential functions of a particular job. The law also
requires new buses and trains, as well as public buildings, to be accessible to the
disabled, and it mandates communications companies to operate relay systems that
will allow speech and hearing-impaired persons access to telephone services.

As with the concepts of rape and sexual harassment discussed earlier, the
concept of disability has undergone a definitional expansion to cover not only
the lame, the halt, and the blind, but a plethora of claims of learning disabilities
and other dysfunctional attributes beyond the universally recognized and classically defined mental disorders, such as schizophrenia and depression. The Equal
Employment Opportunity Commission announced a ruling that the ADA will
cover not only physical but also mental disabilities, including a range of learning
disorders. There are limits to this expanded coverage, however. The ADA does
not cover substance abuse or transsexuality, for example. For many of the newly
claimed learning disabilities, there are no standard tests or indicators. The Act
defines learning disabilities as "a disorder in which one or more basic psychological processes involved in understanding or using language . . . may manifest itself
in an imperfect ability to listen, think, speak, read, write. . . ." Accommodations
have been mandated to covered individuals. For example, a college was required to
waive a math requirement for a business major who was afflicted with dyscalculia—
a math disability. The New York Board of Law Examiners was required in
July 1997 to provide one Marilyn Bartlett unlimited time to take the bar exam,
a special private room, and other amenities because she was putatively afflicted
with a reading disability called phonological processing. The issue here is whether
a person who, for whatever reason, cannot read at a normal level should be certified as a competent attorney. Secondly, critics fear that failure and mental incom-
petence now have to be accommodated because it has been redefined in clinical

terms. For example, "premature closure, belief perseverance, resistance to new ideas, dogmatism about beliefs," have been identified as "dysrationality" in the October 1993 *Journal of Learning Disabilities*. Professionals in the field disagree as to the reality of these newly conceptualized pathologies. Would such a person simply be close-minded? The expansion of the conceptualization of a handicap to which society is commanded to provide accommodations is, to the critics of this trend, a way of shifting blame and responsibility for failure. It is less humiliating to claim that you are a victim of dysgraphia than to admit that you are poor at grammar.[30]

Native Americans.   Native Americans constitute another group that has historically been subject to oppression by the dominant culture. From Plymouth, Massachusetts, to Wounded Knee, South Dakota, their numbers were systematically reduced, and they were forced onto desolate and often infertile reservations. They were caricatured as malevolent and ignorant savages in countless Western films. Their standard of living is substantially below the national norm, and they are beset today by structural unemployment, alcoholism, and other symptoms of alienation.

   In 1991, Native Americans took up as a target of protest the names of certain athletic teams. They organized demonstrations when the Atlanta Braves played in the World Series and in early 1992, when the Washington Redskins went to the Super Bowl. In 2007, the University of Illinois was forced to abandon its traditional mascot, Chief Illiniwek, who had been a central part of the University's athletic tradition since 1926. Defenders argued that the team names had never been meant to disparage, and that, in any case, the protests were a distraction from addressing the undeniably deep social and economic problems of the Native Americans. The 500th anniversary of Christopher Columbus's voyage also became an opportunity to debate the effect of American society on the original population.

POLICY EVALUATION: THE DRIVE FOR PROPORTIONAL EQUALITY

The impact of public policy on the issues of inequality examined in the preceding section is complex, but focusing on racial preference programs will tell us much about present general trends.

Busing for Racial Balance

Busing children to achieve racially balanced schools historically generated intense social and political conflict. However, busing for racial balance has become increasingly rare on the American political landscape: it has been replaced by other programs such as magnet schools or the Seattle program discussed in Recent Assaults on Racial Preference. Opposition to busing stemmed from several causes.

First, there is a cost to busing for racial balance. Furthermore, an important policy question is whether or not such busing produces social benefits that can justify the social cost. Busing can bring about racially balanced schools but without creating actual integration. Frequently, students are grouped in classes according to previous test scores or grades (tracking) so that the higher-achieving, middle-class students will take college preparatory academic subjects, and lower-achieving, minority students will take vocational education or remedial courses. This practice, of course, defeats the purpose envisioned by believers in the Coleman Report, the intermingling of high and low achievers. As to whether busing has had any impact on academic performance, the evidence is at best mixed and inconclusive.[31] It seems fair to say that busing has not yet provided the educational panacea for underachieving minorities that its supporters may have hoped for.

The impact of such de facto segregation is even greater today than it was in the 1960s, at least legally speaking, as the effectiveness of busing as a tool to achieve racial balance in the schools of many Northern urban areas was severely curtailed by the more conservative Burger Court in the mid-1970s. In *Milliken v. Bradley* (1974), the Court held that busing could not be required across school district lines.[32] In many metropolitan areas, whites have moved to the suburbs with their own independent school districts, and so African Americans now dominate the population of the city proper, a phenomenon known as white flight. Trends and projections show that the inner cities are becoming populated overwhelmingly by African Americans, and the suburbs remain overwhelmingly white. Thus, because city boundaries frequently constitute the school district boundaries, moving students about within mostly African American cities or nearly all-white suburbs will not contribute much to the racial balance of the schools. Moreover, some scholars express doubts that racial balance is the most important goal in engineering better schools. A majority of white parents and nearly half of the African American parents in polls express a preference for the school closest to home to better facilitate parental involvement in their child's education.

Whether or not it is actually a cost-efficient means of achieving widely agreed-upon goals of public policy, reliance on busing to achieve racial balance has declined in recent years in favor of alternative methods, such as the use of magnet schools. Magnet schools are schools in target group neighborhoods that offer special or enriched programs and activities to attract students from outside those neighborhoods. The trend appears to be away from court-ordered busing as a remedy for racial imbalance in the schools.

Retreat on Racial Preference Programs: *Weber* and Title VII

The *Bakke* case, discussed earlier, appeared to cast doubt on the validity of direct quotas in educational admissions. In *Kaiser Aluminum v. Weber* and *United Steelworkers of America v. Weber* (1979), the Court confronted the legality of a voluntary quota to balance racially a training program leading to promotion at Kaiser Aluminum.[33] Brian Weber's allegation was that Title VII of the 1964 Civil Rights Act forbade the company, with the union's concurrence, from voluntarily adopting such a racially preferential program that involuntarily excluded Weber from an opportunity to which he otherwise would have been entitled. That law forbade a covered employer from discriminating

> against any individual with respect to his compensation, terms, condi-
> tion, or privileges of employment because of such individual's race,
> color, religion, sex, or national origin; or to limit, segregate or classify
> his employees . . . in any way which would . . . adversely affect his
> status as an employee because of such individual's race, color, religion,
> sex, or national origin.

The Kaiser program, which led to promotions, selected individuals on the basis of seniority. However, for every white selected, one African American had to be selected, regardless of seniority. Thus, though Weber was excluded, some African Americans with less seniority than Weber were selected. There was no evidence or allegation of previous discrimination by either Kaiser or the union.

In holding that Title VII did not prohibit Kaiser's racial preference program, Justice Brennan, speaking for the Court, distinguished between the literal meaning of the law and the purposes that he inferred Congress had in mind in adopting that law. Brennan saw the purpose of Congress as correcting the problems of African American unemployment and African American underrepresentation in management or higher-status jobs. He reasoned that because the program is aimed at this purpose, Congress could not have intended Title VII to preclude the program, even though that is what the words of the law say.

The Weber case focused on whether the Civil Rights Act banned discrimination when whites were the victims. This question was revisited in the 2009 case of *Ricci* v. *DeStefano*, a case involving a test for promotion in the New Haven Connecticut fire department.[34] Frank Ricci, afflicted with dyslexia, had gone through considerable personal effort and expense to prepare himself for the test which he passed along with 116 other whites. However, when no African Americans scored high enough for promotion, the city, fearing a lawsuit on behalf of the African Americans, threw out the test denying promotion to the successful whites. The Court in June, 2009 ruled that the action of New Haven discarding the test, violated the Civil Rights Act of 1964.

The same question, did the Civil Rights Acts protect whites, arose when two men, dressed in combat gear and wielding clubs intimidated white voters at a Pennsylvania polling place in the 2008 presidential election. The justice department prosecuted the two men, members of the New Black Panther gang, for violation of the Voting Rights Act of 1965 but Attorney General Eric Holder quashed the prosecution. Members of Holder's department testified that they were told that it was policy not to use the act to protect whites.

Careful examination of the legislative debate over the adoption of the 1964 law may lead to the conclusion that Congress intended Title VII to prevent race from being used as a basis for hiring, firing, or employment status whether for or against target group interests, and at least one scholar, quoting the leaders of the House and Senate in this debate, made a powerful case for that interpretation.[35]

This trend of undermining judicial support for affirmative action policies was reinforced in two 1989 decisions (*Richmond v. Croson* and *Wards Cove Packing Co. v. Antonio*),[36] in which the Rehnquist Court moved to limit the force and effectiveness of affirmative action. The *Croson* case concerned a Richmond, Virginia, statute requiring that 30 percent of all city contracts go to firms in which a targeted minority had at least 51 percent ownership. These targeted groups, according to the statute, include "citizens of the United States who are African American, Spanish-speaking, Oriental, Indians, Eskimos, or Aleuts," although groups other than blacks amounted to just 1.82 percent of Richmond's population. The statute was clearly aimed at African Americans, who account for about half of that city's population. The J. A. Croson Company challenged the law, and the Supreme Court overturned the law. In July 1995, the Court reinforced *Croson* with its ruling in *Adarand Constructors v. Peña*.[37] A 5–4 majority, speaking through Justice O'Connor, held that an affirmative action plan must be shown to satisfy a "compelling public interest." That interest must be directed at redressing specific discrimination by the parties involved. Merely creating "a more diverse society" will not pass the rigorous "strict judicial scrutiny" demanded by the compelling public interest test. This criterion placed much of the network of affirmative action programs in constitutional jeopardy because in recent cases diversity was the value that justified race-based selection. The *Adarand* case concerned a business challenging a construction contract awarded to a contractor that subcontracted guard rail construction to a black-owned firm that was not the low bidder. (Ironically, the challenger in this case was Hispanic.) The presumption underlying minority set asides (giving a fixed percentage of public contracts to minority-owned businesses regardless of who is the low bidder) is that minority-owned businesses are necessarily disadvantaged. Thus, white-owned businesses may try to refute the presumption by showing they are more disadvantaged, a difficult task considering the ambiguous definition of the concept of "disadvantaged." The Court rejected that presumption.

The 1991 Civil Rights Act and the Judicial Assault on Racial Preference. The issue of affirmative action remains far from settled. The key issue that emerged from the *Croson* case is whether racial preference plans may be implemented in the absence of evidence of specific discrimination by the firm or institution instituting the plan and, if past discrimination must be shown, what kinds of evidence must be used as the basis of that conclusion. The *Croson* and *Wards Cove* cases showed that the Court was unprepared to accept simple statistical evidence to justify racial preference policies.

Congress sought legislative reversal of the *Croson* and *Wards Cove* decisions in the *Civil Rights Act of 1991*. The essential provision of the Act is to reverse the burden of proof in charges of employment discrimination and thereby to render it easier for minorities to initiate and win litigation in such disputes. The law requires employers charged with discrimination on the basis of a statistical underrepresentation of targeted groups in their work force to justify their hiring criteria in terms of job relevance or "business necessity," a requirement that effectively negates the *Wards Cove* decision.

Critics branded the legislation "a quota bill," a charge its supporters denied. The bill specifically outlaws quotas. However, it made statistical disparities in the workforce prima facie evidence of employment discrimination and placed the burden of proof on employers to show business necessity for hiring qualifications that lead to such disparities. The underlying assumption of using statistical disparities as evidence of discrimination is that in the absence of such discrimination all groups would be proportionately represented in each social or economic role; an assumption that certain people from certain kinds of cultural or religious backgrounds, for instance, are not more or less disposed than people from other backgrounds to pursue certain social or occupational roles. This may not be true. The effect of the provision putting the burden of proof on the employers to justify statistical imbalance, opponents of the bill argued, is to invite a deluge of litigation against employers in whose workforce target group members are statistically underrepresented, lawsuits that are expensive, time-consuming, and stressful even if one wins. Therefore, it would be rational for employers to try to avert the increasing prospect of being sued by avoiding statistical disparities in their workplaces, in other words, to institute voluntary quotas. In effect, the *Wards Cove* and *Croson* decisions have been overturned, and the burden of proof is upon employers to justify any statistical discrepancies in their workforce.

Recent Assaults on Racial Preference

The racial preference plans implicitly approved in the *Bakke* decision were challenged in a case emanating from the University of Texas Law School and resolved at the Circuit Courts of Appeals level and therefore binding only on the fifth judicial circuit (applying to Texas, Louisiana, and Mississippi). In that case, Cheryl Hopwood and four others claimed the school's admission policy discriminates against whites.[38] The case grew out of the following facts: The Law School, with many more applicants than it can accept, is highly selective. The median Law School Admission Test (LSAT) score of white students admitted is in the 93rd percentile and the mean GPA is 3.5. As of 1992, the median LSAT score for African Americans was in the 78th percentile. The white student criteria would have admitted only 1 out of 280 African American applicants, resulting in a virtually all-white student body. Nearly 700 higher scoring white applicants were passed over before the first blacks were denied admission; therefore, race was clearly the deciding factor in selecting African Americans over whites. The school set a different set of criteria for target group members in order to meet a goal of 10 percent Mexican Americans and 5 percent blacks and to ensure racial and ethnic diversity. Although race was one factor in the admissions process for the University of Texas Law School, the school insisted that it admitted blacks who were qualified to meet the academic demands of a legal education. Yet while some 90 percent of the non-target group passed the bar exam on the first try, the corresponding rate for the African Americans admitted under the race-sensitive selection criteria was a pass rate of less than 50 percent. Without race as a decisive factor, the University of Texas Law School soon became virtually an all-white institution, as even the most well-qualified African American students elected to apply elsewhere.

The *Hopwood* principle was challenged in two Supreme Court cases involving the University of Michigan decided in June 2003, *Grutter v. Bollinger* and *Gratz v. Bollinger.* The former case emanates from the law school while the latter case concerns undergraduate admissions. The law school took race into account for each individual in an imprecise way that the Supreme Court found did not isolate the target group applicants from competition with other applicants, but considered all in the same applicant pool. Moreover, the Court found that the policy was "narrowly tailored" to the public purpose of achieving a diverse student body. However, in practice race had a decisive weight. The university, however, admitted undergraduate students on a point system. An excellent essay on the admission form was worth three points and an SAT score over 1360 out of a possible 1600 was worth twelve points, but being a member of the right target group was worth twenty points, more than any other single factor except the twenty points given to scholarship athletes. The precise weighting given race in undergraduate admission was rejected by the Court in *Gratz*, but taking race into account in law school admissions was upheld in *Grutter,* a decision that effectively overruled *Hopwood.*[39]

The "compelling public interest" used to justify race-based selection, the criterion discussed previously for overriding the principle of equality under law and using the suspect category of race, has been diversity defined in terms of race. Critics charge that other possible criteria of diversity, such as religion, socioeconomic background, or even ideas are ignored by race-based selection. Eminent social scientist James Q. Wilson recently reported a body of research that found that, contrary to current conventional wisdom, people were better off "by every measure of social well-being" in racially homogeneous neighborhoods rather than ethnically diverse ones.[40] The Court followed such critics of race-based selection in a landmark case in 2007, *Parents Involved in Community Schools v. Seattle School District Number 1,* in which the school district assigned students to public schools specifically to keep the racial mix within specified limits. This case was merged with a case posing the same question emanating from Louisville, *Meredith v. Jefferson County.*[41] The Court struck down the Seattle plan for racially balancing its schools, stating that diversity as conceptualized above was not a compelling enough public purpose to justify the use of the suspect category of race. This decision casts doubt on the legality of most affirmative action plans in the country to engineer a racially diverse student body.

Meanwhile, another far-reaching assault on race-based selection, led by African American entrepreneur Ward Connerly, was in the form of a constitutional referendum that handily passed first in the state of California in 1996 and was upheld by the Supreme Court in 1997. His claim as an African American is that such policies demean the many blacks who achieve on merit and ability and they exacerbate the opposition to other legitimate claims of the civil rights movement. Proposition 209, known as the California Civil Rights Initiative, reads as follows:

> Neither the State of California nor any of its political subdivisions or
> agents shall use race sex, color, ethnicity or national origin as criterion

for either discriminating against, or granting preferential treatment to, any individual or group in the operation of the state's system of public employment, public education or public contracting.[42]

Nebraska adopted a similar civil rights initiative" in 2008 and Michigan adopted one in 2006, possibly indicating a trend away from race-based selection. Each of these propositions had the support of an overwhelming majority of voters in their respective states. Clearly, the California proposition effectively ends affirmative action in its most recognized forms (either quotas or racial preference plans for hiring and firing in state agencies) by the state of California and nationally if it is adopted in other states. Some argue that to increase target group numbers without using either quotas or racial preference plans, state agencies will have to substantially lower their selection criteria. California has in the past been a bellwether for the rest of the country; hence, it was not surprising that Connerly was able to successfully take his crusade to other states. In 2006, he was able to get the voters of Michigan to ban the use of race in university admissions. Partly in a reaction to the *Grutter* decision, which the vote effectively nullified, the Michigan Civil Rights Initiative (MCRI) received nearly 60 percent of the votes despite a strong campaign against the MCRI by most of the state's political elites. Michigan thus joined California, Florida, Nebraska, and Washington in banning race-based school assignment. However, Connerly's quixotic crusade may have been rendered superfluous by the Seattle case.

The Impact of Challenging Race-Based Selection. An empirical study by Linda Wightman on the effect of race-based selection on diversities in our nation's law schools reveals that in 1990–1991, of the 3,435 blacks admitted to law schools that year, only one-fifth would have been admitted to the schools that accepted them without racial preference. Among the more prestigious law schools, 17.5 times as many black students were admitted as would have gotten in if race had not been a factor.[43] Advocates of affirmative action argue that many target group members who would not have had the opportunity to attend law school without race-based selection will now do so, creating a more ethnically diverse student body and profession. Critics of affirmative action argue that these data confirm that people who get in by race-based selection must compete against students who have much higher grade point averages and test scores; hence, they fail or drop out from these prestigious schools. They could have succeeded in good, but less-selective schools where their records would have earned them admittance. Therefore, paradoxically, critics of race-based selection point to research by UCLA Professor Richard Sandar that shows that these plans result in fewer black lawyers. The data on differential rates of passing the bar exam suggest that the weaker levels of preparation are handicaps that race-based admittees do not frequently succeed in overcoming. Supporters of California's Proposition 209 argue that minority students who can no longer get admitted to the highly selective programs under a racial preference plan can enroll in a less-selective institution where their chances of failure will be substantially reduced. It is a fact that while the percentage of African Americans being admitted to higher education has greatly increased under affirmative action plans, African Americans tend to drop out without getting their degree at a much greater rate than whites. It is uncertain what psychological costs are incurred by the individual who enters a program beyond his or her abilities and skills and consequently fails.

FUTURE ALTERNATIVES: THE CHANGING CONCEPTION OF EQUALITY

The Debate over Affirmative Action

These racial preference plans are part of the entire spectrum of affirmative action programs that date from the late 1960s, when government instituted a number of specific policies to redistribute social benefits to those groups who had less than their share—the goal of proportional equality.

Affirmative action describes a series of policies or active government efforts to bring into valued roles members of designated disadvantaged groups in rough proportion to their percentage of the population at large. It is defended primarily in terms of compensatory justice. That is, justice requires that these groups be given compensation for the harm done to them by previous social policies. It announced the intention of the national government no longer to be neutral toward disproportionate distribution of society's values, whether among racial or ethnic groups, between the sexes, or in the sense of underrepresentation of these groups in valued social roles. Sometimes affirmative action has taken the form of direct government action, as in the preferential hiring or promotion of government employees from among the groups designated for such benefits. More often it has been the encouragement of others to take such steps, by the promise or threat of granting or withholding federal funds or by direct government order.

Affirmative action includes a number of government actions, regulations, and judicial decisions. The idea most that is the most controversial manifestation of affirmative action is quotas, the setting aside a fixed percentage of social values for members of the target group, such as the requirement that a given percentage of those hired, promoted, or admitted to desired roles must be from designated groups. Members of the target groups pursue these values as members of a separate applicant pool.

Secondly, affirmative action may mean granting some form of preferential consideration to members of target groups. In such racial preference plans, target group members would be chosen for benefits over nontarget group members only when other qualifications were approximately equal. The possibility would still exist that no members of target groups would receive the values in question. Such racial preference plans were the most commonly used form of affirmative action but both quotas and racial preference plans—since they both use race to allocate values—have apparently been rendered illegal by the Seattle case discussed previously, at least in public school student assignment.

Thirdly, the meaning of the term can even be extended to include a readjustment of standards to accommodate the inability of a proportionate number of targeted groups to meet those standards as was done in the Ricci case A 1979 California case, *Larry P. v. Riles,* banned the use of IQ tests for blacks in the public schools when the judge reasoned that "Black children's intelligence may be manifested in ways that the tests do not show. . . ."[44] Another illustration is the court challenge to the tests of reading skills, passage of which is required for a high school diploma irrespective of high school grades. Most states now require minimum competency tests for students and teachers (discussed in Chapter 9). African Americans and Hispanics fail such tests at a disproportionate rate.

This implicit assumption that it is unfair to hold African Americans to the standards of the European or Western-based civilization on which this nation has operated also underlies the rationale for Afrocentrism, a movement that goes beyond stressing the role of blacks in American history and culture to the claim that most of the great cultural, philosophical, and scientific advances in the world originated with black Africans and were stolen by Alexander the Great from a library in a black-dominated Egypt. Designed to enhance the self-esteem of African American students accustomed to failure, Afrocentrist curricula have come to dominate the educational experience of a growing number of young blacks in America. Critics express concern that is done at the expense of those students acquiring the skills and knowledge they will need to function in this society. The academic qualifications of the leaders of these programs have been called into question. For example, Hunter Adams, who wrote the essay on science in the most widely used Afrocentric textbook, *African-American Baseline Essays,* has only a high school diploma. Abena Walker, who was paid $165,000 to train Washington, DC, teachers in Afrocentrism, had only a degree that she created herself from a bogus university. Critics of the Afrocentric curriculum also express concern that at its root, Afrocentrism constitutes an attack on the fundamental Western concept that facts and science possess an objectivity that is independent of culture. As Marimba Ali writes in *Yurugu: An African Centered Critique of European Cultural Thought and Behavior,* "Our task is to throw into question European . . . scientific epistemology." Martin Bernal of Cornell argues that evidence from cults and legends "is not categorically less valid than from archeology." Thus, instead of imparting the tools and the ability to use them that young blacks will need to function in a modern Western society, Afrocentrists choose to use scarce educational resources attacking the validity of those tools.

Support for Affirmative Action. Those who challenge traditional performance standards claim that they do not really measure what they purport to measure. It is frequently charged that such standards are attributes of the dominant groups in society. These standards perpetuate the existing stratification system. For instance, critics express skepticism that college grade point averages really show one's potential for becoming a good doctor, lawyer, businessperson, or scientist or that the general abilities test given as part of the civil service examination measures one's potential for becoming a good bureaucrat. In other areas, such performance standards have been challenged in court, including whether a score on an IQ test is relevant to selecting a good police officer, whether a high school diploma is relevant to selecting power company employees,[45] or whether publications and prestigious degrees are relevant to selecting college teachers. These requirements are being questioned in the first place because the targeted disadvantaged groups fail in disproportionate numbers to meet these performance standards, and the gap between those who have more and those who have less widens still further.

Today's underclass is held to need special help not required by the waves of earlier immigrants because today's high-tech economy has a dearth of entry-level semi- and unskilled jobs. A generation ago it was easer for a healthy person to find work, save, and attend or send one's children to college, and attain upward mobility. Moreover, it is harder for today's underclass to find acceptance because, being ethnically or racially distinct, it is more difficult for them to blend in and assimilate.

The basic defense of affirmative action rests on the continuing impact of previous discrimination. Because it is now recognized that poverty is self-perpetuating both for individuals and across generations, policies that place a group in a disadvantaged position can be blamed for that group's continuing disadvantaged position even after the discriminatory policies themselves have ended.

Another justification for affirmative action policies designed to place a number of members of targeted minorities in valued roles is that they become role models for the youth of their group. Young African Americans, for instance, may be motivated to aim higher if they can see African American doctors, attorneys, teachers, and executives. Such role models may provide hope of redemption within the confines of the system and thereby head off pervasive alienation.

The zero-sum aspect of affirmative action programs, the fact that resources assigned to targeted groups must be taken from nontargeted groups (for instance, white men), is defended by claiming that the dominant position of the nontargeted groups was attained at the expense of the subordinate target groups. In other words, whites have become dominant by exploiting African Americans and Hispanics, and so whites should pay the cost of correcting the consequences of that exploitation.

Affirmative action programs at professional schools and universities create a racially and ethnically diverse student body that more closely mirrors that ethnically diverse population with whom the graduates of these schools will have to work and interact. That very process of interaction should lessen the tendency of people from different backgrounds to perceive one another in terms of stereotypes.

Opposition to Affirmative Action.   Despite the compelling logic of the case for affirmative action, such policies remain among the most controversial of our time and generate persisting and often bitter opposition, which sometimes comes from the very people who supported the civil rights movement when its goal was primarily legal equality. The case against affirmative action has been based on both logical arguments and the self-interest of groups not favored by the policy.

Perhaps the main logical or philosophical objection to affirmative action is that it seems to deny the principle of equality under law. In the final analysis, affirmative action policies reward or penalize individuals on the basis of who they are—their racial, ethnic, or sexual attributes—rather than on the basis of what they do. Furthermore, this aspect of affirmative action reintroduces the relevance of racial and ethnic categories as permissible in American legislation. Yet, as was noted in the discussion of equality under law, the struggle to label certain categories as suspect has been viewed as a liberal and progressive struggle, and the triumph of meritocracy over privilege based on the accidents of birth has been traditionally seen as one of the attributes of both a liberal and a more developed society. Some opponents of affirmative action warn that if race can be used for benign purposes, it will henceforth be more difficult to prevent race from being used in other ways. After all, defining what constitutes a benign policy becomes a judgment by those in power. Thus, critics claim, affirmative action works against the principles of individualism and meritocracy. Moreover, in technologically advanced societies with the high skill levels required to fill more complex social and economic roles, modification of the principles of meritocracy seems to threaten overall productivity.

Some opponents of affirmative action question the selection of its beneficiaries. They argue that many groups have suffered serious discrimination. It was described earlier how Asian immigrants once suffered worse discrimination and more disadvantages than Mexican immigrants did; yet the latter are designated as affirmative action beneficiaries, while the former are frequently classed with the white majority. Poles, the Irish, Jews, and Italians all in their turn suffered social and legal discrimination, yet none of these groups is targeted for affirmative action benefits. By what criterion, affirmative action opponents ask, are some groups selected for benefits?

The attribute that distinguishes the target groups seems to be that statistically they have lower success levels than other groups do; they have lower mean incomes, lower mean indices of socioeconomic status, and higher levels of poverty. In other words, the recipients of affirmative action benefits are members of groups that, in the aggregate, have been unable to overcome the impact of discrimination. It is a policy that rewards the lack of competitive success and achievement.

This generally agreed-upon definition of affirmative action recipients raises two key observations from critics. First, individual members of groups not targeted by affirmative action often suffer real penalties as compensations are awarded to the disadvantaged group. The resources of society are finite; when a resource is assigned to one who would not have earned it by meeting society's performance standards, it must be denied to another who would have met them, an unintended but very real consequence. For each African American, Hispanic, or other designated beneficiary admitted to law school, medical school, a management training program, or some other upward-mobility program to which that person would not otherwise have been admitted, a member of a nontargeted group who may otherwise have earned admission must be kept out. This concept of finite values so that values given to some must be taken from others is called a "zero-sum" society. To members of nontargeted groups who also see themselves as victims of systematic persecution, such as Jews and Asians, such policies generate particular hostility, especially since being disproportionately successful, they are disproportionately among those displaced. These people see their group as being in effect penalized for its success in overcoming the effects of past discrimination. This would seem to be inconsistent with the approval of competitive success that has been widely identified as a basic attribute of American culture and a key feature of equality of opportunity.

Members of such groups deny that their success is simply a result of exploiting African Americans and Hispanics. As we pointed out, many of the more successful groups have themselves suffered discrimination. Moreover, the cultural dispositions of some groups are more conducive to success in this system than others. For example, David McClelland notes that the child-rearing patterns of some groups foster an "achieving personality."[46] In recent years, an explosion of illegitimate teenage pregnancies among members of the *underclass* (the unskilled and unemployable) in urban slum neighborhoods has been identified as both a social tragedy and a major impediment to upward mobility among members of the underclass. Former Harvard sociologist and then undersecretary of labor Daniel Patrick Moynihan issued a fifty-three page analysis in 1965, "The Negro Family: The Case for National Action" that identifies the skyrocketing rate of illegitimacy among Negros (which has now reached 70 percent nationwide from the 24 percent at the time of Moynihan's report) as a major cause of black poverty: "a social catastrophe." Initially, Moynihan was accused of "blaming the victim," but research shows that children raised in an intact two-parent family fares better in academics and in life.[47] Meanwhile, in the same period illegitimacy among whites rose from 3 percent to 24 percent.

Thus, some conservatives argue that persisting marginal socioeconomic status of the underclass is now more a function of their own behaviors than of past social oppression.[48] If so, the argument for privileges to target groups in the name of compensatory justice is weakened.

Many critics ask whether affirmative action policies actually help those members of targeted groups who are most disadvantaged. Affirmative action programs, being race-based, assume a perfect correlation between race and other attributes such as socioeconomic status and the ability to compete. Affirmative action policies stipulate that members of certain groups be selected for desired roles without specifically stipulating which individuals may be chosen or what attributes they may or may not possess; that is, these policies tend only to say that they must be members of the designated group. Because those who design and administer affirmative action programs are reluctant to abandon performance standards entirely, those members of the designated groups who are the best qualified by traditional performance standards tend to be the ones selected for desired roles. This means that middle-class African Americans and Hispanics, not unemployed school dropouts (who are mainly responsible for their group's statistically disadvantaged status) are often the ones who benefit most from affirmative action. This fact illustrates the often-observed weakness of the assumption that what is true for relationships among groups (the white race is better off than the black race as a whole) holds true for individuals within those groups. It is, in fact, quite likely that the best nonwhites selected for affirmative action positions may come from less-disadvantaged backgrounds than do those whites they displace, whites who would have only marginally succeeded in being selected by conventional performance standards. Moreover as explained earlier, in moving the best target group members into roles higher than they would have achieved by performance standards, these capable young people are taken from probable success into frustrating failure.

Stephen and Abigail Thernstrom, in a 1997 book on America's race problem, present data indicating a very large measure of African American progress by social and economic criteria, progress that to a large measure antedated affirmative action. According to the Thernstroms, this progress indicates that African Americans are capable of effectively competing with whites. For example, they note that in 1940, the median annual income for black males was 41 percent that for white males, while by 1970 it had risen to almost 60 percent. The corresponding figures for black women are 36 percent and 73 percent. Most of this progress antedated affirmative action, which was instituted in the mid-1960s. Moreover, while black families as of 1995 had only 61 percent of the income level of white families, if one includes only intact or two-parent families, blacks had 87 percent of the income of whites.[49] Hence, one might infer that the greater tendency toward family instability might account for much of the gap between blacks and whites as argued by Moynihan almost half a century ago, rather than the lack of a level playing field and the residual racism that affirmative action programs are designed to rectify.

Underlying the goal of proportional equality that is at the heart of affirmative action is the presumption that in the absence of pervasive and continuing discrimination against target group members, they would attain a proportionate representation in valued social and economic roles. Yet others suggest that different groups have cultural backgrounds and widely held values that dispose their members to seek certain roles more than others. Without denying that cultures are equally valid and of value, they are not identical and do not disseminate the same values, attitudes, and skills to their progeny.

It should be noted that some of the opposition to affirmative action programs is based in part on grounds of self-interest rather than principle. Those who are not members of the designated beneficiary groups, such as white men, find that with selected social rewards being set aside for members of designated minority groups, there are fewer rewards for white men to allocate among themselves.

African Americans and Jews: A Broken Alliance. American Jews epitomize this phenomenon. They populate high-status roles well in excess of their proportion of the population. For example, although making up only one-and-one-half percent of the total population, Jewish teachers constitute nearly half of all Ivy League faculties. Thus, when white men in general are restricted (by quotas favoring minorities) from competing for a stipulated number of academic positions, Jewish men are disproportionately excluded, as they are being partially barred from an area of traditional high employment. Therefore, although Jews helped lead the struggle for legal equality of African Americans—as many legally supported restrictions applied to them as well—Jewish writers and publications have often taken strong editorial stands against the affirmative action direction of the African American civil rights movement. This opposition has generated tension between these formerly allied ethnic groups. African Americans currently manifest more anti-Jewish attitudes than do any other American ethnic or racial group, and these attitudes are more common among the younger and better-educated African Americans.[50] However, American Jewish voters gave Barack Obama 77 percent of their vote in 2009. Anti-Semitism in other groups generally is found in older and less well-educated people; among African Americans, such attitudes are strengthening over time, whereas they are fading among other groups. It appears that the difference in interests between these two former allies is growing into an emotional, deeply felt antipathy between them.

The mutual hostility was highly visible in the 1990s. At the City University of New York, paired incidents occurred: The chair of the Black Studies Department, Leonard Jeffries, Jr., in the course of several anti-Semitic speeches, claimed that Jews had financed the slave trade and that Jews controlled the American media and film industry and conspired to exclude African Americans from both. A philosophy professor, Michael Levin, had been telling his classes that African Americans are for genetic reasons less intelligent than whites and that African Americans should be segregated in the New York subways for reasons of public safety. Neighborhood tensions were high in several cities, most notably in the Crown Heights section of Brooklyn, where large African American and Hasidic Jewish neighborhoods intersect. Violent demonstrations took place after an African American child was struck and killed by a van driven by a Hasidic Jew. A young Hasidic scholar from Australia, Yankel Rosenbaum, was killed by a roving mob, and Lemrick Nelson, who bragged about killing Rosenbaum, was released by an all-black jury.[51] This mutual antipathy continued in November 1993 when a Nation of Islam leader gave a much-reported speech at Kean College in New Jersey in which, among other things, he claimed the Jews owned 75 percent of the slaves in the Old Confederacy, that the Holocaust was justified by the actions of the Jews, and that Jews were "the bloodsuckers of the Black nation."These views were repeatedly espoused by President Obama's pastor, Jeremiah Wright; however, Obama's strong Jewish vote indicated a Jewish perception that he had disassociated himself from those views. However, polls taken in the late spring of 2010 indicate a weakening of that support, as President Obama was perceived as hostile toward Israel.

Race and Equality

The most clearly discernible trend in the struggle for equality is the evolution of the generally understood meaning of the term, which has changed its goals and issues. The meaning of the term once referred to the struggle for eradication of discrimination, based on racial, religious, sexual, or ethnic attributes, and of laws or social policy that burden or penalize people on the basis of such attributes. It has, in recent decades, come to imply that each identifiable racial or ethnic group and each sex has a right to a proportionate share of the benefits of society. The legitimacy of an uneven distribution of material well-being and of the dominance of certain groups over others has increasingly come under attack.

The changing conception of equality has been accompanied by a changing conceptualization of racism. More recently, supporters of target groups have been using the term *symbolic racism* to refer to opposition to programs and policies advocated by target group leaders or to statements not overtly racist as a racial or ethnic slur, but statements to which target group members nonetheless take offense as "insensitive."[52] Thus, someone who criticizes busing for racial balance or some affirmative action policy may be accused of using such critiques as a cover for deeply held racist attitudes. Of course, the charge of symbolic racism is hard to avoid. One can with care avoid using direct racial slurs, but one may find it more difficult to anticipate those statements or opinions to which some target group member may take offense or regard as insensitive. For example, at the University of Pennsylvania in early 1993, a graduate student, an Israeli named Eden Jacobowitz, shouted to a group of African American women celebrating beneath his dorm window, "Shut up, you water buffalo!" Jacobowitz had translated an Israeli term that connotes coarseness or crudeness, but has no particular racial connotations. Still, Jacobowitz was pursued for an entire semester with charges of racist insults under Penn's rigorous speech code.

Clearly, there are arguments to be made for some form of compensatory justice in view of the history of discrimination against certain groups. However, because of the confusion between the bigotry or discrimination of groups and those of individuals within those groups, the justice of the matter becomes muddled. The white race may, in the aggregate, be guilty of discrimination; however, individuals—Brian Weber, Cheryl Hopwood, or Alan Bakke—pay the debt, even though they may not personally have so discriminated. To change the rules of the game and deny benefits to the Hopwoods, Webers, and Bakkes of society, benefits to which they were entitled under the old rules, is perceived by some as a denial of their rights.

Yet minorities do have a right to combat the persisting impact of the history of social discrimination. The point is that rights conflict. The intractable difficulty of the equality issue is that it is not a clear case of right and wrong, but one of conflicting rights. Plausible ethical arguments can and have been constructed to support conflicting claims based on powerful interests. In addition, in an economy in which hopes of perpetual economic growth confront the reality of scarcity and the finite supply of resources, society is increasingly in a zero-sum situation. Members of nontargeted groups increasingly perceive that they cannot help target groups without giving up something themselves. Thus, the strongest opposition to affirmative action frequently comes from those segments of white society most likely to be displaced by members of target groups, the middle or lower-middle classes. Members of the upper class are less likely to be so displaced, and therefore the support for affirmative action by so-called limousine liberals is without cost. Because of this conflict among plausible rights, issues concerning equality promise to continue to be among the most intractable and divisive of issues facing the country for the indefinite future. The issue of racial equality in higher education was given new life in a 1992 case in which the

Supreme Court ruled that Mississippi's system of predominantly African American and white universities is discriminatory. Similar systems in nineteen other states were strongly affected by this ruling.

The struggle for equality by African Americans has resulted in an inevitable rise in tensions between African Americans and the rest of society, many of whom perceive the progress of the targeted groups toward greater material well-being as coming at their expense. In particular, racial, ethnic, or gender preference plans are deeply resented. A new phase of the struggle of the less well-off groups has been entered, in which it is perceived that the goal of such groups has shifted from seeking integration or assimilation in the liberal democratic system, as symbolized by the renowned "I Have a Dream" speech of the Reverend Dr. Martin Luther King, Jr., to challenging the legitimacy of the system itself. Thus, the sympathy of such current African American leaders as the Rev. Jesse Jackson, singer Harry Belafonte, or the Reverend Jeremiah Wright for third-world anti-democratic leaders such as Fidel Castro or Hugo Chavez is perceived as a threat to the dominant system in a way that King's goals of assimilation were not. Thus, despite all of the progress toward equality documented throughout this chapter, tensions between the targeted less well-off groups and the rest of society remain high. These racial tensions are exacerbated by highly publicized incidents, such as the conflict between African Americans and Jews discussed earlier. The question of whether African Americans can receive equal justice in the American judicial system is likely to remain salient for the foreseeable future.

Just how difficult it is for African Americans and other racial minorities to achieve just treatment is dramatically revealed by periodic housing studies. A study conducted for the Department of Housing and Urban Development by Syracuse University in the early 1990s employed 3,000 paired African American, white, and Hispanic prospective homebuyers and renters. It found that African Americans experienced some form of discrimination 56 percent of the time they sought to buy and 59 percent of the time they sought to rent a house. Comparable figures for Hispanics were 50 percent and 56 percent.[53] Follow-up studies by the Fair Housing Alliance used a similar methodology and discovered the same patterns of discrimination as recently as 2006.[54]

The levels of racial antagonism and African American alienation from American society were shown in the celebration of the acquittal of accused murderer O. J. Simpson in 1995. Simpson's attorney Johnny Cochran had urged the jury to send a message to the white community in the face of a mountain of incriminating evidence. The right of a jury to return a verdict in the face of contradictory evidence is known as jury nullification, an option that was frequently used by Southern white juries to free whites who committed crimes against blacks. Now it was being used in defiance of the white criminal justice system. It had also been used in acquitting Lemrick Nelson, despite his admitted role in the murder of Yankel Rosenbaum (discussed earlier). Not only was there generalized outrage at the criminal justice system and at the living conditions of many African Americans in urban America, there was specific hatred directed at whites, Hispanics, and Asians.

ENDNOTES

1. Stephen and Abigail Thernstrom, *America in Black and White: One Nation Indivisible: Race in Modern America* (New York: Simon & Schuster, 1997), 14.

2. Michael Lewis Beck, Charles Tien, and Richard Nadeau, "Obama's Missed Landslide: A Racial Cost," *PS: Political Science & Politics*, Vol. 43 (January 2010): 69–76.

3. *The Civil Rights Cases*, 109 U.S. 3 (1883).

4. For a detailed account of admissions policies at Harvard, see Alan Dershowitz, *Chutzpah* (Boston: Little Brown, 1991), 66–74.

5. For a full treatment of Berkeley's policies to restrict the admission of Asians, see Dinesh D'Souza, *Illiberal Education* (New York: Free Press, 1991), Chapter 2.

6. Peter Uhlenberg, "Demographic Correlates of Group Achievement: Contrasting Patterns of Mexican Americans and Japanese Americans," in Robert K. Yin, ed., *Race, Creed, Color or National Origin* (Itasca, IL: Peacock Press, 1973), 86.

7. Colin Powell, *My American Journey* (New York: Random House, 1995), 72.

8. Elizabeth Koontz, "Women as a Minority Group," in Yin, ed., *Race, Creed*, 288–289.

9. Richard Hernnstein and Charles Murray, *The Bell Curve: The Reshaping of American Life by Differences in Intelligence* (New York: Free Press, 1994).

10. Stephen Thernstrom, "The Scandal of the Law Schools," *Commentary*, 104 (December 1997): 27–31.

11. *The Civil Rights Cases*, 109 U.S. 3(1883).

12. *Plessy v. Ferguson*, 163 U.S. 537(1896).

13. *Brown v. Board of Education of Topeka, Kansas*, 347 U.S. 483(1954). The Court also struck down the constitutionality of government-required segregation in federally controlled territory, in this case Washington, DC, in *Bolling v. Sharpe*, 347 U.S. 497 (1954). Recall that the Fourteenth Amendment only restricts state government; hence, the *Bolling* case was decided under the due process clause of the Fifth Amendment.

14. *Brown v. Board of Education of Topeka, Kansas*, 349 U.S. 294 (1955).

15. *Alexander v. Holmes County Board of Education*, 396 U.S. 19 (1969).

16. James Coleman, *Equality of Educational Opportunity* (Washington, DC: U.S. Government Printing Office, 1966); and U.S. Commission on Civil Rights, *Racial Isolation in Public Schools* (Washington, DC: U.S. Government Printing Office, 1967).

17. *Green v. School Board of New Kent County*, 391 U.S. 430 (1968).

18. *Swann v. Charlotte-Mecklenburg Board of Education*, 402 U.S. 1 (1971).

19. See the discussion of specific cases in Nathan Glazer, *Affirmative Discrimination* (New York: Basic Books, 1975), 100ff.

20. *Heart of Atlanta Motel v. United States*, 379 U.S. 241 (1964); *Katzenbach v. McClung*, 379 U.S. 294 (1964).

21. *Washington v. Davis*, 426 U.S. 229 (1976).

22. Alan Sindler, *Bakke, DeFunis, and Minority Admissions* (New York: Longman, 1978), 59.

23. *Craig v. Boren*, 429 U.S. 190(1976).

24. *Rostker v. Goldberg*, 453 U.S. 57 (1981).

25. *New York State Club Association v. City of New York*, 108 S. Ct. 2225 (1988).

26. *The New Republic* (June 23, 1997).

27. Katherine Roithe, *The Morning After* (Boston: Little Brown, 1993).

28. *Boy Scouts of America v. Dale*, 530 U.S. 640 (2000).

29. *Bowers v. Hardwick*, 106 S. Ct. 2841(1986); *Lawrence v. Texas*, 539 U.S. 558 (2003).

30. This discussion of disability is drawn significantly from Ruth Shalit, "Defining Disability Down," *The New Republic* (August 25, 1997): 16–22.

31. David Armor, "The Evidence of Busing," *The Public Interest*, 28 (Summer 1972): 90–126.

32. *Milliken v. Bradley*, 418 U.S. 717 (1974).

33. *Kaiser Aluminum v. Weber* and *U.S. Steelworkers of America v. Weber*, 443 U.S. 193 (1979).

34. Ricci v. DeStefano, 567 US 129 S. Ct. 2658

35. Carl Cohen, "Justice Debased: The Weber Decision," *Commentary*, 68 (September 1979): 43–53.

36. *Richmond v. J. A. Croson Co.*, 488 U.S. 469(1989); *Wards Cove Packing Co. v. Antonio*, 493 U.S. 802 (1989).

37. *Adarand Constructors v. Peña*, 515 U.S. 200(1995).

38. *Hopwood v. Texas*, 78 F.3d 932(1996) and 116 S. Ct. 2580 (1996).

39. *Grutter v. Bollinger*, 539 U.S. 306(2003); *Gratz v. Bollinger*, 539 U.S. 244 (2003).

40. James Q. Wilson, "Bowling with Others," *Commentary*, 124, No. 3 (October 2007): 34–38.

41. *Parents Involved with Community Schools v. Seattle School District No. 1*, 551 US 701, 127 S. Ct. 2738 (2007).

42. Quoted from *The New Republic* (January 30, 1995): 18.

43. Linda Wightman, "The Threat to Diversity in Legal Education: An Empirical Analysis of the Consequences of Abandoning Race as a Factor in Law School Admissions Decision," *New York University Law Review* 72 (April 1997): 1–53.

44. *Larry P. v. Riles*, 495 F. Supp. 926 (1979).

45. *Washington v. Davis* and *Griggs v. Duke Power Co.* 401 U.S. 424 (1979).

46. David McClelland, *The Achieving Society* (New York: Free Press, 1967).

47. James T. Patterson, *Freedom Is Not Enough: The Moynihan Report and America's Struggle over Black Family Life from LBJ to Obama* (New York: Basic Books, 2010).

48. For a famous but much criticized exposition of this perspective, see Edward Banfield, *The Unheavenly City: The Nature and Future of Our Urban Crisis* (Boston: Little Brown, 1970), esp. pp. 53ff.

49. Thernstrom and Thernstrom, *America*, 194–195.

50. See the A.D.L. surveys cited in Nathan Perlmutter and Ruth Ann Perlmutter, *The Real Anti-Semitism in America* (New York: Arbor House, 1982), Chapter 8. See also Arthur Liebman, *Jews and the Left* (New York: Wiley, 1979), 564–568. The 1978 Harris Survey also found anti-Semitism higher among African Americans than among other groups.

51. A detailed account of these events may be found in *The New Republic* (October 14, 1991): 21–31.

52. Paul Sniderman, "The New Racism," *Journal of Political Science*, 35 (May 1991): 423–424.

53. *The Baltimore Sun*, August 31, 1991.

54. National Fair Housing Alliance, Unequal Opportunity—Perpetuating Housing Segregation in America: 2006 Fair Housing Trends Report, www.nationalfairhousing.org/resources/newsArchive/resource_24256802754560627686.pdf; Accessed October 10, 2010.

RESOURCES

Books

Banfield, Edward. The Unheavenly City: *The Nature and Future of our Urban Crisis*. Boston: Little Brown, 1970.

Bernstein, Richard. *The Dictatorship of Virtue: Multiculturalism and the Battle for America's Future*. New York: Knopf, 1994.

D'Souza, Dinesh. *The End of Racism: Principles for a Multiracial Society*. New York: Free Press, 1995.

D'Souza, Dinesh. *Illiberal Education: The Politics of Race and Sex on Campus*. New York: Free Press, 1991.

Dworkin, Ronald. *A Matter of Principle*. Cambridge, MA: Harvard University Press, 1985.

Edsall, Thomas B. *The New Politics of Inequality*. New York: Norton, 1984.

Dworkin, Ronald. *Taking Rights Seriously*. Cambridge, MA: Harvard University Press, 1977.

Glazer, Nathan. *Affirmative Discrimination*. New York: Basic Books, 1975.

Greer, Germaine. *Sex and Destiny*. New York: Harper & Row, 1984.

Hacker, Andrew. *Two Nations: Black and White, Separate, Hostile, Unequal*. New York: Scribner, 1992.

Kristol, Irving. " About Equality." *Commentary*, 54 (November 1972): 41–47.

Lefkowitz, Mary. " Not Out of Africa." *The New Republic* (February 10, 1992).

Millet, Kate. *Sexual Politics*. New York: Doubleday, 1969.

Rawls, John. *A Theory of Justice*. Cambridge, MA: Harvard University Press, 1971.

Roithe, Katherine. *The Morning After*. Boston: Little, Brown, 1993.

Shipler, David. *A Country of Strangers: Blacks and Whites in America*. New York: Knopf, 1997.

Thernstrom, Stephen, and Thernstrom, Abigail. *America in Black and White: One Nation Indivisible: Race in Modern America*. New York: Simon & Schuster, 1997.

Websites

American Civil Liberty Union's Lesbian Gay Bisexual Transgender Project: **www.aclu.org/lgbt/index.html**

Center for Equal Opportunity: **www.ceousa.org/**

Center for Race and Ethnicity at the Manhattan Institute:
www.manhattan-institute.org/html/cre.htm

Feminist Majority Foundation: **www.feminist.org/**

National Association for the Advancement of Colored People (NAACP):
www.naacp.org

National Organization for Women (NOW): **www.now.org**

U.S. Supreme Court Multimedia Database: **www.oyez.org/**

Chapter 11

Immigration Policy:
The Barely Open Door

The romanticized notion of America is that anyone could come to the United States and succeed through hard work. *Immigrants* helped the nation's westward expansion and helped fuel the industrial revolution that defined the U.S. economy for over a century. Beneath the romanticization of immigration, however, there always lurked some fears of the impact of immigrants on the social, cultural, economic, and political fabric of the country.[1] Even in colonial days, the nation's founders feared that immigrants might foster challenges to the political system being developed in the new country.[2] Nonetheless, it was not until the late nineteenth century that significant debate developed over immigration, and since that time the issue has waxed and waned as a major concern. Since the 1970s, immigration policy has commanded a great deal of attention in political debate, as it has been tied to issues of the rate of flow of immigrants, effects on racial/ethnic mix of the population, economic well-being of citizens, and demands for public services. Since the early 1990s, the issue dominated public policy debates in many parts of the country and in national elections.

Michael LeMay notes that every shift in immigration policy followed a major recession or depression and came during a period of social unrest and turmoil.[3] According to LeMay, each major shift also resulted from one or more of the major political parties including such a change in policy as part of its party platform and after the formation of interest groups focusing on the issue. In most instances, groups used immigrants as scapegoats for the problems they identified, although, on occasion, the groups advocated greater support for immigration. This chapter examines immigration policy in light of the forces advocating either opening the doors to or advocating limitations on immigration.

ISSUE BACKGROUND: FROM AN OPEN DOOR
TO INCREASING LIMITS

The Open Door

Traditionally, people viewed the United States as a nation of immigrants, implying that it is open to immigrants from around the world. As part of that view, the expectation arises that immigrants are part of the social contract the nation has with its citizens. The social contract "implies that citizens (and, in certain instances, other residents) who work hard and obey the law are eligible for government assistance in the form of health and education benefits and other social services at certain points in their lives, including those times when they are especially economically vulnerable."[4] The poem by Emma Lazarus inscribed inside the pedestal of the Statue of Liberty symbolizes the values of liberty and opportunity that attract many immigrants and that reflect the openness of American society:

> Give me your tired, your poor,
> Your huddled masses yearning to breathe free,
> The wretched refuse of your teeming shore.
> Send these, the homeless, tempest-tost to me,
> I lift my lamp beside the golden door.

For most of its history, U.S. government policy officially reflected these ideals. Nonetheless, implementation of policy did not always live up to the ideal, and there always has been sentiment to restrict entry.

Although some founders of the nation expressed concern about the effects of immigration, such as the potential for undermining the political values of the new nation, little formal policy emerged during the developing years of the United States. Instead, immigrants were welcomed to populate the country and aid in its economic development. Early concerns focused mostly on moral character and loyalty to the country. Some of these concerns arose from colonial days, when authorities objected to acceptance of criminals, paupers, or others of undesirable character. For example, in 1717, the Pennsylvania Colony imposed a fine of five pounds on every criminal brought in and made shipmasters post a year's bond for the good behavior of some passengers. Religious compatibility also affected colonial acceptance of immigrants. Beginning in Massachusetts in 1637, all colonies but Rhode Island imposed limits on settlers based on religious belief. Massachusetts, for example, restricted settlement of non-Puritans. Still, economic development and the abundance of land overshadowed these concerns and little regulation took place.[5] Citizenship could be acquired in state courts after five years of residence. This laissez-faire approach to immigration held until the mid-nineteenth century.

Use of Quotas

From the 1780s until 1819, approximately 250,000 immigrants arrived in the United States. Beginning in 1820, the pace of immigration quickened, with over 140,000 arriving during the 1820s and an annual average of almost 164,000 from the 1830s until 1860. A total of 5.1 million arrived during the 1860s and 1870s.[6] The increasing pace of immigration created the conditions for opposition to arise. However, since more than 80 percent of the immigrants came from Western and Northern Europe, opposition was not widespread before 1820. Because most immigrants who came after 1820 looked for work in the developing factories and textile mills, they tended to settle in the Northeast, especially in New York and Pennsylvania. Because many of these immigrants were different from the existing population, coming from southeastern Europe, being non–English speaking, and being predominantly Catholic and Jewish, opposition began to arise and quotas were imposed.[7]

Immigrants became "ghettoized" and many urban pockets of poverty developed. To many of the "native" population, these ghettos were spawning grounds for social problems, such as poverty, housing deterioration, lack of social cohesion, and crime.[8] Violence erupted in some places, such as in Philadelphia, which experienced a riot in 1844. The Native American Party (also known as the Know Nothing Party) arose in the 1850s out of anti-immigrant sentiment and enjoyed success in electing governors and members of Congress in the northeastern states. The party built on the beliefs of many native-born citizens that immigrants were a threat to their job security and threatened their religious foundations and the political culture.[9]

After the 1850s, negative responses of native-born citizens continued to build, and states expanded their exclusionary policies. The Civil War created a temporary diversion from the immigration issue and split the Know Nothing Party, but after the war, sentiment against immigrants grew again. California, in particular, excluded people based on their nation of origin, focusing on the Chinese, who arrived in large numbers in the West. California also imposed fees on Chinese immigrants, but this policy and all other state laws restricting immigration were invalidated by various decisions of state and federal courts based on the fact that immigration was a national and not a state issue. In 1882, the U.S. Congress acceded to the pressure from California and the Asian Exclusion League by passing a law setting a *quota* on the number of Chinese who could immigrate to the United States, and in 1888 further targeted Chinese immigrants through the Chinese Labor Exclusion Act. Congress also established a national policy on immigration through the Immigration Act of 1882, excluding ex-convicts and the mentally ill. These policy initiatives foreshadowed the bases for future limitations to immigration. The notion of excluding undesirables led to a long list of those to be excluded. Subsequent laws restricted polygamists, those convicted of crime, and those with certain illnesses.[10] Congress also responded to the concerns of organized labor with the Alien Contract Labor Act of 1885, banning the importation of contract labor, which often commanded lower wages than domestic labor.

By the end of the nineteenth century, Japanese immigration to the United States emerged as an issue, again in California. Efforts to limit Japanese immigration resulted in cities, such as San Francisco, segregating Japanese from the white population in schools. California again turned to the national government to stem the tide of Japanese immigrants. With pressure from President Theodore

Roosevelt, Japan agreed to limit issuance of passports for nonlabor individuals going to the United States.[11] California went so far as to prohibit Japanese residents from owning agricultural land, and eventually, even from owning leases or any other real estate interests. Other states, such as Arizona, Texas, and Washington, followed suit.

In 1881, Congress established the Office of Immigration in the Treasury Department to coordinate the evolving immigration policies. The 1906 Naturalization Act renamed the office to the Bureau of Immigration and moved it to the Commerce and Labor Department. The act also established the requirement that immigrants be able to speak English to gain citizenship. Reflecting continuing growth of anti-immigrant sentiment, Congress passed the 1917 Immigration Act, which incorporated all the earlier exclusions, required a literacy test, and specifically banned immigration of most Asians and Pacific Islanders. During the first two decades of the twentieth century, immigration averaged over 700,000 per year. During World War I, immigration dropped off, but it resumed at a higher pace after the war (see Figure 11.1).

Social problems, such as unemployment, economic sluggishness, and a shortage of housing, fueled anti-immigrant sentiment. Groups such as the Ku Klux Klan, the American Coalition, the Immigrant Restriction League, and the American Protective League of True Americans arose to advocate greater restriction on immigration. At the same time, others, such as the Hebrew Sheltering and Immigration Aid Society and the Anti-National Origins Clause League, opposed the restrictions. Congress passed the 1921 Quota Act, restricting the number of immigrants, and also established a quota limiting immigrants of any given nationality to 3 percent of those of the same nationality living in the country in 1890 as the base year for the quotas. The National Origins Quota Act of 1924

FIGURE 11.1 Legal Immigration Trends

SOURCE: http://www.dhs.gov/xlibrary/assets/statistics/yearbook/2009/table01.xls; Accessed June 25, 2010.

helped enforce the provisions by requiring immigrants to obtain visas from U.S. embassies in their native country. These acts attempted to maintain the ethnic balance of the United States and made it especially difficult for people from Italy, Spain, Russia, and Africa because their proportions in the population already living in the United States were small compared to Western or Northern Europeans. Thus, the intent of the act was to shift the balance of immigration flow back to northwestern Europe by establishing low quotas for others. An unintended consequence of these new policies emerged as *illegal immigration* through Mexico and Canada by those from countries with very low quotas, because they had no other way of entering the country. Unlike the economies of the affected nations, the economy of the United States was very strong and opportunities abounded. The increase in illegal immigration prompted the Bureau to create the Border Patrol.

Because of the Depression, immigration declined dramatically in the 1930s. Most people seeking residency in the United States during this time were attempting to flee Germany and other Nazi-dominated countries, although the quota acts led to restrictions on the number who could be admitted. By 1940, national security concerns further limited immigration and Congress passed the Alien Registration Act, which required fingerprinting and registration of new immigrants. It also required that criminals and subversives be deported. The bombing of Pearl Harbor by Japan led to relocation of many Japanese living in the United States. Whether they were new immigrants, long-time residents, or citizens, public officials considered Japanese potentially disloyal. The national government moved them from the West Coast to internment camps. Many of them lost their property because they defaulted on property taxes while in internment or were unable to secure it. Many were imprisoned. Also in 1940, the Bureau of Immigration was moved to the Department of Justice and renamed the Immigration and Naturalization Service (INS).

World War II and the draft created shortages of labor resulting in a policy allowing temporary workers (especially from Mexico) to enter the country. The lower wages paid copy these workers led to industries pressuring for continuation of the program after the war. The United States and Mexico signed a Migrant Labor Agreement in 1951 making the program permanent. Called the *Bracero Program*, it survived until 1964. In 2001, some businesses and political leaders, especially in the Southwest, argued for a return to allowing temporary workers to enter the country. The recession of 2001–2002 temporarily eliminated the support for such programs; the recession of 2007–2009 again dissipated support.

In 2004, President Bush proposed a plan for a temporary worker program that included provisions for immigrant workers to be matched with employers willing to hire them. Permits could be renewed for up to three years. A bipartisan group spearheaded by Senators John McCain and Edward Kennedy drafted legislation to address the issues in 2005. Again in 2007, a bipartisan group of senators proposed comprehensive reform that was also supported by President Bush. Controversy arose over whether a *guest worker* program (a revived Bracero Program) should be included and over a proposed pathway to citizenship for those already here. Rhetoric cast the debate in terms of amnesty versus deportation of immigrants.

Despite the bipartisan support, the effort failed by a small margin and reform appeared to be dead. After the failure of the proposed legislation, the administration decided to aggressively enforce sanctions against employers who knowingly hire illegal immigrants thus stirring up new controversy. The Obama administration promised to push for comprehensive immigration reform.

The many applications of *refugees* just prior to and during World War II called attention to the problem of refugees and the fact that the United States did not differentiate among potential immigrants. Eventually, the 1948 Displaced Persons Act addressed the issue by setting up a separate refugee system. During the 1950s, the act accommodated those fleeing communist countries. The refugee system permitted people to be accepted outside the quota system for their nations of origin. These refugees were granted *permanent resident* status and were permitted to apply for citizenship. The Cold War and anti-Communist frenzy stimulated closer scrutiny of immigrants as well to ensure exclusion of suspected subversives. After the terrorist attacks of September 11, 2001, similar pressures led to measures imposing greater scrutiny of immigrants and visitors.

Transition to a Preference System

In 1952, Congress enacted the Immigration and Nationality Act, which consolidated much of the earlier policy into one general policy. The act maintained the quota system and alien registration. It also gave preference to skilled labor and relatives of citizens and resident aliens. Later, the Immigration and Nationality Act of 1965 abolished the national origins quota system and established numerical limits in order of preference to:

1. unmarried children of U.S. citizens,
2. spouses and unmarried children of permanent resident aliens,
3. people in the professions and exceptional scientists and artists,
4. married children of U.S. citizens,
5. siblings of U.S. citizens,
6. workers with skills needed in the U.S. labor market, and
7. refugees.[12]

The act set a limit of 170,000 annually from the Eastern Hemisphere. It also established a limit of 120,000 annually for the Western Hemisphere after July 1968. The new policies resulted in large increases in illegal immigration and mounting pressure within the country for policies dealing with it. Much of the illegal immigration increase resulted from the fact that many of the Braceros who worked legally in the United States until the unilateral termination of the program by the United States still were welcomed by employers, especially in the agricultural sector. The workers now just came across the border illegally to work in the same jobs. The deterioration of the Mexican economy also contributed to the increase.

After 1965, immigration again surged and backlogs developed in applications because of the ceilings imposed, especially on immigration from the Western Hemisphere. To some, the reforms of 1965 represented a method of maintaining the same effect of the national origins quota system without being overt about it, since Asians and Africans would still find it difficult to immigrate because relatively few of them had relatives here.[13] The concept of *family reunification* drove the development of the new system that still underpins much of today's policy. The huge backlogs led to long waits for applicants, especially from Mexico. In 1976, Congress responded by creating the appearance of equality of treatment by establishing a limit of 20,000 immigrants from each country in the Western Hemisphere. Another change in 1978 imposed a ceiling of 290,000 visas per year for the world as a whole, thus deleting the differentiation between the Eastern and Western Hemispheres. The preference categories established in 1965 provided the basis for immigration under the 1978 policy.

Congress addressed the refugee issue again in 1980, separating refugee policy from overall immigration policy. The Refugee Act of 1980 created a separate admissions process for refugees and established a ceiling of 50,000 per year. It also gave the president, in consultation with Congress, the power to act in emergency situations involving refugees.

In 1986, Congress confronted the illegal immigration issue through the Immigration Reform and Control Act of 1986. The act granted *amnesty* and temporary resident status to illegal immigrants who had lived in the United States continuously after January 1, 1982. It also attempted to address the employment of illegal aliens by banning employment of *undocumented workers* and imposing sanctions on employers who knowingly hired illegal aliens. It created a program to help alleviate labor shortages, which might result from the sanctions on employers. Border patrol and inspection were strengthened by the act as well.

The Immigration Act of 1990 built upon the 1965 reforms and serves as the foundation for current policy. The act provided that, after 1995, immigration would be limited to 675,000 per year for all types of immigration. Family reunification remained the primary criterion for the policy, but some new categories also were created. For example, those who would invest $1,000,000 in urban areas or $500,000 in rural areas and create at least ten new jobs would be eligible above the overall ceiling. The act created a classification of *diversity immigrants* to allow people from countries with very low representation in the U.S. population to immigrate through a lottery process.

Illegal Immigration

The Illegal Immigration Reform and Immigrant Responsibility Act of 1996 addressed numerous issues concerning illegal immigration. The act responded to growing pressures among the public, especially in states along the Mexican border, to stem the flow of illegal immigration. To achieve that objective, the act almost doubled the size of the Border Patrol and provided resources to acquire sophisticated technology and otherwise improve the tools for securing the border and for detection and apprehension of those entering the country illegally. Stiffer penalties were enacted for smuggling illegal persons into the country and for production and use of fraudulent documents. Illegal immigrants caught also face stiffer penalties under the law.

The 1996 reform also attempted to deal with the problem of employment of undocumented workers. Specifically, the act provided sanctions for knowingly employing illegal immigrants and created some pilot projects to assist employers in confirming the eligibility of the employee to be hired. The programs emphasize the need for the Immigration and Naturalization Service, Social Security Administration, and the attorney general to work together and to develop systems for speedy confirmation of information to employers. They developed the E-Verify system for employers to check the eligibility of applicants to work in the United States.

The 1996 law requires family members who sponsor immigrants to earn 125 percent of the federal poverty income guideline in order to sponsor a relative. The law also addresses some of the provisions of the 1996 welfare reform affecting immigrants. In particular, the provisions make clear distinctions between legal and illegal immigrants relative to benefits that states can or may provide. Generally, illegal immigrants may be denied benefits, but some benefits also will be denied to legal immigrants. Specifically, Social Security benefits may not be paid to immigrants not legally present in the country; higher education benefits to illegal aliens are restricted; food stamps and Supplemental Security Income are phased out for most noncitizens; and states are permitted to deny benefits, such as nonemergency Medicaid to illegal aliens and sometimes to legal permanent residents. By 1997, Congress and the president faced pressure to change some of the provisions to assure benefits to immigrants in the country legally and who worked and paid taxes. SSI benefits were restored for legal immigrants in the country prior to enactment of the 1996 reforms. Congress also approved changes that allow immigrants with *green card* applications filed by January 4, 1998, to remain in the country while the application paperwork is processed. Congress also passed legislation making Nicaraguan and Cuban refugees automatically eligible for permanent status and allowing refugees from El Salvador, Guatemala, and Eastern Europe to apply for suspension of deportation under pre-1996 provisions less stringent than those in the 1996 act.

CONTEMPORARY POLICY: RESPONDING TO CHANGING IMMIGRATION DYNAMICS

As with all public policies (see Chapter 1), contemporary immigration policy serves diverse purposes. Most pieces of immigration policy reflect attempts to deal with a particular concern rather than a comprehensive approach, thus resulting in a complex patchwork of items. Thus, efforts to limit immigration often are justified in terms of meeting security and prosperity needs of people. Specifically, many opponents of immigration argue that immigration is an internal threat to the extent that it is related to social problems, such as crime and poverty, and to the extent that it undermines the political and social covenants on which American society is built. At times immigration also is linked to external threats, such as terrorism or, as during the Cold War, to subversion. These threats to security provide one rationale for limiting immigration. The threats became very real with the September 11, 2001, terrorist attacks in New York, Pennsylvania, and Washington, DC. In response, Congress passed the USA Patriot Act of 2001, officially known as the Uniting and Strengthening America by Providing Appropriate Tools Required to Intercept and Obstruct Terrorism Act of 2001. The act enhanced immigration enforcement with particular attention to potential terrorist threats. Many calls for even more restrictive policies use the terrorist threat as a rationale.

The Homeland Security Act of 2002 created the Department of Homeland Security and integrated immigration services and programs into the department. Specifically, the act created the U.S. Citizenship and Immigration Services (USCIS). In March 2003, USCIS fully absorbed INS and renamed it the U.S. Immigration and Customs Enforcement (ICE). The Homeland Security Department also includes U.S. Customs and Border Protection (CBP).

Regulation of immigration is often based upon prosperity needs. Many of the arguments against immigration are couched in terms of economic impact. Opponents argue that immigrants take away jobs of native-born citizens and put downward pressure on wages and the standard of living. Others contend that immigration should be encouraged because our economy needs people to take jobs that native-born citizens are unwilling to take. Also, many supporters of immigration point to the many highly skilled immigrants in technical fields as important to our ability to compete in the global economy. Thus, both proponents and opponents of immigration point to effects on the prosperity needs of the society to support their positions.

Policies on illegal immigration also rest on arguments about security and membership purposes. The same contentions as those regarding immigration generally are used, but others emerge as well. Membership is used as a basis for limiting access to various social programs. For example, denying noncitizens and illegal immigrants education and welfare benefits is based on membership as defined by citizenship.

The myth of immigration in United States history claims that the country opens its doors to the world and represents the best and most generous aspects of humankind. It has become a part of what is known as the American spirit. Some label it a myth because the specifics of immigration policy, as they developed, support anti-alien sentiment arising from people's anxieties and self-interest.[14] Despite restrictions, the United States ranks "as the principal immigrant-receiving nation in the world."[15] Others, however, argue that while absolute numbers of immigrants place the United States at the top, other nations, such as Australia, Canada, and Germany, admit more immigrants as a ratio of their total population.[16]

Part of the debate over immigration policy emanates from the national origin of immigrants and the large concentrations of some ethnic groups. Current policy gives preferences to those who have family already in the country, reflecting the family reunification philosophy of the policy. The family reunification policy supports maintaining the ethnic balance of the country and makes immigration from Africa particularly difficult. Furthermore, perceptions are that the number of Hispanics, and especially Mexican Americans, has increased dramatically in recent years. Data indicate that immigration from Mexico and other

Latin American countries remained stable from the 1920s to 2000 at 35 to 45 percent, but then increased to 54.6 percent by 2007 with more than 31 percent coming from Mexico.[17] The concentration of immigrants from Central America and Mexico in the Southwest and of Cubans in Florida gives the appearance of huge waves of immigrants from these areas and results in their being targets for the frustrations of native-born citizens.

Current policy is based on the 1965 Immigration and Nationality Act with modifications made in the 1990 Immigration Act and the Illegal Immigration Reform and Immigrant Responsibility Act of 1996. The policy establishes family reunification as the primary criterion for immigration and sets limits on the flow of immigrants. The 1996 act, in particular, attempts to control the influx of illegal persons and imposes penalties on employers of illegal immigrants. Immigration to the United States reached an all-time high of 1.8 million in 1991. Tougher policies reduced those numbers dramatically in succeeding years. The reforms of 1990 provided a ceiling of 675,000 beginning with fiscal year 1995. The ceilings have been exceeded because of various exceptions granted and because the family reunification philosophy allows immigrants to include their immediate families beyond the limit. In 2001 and 2002, for example, total immigration numbered 1.1 million; it dipped to 705,827 in 2003, and then gradually rose again to 1.27 million in 2006. It leveled off to 1.1 million in 2009 (see Table 11.1). Family-sponsored immigrants account for roughly 66 percent. Included are parents and children of U.S. citizens and resident aliens and siblings of U.S. citizens.

Approximately 12.7 percent of immigrants are admitted under *employment-based preferences*. These include people with advanced degrees or of exceptional ability, skilled professionals, unskilled workers filling special needs, and other special categories, including students covered under the Chinese Student Protection Act who might face persecution if they return to China. The category also includes *investor immigrants*, who receive admission to the United States based on their investing large sums of money into the economy. Employment-based immigration often is justified in terms of the increasingly global economy and the need for the United States to remain competitive. Often, highly technical skills are available in other nations and the ability to communicate and penetrate other economies through language and culture also are addressed in these approaches.

Refugees and *asylees* constitute another category. These are people who face persecution in their native countries. Refugees are usually people displaced from their countries because of political instability or persecution by a political regime against a particular group. Asylees claim political persecution for their ideas or political activities. They may be granted political asylum because of the harm they face by going back to their native countries. Refugees and asylees made up about 15.7 percent of immigrants in 2009 and diversity immigrants represented approximately 4.2 percent.

The top countries from which immigrants came in 2006 were Mexico, China, Philippines, India, and Dominican Republic (see Table 11.2). Until the 1960s, Europe dominated in sending immigrants to the United States. With the new face of immigrants, especially the large numbers of Asians and Hispanics, public attitudes have changed. Assimilation is not as easy as it was for the

TABLE 11.1   Immigration since 1990

Year	Number of Immigrants Admitted
1991	1,826,595
1992	973,445
1993	903,916
1994	803,993
1995	720,177
1996	915,560
1997	797,847
1998	653,206
1999	644,787
2000	841,002
2001	1,058,902
2002	1,059,356
2003	703,542
2004	957,883
2005	1,122,257
2006	1,266,129
2007	1,052,415
2008	1,107,126
2009	1,130,818

SOURCE: U.S. Department of Homeland Security, *2009 Yearbook of Immigration Statistics*, Table 1, http://www.dhs.gov/xlibrary/assets/statistics/yearbook/2009/table01.xls; Accessed June 25, 2010.

TABLE 11.2   Legal Immigrants by Top Ten Countries of Origin, Fiscal Year 2009

All Countries	1,130.818
Mexico	164,920
China	64,238
Philippines	60,029
India	57,304
Dominican Republic	49,414
Cuba	39,954
Vietnam	29,234
Colombia	27,849
South Korea	25,859
Haiti	24,280

SOURCE: U.S. Department of Homeland Security, *2009 Yearbook of Immigration Statistics, Table 2,* www.dhs.gov/xlibrary/assets/statistics/publications/pr_fr_2009, Table 3; Accessed June 25, 2010.

Europeans of early immigration waves. Resentment grows and is exploited by many interest groups and political opportunists. Anti-immigrant sentiment peaked in 2001. Polls in 2001 found that 59 percent of Americans believed that legal immigration should be reduced; by 2007, only 35 percent responded that way, and in 2010, 11 percent said legal immigration should be decreased.[18]

Immigration patterns are different today than they were prior to the 1970s.[19] As noted before, most immigrants during the nineteenth century and into the 1960s came from Europe, primarily Northern and Western Europeans, followed by Southern and Eastern Europeans. Generally, they settled in the Northeast and Midwest. They were attracted by the urban areas, which had jobs in the industrial sector. Since the 1970s, however, more immigrants come from Asia and the Caribbean and Latin American countries. Their settlement patterns are different. Generally, they settle in the coastal states, with the Pacific states and Southwest attracting Asians and Mexican Americans. Florida and the Northeast coast are the destinations of most of those from Cuba and the Caribbean. Currently, California, New York, Florida, Texas, New Jersey, and Illinois attract the largest numbers of foreign-born people (see Table 11.3).

Racial and ethnic origins of immigrants also have changed over recent decades.[20] Prior to 1970, 86 percent of the foreign-born population was white, while in 2003, only 46.7 percent of those arriving were white. Hispanics increased from 32 percent pre-1970 to 53.3 percent in 2003 and then to 47.5 percent in 2007. Asians increased from 9 to 26.8 percent of the foreign-born population in the same time period. Blacks represent about 8.1 percent of the foreign born.[21]

The education level of immigrants varies somewhat from the native-born population as well. Interestingly, almost four times the percentage of foreign born (29 percent) than native born (7.5 percent) lack a high school degree, but

TABLE 11.3   Concentration of Legal Immigrant Populations by Top Ten States of Residence, Fiscal Year 2009

California	227,876
New York	150,722
Florida	127,006
Texas	95,384
New Jersey	58,879
Illinois	41,889
Massachusetts	32,607
Virginia	28,825
Georgia	28,396
Maryland	27,562
All states	1,130,818

SOURCE: U.S. Department of Homeland Security, *2009 Yearbook of Immigration Statistics*, Table 4, www.dhs.gov/xlibrary/assets/statistics/publications/pr_fr_2009.pdf, Table 4; Accessed June 25, 2010.

approximately 11 percent of foreign born have graduate or professional degrees compared to about 10 percent of native born. Immigrants are a little less likely to have a bachelor's degree (17.4 percent) than are native born (20.8 percent). Native born are more likely to have graduated high school and have some college (51.5 percent) than foreign born (35.1 percent).[22] Data indicate that the education level of immigrants overall is dropping.[23]

The Illegal Immigration Reform and Immigrant Responsibility Act of 1996 addresses the problem of illegal immigration, which reached a peak in 2007 at 11.8 million. Much of the pressure for reform of immigration arose out of the frustration that many people felt about illegal immigration and their beliefs that illegal immigrants are the cause of many of the country's social ills. The 1996 reforms addressed this problem directly. Figures on illegal immigration are difficult to ascertain with accuracy, as illegal immigrants shy away from census takers. In 2009, the Department of Homeland Security estimated that there were 10.8 million illegal immigrants residing in the United States.[24] As Table 11.4 indicates, estimates of the number of unauthorized immigrants grew steadily between 2000 and 2007 and has since been leveling off. The number of illegal aliens apprehended (currently approximately 725,000 per year) by the ICE serves as one measure of the magnitude of the problem. ICE apprehensions increased steadily from the 1960s to 2000, and have been declining since. Increased enforcement and Mexico's improving economy and fewer economic opportunities in the United States are pointed to as reasons for recent declines, along with the 1996 act and stricter border controls under the 2001 USA Patriot Act. Apprehensions grew from a little more than 1.5 million during the 1960s to over 8 million in the 1970s to 14.6 million in the 1990s. More than 6 million were apprehended from 2001–2008. Illegal immigration is a very emotional issue as many Americans are convinced that illegal immigrants are a burden to society and create economic problems by taking jobs away from native workers. Additionally, the distinction between legal and illegal immigration is not always clear. Past law has allowed illegal residents to become legal; many families in the

T A B L E 11.4   Estimated Unauthorized Immigrants in the United States

Year	Number
2000	8,500,000
2005	10,500,000
2006	11,300,000
2007	11,800,000
2008	11,600,000
2009	10,800,000

SOURCE: U.S. Department of Homeland Security, *2009 Yearbook of Immigration Statistics,* http://www.dhs.gov/xlibrary/assets/statistics/publications/ois_ill_pe_2009.pdf; Accessed June 25, 2010.

United States contain some legal and some illegal members; and the status of many is unclear, awaiting adjudication. The next section explains the different views about the effects of current immigration policy.

POLICY EVALUATION: CONTRASTING PERCEPTIONS

Current Policy Concerns

Immigration policy is a very emotional issue that does not lend itself easily to ideological splits. Instead, people's views are shaped by their family ties, their experiences with immigrants, their fears of the impact of immigration, and the areas of the country in which they live, to name a few. LeMay argues that economics, race, nationalism, and foreign policy play pivotal roles in all U.S. immigration policy.[25] The opposing perspectives presented in the following discussion bear out LeMay's contention. Negative or positive perspectives on immigration revolve around several issues, including the impact on the economy, with special emphasis on employment, dependence on public services (such as welfare and education), quality of life, and impact on the social and political culture.

Economic Concerns

Much of the debate over immigration policy focuses on its impact on the economy, with those favoring a more restrictive policy claiming that immigrants are a drain on the economy and take jobs away from the native population.[26] Those who support immigration and even argue for more immigration point to many positive effects on the economy and the need for the labor provided by immigrants.[27] Certainly, traditional immigration provided a supply of labor that helped develop the United States into a leading economic power. Even during the nineteenth and early twentieth centuries, however, the arrival of many immigrants led to resentment and policy changes attempting to limit or exclude some groups, as noted in the first part of this chapter. During economic boom times, the issue usually is not as visible as during periods of economic sluggishness.

Opponents of immigration argue that immigrants take jobs held by natives or are willing to work at very low wages, thus depressing the income of the native population.[28] This argument has considerable emotional appeal and seems very logical. Examples of the Vietnamese who fish on the Gulf Coast of Texas or the prevalence of Hispanics in hotel and food service industries in Florida and California support critics' contentions that immigrants take jobs from native born citizens. While these examples illustrate real problems in specific locales, they do not reflect the overall impact on the labor market. Critics of immigration argue that the unemployment rate is evidence of the availability of native-born labor. Some cite the inability of people to live on the minimum wage and blame immigrants for depressing wages because of their availability in the workforce.

Traditionally, labor unions have opposed immigration as a means of protecting their own interests. Cheap labor might undermine the efforts of labor unions to share in the profits of business. Additionally, they argue that the cheap labor does not reflect the type of skills that the United States should be encouraging to help it in global competitiveness.[29] Nonetheless, some unions now embrace immigration as they have seen their numbers grow with the addition of immigrant workers to union rolls.[30]

People on the other side of the issue argue that immigration has negligible impact on the labor market and that rather than taking jobs from others, immigrants actually help create jobs.[31] Immigrants are still attracted by employment opportunity. As they take jobs, they become productive participants in the economy and spend money, thus helping to create demand for more products and thus more employment. Proponents of immigration also note that immigrants tend to have a very strong work ethic because they were motivated to come to the United States to seek opportunity. They have not differed from nonimmigrants in their rates of unemployment until the recession of 2007–2009, which seems to have had a larger effect on immigrants.[32]

Proponents of immigration also cite the entrepreneurial activities of immigrants and how those activities contribute to the growth of the economy and employment. Julian Simon refers to Canadian studies, which suggest that nearly 5 percent of immigrants to Canada started businesses within their first three years in Canada, creating nearly 30 percent more jobs than all the immigrants held during that time.[33] U.S. data indicate that minorities and immigrants start businesses at a much higher rate than members of the native population.[34] Though the enterprises tend to be small, small enterprises are the source of nearly a quarter of new jobs since the early 1970s.

Although many immigrants work in low-wage jobs, many also are highly talented and skilled professionals. Clearly, many industries depend upon the unskilled laborers who harvest produce and work in the garment, restaurant, and hotel industries. Significant numbers of immigrants also are scientists and engineers and have been important parts of the success of high-tech industries.[35] Additionally, as noted earlier in the chapter, the children of immigrants tend to achieve college education and enter the professional ranks at very high rates. Asians appear to be the most successful and arrive with high levels of education and skills. Indians and Arabs also tend to be highly educated and skilled. Not surprisingly, Mexicans tend to be less educated and more unskilled as they generally are immigrating to escape poverty and the lack of opportunity in their society. Generally, facts suggest that immigration has positive impacts on the economy. At the same time, the negative impact in a given community with high concentrations of immigrants can be very significant and can put a strain on resources in that community.

Impact on Public Services

Opponents of immigration raise the specter of overloaded public services as another major issue. They argue that our schools are overrun with children of immigrants, and that immigrants burden the welfare system. The issue created much pressure in many states and in national politics to limit the access of immigrants, especially illegal immigrants, to these governmental benefits. Several states passed laws, often citizen initiatives, to prohibit illegal immigrants from receiving benefits such as publicly funded health and welfare benefits and in-state tuition at institutions of higher education. All but a few states now prohibit illegal immigrants from having driver's licenses. Some municipalities have adopted ordinances prohibiting landlords from renting to illegal immigrants, but a court in Pennsylvania found such an ordinance in Hazelton, Pennsylvania, unconstitutional, saying that immigration is a federal government responsibility. Thus, other such laws are certain to face challenge.

Immigration poses many challenges to public school systems in the areas in which there are large concentrations of immigrants. Clearly, these challenges have existed for long periods of time in the major cities, such as New York and Chicago. Recent immigration patterns, however, have brought the challenges to new areas, especially in Florida, Texas, California, and generally the Southwest.[36] School districts in these areas experience difficulty in handling the numbers of students and in meeting their needs because of the language barriers and the lack of resources to serve many of their students, immigrant or nonimmigrant. Typically, the most affected school districts are the large urban districts that long have suffered the most from lack of adequate funding and from overcrowding in poorly maintained facilities. These problems mean that they cannot meet the educational needs of immigrant and native-born children alike. All the problems of large urban school districts make the assimilation of immigrant children more difficult than it otherwise would be. Because immigration law, specifically the 1996 act, permits states only to limit higher education benefits, public schools are required to provide education for immigrant students. The Supreme Court in *Plyler v. Doe* (1982) ruled that illegal immigrants could not be denied public education. Restrictions do apply, however, to some students, particularly those who live on the Mexican border and enter the United States for their education. Under visa restrictions, they are denied access to public schools. Nonetheless, studies indicate that children of immigrants have better attendance, are less likely to drop out, and are more likely to do better in school than U.S.-born children.[37] While not much research exists on the subject, a few studies indicate differential performance by immigrant groups. A study of San Diego high school students indicated that, with the exception of Hispanics, performance of children of non–English speaking immigrants had higher test scores than all other students. Other studies indicate that students of immigrant families from China, Korea, Japan, Vietnam, the Philippines, Laos, and Cambodia outperform native-born students. Also, Mexican-born immigrant students tend to outperform U.S.-born students of Mexican descent.[38]

According to many opponents of immigration, the welfare state is a major attraction of immigration to the United States. Many of the concerns are raised by state government officials because state and local governments bear much of the cost of social services, especially as the national government has cut back in recent years (see Chapter 2). Studies indicate that recently arrived immigrants are slightly more likely to use public services than is the general population, but that over time, they are less likely to do so.[39] More recent research, however, suggests that immigrants are more likely than the rest of the population is to use social services.[40]

All immigrants are eligible for public school education, but eligibility and use of other benefits differs somewhat by category. Until 1996 reforms in welfare and in immigration, most legal immigrants were eligible for most benefits. With the 1996 reforms, higher education benefits and welfare benefits, such as food stamps and disability benefits, are denied to some legal immigrants. Children born in the United States of illegal parents, however, are eligible for benefits. Some states are considering legislation to ensure medical and financial assistance to legal immigrants by replacing the federal funds with state money. Refugees and asylees generally are treated like legal immigrants when it comes to benefits. Illegal immigrants, however, are unlikely to see much support for their access to services.

Proponents of immigration also present data on the taxes paid versus the costs of services. By these calculations, immigrants represent a positive investment for the country. Immigrants contribute more to the system in taxes than they use in benefits and thus pay their own way. Ironically, illegal immigrants contribute at an even higher rate than others because they work and pay taxes, but are less likely to be eligible for or to apply for public services because they fear deportation.[41] A disproportionate share of the taxes, however, is paid in income tax to the national government while the burden of providing services falls to state and local governments.

Much has been made of older relatives of immigrants coming to the United States to take advantage of Social Security or SSI benefits (see Chapter 7). After the 1965 reforms, it appears that there was an increase in such immigration, but some observers suggest that immigrants actually provide support for the survival of Social Security programs. Given the fact that the native population is aging and increasingly qualifying for Social Security benefits, workers are faced with increasing taxes to support the system. Many argue that the system will be bankrupt by the time the baby boomers retire. Some scholars argue that immigrants usually come to the country while they are in their prime working years and that they help ensure the survival of the Social Security system by their contributions to the trust fund.[42]

Clearly, many state and local governments feel the pressures of immigration, both legal and illegal. The pressures on social services, roads, and bus systems can be very heavy, leading to frustration on the part of the taxpayers who have to pay for the services and for those needing the services when they are unavailable. The burden is distributed unevenly. Because of large numbers of immigrants in states such as Florida, California, Arizona, and Texas, and especially in major cities, such as Miami, San Diego, and Los Angeles, the pressures on these states and cities are especially large. At the same time, the contributions of working immigrants to the tax base support the economy and society as a whole. Both supporters and opponents of immigration have pointed out the uneven distribution of the costs and make suggestions for federal government support for services that cannot be denied because of the Constitution or other federal policy. The restriction of many benefits to citizens or legal immigrants resulted in part from this pressure as well.

Quality of Life

Quality of life issues arise relative to immigration mostly among those who oppose more immigration. They argue that continued immigration will lead to overpopulation of the country, resulting in increasing poverty and harm to the environment. Opponents also argue that the culture of the society is being changed and that the social fabric is being destroyed. In particular, they hearken back to the idea that the United States has been a melting pot, but that with the new waves of immigration, the society is being fragmented. Assimilation occurs more slowly because larger concentrations of people of similar background sustain old customs and traditions. Some suggest that the United States no longer is a melting pot but a pluralism of ethnic groups that do not become assimilated.[43] In recent years, many new groups have tried to preserve their ethnic identities by celebrating their ethnic and cultural traditions. These developments lead to resentment by many people who believe they should make efforts to assimilate more fully. Immigrants often become scapegoats for many of the problems of society.[44]

Overpopulation.   Overpopulation is often cited as a problem by those opposing more immigration. Some people fear the sheer growth in numbers of population as putting a strain on all aspects of American society.[45] Many social critics blame immigrants for the decline of some of the major cities, citing crime statistics, exodus of whites to the suburbs, housing deterioration, poverty, and loss of business and jobs in the central cores at the same time that immigrants are moving into those areas.[46] The rhetoric often is very inflammatory and leads to policy proposals that might not necessarily address the real problems. Blaming immigrants for threats to economic security, for example, diverts attention away from the causes of the slow wage growth, as the data indicate that immigrants have little overall impact on the issue. Closing the doors to immigrants seems like an easy solution, but the problems of America's major cities are much more complicated than immigration.

One of the issues raised concerning population growth is the impact on the environment. Some critics suggest that the pressures on production of food and the waste produced will lead to effects such as global warming, air pollution, water pollution, and the destruction of the physical environment (see Chapter 5).[47] There is no question that increasing population puts a strain on many environmental features. What those on the other side of the issue say, however, is that the United States is nowhere near its capacity to handle the population and that efforts should be made to improve environmental policy to protect the environment rather than using immigrants as the scapegoat. They also counter that the native birthrate is declining, and that immigration is barely replacing the decrease in population due to this decline.[48]

Crime.   Crime is another issue used by opponents of immigration to get the attention of the populace. They blame immigrants for a high crime rate, especially in the major cities and along the border with Mexico. Although immigrants themselves appear to be less likely than the rest of the population to be involved in crime, critics still blame them for crime by their argument that they take the jobs of U.S.-born natives, thus increasing the unemployment rate. High unemployment in the urban centers then contributes to a life of crime by people who are disenfranchised from the system.[49] Given the evidence that immigration has a negligible impact on employment issues, proponents of immigration note that the argument does not follow. They also cite the vitality of many ethnic neighborhoods fostered by immigrant groups and that those neighborhoods foster a sense of community, which helps discourage crime.[50]

Social and Political Culture.   Perhaps the most controversial issue raised about the impact of immigration on the quality of life is the impact on social and political culture.[51] Many opponents of immigration claim that it is threatening the values of our society and that ethnic groups have separatist notions, which lead to balkanization of American society. Some claim that these developments are leading to culture wars, and that our borders must be closed to stop the march to disappearance of America's distinctive social and political culture.[52] These arguments are not new. The founders of our nation raised the issue at the very beginning, as did many of the colonists. The Know Nothing Party of the 1850s and 1860s brought the ideas to the electorate. Depending on the time and circumstances, critics perceived threats to religious homogeneity, the family structure, and social cohesion of communities, to name a few. Thus, these critics of immigration continue a long tradition of appealing to the fears and anxieties of citizens. Clearly, the concentrations of Mexican Americans in the Southwest and Haitians and Cubans in Miami are examples for many people of the ability of new immigrants to hold on to their cultures. Because they have distinct cultures, they are easy targets for those who have an idealized view of Americans as a homogeneous culture. Sometimes it is easier to strike out at the identifiable group than to accept that society evolves constantly. There is much evidence of identifiable ethnic groups attempting to continue their homeland cultural traditions, but there is no evidence that it undermines the political democracy of the United States.

Because of the cohesion of some groups, critics also fear the political power they represent. These fears helped proponents in their efforts in Arizona in 2004 to pass Proposition 200, which required proof of citizenship to vote. Similar measures have passed in other places. Of course, immigrants in the past helped political machines of both political parties in many of the major cities. Their support was given in return for services provided by the machines, and the process helped assimilate many immigrant groups into the political culture. Modern-day immigrants are unlikely to have the same close relationship with political leadership, but political parties certainly can exploit the opportunity to address their interests in hopes of gaining their support. It is unlikely, however, that the type of patronage that the nineteenth and early twentieth centuries witnessed will arise. Politicians, however, will pay attention to issues that affect new citizens. President George W. Bush and others, for example, were criticized for their support of a path to citizenship for those here illegally. It also is an issue that continues to derail comprehensive reform efforts.

Some proponents of immigration charge that the culture issue is a code for racism.[53] They are concerned that opponents are worried primarily that the white majority is declining and that opponents fear competition with the many ethnic groups emerging as serious social and political forces. They claim that the effects of immigrants on jobs and on public services create divisiveness and pit groups against one another.[54] These efforts create what the opponents of immigration claim is a culture war, but in many ways the opponents themselves provide the fuel for the culture wars through the rhetoric they use to support their positions.

FUTURE ALTERNATIVES: OPENNESS OR RESTRICTION?

Although there is much disagreement about whether immigration *per se* is a problem, there seems to be consensus that immigration policy needs improvement. Depending upon whether people believe that there is too much or not enough immigration or somewhere in between, views on future policy options range from closing down immigration to encouraging more immigration, with options between the two extremes as well.

Some people argue that immigration should be stopped completely. Pat Buchanan spoke for them when he suggested that the borders of the United States be closed down and that the military be used to enforce the policy. In some instances, he seemed to support a temporary suspension; at other times, he seemed to be suggesting a permanent closure to immigration. His arguments usually focused on preserving the national culture and on preserving jobs for the native born. Congress did pass legislation to secure the border with fences or walls and technology, and the National Guard has been sent to help the Border Patrol do its job. Many critics of militarizing the border claim that the military is not equipped for law enforcement. The terrorist strike of September 11, 2001, however, led to the military being involved in many activities to deal with terrorist activities as well as border security.

Most people recognize that a complete stop to immigration is impractical and maybe impossible even if they are troubled by the degree of immigration at present. Thus, they advocate a moratorium[55] or a reduction.[56] The reasons vary according to the way in which they define the problem. For the most part, advocates of a moratorium or a reduction in immigration believe that the nation needs to catch up with the absorption of those who have already arrived. They also see a moratorium or reduction as an opportunity to consider improvement in immigration policies to deal with the problems they believe immigration has created. Reforms have attempted to address concerns about the numbers of immigrants entering the United States; thus, taking some cues from advocates of reductions.

Some of the specific recommendations for limiting immigration suggest that the policy should focus on what needs the country has, especially in job skills.

They argue that the majority of immigrants are unskilled and do not help revitalize the economy or support U.S. competitiveness in the global economy.[57] To correct this perceived problem, it is suggested that immigrants be allowed in, based primarily on having skills that will contribute to advancing the economy. Others argue that economic policy, not immigration, is the issue and that the United States needs to align its immigration policy with its trade policies, which focus on opening borders to trade.[58]

Others argue that immigration should focus primarily on people who are committed to becoming U.S. citizens.[59] Applications for citizenship give some indication of the prevalence of commitment to citizenship. After enactment of the Immigration Reform and Control Act of 1986, granting amnesty to illegal aliens who had lived in the United States continuously since January 1, 1982, and providing for restrictions and renewal of green cards allowing employment, applications for citizenship increased. Similarly, when Proposition 187 was being proposed in California, many people applied for *naturalization* so that they could vote in the election. Applications for citizenship numbered 206,668 in 1991 and peaked at more than 1.4 million in 1997. They decreased to 932,957 in 1998 and 523,370 in 2003 and were back up to 1,382,993 in 2007. They dropped off again in 2008 (525, 786) and 2009 (570,442).[60] The concern of people arguing that citizenship should be the focus is that most debates over immigration take a short-term perspective on the problems and contributions of immigration. The long-term view considers the assimilation of immigrants and their becoming citizens as having positive outcomes because they imply commitment to the system and greater likelihood of learning the language and culture of the United States. Most studies indicate that the issue of language and culture is not nearly as important as many critics of immigration contend. In fact, children of immigrants prefer English and adapt very quickly to American culture.[61] It appears that those groups that come to the United States with little hope or intent of returning to their native lands (e.g., the Vietnamese, Laotians) achieve citizenship and adapt to the culture more quickly, while those who expect to return to their homelands someday are less likely to do so (Central Americans and those from the Caribbean, for example).[62]

Still others contend that the various criteria for determining who can immigrate are not realistic and that immigration should be based on a "first come, first served" basis.[63] People taking this position suggest that some spots should be reserved for family reunification and other criteria, but that the majority of slots should be based on review of applications as they are received. The position harkens back to the ideological basis for immigration; namely, that the country opened its doors to people from around the world primarily because Americans believed that everyone should be given a chance. Proponents of this position contend that other bases for including or excluding immigrants have not worked and should be scrapped for this more rational approach, which does not accept the premises of the proposals at either extreme of the debate.

The arguments over immigration often appear to be driven by anxieties that actually have nothing to do with immigrants. Immigration is easy to exploit as the cause of many of the nation's problems because immigrants are an easily identifiable and usually relatively powerless element of society. The nativist arguments resonate with people who fear what they do not know or understand. Those who suffer economic dislocation or fear poverty and crime find an easy target in immigrants. Immigrant rights groups also often oversimplify the issues and see immigrants as victims in every effort to gain some control over the problems related to immigration. Most observers of immigration policy recognize that some regulation of the flow of immigration is desirable. How to achieve that regulation and how to ensure fairness and humane considerations are at the root of the controversies over immigration policies.

President Bush and a bipartisan coalition of senators proposed a bill that would have granted immediate probationary legal status to illegal immigrants who were in the United States before January 2007. They would be able to work and travel if they passed a legal background check. The proposed law also would have established a new Z visa that would allow undocumented immigrants and their families to stay for four years if they paid a $5,000 fee. The visa could be renewed indefinitely and after eight years, the immigrant could apply for permanent residency; however, that person would have to return to his or her home country and pay another $4,000 to do so. An additional 400,000–600,000 guest workers would be allowed to come each year to work for two years on a new Y-1 visa. After two years, they would have to return home for a year and could apply for another two-year Y-1 visa. The process could be repeated once more for a total of six years of work in the United States.

The proposed legislation also focused on border security and immigration enforcement before the Z and Y-1 visa provisions took effect. The proposal called for increasing the Border Patrol by 18,000 agents and construction of 200 miles of border fence to help keep illegal border crossers out.

Under the proposed legislation, employers would have been required to verify eligibility of applicants through an electronic system and would face stiff penalties for knowingly hiring illegal immigrants. A new system for granting legal immigration would be created that used a new point system granting credit for English proficiency, job skills, education, and family ties.

These and other provisions were proposed to broaden potential support by including something to satisfy many different perspectives. What happened, however, was that people opposed to various provisions campaigned against the entire legislative package, since neither extreme found it acceptable. Conservatives wanted border security and criticized the proposal as giving amnesty to illegal immigrants. Liberals wanted a way for undocumented workers already here to have a path to permanent residency and citizenship, while they decried what they considered draconian border security measures and hardships for families. In the end, the proposal failed to secure enough votes to pass the Senate, and comprehensive reform died.

After the proposed reform failed, some on each side of the issue proposed specific, narrower policies focusing on their issues, but found little enthusiasm for dealing with the issue before the 2008 elections. Seeing that Congress could not agree on a policy, many state and local governments stepped into the fray. Some states have adopted policies denying illegal immigrants access to social services and in-state tuition, among other benefits. Some have adopted stiff sanctions on employers that employ illegal immigrants. Some local governments have adopted ordinances banning landlords from renting to illegal immigrants and requiring local police to arrest and deliver illegal immigrants to the U.S. Immigration and Customs Enforcement (ICE). The patchwork of policies concerns employers and others who have to deal with conflicting policies. Cases have been filed in court, and there are conflicting decisions as well. Eventually, the national government will have to develop a national policy. The Bush administration started stricter enforcement of policy to arrest and detain illegal immigrants and stepped up enforcement against employers who hire undocumented workers, and the Obama administration generally followed suit.

In the 2008 presidential election, Obama called for comprehensive immigration reform, but he did not push it aggressively early in his presidency. In the meantime, a strong advocate of comprehensive reform, Senator Edward Kennedy, died; another strong advocate, Senator John McCain, changed his stance as he faced a very strong anti-immigration candidate in his Republican primary in Arizona. Because the national government failed to act, anti-immigration forces gained support, especially in places like Arizona, where Senate Bill 1070 was passed by the legislature. This law made it a crime to be in the state without legal documents, among other provisions. The author of the legislation, State Senator Russell Pearce, boasted that one purpose of the legislation was to make it so uncomfortable for illegal immigrants that they would leave the state. At this writing, he is crafting legislation to deny citizenship to babies born in the United States to illegal immigrants, seemingly in direct violation of the Fourteenth Amendment to the U.S. constitution. The Arizona law reinvigorated the debate on illegal immigration and generated lawsuits against it by numerous organizations, including the U.S. Justice Department. It also rekindled interest in comprehensive reform: President Obama renewed a call for comprehensive reform in July 2010. He stated that securing the border is necessary, and noted that he was committing to adding 1,800 national guard troops to assist in doing so in June 2010. However, Obama also indicated that to be effective, reform needs to include a pathway to citizenship for illegal immigrants already here. They would be required to admit that they had broken the law, and they would need to learn English, pay fines and back taxes, and perform community service before being eligible for citizenship. Reflecting the deep divisions on the issue, critics immediately rejected Obama's plans for citizenship as amnesty and repeated their call for securing the border before anything else could be done. It is unlikely that any reform is possible before the mid-term elections of November 2010, as immigration is a major issue and anti-immigration sentiment is running high.

Immigration policy will remain a controversial issue for the foreseeable future. It is an emotional issue that does not lend itself to consensus.

ENDNOTES

1. Kevin R. Johnson, *The Huddled Masses Myth: Immigration and Civil Rights* (Philadelphia: Temple University Press, 2004) and Aristide R. Zolberg, *A Nation By Design: Immigration Policy in the Fashioning of America* (Cambridge, MA: Harvard University Press, 2008).

2. The CQ Researcher, "Immigration Policy: A Historical Overview," in Scott Barbour, ed., *Immigration Policy* (San Diego: Greenhaven Press, 1995), 11–16.

3. Michael LeMay, *From Open Door to Dutch Door: An Analysis of U.S. Immigration Policy Since 1820* (New York: Praeger, 1987), xiii–xiv.

4. Frank D. Bean, Robert G. Cushing, Charles W. Haynes, and Jennifer V. W. Van Hook, "Immigration and the Social Contract," *Social Science Quarterly*, 78 (June 1997): 263.

5. Chilton Williamson, Jr., *The Immigration Mystique: America's False Conscience* (New York: Basic Books, 1996), 24–27.

6. Phillip Q. Yang, *Post-1965 Immigration to the United States: Structural Determinants* (Westport, CT: Praeger, 1995), 10.

7. LeMay, *From Open Door to Dutch Door*, xiii.

8. Barry Edmonston, ed., *Statistics on U.S. Immigration: An Assessment of Data Needs for Future Research* (Washington, DC: National Academy Press, 1996), 10–11.

9. David Bennett, *The Party of Fear: From Nativist Movements to the New Right in American History* (Chapel Hill: University of North Carolina Press, 1988); Vernon M. Briggs, Jr., *Immigration Policy and the American Labor Force* (Baltimore: Johns Hopkins University Press, 1984), 19–22; Thomas J. Curran, *Xenophobia and Immigration, 1820–1930* (Boston: Twayne Publishers, 1975), 21; James Lincoln Collier, *The Rise of Selfishness in America* (New York: Oxford University Press, 1991); and Cheryl Shanks, *Immigration and the Politics of American Sovereignty, 1890–1990* (Ann Arbor: University of Michigan Press, 2004).

10. U.S. Immigration and Naturalization Service, *An Immigrant Nation: United States Regulation of Immigration, 1798–1991* (Washington, DC: Immigration and Naturalization Service, 1991).

11. Williamson, *The Immigration Mystique*, 47–49.

12. LeMay, *From Open Door to Dutch Door*, 111–112; Michael LeMay, *U.S. Immigration: A Reference Handbook* (Santa Barbara, CA: ABC-CLIO, 2004).

13. Vernon M. Briggs, Jr. and Stephen Moore, *Still an Open Door? U.S Immigration Policy and the American Economy* (Washington, DC: American University Press, 1994), 16–17.

14. Aviva Chomsky, *"They Take Our Jobs!" and 20 Other Myths About Immigration* (Boston: Beacon Press, 2007); Johnson, *The Huddled Masses Myth*; Armando Navarro, *The Immigration Crisis: Nativism, Armed Vigilantism, and the Rise of a Countervailing Movement* (Lanham, MD: Altamira Press, 2009); and Williamson, *The Immigration Mystique*, 47–49; Zolberg, *A Nation by Design*.

15. Michael Fix and Jeffrey S. Passel, *The Door Remains Open: Recent Immigration to the United States and a Preliminary Analysis of the Immigration Act of 1990* (Washington, DC: Urban Institute, 1991); and Michael Barone, *The New Americans* (Washington, DC: Regnery, 2001).

16. Stephen Moore, "Part Two: The Economic Case for More Immigrants," in Briggs and Moore, *Still an Open Door?*, 84–85; and Julian L. Simon, *The Economic Consequences of Immigration* (Cambridge, MA: Blackwell, 1990).

17. Steven A. Camarota, *Immigrants in the United States, 2007: A Profile of America's Foreign-Born* Population, Center for Immigration Studies, http://www.cis.org/articles/2007/back1007.html: Accessed June 20, 2010; Luke J. Larsen, *The Foreign Born Population in the United States: Current Reports, P20-551* (Washington, DC: U.S. Census Bureau, 2004); Moore, "Part Two: The Economic Case for More Immigrants," 87; and U.S. General Accounting Office, *Immigration: The Flow of Legal Immigration to the United States* (Washington, DC: U.S. Government Printing Office, 1988).

18. CNN/Opinion Research Corporation Poll, May 23, 2010, http://www.polingreport.com/immigration.htm; National Public Radio (NPR), the Henry J. Kaiser Family Foundation, and John F. Kennedy School of Government, *NPR/Kaiser/Kennedy School Immigration Survey*, www.npr.org/templates/story/story.php?storyId=4062605: Accessed January 5, 2005; CBS News/New York Times Poll, May 18–23, 2007, p. 4, http://pollingreport.com/immigration.htm; Accessed August 17, 2007.

19. Aviva Chomsky, *"They Take Our Jobs!"*; Heather Dewar, "Wave of Immigration Altering Nation's Face," *The Arizona Republic*, June 16, 1997, pp. A1–A2; Armando Navarro, *The Immigration Crisis*.

20. Barone, *The New Americans*; and LeMay, *From Open Door to Dutch Door*.

21. Camarota, *Immigrants in the United States;* Pew Hispanic Center, *Statistical Portrait of the Foreign-Born Population in the United States, 2008* http://pewhispanic.org/files/factsheets/foreignborn2008/Table%07; U.S. Census Bureau, *Race and Hispanic Origin of the Foreign-Born Population in the United States: 2007*, http://www.census.gov/prod/2010pubs/acs-11.pdf; Accessed June 29, 2010.

22. Moore, "Part Two: The Economic Case for More Immigrants," 115–118; Luke J. Larsen, *The Foreign Born Population in the United States: 2003*, www.census.gov/; Accessed August 20, 2007.

23. Dirk Chase Eldredge, *Crowded Land of Liberty: Solving America's Immigration Crisis* (Bridgehampton, NY: Bridge Works Publishing, 2001); U.S. Census Bureau, *Selected Characteristics of the Native Foreign-Born Populations*, www.factfinder.census.gov; Accessed August 20, 2007.

24. Michael Hoefer, Nancy Rytina, and Bryan C. Baker, *Estimates of the Unauthorized Immigrant Population Residing in the United States: January 2009*, http://dhs.gov/xlibrary/assets/statistics/publications/ois_ill_pe_2009.pdf: Accessed June 25, 2010; and Jeffrey S. Passel, Randolph Capps, and Michael E. Fix, *Undocumented Immigrants: Facts and Figures* (Washington, DC: Urban Institute, 2004), www.urban.org/UploadedPDF/1000587_undoc_immigrants_facts.pdf; Accessed January 13, 2005.

25. LeMay, *From Open Door to Dutch Door*.

26. Roy Beck, *The Case against Immigration* (New York: Norton, 1996), especially chapters 5 and 6; Otis L. Graham, *Unguarded Gates: A History of America's Immigration Crisis* (New York: Rowman & Littlefield, 2004); and Otis L. Graham, "The Unfinished Reform: Regulating Immigration in the National Interest," in Roger Daniels and Otis L. Graham, eds., *Debating American Immigration, 1882–Present* (Lanham, MD: Rowman & Littlefield, 2001); Reclaim American Jobs Caucus, http://www.numbersusa.com/content/news/march-19-2010/reclaim-american-jobs-caucus-introduction.html; Accessed June 30, 2010.

27. Randolph Caps, Everett Henderson, John D. Kasarda, James H. Johnson, Jr., Stephen J. Appold, Derek L. Croney, Donald J. Hernandez, Michael E. Fix, *A Profile of Immigrants in Arkansas* (Washington, DC: The Urban Institute, 2007); Aviva Chomsky, *"They Take Our Jobs!"*; Elzbieta M. Gozdziak and Susan F. Martin, *Beyond the Gateway: Immigrants in a Changing America* (New York: Lexington Books, 2005), Chapter 10; Roger Daniels, "Two Cheers for Immigration," in Daniels and Graham, eds., *Debating American Immigration*, 5–69; and John R. Logan, Richard D. Alba, and Michael Dill, "Ethnic Segmentation in the American Metropolis: Increasing Divergence in Economic Incorporation, 1980–1990," *International Migration Review,* 34 (Spring 2000): 98–132.

28. George Borjas, *Friends and Strangers: The Effect of Immigrants on the U.S. Economy* (New York: Basic Books, 1990); Graham, "Unfinished Reform"; and Lawrence E. Harrison, "Immigration Should Be Reduced to Strengthen U.S. Competitiveness," in Barbour, ed., *Immigration Policy*, 34–37.

29. Harrison, "Immigration Should Be Reduced"; and Julie R. Watts, *Immigration Policy and the Challenge of Globalization* (Ithaca, NY: Cornell University Press, 2002).

30. "Split in Organized Labor Over Immigration," MSNBC, www.washingtonpost. com/wp-dyn/content/2007/01/26AR2007012601635.html; The Migration Policy Institute, *Immigrant Union Members, Numbers and Trends,* http://www.migrationpolicy.org/7_Immigrant_Union_Membership.pdf: Accessed June 30, 2010.

31. Edmonston, ed., *Statistics on U.S. Immigration,* 19–29; Johnson, *The Huddled Masses Myth*; Moore, "Part Two: The Economic Case for More Immigrants," 77–80; and Julian L. Simon, "Immigration to the United States Should be Increased," in Barbour, ed., *Immigration Policy*, 55–66.

32. Steven A. Camarota and Karen Jensenius, *Trends in Immigrant and Native* Employment, Center for Immigration Studies, http:www.cis.org/FirstQuarter2009Unemployment: Accessed August 24, 2007; Aviva Chomsky, *"They Take Our Jobs!"*; Chris Isidore, "Jobless Rate Higher for U.S.-born than Immigrants," CNNMoney.com, http://money.cnn.com/2006/04/05/news/economy/jobs_immigrants/index.htm: Accessed August 24, 2007; David M. Kennedy, "Can We Still Afford to Be a Nation of Immigrants?," *The Atlantic Monthly Atlantic Unbound,* www.theatlantic.com/atlantic/issues/96nov/immigrant/kennedy.htm: Accessed January 13, 2005.

33. Simon, "Immigration to the United States Should Be Increased," 60–61.

34. Richard T. Herman and Robert L. Smith, *Immigrant, Inc.: Why Immigrant Entrepreneurs Are Driving the New Economy (and How They Will Save the American Worker)* (Hoboken, NJ: Wiley, 2009); Kauffman Foundation, *Kauffman Foundation Study Points to "Brain Drain" of Skilled U.S. Immigrant Entrepreneurs to Home Country*, www .kauffman.org/items.cfm?itemID=906: Accessed August 23, 2007; Alejandro Portes and Ruben G. Rumbaut, *Immigrant America* (Berkeley: University of California Press, 1990); Vivek Wadhwa, Anna Lee Saxenian, Ben Rissing, and Gary Gereffi, *America's New Immigrant Entrepreneurs 2007*, http://papers.ssrn.com/so13/papers.cfm? abstract_id=990152: Accessed June 30, 2010.

35. Elizabeth Corley and Meghna Sabharwal, "Foreign-Born Academic Scientists and Engineers: Producing More and Getting Less Than Their U.S.-Born Peers?" *Research in Higher Education*, 48 (December 2007): 909–940; Lynn A. Karoly and Constantin W. A. Panis, "Supply and Demand for Skilled Labor in the United States," in Jagdish Bhagwati and Gordon Hanson, eds., *Skilled Immigration*

Today: Prospects, Problems, and Policies (New York: Oxford University Press, 2009); Wadhwa et al., *America's New Immigrant Entrepreneurs*.

36. Camarota, *Immigrants in the United States*; Lorraine M. McDowell and Paul T. Hill, *Newcomers in American Schools* (Santa Monica, CA: Rand, 1993).

37. Jorge Ruiz-de-Velasco and Michael Fix with Beatriz Chu Clewell, *Overlooked and Underserved: Immigrant Students in U.S. Secondary Schools* (Washington, DC: Urban Institute, 2000); and Ruben G. Rumbaut, *Immigrant Children in California Public Schools: A Summary of Current Knowledge* (Baltimore: Center for Research on Effective Schooling for Disadvantaged Students, Johns Hopkins University, 1990).

38. Alejandro Portes and Ruben G. Rumbaut, *Immigrant America: A Portrait* (Berkeley: University of California Press, 2006); and Rumbaut, *Immigrant Children*.

39. Randolph Capps, Michael E. Fix, Everett Henderson, and Jane Reardon-Anderson, *A Profile of Low-Income Immigrant Families*, Urban Institute, http://www.urban.org/publications/311206.html: Accessed July 1, 2010; Moore, "Part Two: The Economic Case for More Immigrants," 81–90; National Immigration Law Center, *Facts About Immigrants' Low Use of Health Services and Public Benefits*, http://www.nilc.org/immspbs/research/imms&publicservices_2006-9-12.pdf: Accessed July 1, 2010.

40. Borjas, *Friends or Strangers?*; Steven A. Camarota, *Economy Slowed, but Immigration Didn't: The Foreign-Born Population, 2000–2004* (Washington, DC: Center for Immigration Studies, 2004); Steven A. Camarota, *The High Cost of Cheap Labor: Illegal Immigration and the Federal Budget,* 2004, http://www.cis.org/articles/2004/fiscal.pdf (accessed 07-01-10); Hiromi Ono and Rosina M. Becerra, "Race, Ethnicity and Nativity, Family Structure, Socioeconomic Status and Welfare Dependency," *International Migration Review,* 34 (Fall 2000): 739–765; Ellen Seghal, "Foreign Born in the US Labor Market: Results of a Special Survey," *Monthly Labor Review* (July 1985): 18–24; and Simon, "Immigration to the United States Should Be Increased."

41. Randy Capps, Michael Fix, Jason Ost, Jane Reardon-Anderson, and Jeffrey S. Passel, *The Health and Well-Being of Young Children of Immigrants*, Urban Institute, http://www.urban.org/publications/410412.html: Accessed July 1, 2010; Chomsky, Aviva, *"They Take Our Jobs!"*; Roger Mahony, "Roman Catholics Should Work for Liberal Immigration Policies," in Barbour, ed., *Immigration Policy*, 95–99; and Simon, "Immigration to the United States Should Be Increased," 60.

42. Camarota, *The High Cost of Cheap Labor*; Moore, "Part Two: The Economic Case for More Immigration," 95–96; and Simon, "Immigration to the United States Should Be Increased," 62.

43. Patrick J. Buchanan, *Day of Reckoning: How Hubris, Ideology, and Greed Are Tearing America Apart*, reprint ed. (New York: St. Martin's Griffin, 2009); Graham, *Unguarded Gates*; Samuel P. Huntington, *Who Are We? The Challenges to America's National Identity* (New York: Simon & Schuster, 2004); Arthur Schlesinger, Jr., *The Disuniting of America: Reflections on a Multicultural Society (Revised and Enlarged Edition)* (New York: Norton, 1998).

44. Patrick J. Buchanan, *State of Emergency: The Third World Invasion and Conquest of America* (New York: Thomas Dunne Books, 2006); Graham, *Unguarded Gates*; Elizabeth Martinez, "The U.S. Should Not Make Immigrants Scapegoats," in Barbour, ed., *Immigration Policy*, 17–20; and La Resistencia, "Ethnic Cleansing by Attacks on Immigrants Must Be Stopped," in Barbour, ed., *Immigration Policy*, 108–111.

45. George F. Kennan, "Immigration to the United States Should Be Reduced," in Barbour, ed., *Immigration Policy*, 17–20; and Dan Stein, "The Federal Government Should Enact a Moratorium on Immigration," in Barbour, ed., *Immigration Policy*, 21–24.

46. Gregory Fossedal, "Immigration Juggernaut," *San Francisco Chronicle*, March 28, 1990; Daniel James, "Big Immigrant Wave Swamps Assimilation," *Wall Street Journal*, July 2, 1992, p. A9; and Michael Myer, "Los Angeles 2010: A Latino Subcontinent," *Newsweek*, November 9, 1992.

47. Leon F. Bouvier, "Immigration Should Be Restricted for Environmental Reasons," in Barbour, ed., *Immigration Policy*, 38–40.

48. Moore, "Part Two: The Economic Case for More Integration," 82–84; and John Isbister, *The Immigration Debate: Remaking America* (West Hartford, CT: Kumarian Press, 1996), especially Chapter 5.

49. Louis Uchitelle, "America's Army of Non-Workers," *New York Times*, September 17, 1987, pp. F1, F6; and William Julius Wilson, *The Truly Disadvantaged: The Inner City, the Underclass, and Public Policy* (Chicago: University of Chicago Press, 1987).

50. Elizabeth Bogen, Testimony before the Joint Economic Committee, U.S. Congress, *Hearings on the Economic and Demographic Consequences of Immigration* (Washington, DC: U.S. Government Printing Office, 1986).

51. Huntington, *Who Are We?*

52. Patrick J. Buchanan, *The Death of the West: How Dying Populations and Immigrant Invasions Imperil Our Country and Civilization* (New York: Thomas Dunne Books, 2001); and Huntington, *Who Are We?*

53. Simon, "Immigration to the United States Should Be Increased"; Martinez, "The U.S. Should Not Make Immigrants Scapegoats"; and La Resistencia, "Ethnic Cleansing by Attacks on Immigrants Must Be Stopped."

54. Beck, *The Case against Immigration*, chapter 8.

55. Eldredge, *Crowded Land of Liberty*; Federation for American Immigration Reform, *Why America Needs an Immigration Time-Out*, http://www.fairus.org/site/PageServer?pagename=iic_immigrationissuecentered1994; and Stein, "The United States Should Enact a Moratorium on Immigration."

56. Kennan, "Immigration to the United States Should Be Reduced"; Harrison, "Immigration Should Be Reduced to Strengthen U.S. Competitiveness"; Bouvier, "Immigration Should Be Restricted for Environmental Reasons"; and Beck, *The Case against Immigration*.

57. Graham, "The Unfinished Reform"; Harrison, "Immigration Should Be Reduced to Strengthen U.S. Competitiveness"; and Beck, *The Case against Immigration*.

58. Walter A. Ewing, "From Denial to Acceptance: Effectively Regulating Immigration to the United States" (Washington, DC: The American Immigration Law Foundation, 2004), http://www.ailf.org: Accessed January 18, 2005.

59. John Kotkin, "U.S. Immigration Policy Should Be Based on Citizenship," in Barbour, ed., *Immigration Policy*, 84–89.

60. Department of Homeland Security, *2009 Yearbook of Immigration Statistics*, Table 20, www.dhs.gov/xlibrary/assets/statistics/yearbook2009/table20.xls: Accessed June 25, 2010.

61. Portes and Rumbaut, *Immigrant America*.

62. Rumbaut, *Immigrant Children*.

63. Peter D. Salins, "U.S. Immigration Policy Should Not Discriminate," in Barbour, ed., *Immigration Policy*, 72–76.

RESOURCES

Books

Bhagwati, Jagdish, and Hanson, Gordon, eds. *Skilled Immigration Today: Prospects, Problems, and Policies*. Boston: Beacon Press, 2007.

Bloemread, Irene. *Becoming a Citizen: Incorporating Immigrants and Refugees in the United States and Canada*. Berkeley: University of California Press, 2006.

Borjas, George J., *Heaven's Door: Immigration Policy and the American Economy*. Princeton, NJ: Princeton University Press, 2001.

Briggs, Vernon M., Jr. *Mass Immigration and the National Interest*, 3rd ed. Armonk, NY: Sharpe, 2003.

Buchanan, Patrick J. *Death of the West: How Dying Populations and Immigrant Invasions Imperil Our Country and Civilization*. New York: Thomas Dunne Books, 2002.

Chomsky, Aviva. *"They Take Our Jobs!" and 20 Other Myths About Immigration*. Boston: Beacon Press, 2007.

Daniels, Roger, and Graham, Otis L. *Debating American Immigration, 1882–Present*. Lanham, MD: Rowman & Littlefield, 2001.

Eldredge, Dirk Chase. *Crowded Land of Liberty: Solving America's Immigration Crisis*. Bridgehampton, NY: Bridge Works Publishing, 2001.

Huntington, Samuel P. *Who Are We? The Challenges to America's National Identity*. New York: Simon & Schuster, 2004.

Johnson, Kevin R. *The Huddled Masses Myth: Immigration and Civil Rights*. Philadelphia: Temple University Press, 2004.

LeMay, Michael. *Guarding the Gates: Immigration and National Security*. Westport, CT: Praeger, 2006.

LeMay, Michael. *Illegal Immigration: A Reference Handbook*. Santa Barbara, CA: ABC CLIO, 2007.

Navarro, Armando. *The Immigration Crisis: Nativism, Armed Vigilantism, and the Rise of a Countervailing Movement*. New York: Altimira Press, 2009.

Ruiz-de-Velasco, Jorge, and Fix, Michael, with Beatriz Chu Clewell. *Overlooked and Underserved: Immigrant Students in U.S. Secondary Schools*. Washington, DC: Urban Institute, 2000.

Zolberg, Aristide R. *A Nation by Design: Immigration Policy in the Fashioning of America*. Cambridge, MA: Harvard University Press, 2008.

Websites

Center for Comparative Immigration Studies: **www.ccis–ucsd.org**

Center for Immigration Studies: **www.cis.org**

Center for Migration Studies: **www.cmsny.org**

Center for Research on Immigration Policy, Population and Public Policy:
   http://www.cri.uci.edu

Ellis Island National Monument: **http://www.ellisisland.org**

Federation for American Immigration Reform: **www.fairus.org**

U.S. Department of Homeland Security: **www.dhs.gov**

Chapter 12

Foreign and Defense Policy: Security and Interests in a Dangerous World

The events of September 11, 2001, brought home to America the realization that retreat to a fortress America, the recurring isolationist approach to foreign policy in American history, is no longer (if it ever had been) a realistic option. The ongoing threat of massive terrorism cast this country into the maelstrom of world conflicts suddenly and to a degree for which the nation was quite unprepared and unwilling to support on a long-term basis. The catastrophic destruction of the World Trade Center on September 11 was but the most destructive of a number of terrorist attacks on American lives and properties perpetrated in recent years by militant Islamist groups. Some commentators, comparing these attacks to the Japanese assault on Pearl Harbor in 1941, have declared that America has been propelled into World War IV, a conflict that these commentators claim is directed against Western Civilization as we know it.[1] Others disagree that America faces such a direct threat, especially from those opposing American efforts to reshape Iraq, and advocating a withdrawal of American troops from the Middle East.

The natural borders on the east and west coasts of the United States, provided by two major oceans, together with nonthreatening neighbors on the northern and southern borders, seemed for much of U.S. history to insulate the country from the need for active involvement in the affairs and conflicts of the world outside of the Western Hemisphere. Two world wars in the twentieth century did much to puncture belief in such insulation. The Cold War with the Soviet Union left the U.S. feeling uniquely vulnerable to the Soviet's intercontinental thermonuclear capacity (what the aforementioned commentators call World War III).

The seizure of fifty-two American Embassy workers in Teheran, Iran, by militants loyal to Ayatollah Khomeini precipitated a hostage crisis lasting throughout the last year of the Carter administration (1979). In other attacks through the Reagan and Clinton administrations, America experienced a wave of violent assaults on its personnel and property by militant Islamist groups, including an April 1983 car bombing of the U.S. embassy in Beirut, killing 63 another car bombing in October 1983 of the Marine barracks in Lebanon, killing 241 sleeping marines; a bombing of the U.S. Embassy in Kuwait; the kidnapping and murder of CIA station chief William Buckley in Beirut; a 1993 attempt to car bomb the World Trade Centers in New York; the December 1984 hijacking of a Kuwaiti airliner, in which two Americans were murdered; the June 1985 hijacking of a TWA airliner, in which an American naval officer was killed; and the seizure of a cruise ship, in which a wheelchair-bound American was killed. America, unprepared for this wave of assaults on its people and property around the world, did not treat these attacks as enough of a threat to its vital interests to mount a serious response until President Reagan, in the wake of a 1986 bombing of a German discotheque patronized by American servicemen, ordered the bombing of Tripoli, based on evidence that Libya had sponsored this and other assaults. In the wake of the bombing of Tripoli, Libya refrained from sponsoring terrorist attacks for three years until the downing of a U.S. airliner over Scotland that killed 271 people, mostly Americans. The wave of assaults by militant Islamists continued through the administration of Bill Clinton after the February 1993 car bombing of the World Trade Center in New York that killed six and wounded over one thousand people. In June 1996, the Khobar Towers housing American military personnel in Saudi Arabia were destroyed by a truck bomb, killing 19 Americans and injuring 240 others. The wave of unanswered assaults continued in 1998 with the bombing of the U.S. embassies in Kenya and Tanzania, killing over 200 people, including 12 Americans. The wave of assaults (successful and unsuccessful) on American lives and property continued in the aftermath of the September 11, 2001, attacks through spring 2010. In November 2009, U.S. Army Major Nidal Malik Hasan began randomly shooting personnel at Fort Hood, Texas, while shouting the Muslim cry of "Allah Akbar" (God is great), killing 13 people and wounding another 30. On December 25 of that year, Umar Farouk Abdulmutallab boarded a flight to Detroit with a bomb in his underwear. Fortunately, the bomb failed to detonate and merely singed Farouk. In May 2010, Faisal Shahzad parked a van with a home-made bomb inside in Times Square, New York. The bomb failed to detonate; Americans were fortunate again. In each of these incidents, the government initially claimed that the perpetrators were isolated and deranged individuals without ties to external forces. In each case, however, it was established that the perpetrators had direct contact with, and trained with, Al Qaeda forces, Umar in Yemen and Shahzad in Pakistan. These events triggered a debate among America's political and journalist elites as to whether we should consider ourselves in a state of war with an extreme and militant segment of the Islamic world or whether we should regard these events as criminal acts. The Obama administration, concerned with provoking the rest of the vast Muslim world, decided to eschew the terms terrorism, *jihad*, or Islamic extremism and to refer to these acts as "overseas contingency operations." Attorney General Eric Holder, testifying before Congress in May 2010, refused to suggest that the perpetrators of the attacks of 2009 through 2010 might have been motivated by a connection to Al Qaeda. The slaughter of Americans and other bystanders and an unvarnished assault on American interests appeared to be a cost-free activity.

The bombing of Tripoli was an isolated response; it was the last serious response to the wave of assaults from militant Islamists until 2002 when President Bush mounted an armed offensive aimed at removing the Taliban regime from power in Afghanistan. The Taliban had provided a safe haven for the militant Islamist group, Al Qaeda, which mounted the devastating attack on the World Trade Center in 2001. The World Trade Center had already been the target of a terrorist bombing in 1993. Before a replacement regime could attain legitimacy in Afghanistan, in spring 2003 America launched a preemptive strike (attacking them before they could attack) at Saddam Hussein's Iraqi regime. The war in Iraq, and the entire concept of preemptive war on which it was based, has generated some of the most bitter political controversy in decades, a topic examined in this chapter.

ISSUE BACKGROUND: COMPETING APPROACHES TO FOREIGN POLICY

Realism or Classical Diplomacy

There is a style in the conduct of international diplomacy that characterized relations among European and other Western powers for much of the modern era. This style, based upon a set of assumptions about the nature of the world order and about the nature of humanity, is widely known as *classical diplomacy*. This approach to foreign policy is also known as political *realism* or power politics. Scholars such as Hans Morgenthau, E. H. Carr, and Kenneth Thompson were leading proponents of this approach.[2] This chapter will show that a perspective different from realism has primarily influenced the foreign policy of the United States in the twentieth century.

The first premise of classical diplomacy is that there are no universally self-evident principles of justice, right and wrong, or truth that nations are morally obligated to pursue. Hence, the national interest is not only a legitimate goal of foreign policy, but, in the view of political realists, the only defensible goal. States function and are morally obligated, in this view, to protect the interests of their societies. Realists point to the widespread public support that has existed for policies that the mainstream West regards as obscene, such as genocide (the systematic slaughter of an entire racially, religiously, or ethnically defined people).[3] Regimes based on widespread public support carried out such genocide not only in World War II, but in the former Cambodia (now called Kampuchea), in the former Yugoslavia, and in Rwanda since World War II. The defiant lack of remorse by Slobodan Milosevic, the former president of Serbia, during his trial in an international tribunal for a policy of ethnic cleansing against Bosnian Muslims, the growing popularity among Islamist militants of using their children as suicide bombers to maximize slaughter and mayhem among civilians, the deliberate starvation and slaughter of tens of thousands of black Sudanese by their militant Arab government, as well as the aforementioned other acts of modern genocide, cast doubt on the assumption that universal principles of justice are self-evident to all reasonable persons.

Because of considerations of geography, demography, resources, and history, each nation develops a set of objective and perceived interests, some of them considered vital, that are unique to that nation. Moreover, the interests of nations naturally come into conflict. Hence, conflict among nations is normal. What is good for some nations logically conflicts with what is in the interests of other nations. The goals of foreign policy to the realist, therefore, ought to be framed in terms of such interests, rather than in terms of abstract principles of justice or universal morality. Thus, some critics of President Obama argue that his stated aim of being universally liked as a "citizen of the world" conflicts with his first duty, to represent and defend his country's national interests.

For example, contrary to realist principles, the American *Cold War* policy of *containment*, the resistance to any expansion of communist control or influence between World War II and 1990, was based more on the presumption that communism was a bad thing, and the antithesis of many of the fundamental values of the West, than upon any consideration of how much a particular expansion of communist influence affected our national interests. Many realists criticized our involvement in the Vietnam War on the basis that we did not have enough at stake in who controlled the Indochinese Peninsula to justify the costs of keeping South Vietnam in the hands of an anti-communist regime. Similarly, the brutality with which Saddam Hussein treated his Iraqi subjects, including torture and mass murder, would not for the realist constitute an adequate justification of our invasion of that country unless the invasion could be justified in terms of American interests. Imposing our values, such as Western-style civil liberties, on another country ought not to be a goal of foreign policy. Foreign policy goals, in the realist perspective, can be framed in terms of whether the national interests in question are achievable and in terms of an analysis of the costs of achieving them in relation to the benefits to be derived. Thus, the question is not whether we are better off with Saddam Hussein not in power, defying the international community, funneling money to terrorist groups, and threatening his neighbors. The question is whether the benefit to our interests is worth the considerable cost in blood and treasure to remove his regime (about 4,400 American lives as of May 2010, a little more than half the number of troops lost in the first day of the Normandy invasion in World War II). The aims of foreign policy, to the realist, should not be separated from consideration of the relative power of the concerned nations and the costs of achieving one's goals.

Power Politics.   Force, in this classical or realist perspective, is neither moral nor immoral in itself, but rather an extension of diplomacy intended to pursue the national interest. Power is a central concept in the realist perspective.[4] *Power* is defined here as a relationship between two or more actors such that the power wielder can get others to do what the power wielder wants them to do and which they otherwise would not have done. The powerful accomplish this by manipulating the threat or promise of potential rewards and punishments to make the others perceive that they would be better off doing what the power wielder wants. Such use of power is the essence of politics.

Realists define broadly the resources involved in creating the threat of rewards or punishments; they may include such things as economic power, the appeal of one's principles, or the intensity or degree of one's commitment to the goals in question, as well as military might. Power in the realist perspective is therefore based in large part on a country's reputation for using its strength in the pursuit of its interests; a nation that is perceived as relentless in the use of power to pursue its interests is less likely to have those interests challenged. Therefore, President Obama's apologies to numerous segments of the world community for America's alleged sins was widely perceived as conveying an image of weakness, making it more difficult for America to assert its national interests.

Given the natural conflict of interests among nations, politics or the use of power is inescapable in this perspective. Diplomacy or negotiation is not a substitute for the application of power or force, because diplomacy without an understood ability and willingness to back up one's goals with force or power becomes equivalent to supplication (begging). Nations, in this view, must be perceived as willing to use force or power to pursue their interests to the extent that the likely benefits of achieving one's goal exceed the costs. This cost–benefit analysis does not include a moral judgment of the inherent goodness or evil of one's opponents. Realists, therefore, are willing to engage in limited war for limited objectives, something with which Americans have traditionally felt uncomfortable, preferring to define conflicts in moral terms. Thus, in the case of the Iraq crisis of 2003, the United States led a movement in the United Nations (U.N.) to pass a number of Security Council Resolutions regarding such concerns as cooperation with the U.N. weapons inspectors, adherence to the no-fly zone over Kurdistan and southern Iraq, and allocation of the revenues from the oil for food program, resolutions that were defiantly ignored or rejected by Saddam Hussein. There was concern that an unwillingness to back up these resolutions with force in the face of that defiance would have left the United States with an image of impotence, rendering it unable to defend its interest in that part of the world.

Spheres of Influence. Since principles of justice are not universal, the legitimate interests of nations are greater in some parts of the world than in others. Normally, nations have a greater interest in territories contiguous to their borders than in other parts of the world. Hence, in the Monroe Doctrine, the United States proclaimed to the world that it had a vital interest in the politics of the Western Hemisphere. Similarly, near Yalta at the end of World War II, Roosevelt yielded to the claims of the Soviet Union that they had a greater interest in the affairs of Eastern Europe than did the United States. This was not, as critics of the Yalta agreements charge, a case of selling out the freedom of Eastern European people as much as a case of not having as great an interest or a willingness to expend as many resources in shaping the politics of that region as did the Soviets. Similarly, opponents of the second Iraq War argued that the U.S. did not have enough interests in shaping the character of that country to justify the cost in blood and treasure to achieve that goal.

In a reaction against American participation in the Vietnam War, many people identified the lessons of Vietnam as indicating that the United States ought not to attempt to shape the internal politics of other countries as they did in trying to prevent South Vietnam from becoming part of the communist orbit. These lessons were the basis of a scathing critique of U.S. opposition to the pro-Marxist Sandinista regime in Nicaragua during the 1980s. Yet the sphere of influence principle was also used to argue that America had a legitimate interest in the affairs of Central America that it did not have in the affairs of Indochina. After all, an anti-American regime in Central America, able to influence if not subvert other regimes in the region, including Mexico, which shares a long, porous border with the United States, could pose a realistic threat to American interests that did not exist from a small, nonindustrialized country in Southeast Asia.

It seemed heartless, or at least ethnocentric, that the U.S. did not commit blood and treasure to intervene in the mass slaughter between the Hutu and Tutsi tribes in Rwanda in Central Africa in the early 1990s, or the mass slaughter of black Sudanese beginning in 2004 by the Muslim government in Khartoum, while it did commit such resources to halt ethnic cleansing in the former Yugoslavia. Critics of the failure of America to act more decisively to halt the slaughter in Africa have suggested it was because the victims were black. Yet realists make the argument that the United States had more interests at stake in the affairs of central Europe, a region that provided the spark to ignite the two world wars in the twentieth century, than it did in Rwanda or the Sudan. Such a conclusion would be an implementation of the concept of spheres of influence as opposed to the idealist conception that America should fight injustice with equal vigor wherever it occurs. The spheres of influence argument could also be used to add to the criticism of U.S. efforts to impose a multidenominational, pro-Western government in Iraq.

The concept of spheres of influence provides a criterion for rationing the expenditure of scarce resources. Political realists argue that if the United States appointed itself as a world police force or guardian of international justice, it would have to raise and support a considerably expanded defense and military establishment. By confining efforts to the protection of one's own vital interests, the expenditure of resources becomes more manageable. George W. Bush may have been articulating this position in the 2000 presidential campaign when he argued against our assuming the role of the world's policeman. He was reacting to the unsuccessful insertion of our military forces in Somalia during the Clinton administration. The apparent inconsistency between this position and his later action in Iraq may be explained for some by the enhanced awareness of the terrorist threat after the events of September 11.

This kind of realism in Bush's 2000 position is not equivalent to the isolationist sentiment of the inter-war period (between the two world wars), which asserted that events outside of our borders were none of our concern. The spheres of influence concept acknowledges American vital interests at stake in the Western Hemisphere and Western Europe, among other places. However, due to modern technology, U.S. interests are no longer defined only geographically. The affairs of an economic superpower like Japan may have a serious economic impact on Americans.

The Balance of Power

Another major concept of this realist, or power politics, approach to foreign policy is that of the *balance of power*. The key principle of this concept is that no one power or coalition of powers should be allowed to gain such dominating power as to be able to dictate terms of the relationships among nations without having to compromise its interests with the demands of competing interests. *Hegemony* designates a situation in which one state so dominates other states that it may dictate the terms of the relationship between them without the need to compromise its interests. When one nation acquires hegemonic power over other nations, the other nations lose their ability to protect the vital interests of their citizens.

Nations that pursue the balance of power strategy do so by shifting alliances so that one power always allies with the weaker of competing states or alliances. If a nation joined the stronger alliance, once that alliance eliminated the competing weaker alliance, the strongest power in the victorious alliance would have hegemonic power. However, by joining the weaker alliance or power, and thereby increasing the strength of the weaker forces or diminishing the strength of the strongest power, the balancing nation could force the strongest power in the stronger alliance to bargain and come to terms with competing powers and interests.[5] The idea is to check the imposition of the goals and values of the strongest and potentially hegemonic powers by establishing equilibrium among the nations.[6] Consistency in the balance of power strategy does not mean you always either support or oppose a given regime. Thus, in the first Gulf War, the United States sided with Kuwait against Saddam Hussein to prevent Iraqi hegemony in the region, even though it had sided with Hussein's regime in its earlier war against Iran when it perceived the latter country was threatening to achieve hegemony in the region.

For several centuries in European history, beginning at about the sixteenth century, Great Britain played the balancing role in the recurring conflicts involving France, Spain, and the Holy Roman Empire. Henry VIII, who allegedly said, "He whom I support will prevail," and Elizabeth I played this role especially well. The balancing power has as its objective maintaining a balance or equilibrium irrespective of concrete policy considerations. This balancing power has neither permanent friends nor permanent enemies and is thus in a state of self-imposed "splendid isolation."[7] Britain thus allied itself with the Low Countries, especially the Netherlands, and the Hapsburgs of the Holy Roman Empire against the powerful Louis XIV of France, most notably in the War of the Spanish Succession (1702–1713). The roles of Britain and eventually the United States in World War I were an exercise in balance of power politics with the goal of checking Germany's Second Reich under Kaiser Wilhelm from obtaining a hegemonic domination of Western Europe. Thus, Professor Nicholas Spykman, a staunch political realist, wrote that "Twice in one generation we have come to the aid of Great Britain in order that the small offshore island might not have to face a single gigantic state in control of the opposite coast of the mainland."[8] Of course, United States idealists did not see it that way. Instead, they defined the American mission in apocalyptic and idealistic terms, such as "the war to end all wars" and "saving the world for democracy." The balancing strategy epitomizes classical diplomacy in that normative policy considerations are irrelevant and power considerations are everything.

Deterrence.   As opposed to the strategy of avoiding aggressive action by potential foes by reconciling differences and accommodating grievances by negotiation, realists avoid attacks on their vital interests with a strategy known as *deterrence*. Deterrence is a strategy based purely on power politics considerations without concern for the relative merits or justice of the respective policy goals. This strategy involves the possession of sufficient and varied power to survive the best first strike by a potential foe with enough power and willingness to inflict unacceptable damage on such an attacker.

There are psychological dimensions to the strategy of deterrence. The implied threat of the use of power or force against the potential foe must be credible. That is, the potential foe must believe in one's willingness to actually use the deterring force. Thus, the U.S. Cold War strategy of relying on massive nuclear power to deter Soviet encroachment on its vital interests did not deter the Soviets from numerous encroachments on lesser interests, because they did not believe in U.S. willingness to launch a thermonuclear strike and risk nuclear retaliation for any interest short of the very survival of our country. Moreover, the deterrent effect of the undeniably most powerful U.S. armed forces may have been diluted had we been unwilling to exercise force in Iraq without the approval of our reluctant allies. After Saddam's humiliating capture in a hole in the ground, Libyan strongman Kaddafi abandoned his earlier defiance of the United States and United Nations and voluntarily surrendered his nuclear arms program to Western weapons inspectors.

The second psychological dimension is the question of what damage the leadership of a potential foe considers unacceptable. Authoritarian leaders in some countries have shown a willingness to accept a considerable amount of misery and even death among large segments of their citizenry in order to pursue their policy goals. Both Stalin and the rulers of Communist China were willing to accept massive starvation in order to collectivize agriculture. Saddam Hussein of Iraq was willing to accept considerable deprivation among his people to ride out U.N. sanctions and protect his freedom to pursue weapons programs. Iran's Prime Minister Rafsanjani said in 2007 that the loss of two-thirds of ordinary Iranians would be an acceptable price to pay for the extermination of all of Israel in a nuclear exchange, while the Ayatollah Khomeini, the founder of the Iranian Islamic Republic, declared that "We do not worship Iran. We worship Allah … I say let this land go up in smoke …" These leaders have provisions that they could survive even nuclear retaliation against their countries. There is therefore a serious question as to whether the prospect of massive losses among their populations would be enough to deter such leaders.

Nevertheless, deterrence has a record. Despite an announced desire to do so, the Soviet Union never attacked the West directly during the Cold War, the longest period in modern history without a general war in the West. Throughout the Cold War period, however, many American idealists criticized the American arms buildup to implement the deterrence strategy. On the other hand, the strategy used between 1919 and 1939 to avoid future wars was negotiation unsupported by the credible threat of power, combined with mutually negotiated disarmament.[9] World War II attests to the colossal failure of this latter strategy.

The American Style in Foreign Policy: Wilsonian Idealism

The previous discussion of classical diplomacy or power politics implicitly contrasted that approach to foreign policy with a different American style. Scholars characterize that American style as *idealism*. Because President Woodrow Wilson's Fourteen Points speech to Congress in 1918, in which he proposed the League of Nations, epitomized this approach, it is often called *Wilsonian Idealism*. Americans have been more prone to exercise the idealist style in foreign policy than other Western nations; however, the United States has not been consistent in that regard and at times has exercised hardheaded realism in making foreign policy

Universal Justice and the Nuremberg Principle

To the idealist perspective, the pursuit of the national interest is an inadequate justification for resorting to the horrors of armed conflict. There are, for idealists, knowable and universal principles of justice over and above the laws and policies of any particular state. Hence, the governments and people of nation-states can be held accountable for the protection and pursuit of those principles. Thus, the

leadership and even the population of the sovereign nations of the world are
morally obligated to disregard and disobey the laws and policies of their countries
to the extent that these laws and policies violate these knowable principles of
justice. This position is sometimes called the *Nuremberg Principle*, because without
the assumption of such knowable universal principles of morality and justice, the
war crimes trials of top Nazi leadership in Nuremberg, Germany, would have
made no sense. The Nazi elites, after all, were obeying the laws and orders of
their lawful superiors in their nation-state.

The Universal Harmony of Interests.   With this assumption of a knowable
universal good, idealists view human nature as essentially good and cooperative.
Most people, therefore, share basic values (health, prosperity, family). President
George W. Bush, in defense of his policy to import democracy to Iraq, claimed
that given the choice, any man would choose freedom. The world, therefore,
possesses a universal harmony of interests marred only by the selfish motives of a
small group of unaccountable rulers. Thus, in their concern for just treatment of
Muslims (alluded to above), American leaders reassured the American public in
the wake of the attacks on the World Trade Center and Pentagon of September
11, 2001, that these events were the work of a few extremists who distort
Muslim principles and that the vast multitudes of ordinary people in the Muslim
world would never condone such attacks. Thus, following the events of
September 11, students at a number of major universities, for example at the
University of North Carolina, were required to read accounts of Islam that
treated it as an essentially peace-loving faith. In positing the clear distinction
between the allegedly selfish and out-of-touch rulers and their ordinary masses,
the idealist perspective rejects the claim of realist scholars, like Harvard's late
Samuel Huntington, that Islamic civilization has been based upon and has pursued values and goals in direct conflict with the West for 1,400 years, and that
the Muslim masses increasingly see the West as "materialistic, corrupt, decadent
and immoral."[10]

Because of this universal harmony of interests, calm reasoning or negotiation
can generally resolve conflicts, and war is usually wrong and unnecessary. When
war becomes unavoidable, however, it becomes a crusade against these selfish
and autocratic rulers. War is never justified in terms of a pursuit of the national
interests alone, but only as a moral crusade. President Bush, in his 2002 State of
the Union speech, defined conflict in such moral terms when he characterized
Iran, Iraq, and North Korea—nations whose professed aims and whose potential
weaponry render them a threat to the vital interests of the United States—as "the
axis of evil." When one defines conflicts in such normative terms, the goals of
the utilization of force frequently become unconditional surrender or the total
destruction of one's opponents. After all, one does not bargain and compromise
with pure evil. When it was obvious by the fall of 1918, following America's
1917 entry into World War I, that Germany would be unable to obtain the
hegemony that it sought over Europe, Germany sought a negotiated peace.
The American president, however, insisted upon the abdication of the "evil"
Kaiser Wilhelm and the creation of a democratic republic completely incongruent

with the German culture and experience. The war dragged on for another year before the capitulation of the Second Reich. The inevitable failure of the Weimar Republic that followed created a power vacuum in Central Europe that would be filled by Hitler's Third Reich some fourteen years later.

Because they see principles of justice as universal, idealists reject the premise of the spheres of influence principle of classical diplomacy. Thus, to the idealist, this assumption of universal justice is that the same moral imperatives that led to our intervention in the former Yugoslavia against the Serbian "ethnic cleansing" should have led to our intervention in the mass slaughter in Rwanda or the Sudan. Evil is evil, whether it occurs in central Europe or in Africa.

Diplomacy, Force, and American Optimism

In the American idealist perspective, diplomacy is an alternative to the use of force. Since people are essentially cooperative by nature and motivated by the same basic values, mutual reasoning and persuasion can resolve differences among peoples. From the Kellogg–Briand Pact of 1928 that renounced war as an instrument of national policy and the mobilization of anti-war sentiment by Charles Lindbergh and others on the eve of World War II, to the mobilized opposition to the Vietnam War, our entry into the 1991 Gulf War, the U.S. intervention in the former Yugoslavia, and the war in Iraq in the first decades of the twenty-first century, Americans have been reluctant to commit military force for any purpose short of the survival of the country. The disappointing outcome of U.S. intervention in the Vietnam War reinforced this reluctance to the point where American hesitancy to use force has sometimes been called the Vietnam syndrome. President Obama's oft-pronounced willingness in his presidential campaign to sit down and talk without pre-conditions with the leaders of the most aggressively anti-American countries in the world, such as the Islamic Republic of Iran and the government of North Korea, epitomizes this belief that talks unsupported by power can productively resolve issues with such countries that do not share our most fundamental values. This faith in the ability to resolve conflict with reasoned negotiation downplays the significance of conflicts of interest.

This persisting faith in diplomacy rests upon the deep-seated American faith that all conflicts are ultimately resolvable by reasoned negotiation. Former Secretary of State Henry Kissinger has written of the American confidence in the bargaining process in which our diplomats view themselves as mediators between Washington and the country with which they are negotiating.[11] All of this presumes that there is a scenario to which all parties, given their values and goals, can plausibly agree. For example, it will be shown that advocates of the Middle East *peace process*, in which America has been so heavily engaged, assume that all of the major parties ultimately would be satisfied with a two-state solution. This perspective also assumes that the conflict is really about borders rather than mutual acceptance by Palestinians and Israelis of the right of the other to exist. Yet, it is doubtful that all relevant parties would agree to such an outcome regardless of the borders.

Besides divorcing diplomacy from power, idealists tend to divorce the formulation of foreign policy goals from the costs and possibilities of achieving them. Our

Cold War goal of containment, the policy of resisting any further encroachment of governments labeled communist in whatever form or context, framed foreign policy in terms of the moral presumption that communism was a bad thing. Although, other things being equal, the United States may have been better off with a noncommunist government in place in a given country than an avowedly communist one, it was not clear that all regimes labeled communist posed an equal threat to American interests. Therefore, the costs of preventing the expansion of a particular communist regime may or may not have been justified in terms of those interests.

Moreover, aside from considerations of cost, it is not clear that all foreign policy goals are ultimately achievable. Regardless of the desirability of having a stable and legitimate noncommunist and pro-Western government ruling South Vietnam, knowledge of the history of Vietnamese nationalism suggests that goal was never achievable. It remains to be seen whether that judgment also applies to Iraq, although by 2010, the achievement of that goal began to look promising. At this writing however, that goal with respect to Afghanistan appears uncertain.

This disposition to define foreign policy goals independently of the costs and possibility of achieving them is a result of defining international conflict in terms of the pursuit of some conception of universal justice, rather than in terms of the national interests. American idealists have tended to seek an alternative to power politics and to define military conflict as "a holy crusade against evil incarnate ... holy wars of 'unconditional surrender' against solitary infidels ..."[12]

Collective Security and Institutional Solutions to World Conflict

Idealists reject the balance of power strategy for deterring aggressive behavior and its underlying premise that war is a normal instrument of policy. Among the institutional means of preventing conflict offered by idealists is the principle of *collective security*. This system assumes that the preponderance of states in the world share values of peaceful coexistence and wish to prevent aggression by one state on another. It assumes that the states in the system will subordinate their particular national interests to the collective good. It further assumes that there is agreement among the states as to the status quo that is to be preserved. It also assumes there is agreement about what constitutes an act of aggression.[13] Given that the term is normative (the other fellow's military action is aggression; mine is self-defense), identifying acts of aggression could be a problem. Is an act of violence terrorism, aggression, self-defense, or an act of war? Such regional alliances as the North Atlantic Treaty Organization (NATO) and the Southeast Asia Treaty Organization (SEATO) are examples of the principle of collective security, where each participant declares that an attack on one is an attack on all. With the end of the Cold War, the purpose and future of such collective security arrangements has been rendered uncertain. The September 11 attacks on the United States did not bring a collective security response from the other NATO members. Surveys showed that a majority of the European populace believed the claim that attacks were carried out by Americans to justify the U.S. attack on Iraq and Afghanistan or by the Israeli Mossad. Indeed, a book making this claim was the best-selling book in France for part of 2007.

One of the critiques of the second Bush administration's attack on Iraq has been that it was virtually an act of *unilateralism*, policies undertaken without first obtaining political and material support from most major allies. The converse concept, *multilateralism*, means that serious foreign policies ought to be implemented in concert with and presumably with the blessing of one's major allies. If one cannot obtain the cooperation of major allies for a foreign policy operation, the policy may lack justification according to widely accepted standards of international justice and morality. Critics of multilateralism claim it gives other countries a veto over our foreign policy options. Unilateralism implies that a country is acting according to its own narrow (and, by implication, selfish) conception of its national interests, virtually the epitome of classic realism. President Bush was criticized for launching the attack on Iraq without getting U.N. approval and especially without the approval or cooperation of France and Germany. However, defenders of the war in Iraq point out that France and Germany each imported a substantial share of their oil from Iraq and that these governments had special arrangements for obtaining Iraqi oil that substantially enriched the leadership of these three countries. Then-President Jacques Chirac reportedly received substantial sums of money from the Iraqi oil for food program, giving him and France a particular interest in preserving Saddam's regime.[14] The United States, by contrast, gets most of its imported petroleum from Mexico, Canada, and Venezuela. Hence, the lack of cooperation on Iraq between the United States and its allies stems largely from the fact that their interests diverged. Unilateralism is based on the principle that each nation is responsible for defining and acting to preserve its own national interests, the essence of the realist or classical style in foreign policy.

Policymakers in the American idealist tradition have thus often sought an alternative to what they regard as the corrupt power politics of classical diplomacy. We will now turn to how the formulation and implementation of major foreign policies in the post–World War II world reflected these assumptions and dispositions and how these policies differ from the classical style of diplomacy.

POLICY PAST AND PRESENT:

COLD WAR, CONTAINMENT, AND AFTER

The alliance of the United States and the Soviet Union quickly fell apart at the close of World War II, when the Soviets engineered the installation of regimes in Eastern and Central Europe hostile to the West and its values. What Winston Churchill called "the iron curtain" descended across Europe, separating the democratic states of Western Europe from these Soviet puppet regimes united in a collective security arrangement called the Warsaw Pact. Meanwhile, the Western democracies formed their own collective security arrangement, the North Atlantic Treaty Organization (NATO).

This arrangement seemed necessary in light of the failure of the collective security provisions of the newly established United Nations. Collective security in the United Nations depended upon the unanimous agreement of the great powers (as noted earlier in the discussion of collective security). The effective veto power of the Soviet Union over decisions of the U.N. Security Council meant that organization could not mobilize a response to Soviet aggression.

The success of the communist revolution in China and other parts of Asia did not seem initially in the early postwar era to alter the apparent bipolar nature of the postwar world order. The essential nature of that order was perceived in the West as the freedom-loving, democratic states of the West threatened by a monolithic bloc of communist nations directed from the Kremlin in the Soviet Union.

The reality of the Chinese–Soviet split and the emergence of a wave of newly independent nations in Africa and Asia in the 1950s and 1960s following the breakup of European-dominated imperialistic empires challenged this perception of a bipolar world. These newly emergent states, however, appeared to many Americans as a similarly monolithic third world independent of the communist and noncommunist blocs of nations.

Nevertheless, the United States viewed the postwar world as dominated by the threat of the aggressive communist bloc of nations to the security of the democratic West. Although ideological tension between the putatively capitalist West and what the Soviets called communism goes back to the Bolshevik Revolution of 1917, these ideological stances were more of a justification for action in pursuit of national interests than a cause of conflict. The ideological conflict, however, took on a life of its own once the Cold War became a reality.[15] Fear of communist expansion and assaults on the vital interests of Western nations was not unrealistic in this early Cold War period. Aggressive action by communist bloc nations did occur (for example, the invasion of South Korea by its northern neighbor in 1950), as did instances of Soviet-directed espionage and undermining of noncommunist regimes. However, this bipolar view of the world dominated all other interests and became normatively defined as a struggle against what President Ronald Reagan called "the evil empire."

It was clear that the publics of the West were not ready to undertake military action to wrest control of the communist bloc nations from the Soviets, especially when it became clear that the Soviet Union had acquired the capability to manufacture and deliver nuclear weapons. The alternative adopted as the defining principle of American foreign policy during the Cold War was what George Kennan, a diplomat in the U.S. embassy in the Soviet Union, called *containment*.[16] Kennan and those who thought like him believed that the Soviet Union was going to be an aggressively expansive power, a conclusion reinforced by Soviet leader Joseph Stalin's speech in February 1946, in which he discussed "the inevitability of conflict with capitalist powers."[17] The essence of the concept of containment was that the United States would act to resist the expansion of the influence of communist powers over previously noncommunist powers. The policy glossed over the distinctions among the nation-states in each of these broad categories. Clearly, some structures bearing the label communist posed a very different level of threat to American interests than other such structures. Hence, a hard-line Stalinist regime, such as the one that headed the Democratic Republic of Germany (East Germany), would challenge American interests much more than a nominally communist party that had declared its independence of the Kremlin line, such as the Italian Communists. Moreover, noncommunist states varied greatly with respect to whether they supported or challenged American interests. The United States supported some very authoritarian and unsavory regimes during the Cold War because such regimes identified themselves as being anti-Communist. For example, it supported a military junta in Greece headed by an autocratic Colonel Papadopoulos because the elected previous Greek head of government was a leftist too closely associated with a Marxist point of view. This simplistic division of the world into the good-guy capitalists and the bad-guy communists reflects a characteristically American moralistic perspective that ignores the national interest in particular cases.

The war in Korea that began when the North Korean regime invaded the South in 1950 was a classic implementation of the principle of containment. When Communist North Korea launched its invasion, President Truman, under U.N. auspices, ordered American forces into battle to save South Korea. There was little or no discussion of how communist control of the Korean peninsula would affect American interests, other than to invoke the Munich analogy. Munich refers to the infamous appeasement of Adolf Hitler on the eve of World War II. Appeasement means accommodating the announced grievances of aggressive leaders in the hope that they will then abandon their aggressive behavior. At Munich, British Prime Minister Neville Chamberlain gave Hitler the Sudetenland, the German-speaking part of Czechoslovakia, in return for empty promises of peace. The analogy presumes that Europe under the control of the Nazi war machine posed no greater threat to American interests than the Korean peninsula under the control of the less-modernized North. The American effort was successful in saving the noncommunist status of South Korea, because its military had a legitimate political system to defend. We will see that was not the case in the next major American military commitment in Vietnam.

The Failure of Containment in Vietnam

The success of the individual known as Ho Chi Minh in gaining control of first the government of the North and the support of much of the population of the South was that he co-opted the strong nationalist and anti-imperialist passion among the Vietnamese people for his political and communist purposes.[18] Indeed, the success of the Communist movement in Southeast Asia was proportional to its ability to become identified with the struggle for national independence.[19] While we perceived the struggle there as between the yoke of communist oppression and the freedom of the noncommunist world, many Vietnamese saw the struggle as between Western imperialism and national liberation.

The Leninist modifications of Marxism in fact offered an ideal ideological vehicle for mobilizing movements of national liberation. Lenin explained the failure of capitalism to collapse as Marx predicted by imperialism. Imperialism, he argued, gave capitalism artificial life by providing cheap foreign raw materials and captive markets to siphon off the surplus value that Marx predicted would bring down capitalism. It was therefore not hard to combine a passion for Marxism–Leninism with a nationalist opposition to Western colonialism. In this way, Ho Chi Minh was able to co-opt the Vietnamese nationalist front, the Viet Minh, for the goal of a communist dictatorship.

The Japanese in World War II had thrown the French out of Indochina. Because it identified Ho Chi Minh as a Communist, the United States financed and supported a French invasion of Indochina to resume French colonial control after the war. When the French armies were defeated, the United States gradually assumed the role of fighting the Viet Minh for control of South Vietnam under the presumption that we were fighting communism. Many of the Vietnamese, however, saw our role as a defense of Western colonial control of their homeland.

At that point in history, Western imperialism was not a defensible system; however, that defense appeared to be the American role in Vietnam. Because much of the native population perceived South Vietnam as an instrument of Western colonialism, it lacked internal legitimacy. Our military can certainly defend a sovereign, legitimate government, but it cannot as readily create one. This may also speak to America's difficulty in creating a stable post–Saddam Hussein regime in Iraq, although in spring 2010 that effort appeared on the brink of success. In any event, the putative goal of participation in the Vietnamese War, the maintenance of a stable, effective, noncommunist, and pro-Western government in South Vietnam, was possibly never attainable.

American political leaders in the Post War world seldom asked questions about the feasibility and costs of our goals. Southeast Asia experts, whose sense of history made them skeptical about America's policies, had been squeezed out of the State Department by young, inexperienced people characterized by the typically American unbounded optimism that any goal could be achieved with sufficient commitment.[20] The realists' position that some goals are unachievable seems to be supported by the frustrating outcome of American policy in Vietnam, the loss of South Vietnam to the North in the mid-1970s.

The Search for a Comprehensive Peace in Palestine

Foreign policy idealism appears also in the active engagement of the United States on several occasions to broker a comprehensive peace agreement between the state of Israel, the various Arab and Muslim countries in the area, and the various groups that support the nationalist aspirations of the people known as the Palestinians. From the active role played by President Carter to engineer a peace agreement between Israel and Egypt, and the intense effort by President Clinton in 2000 to broker a comprehensive settlement between Israel and the Palestinian Authority represented by the late Yasser Arafat, to the U.S.-sponsored conference in Annapolis in November 2007, the United States has expended considerable diplomatic capital on this effort. President Obama has further pursued this elusive goal with the appointment of Dennis Ross and former Senator George Mitchell as permanent negotiators for an Israeli–Arab peace process. This tradition re-emerged in the second Bush administration with its declaration of a *Road Map to Peace* between the Israelis and Palestinians. This Road Map consists of a tentative plan outlining the steps toward a final settlement, the two-state resolution (separate states of Israel and Palestine peacefully coexisting side by side). This effort is justified by the recognition of having important American interests in the region, by the presumption that a settlement is desired by both parties and is possible, and by an American disposition to end violence and correct perceived injustices throughout the world. Furthermore, the ongoing conflict between the Palestinians and Israel is perceived by President Obama as a major obstacle to the goal of reaching out for friendlier relations with the Muslim world, a goal clearly stated in a speech from Cairo early in his presidency.

POLICY EVALUATION: REALISM VERSUS IDEALISM IN THE MIDDLE EAST

The contemporary foreign policy challenges that stem from American policy in the Middle East particularly involve the conflict between Israel and the Palestinians, the politics of oil, and the terrorism directed at the United States and its allies. Realism and idealism seem intertwined in the policies of the United States toward the region.

America perceives that it has several important interests at stake in the region, interests that could be threatened by an eruption of the tension into a general conflict. These interests include access for the United States and its Western allies to the world's largest proven reserves of crude petroleum; hence, it feels the need to maintain a working relationship with those Arab and Muslim states in the area that control those reserves. Actually, our European and Japanese allies are even more dependent on Middle East oil than the U.S. is, but it has an interest in the health of their economies. Secondly, the Middle East is geographically at a strategic crossroads in the world (see Map 12.1). It therefore is to America's benefit to have a reliable ally who can provide logistical support for American military forces, such as facilities to land and refuel planes, store supplies, dock ships, and give liberty to crews, as well as to share intelligence about movements and forces in the area that affect our interests. For example, the United States used bases in Saudi Arabia during the Gulf War of 1991. Middle East policy, then, tests the limits of classical diplomacy and of foreign policy idealism. The American pursuit of peace (the absence of open warfare) in the area may be in conflict with the American interest in preventing the vigorously anti-American regime in Iran from becoming a nuclear power, which would give Iran hegemonic control over other states in the region. As of spring 2010, Americans seem unable to get Russia and China to cooperate with serious sanctions to prevent Iran from acquiring nuclear weapons; hence, an attack on Iranian nuclear facilities may soon be the only way to prevent Iran from getting the bomb. However, many people feel that such an attack would lead to the outbreak of general war in the region.

MIDDLE EAST

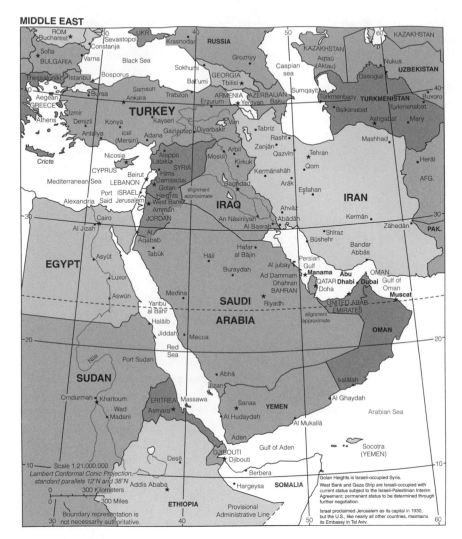

M A P 12.1   Nations of the Middle East

The Emerging Threat of Iran's Nuclear Ambitions

American interests have been threatened in recent years by the increased radical-
ization of the Islamic regime governing Iran, while that regime appears to be
acquiring the ability to deliver nuclear armed missiles in the near future. Iranian
President Mahmoud Ahmadinejad has asserted his intention to "wipe Israel off
the map" and claims to envision a possible world without the United States.
Claiming to be driven by an eschatological vision of a world dominated by the
Shiite version of Islam, Ahmadinejad threatens to establish Iranian hegemony
(unchallengeable domination) over the entire Middle East region, while his
regime remains militantly hostile to the West and the values it entails.

This emerging situation has presented the United States with policy dilemmas and strained relations between it and other industrialized countries who appear to be reluctant to cooperate in imposing sanctions on Iran strong enough to cause Iran to abandon its nuclear ambitions. Several of these countries are heavily dependent on Iranian oil. Yet, if Iran is allowed to acquire a nuclear capability, Western interests and the very survival of America's formerly close ally Israel will be in grave jeopardy.

This situation has caused some speculation about a possible military strike to destroy or at least delay Iran's capability to acquire usable nuclear weapons.[21] The total elimination of all of Iran's nuclear operations is apparently unfeasible; however, some argue that key links in the chain needed to produce the weapon could be put out of commission for a period of time. It is rumored that Israel has been actively training for such an operation. Such a strike would fall under the concept of preemption discussed later with reference to the second Iraq War. Meanwhile, the immediate need for such a strike may be less pressing as a computer virus, reportedly developed by Israelis, invaded computers used in Iran's nuclear program in October, 2010.

Oil, U.S. Foreign Policy, and the Middle East

The idealist position assumes that there is a just and legitimate Palestinian nationalism and a just and legitimate Israeli nationalism. Under this assumption, the goal of a peace process is a Palestinian state that would coexist with the Jewish state of Israel, and this goal can be achieved by trading for peace land that Israel seized in the 1967 war. Therefore, efforts to broker peace presume that the issue is where to draw the borders between a Jewish and a Palestinian state. These efforts further presume that there is some scenario or outcome to which all contending parties might conceivably agree. This presumption was dealt a serious blow at the Annapolis Conference of November 2007, when Israeli Prime Minister Olmert declared that Arab recognition of Israel *as a Jewish state* is a prerequisite for any further concessions. All of the Arab leaders immediately and unequivocally responded that they would never consider such recognition. Together with their insistence on a right of return for some six million descendents of the Palestinian refugees, that refusal reveals that the intention of these Arab leaders is to undermine the Jewish character of Israel which, after all, was the whole point of the Zionist enterprise. This reaction presumes that the preservation of a Jewish-free East Jerusalem could be the foundation of a Palestinian state, which could lead to the end of the Israeli–Palestinian conflict. Yet the Arab leaders have been repeatedly saying for the past sixty years that they are not interested in any state living peacefully with Israel. This illustrates the American refusal to conclude that there is no possible scenario for a settlement of the dispute.

The Obama administration operates under the apparent assumption that if Israel makes enough concessions to the Arabs, such as giving them more land or in unilaterally disarming themselves (as in Obama's push in spring 2010 to pressure Israel to dismantle its nuclear capability under the terms of the Nuclear

Non-Proliferation Treaty), that the Arabs would agree to live peacefully with Israel. This assumption by the Obama administration was illustrated by its publicly expressed anger in May 2010 at Israel's plans to build apartments in a Jewish neighborhood in East Jerusalem, because the Arabs insist that the entire eastern and holy parts of Jerusalem be reserved as the capital of a future Palestinian state. These strained relations were further manifested in a lengthy and angry phone call by Secretary of State Clinton to Israeli Prime Minister Netanyahu that took on the nature of a scolding.

This strained relation was further manifested and magnified by America's public neutrality over an anti-Israeli group (HHI, operating out of Turkey with ties to Al Qaeda) that attempted to break a blockade of Gaza in June 2010. Blockades are an accepted tactic under the rules of war. Lincoln's blockade of the American South probably hastened the victory of the Union in the Civil War; America blockaded German and Japanese ports in World War II; and John F. Kennedy's blockade of Cuba in the 1960s resolved the "missile crisis." The Israeli blockade is intended to separate out materials (e.g., arms and weapons) that could be used in that war. After the separation of potential war materials, hundreds of thousands of pounds of humanitarian aid (mostly food and medicine) was delivered by Israel to Gaza in the first half of 2010. Critics of Israel complained that building materials that would be used to construct schools and hospitals were also withheld. Israel argues that these materials could also be used for such military purposes as barricading missile launching sites.

When Israeli special forces boarded a ship trying to run the blockade in June 2010, they were set upon by people armed with steel pipes and knives. Several Israelis were seriously injured. The Israelis responded, and several blockade runners or "peace activists" were killed. Israeli use of "disproportionate force" was strongly criticized around the world, including by the Obama administration; however, supporters of Israel insist that the right to institute a blockade of enemy ports is an established principle of the laws of war. It turned out that the ship was not carrying military supplies, but the Israelis could not know that until they had boarded the ship.

The value at stake here is Western access to the oil reserves of the Middle East. How an American-brokered settlement would enhance that access or whether the continued tension between the parties would impair that access is a key unanswered question. The Arab world has sold oil to the West since the value of that resource became manifest. This has occurred despite the fact that the 1,400-year history of relations between the Muslim world and the West has been one of tension.[22] The Arabs sell oil to the West because that is the only way that resource is of such value to them, not because they like the West. Iraq, despite the Gulf War of 1991 and the continued tensions between that country and the West, fought for the right to sell its petroleum to the West.

Moreover, supporters of Israel argue that the United States has an interest in the preservation of the one nation in that part of the world that is democratic and has been consistently pro-Western. With the possible exception of Iraq, the Arab world has yet to produce a single transition to democracy, despite waves of such transitions in other parts of the world. America, partly out of a feeling of kinship to a Western-style democracy, partly out of sympathy for a nation born out of the Holocaust, and partly out of the domestic power of the American Jewish community, has felt obliged to offer considerable financial support to the beleaguered state of Israel, without which that nation could not survive. This support angers the Muslim world, which refers to the establishment of the Jewish state as the *nakba* (catastrophe), hardly an orientation implying either recognition of or a propensity to live peacefully with that state.

Meanwhile, Israel has come under almost universal condemnation from elites throughout the Western world. This condemnation, which included a boycott of Israeli products urged by the British National Union of Journalists and a boycott of Israeli academics voted by their union of university faculties, is largely based on a perception that Israel is illegally occupying Arab land with its settlements on the West Bank and its control of Jerusalem. Occupation implies that one is on land belonging to someone else. The alleged Jewish occupation of Arab land is held as a justification for Arab violence against Jews. However, the question of who has a claim to the land known as Palestine is more complex than commonly assumed (see Map 12.2). The Jewish state lasted from the conquest of Canaan in about 1200 B.C. until the Babylonian conquest in 587 B.C. and then again until it was destroyed by the Romans in A.D. 70. Over the years, the land was controlled by the Egyptians, Seleucids, Crusaders, Mamelukes, and Byzantines. The Ottoman Turks controlled it from 1517 to 1917, when it fell under the control of the League of Nations as a result of World War I. The Arabs had a caliphate there under the Omayyad Dynasty from 638–1099, a total of less than 500 out of over 3,000 years, but have not had political control over the area since. This raises the question for some of under what rules of international law is the territory considered to currently be Arab land, rendering Jewish presence there an occupation. Still, for the reasons previously stated, America seeks to maintain a working relationship with the Muslim nations of the Middle East as well as Israel. President Obama has made a concerted effort to extend the hand of American friendship to the Muslim world, beginning with a major speech from Egypt shortly after he was inaugurated. This has led to an effort to distance America from its formerly close ally, Israel.

There is a growing and increasingly aggressive segment of American society that argues that it is not in America's interest to continue its level of support for Israel. This segment of our society, which is joined by most of the leadership of other Western societies, characterizes Israel as an oppressive society that is largely to blame for the tensions in the Middle East and is therefore a major threat to peace in the region. This point of view, found largely among left-oriented academics, was epitomized in a set of highly controversial essays published by two of America's preeminent political scientists, John Mearsheimer of the University of Chicago and Stephan Walt of Harvard, arguing that a disproportionately strong Israeli lobby (AIPAC, or the American-Israeli Political Action Committee) distorts American foreign policy to serve Israeli interests at the expense of American interests.[23] Former president Jimmy Carter published a bitterly anti-Israeli book, comparing the Israeli treatment of its Arab subjects to the brutal and oppressive treatment of South Africa's blacks by that country's

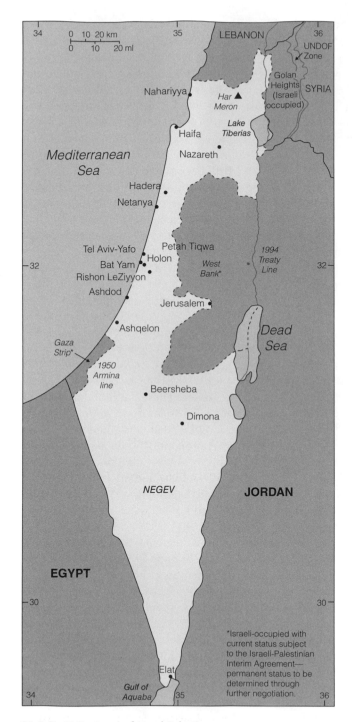

34

0   10 20 km
0   10   20 ml

35   LEBANON   36
                                   UNDOF
                                   Zone
                          Golan
                          Heights
                          (Israeli
              Har ▲   occupied)   SYRIA
Nahariyya   Meron
                          Lake
                          Tiberias
           Haifa
                    Nazareth

Mediterranean
Sea
         Hadera
       Netanya

   Tel Aviv-Yafo   Petah Tiqwa
           Holon   *West*   1994
   Bat Yam   *Bank**   *Treaty*
   Rishon LeZiyyon   *Line*
      Ashdod
                   Jerusalem

        Ashqelon   *Dead*
                                  Sea
Gaza
Strip*   *1950*
                 Armina
                 line
              Beersheba

                   Dimona

          NEGEV   **JORDAN**

EGYPT

32   32

30   30

              Elat   *Israeli-occupied with
                          current status subject
  Gulf of   to the Israeli-Palestinian
  Aquaba   Interim Agreement—
34   35   permanent status to be   36
                          determined through
                          further negotiation.

M A P 12.2   Land of Israel-Palestine

apartheid regime.[24] Given that Israel's Arabs vote, hold office, and have full political rights, the comparison seems unfair to Israel's supporters. Even Jewish Americans have actively joined in the condemnation of Israel as an aggressive rogue state. J-Street is an organization of Jewish academics whose purpose is to paint Israel as the main impediment to Middle East peace. Anti-Israeli feelings have been particularly strong on the campuses of America's top tier universities. The Israeli ambassador to the U.S. was even barred from giving the May 2010 commencement address at Brandeis University, a Boston-area school under Jewish auspices.

Critics of the Walt and Mearsheimer perspective argue that it exaggerates the influence of AIPAC, which cannot even get the United States to recognize Israel's capital of Jerusalem and move its embassy there accordingly. Mainly, they argue that the interests of America and Israel are largely compatible and aligned against anti-democratic, aggressive regimes, especially aggressive Islamist movements. Yet, the anti-Israeli chorus continues to be strong.

Palestinian Nationalism

Numerous American political figures and observers of the political process urged President Bush to re-engage the administration in the peace process. The question for American interests in the area is what can the American government do to reduce the likelihood of renewed war? It is assumed by many that America also has a realist or pragmatic interest in the survival of the pro-American state of Israel within the bounds of acceptable costs. Yet American pressure on Israel to make unilateral concessions, rather than produce a settlement, may likely increase the odds of war or at least of continued violence by making Israel appear more vulnerable. The Arabs have used their acquisition of control of Gaza in 2006 to launch an unrelenting barrage of missiles and rockets into southern Israeli towns. Arab control of the entire West Bank would place Israel's major population centers within rocket and even mortar range. The barrage from Gaza was so intense that the Israel Defense Force (IDF), in Operation Cast Lead, invaded Gaza in 2009 to seek out and eliminate the sources of these rocket attacks. Israel was roundly condemned in the world community for this operation. Despite efforts of the IDF to minimize collateral damage to civilians, casualties did occur among civilians fueling this condemnation.

The idealist argument for the Palestinian cause reflects an assumption that the Israelis are settlers who have occupied land that has been Arab or Palestinian since "time immemorial." This widely held assumption about that area was most succinctly stated by author Joan Peters. She refers to "the myth that 'the Jews arrived only in 1948 where they displaced a teeming Arab population from its rooted homeland since time immemorial.'"[25] In a profusely documented work culminating years of research, Peters came to a different conclusion than the one she set out to prove. She found that while some Arabs and some Jews had always lived in the area of the Palestine Mandate, it was sparsely settled and run down. Many of the people we call Palestinians descend from people who migrated to the area about the same time, as the Zionists in the early twentieth century, taking advantage of an expanding Westernized economy.[26] (The late Palestinian Authority Chairman Yasser Arafat himself was born and raised in Egypt.) Critics of Israel reject Peter's research and conclusions as flawed, however.

Moreover, the argument for the justice of a borders-based settlement to the conflict reflects the widespread belief that this particular self-proclaimed nation deserves self-determination and a sovereign state that allows it to act in the world as an identifiable people. However, there are numerous national groups whose stateless conditions do not seem as pressing to the world as that of the Palestinians (e.g., the Kurds, the Chechens, the Basques, the Catalonians, the Armenians, and the Tibetans). The irreconcilable positions taken at Annapolis in 2007 suggest that a resolution in the short run may not be possible; America may have to live with continuing tension. Given the Palestinian determination to settle for nothing less than the elimination of Israel, America's pushing Israel to make territorial concessions may encourage the Arabs to aggressively pursue that goal. In other words, it may make war more likely, which is not in America's interest. The status quo may not make life pleasant in Israel but it may be the option that least threatens American interests. The Palestinian determination to exterminate Israel as a Jewish state may be inferred from their repeated eschewal of a two-state solution described in the following historical summary.

When the British abandoned its mandate after World War II, the United Nations Security Council voted to partition the mandate into three states: a small Jewish state on the shores of the Mediterranean, an Arab state east of the Jordan River called Trans Jordan to be governed by the Hashemite monarchy, and another Arab state between the west bank of the Jordan River and Israel. Israel and Trans Jordan accepted the partition and declared their states. The rest of the Arab world rejected the partition and mobilized to destroy the Jewish state by armed force. The point here is that a Palestinian state was formally offered by the United Nations and Israel and rejected by Arab leaders. This is the second of four times that a formal offer of a Palestinian state was rejected, the first being the Arab rejection of the 1938 Peel Commission Report by the British as a proposal to dispose of its League mandate. Although the Arab attempt to destroy the Jewish state did not succeed, Jordan occupied the West Bank, leaving the Jewish state eight to twelve miles wide at its neck, not a defensible position.

The third rejection of such an offer came in the wake of the 1967 Six Day War. Declaring once again their intention to destroy the Jewish state, the Muslim states massed their troops on its borders. Israel's ports were blockaded, an act of belligerency under international law. Facing this situation and with their indefensible borders, Israel launched a preemptive strike (a concept discussed later in the context of the second U.S.–Iraq War), destroyed the Egyptian air force on the ground, and defeated the combined Arab powers in six days. The Israelis now controlled the *West Bank*, the Sinai Desert through which the Egyptians had launched three armed attacks against Israel in twenty years; the area known as *Gaza*; and the Golan Heights, through which Syria had launched its assaults on Israel. Although Israel now had defensible borders, its government offered to return the territories it had captured in return for peace treaties and formal recognition from its neighbors. The immediate Arab response was the so-called

Khartoum Doctrine: "no negotiation, no recognition, no peace." However, after Egyptian president Gamal Abdel Nasser died, President Anwar Sadat negotiated a peace treaty with Israel. The entire Sinai, with its valuable oil reserves and strategic passes, was returned to Egyptian control. Relations between the two states, however, remain cold and hostile.

The fourth refusal of an explicit offer of a state for the Palestinians came after weeks of intense negotiations under the mediation of President Bill Clinton in 2000. The offer included the return to Palestinian control of over 95 percent of the West Bank, the Gaza Strip, and the holy parts of old Jerusalem, which are highly sacred to Jews and Muslims. This offer went further than anyone familiar with Israel thought its government would ever go. Nevertheless, Chairman Arafat of the Palestinian Liberation Organization refused the offer, believing that the offer did not include a right of return for all of the descendents and their relatives of the 700,000 or so Arabs who fled to escape the oncoming war. This would amount to some six million Arabs flooding into Israel, which would of course render the Jews a second-class minority in their own land; thus, Israel would no longer be a Jewish state. Subsequently, Arafat either ordered or permitted his followers to launch a new wave of intense violence against Israeli civilians, following various perceived injustices on the part of the Israeli occupation of parts of the West Bank and the Gaza Strip.

The Clinton-led negotiations were the culmination of a lengthy process known as the Oslo Peace Process after an agreement negotiated in that city. The agreement committed the Israeli and Palestinian parties to a land-for-peace process. The Palestinians committed themselves in this pact to recognize Israeli's right to exist and to curb violence against Israeli citizens. The Israelis committed themselves to withdrawal from territories occupied in the 1967 war. (The Israelis argue such a withdrawal should be tied to the aforementioned Palestinian Authority steps while the Arabs argue withdrawal should be total and precede any negotiation.)

The Palestine Authority (PA) charter, committing the organization to the destruction of Israel, has not been changed. Moreover, in mid-May 2004, the late chairman of the PA, Yasser Arafat, ordered an escalating wave of violence following the announcement of Bush's Road Map, involving numerous suicide bombers in public places. In the first eleven weeks following the announcement of the Road Map, there were 321 attempted suicide attacks resulting in 51 murdered civilians and 317 serious injuries. Following a bus bombing in September 2004 that killed sixteen Israelis, the PA turned out 20,000 individuals to dance in celebration while Arafat told the crowd, "We will march to Jerusalem; we will sacrifice millions of martyrs."[27] The hoped-for negotiated reconciliation between Israel and the PA has been rendered more difficult by the election of Hamas to lead the PA. While *Fatah*, the faction headed by the late Arafat, occasionally hinted at a willingness to negotiate, *Hamas* has been unambiguous about its goal of the elimination of Israel. Meanwhile, the current (as of June 2007) speaker of the PA legislature has publicly called for "the extermination of all Jews and Americans."[28] Supporters of the peace process argue that such statements are mere rhetoric for local consumption. Israelis, however, take promises to exterminate them seriously.

Meanwhile, the Israelis have withdrawn from over 90 percent of the West Bank. Israeli Prime Minister Ariel Sharon, in a move drawing strong opposition from within his own country, ordered an Israeli retreat from and abandonment of its remaining settlements in Gaza as well as some of its remaining West Bank settlements in order to unilaterally establish defensible borders for the Jewish state. The forced evacuation of all Israelis from Gaza, some of whom had lived there for three generations and had built thriving cities and businesses, caused intense controversy among Israelis. The Israeli government apparently concluded that the costs of protecting a few thousand Jews living in Gaza among over a million hostile Arabs were excessive. Rather than govern their newly acquired Jew-free territory, the Arabs have chosen to turn it into a platform for the daily launching of Kassam rockets into southern Israel and a base for the collection of arms and explosives; meanwhile, armed gangs roam Gaza, killing and terrorizing local inhabitants in pursuit of the deadly conflict between the Fatah and Hamas factions of the Palestinians. The latter group, being more explicit in its genocidal aims regarding Israel, is regarded by the United States as more militant. Hence, the United States in mid-2007 pressured the Israelis to allow the importation of thousands of assault rifles, RPGs, anti-tank missiles, and hundreds of armored personnel carriers into Gaza to support Fatah. However, Fatah is so weak that many of these weapons would fall into the hands of Hamas.

In June 2007, the victory of Hamas over Fatah was complete. Gaza fell into chaos as armed gangs roamed, killing children (in front of their parents), doctors working in hospitals, and other civilians, while Israel continued to provide essential water and electricity to Gaza for humanitarian purposes. At the same time, Fatah was killing Hamas people in the West Bank. The implication for U.S. policy is that continuing pressure on Israel to make further concessions is not likely to produce a peace agreement. Rather, such concessions would be perceived by Arab militants as a sign of weakness of Israel and its American supporters and an incentive to increase efforts to eliminate Israel.

Apparently, Israel's strategy is to unilaterally set what it determines is its defensible borders in the absence of a serious negotiating partner. In order to carry out this decision that six million Jews cannot indefinitely govern thirty million Arabs, the Sharon forces decided to voluntarily relinquish control of most of the disputed territories. Although Sharon was felled by a stroke that left him comatose, his successor, Ehud Olmert was determined to carry out the plan of Sharon and his *Kadima* (Forward) *Party*.

To curb the almost daily slaughter of its civilians, Israel has undertaken the construction of a wall or fence along these unilaterally declared borders. In the first four years after the current *Intifada* was launched, after the failure of the summit at Camp David and Taba, 1,017 Israelis have been killed, 70 percent of whom were civilians, and 5,600 injured, 83 percent of whom were civilians.[29] At this writing (in the summer of 2010), the wall has been completed on the northern border between Israel and Samaria (the Israeli name for the northern West Bank) and construction continues along the border with Judea (the Israeli name of the southern West Bank). Since the construction, successful suicide bombings in Israel have been reduced by over 90 percent. A suicide bombing occurred in September 2004, allegedly in retaliation for the targeted assassinations of the last two well-known leaders of the radical group Hamas, Ahmed Yassin and Abdel Rantisi, six months earlier. It took that long for Hamas to launch a successful attack, and these killings occurred south of the completed wall between Israel and Judea. Meanwhile, life in Israel has returned to near normal. The economy grew in 2004 at 4 percent a year and Jerusalem's King David Hotel has reached full occupancy.[30] Israel, however, remains a garrison state under siege with armed soldiers patrolling throughout Israel, with armed checkpoints along every major roadway, and guards questioning and searching patrons to virtually every restaurant, examinations based upon unabashed ethnic profiling.

In light of widespread condemnation of the wall, the International Court at The Hague issued a judgment that the wall is illegal based on the premise that the West Bank is legally Arab land, an assumption addressed earlier in this chapter. The Court ruled that Israel could not claim the right of self-defense because that right only applies to attacks from a state, and the Palestinian Authority is not a state. The Court further ruled that the wall illegally encroaches on the sovereign territory of Palestine. Sovereignty presumes statehood, creating the impression of internal inconsistency in the Court's ruling. President Bush took the position that the wall is a legitimate exercise in self-defense and advised Israel to ignore the ruling. Numerous other states use a wall to protect one or more of their borders (including Saudi Arabia on its border with Yemen). The wall apparently presents a major obstacle to the goal of Hamas, Islamic *Jihad*, and the PA to destroy the fabric of Israeli society, with an intolerable level of killing of innocent men, women, and especially children. Possibly that is why its construction has generated so much anger among the PA and its sympathizers.

A number of Israeli settlements remain in this contested territory. Some of these are quite large with elaborate, modern edifices and are generally surrounded by a wall. These settlements in this unincorporated territory, the refusal of the Israel government to permit some Palestinian building in territories under dispute, and the strikes ordered by former Israeli Prime Minister Ariel Sharon against leaders of groups claiming credit for the suicide bombings in Israel (discussed later in the section on terrorism) are regarded by the Palestinian leadership as provocative. But as discussed earlier and reinforced by their reaction to the pull-out from Gaza and large parts of the West Bank, the decisive grievance of most Arab elites is not the settlements or the retaliation against terrorist leaders and the launchers of rockets, but the existence of the Jews themselves, especially in the Middle East.

Given the offer rejected in 2000, it is hard to see any plan on which the parties can agree. While classical diplomacy involved mutual concessions in which no party got all of what it wanted, the Arab position, in the wake of Arabs having launched and lost at least three wars in less than half a century, seems to demand that the victorious target of those attacks surrender to Arab demands unconditionally. Moreover, several strong and well-armed Palestinian groups have never wavered in their declared intention to completely destroy the Jewish state: Hamas, Islamic Jihad, Hezbollah, the Popular Front for the Liberation of Palestine, Black September, and even Arafat's Fatah movement, although the Fatah made some conciliatory statements in its discussion with

Western leaders and media. The supposedly moderate president of the PA, Mahmoud Abbas, has made it clear that he has neither the power nor the will to compel the Hamas prime minister to eschew continued violence against Israeli civilians. On the other side, a vocal but tiny orthodox Jewish minority claims the right of Israel to the entire territory of Palestine as a biblical mandate. (This position was represented by the National Religious Party, which received 7.9 percent of the vote and 9 of 120 seats in the Israeli Knesset in 2006.)

The Saudis floated a peace plan that demands that Israel retreat to the pre-1967 borders prior to negotiations to essentially get their way before rather than as a result of negotiations, a demand echoed by the PA's Abbas. These, however, are indefensible borders, as noted earlier. Given the fears about the intentions of the several Arab states and assorted militant groups previously discussed, it is almost inconceivable that Israel would ever accept such a demand. In fact, were Israel to withdraw to such borders, the temptation would be great for some Arabs to take advantage of the situation and to attempt to eliminate the Jewish state entirely. American realist interests are to reduce the likelihood of war in the area. Such an Israeli concession would make Israel appear vulnerable and hence war more likely. Given that American interests in the area include the relaxation of tensions between the Palestinian leadership and Israel, leaning on Israel to make concessions in the absence of a change in the attitudes of Palestinian leaders would seem counterproductive.

American Options in the Area: A Ray of Hope Dashed

It therefore has been hard to imagine the basis for any conceivable settlement. Yet the American government continues to dispatch representatives to the region, including the November 2007 Conference at Annapolis, in which several major Arab and Israeli leaders, Secretary of State Condoleezza Rice, and even President Bush convened at America's insistence to try to broker a settlement based on President Bush's Road Map plan leading to the two-state solution. Israel had seemed most amenable to American pressure, so the temptation was to lean on the country to make additional concessions. Since the ascension of harder line Binyamin Netanyahu of the hawkish Likud Party to the prime minister's office in Israel, Israel has been less amenable to American pressures, despite such pressures being pursued more vigorously by the Obama administration than by its predecessor. Indeed, Prime Minister Netanyahu defied the Obama administration's demand that he extends a moratorium on the construction of Jewish housing in East Jerusalem in September 2010 prompting a forty-five-minute scolding phone call from Secretary of State Clinton.

Before the 2007 conference and 2010 meeting, a ray of hope emerged in late October 2004, when Chairman Arafat died rather suddenly of still undisclosed causes and was succeeded by Mahmoud Abbas as president of the PA. Abbas had been identified as a Palestinian moderate. Of course, moderate is a relative term. Abbas earned the designation by stating that the Intifada was a tactical mistake (not a moral one). Nevertheless, he also said that "a crackdown on Hamas (the main perpetrator of suicide bombings) ... is not an option." Abbas said that he would never compromise on an unlimited right of return, and authored a book denying that the Holocaust occurred. Abbas won the weakly contested Palestinian election in January 2005. The content of his mandate remains uncertain, especially in light of the fact that Hamas—explicitly rejecting negotiations with or recognition of Israel—now controls the PA legislature. The substantial reduction in Israeli casualties (over 90 percent) from the Intifada in the last half of 2004 since the erection of the security fence and the targeted killing of terrorist leaders could have rendered the continuation of the killing option less attractive and further encouraged the emergence of a more moderate Palestinian leadership. Such an outcome could have introduced a new, more hopeful dynamic to the prospects of a settlement between these bitter enemies. However, these hopes have been dashed by the maximalist rhetoric by the Hamas leadership of the PA and the outbreak in 2006 of renewed fighting in southern Lebanon. This fighting came in response to Hezbollah (the Party of God) kidnapping two Israeli soldiers from Israeli soil and the raining of Katyusha rockets on Israel's northern cities, killing forty-four civilians. Meanwhile, tensions in the area have been further exacerbated by the aforementioned rain of Kassam rockets from Gaza. This fusillade of rockets left the Israeli town of S'derot virtually uninhabitable.

Meanwhile, American aid to Israel is crucial in enabling that state to survive. The continuation of tension and stalemate between Israel and the Palestinian and opposing Arab forces do not in themselves harm American interests, which consist of access to Middle East petroleum reserves and maintaining the existence of the single consistently pro-Western democratic state in the area. Given the unyielding refusal of Arab leadership and of the majority of Palestinian people to accept a Jewish state in the area, America's acceptance of that stalemate while ensuring Israel's ability to defend itself may be America's only realistic option in the immediate future.

FUTURE ALTERNATIVES: RESPONDING TO TERRORISM AND NUCLEAR PROLIFERATION

The events of September 11, 2001, brought the specter of terrorism to the forefront of American consciousness to a greater extent than ever before. Although Americans have suffered acts of terrorism on several occasions in recent years, as noted at the outset of this chapter, foreign terrorism had never struck so violently so close to home. Moreover, the threat of large-scale terrorism against Americans appears to be an ongoing danger. In 2007, the United States and British agents uncovered plots to blow up ten U.S. airliners carrying hundreds of passengers over the Atlantic, to slaughter as many GIs as possible at Fort Dix, and to cause massive explosions at Kennedy Airport in New York. More recently, there were shootings at Fort Hood and the failed underwear and Times Square bombings mentioned at the outset of this chapter. Terrorism appears to be an increasingly popular tool for militarily weak, but disaffected, forces against the democratic West, today a tool almost exclusively used by young and radically religious

Muslims. In the wake of the events of September 11, our government fully committed itself to a war on terror. In order to assess the effectiveness of that war, we need to examine the nature of terrorism and the policy options for confronting it.

Defining Terrorism

Terrorism has acquired an ideological connotation: what your enemy does is terrorism, while your perpetrators of political violence are called freedom fighters, or some equally positive term. Terrorism, however, has a particular meaning. Terrorism is not merely violence to achieve political objectives. Wars, and even guerilla tactics by irregular troops, use violence for political goals, but these are not normally designated as terrorism. Rather, *terrorism* consists of random violence against civilian or noncombatant populations to compel another power to change its policies by generating widespread anxiety or fear among its people. The randomness of the violence is a function of the soft or indefensible nature of the targets. Even the victims of the Fort Hood shootings were impersonally and randomly selected. Thus, the events of September 11 were clearly terrorism, as was arguably the June 1996 attack on the Khobar Towers in Saudi Arabia, where military personnel in a noncombatant mode were sleeping. A major attempt to explode bombs in the London Underground in July 2005 was partially successful, and inflicted numerous casualties. Because it is virtually impossible to avoid being a potential target, terror can paralyze the ordinary daily life of the target population. For example, many Israelis routinely ride the bus to school or work; hence, after several attacks killed the occupants of buses, Israelis were afraid to put their children on the bus to school or to commute to work. Even those who were not killed or maimed were unable to carry on their ordinary life. Thus, terrorism, if successful, paralyzes the ordinary life of the target society. This tactic appeals to weaker forces with grievances against stronger powers, because such acts have been almost unpreventable. No nation can constantly guard every possible target of such attacks. Moreover, when terrorists are willing, as they frequently are, to risk or sacrifice their own lives, it is very difficult to prevent these tactics. Hence, as detailed at the outset of this chapter, America as the world's strongest power has been the target of terrorist tactics numerous times in recent decades.

Options for Confronting Terror

Some policy analysts and political activists from the idealist perspective urge that we try to address and remedy the grievances of those who commit or are likely to commit such acts, a strategy that realists give the now pejorative name of appeasement, as explained earlier. Idealists argue that although we cannot stop people from committing acts of terror if they are determined to do so, we can remove the incentive by remedying the alleged injustices and the poverty that breed suicidal rage at American interests. From this perspective, a just peace in the Middle East and economic development in the Islamic world would reduce the conditions of terrorism.

Realists, however, dispute this. They note that the head of the leading Islamist terrorist organization, Osama bin Laden, came from a wealthy family and that most of the perpetrators of the events of September 11 were not poor.[31] (*Islamism* refers to the radical and militant aspects of Islam, not to the entire Muslim world.) A typical suicide bomber, Zainab Al Issa Abu, who blew herself up in Jerusalem in mid–September 2004, came from a wealthy family whose parents owned a television station. Ms. Abu, one of an increasing number of women suicide bombers, was the hostess of a children's show on that station. These realists argue that one should never grant the grievances of terrorists, even to the extent of not doing something one might have been disposed to do if such policy were a terrorist demand, and even to the extent of refusing to negotiate with the terrorists or discuss their grievances because America must not let the terrorists perceive that their tactics are achieving their objectives.

Despite the tactical reasons for Israel's withdrawal from Gaza discussed above, Islamist groups have claimed that they have driven the Jews out of Gaza; they have argued that terrorism is working and ought to be stepped up. They made this same argument after the unilateral Israeli withdrawal from Lebanon after both incursions into that country. For example, in the *Al Ahram Weekly* of September 30 to October 6, 2004, Yasser al-Zaatrah argued that Islamist groups had made good their pledge to drive Israel out of Lebanon, and they have driven them out of Gaza. The realists argue that the first principle in preventing acts of terror is to remove the incentive to commit them by making it clear that the potential terrorists cannot realize their agenda with these acts. They further argue that the strategy of granting their demands and remedying their grievances is impossible, because such grievances tend to be infinitely expansive and to conflict with the vital interests of the stronger power. Thus, Daniel Pipes argues that the agenda of the Islamist militants (not all Muslims) is to impose an Islamic theocracy on the United States with Islamic law (Shira) trumping American law, obviously not a viable policy option for most Americans.[32] The impression that weaker powers can advance their agenda by committing acts of terror invites such acts in the future, according to the realist position. Hence, some analysts fear that the shift in election results in Spain from the pro-Western conservative government to the anti-U.S. socialist government in 2004 following the deadly attack on a Spanish railway facility just prior to the election will prompt terrorists to attempt such attacks prior to elections in other countries.

To take this position means that the potential target nation must consider victims and potential victims of terror as expendable. When terrorists seize hostages, the media always consults the families of the hostages, who urge meeting the terrorists' demands. Realists argue that these are the last people to have any perspective on balancing the concern for the victims with the interests of the whole nation and the prevention of future acts of terror.

The second realist principle in fighting terrorism is to impose costs on those who make the decision to commit such acts and who plan and support them. This means that one should hold accountable not merely the perpetrator, such as the suicide bomber, but the states or large organizations who increasingly plan and sponsor such acts. Until the 2001 war on terror, the United States was reluctant to take action against such states or organized terrorist networks.[33] The United States had known for some years about the Al Qaeda network that planned and sponsored not only the September 11 attacks but also a number of the other acts against the United States previously discussed. Increasingly, complex acts of terror involve either the sponsorship of nation-states or well-organized networks like Al Qaeda. This is a phenomenon known as state-sponsored terrorism. A related version of this has been terrorism sponsored by the governing authority in the Palestinian-controlled territories or the organizations affiliated with them, such as Hamas, Islamic Jihad, and Black September. These organizations, including an arm of the late Chairman Arafat's own Fatah group, the al-Aqsa Martyrs' Brigades, unleashed a rash of nine suicide bombings in nine days in the heart of Israeli cities, killing dozens of men, women, and children in March 2002. A sense among the Arab world that such a strategy is effective was encouraged by a wave of anti-Israeli and anti-Semitic violence throughout Europe. Israel, following the realist formula, responded with a military push into the West Bank town of Ramallah against the headquarters and leaders of these groups. Further seeking to impose costs on the leaders of this new Intifada, Israel began a policy of targeted assassinations of the leaders of Hamas, the group behind most of the recent attacks and more recently the leaders of the Islamist Taliban in Afghanistan using pilotless drone aircraft. Using helicopter-launched missiles, the Israelis killed Ahmed Yassin in spring 2004, and then two weeks later killed his successor, Abdel Aziz al-Rantisi. No visible Hamas leader willing to be publicly identified emerged for some months; after the almost-daily attacks, six months passed before the next Hamas attack. The Israelis, meanwhile, even attacked the sense of a safe haven for terrorist leaders by killing another Hamas leader, Izz al-Din al-Sheikh Khalil, in Damascus, Syria in September 2004. The sharp reduction in the incidence of successful suicide bombings in 2004 suggests to some scholars that the policy of targeted assassinations of Hamas leaders caused the group to become more cautious in their attempts to paralyze Israeli life. Tourism was up sharply in Israel; the economy grew in 2004 at around 4 percent, and life returned to a kind of well-guarded normalcy.[34] The result of imposing costs on terrorists and those who sponsor terrorism may be seen in the actions of Libyan leader Qadaffi voluntarily surrendering his nuclear weapons program after seeing the spectacle of Iraqi leader Saddam Hussein reduced to rags when he was taken into custody. Yet, some argue that the Obama administration has weakened the deterrent effect of swift justice for terrorists by treating them as ordinary criminals entitled to all the procedural rights afforded such accused perpetrators of ordinary crime. In particular, such critics of our treatment of captured jihadists object to the practice of affording them "Miranda rights," with a state-appointed lawyer advising his/her client of a right to silence and cutting off a potentially valuable source of intelligence about other terrorist plans. Defenders of the administration argue that harsh treatment of jihadist prisoners is a "recruiting tool" causing Muslim individuals to join terrorist organizations. The alternative to affording jihadists "due process of law" is military tribunals, a process that was used against Nazi saboteurs in World War II.

Such interrogation of prisoners is part of another option in the struggle against terrorists, to try to uncover and foil terrorist plots before they occur.

To this end, the USA Patriot Act authorized a variety of intelligence-gathering techniques, including the interception of phone calls from suspected militants and other Muslims to overseas recipients without prior judicial authorization. Critics of the USA Patriot Act raise privacy issues and paint the specter of a police state. Defenders of the act claim that exigencies often do not permit the luxury of hunting down a judge without losing the opportunity for crucial information. The USA Patriot Act was scheduled to sunset and had to be reauthorized in 2005 in the Senate and 2006 in the House with amendments. The amendments now require high-level (FBI director or deputy director or official in charge of intelligence) approval of requests for sensitive information, such as library or medical records, and require court notification within ten days of surveillance of new objects. Supporters of the administration policy point out that no successful terrorist plots were carried out in the United States since the events of September 11, while several major attempts have been foiled. Occurrences such as the underwear bomb attempt or the foiled Times Square truck bombing reminds us that plotting such mass murder is an ongoing enterprise. Some defenders of civil liberties on the left argue that threat of terrorism is exaggerated and is used as an excuse to infringe on those liberties. Israel also refuses to discuss the grievances of the Palestinians while the suicide attacks continue, because it does not want to appear to reward this kind of terrorism.

Idealist attempts to remedy the grievances of the Islamists may be frustrated by the depth of their hatred of Western civilization itself. It has now been reported that Islamist academies not only in the Middle East, but in the United States and other Western countries as well, are teaching children that it is their sacred duty to kill Jews and convert other Americans. These academies are run by the militant Wahabi wing of Islam, financed by our putative ally, Saudi Arabia. Muslim schools in the territories and even a Muslim Mickey Mouse preach hate and the glory of *shahada* (dying for Islam) to very young children.[35] Bernard Lewis, perhaps the leading Western authority on Islam, stated on July 28, 2004, that Europe would be Islamic by the end of this century at the latest, a recognition of the intensity of the commitment of the Islamists to convert or exterminate the infidels of the Western world.[36] Some may view terrorism as an essentially rational act to achieve certain goals. However, it may be that such acts are just as much an expression of raw hatred and shame at one's powerless situation. The danger here is magnified by recent efforts by the leaders of states and organizations sponsoring terrorism to acquire chemical, biological, and nuclear weapons of mass destruction.

The War in Iraq and the Struggle with Terror

America's first response to the events of September 11, 2001, was to invade Afghanistan and militarily bring down the Islamist Taliban regime that had been providing a territorial haven for the Al Qaeda group responsible for those events. There was little quarrel with this response. However, while a number of Al Qaeda leaders were captured, the top leadership, including Osama bin Laden, the head and main financial support of that group, escaped capture. With these leaders still at large, President Bush ordered a U.S.-led invasion of Iraq in March 2003, a move that generated intense domestic criticism.

This criticism had two targets. First, critics questioned the decision to go to war in the first place, a decision that was in part justified by the claim that Saddam Hussein had weapons of mass destruction (WMD) that included chemical, biological, and nuclear weapons. When no stockpiles of these weapons were found after the collapse of Hussein's regime, critics of the war alleged that Bush had deceived the nation to justify a war either for oil or to settle old scores for his father. Second, critics claim that the aftermath of the war—the occupation and rebuilding of Iraq after the fall of Saddam's regime—was handled badly, with unrealistic expectations for the ability of the Iraqis to govern themselves along democratic lines. Some people who had supported the initial decision to invade Iraq agree with this second critique of President Bush's handling of the war.

The major justification for this invasion was Iraqi leader Saddam Hussein's repeated noncooperation with a U.N.-sponsored weapons inspection regime and his defiance of several U.N. resolutions demanding his cooperation and an accounting of his weapons programs. These inspectors and resolutions were instigated by the fear that Saddam Hussein had WMDs that he could and would eventually use against Western targets. President Bush argued that given the destructive power of such weapons, he could not rely on deterrence and retaliation, granting Hussein the first shot. This is the newly asserted doctrine of *preemptive war*; it replaced the old doctrine of deterrence because we can no longer rely on a second strike in this era of WMDs. It turned out, however, that after we toppled Hussein's Baath Party regime, no stockpiles of WMDs were found. Moreover, readers of an investigative report on the justification for our invasions argued that the report found no support by Hussein for the Al Qaeda perpetrators of the events of September 11. President Bush, however, ordered the preemptive attack based on the intelligence available to him prior to the attack, intelligence that in retrospect appears to have been flawed. Critics of the attack argue that we should have given the process of inspections and negotiations more time. These critics argue that the threat that Hussein's regime posed to the United States was not clearly imminent. Moreover, they argue that we should have assembled more international support for our actions to clothe them with international legitimacy. Realists respond by saying that we cannot give other nations an effective veto on how we defend our national interests. Idealists also question the morality of the doctrine of preemptive war and the use of force based upon the unproven inference that the object of the attack is likely to threaten one's vital interests.

Prewar Intelligence on WMDs and on a Connection Between Iraq and Terrorism

The United States knew that Saddam's regime had chemical weapons and had used them in the 1980s to kill millions of Iranians in the Iraq–Iran War and thousands of its own Kurdish citizens. Saddam's son-in-law briefly defected to the West and told of a chemical weapons plant at which he had been employed in the late 1990s. Clearly, Saddam had the know-how to replenish his supply of chemical weapons. Moreover, it is clear that Saddam had sought and acquired some technology and material used in the development of a nuclear weapons program, but it is not clear how far he had progressed on that quest. Further, it is clear that he had gone to considerable length to frustrate and harass members of the weapons inspection team when it would have been to his advantage to cooperate when he had nothing to hide. In the month and a half between the U.S. announcement of its intention to attack after exhausting the U.N. options, intelligence satellites picked up a heavy increase in truck convoy traffic between Iraq and Syria. We do not know what these trucks were carrying, but WMDs are among the possibilities. The head of Israel's Mossad claimed that his organization could confirm that shipment of WMDs to Syria, according to Carolyn Glick in her *International Jerusalem Post* column of April 23, 2006. Moreover, memos from Saddam to his associates discussed restarting chemical weapons programs as soon as the inspections ended. Given the fact that he had the knowledge and technology to acquire such weapons, he could have had a small stockpile in a matter of months. However, in hindsight, it may simply be that the intelligence available to President Bush prior to the attack on Iraq, suggesting that Saddam Hussein had recently been involved in the acquisition of WMDs, was flawed.

Saddam had supported terrorism in a variety of ways. He sent large cash payment to the families of Palestinian suicide bombers to encourage that activity. He offered his country as sanctuary to a number of prominent terrorists. The late Abdul Nidal, for example, was a long-time guest in Iraq. Moreover, despite the denials by many of the critics of the war, there were ongoing and repeated, although not formal and institutionalized, connections between Saddam's regime and Al Qaeda leadership. We know that these contacts were discussed in a memo from Undersecretary of Defense Douglas Feith to Jay Rockefeller and Pat Roberts of the Senate Intelligence Committee dated October 27, 2003. Between 1992 and 1995 meetings were held in Khartoum, Sudan, between Iraq Intelligence officials and Al Qaeda leader Faruq Hijazi. Iraqi Intelligence officer Ahmed Hikmat Shakir facilitated the entry of several September 11 hijackers through customs in Kuala Lumpur, Malaysia, in January 2000 and attended a meeting with them. We do not know what they discussed, but it is reasonable to infer terrorist activities were mentioned. There was an ongoing if unofficial pattern of contact and support between Iraq and terrorists, including Al Qaeda.[37]

Moreover, Laurie Mylroie wrote in the *New York Sun* on October 19, 2004, that the Iraqi Survey Group went into Iraq immediately after the fall of Saddam's regime and found a base at Sulman Pak just south of Baghdad that they knew had been used to train terrorists. The base even had an old airplane that had been used to train for hijacking airliners. While there is no evidence that Hussein was involved in planning the events of September 11, there is no doubt he supported radical Islamist terrorism in general. The question is whether this connection in and of itself justifies a preemptive invasion of Iraq. Idealist critics of the war strongly argue against the morality of initiating the horrible human cost of war without a direct and imminent threat to a nation's vital interests.

It is, however, too late to argue whether we should have invaded Iraq. Now that we have overthrown Saddam's regime, our options are different and difficult. At this writing, U.S. forces in Iraq and Iraqi civilians are being killed and wounded although at a much reduced rate since a "surge" of twenty thousand additional troops were deployed in 2007. However, a persisting insurgency of former Baathist militants and itinerant Islamist fighters remained. This violence is exacerbated by internal warfare between armed gangs of Sunnis, the minority sect that had ruled Iraq under the aegis of Saddam's regime, and armed Shiite militias bent on exacting revenge upon their former Sunni oppressors. Some call this a civil war with American and allied troops caught in the middle. We have been restrained in our response to these attacks on American troops (frequently improvised roadside bombs) for fear of alienating "the Arab street." Critics of the war argue that our aggressive use of force alienates ordinary Arabs, facilitating the recruitment of additional terrorists to bin Laden's cause. These critics argued vociferously, but erroneously, that the surge would fail. Thus, they press for a publicly announced timetable for the withdrawal of American troops from both Iraq and Afghanistan. This, they argue, will force the Iraqis and the Afghan leaders to take the responsibility to quit their infighting and to govern themselves. War critics demand that we have an exit strategy for terminating our participation in the war (which, war hawks point out, is not the same as the goal of victory).

Realists respond that if we withdraw from Iraq without realizing our objective, the Islamists would likely convince themselves that they had driven us out, thereby justifying a renewed commitment to terrorism. Moreover, they point out that an announced timetable for the withdrawal of allied troops will tell the insurgents and other Islamist opponents of the pro-American forces that they only need wait us out. Potential friends among Iraqis or in Afghanistan will know that the Americans will not protect them after that date. It would in fact become an unconditional surrender to those who wish to end American influence in that country. These realists further argue that the hostility of the Arab street to the West exists independently of our policy. While the death of any American serviceperson is a tragedy and an unbearable loss to his or her loved ones, in perspective, we lost twice as many troops on D-Day alone in World War II as we have lost in four years of fighting in Iraq. Supporters of the war argue that the assertion of our national interests sometimes requires such tragic cost.

War hawks advocate that the U.S. sent enough troops in Iraq to decisively defeat the insurgents. A surge of some 20,000 additional troops were deployed in Iraq in the summer of 2007. The idea of the surge is to allow the allies to clear a contested area of insurgents and then have enough personnel to hold that area, where previously, when the allies drove the insurgents out, they would soon have been redeployed and the insurgents would have moved back into the area. As of spring 2010, experts agree that the surge is helping to stabilize Iraq. However, the antipathy between the Shiite Muslims, the Sunni Muslims, and the Kurds override a widespread sense of an Iraqi nation. President Bush's goal of legitimizing an effective pro-Western regime in Iraq continues to appear elusive due to those divisions. The distinguished scholar and expert on the concept of community, Amitai Etzioni, has argued for a communitarian solution to the question of how such a segmented society could provide essential security. He advocates that the three geographically defined subcultures—Sunni, Shia, and Kurd—each provide security for its own people and area.[38] Yet, realists argue that failure to achieve some plausible approximation of our goals would render it difficult for America to assert its interests in that region for many years.

Rogue Regimes and WMDs

The threat posed by countries who challenge American vital interests is infinitely exacerbated when *rogue states*, states that operate outside acceptable patterns of international behavior, acquire the capacity to build and deliver WMDs. In the era of widespread availability of information, it is increasingly difficult to contain that capacity. A less-developed and otherwise weak country could deliver devastating carnage and destruction to the strongest of nations, a development that renders the second strike capacity of deterrence unacceptable. Hence, President Bush argued that the United States must consider preemptive action against hostile nations on the verge of acquiring that capacity. It will be recalled that Israel took such preemptive action in destroying Iraq's nuclear reactor in 1983.

Such is the case today with Iran, a nation with a nuclear program close to having the ability to use that power to produce nuclear weapons, and with North Korea, a nation that already has such weapons and some capacity to deliver them. Iranian medium-range missiles could easily reach Israel as well as parts of Europe with a nuclear warhead. It is uncertain how effective the Arrow anti-missile system fielded by the United States and Israel would be against such an Iranian strike.

Iran is controlled by radical Muslim clerics, while North Korea is a hard-line communist state. Obviously, it would be much more difficult and dangerous to confront North Korea with its existing nuclear capacity and its massive, well-armed military. Talks with North Koreans have resulted in it breaking promises not to push ahead with its nuclear program, which directly threatens South Korea. North Korea has, in the past, shared its nuclear and missile technology with anti-American forces such as Iran and could provide a nuclear capability to terrorists. While many strategists and scholars such as Zbigniew Brzezinski and Brent Scowcroft point out the possible calamitous consequences of alienating the Arab world with such a strike, Israel may also be considering another preemptive strike as it did in Iraq if Iran nears success in producing deliverable weapons, but its task would be much harder this time without the benefit of surprise and because Iran's program is spread to several sites. However, some experts, including some Arab leaders, encourage the possibility because of the equally dire consequences of a nuclear armed Iran and its ability to "Finlandize" the region (or politically dominate the region so that other countries could not act contrary to Iran's wishes).[39]

A pair of MIT scholars has presented research on the feasibility of such an operation given the status of Israeli military capability and Iranian defenses against such an attack. They conclude that "... the IAF now possesses the capacity to destroy even well-hardened targets in Iran with some degree of confidence. The operation appears no more risky than the earlier attack on Osirak."[40] Two scholars, one a nuclear engineer and the other a political scientist, concluded that the Israelis would have a reasonable chance of successfully accomplishing that task by concentrating on three key links: the heavy water plant at Arak, a uranium conversion facility at Ishfan, and a uranium enrichment facility at Natanz. A successful Israeli operation would clearly be in America's interest. Not only has Iranian President Mahmoud Ahmadinejad promised to wipe Israel off the map but has stated the eventual goal of a world without the United States. Therefore, while it would be very difficult to completely destroy Iran's widely dispersed nuclear program, some think that Israel could prevent Iran from assembling a bomb by taking out key links in the nuclear chain. Other Arab states feel threatened by the prospect of a nuclear Iran. Saudi Arabia, for example, has granted Israel permission to use its air space en route to such a raid.

The United States has tried to engineer an economic boycott of Iran to pressure it to abandon its nuclear program, but America's European allies have eschewed support for such a boycott, thereby rendering such an effort ineffective. Hence, American options regarding this problem are limited. However, Seymour Hirsch, writing in the *New Yorker* in late January 2005, charged that the United States had special operations units infiltrating Iran to determine the location of that nation's nuclear facilities (possibly for an air strike on said facilities).

Future Issues on the Foreign Policy Horizon:
Globalization and National Interests

Americans hoped that the demise of the Soviet Union would end the decades of tension between the democratic West and Russia, perhaps forgetting the foreign policy goals of the Soviet Union reflected the long-standing foreign policy interests of Russia. Although Russia flirted with democratic institutions for a while under President Boris Yeltsin, a colorful character who had been instrumental in bringing about the collapse of the Soviet Union, a former hard-line MKVD (an espionage and police agency) leader, Vladimir Putin, succeeded Yeltsin in the Russian presidency. On a range of issues, such as backing sanctions and embargoes on Iran and North Korea to keep them out of the nuclear club, Russia has been very noncooperative. Meanwhile, Putin has been suppressing opposition to his rule within Russia and aggressively suppressing a separatist movement in the province of Chechnya. Meanwhile, former Communists have been emerging in key leadership posts, such as Gennady Seleznev being elected Speaker of the Russian parliament. With Russia suffering deplorable economic and social conditions, it is apparent that the Russian people value a strong and effective government more than they do civil liberties, making the emergence of a Western-style democracy disappointingly unlikely.

The other great communist power, China, has been rapidly growing from a less-developed country to a military and economic superpower. With very cheap labor, China has become a major exporter of consumer goods, creating a massive trade imbalance with the United States. This means we buy far more from China than it buys from us, weakening the value of the dollar. As China becomes an industrial power, it adds significantly to the body of pollution that threatens the air and seas of the world. This is an age of what is called *globalization*, the fact that we live in world economic and industrial systems in which the impact of economic and other activities transcends international borders. The United States has little if any control over the activities of this Chinese monolith, whose activities pose a threat to our interests. This is especially true as China has become th creditor for much of the enormous debt the U.S. has amassed in the first decade of the twentieth century.

Similarly, the West is virtually without leverage in protecting its security interests in the face of an expanding nuclear club. Countries such as Iran and North Korea that do not share basic Western values have or are about to acquire the means to wreak devastating destruction on their foes. While President Obama claims to envision a world without nuclear weapons, any action toward that goal seems to be unilateral with the United States relying on a reduced supply of over-aged and untested weapons. Some feel that weakens the deterrent effect of our nuclear capability in the face of the threat of nuclear power in the hands of powers that do not like us. Clearly, America faces unprecedented challenges from the globalized world system. The solutions to these challenges are still being sought as the nation attempts to cope with a perilous future.

Conservatives and liberals differ from one another with respect to the issue of unilateralism and the defense of national sovereignty versus globalism and transnationalism. While conservatives are generally more concerned with the defense of sovereignty and the capacity of unilateral action without the approval of allies, liberals are inclined to favor a global or transnational approach. This issue emerged in August 2007 in the meeting of the heads of government from the United States, Canada, and Mexico in Montebello, Canada, to "harmonize" their respective economies, regulatory systems, and policies through what they call a Security and Prosperity Partnership (SPP), which is an umbrella for two dozen trilateral working groups. Professor Robert Pastor, a former Clinton administration insider now working with SPP, has already come out in favor of a common currency that he would call "the Americo," a proposal sure to offend conceptions of American national sovereignty.

ENDNOTES

1. For example, Norman Podhoretz, "World War IV: How It Started, What It Means, and Why We Have to Win," *Commentary*, 118, No. 2 (September 2004): 17–80.

2. Hans Morgenthau, *In Defense of the National Interest* (New York: Knopf, 1951); Edward H. Carr, *The Twenty Years' Crisis, 1919–1939*, 2nd ed. (New York: St. Martin's Press, 1964); and Kenneth Thompson, *Political Realism and the Crisis of World Politics* (Princeton, NJ: Princeton University Press, 1960).

3. Daniel Jonah Goldhagen, *Hitler's Willing Executioners: Ordinary Germans and the Holocaust* (New York: Vintage Books, 1997), documents that the Nazi's systematic extermination of the Jews in World War II was not only widely known but enthusiastically supported by millions of ordinary Germans.

4. On the concept of power in political science, see Harold Lasswell and Abraham Kaplan, *Power and Society* (New Haven, CT: Yale University Press, 1950); and Harold Lasswell, *Politics: Who Gets What, When, How* (Cleveland: Meridian Books, 1958).

5. See Hans Morgenthau, *Politics among Nations: The Struggle for Power and Peace*, 3rd ed. (New York: Knopf, 1962), Chapter 12, 178ff.

6. See the discussion of balance and equilibrium in Ernst Haas, "The Balance of Power: Concept, Prescription, or Propaganda," *World Politics*, 5 (1953): 459–474.

7. Morgenthau, *Politics among Nations*, 194.

8. Nicholas J. Spykman, *America's Strategy in World Politics* (New York: Harcourt Brace, 1942), 460.

9. The failure of American policy during this period is the theme of Carr's classic, *Twenty Years' Crisis*.

10. Samuel Huntington, *The Clash of Civilizations* (New York: Simon & Schuster/ Touchstone Books, 1997), 209–213.

11. Henry Kissinger, *American Foreign Policy*, expanded edition (New York: Norton, 1974), 31–32.

12. Thompson, Political Realism, 68.

13. Morgenthau, *Politics among Nations*, 414ff; Thompson, *Political Realism*, 189–197.

14. Kenneth Pollock, "Saddam's Useful Idiots," *Wall Street Journal*, March 15, 2004.

15. John Lewis Gaddis, *The United States and the Origins of the Cold War, 1941–1947* (New York: Columbia University Press, 1972).

16. Kennan first stated the doctrine of containment in a now celebrated "anonymous" article, X, "The Sources of Soviet Conduct," *Foreign Affairs*, 25 (July 1957): 566–582; see also Kennan, "The United States and the Soviet Union, 1917–1976," *Foreign Affairs*, 54 (July 1976): 570–590.

17. Reported in Charles Kegley and Eugene Wittkopf, *World Politics: Trend and Transformation*, 4th ed. (New York: St. Martin's Press, 1993), 93.

18. Sir Malcom Kennedy, *A Short History of Communism in Southeast Asia* (London: Wiedenfeld & Nicolson, 1957), 19, argues, "Communism and Nationalism in South and East Asia have become so intertwined as to be almost indistinguishable one from the other."

19. Virginia Thomson and Richard Adloff, *The Left Wing in Southeast Asia* (New York: Sloan for the I.P.R., 1950), 205.

20. James Thompson, Jr., "How Could Vietnam Happen: An Autopsy," in Charles Kegley and Eugene Wittkopf, eds., *Perspectives on American Foreign Policy* (St. Martin's Press: New York, 1983): 379ff.

21. For example, Norman Podhoretz, "The Case for Bombing Iran," *Commentary*, 123, No. 6 (June 2007), 17–23.

22. The strongest case for this conclusion is made by Huntington, *The Clash of Civilizations*, 209ff.

23. John Mearsheimer and Stephan Walt, "The Israeli Lobby," *London Review of Books*, 28, No. 9 (May 11, 2006). Compare a more extensive version, John Mearsheimer and Stephan Walt, "The Israeli Lobby and American Foreign Policy," *Middle East Policy*, 13, No. 3 (Fall 2006), 1–59.

24. Jimmy Carter, *Palestine: Peace Not Apartheid* (New York: Simon & Schuster, 2006).

25. Joan Peters, *From Time Immemorial: The Origins of the Arab–Jewish Conflict over Palestine* (New York: Harper & Row Perennial Library, 1984), 221.

26. Peters, *From Time Immemorial*, especially Chapters 11–14.

27. Near East Research Inc., *Near East Report*, September 13, 2004, p. 4.

28. *The International Jerusalem Post*, June 17, 2007, p. 17.

29. Jerusalem Centre for Public Affairs, "Israel Campus Beat," www.cpa.org; (Accessed October 4, 2004).

30. Yossi Klein Halevi and Michael B. Oren, "Israel's Unexpected Victory over Terrorism," *New Republic* (September 27, 2004): 19–20.

31. Daniel Pipes, *Militant Islam Reaches America* (New York: Norton, 2002), 52–64.

32. Daniel Pipes, "Who Is the Real Enemy," *Commentary*, 113 (January 2002).

33. See the analysis of this trend in Norman Podhoretz, "How to Win World War IV," *Commentary*, 113 (February 2002): 19–30.

34. Halevi and Oren, "Israel's Unexpected Victory over Terrorism," 19–23.

35. *The International Jerusalem Post*, June 17, 2007, p. 17.

36. Christopher Caldwell, "Islamic Europe," *The Weekly Standard* (October 4, 2004): 15–16.

37. Stephen Hayes, "Case Closed: The U.S. Government's Secret Memo Detailing Cooperation between Saddam Hussein and Osama Bin Laden," *The Weekly Standard*, 9, No. 11 (November 24, 2003). In this and in a subsequent book, Hayes details the ongoing pattern of meetings between Iraqi intelligence officials and military leaders and leading Al Qaeda operatives.

38. Amitai Etzioni, *Security First: For a Muscular, Moral Foreign Policy* (New Haven: Yale University Press, 2007).

39. E.g., Norman Podhoretz, "The Case for Bombing Iraq," *Commentary* (June 2007).

40. Whitney Raas and Austin Long, "Osirak Redux: Assessing Israel's Capacity to Destroy Iranian Nuclear Facilities," *International Security*, 31, No. 4 (Spring 2007): 7–33.

RESOURCES

Books

Albright, Madeleine. *The Mighty and the Almighty: Reflections on America, God, and World Affairs*. New York: Wadsworth, 2007.

Huntington, Samuel. *The Clash of Civilizations*. New York: Simon & Schuster, 1997.

Kegly, Charles W., and Blanton, Shannon L. *World Politics: Trends and Transformations*, 12th ed. New York: Wadsworth, 2009.

Morgenthau, Hans. *Politics among Nations: The Struggle for Power and Peace*, 3rd ed. New York: Knopf, 1963.

Oren, Michael B. *Power, Faith, and Fantasy: America in the Middle East: 1776 to the Present*. New York: Norton, 2008.

Chapter 13

Private Morality and Public Policy: Moral Values, the Constitution, and the Open Society

The concept of the open society, which provides for tolerance and diversity of all political, social and religious points of view, is a philosophy that the United States Supreme Court has appeared increasingly more willing to side with when interpreting the constitutional rights of individuals. Yet this idea of the open society sometimes runs counter to the moral values and public policy of groups on both the left and the right of the political spectrum.

The 1960s brought tremendous social change in the United States, and in many respects, the United States Supreme Court was in the middle of this change. During this time, the Court became more involved in upholding the ideals of individual liberty that flow from our Constitution, particularly in the area of rights of crime suspects, rights to privacy, and freedom of speech. Even before the 1960s, the Court had been moving toward greater involvement in protecting individual liberties and away from the New Deal controversies of government regulation of the economy. The Court's move to protect such individual rights precipitated a backlash among conservatives (both conservative Republicans and Southern conservative Democrats). In a speech in 1969, President Richard Nixon appealed to the "silent majority" in the hope of uniting conservatives against the permissiveness of the more liberal counterculture of the 60s. In 1973, the Supreme Court ruled in *Roe v. Wade* that the constitutional right to privacy included a woman's right to an abortion, providing an even greater rationale for Southern Democratic conservatives to begin uniting politically with conservative Republicans. Christian evangelist Jerry Falwell created the Moral Majority in the late 1970s as a conservative political movement designed to promote Christian family values and fight the open society. The Moral Majority heavily supported Ronald Reagan in the 1980 presidential election.

Ronald Reagan's election in 1980 heralded a process of transformation of the American right that had been occurring for decades (as Reagan captured a large portion of the Southern conservative Democratic vote). The traditional Republican Party of Calvin Coolidge, Herbert Hoover, and Robert Taft, a party whose principles included a hierarchical sense of human nature and a commitment to neo-classical (free market and pro-business) economics, was partially transformed into a neo-populist party of the right. This blue-collar Republicanism reflects a well-established populist tradition in American history and transformed the issue focus of the American right from a preeminent concern with the protection of the self-regulating market and the interests of the business and capitalist classes of society to a preeminent concern with social issues and the protection of their view of public morality.

Social conservatives are not the only group opposing the concept of an open society. In recent decades, some on the political left have also begun to oppose this concept through their support of laws designed to promote morality in the area of racial and cultural tolerance.

THE IDEA OF THE OPEN SOCIETY

The Neo-Populism Emergence on the Right and
Its Challenge to the Open Society

Populism is one of those social science terms without precise meaning or content; however, there is widespread agreement on several attributes associated with the concept. Rather than accepting the hierarchical view of human nature associated with traditional conservatism, populism presumes a commonsense wisdom of the working class and average person. Thus, Pat Buchanan, a well-known figure of the populist right, alluded to being backed by "the peasants with their pitchforks," while Bill O'Reilly of Fox News claims to be "looking out for the folks." Populism is not confined to the ideological right. From the political center, billionaire presidential candidate Ross Perot ran a populist campaign for president and later turned his populist rhetoric to fight against the adoption of the North American Free Trade Agreement, claiming it would hurt the regular working American. On the political left, John Edwards ran a populist campaign for president in 2008 with a theme about "Two Americas." Also on the political left, Ralph Nader has made a career out of claiming to protect the interests of working Americans against what he perceives as big corporations trying to take advantage of them. In this respect, populism further perceives that the interests of these common people are opposed by conspiratorial elites such as bankers, big business, bureaucrats, and politicians. This anti-elitist faith in the commonsense wisdom of the masses frequently degenerates into anti–intellectualism.

The populist tradition in the United States mobilized in the 1890s with the first nominating convention of the People's Party in 1892. Then it was basically a movement of Midwestern and southern farmers. It eventually became expressed through such charismatic mobilizers of the marginalized masses as Democrats Huey Long, William Jennings Bryan, and Tom Watson. The populist tradition appealed to marginalized individuals such as unskilled workers, small shopkeepers, smaller farmers, and others whose economic roles and well-being seemed threatened by the forces of modernization. These people evolved into a new right which was distinct from the old Republican conservatism of people like Calvin Coolidge. The clientele of the old right was dominated by big business, professionals, and other examples of the social and economically successful in our society. These well-educated members of the classic right tend to be more tolerant on social issues such as moral questions or civil rights. With the new clientele of the right, evangelical and fundamentalist Protestants and traditionalist Catholics joined such mainstream Protestants as Congregationalists, Episcopalians, and Presbyterians as the core support of the GOP. The relationship between the new and old right may be seen graphically in Figure 13.1.

The populist revolt on the American right was to a large extent a revolt against the secularization and increasing social permissiveness of the American culture. In particular, the evangelical and fundamentalist clientele of the new populism were offended by the extent to which this secularization became a

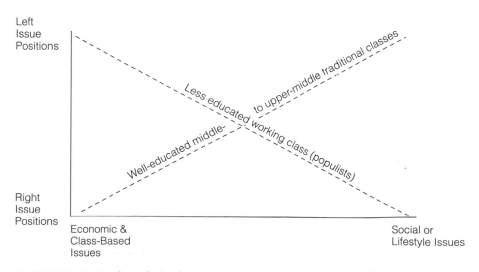

FIGURE 13.1 The Relationship Between the Old and the New Right

goal of official policy. Much of the new right's outrage is directed at *Roe v. Wade*, which created a right to an abortion, but their angst extends to other areas as well. Thus, we saw in Chapter 10 that the religious right is not so much offended by the fact that some people are homosexual as by official policy equating and legitimating the formal union between gays and lesbians as the moral equivalent of conventional heterosexual marriage. The GOP was transformed from the party of big business, the well-to-do, and the professional classes to a party whose clientele is more middle class and to a party that emphasizes social issues and government-mandated restoration of traditional Christian morality. Along with social issues, the emerging threat of militant Islamism brought foreign policy and national security issues to the forefront as discussed in the previous chapter, issues that differentiated what we have called the old right from the populist new right. The old right tends to emphasize tolerance, cosmopolitanism, openness toward other cultures and a belief that most international issues can be resolved through diplomacy. The new right is more chauvinistic and hawkish toward potential foes, bringing these social issues to the forefront of the American political agenda.

The importance of these social issues to the Republicans, as well as the tensions they cause with the economic conservatives of the party, played out in the 2007–2008 presidential primary campaign for the Republican nomination. Many social conservatives supported former Arkansas governor and one-time Baptist preacher Mike Huckabee. However, economic conservatives in the party balked at some of Huckabee's economic views and his record on taxes while governor of Arkansas. Huckabee ran somewhat of a populist campaign in the party nomination battle, appealing to the average working American while making opposition to abortion and same-sex marriage pivotal foundations of his campaign. While Huckabee lost the Republican nomination, the eventual winner of the Republican nomination John McCain reached out to social conservatives by picking Alaska governor Sarah Palin as his running mate. As a devout Christian, Palin made it a point in the campaign to voice her opposition to abortion by way of illustrating how she had elected not to have an abortion after she discovered during her last pregnancy that her soon-to-be child had been diagnosed with Down syndrome. Although some mainstream traditional economic conservatives do not take Palin seriously, she has attracted large crowds and lots of media attention and is seen as a potential presidential contender at some point in the near future.

Challenges to the Open Society on the Left

As noted earlier, challenges to the concept of an open society are not confined to populists on the new right. Some feminists, civil rights activists, and communitarians on the left have sought to impose their own moral values by promoting the regulation or abolition of speech or conduct that they believe is offensive, insensitive, or intolerant toward women or people of other races or cultures. Somewhat ironically, these groups seek to enforce the value of respect for tolerance of all peoples and views by regulating or criminalizing expressions of views that they consider to be intolerant or offensive. In this respect, these groups have advocated hate crimes legislation, laws against hate speech, and laws against speech that might be considered sexual harassment in the workplace. Other examples include the rise in speech codes on university campuses. In some instances, those on the left have resorted to protests and other political tactics to stop someone they believe is intolerant from speaking. When former Colorado Congressman Tom Tancredo, a strong conservative opponent of illegal immigration, attempted to give a speech at the University of North Carolina–Chapel Hill in the spring of 2009, hundreds of student protesters showed up, forcing university officials to shut down the speech before it even started. One student activist told the *Raleigh News and Observer*, "We don't think Tom Tancredo has the right to go around spewing his hate speech."[1] Many of these groups support laws making hate speech a crime. Thus, some liberal communitarians, like some social conservatives, seek to promote public policy that enforces their moral view of the world on others, in contradistinction to the idea of an open society, where all lifestyles and points of view are respected.

The Open Society and Tolerance of Diverse Ideas

The emerging importance of these social issues exists in a state of tension with another emerging force in American politics: the legitimation of a diverse and open society. The concept of the *open society* entails tolerance of diversity in *all* social, political, and religious points of view, that is, acknowledgment that different judgments on these subjects all have a right to be held and advocated. Democratic political institutions in the modern world are characterized, at a minimum, by genuine, regular competition among alternative political elites for the occupancy of decision-making roles.[2]

It is therefore presumed that the different conceptions of the public good, emanating from different interests, will be resolved by a process of bargaining and compromise in which no one group or interest will completely get its way. Each will be restrained by competing interests. The concept of an open society thus means that in matters of social, political, or ethical judgments, no one has a monopoly on truth or wisdom; therefore, it makes sense to leave the channels of communication open. As Justice Oliver Wendell Holmes said in perhaps one of the most eloquent of all expositions on the concept of freedom of thought:

> Persecution for the expression of opinions seems to me perfectly logical. If you have no doubt of your premises or your power, and want a certain result with all your heart, you naturally express your wishes in law, and sweep away all opposition. To allow opposition by speech seems to indicate that you think the speech impotent, as when a man says that he has squared the circle, or that you do not care wholeheartedly for the result, or that you doubt either your power or your premises. But when men have realized that time has upset many fighting faiths, they may come to believe more than they believe in the very foundations of their own conduct that the ultimate good desired is better reached by free trade in ideas—that the best test of truth is the power of thought to get

itself accepted in the competition of the market, and that truth is the
only ground upon which their wishes safely can be carried out. That,
at any rate, is the theory of our Constitution.[3]

The notion here is that if opinions or philosophies are untrue or pernicious,
they will be rejected in an open society aware of competing ideas. It should not
be necessary to use the enforcement machinery of the state to repress any set of
ideas, even if such ideas are considered immoral by conservatives or intolerant by
liberals. Rather, differences in opinion should be dealt with by discussion—the
interchange of ideas. The open society further entails the principle that each perspective on these essentially subjective matters on which reasonable people will
always disagree is equally legitimate—that there is no official position on matters
of morality and religion. The open society refers to a libertarian view of how
government treats morality. The new politics of social issues, however, centers
on such concepts as family values, community, and political correctness that entail the assumption that some positions on such issues are preferable to competing
positions and thus ought to be protected or encouraged with public policy.
More importantly, competing positions are penalized and therefore not tolerated
by public policy. The principle that all perspectives on religious, philosophical,
and political positions are equally legitimate was tested in the 2008 campaign of
Mitt Romney, a Morman, for the Republican presidential nomination. Some
religious Christians said they could never vote for a person of the Morman faith,
which they dismiss as a cult.

The open society position—that all political and social points of view should
not only be tolerated but may be advocated—has been put to the test in the first
decade of the twenty-first century by the widely perceived threat of militant
Islam to perpetrate acts of terror in the United States. There have been calls to
silence radical mullahs who allegedly preach to their young followers in their
madrasses (Muslim day schools) the duty to carry out violent attacks on
Americans. Here, the value of the open society comes into tension with the
need to provide the security that would prevent random killings of civilians. This
tension was epitomized in the controversy surrounding the U.S. Patriot Act. The
Patriot Act was enacted in 2001 in the wake of the events of September 11 of
that year: it authorized the gathering of data about potential terrorists, including
the interception of phone calls from known Islamist radicals to other Islamists
overseas; Section 215 authorized access to such sensitive data as library and medical
records. This bill was widely attacked by liberals as an invasion of the right of
privacy but defended by conservatives as a necessary tool to allow the government
to protect the lives and property of its citizens against a severe and ongoing threat.
The law was scheduled to sunset (expire) in 2005 unless renewed. The law was
renewed in March 2006, but only after compromises which now require
high-level approval of requests for Section 215 data.

The various parts of the First Amendment all may be seen as protecting the
concept of the open society, that some perspectives and values may not be
suppressed by dominant majorities. The whole point of the concept of civil liberties is that there are some things that majorities may not do, no matter how

politically dominant they are. This position that majorities may need to be suppressed is in a state of tension with the populist perspective, which places great faith in the wisdom of the masses and generally seeks procedures to guarantee that majorities of the moment can determine the course of public policy.

Community and Family Values versus the Open Society

The central precepts of the open society and of multiculturalism, that all perspectives are equally legitimate, exist in a state of tension with the recently rediscovered concept of community. The principle of community, as advocated by such communitarian spokespersons as Amitai Etzioni, entails the idea that the essential nature of a society is defined by a set of shared values and assumptions.[4] Thus, it may be argued by conservative communitarians that the United States is a Western society defined by the traditions of Western political thought and the Judeo-Christian religious tradition and that competing religious and philosophical perspectives, while tolerated, are not equally legitimate in defining this social system. There has been a widespread perception among conservative communitarians that the radical Islamist movement poses a direct threat to Western civilization and its values. This perception created a challenge for the multiculturalist view that all religious perspectives are equally valid and should be given equal tolerance. Thus, some scholars since at least the mid-1990s have been arguing that radical Islam is an enemy of the West—that a clash of civilizations is inevitable—while other scholars have cautioned that we should avoid stigmatizing Muslims.[5]

Conservative communitarians in general argue that these shared Judeo–Christian Western values are the cement that binds the social system together as a coherent entity and gives it meaning. America, in this perspective, stands for something; it is not merely the collection of individuals who happen to reside there. Moreover, it is argued that multiculturalism carried to its logical conclusion can lead to a *segmented society*—a society in which the different cultural segments are mutually isolated from one another. Such societies in the world with mutually isolated and alienated segments have not generally fared well as coherent entities able to effectively resolve issues. Our neighbor Canada has been beset with secessionist sentiment among its French-speaking subculture for some time. Belgium, where the Flemish and French-speaking Walloons have often been at odds, has gone from a unitary state to a confederation. Nigeria has experienced a civil war between its Muslim elite and one of its Christian tribes and is proving ungovernable. The list could go on, but the message is that some level of community may be necessary in order for a political system to retain stability and effectiveness. The Christian right in the United States, although in disagreement with the communitarians on a number of issues, has advocated widespread acceptance of traditional, bourgeois moral values—what are referred to as family values—as precisely the kind of social cement of which we have been speaking. Moreover, political scientist Robert Putnam of Harvard finds in a recent five-year study that a culturally diverse and segmented society weakens the institutions that sustain communities and increases interpersonal distrust.[6]

Family values is a somewhat imprecise term that has acquired a great deal of symbolic content as a code word for many of the values that are held to delineate America as a community defined by its Western heritage. It appears to refer to many of the principles of the Judeo–Christian tradition that underlies the sense of America as a community. Family values has therefore been used to advocate against equal moral and social status for gays and lesbians; against redefinition of appropriate gender roles, and therefore for the traditional two-parent family with a male breadwinner and a female bearer and nurturer of children; and even against the promotion of effective contraception. In other words, family values has come almost to symbolize a defense of middle-class morality against the forces of secularization and change that seem to accompany modernization. To its opponents, the concept of family values suggests a kind of monism as opposed to pluralism and the open society—the idea that only a particular set of values are legitimate and that there are distinct limits to the extent to which contradictory values will be tolerated. The issues generated by the defense of family values are particularly divisive in the United States because the process of *secularization*— defined by decline of conventional religion and of regular church attendance and professed belief in traditional religious doctrines, along with restriction of religion to private spheres of life—has affected the nation to a significant extent, but much less than in other Western nations. Thus, while about 42 percent of Americans attend church weekly according to one 2008 Gallup survey, regular attendance in the United Kingdom and other Western European countries is less than half that number. A 2009 Gallup Poll indicated that less than half of all Americans believe in evolution. Thus, Americans are more likely to be committed to support policies designed to reinforce Christian doctrine symbolized by the concept of family values.

On another front, the partial secularization of American society has emboldened many gays and lesbians to ask for equal treatment from the government in various walks of life, a movement discussed in some detail in Chapter 10. For example, gays and lesbians have asked that they be allowed to serve in the armed forces without regard to their sexual orientation, and they have also pursued the right to be treated equally in marriage—working for the legal recognition of same-sex marriage. For our purposes here, it is important to note that the goal of the gay and lesbian equal rights movement (also known as the Human Rights Campaign) is to receive equal treatment from the government. This goal offends supporters of family values, resulting in such phenomena as the constitutional referendum in Colorado banning laws and actions that forbid discrimination against homosexuals, a referendum subsequently struck down by the Supreme Court in the *Roemer* case.

The concept of the open society is therefore in logical conflict with the support of family values. A theme of this chapter will be how this tension generates political issues. Among these issues, the following ones will be dealt with: reproductive freedom, including access to effective contraception and medically supervised abortion; the suppression of pornography and the pursuit of sexual pleasure; the right to die and end-of-life care; and the protection of the practice of traditional institutional religion. Also included in this chapter is the conflict between the open society and efforts to suppress hate speech, offensive conduct, and other points of view that some on the left believe are morally intolerant and unworthy of expression.

Meanwhile, it is important to recognize that the concept of the open society is not merely of philosophical value, but is an important bulwark for the structure for democracy itself. Without acceptance of the legitimacy of positions with which one disagrees, those in power will tend to use the powerful administrative tools at their disposal (e.g., command of law enforcement and the tax structure) to suppress those who advocate those positions and thereby to suppress political opposition itself. But democracy by definition entails regular and meaningful competition for political office. *Therefore, governmental imposition of a given perspective on social and moral issues is held by libertarians to threaten the political competition that is one of the cornerstones of a democratic system. Yet granting equal status to all perspectives on such issues is held by conservatives and some liberals to threaten the sense of community that is the glue that binds society and enables it to function as a coherent entity.*

The Role of the Court and the Presumption of Constitutionality

There exists in our society a restraintist philosophy concerning the role that the law and courts ought to play in the democratic political process. The philosophy grows out of the reality that the U.S. Constitution and fifty state constitutions are regarded as higher laws than ordinary legislation; hence, any *statute* (a law passed by a legislature) or government action inconsistent with that system's constitution is null and void. Courts determine such inconsistencies by interpretation of the relevant laws and constitutional provisions. But sometimes, the answer as to whether a statute or government action violates the Constitution is unclear. The philosophy of restraint holds that when there is doubt about the legality or constitutionality of the actions of the political process, judges ought to interpret the Constitution and laws so as to uphold that political action rather than impose their own values on society. In other words, when there is doubt as to whether the actions of the political or administrative sectors of society are constitutional, such doubt should be resolved in favor of these actions. This restraintist position is called the *presumption of constitutionality*.[7]

This presumption conflicts with the judicial activist idea that the Constitution entails unambiguously discernible principles and values that the Court is duty-bound to protect against intrusion by a government reflecting a current of popular opinion. Judicial activists look to the courts to protect the interests and values of individuals against an abusive majority by stipulating that there are some things a government may not do regardless of its support or of public opinion. When a court, using an interpretation of the Constitution on which reasonable people might disagree, nullifies a law or governmental action, we say the court is practicing *judicial activism*. Both conservatives and liberals have relied upon an activist court to protect principles that they regarded as fundamental to the American system against governments with which they disagreed. Conservatives relied on the Court to protect a nearly absolute right of property from our founding to the late 1930s. In the post–World War II era, liberals relied upon the Court to protect individual values such as First Amendment freedoms or racial equality. Limits on what government may or may not do to people are often referred to as *rights*. Controversy arises when the finding of such rights is not based on an unambiguously stated constitutional principle.

Of course, judges have a choice in how to interpret the laws or the Constitution. Otherwise, all the decisions of the Court would be unanimous, which is emphatically not the case. Presidents therefore appoint justices to the Court who, they predict, will reflect the values that the president purports to represent. The importance of who controls the presidency is magnified by the power to shape the direction of the Court even long after that president leaves office. President George W. Bush, for example, altered the ideological makeup of the Court by appointing the conservative Samuel Alito to replace the more moderate Sandra Day O'Connor. President Barack Obama has not had a chance yet to change the ideological direction of the court, as the only justices who have retired are liberal justices, and Obama has replaced them presumably with more liberals. In 2009, liberal Justice David Souter retired, and President Obama replaced him with another liberal, Sonia Sotomayor. When liberal justice John Paul Stevens retired in 2010, he was replaced by Elena Kagan, another liberal. As of summer 2010, the makeup of the Court is shown in Table 13.1.

A consistent practitioner of judicial restraint will assume the limits that the Constitution places on government actions are usually unclear and therefore he or she will tend to uphold the government actions whether he or she approves of them or not. The political preferences of the consistent restraintist are irrelevant. During the middle of the last century, liberal Justice Felix Frankfurter was a consistent restraintist on the Supreme Court who opposed the idea of the Court regularly striking down the actions of a democratically elected legislature or the executive branch. An activist, on the other hand, assumes that the Constitution places more clear limits on what government may do. Therefore, the activist is more prone to nullify what government has done. The choice of what to nullify will normally be affected by the justice's own political preferences. Hence, activists may use their judicial role to impose their own policy preferences on the country. Activists are therefore either liberal or conservative activists.

While the Supreme Court's liberals in the 1960s were perceived as activist, interpreting the Constitution to provide various rights not directly found in the Constitution, such as the right to abortion, the conservative majority on the

T A B L E   13.1   The Supreme Court in 2010

Conservative	Liberal
John Roberts, Chief Justice	Ruth Bader Ginsburg
Antonin Scalia	Elena Kagan
Samuel Alito	Sonia Sotomayor
Clarence Thomas	Stephen Breyer
Swing Vote: Anthony Kennedy	

Supreme Court in the 1990s were perceived as activist, striking down laws of Congress where they believed Congress had exceeded its authority under the commerce clause of the constitution. With the appointments of conservatives Alito and Roberts under the Bush administration, it is unclear whether these two conservatives will be restraintist or activist. It is also unclear whether Justice Sonia Sotomayor, President Obama's 2009 appointee, will turn out to be restraintist or activist. Oftentimes, conservatives on the court appeal for "restraint" when reviewing a law or action favorable to conservatives, while liberals appeal for "restraint" when reviewing a law or action viewed as favorable to liberals. Thus, in reality, there appear to be few true restraintists on the current court.

Rights are legally or constitutionally imposed limits on what government may choose to do. Government actions to encourage and protect family values have come into conflict with variously interpreted rights from the First Amendment, as well as with the right of *privacy*, a right not expressly stated as such in the Constitution but inferred by judicial interpretation. The fact that the exercise of the right of privacy is based upon judicial inference has been used by some conservatives as a point of argument to claim that the Constitution does not explicitly guarantee such a right. The inferential basis of the right of privacy is in the Fourth Amendment protection against "unreasonable searches and seizures," in the Fifth Amendment Due Process Clause, and in the much-overlooked Ninth Amendment that tells us "the enumeration in the Constitution of certain rights shall not be construed to deny or disparage others retained by the people." The origins of the Ninth Amendment arise out of the founders' natural law view of rights—that rights are derived from God, not from government, and thus are unalienable. The Constitution conferred limited powers upon the federal government, as designed by its original drafters. There was a fear at the time of its drafting that if explicit rights were listed in a bill of rights, there would be the assumption by implication that those rights not listed could be regulated by the government. The Ninth Amendment was placed in the bill of rights as a catch-all phrase for our rights, designed to check the federal government from regulating rights which may have been inadvertently omitted from the Constitution. Thus, the Ninth Amendment essentially reiterates the premise that the Constitution confers limited powers on the federal government and that the people retain all of their rights. The conceptual problem with the amendment is about who decides what these other rights are that are not listed. This is nothing less than an invitation for future generations and courts to find unlisted rights by inference, an elastic clause for the Bill of Rights. Yet the concept of a right of privacy—that some areas of behavior or life are none of the government's business—is one of the core attributes by which a relatively liberal society is differentiated from one with totalitarian tendencies and aspirations.

Among the purposes for which the right of privacy has been used are to protect access to information and technology for effective contraception and to professionally performed abortions, goals that conflict with the principle entailed by the family values belief that human sexuality should primarily be confined to the instrumental goal of reproduction within the bonds of marriage. The privacy right was first explicated by the Court in *Griswold v. Connecticut*, a case that struck down Connecticut's ban on the practice of artificial contraception (contraception using chemical or barrier methods). When the Court later used this inferred right to resolve the sensitive and controversial issue of the legal status of abortions by judicial fiat, this resolution proved unacceptable or illegitimate to the anti-abortion or pro-life forces on the losing side. The legal status of abortion is perhaps the issue that generates the most passion and intensity of conflict of all the issues that involve the clash of inviolable moral principles of conservatives on the one hand, and the secularized, more libertarian concept of the open society on the other.

ABORTION, BIRTH CONTROL, AND THE LAW

Prior to 1973, most states criminalized abortions. The common exception was an abortion permitted when necessary to save the life of the mother. As noted earlier, *Roe v. Wade* (1973) overturned these laws as a violation of the right of privacy, a right not specifically mentioned in the Constitution, but inferred from the Fourth, Fifth, and Ninth Amendments and applied to the states through the Fourteenth Amendment.[8] Specifically, the opinion said that states are forbidden to ban abortions in the first trimester (three months) of pregnancy; states may regulate abortions in the interest of the health of the mother in the second trimester; and the state may choose to ban abortions in the final trimester unless the health (broadly considered) of the mother is in danger. The Court found that states had no "compelling interest" to intervene during the first trimester in the private decision of a pregnant woman to abort. Abortions are statistically safer than childbirth for the mother during the first trimester, when performed by competent medical personnel in sanitary surroundings. However, abortions become progressively more dangerous during the second trimester; this gives states a compelling interest in protecting the health of the mother. At around the beginning of the third trimester, the fetus becomes viable outside the womb, and the now potentially independent new life becomes another compelling interest. These three legal distinctions in time are, of course, approximations. Fetuses born in the second trimester have survived, and fetuses born after the second trimester sometimes do not live. Moreover, the trimester division comes increasingly under question as medical advances place the viability of fetuses earlier in pregnancy. A Missouri law upheld in 1989 requires fetal viability tests on any fetus over twenty weeks old.[9] Critics argue that no fetus could survive at that early age and that the tests are dangerous and inconclusive. However, anti-abortion (or pro-life) forces view the fetus, no matter how small, as no different from a baby. Pro-life forces often use graphic images of aborted fetuses in protests to make their point. The recorded rate of abortion has almost doubled since *Roe v. Wade* from about fifteen per 100,000 live births to about twenty-six. However, it should be noted that the pre-*Roe* figure may be low because illegal abortions were not accurately recorded.

Despite charges that *Roe* grants the right to abortion on demand, that case affords no absolute constitutional right to a third-stage abortion. And despite the imagery employed by pro-life forces, as in Bernard Nathanson's film, *The Silent*

Scream, well over 95 percent of all abortions are performed in the first trimester. Second-trimester abortions occur principally because of the availability of amniocentesis, a procedure that shows whether a fetus (or unborn child) is seriously flawed, as with spina bifida. Amniocentesis is possible only in the fourth month of the gestation period. Although hundreds of third-trimester abortions do take place, it is difficult to find physicians willing to perform them, as a recent *Los Angeles Times* notes, and those that do are subject to violent threats from extremists on the pro-life side. In 2009, Dr. George Tiller, a provider of late term abortions in Kansas, was gunned down inside his own church by a pro-life extremist.

Despite the rarity of late term abortions, attention in the late 1990s began to be focused on a particularly brutal form of late-stage abortion known as partial birth abortion, a procedure in which the unborn baby is extracted from the womb except for the head. The base of the baby's skull is pierced and the brain is sucked out, collapsing the size of the head, at which point the head is removed from the woman. This procedure is defended as being less threatening to the health and well-being of the mother, although these details do not serve to enhance public support of the pro-choice positions. Proponents of the availability of this procedure argue that there may be circumstances in which the health problems of the pregnant woman could not have been known until too late in the pregnancy and that alternative methods are effectively unavailable or unnecessarily risky to the pregnant woman. However, even many of those who support a woman's right to choose to have a legal abortion were repulsed by the details of this procedure, as well as by the claim that many of these procedures are performed on healthy women bearing healthy fetuses. Disagreements exist as to the frequency with which this procedure occurs; estimates range from a few hundred to a few thousand. The widespread public revulsion to partial birth abortion has led to repeated attempts to ban the procedure.

An attempted federal ban on this procedure was vetoed by President Clinton; however, the state of Nebraska passed such a ban in 2002. This ban was struck down in the case of *Stenberg v. Carhart*. However, with the recent changes in the makeup of the Court, a federal ban on the procedure, the Partial Birth Abortion Act signed by President George W. Bush, was upheld in *Gonzales v. Carhart* in April 2007.[10] The Supreme Court was bitterly divided in a 5–4 vote with the two new Bush appointees effectively reversing the majority in the *Stenberg* case and upholding the ban. It is not clear that this more conservative court would overturn *Roe*, however, as Chief Justice Roberts has stated his respect for precedent and "settled law."

The ease by which a pregnancy may be terminated was enhanced by the development of a pill (RU–486) in France in 1988 that induces a spontaneous expulsion of a newly implanted embryo without the necessity of any further medical procedure. The Roman Catholic Church in France forced the pharmaceutical firm that produced the pill, Roussel-Uclaf, to withdraw it from the market, but then-President Mitterrand ordered the pill placed back on the market. Faced with a threatened boycott of its other pharmaceutical products organized by the American pro-life forces, the firm was reluctant to introduce the pill into the United States. However, it was finally persuaded to donate the patent on the pill to the New York–based World Population Council, a contraceptive research group. The Food and Drug Administration has approved the pill as safe and effective and it is now widely available. President George W. Bush angered feminist and abortion rights groups by delaying a decision allowing Medicaid coverage of a morning-after pill known as Plan B that the FDA in 1996 had found "safe and effective" (a pill that prevented the implantation of a fertilized egg in the womb). The pill is currently available. Yet the administration had Medicare cover the costs of anti-impotency pills such as Viagra or Levitra. The Obama administration has reversed some of President Bush's policies on this issue, such as requiring military hospitals and clinics to carry the morning-after pill. Dr. Nancy Jasper of Columbia University Presbyterian Hospital claims that the pill is 89 percent effective in cutting down unwanted pregnancies when used within seventy-two hours of intercourse. However, Patricia Lamantia, director of the University of Pittsburgh at Greensburg Student Health Center, argues that making the pill available "makes it too easy to have unprotected sex," an argument that indicates greater concern with deterring the sexual activity than with the prevention of unwanted pregnancies.

The Supreme Court's *Roe* decision does not require any physician to give an abortion or require any medical personnel to participate in the procedure. Rather, it says in effect that when physicians decide to give abortions to patients who freely seek them at a time when the procedure is safer than childbirth itself, it is none of the state's business. Hence, the agenda of the pro-life forces is to prevent others from violating what they regard as the moral principles of the right to life. Many hospitals, especially religiously sponsored ones, refuse to permit abortions to be performed in their facilities. In some areas, this makes legal abortions unavailable to persons who want them and who are willing and able to pay.

Meanwhile, Pennsylvania enacted a law erecting a number of barriers to the exercise of abortion rights: a mandatory twenty-four-hour waiting period for women seeking abortions, a requirement that a doctor inform the patient of the development of the fetus and of alternatives to abortions, and that minors seeking an abortion obtain the consent of one parent or a judge. The constitutionality of the law was challenged, and both pro-choice and pro-life forces saw the case as providing an instrument for the Supreme Court to issue a definitive reevaluation of the constitutionality of *Roe*. In June 1992, the Supreme Court upheld the Pennsylvania law's abortion restrictions, with several justices citing an "undue burden" standard that Justice Sandra Day O'Connor had urged be adopted in an earlier case. This standard stated that restrictions on abortions were constitutional if they did not place "an undue burden" on women seeking abortions. The Court also, however, explicitly upheld *Roe's* right to abortion.[11]

Of course, abortions are not cheap, and economic considerations limit their availability to the poor. Congress has perpetuated this situation by forbidding the use of Medicaid funds for abortions (which during much of the 1970s were provided under the program) except to save the life of the mother, even in cases of rape or incest. However, it is important to note that one study showed that the cutoff in Medicaid funds has not substantially reduced the incidence of legal abortions. Apparently, women who want legal abortions will undergo other sacrifices or find other means to pay for them.

Access to abortion is not merely a matter of the legal right to abortion, but of having in fact access to medical personnel and facilities willing and able to perform them. Clinic access has become a contentious political issue. An aggressive pro-life movement has been led by such groups as Operation Rescue, whose tactics include the physical obstruction of clinics performing abortions, and a "Nuremberg Files" website inciting viewers against 225 identified physicians who performed abortions. Two operators of abortion clinics sought injunctive relief from the website-induced harassment under the RICO (antiracketeering statutes) while the demonstrators claimed their right to such activity was protected by the freedom of speech clause of the First Amendment. In *Planned Parenthood of Columbia v. American Coalition of Life Activists*, the Ninth Circuit Court of Appeals upheld the freedom of speech claims against a court injunction prohibiting harassment in the form of mobilizing hatred of abortion providers through the Internet.[12] Congress and some states in the early 1990s enacted laws designed to protect access to abortion facilities by restricting the activities and distances of protesters. The Supreme Court in *Hill v. Colorado*[13] had upheld a state law establishing restrictions on anti-abortion protesters within 100 feet of the clinic, commanding an eight-foot space between the protester and the abortion clinic client. The difference between the cases is that the Colorado law involved physical impediments to abortion clinic clients while the Columbia case did not involve physical force, a distinction that the Court has long used.[14]

Pro-life forces have responded in many cases by escalating their tactics, including resorting to violence against medical personnel performing abortions. Since 1993, five people, including two physicians, were murdered at abortion clinics by three individuals who at some point have been associated with the organized harassment of abortion clinics and their patrons. In 1993, Dr. David Gunn was shot and killed by Michael Griffen of Rescue America; in 1994, Dr. John Britton and his escort were murdered by Paul Hill; and in 1995, two receptionists at abortion clinics in Massachusetts were slain by an individual who had been associated with picketing abortion clinics. Pro-choice people were outraged that a number of people in the pro-life movement suggested that these killings were somehow justified in the light of the many unborn children killed by abortion. John Burt of Rescue America said that the shootings were "unfortunate" but a large number of "babies' lives will be saved." Mainstream pro-life groups strongly condemned such killings. Many medical personnel offering abortion services saw these events as an implicit threat to the health and safety of themselves and their families. In some cases, the threats were explicit. This violence continued through 1996 with the bombing of a Planned Parenthood clinic that performed abortions in Spokane, Washington, and a fatal bombing in Birmingham, Alabama, in early 1998. As mentioned earlier, in 2009 Dr. George Tiller, a provider of late-term abortion services, was killed inside his own church in Kansas. As a result of such violence, numerous doctors who were performing abortions are no longer willing to do so. Fewer medical students are electing to learn the procedure, although a couple of states now require that medical residents in obstetrics-gynecology be trained in abortion procedures. It is still true, however, that while abortion may be technically legal, in many parts of the

United States it is difficult to find medical personnel willing and able to perform the procedure. This is particularly true in rural areas.

Access to abortion continues to be a source of contention in politics at the national level. The debate over access to abortion became heated in Congress while lawmakers were considering President Obama's health care reform bill in 2010. Many pro-life Democrats in the House of Representatives, led by Bart Stupak of Michigan, held up agreement on the health care bill because the language in the proposed legislation could allow individuals to use federal funds to buy health insurance plans that covered abortion procedures. Only after President Obama issued an executive order prohibiting federal funds for use in elective abortions did pro-life Democrats agree to support the bill, thus allowing its passage. But the legislation did not survive the vote without controversy, as conservatives argued that the executive order did not adequately safeguard against the use of federal funds for abortion, and that the current president or a future president could do away with the order at any time. During the final vote on passage, as Congressman Stupak was giving a speech at the podium defending his deal with the President, Republican Congressman Randy Neugebauer of Lubbock, Texas yelled out "Baby Killer," to the shock and astonishment of his colleagues at this breach in etiquette on the House floor.

Contraception.   The same logic that impels concern over the availability of safe, legal abortion applies to the availability of effective contraception. The argument of pro-life forces that abortion should not be used for birth control is strengthened if effective contraception is realistically available. Yet some conservative forces have opposed the promotion of effective contraception. One example of this is the opposition of such groups to sex education in school on the grounds that it encourages promiscuity. Another is the example of the so-called "squeal rule" established by the Reagan administration and avidly supported by forces of the religious right. This was the executive order denying federal funds to any clinic that provided contraception aid to minors unless the parents of such minors were notified. Supporters pointed to the value of parental responsibility and control of minors, a quintessential *family values* position, involving not only parental control but also the protection of middle-class moral principles, especially with regard to extramarital sexual activity. Opponents argued that such a rule would only discourage minors from seeking such aid, not from engaging in sexual activity.

This conclusion is supported by an early 2005 study done in Texas on the impact of abstinence-only programs. The study found that subjecting that state's teenagers to a systematic abstinence-only course did not reduce the probability of their engaging in sexual activity. Such uninformed and unprotected sexual activity would result in exacerbating the already critical level of unwanted teenage pregnancy. Supporters of the abstinence-only program argue that the study was flawed but doubts about the effectiveness of such programs have been widespread for some time. A national study in 2007 reached the same conclusion.

The conservative assumption appears to be that the ability to have illicit sex without the risks of pregnancy encourages promiscuity. The liberal position is that sexual activity is inevitable; therefore, denying access to abortion and birth control will merely produce the spillover effect of unwanted pregnancy. This liberal position was manifested in a compulsory school assembly in a Boulder, Colorado, high school in spring 2007 in which several speakers advocated the use of condoms, masturbation, same-sex activity, and experimenting with certain illegal drugs, causing an outraged response from conservative political commentators who resented the school sponsoring an assault on their deeply held values. Meanwhile, some spokespeople on the religious right apparently regard as immoral anything that enables people to engage in sexual activity for mere pleasure while avoiding its natural consequences. Promotion of family stability and traditional sexual morality are inseparable, they argue. Supporters of the policy of encouraging condom use, many of whom also are concerned with the availability of safe, legal abortions, argue that abstention from sexual activity may be desirable, but that it is not realistic to expect it.

The Moral Issue.   Opponents of abortion base their opposition mainly on the premise that the fetus is in fact a human being; therefore, legal abortions are tantamount to the legalization of murder. The point of disagreement is whether life begins at the point of conception. Many aver that human life commences at birth or when the fetus becomes viable outside the womb. Opponents of abortion—led by many New Right conservatives and religious groups—argue that legalized abortions encourage greater use of this procedure, to the point that the procedure becomes a form of birth control. Moral considerations require the state to take a stand against what these opponents see as legalized killing. The data seem to support the claim that the number of abortions has increased considerably since abortion was made legal (though the last two decades have seen a decline in the abortion rate), and it is undeniable that many fetuses are aborted by pregnant women simply because they do not want the child, rather than for reasons of health.

However, supporters of legal abortion (i.e., pro-choice groups)—who tend to be liberal and religiously secularized—object to the contentions of pro-life groups on two grounds. First, whether legal or not, women who need abortions will seek them out. Second, pro-choice groups argue that the availability of legal abortions is fundamentally an issue of protecting the civil right of women to make their own decisions about themselves—in this case, that is, the right not to allow the state to dictate what choices they may make about their own bodies.

Pro-choice activists point out that abortion has long been a widespread reality, legal or otherwise. By criminalizing the procedure, the state may reduce the number of abortions, but it cannot prevent many abortions from occurring. Criminalizing abortion may have the impact of driving many pregnant women to incompetent and untrained abortionists, with disastrous effects on the lives and health of the women involved, although pro-life forces dispute these claims. When abortion was against the law, many women died each year, from crudely performed, unsanitary, illegal abortions—women who in many cases would have lived had legal abortions been available. The government of Ecuador, for example, where abortion is completely criminalized, complained in early 2005 of a high and rising number of women dying from incompetently performed illegal abortions. Therefore, supporters of legal abortion emphasize that the number of unborn children saved by criminalizing abortion must be balanced against the number of pregnant women killed or seriously maimed.

To pro-life groups, these considerations pale in the face of their strongly held beliefs that readily available, affordable, and safe abortion (1) constitutes a form of murder, and (2) encourages sexual promiscuity. Here again we find a concern with deterring the promiscuous activity overriding the prevention of unwanted pregnancies, which clearly exacerbates the demand for abortion. The feelings here are so strong that the arguments on this issue are antithetical moral assumptions that cannot be resolved by discussion. What pro-choice groups call choice or freedom, pro-life groups call promiscuity or irresponsibility. Yet both groups are referring to the ability to engage in sexual activity without suffering undesired consequences. The essential facts are not in dispute; rather, the moral interpretation of such facts is the essence of the issue.

Moreover, the issue of legalized abortion is perceived as a matter of equality for women, as the legal availability of abortions gives women greater decision-making power over their lives. They have greater freedom to pursue sexual activity—as men do—without suffering the consequences of childbearing, and they need not retire from economic pursuits to raise children from unwanted pregnancies. Abortion and birth control offer greater alternative possibilities to women beyond their traditional roles of homemaker and raiser of children. On the other hand, many opponents of abortion see such greater sexual freedom as leading to sexual irresponsibility and increased rates of adolescent pregnancy. It should also be noted that the issue of legalized abortion is not seen by everyone as a woman's equality issue. The opponents of legalized abortion see it as a fundamental moral issue, a question of human life and dignity and a defense of the family values that defined the United States as a community.

The Supreme Court, as constituted at this writing, does not appear disposed to reject the right to abortion as such but, with a current 5–4 conservative majority, the Court may act to further restrict that right. If *Roe* were to be reconsidered by the Court, however, the decision would be vulnerable on the inferential nature of the right of privacy that underlies it and on the justification of when the fetus acquires life. The Court's justification for allowing states to ban abortion in the third trimester is based on the presumed point at which the fetus becomes independent of the mother in the sense of survival outside the womb. However, since the decision was handed down in 1973, medical technology has enabled fetuses to survive miscarriage in the second trimester, in rare cases as early as twenty-three weeks. The National Abortion Rights Action League (NARAL) estimates as of 2005 that should *Roe* be overturned, pro-life forces in thirty-eight states have the power and determination to again criminalize most or all abortions throughout the gestation period.

The determination of pro-life forces to criminalize abortion remains unabated despite opinion polls indicating that a majority of Americans support access to legal abortion in some circumstances. The incidence of direct physical impediment to the operation of clinics or medical facilities performing abortions intensified during the 1990s coordinated by Operation Rescue, and employed tactics of sit-ins at abortion facilities. Pro-choice forces have responded by advocating laws and injunctions severely restricting pro-life speech and demonstrations near abortion facilities. The Supreme Court, it will be recalled, upheld such a law in the *Hill* case but also upheld the free speech rights of pro-life activists to mobilize opposition to abortion providers through their website. Pro-life forces argue that this is an assertion of their free speech rights, a right that is asserted on both sides of the morality and family values debate.

End-of-Life Care, Assisted Suicide, and the Preservation of Life

The moral perspective underlying the religious right's position on contraception and abortion, the perspective that elevates the preservation of life, regardless of its quality, to a moral absolute, emerged in the related issue of assisted suicide or euthanasia. Most states do not allow assisted suicide, but currently three states allow physician-assisted suicide (Oregon, Washington, and Montana). The debate of what rights people have toward the end of life reached the Supreme Court in 1990 in the case *Cruzan v. Director, Missouri Department of Health*. In that case, Nancy Cruzan suffered injuries in a car accident which caused her to be in a persistent vegetative state, and her family requested that life support be turned off. However, the state of Missouri objected, and the Supreme Court ruled that her family must present "clear and convincing evidence" that Ms. Cruzan would have wanted to refuse medical treatment and have life support turned off in this situation. To satisfy the Supreme Court's new legal standard clarifying the rights of persons in a coma or a persistent vegetative state, the family then returned to the trial court with more evidence to support their claim that Ms. Cruzan would not have wanted to remain on life support.

Questions about how someone wants to be treated near the end of life or while in a permanent coma can be addressed using a living will. However, most people never take the time to draw one up. Thus, questions over the right to terminate life-sustaining treatment (if the person is unable to speak for themselves) often depend on what statements the person in question may have made earlier in life about their intentions. This debate attracted national attention in the case of Terry Schiavo, a Florida woman who had been in a persistent vegetative state for years. Her husband filed legal action to have her feeding tube removed, but Ms. Schiavo's parents fought their son-in-law in court for years to keep their daughter alive. After Ms. Schiavo's feeding tube was removed for a second time by a state judge in 2003, the Florida legislature got involved in an emergency session, passing "Terri's Law," which gave Florida Governor Jeb Bush authority to intervene. However, the Florida state courts struck down the law, and by January 2005, the parents had taken the case all the way to the U.S. Supreme Court. The Supreme Court refused to hear the appeal, and so a Florida state judge once again ordered Ms. Schiavo's feeding tube to be removed. Shortly thereafter, the U.S. Congress became involved, with conservatives passing a bill that allowed the case to move to federal court—a bill which President

Bush promptly signed into law. But the federal courts refused to reinsert the feeding tube, and Ms. Schiavo died. In the wake of this dispute, a number of states have sought to clarify people's rights to life and end-of-life care.

Of a slightly different concern is the issue of whether a conscious person, who is near death and is suffering, can request help in terminating her life early (i.e., assisted suicide). The issue of the right to die and assisted suicide gained wider attention in the 1990s through the efforts of Dr. Jack Kevorkian (otherwise known as "Dr. Death"). Dr. Kevorkian believed in helping terminally ill patients die when they are in pain and express a desire to die. Although Michigan revoked Dr. Kevorkian's medical license, he assisted nearly one hundred presumably terminally ill people in dying during the 1990s. In Oregon in 1994, voters approved an initiative legalizing physician-assisted suicide. The law allows physicians to prescribe drugs to hasten death for patients who have been confirmed to be suffering from a terminal illness and are undergoing considerable pain waiting for their inevitable death. In 2001, the Bush administration challenged the state law, saying it violated the federal government's Controlled Substances Act (CSA). However, the Supreme Court, in *Gonzales v. Oregon* (2006), upheld the state law, stating that the CSA had to do with drug dealing and that the federal law could not be used to dictate the standards of medical practices in states.[15] As in the cases of abortion and contraception, the religious right opposes the right to terminate life, while the secular left supports the Oregon law. Aside from the moral issues involved, some argue that legalizing assisted suicide or euthanasia could result in terminally ill patients being pressured to end their life (or even being involuntarily euthanized) for the purposes of harvesting their organs or cutting down on health costs.

THE FIRST AMENDMENT AND PUBLIC MORALITY: SUPPRESSING OBSCENITY AND OFFENSIVE SPEECH

Freedom of Speech

The attempt by socially conservative forces such as the Christian Coalition to defend if not impose a set of values reflecting middle-class morality, the so-called family values issues, was further manifested in the attempt of those forces to reverse the liberalization of laws permitting the distribution of literature, films, and other materials with strong sexual content, material they regard as obscene and that is generally referred to as pornography. Liberals have also sought to impose their values of tolerance on society by pushing for laws that prohibit speech that they regard as intolerant, hateful or sexist. First, we take up the issue of obscenity raised by social conservatives.

The concept of *obscenity* refers to that which offends widely accepted basic values or a sense of decency. In the American context, obscenity has for the most part been applied to sexual content, although more recently liberal forces have been trying to stress the graphic display or depiction of violence as obscene. Of course, the attempt to suppress material on obscenity grounds comes into conflict with the constitutional protection of freedom of speech as well as with the concept of the open society. The extent of that conflict depends on the interpretation that the courts give to the phrase "freedom of speech." Judges have developed a set of principles or criteria by which they may consistently interpret that phrase.

The absolutist position on free speech holds that the freedom of speech clause constitutionally protects all utterances or published material, regardless of their worth. The Supreme Court has rejected the absolutist interpretation. In lieu of such an interpretation, the Court has had to develop criteria or standards by which some categories of speech or expression are deemed unworthy of constitutional protection and are considered outside the bounds of the concept of free speech as contemplated by the Constitution.

Traditionally, in English common law, the concept of freedom of speech merely entailed a restriction on the right of government to suppress what was being said or written in advance of the utterance; in other words, it prohibited *censorship*.[16] Legal scholars refer to this as the doctrine of *prior restraint*. The doctrine of prior restraint under English common law equated freedom of speech as the right to publish something without the government prohibiting or restraining you before you even publish. However, even though people are not censored from writing something before it is published, this doctrine leaves open the possibility that government may punish speakers after the material becomes published. Historically, speakers in England might have faced punishment for seditious libel, that is, false criticism of the government.

Freedom of speech now means more than the absence of prior restraint, but the concept has always meant at least that much. In that sense, the absence of prior restraint represents a floor in one's rights to free speech. Thus, when a government moves to shut down a publication or censor material, the government faces a heavy burden to show that such an exercise in prior restraint is justified under the Constitution. Denial of licenses to speak, injunctions not to publish, and the like are strongly presumed to be unconstitutional unless the government can justify their actions based on an extremely compelling interest (and that is usually very difficult to do). But even prior restraint is not an absolute doctrine. The burden of proof, however heavy, may be satisfied. One such example might be the publishing of current troop movements during wartime. During the Iraq War in 2003, the military expelled Geraldo Rivera of Fox News from Iraq after he broadcasted details of future troop movements. While the Courts would probably allow the government to censor the publication of current troop movements based on national security and the safety of U.S. troops, the government cannot use national security as an excuse to censor anything related to war activities. In the case of the *Pentagon Papers*, the government was not allowed to stop the *New York Times* from publishing a classified study which revealed that the government had secretly expanded the Vietnam War into bombings of neighboring Cambodia, without the knowledge of the American people. In this case, the Supreme Court refused to uphold the Pentagon's request for a prior restraint, as it found that the material in the secret study was information about the war that the American people had a right to know, and that such information would not endanger current troop operations. As the *Pentagon Papers Case* suggests, there is a strong presumption in the law against censorship. This is significant because policy to protect public morality has frequently involved censorship of materials thought to be obscene and morally corrupting.

It is, however, especially difficult to reconcile censorship with the concept of an open society presented in these pages. Censorship, after all, pertains to a small elite, often self-designated, telling the general population of presumably rational adults what they are to be permitted to read, hear, or view and to what values or thoughts they may be safely exposed without being morally corrupted. But the concept of an open society entails the assumption that rational adults are the best judges of their own interests, that they are able to choose among the many ideas and values to which they are exposed. Here again we see that the concept of the open society comes into apparent conflict with protection of family values and public morality.

The courts and legal profession have often viewed the free speech clause as primarily protecting political discussion. Beyond that, the courts have defined categories of speech whereby certain expressions are allowed to be regulated by the government. These categories include such expressions as fighting words; commercial speech; libel or slander of private individuals; speech that might cause an immediate breach of the peace; speech or expression deemed obscene; and speech subject to reasonable time, place, and manner restrictions (such as noise restrictions that would disallow a political protest at 3 a.m. in the morning, or university rules that would prohibit a student from standing up in the middle of astronomy class and talking about abortion). The Supreme Court case of *Chaplinsky v. New Hampshire* (1942), a case which has never been reversed, suggests that there are certain categories of speech that are outside the bounds of what people consider to be free speech protected by the Constitution:

> There are certain well defined and limited classes of speech, the prevention and punishment of which has never been thought to raise any Constitutional problem. These include the lewd and obscene, the profane, the libelous and the insulting or "fighting" words—those that by their very utterance inflict injury or tend to incite a breach of the peace. It has been well observed that such utterances are no essential part of any exposition of ideas and are of such slight value as a step to the truth that any benefit that may be derived from them is clearly outweighed by the social interest in order and morality.[17]

The historical trend in behavior by the courts suggest that they are more likely than not to end up siding with the concept of an open society when interpreting the Constitution, but there is some room for government to engage in public policy in limiting expression which the majority finds immoral. The courts often consider the right of expression in terms of democracy and whether the speech or expression contributes to a free exchange of ideas or infringes on the rights of others. In the next two sections, we'll discuss how two categories of speech—fighting words and obscene speech—have an impact on the regulation of moral values within the context of an open society.

Fighting Words and Regulating Insensitive Speech

With the passage of Civil Rights legislation in the 1960s, the United States gov-ernment finally began addressing the wrongs committed against racial and ethnic minorities throughout our history. Congress has continued to pass additional Civil Rights bills in order to further address issues of inequality. While these laws sought to outlaw discrimination and provide opportunities for minority groups, an important component for making these laws more effective is chang-ing the hearts and minds of people and ending a culture of racism. To deal with this concern, some on the left have advocated laws which regulate or prohibit insensitive speech or intolerant expression, including racial or religious slurs. The argument by those on the left is that such speech or expression is unaccept-able in public discourse and has no value for the free exchange in ideas. To this end, some communities have enacted laws that specifically banned speech that incites racial or religious hatred, so-called hate speech laws. Another variant of this effort are hate crimes legislation. Hate crimes laws provide for additional punishment to people engaging in a criminal act, if their motives behind the act were based on ill-will toward a specific minority group or religious group or based on a person's gender or sexual orientation.

Critics claim that the behaviors that such laws are intended to proscribe are rendered punishable under other existing, conventional statutes such as those penalizing destruction of property, incitement to violence, and so on. Further-more, in the context of hate speech, the determiner of whether the speech or expression is considered "hate" will be the government. Thus, the concern by critics is that a current majority who controls government will broaden the defi-nition of hate speech and use these laws as an excuse to punish speech with which the majority ideologically disagrees. For example, would expressing oppo-sition to affirmative action policies be considered hate speech? In the San Francisco Bay Area in 2010, a high school principle sent several students home for wearing T-shirts showing the American flag on Cinco de Mayo day, a national holiday in the country of Mexico.[18] The principle said that the students could wear the T-shirts on any other day, but not on Cinco de Mayo, because such an action was insensitive to Mexican Americans. Some Mexican American students had said that they were offended that these boys would wear the red, white, and blue on a Mexican holiday. Generally, most advocates of hate speech laws would not consider such expressions hate speech, and it is highly unlikely the courts would uphold such an interpretation under the First Amendment. But, even more gener-ally, it is doubtful the Supreme Court would uphold *any* hate speech law as consti-tutional, unless it could be shown that such a law falls within the category of unprotected speech known as fighting words.

The problem with using the fighting words doctrine to outlaw hate speech is that the Supreme Court has weakened this doctrine over the years, and has permitted a wide array of intolerant speech to occur on the basis that such speech is protected by the Constitution. In the *Chaplinsky* case, the Supreme Court up-held the conviction of Chaplinsky, a Jehovah's Witness, because in essence, he had yelled at a police officer, calling him a "damned fascist" and "a God-damned

Racketeer." The state law under which Chaplinsky was tried prohibited "any offensive, derisive, or annoying word to any other person who is lawfully in the street." If this law was upheld, one might assume that laws prohibiting hate speech could also be upheld.

But hate speech laws are unlikely to benefit from the *Chaplinsky* case. The only reason that the U.S. Supreme Court upheld the law was because the state of New Hampshire limited the regulation of the speech in three important ways. First, in order to be prosecuted under this law, the forbidden word had to be directed at a specific person. Second, the word had to "have a direct tendency to cause acts of violence by persons to whom . . . the remark is addressed." Third, the definition of "offensive" could not be defined simply by whether the "addressee" was offended. In other words, just because someone is offended by a remark does not mean the state could punish the person making the remark. Rather, the Court said that "the test is what men of common intelligence would understand would be words likely to cause an average addressee to fight." Interpreted in this way, the fighting words doctrine would not cover many facets of a hate speech law. For example, publishing a racially intolerant book or having a parade to promote one's intolerance against gays and lesbians, or yelling out racial epithets to oneself on the street could not be prohibited by the government because one is not directing the speech specifically at an individual. On the other hand, one could be prosecuted under the fighting words doctrine for yelling racial epithets specifically at another individual.

The idea that one's offensive statements must be directed at a particular individual was further supported by the Supreme Court in the *Cohen v. California* case (1971). In this case, the Court overturned Cohen's conviction for inciting a disturbance of the peace (Cohen had worn a jacket in the halls of the Los Angeles County Courthouse bearing the epithet, "Fuck the draft"). In this case, no disturbance actually ever occurred. There was no evidence that Cohen intended to offend anyone or that anyone was actually offended. The Court held that times change and that words that offend at one time and place may not offend elsewhere; in other words, no phrase is inherently and necessarily beyond First Amendment protection.

The problem of prohibiting hate speech was most aptly demonstrated by the 1978 case of the American Nazi Party's request to conduct a parade and rally, complete with swastikas, SS uniforms, and jackboots, down the streets of Skokie, Illinois, a community with a preponderantly Jewish population and numerous survivors of Nazi extermination camps. Clearly, no persuasion was likely to take place in this context. What was being protected was the Nazi party's right to symbolically and explicitly express its racist and anti-Semitic ideology. The city of Skokie had attempted to prevent the march by several means, including the requirement of a confiscatory bond against potential damage and, perhaps more significantly, an injunction against utterances that castigated any racial or religious group. The U.S. district court held that racial slurs are a protected form of speech under the Constitution, and the Illinois Supreme Court held that ". . . the display of the swastika in Skokie cannot be enjoined under the fighting words exception to free speech, nor can the anticipation of a hostile reaction justify prior restraint."

This case showed that if a parade of anti-Semitic slurs by avowed Nazis through the neighborhood of concentration camp survivors is not fighting words in the *Chaplinsky* sense of the term, it is hard to imagine any other utterance that would so qualify. In striking down the injunction against racial slurs, the U.S. district court reasoned as follows:

> The question is not whether there are some ideas that are unacceptable in a civilized society. Rather the question is which danger is greater: the danger that allowing the government to punish "unacceptable" ideas will lead to the suppression of ideas that are merely uncomfortable to those in power; or the danger that permitting free debate on such unacceptable ideas will encourage their acceptance rather than discouraging them by revealing their pernicious quality.

The district court found the former danger to be greater, a decision affirmed by the U.S. Supreme Court.

The *Cohen* and *Skokie* cases have very nearly transformed the interpretation of the freedom of speech clause to embrace any politically based form of expressive utterance, and the Supreme Court has continued this libertarian view of free speech rights. In a 1992 case involving the burning of a cross on the lawn of an African American family, the Court struck down a Minnesota hate speech ordinance banning speech that "arouses anger, alarm or resentment in others" as an overly broad infringement on freedom of speech.[19] Obviously, speech that arouses anger or offends is exactly the kind of speech that the First Amendment is designed to protect; one does not need constitutional protection to say what everyone wants to hear.

The Political Correctness Controversy.   Still, these court cases have apparently not laid to rest the issue of the constitutional protection of inflammatory speech, especially with regard to the protection of racial slurs. Colleges and universities have taken the lead in the attempt to suppress speech that is regarded as insensitive to targeted racial and ethnic groups. The campaign to suppress speech offensive to some oppressed groups arose from a spate of racial insults on American college campuses. At the University of Michigan, for example, in 1987, a radio talk show host at the university-run station called for listeners to contribute their favorite racial jokes. In 1988, at Yale University, someone painted a swastika and the phrase "white power" on the Afro-American Center.

The University of Michigan took the lead in late 1988 in adopting a rule restricting speech that members of targeted groups found offensive, again raising the question posed earlier with regard to hate speech laws, whether one can, consistent with the concept of freedom of speech, grant anyone the right not to be offended. The policy adopted defined as punishable "any behavior, verbal or physical, that stigmatizes or victimizes an individual on the basis of ethnicity, religion, sex, sexual orientation, creed, national origin, ancestry, age, marital status, handicap, or Vietnam-era veteran status." University officials averred that freedom of speech does not include the right to harass or injure others. Harassment or injury is further described as a situation in which a person perceives that

he or she is in "a hostile learning environment." Sanctions may vary from repri-
mand to expulsion. The significant departure in such policies on "insensitive
speech" is to define the offense as how the listeners perceive or react to the
speech rather than the content of what is said or the tone and style of the writer
or speaker. The punishing of speech because of the way others perceive it or
react to it violates an established rule of law called *scienter* (roughly, "knowledge
of wrongdoing")—that the distinction between what is permissible and what is
sanctioned must be specified in advance of the act in question. One cannot be
sure at what others will take offense. Several other schools have adopted policies
of speech censorship patterned after the Michigan model, including Middlebury
College, Brown University, Pennsylvania State University, Tufts University,
Stanford University, and the Universities of California, Connecticut, North
Carolina, Pennsylvania, and Wisconsin.[20] Some of these speech codes, however,
could be unconstitutional if enforced by a government-run state university. For
the state university speech code to be constitutional, it has to be seen as outlaw-
ing only fighting words directed at a specific individual.

In some cases, conservative critics of such suppression charge that the leaders
in academic communities and the media have imposed a criterion of political
correctness on permissible expression. The vagueness of the definition of racial
or ethnic insensitivity is seen by some as allowing its use as a tool to limit the
expression of positions that contradict a liberal perspective. In some instances it
has virtually come to include anything to which the target group members take
offense.

For example, Harvard University defined racial harassment as any actions or
words "which cause another individual or group to feel demeaned or abused
because of their racial or ethnic background." The offense, in this reading, consists not in what the speech in question actually says, but how some people feel
about it. In February 1988, Stephan Thernstrom, Winthrop Professor of History
at Harvard, was charged with racial insensitivity because he had quoted southern
plantation owners on the subject of black character during his lectures. Although
his tenure was not threatened, Thernstrom was chastised by university officials
and warned to avoid "possible insensitivity in lecturing." He claimed that he
was quoting for analytical purposes, not expressing his own views, and that he
was unaware of having given offense. A similar event occurred at the University
of Maryland when a professor of Latin American History read to his class a
description of Native Americans written by Spanish conquistadors. The professor
was required to read a formal apology to his class for "racist speech." Such accusations of alleged insensitivity are based upon subjective perceptions of those
most easily offended and appear to be impermissibly vague by any interpretation
of the First Amendment.

Similarly, an editor of the student newspaper at California State University at
Northridge was suspended from school for printing a political cartoon critical of
affirmative action, and another student was suspended for writing a letter to the
paper criticizing the editor's suspension. There was no suggestion that either the
letter or the cartoon was outside the bounds of taste and propriety or unduly
inflammatory; rather, the sin seems to be the substance of the position.

Militant Muslims have added their group to the list of people demanding protection from being offended. In 2006, militant Muslims staged violent riots worldwide to protest cartoons published in a Danish newspaper making fun of the prophet Mohammed. Some devout Muslims stated that it brings great offense to their religion to see printed cartoon images of the prophet Mohammed. In Syria, Muslim protesters burned down the Danish and Norwegian embassies.[21] Norway was targeted simply for re-publishing the cartoons.

In 2010, Comedy Central Network censored portions of an episode of the cartoon *South Park* that showed the prophet Mohammed dressed up in a bear costume. *South Park*'s creators Trey Parker and Matt Stone have often poked fun at various organized religions, from Scientology to Buddhism to Christianity. In fact, in one *South Park* cartoon episode, Jesus Christ is depicted defecating on President Bush and the American flag. Previously in 2006, Comedy Central had refused to allow Parker and Stone to include an image of Mohammed in their cartoon. In the 2010 episode, all the previously offended icons (from religious figures to celebrities) file a class action lawsuit against the town of South Park. To get around the problem of displaying Mohammed's image and to call attention to the issue of censorship, Parker and Stone decided to depict Mohammed dressed up in a bear costume throughout the entire cartoon (so that no actual image of the prophet would ever be shown, only the caricature of a bear costume). But ironically, after Comedy Central received threats from a radical Muslim website, they engaged in censorship by bleeping out all references to the prophet before showing the episode. The *L.A. Times* couched the issue as one where "media conglomerates are still struggling to balance free speech with safety concerns and religious sensitivities."[22] UCLA law professor Eugene Volokh told the *L.A. Times*, "The consequence of this position is that the thugs win and people have more incentive to be thugs. There are lots of people out there who would very much like to get certain kind of material removed, whether religious or political. The more they see others winning, the more they will be likely to do the same." In a demonstration of solidarity, *The Simpsons* TV show on the FOX Network showed Bart Simpson writing 100 times on the chalkboard in the opening scene of a 2010 program, "*South Park*—We'd stand beside you if we weren't so scared."

Great effort continues to be made to avoid offending certain groups, as exemplified by the British Broadcasting Company's (BBC) banning the use of the term *terrorists* to refer to the perpetrators of the 2007 London Tube bombings, referring to them instead as "misguided criminals." Dr. Paul Payek, president of the Global Language Monitor, claims "in 2006, the Political Correctness Movement continued to gain momentum. . . ." Clearly, the protection of minorities against being offended by hate speech is taking priority over more rigorous interpretations of freedom of speech. Moreover, the diversity sought by proponents of race-based college admissions (discussed in Chapter 10) apparently does not include diversity of opinion. The political correctness movement is designed to guard against insensitivity to the feelings of affected minority groups. Carrying this goal a step further, a movement known as *multiculturalism* seeks as a goal the protection of the self-esteem of members of these groups, especially through changes in curricula to reflect the contributions of such groups. (Multicultural issues in education are discussed in Chapter 9.)

The campaign to restrain expression is not limited to insensitivity to racial and ethnic groups but has at times required conformity to the values of the intellectual left in general. During the 1991 war in the Persian Gulf, for instance, administrators at the University of Maryland ruled that students may not fly the American flag in support of the war effort because such displays might offend those (including many administrators) who opposed the resort to arms. Expressed antipathy to homosexuals is similarly forbidden. A University of Connecticut student was banned from her dormitory and dining hall for displaying a poster on the door of her room referring to gays and lesbians as "homos," a pejorative epithet.

Many charge that the nation's universities, heretofore counted on to defend the unfettered exchange of ideas, have now taken the lead in suppressing the expression of ideas that are regarded as politically incorrect. The range of what is considered too insensitive to be permitted is both broad and expanding.

It may be inferred, in light of the Skokie incidents, that the First Amendment protects the right to express pejorative claims about a group in general; therefore, many state university speech codes are carefully drawn to proscribe only insults directed at individuals. Yet the incidents that gave rise to these codes frequently involved insults to groups as a whole. Few people would claim that a Nazi's bigoted speech is worth much of anything, but the Constitution does not allow for the prosecution of one's beliefs, even if those beliefs are intolerant and despicable.

Obscenity and the Marketplace of Ideas

While some liberals tend to promote the idea of censoring offensive hate speech, conservatives tend to advocate censoring what they see as sexually obscene expression. It should be noted that the material in question in obscenity legislation rarely contributes to the free exchange of ideas. Much of it does not even qualify as worthwhile artistic expression by the standards of most critics. Controversial examples include Andres Serrano's photograph of a crucifix in a glass of urine, nude dancer Karen Finley smearing herself with chocolate and moving her hands on her body in a highly suggestive fashion, and performance artist Annie Sprinkle, who invited the audience to closely examine her sexual organs. But a great deal of material that is regarded as artistically valuable has in some places been suppressed on obscenity grounds, some of which are listed in the following discussion. Good literature, attempting to deal with life in a realistic way, does not ignore the reality of human sexuality. The origin of obscenity legislation, however, never rested on critical measures of aesthetic worth; instead, it sought to protect communities from the perceived social evils of sexually explicit material in any context. Essentially, such legislation had two goals: the reduction of sexual stimulation and the perpetuation of the view sometimes found in Christianity that sex for pleasure is an avoidable and undesirable aspect of human personality and interaction. The Puritan tradition in America, once characterized by H. L. Mencken as the nagging fear that somewhere someone may be enjoying himself, was the heir of this view. The suppression of information about sex, however, has been a spillover effect of obscenity legislation.

One source of controversy in this arena is that different individuals have differing levels of tolerance for sexually related material. Some are greatly offended by any four-letter expletive; others are untroubled by graphic depictions of sex acts. Those who are most easily offended tend to be the most active in trying to obtain legislation and ensure its enforcement of their more restrictive moral standards on others. People who are less easily offended are generally less concerned about pornography, and they have left the field to the wishes of the moralists. Moreover, there is an additional pressure that tends to prevent those with a more tolerant attitude from defending pornography too vigorously, for there is a certain stigma attached to taking such a position; one risks being identified as a consumer of pornography and an oversexed deviant. Thus the censor's position seems more legitimate than that of the defenders of freedom of speech and expression.

Obscenity and the Law: The *Roth* Rule

The courts have never taken the position that obscenity, defined here as materials of a graphic nature that have the primary purpose to arouse erotic impulses, should itself be granted First Amendment protection. The difficulty is that much material that might otherwise be deserving of such protection contains sexually explicit elements. The constitutional problem has been to devise principles that will allow society to shield its citizens from being unduly sexually stimulated or offended without closing off their access to art, literature, and ideas that are protected by the freedom of speech clause. The common-law interpretation of the freedom of speech clause gave wide latitude to the discretion of government censors in the suppression of sexually relevant material. The nineteenth-century *Hicklin* test (1868) judged matter to be obscene if any isolated passage in the material has a "tendency to corrupt and deprave those who are open to such immoral influence. . . ."[23] In other words, material may be censored if it contains any passage that is likely to arouse someone who is particularly susceptible to being so aroused. Because it is possible to find some individuals who are offended and aroused by the most innocuous material and because many pieces of serious writing contain some isolated passage that may offend such people, the *Hicklin* test puts freedom of speech on very tenuous grounds. Consequently, there was pressure to liberalize this standard to afford greater protection to art and literature against suppression by the censors.

A more permissive standard was finally handed down in the *Roth* case in 1957. The so-called *Roth* rule has become the standard that subsequent obscenity court decisions either assume or modify. It modified the *Hicklin* test in three important ways: First, the test no longer focused on any isolated passage or words, but rather on whether "the dominant theme of the material, taken as a whole, appeals to prurient (sexual) interests"; second, its standard of measure became whether the material appeals to the prurient interests of the "average" person, not a particularly susceptible segment of society; third, the treatment of sex in the material under question was not to justify censorship unless it was "utterly without redeeming social importance."[24]

Now material can no longer be censored because of some isolated passage or because some individual can find a sexual innuendo where the thought would not occur to most people. Of course, the stipulation that the government can only censor works "utterly without redeeming social importance" opens the door for a wide range of material to be protected from the censors, because even material that most people would find to be predominantly trash may have some small measure of social value. Although *Roth* suggests that a small, peripheral part of sexually relevant material would not condemn a work, it also appears to say that a small, peripheral amount of worthwhile material might save an otherwise worthless piece of sexual exploitation. This part of the *Roth* rule appears inconsistent with its dominant theme.

The *Roth* rule was later modified in two important ways in the *Miller v. California* case (1973).[25] The Supreme Court dropped the key problematic phrase in favor of saying that, in order to be legally censored, material must lack *serious* literary, artistic, political, or scientific values (LAPS values). This seems more in line with judging the work as a whole rather than on the basis of some isolated passages. Presumably, under the *Miller* criterion of serious LAPS values, an isolated article in an otherwise provocative and graphic girlie magazine would not, in and of itself, save such material from censorship.

The second way in which the *Miller* case modifies the *Roth* rule is by defining obscenity based in part on local community standards rather than national. The Court explicitly rejected the idea that there can or should be a national standard for what can or cannot be censored. This portion of the ruling appears incongruent with the purpose of the First Amendment to provide some national standards for freedom of speech. The Constitution cannot mean one thing in one state and something else in another state or it would not be law.

Publishing, film, and broadcasting are examples of national commerce, and the legal status of their enormous investments must be predictable throughout the country. Without national standards, the standards for the nation as a whole become the standards of what the most prudish local prosecutors or juries are wont to censor, the lowest common denominator; in effect, this completely negates the average-person criterion of *Roth*. By the *Miller* standard, any community should be able to censor whatever sexually explicit material dominant groups choose to censor without violating the Constitution.

The Court backed off from the implications of the local community standard in *Jenkins v. Georgia* (1974) when it ruled that Georgia could not ban the critically acclaimed film *Carnal Knowledge* on obscenity grounds. The Court rejected a reading of *Miller* "that juries have unbridled discretion to determine what is 'patently offensive.'"[26] Thus a community is not free to censor the mere depiction of sex; the material had to be "patently offensive." The Court even offered a list of the kinds of things that may be censored. But this implies national standards that constrain community discretion. In 1987, the Court backed further away from community standards, substituting a "reasonable man" test, a criterion that would allow the repression of speech that is obscene to ordinary, sane individuals.

There may be a useful distinction between obscenity and pornography. One may accept the concept that the avoidance of sexual stimulation is not a value of sufficient weight to justify the discretion given to censors; yet one may still argue that there remains a category of material that is beyond mere salaciousness: it is "patently offensive." In 1989, the Court further elaborated on the distinction between what may be censored in obscenity cases and what is protected from such challenges by the First Amendment in the dial-a-porn case, *Sable Communications v. Federal Communications Commission*. The Court struck down an amendment to the communications act that banned "indecent" interstate calls. The Court said that while obscene calls may be banned, the denial to adults of access to calls that are merely indecent violates the First Amendment.[27] The same logic was extended in *Reno v. ACLU* to the regulation of the Internet by the Communications Decency Act, signed into law by President Clinton and designed to control children's access to sexually explicit material on that medium. The Court found that the proscribed categories, indecent and patently offensive, were unconstitutionally vague.[28]

There is, of course, a problem in drawing the line between what is obscenity and what is not, but most know intuitively where it is. Justice Stewart put it best in *Jacobellis v. Ohio* (1964):

> I have reached the conclusion that . . . under the First and Fourteenth Amendments, criminal laws in this area are limited to hard-core pornography. I shall not today attempt to further define the kinds of material I understand to be embraced within that short hand description; and perhaps I shall never succeed in doing so. But I know it when I see it. . . .[29]

Censorship, Sex, and the Arts.   The expansion of the concept of protected expression generated controversy over government funding of artistic work with sexual content that was offensive to the moral sensibilities of significant segments of the population. Here the issue was one of government funding, not government suppression. In the one instance, the government funded a photographic exhibition produced by a well-known photographer, Robert Mapplethorpe, including some explicit homoerotica and some photographs involving the genitalia of children. Other funded projects that were offensive to many Americans include the Serrano, Finley, and Sprinkle works mentioned earlier.

The debate over funding such projects demonstrated the absence of any objective criteria over what constitutes artistic merit that would override the public interest in the preservation of public morality. Article I Section 8 of the Constitution says Congress is empowered "To promote the Progress of Science and useful Arts," but of course, what is "useful" is not defined in the document. Those who opposed funding these projects argued that they went beyond the bounds of common perceptions of artistic value and that, in any event, whatever rights may exist to freedom of expression do not extend to a right to public funding, especially when the material in question is deeply offensive to a majority. Those who supported funding of these projects argued that representatives of the artistic community should determine what is art and what deserves to be funded. Since market forces are not presumed to identify and reward genuine artistic merit, the issue of public funding is an important one. A heavy metal rock band will sell many more recordings than a classical violinist. Without public subsidies, many widely respected creators of classical music, dance, drama, and the like could not survive. Congress has debated cutting off funding to the arts through the National Endowment for the Arts (NEA), or at least severely limiting such arts funding. The NEA narrowly escaped fiscal death in 1997. It becomes apparent that as the frontier of what is perceived as having artistic value is expanded further, public tolerance of extending funding or protection to such expression may continue to weaken.

The Conflict Between Pornography and Public Morality

A lingering question in the ongoing controversy over obscenity legislation is what social value is preserved by allowing the censorship of patently offensive, hard-core pornography, even assuming that such material can be adequately distinguished. Is the goal of obscenity legislation to protect people from being offended, or is it assumed that certain preventable, harmful behavior and events would be the consequence of the unrestricted dissemination of hard-core pornography? If the former is the value being guarded, government is in the business of controlling thought rather than restricting itself to the control of behavior.

Of course, child pornography, the use of children to produce pornographic books and films, goes beyond thought control, raising issues of the exploitation of those unable to exercise independent judgment. The law has always distinguished the protection needed by children from the needs of adults. Can the law also proscribe computer-generated child pornography? In 2002, the Supreme Court answered this question in *Ashcroft v. Free Speech Coalition* by striking down a ban on computer-generated virtual reality images of children in sexually suggestive depictions. The constitutional basis for banning child pornography concerns the underlying illegal act of exploiting real children in the making of it, whereas in the case of the virtual reality images, the Court claimed the ban "prohibits speech that records no crime and creates no victims by its production."[30] One of the public policy questions raised in the case was whether expression using virtual images of children might increase the tendency of pedophiles to go out and engage in child molestation. But the Court was unpersuaded, responding that "the mere tendency of speech to encourage unlawful acts is not a sufficient reason for banning it."

A principle concern expressed by the Court in the *Ashcroft* case was the fact that the federal law banning virtual images included images of persons who merely appear to be under the age of eighteen, even if they are not. And, there was no exception in the law for work that had a serious literary, political, or scientific value. The Court noted that movies telling the story of William Shakespeare's *Romeo and Juliet*, a literary classic involving a story of a relationship between two teenagers, where Juliet is only thirteen years old, could fall under the scope of this federal ban. As the Court noted, "The work has inspired no less than 40 motion pictures, some of which suggest that the teenagers consummated their relationship."[31]

Some decades ago, Justices Black and Douglas took the position that control of thought is not compatible with an open society. In their dissent from the *Roth* decision, they attacked the central premise of obscenity legislation, that it is permissible to "punish mere speech or publication that the judge or jury thinks has an undesirable impact on thought but is not shown to be part of any unlawful action. . . ." They disagreed with the *Roth* rule because it permits the state to censor material that arouses sexual impulses, whether or not it results in particular forms of behavior. They were suggesting that utterances or ideas that have not been shown to have a likely impact on some unlawful behavior or to cause the physical impeding of some lawful activity are protected by the First Amendment, no matter how much they may offend the moral standards of any particular part of the community. They were essentially rejecting the inferred right not to be offended that we discussed earlier.

The distinction between the impact of material on thought and its impact on action is easier to make in practice than that between hard-core pornography that is patently offensive and soft-core pornography that is mildly offensive. Because these two liberal justices did not believe that material can be censored on the basis of its content, they were the only justices who did not read or review the material at issue in obscenity cases. To them, the material was constitutionally protected, regardless of what it contained.

Some data are available on pornography's impact on behavior. A commission established under President Johnson and reporting years later during the Nixon administration systematically searched for a causal connection between exposure to sexually explicit material and the disposition to engage in antisocial behavior.[32] It failed to find any systematic evidence of such a connection. The presidential commission recommended the abolition of all laws that proscribe the dissemination of sexually explicit material among consenting adults.

Arguments for Censorship.   Opponents challenged the commission's findings on several grounds. The commission's studies were carried out on volunteers who were unrepresentative of the population at large. The effects on children were not considered, nor were long-term effects taken into account. Sociological and anthropological research on the long-range effects of sexual permissiveness leans toward the conclusion that such permissiveness is dysfunctional for creative energy and cultural development.[33]

In 1985, Attorney General Edwin Meese of the Reagan administration released a Justice Department–sponsored study purporting to show the harmful effects of pornography. Critics charged that it lumped together a wide range of sex-related material and did not prove the connection it alleged between pornography and criminal actions. It seems fair to say that there is some evidence that ordinary pornography does not produce undesirable behavior, but that the evidence is not without flaws and there is a fair amount of thought to the contrary. The issue has not been resolved.

Despite such data, a large segment of the population clings to the belief that pornography leads people to commit sex crimes. A poll taken in 1985, the same year as the Attorney General's report was released, showed that 73 percent of those surveyed believed that "explicit sexual magazines, movies and books . . . lead some people to commit rape or sexual violence."[34] By 1994, while that number had declined to a plurality of 48 percent who believed that sexual materials lead people to rape, it was still higher when compared to 42 percent who did not believe such materials lead to rape.[35] These findings are consistent with the popularity of the solicitor general for the county encompassing Atlanta, Georgia, who defended his concentrating the resources at his disposal on driving pornography out of the city with the bald assertion, "I'm convinced that the use of obscene materials results in many antisocial acts . . . rape, sodomy, and the molesting of young children."[36] Such persistent beliefs are a political reality that can both affect and undermine whatever legal principles may protect sexually relevant material. Here again, commitment to community moral standards conflicts with belief in an open society.

There is another argument against pornography which stems from quality of life issues in the neighborhoods where sex shops, topless bars, and X-rated movie theaters reside. Neighborhoods that contain such adult businesses are normally associated with increased crime rates and declining property values. Hence, the Supreme Court upheld the constitutionality of municipal zoning restrictions on such industries in a case involving the City of Los Angeles after the city produced a study indicating that high concentrations of adult entertainment establishments are associated with higher crime rates in surrounding communities.[37]

Arguments against Censorship.   Given the weakness of evidence to support an alleged causal effect of pornography on antisocial behavior, liberals argue that what consenting adults read or view is none of the state's business. This concept of the consenting adult implies that people do not have such material involuntarily foisted on them and that the probability is very remote that they could naively or unwittingly place themselves in contact with such material. For example, a theater showing X-rated films should be clearly so identified, and no one should be pressured or even implored to enter. The notion of consenting adults also implies a distinction between what is available to adults and what is available to minors, a distinction the Court clearly upheld when it struck down a law banning the sale "to the general reading public" of any book "tending to incite minors to depraved or immoral acts" or "tending to the corruption of the morals of youth." The Court held that this law reduced the adult population of Michigan to reading only what is fit for children.[38] The argument that individuals must be presumed able to decide for themselves what material is fit for them to read or view does not apply with equal force to minors.

Assuming that the availability of sexually explicit materials is effectively limited to consenting adults and that there is no demonstrated causal connection between adult exposure to pornography and socially disruptive behavior, why not allow rational adults to choose for themselves what materials they can view without becoming morally offended or depraved? The Supreme Court came close to this position in *Stanley v. Georgia* (1969), which involved the seizure of sexually explicit films in a private home. The Court held that "if the First Amendment means anything, it means that a state has no business telling a man, sitting alone in his own house, what books he may read or what films he may see."[39] One may read into this decision the principle that consenting adults have the right to read or view whatever they choose as long as they do not force such material on unwilling adults or allow its availability to minors. The Court, however, refused to adopt this logical entailment of *Stanley* when in the *Reidel* case (1971) it upheld a state ban on the buying and selling of pornography by consenting adults.[40] The Court explicitly rejected the position that if someone has a right to read what he or she wants in private, he or she also has a right to buy it from someone willing to sell it. Because it was also held in the court case of *Twelve 200 Foot Reels* (1973) that one may be prosecuted for importing salacious materials for one's own personal use, one has no right legally to acquire the materials that *Stanley* gives that person a right to read or see.[41]

The consenting adults argument was more explicitly rejected in *Paris Adult Theater v. Slaton* (1973), in which the Court upheld the right of the state to close down a theater specializing in X-rated films.[42] It was admitted that the theater was so clearly marked that it was impossible to enter it unaware of the sexual nature of the films being shown. It was further admitted that minors were effectively excluded. Nevertheless, the Court still perceived some legitimate state interests in permitting censorship to override any First Amendment values involved. These state interests include "the interest of the public in the quality of life and total community environment, the tone of commerce in the great city centers and, possibly, the public safety itself." The Court further held that even though it had not been shown that there is a causal relationship between exposure to pornography and deviant or objectionable behavior, a state may nevertheless reasonably assume that such a relationship exists in asserting a legitimate interest in regulating what consenting adults may view or read. Why a state may "reasonably assume" something to be true contrary to available evidence was not discussed.

Supporters of censorship correctly point out that much of the material in obscenity cases is obviously pornographic trash and hardly worth protecting. Indeed, despite the Supreme Court's obscenity rulings, opponents point out, all forms of mass entertainment have become far more sexually explicit. Such material contributes very little if anything to the political purpose of the First Amendment, the free trade in socially relevant ideas. Moreover, although censorship in effect imposes the moral standards of dominant groups on other members of society, such principles may be part of the essence of that society. Even if unwilling adults do not actually see pornography, its very presence is held to lend an unsavory moral climate to the environment. As previously noted, in neighborhoods characterized by widely available pornography, crime rates tend to be significantly higher than average. Furthermore, the suppression of pornography would, many believe, bring about the diminishment if not the disappearance of some notorious abuses associated with the production of pornography. Child pornography is one of the more egregious examples of such abuses.

Feminist Concerns about Pornography. A different kind of campaign against pornography has been mounted by a group of feminists, led by law professor Catharine MacKinnon and the late Andrea Dworkin, involving the strategy of obtaining legislation to the effect that such material demeans women, is a form of sex discrimination, and thereby violates their civil rights.[43] The remedy invited by such legislation is civil action against either the producers or the distributors of such material, including the bookseller. Because the criminal process is not involved, the burden of proof is altered from previous strategies of criminalizing the production and distribution of sexually explicit material.

The first example of this was a 1984 law passed by the Minneapolis city council, but vetoed by the mayor. Other such ordinances were introduced in Indianapolis and Los Angeles. These ordinances came under severe criticism on freedom of speech grounds. The critics charged that the standards for determining what may be considered demeaning to the dignity of women are left very imprecise and therefore any bookseller, publisher, or other disseminator of sexually relevant material may find himself or herself the defendant in a lawsuit initiated by any woman who might be so offended. Even if the defendant wins, the costs of being party to such litigation would be great, and so such litigation could cause a severe chilling effect on the willingness of people to handle any sexually relevant material that may offend those most easily offended. The public would then almost be limited to having access only to material inoffensive to the most sensitive women. Laws granting women the right to sue booksellers who distribute salacious material that the plaintiff believes demeans women were tested in *The American Association of Booksellers v. Hudnut* (1984), a case challenging the Indianapolis law. The district court judge, a woman, found that the law presented an unconstitutional deterrent to free speech.

It is argued, on the other hand, that pornography does promote and legitimate the image of women merely as sex objects rather than as complete and equal persons. Moreover, some sadomasochistic, hard-core pornography fosters the idea of the physical abuse of women as a manly thing to do. Such material characterized by simulated rape and violence toward women is typical of hard-core pornography today. The dissemination of such sadomasochistic material thus may actually pose a physical danger to women. Pornography in general depicts sex as a conquest, something that men do *to* women rather than as a mutual expression of affection that men and women do *with* each other. Studies after the 1970 President's Commission Report discussed earlier do indicate that exposure to the new violent, hard-core pornography does soften attitudes toward rape and the sexual exploitation of women. Indeed, men exposed to such material become more tolerant of sexual violence. Of course, to the extent that it can be shown that the violent forms of pornography make men more tolerant of such violence, the argument is no longer simply one of competing moral perspectives but rather a question of the right of the state to protect the well-being of its female citizens. Whatever the case for censorship on moral grounds, censorship of the kinds of material that can be shown to pose a physical danger to women is another matter.

The concept of blaming the source—producers or sellers of reading or viewing material—for the acts performed by consumers of such material, which was struck down in the *Hudnut* case, was resurrected in 1992 by Senate sponsors of the Pornography Victim's Compensation Bill, which would allow civil litigation against the purveyors of pornography by the victims of sexual violence. The bill makes three assumptions. First, as in the MacKinnon–Dworkin laws struck down in *Hudnut*, it assumes that sellers of books, magazines, or video cassettes should be acquainted with the content of everything they sell. A second assumption is that the material in question may incite lust, a charge that could be made of much serious adult material. Third, the bill assumes that violent sex crimes are an expression of uncontrollable lust. Current research indicates, however, that such crimes are expressions of hatred of women (misogyny) and a desire for power over them. If so, the bill would be useless in curbing this tragic social malady whose incidence is growing. This bill has not been passed by Congress.

Censorship and the Open Society.   The problem with censorship on the grounds that material is immoral or offensive is that one has to trust that the censor can selectively stamp out this particular worthless piece of trash or that particular despicable point of view. Censorship is, by definition, delegating the power to one or more persons to decide for everyone else in the jurisdiction which of all future utterances people may see, hear, or read. The adult members of society lose the right to decide for themselves what material is trash and what materials have value, what ideas are legitimate and worthy of consideration, and what ideas are so heinous as to be outside the democratic political arena.

The historical record does not support the idea of government censors using discretion judiciously. Although most Americans can agree that some materials are offensive and worthless, the record is replete with examples of overzealous censors suppressing material that most Americans would find harmless and often of considerable artistic value. The critically acclaimed films *Midnight Cowboy* and *Carnal Knowledge* were censored in some places. Another critically acclaimed film, *Paper Moon*, a comedy involving very little that was even implicitly sexual, was censored because of the use of profane language. The 1960s saw numerous attempts to ban the well-respected novel *Catcher in the Rye* from school libraries. John Steinbeck's *East of Eden*, *The Grapes of Wrath*, *The Red Pony*, and *Of Mice and Men*, and the Tarzan series have all been banned in various places in the United States on obscenity grounds, as were several Hemingway novels.

Informal Censorship: Boycotts, Threats, and Public Pressure.   One tactic used to protect society from putatively salacious material is not direct censorship by a public official but rather a boycott of the products of firms that sponsor shows on television allegedly containing such material, a *boycott* organized and promoted by a nongovernmental source. The chilling effect of the threat of such a boycott has caused sponsorships to be withdrawn in more than one instance. The extent to which the selection and content of shows have been altered because of the boycott threat is unclear. These boycotts are not formally censorship in the traditional sense of a public official banning the dissemination of certain material by law or edict; instead, they constitute a less formal kind of censorship, whereby materials are eliminated from dissemination through the mechanism of socioeconomic pressure.

Another informal tactic simply relies on violence and intimidation by those claiming offense. Comedy Central's response to threats from a radical Muslim website by censoring the *South Park* episodes of the prophet Mohammed is not an isolated incident. Fears of violence caused the New York Metropolitan Museum of Art to take down all art in their gallery that depicted Mohammed in any image, and Yale University Press began refusing to print any images of the prophet in any of its books it published.

Another version of these less formal tactics is the pressure to eliminate certain kinds of material from public school textbooks. The testimony at textbook adoption hearings seems to be dominated by those who want material expurgated from the books; live-and-let-live people who welcome new ideas tend to vacate this field. Some people have become almost fixtures at such hearings in the attempt to make textbooks reflect their view of the world. It is the familiar case of a vocal and passionate minority controlling policy over the more passive majority.

During the 1980s, Norma and Martin Gabler of Texas gained considerable notoriety by devoting their lives and fortunes to the cause of having what they consider to be a liberal view of the world expurgated from schoolbooks. They attacked books containing references to sex, evolution, feminist values, or suggestions that the United States may not always have been right in its foreign affairs. In anticipation of such attacks and public pressure, many publishers self-censor their textbooks in advance. For example, Scott Foresman expurgated four hundred lines from its high school version of Shakespeare's *Romeo and Juliet* in an effort to eliminate any suggestion of carnal lust between those star-crossed lovers.

The right wing does not have a monopoly on such attempts to control the content of textbooks. Feminists, for example, show up to complain about demeaning depictions of women. African Americans have caused the censorship of such works as *The Adventures of Huckleberry Finn* and *Gone with the Wind* because they used the "n——" word, and Jews have caused the removal of Shakespeare's *The Merchant of Venice* from school districts because of the portrayal of Shylock as a wicked Jew.

Liberal groups, though less concerned with sexual morality, have tried to pressure the networks to reduce the violent content of television shows. Network executives claim to have reduced such content, although much violence apparently remains in the current programming. There is some circumstantial evidence, mostly of an illustrative variety, that exposure to television violence can result in violent behavior. (A case in point is the man who set fire to his wife in October 1984 after watching *The Burning Bed*.) However, the evidence is inconclusive and the debate continues.

If a major premise of an open society is that reasonable adults are capable of assessing the value of competing ideas, should they also be presumed capable of making moral choices for themselves, provided that such choices do not harm others? When a censor presumes to tell such reasonable, consenting adults what material is too immoral for them to see or read, is that censor not presuming to make moral choices for others? If so, by what criteria can a censor be presumed to be more fit to make moral choices for other people than the people themselves? Thus the central premise of censorship, that reasonable adults cannot be trusted to make social, political, and moral choices for themselves, is a denial of the essence of an open society. Proponents of censorship argue, however, that an unqualified adherence to the principle of an open society may weaken the commitment to moral and family values that define the essence of America as a community.

CONFLICT OVER THE ROLE OF RELIGION
IN THE UNITED STATES

A general trend toward the *secularization* of society in the Western world has been felt less strongly in the United States than elsewhere. While levels of church attendance and beliefs in God have dropped steadily in Western Europe, the United States is rather unique among industrialized countries in its relatively high levels of religious practice and beliefs in a higher power. The continuing relevance of religiosity in American society is fostered by the prevalence of evangelical and fundamentalist churches in America such as the Southern Baptists, Assemblies of God, and smaller Bible Belt churches, while the salience of religiosity in American political life has been reinforced by the emergence of such religious advocacy groups as Focus on the Family and the Christian Coalition, the latter being the creation of former presidential candidate and televangelist Reverend Pat Robertson. While most secularists in America populate the political left, conservatives do not have a monopoly on religion, as even some liberals exhibit a religiosity not seen in Europe.

Still, those on the Christian right feel that their faith and their right to declare it has been under widespread attack by the secular left. From a ban on the employees of Wal-Mart and other stores from wishing their patrons "Merry Christmas" to an effort to have a large white cross on a hill near San Diego removed, secularists have attacked public expressions of Christian faith. In particular, some public displays of the Ten Commandments have come under attack. For example, a judge was prevented from displaying a plaque containing the Ten Commandments in his courtroom. In another incident, Chief Justice Roy Moore of the Supreme Court of Alabama wheeled a 5,280-pound granite monument of the Ten Commandments into the central rotunda of the state supreme court building. A federal judge ordered Moore to remove the huge monument, but he refused, precipitating his removal from the bench by state authorities for disobeying a federal court order and violating the state's canons of judicial ethics. Meanwhile, leaders on the religious right have applied pressure on both Congress and the Republican Party platform writers to incorporate the imperatives of fundamental Christian social doctrine into policy proposals. Their success was manifested in the strong anti-abortion plank in the Republican platform of the last few decades. In addition to efforts to re-criminalize abortion and suppress the encouragement of contraception, the New Christian Right has focused on the re-introduction of devotional observance in the public sector, especially in public schools.

Freedom Of, and From, Religion

Previous sections have shown how the First Amendment protects pluralism, the legitimate coexistence of various points of view and belief systems. The religion clauses of the First Amendment protect the legitimacy of divergent religious orientations, including agnosticism and atheism. If the right to choose one's own views and to evaluate ideas for oneself is a hallmark of the concept of the open society, surely this principle also applies to religion, which touches fundamental and intensely held sets of values and beliefs. It is therefore fitting that the two religion clauses of the Bill of Rights are included in the First Amendment, which is devoted to the protection and legitimacy of pluralism and the open society. Precisely because religious beliefs are so intensely held, however, dominant groups will seek to impose values from those beliefs on their society. Many of the values that the social conservatives and religious right define as part of the essence of the American community are religiously based. The religious right therefore seeks to impose conformity to these values through law and social policy, an objective that comes into conflict with the concept of the open society.

There are two distinct religion clauses in the First Amendment: the establishment clause and the free exercise clause, which read as follows:

> Congress shall make no law respecting an establishment of religion, or prohibiting the free exercise thereof . . .

The *establishment clause* is concerned with preventing the government from promoting or aiding religion; the *free exercise clause* is concerned with preventing the government from interfering with the practice of religion. To the extent that government implements either of these clauses to its logical extreme, it may be held to violate a conception of the other clause. For example, when government does nothing that may indirectly aid religion, such as not permitting religious practices in public schools even when a decisive majority desires such activity, government may be seen as preventing the dominant forces in the community from practicing their religion as they see fit. In short, these clauses may come into conflict with each other; therefore, to uphold one clause absolutely would endanger the other.

The Establishment Clause

Schools.   There is, of course, considerable ambiguity in the phrase "Congress shall make no law respecting an establishment of religion." Reasonable people can and do disagree about precisely what government is prohibited from doing. At a minimum, it is understood that government may not sanction a particular religious sect as the official state religion, a practice common in many European nations. In England, the Anglican Church is the state church; in Scotland, it is the Presbyterian Church; in Spain, the Catholic Church has official status; and in Scandinavia, the Lutheran Church is the official state religion. A state church or religion means that the head of state normally must be a member of that church, that he or she officially appoints the leading clerics in that church (usually on the advice of political and religious leaders), and that the church and its schools receive overt financial support from the state. In some places, it may mean that the religion's moral views are enacted into law, as exemplified by limitations on divorce, contraception, and abortion in some Catholic countries. Although it has meant in the past that members of minority or nonofficial religions lost their religious freedoms and even their property and lives, members of the nonofficial religions are no longer so threatened in Western democracies. The Western world, on the official level at least, is now generally a model of toleration of religious pluralism, despite the continued existence of established churches.

Beyond this prohibition of an official national church, it is generally agreed that the government in the United States may not legislatively bestow advantages on one or more sects over other religions. That is, any government activities that aid one religious sect must similarly aid all religions. This is known as the *accommodationist* interpretation of the establishment clause. If the clause meant no more than this, this interpretation would allow government to promote religion in general as long as one sect was not favored over others.

Another interpretation of the Establishment Clause is sometimes called the *wall of separation* position, using the words of Thomas Jefferson. Not only does this position itself generate controversy, as it is not self-evident that the establishment clause forbids government aid to all religions equally; the wall of separation doctrine also generates controversy even among its ostensible adherents concerning precisely what the government may do without breaching the wall. The Supreme Court has seemingly alternated between the wall of separation and accommodationist interpretations of the Establishment Clause. The Court's first Establishment Clause case in 1899 involved the question of whether the federal government could appropriate money toward a Catholic-run hospital in Washington, DC for the construction of facilities to care for indigent patients. The justices decided that since the money was appropriated for a secular purpose, a hospital, that no violation of the Establishment Clause occurred. Half a century later, in the 1947 *Everson* case, the Court seemed to move toward more of a wall of separation between church and state. Although the Court ruled in *Everson* that it is constitutional to use public money to reimburse parents for bus transportation to both public and parochial schools,[44] Justice Black's opinion explicitly used the wall metaphor in analyzing the case. Four dissenters thought the wall was breached in this instance. The case implicitly established the precedent that the wall of separation doctrine does not prevent some government activities that provide some secondary or spillover benefits to religion if the primary purposes of the policy are secular ones and, in the case of parochial education, if the primary beneficiary is the schoolchild. Thus, the question of where to draw the line went unanswered by the wall of separation position.

The wall of separation interpretation of the establishment clause has been used to oppose public aid to private parochial schools. In general, the Court has taken the principle laid down in *Lemon* that such aid is permissible if the primary purpose is secular (teaching courses like math, language, or science) and the primary beneficiary is the child rather than the church.[45] More recently, the idea of taking a position of neutrality between government and religion has been gaining a majority of the Court, as *Mitchell v. Helms* upheld the distribution to parochial schools of library and media materials, and computer hardware and software on secular subjects.[46] It is likely that this trend will continue, given the conservatives' 5–4 majority on the Court.

Aids to Parochial Schools. The *Everson* case (1947), in upholding the reimbursement of public funds to parents for the costs of busing their children to sectarian schools, laid down the child benefit standard. This means that if the primary effect of the aid is to benefit the pupil in the attainment of a secular education, a spillover effect of some benefit to a religious institution does not in itself rule that legislation unconstitutional.

The Court applied this principle in the *Allen* case (1968) in holding that it is legal for the state to lend textbooks on secular subjects approved by public school officials to pupils in sectarian schools.[47] Although the Court was willing to approve the loan of textbooks, it drew the line in another case, *Lemon v. Kurtman* (1971), on state reimbursement for the purchase of books and payment of teachers' salaries by sectarian schools.[48] The Court established a three-part test for determining if the laws could survive establishment clause scrutiny: (1) The law in question had to have a secular legislative purpose; (2) The law's primary effect could not advance religion, nor could it inhibit religion; (3) The law could not "foster excessive government entanglement with religion." In the *Lemon* case, the Court found that the law had a secular purpose of enhancing education in all schools. However, the law in question violated the third part of the test because the state set up elaborate systems to ensure that teachers at religious schools which qualified for reimbursement of salaries were not teaching religious instruction. The reality was that the state could not ensure the religious neutrality of sectarian school teachers, whose salaries they would be paying, when they worked under independent religious school administrations. The Court felt that the law created excessive entanglement between government and religion. On the other hand, the Court later upheld a Minnesota law allowing parents a state income tax deduction for certain expenses of a private parochial education as well as for public education.[49] In *Zobrest v. Catalina Foothills School District*, the Court held that the establishment clause did not require a school district to deny the services of a sign language interpreter to a hearing-impaired student simply because that student attended a Catholic school.[50]

As it stands, the bulk of the cases indicate that the Court appears willing to allow the state to provide direct aid to parents who then make choices that end up benefiting parochial schools, but the Court draws the line on direct state aid to parochial schools. This point became key to the Court's resolution of whether school vouchers to private schools violated the Establishment Clause. For years, conservatives had been pushing states to adopt voucher programs, where students of public schools could take state money spent on the student and use that money toward tuition costs at a religious school. The Supreme Court addressed the constitutionality of voucher programs in a 2002 case out of Ohio, where the state instituted a voucher program for the Cleveland school system, which had a large population of low-income students, after the school system began failing.[51]

Ohio's voucher program offered several options. It allowed parents of the Cleveland school system to receive a scholarship of $2,250 per year to attend an accredited private nonreligious or religious school. Alternatively, students could remain in the Cleveland school district and receive $500 in tutorial assistance. Or, students could move to another public school district willing to accept Cleveland students, and that public school district would then receive the $2,250 in state aid for accepting the Cleveland student. After the program was enacted, 96.7 percent of students who used tuition vouchers chose to attend religious private schools (although there were also nonreligious private schools that participated in the program that were available to parents). The central question for the Court was whether the law impermissibly advanced religion. In a 5–4 decision, the Court upheld the voucher program, in part, because those tuition scholarships that ultimately went to religious schools were the result of the private choices of parents. The Court reiterated the principle that "government programs that neutrally provide benefits to a broad class of citizens defined without reference to religion are not readily subject to an Establishment Clause challenge."[52]

Arguments for Aid. First, arguments for such aid begin with the fact that sectarian schools do a respectable job in providing a secular education, that is, training pupils in subjects like mathematics, English, science, and geography. In fact, many people feel that, in general, sectarian schools do a better job in that regard than do most public schools. Thus, because sectarian schools perform an important public function, they are said to deserve public support. Moreover, if sectarian schools were to cease to function tomorrow, the existing public school systems would be unable to handle the large population of religious school pupils they would discharge into the public schools. The money not spent on sectarian schools would then have to be spent on a substantial expansion of the public schools.

Second, parents of parochial school pupils carry a double burden: They must pay the property taxes that support public schools and must finance the parochial education of their own children. In effect, they are financially penalized for choosing a religious school education for their children. Therefore it is argued that the lack of public support for parochial education goes beyond neutrality toward religion. Although it is true that parochial school pupils are free to take advantage of the public school system, if any great number of them did so, that system would collapse if not supported by greatly increased taxation.

Third, arguments for aid to religious schools draw upon the desire to return to the traditional value of strong parental responsibility for the education of their children. Because many evangelical and fundamentalist parents believe that modern, secular education in the public schools undermines traditional Christian teachings, they assert a free exercise right to support for their educational duties.

Arguments Against Aid. Opponents of aid to parochial education see such aid as the first potential break in the symbolic wall that separates church and state, a breach that will make subsequent breaches more likely.

Furthermore, in light of the intense emotion surrounding religion, the danger of parochial school aid is that the benefits will not be allocated equally among all religions, not to mention between organized religion and nonreligion. Any aid policy will benefit the members and institutions of some religions to the exclusion of those who do not belong to those religions, as different religions have different levels of commitment to parochial education. Perhaps this is one justification for a secularized school system in a society with a variety of religious orientations.

Prayer in School.   The problem of parochial schools as an alternative to secularized public schools for parents who want religious content in their child's education remains their affordability for most middle-class families. Hence, many parents continue to press for religious content in the public school curriculum. It would seem, however, that such activity is clearly unconstitutional under the Establishment Clause. Presumably, no devotional activity, no matter how voluntary or nondenominational, may be sponsored by the public schools. But, the concepts of devotional activity and school sponsorship are not unambiguous.

In two separate decisions—the Bible-reading cases, *Schempp* and *Murray* (1963), and the New York regents prayer case, *Engle v. Vitale* (1962)—the Court seemed to take an unequivocal position. In the first case, the Court ruled that devotional reading, without comment, from the New Testament is inconsistent with the Establishment Clause, even when objecting students are excused from class.[53] In the second, it ruled that prayer sponsored by school authorities, regardless of who actually reads it and regardless of how nonsectarian or voluntary the prayer may be, is in violation of the Establishment Clause.[54] In striking down such a prayer, the Court made clear that any prayer sponsored by public school officials is on its face unconstitutional. There is no way that any amount of tinkering with the nature of a school prayer or the mode of its presentation can render that prayer logically consistent with the constraints imposed by the school prayer decision. In the summer of 1985, the Court struck down an Alabama law requiring silent meditation or prayer as an organized activity in its public schools. The Court's opinion did hint, however, that some form of silent meditation might pass constitutional muster. The Court has also ruled that it is unconstitutional to distribute Gideon Bibles in public schools, even though students have the right to refuse to accept one. Meanwhile, militant secularists continue to challenge any mention of God or religion in public school classrooms. The case of *Elk Grove Unified School District v. Newdow* (2004) dealt with a challenge by atheist Michael Newdow to saying the Pledge of Allegiance with words "under God" in a public school attended by his daughter, a challenge dismissed by the Court because Newdow, who brought the case, did not have custody over his daughter in the school and therefore lacked "standing to sue" (something personally at stake in the outcome of the case).[55]

The issue of prayer in the schools arose again in *Lee v. Weisman*, this time not inside a classroom, but rather at a school graduation ceremony.[56] Ironically this case involved a challenge by a Jewish parent to a prayer offered at 1991 graduation ceremonies by a Jewish rabbi. Despite this unusual circumstance, in the overwhelming preponderance of cases, such prayers are offered in the dominant religion of the community. In 1992, the Supreme Court decided the case, ruling such graduation prayers unconstitutional, thereby maintaining exclusion of officially sponsored prayer in public schools, including school-sponsored functions outside the classroom.

More recent attempts to insert prayer into the public schools have involved prayer services initiated by students rather than by school officials and instituted at extracurricular functions. This phenomenon came before the Court in 2000 involving the well-established practice in countless small- to medium-sized communities of holding public prayer at high school football games. In *Santa Fe Independent School District v. Doe*, the Court considered a student-led prayer delivered over the public address system prior to each game, a practice approved by a substantial majority of the student body in an annual vote.[57] Community opinion was so strongly supportive of the prayers that the two plaintiffs were permitted by the lower courts to proceed anonymously. Nevertheless, the Court struck down the practice by a 6–3 vote as a violation of the establishment clause. The Court found that in addition to those who had to attend—players, cheerleaders, band members—there is strong peer pressure on others to attend the high school football game in that small Texas town. Once again, the Court was pointing out that in the area of school-sponsored devotional activities, voluntary is not really voluntary due to peer pressure to conform.

To get around the Establishment Clause rulings, both President Reagan and the 1984 Republican Party platform explicitly supported a constitutional amendment to overturn the *Vitale* decision and to establish the right to voluntary prayer in the public schools. In a sense, students still have the right of voluntary prayer. It is important to realize that the courts have in no way limited the right of individuals in school to pray in any private manner they choose. Rather, only organized devotional activity, sponsored by the school, has been banned. Some religious leaders have held that such private prayer is actually more meaningful, as it comes from within an individual by choice rather than being recited by compulsion as part of a group exercise. The advantage of the school-sponsored group prayer that the proposed constitutional amendment would ostensibly protect, according to its supporters, is that it gives official recognition and support to the Judeo-Christian moral values they feel are the core of the American community. This goal assumes greater importance to the more conservative Christians as they perceive those values as increasingly under attack by Islamic militants while liberal secularists strive even harder to take a multicultural approach and thus to avoid offending those who do not share these core American values. More skeptical secular liberals suspect that the dominant group wants the leverage that the amendment would give them to compel others to pray and to do so in a manner determined by the dominant group. As Justice Frankfurter observed in the *McCollum* case, "The law of imitation operates, and non-conformity is not an outstanding characteristic of children."[58] Peer pressure to participate will be strong and accordingly, in the case of organized, school-sponsored religious activities, participation is never really voluntary. Some fundamentalist religious leaders still argue that such organized prayer in the schools is essential to restoring the nation's moral foundations, though other religious leaders contend that prayer must be private and voluntary in order to be meaningful. The Senate has regularly rejected a proposed constitutional amendment to permit such prayer, but the issue is placed back on the agenda by conservative legislators each year.

The prayer and Bible-reading decisions reinforced a tendency for the Court to compel the complete secularization of America's public schools that had previously been apparent in the *McCollum v. Board of Education* case (1948), which had struck down "voluntary" religious training by leaders of the major religions during the school day and on school time. Both the hostile public reaction and noncompliance to this decision and the prayer and Bible-reading cases were extensive in many public school districts throughout the nation. For instance, one national sample of school teachers found that 28 percent continued to recite classroom prayer two years after the *Engle* decision.[59] Noncompliance was heaviest in the Bible Belt South. For example, a survey of 121 of Tennessee's 152 school districts found that only one had eliminated such Bible reading.[60] It has been estimated that almost half of the released time programs continued after *McCollum*, although they were clearly inconsistent with the decision. In the face of such public resistance, the Court backed off somewhat from the implications of *McCollum* and held in a New York case that students could be released for religious instruction during the school day if the instruction took place off the school campus. In doing so, they implicitly rejected much of the logic in the *McCollum* decision.

The trend toward noncompliance with bans on public school religious observances has been a continuous obstacle to the Court-mandated secularization of those schools. Not only were there periods of strife following each of the major policy decisions, but pressures for noncompliance continue today. The theoretically simple solution to the degree of religious activity constitutionally allowable (none) has proved more complex than anticipated.

Other Establishment Clause Issues.   The forces that have promoted the secularization of the public schools have broadened their efforts to promote the secularization of other aspects of public life. These efforts came to a head in the lawsuit challenging the right of Pawtucket, Rhode Island, to display a life-size nativity scene at city expense. The Supreme Court continued its tradition of permitting Christmas pageants, Easter celebrations, and the like in public schools (and therefore presumably in public life) on the grounds that these holidays have become so much a part of the American culture that they have significance beyond their sectarian religious meaning. In *Lynch v. Donnelly* (1984), the Court ruled that the Pawtucket display merely "engenders a friendly community spirit of good will in keeping with the season."[61] However, only a few years later in 1989, the conservative majority (Scalia, Kennedy, Rehnquist, White, and O'Connor) struck down the public display of a nativity scene with overt Christian messages (e.g., "Jesus is Lord"), while in a separate decision it upheld the public display of a Jewish menorah (the candleholder commemorating the Chanukah season) accompanied by symbols of the secular aspects of Christmas in "the spirit of religious pluralism." Thus, the Court seemed to create what some legal scholars refer to as the "and Santa too" rule. The Court will permit religious displays on public property at Christmas time, such as a nativity scene or a menorah, if such religious displays are also accompanied or surrounded by more secular objects, such as a Santa Claus, a Christmas Tree, Candy Canes, Frosty the Snow Man, etc. Clearly, unlike the school prayer decisions, which tacked a more "wall of separation" interpretation of the Establishment Clause, these religious display cases evoke the more accommodationist perspective.

A recurring issue in the area of religious material in public places in general and public schools in particular has been the controversy over the display of the Ten Commandments in public school classrooms and other public venues such as courtrooms or parks. The Ten Commandments are, of course, a nonsectarian symbol of the Judeo–Christian tradition that is an important aspect of our culture. In 1980, the Court struck down a Kentucky law that provided for copies of the Decalogue, financed by private funds, to be placed in public school classrooms.[62] The Court held by a narrow majority that no secular purpose was served by the display. Many religious conservatives have refused to accept that decision and continue to fight to have this, among other religious symbols, displayed in classrooms and other public places. In 2005, the Court permitted a large stone monument of the Ten Commandments to remain in a public park located on the grounds of the Texas State Capitol building and the Supreme Court Building in Austin.[63] However, the same Court rejected the right to display the Commandments inside two Kentucky county courthouses.[64] The difference was in the vote of Justice Breyer, who rejected the right to display the Decalogue in the Kentucky case, but who argued in the Texas case that the monument had gone unchallenged for forty years and had historical value. Breyer also noted that the "physical setting of the monument," which was situated among "17 other monuments and 21 historical markers, all designed to illustrate the 'ideals' of those who settled in Texas" suggested to him "little or nothing of the sacred" in that particular Ten Commandments monument.[65] In a 2010 case, the Court faced an issue involving the constitutionality of a seventy-five-year-old National World War I Memorial containing an eight-foot cross located in the Mojave Desert of California on public land that had been conveyed to a private entity in order to avoid an Establishment Clause issue.[66] In a closely divided Supreme Court, the five-member majority upheld the land transfer (which allowed the Cross to stay put), while Breyer, who sided with the dissenters, thought that there was no need to address the Establishment Clause issue and that the Court should instead focus on the legality of the land transfer.

The Free Exercise Clause

The tension between the establishment clause and the free exercise clause ("Congress shall make no law . . . prohibiting the free exercise" of religion) was discussed at the beginning of this section. In light of this tension, the latter clause is most frequently mentioned in conjunction with values threatened by the vigorous enforcement of the former. Thus the effort to secularize the public schools, an effort justified by the establishment clause, is frequently opposed in the name of the free exercise clause.

In general, the free exercise clause is most often invoked to protect the religious practices of unconventional groups, as the frequency of Jehovah's Witness cases attests. Previously in free exercise cases going back to the late 1930s, over forty of which from 1938 to 1955 involved the Jehovah's Witnesses because of their aggressive proselytizing, the Court decided in favor of the free exercise claim the majority of the time. The clause had been used to protect the right of Jehovah's Witnesses to proselytize door-to-door and to refuse to pledge allegiance to the flag (many of the Jehovah's Witnesses' cases were interwoven with free speech claims, making it easier for the courts to come down on their side).[67]

But despite some of the successes in Court, particularly by Jehovah's Witnesses, religious groups have had mixed success using the clause to exempt themselves from state laws on the basis of their right to practice their religion. For much of the country's history, it was not uncommon for the Supreme Court and other courts to reject claims by groups asking for protection to engage in religious practices that would be otherwise illegal or would violate strongly held moral imperatives. The courts denied free exercise protection to engage in polygamy, sexual license, and exposure to poisonous snakes as a test of faith.[68] In 1955, the Supreme Court held that the free exercise clause does not give parents the right to withhold vaccinations, essential medical care, or education in the name of religion.[69]

But the Court departed significantly from its previous interpretation of the free exercise clause in the 1963 case of *Sherbert v. Verner*, dealing with the question of whether Sherbert, a Seventh-Day Adventist, could refuse to take work on Saturday and still receive unemployment benefits.[70] The Court decided in favor of Sherbert, creating a new test, which stated that if the government passes a law which burdens the free exercise of religion, the government must justify the law based on a "compelling government interest" and must use the least restrictive means possible to further that interest. This test was later used to excuse the Amish from having to attend high school based on religious reasons.[71] The government could still burden one's free exercise rights if it could show a compelling government interest. For example, in 1984, a faith-healing couple from Albion, Indiana, was sentenced to ten years in prison for withholding medical care from their nine-year-old daughter who had died a "preventable death" from meningitis. The superior court rejected their free exercise claim in finding them guilty of reckless homicide.

In 1990, the Court weakened the free exercise rights of religious groups when it essentially did away with the "compelling interest" test in *Employment Division v. Smith*.[72] In that case, the Court upheld the state of Oregon's refusal to provide unemployment benefits to two Native Americans who were fired from their job for using peyote in Indian religious ceremonies. Oregon had argued that because the two individuals were fired from their job for engaging in an illegal activity – that is, smoking peyote, which Oregon law classified as an illegal drug – the state had a right to deny them unemployment benefits. But, the two Native Americans argued that they should be exempted from the law, because they were using peyote as part of their religious practices. Writing for the majority, Justice Scalia said that the "right of free exercise does not relieve an individual of an obligation to comply with a 'valid and neutral law of general applicability." Scalia said to rule otherwise would allow a person "to become a law unto himself" in the name of practicing one's religion. In other words, as long as the law was neutral and applied generally to everyone, individuals could not excuse themselves from having to follow the law by claiming that they are exercising their right to practice their religion. Under this new standard, as long as the law in question is a valid and neutral law of *general applicability*, then the government doesn't have to demonstrate a compelling interest for that law when it burdens the free exercise rights of certain individuals. But, if such practices like smoking peyote are not protected by the free exercise clause, especially when they seemingly hurt no one else, then what is its point?

Supporters of free exercise, including religious groups across the political and theological spectrum, argued that the principle in the *Smith* case would unduly impede the free exercise of religion, views that led both Republicans and Democrats in Congress to pass the bipartisan 1993 Religious Freedom Restoration Act (RFRA). This act forbade policies and rules that burden the exercise of religion unless government can show that the burden furthers a "compelling public interest" and that the challenged action is "the least restrictive means of doing so." Essentially, Congress attempted to overrule the Supreme Court by reinstating the *Sherbert v. Verner* test that had been expressly rejected by the Court in the *Smith* case. After RFRA's passage, prison inmates sued, claiming the right to use drugs as part of their "religious experience," and an Amish group won an exemption from posting orange safety triangles on its buggies. In fear of such a flood of claims, sixteen states joined the City of Boerne in challenging RFRA in a 1997 case that represented a constitutional showdown between Congress and the Supreme Court.

In *City of Boerne v. Flores* (1997), the Supreme Court struck the act down as it related to states, claiming that Congress lacked the authority under the Fourteenth Amendment to require states to accommodate such religious practices, since the Court had already ruled under *Smith* that states were not required to follow the compelling interest test of *Sherbert*.[73] The ruling was somewhat narrow, because the Court allowed for provisions of the act to stand, which required a compelling interest test for federal government actions. In other words, the Court said that Congress could strengthen the free exercise rights of people above the threshold set by the Court in *Smith*, as long as the new standards only applied to the federal government. However, Congress lacked the authority to tell states that they had to provide more rights to practice one's religion above and beyond what was required by the Constitution as interpreted by the Court in the *Smith* case.

Still, conservative and religious groups reacted strongly to this decision, arguing that it was an extreme case of judicial activism and an attempt to impose secularization on all aspects of life. Congress reacted to the Court decision by simply re-passing a scaled-down version of RFRA, which mostly applied to the rights of prisoners in state prison and the regulations of religious land use, and then justified their authority to pass the law under their power to regulate interstate commerce. After this new law was passed, prisoners of the Satanist and Wicca religions, as well as prisoners belonging to a white supremacist Christian sect, sued the state of Ohio under the new congressional law, claiming that they were not allowed access to religious literature or opportunities to worship. The Court found in favor of the prisoners, upholding this revised version of RFRA in 2005.[74]

While the *Smith* case foreclosed religious groups exempting themselves from following generally applicable state laws that were neutral in their treatment of religion, the Supreme Court illustrated that it would not allow a state law to stand which targeted and discriminated against a particular religion just because it was unconventional or unpopular. A 1993 case drew a great deal of attention in this regard when adherents to the Santeria religion set up shop in the City of Hialeah, Florida and began practicing animal sacrifice in their religious ceremonies. City officials and members in the community became alarmed at this development, and the city council passed ordinances banning animal sacrifice in a religious ceremony. However, the law exempted slaughterhouses or the slaughtering of animals for food if "the primary purpose" was for "food consumption." In this case, the *Church of Lukumi Babalu Aye v. City of Hialeah*, a unanimous Court held that the city had singled out that church with the ban on sacrifices; hence, the regulation was not neutral and was a violation of the free exercise clause.[75] But, many of the justices disagreed on exactly why the ordinance was a violation of the free exercise clause. Some wanted to return to the compelling interest test of *Sherbert*, but only a minority of justices wanted to return to that standard.

This neutrality required by government toward regulating religious practices does not apparently apply to government assistance for scholarships. Here, the dual meaning of the religious clauses clashed in one 2004 case in which the Court found that Washington state could exclude "devotional theology" as an acceptable major that could be supported by their scholarship program for gifted students.[76]

Creationism and Secular Humanism.   Supporters of religion in the public schools argue that religion is a necessary part of our heritage and that schools should reflect the dominant culture. They further contend that the secularization of the school is tantamount to teaching a "religion of humanism," a vague concept implying the elevation of humanity to the place of God. The declining importance of religion in the modern world has created a perceived threat of the encroachment of secular humanism on traditional religious values. Secular humanisn's general connotation is that humans can, to some extent, control their fate and are not totally subject to the will of the deity. Moreover, secular humanism implies that it is a legitimate and worthwhile enterprise to strive to improve the quality of life on earth independent of the assistance of God and independent of considerations of salvation.

On the other hand, even the removal of prayer and Bible reading from public schools does not complete their secularization. Public schools still engage in Christmas pageants and related exercises that can readily be viewed as religious. Christmas is clearly a Christian holiday, and other celebrations observed in public schools, such as Halloween and Saint Valentine's Day, have their genesis in Christian traditions. The Court backed off from barring such exercises by ruling that they are more a fixture in the American cultural tradition than strictly religious exercises. Therefore the law now says that although atheists, Muslims, and Jews are protected from being exposed to an innocuous, nonsectarian prayer, they may be compelled either to isolate themselves or to participate in an extensive Christmas pageant under the Court declaration that Christmas is not a religious holiday. Moreover, federal law gives students the right to organize religious clubs and activities on school property outside school hours. Clearly, the establishment clause is imperfectly successful in resisting the inevitable social pressures placed on others to adhere to the imperatives of a dominant religious orientation.

The extent of noncompliance with the Court dictates in the religion cases described earlier illustrates the difficulty in attempting by judicial fiat to secularize the institutions of a nonsecularized culture. Communities have come to expect that the schools that teach their children should reflect the values of the community, and a mere pronouncement by a distant tribunal, a pronouncement that they may well not have heard of and that they almost certainly have not read or studied, is not going to change that expectation. Thus the famous *Scopes* monkey trial involved the question of whether a community can bar the teaching of the theory of evolution—a theory almost universally accepted by the scientific establishment—because it conflicts with the dominant religious doctrine of that community. The Court was forced to rule such efforts unconstitutional as late as 1968, as Arkansas had brazenly passed a law nearly identical with the one challenged in the *Scopes* trial.[77] Despite this, Arkansas and Louisiana passed laws in the early 1980s requiring that scientific creationism be taught. The Supreme Court declared such laws unconstitutional in 1987. Kansas caused a widespread critical reaction in 2000 when its school board forbade the use of the term *evolution* in its public schools. In the face of vociferous protest, the board later dropped the ban. Such establishment clause cases are a classic example of the Court's preventing a clear majority from exercising its strongly felt will. At the very least, such religious majorities feel that the biblical account of creation should be taught in addition to evolution, and they continue to exert pressures to have this done.

MORALITY, THE COURT, AND THE OPEN SOCIETY

With the exception of some of the obscenity cases, the Supreme Court over the last half-century has oftentimes adopted an interpretation of the Constitution that supports the view of an open society. Efforts by conservatives and liberals to impose their visions of morality on the rest of the country have not been particularly successful, as indicated by some of the religious cases and free speech cases mentioned in this chapter. In considering the Supreme Court's actions, it must be remembered that the point of the concept of civil liberties is that there are some things that a majority cannot do to a minority, no matter how strong that majority may be and no matter how intensely it may want to do so. The efforts by conservatives to reverse the Court on the prayer issue and to circumvent rulings on pornography, as well as liberals' attempts to get around the free speech clause in order to impose regulations that punish offensive speech, suggest that no resolution of issues involving morality or religion can be deemed permanent. Such issues will continue to occupy the public in the decades ahead.

ENDNOTES

1. http://blogs.newsobserver.com/campusnotes/unc-students-plan-another-tancredo-protest; Accessed May 1, 2010.

2. This minimal definition may be found expostulated most notably in Joseph Schumpeter's classic, *Capitalism, Socialism and Democracy* (New York: Harper Torchbooks, 1942 and 1962), Chapter 22.

3. Dissenting opinion in *Abrams v. United States*, 250 U.S. 616 (1919), at 630.

4. Amitai Etzioni, *The Spirit of Community* (New York: Crown Publishers, 1993).

5. For example, Samuel Huntington, *The Clash of Civilizations: The Remaking of the World Order* (New York: Simon and Schuster, 1996), 263–272.

6. Robert D. Putnam, "E Pluribus Unum: Diversity and Community in the Twenty-first Century, the 2006 Johan Skytte Prize Lecture," *Scandinavian Political Studies* 30 (2) (2007): 137–174.

7. Justice Stone's now famous footnote 4 in *U.S. v. Caroline Products* 344 U.S. 144 (1938), at 152.

8. *Roe v. Wade*, 410 U.S. 113 (1973).

9. *Webster v. Reproductive Health Services*, 109 S. Ct. 3040 (1989).

10. *Stenberg v. Carhart*, 530 U.S. 914 (2000); and *Gonzales v. Carhart*, 550 U.S. 124 (2007).

11. *Planned Parenthood of Southeastern Pennsylvania v. Casey*, 505 U.S. 833 (1992).

12. *Planned Parenthood of Columbia Inc. v. American Coalition of Life Activists*, 244 F. 3d. 1007 (2001).

13. *Hill v. Colorado*, 530 U.S. 703 (2000).

14. *Adderly v. Florida*, 385 U.S. 39 (1966).

15. *Gonzales v. Oregon*, 546 U.S. 243 (2006).

16. For a scholarly inquiry into the meaning of the freedom of speech clause for its authors, a study that concludes that the authors merely understood it to embrace this common law definition, see Leonard Levy, *The Legacy of Suppression* (Cambridge: Harvard University Press, 1960).

17. *Chaplinsky v. New Hampshire*, 315 U.S. 568 (1942).

18. Lori Preuitt and George Kiriyama, "American Flag Clothing Sparks New Protest," *MSNBC.COM*, http://www.msnbc.msn.com/id/36998746/ns/local_news-san_francisco_bay_area_ca/; Accessed May 6, 2010.

19. *R.A.V. v. City of St. Paul*, 505 U.S. 377 (1992), p. 379.

20. The discussion of the Michigan policy is drawn from Dinesh D'Souza, *Illiberal Education* (New York: The Free Press, 1991), 140–144.

21. "Embassies Burn in Cartoon Protest," *BBC News*, February 4, 2006, http://news.bbc.co.uk/2/hi/middle_east/4681294.stm; Accessed May 1, 2010.

22. Scott Collins and Matea Gold, "South Park Threat No Joke," *Los Angeles Times*, April 23, 2010, A1.

23. *Regina v. Hicklin*, L.R. 3 Q.B. (1868).

24. *Roth v. United States*, 354 U.S. 476 (1957).

25. *Miller v. California*, 413 U.S. 15 (1973).

26. *Jenkins v. Georgia*, 418 U.S. 153 (1974).
27. *Sable Communications of California v. Federal Communications Commission*, 49 U.S. 115 (1989).
28. *Reno v. American Civil Liberties Union*, 521 U.S. 844 (1997).
29. *Jacobellis v. Ohio*, 378 U.S. 84 (1974).
30. *Ashcroft v. Free Speech Coalition*, 535 U.S. 234 (2002)
31. *Ashcroft v. Free Speech Coalition*, 535 U.S. 234 (2002)
32. *The Report of the Commission on Obscenity and Pornography* (Washington, DC: U.S. Government Printing Office, 1970).
33. James Q. Wilson, "Violence, Pornography and Social Science," *The Public Interest*, 22 (Winter 1971): 45–61; and J. D. Unwin, *Sex and Culture* (London: Oxford University Press, 1934). These arguments are well summarized in Harry M. Clor, "Commentary on the Report of the Commission on Obscenity and Pornography," in Clor, ed., *Censorship and Freedom of Expression* (Skokie, IL: Rand McNally, 1971): 119–129.
34. Diana Russell, *Dangerous Relationships: Pornography, Misogyny, and Rape* (Thousand Oaks, CA: Sage Publications, Inc., 1998), 158.
35. Russell, 1998.
36. Quoted in *Newsweek*, May 25, 1981, p. 46.
37. *City of Los Angeles v. Almeda Books*, 535 U.S. 425 (2002).
38. *Butler v. Michigan*, 352 U.S. 380 (1957), at 383–384.
39. *Stanley v. Georgia*, 394 U.S. 557 (1969).
40. *U.S. v Reidel*, 402 U.S. 351 (1971).
41. *U.S. v. Twelve 200 Foot Reels of Super 8mm Film*, 413 U.S. 123 (1973).
42. *Paris Adult Theater v. Slaton*, 413 U.S. 439 (1973).
43. Catharine MacKinnon, *Only Words* (Cambridge: Harvard University Press, 1993).
44. *Everson v. Board of Education*, 390 U.S. 1 (1947).
45. *Lemon v. Kurtzman*, 403 U.S. 602 (1971).
46. *Mitchell v. Helms*, 530 U.S. 793 (2000).
47. *Board of Education v. Allen*, 392 U.S. 236 (1968).
48. *Lemon v. Kurtzman*, 403 U.S. 602 (1971).
49. *Mueller v. Allen*, 463 U.S. 388 (1983).
50. *Zobrest v. Catalina Foothills School District*, 509 U.S. 1 (1993).
51. *Zelman v. Simmons-Harris*, 536 U.S. 639 (2002).
52. *Zelman v. Simmons-Harris*, 536 U.S. 639 (2002).
53. *School District of Abington Township v. Schempp* and *Murray v. Curlett*, 374 U.S. 203 (1963).
54. *Engle v. Vitale*, 370 U.S. 421 (1962).
55. *Elk Grove School District v. Newdow*, 542 U.S. 1 (2004).
56. *Lee v. Weisman*, 505 U.S. 577 (1992).
57. *Santa Fe Independent School District v. Doe*, 530 U.S. 290 (2000).
58. *Illinois ex. rel. McCollum v. Board of Education*, 33 U.S. 203 (1948), at 227.

59. Frank Way, "Survey Research on Judicial Decisions: The Prayer and Bible Reading Cases," *Western Political Quarterly*, 21 (June 1968): 189–205.

60. Cited in Stephen Wasby, *The Impact of the United States Supreme Court: Some Perspectives* (Homewood, IL: Dorsey Press, 1970), 134–135.

61. *Lynch v. Donnelly*, 465 U.S. 668 (1984).

62. *Stone v. Graham*, 499 U.S. 39 (1980).

63. *Van Orden v. Perry*, 545 U.S. 677 (2005).

64. *McCreary County v. ACLU*, 545 U.S. 844 (2005).

65. *Van Orden v. Perry*, 545 U.S. 677(2005), *Justice Breyer's Concurrence.*

66. *Salazar v. Buono*, 559 U.S. No. 08-472 (2010).

67. *Cantwell v. Connecticut*, 310 U.S. 296 (1940); *West Virginia State Board of Education v. Barnette*, 319 U.S. 624 (1943).

68. See, among such cases, *Reynolds v. U.S.*, 98 U.S. 145 (1879); and *Hardin v. Tennessee*, 188 Tenn 17 (1949).

69. For example, *Jacobson v. Massachusetts*, 197 U.S. 11 (1955).

70. 374 U.S. 398 (1963)

71. *Wisconsin v. Yoder*, 406 U.S. 205 (1972).

72. *Employment Division of Oregon v. Smith*, 494 U.S. 872 (1990).

73. *City of Boerne v. Flores*, 521 U.S. 507 (1997).

74. *Cutter v. Wilkinson*, 544 U.S. 709 (2005)

75. *Church of the Lukumi Babalu Aye v. City of Hialeah*, 508 U.S. 520 (1993).

76. *Locke v. Davey*, 540 U.S. 712 (2004).

77. *Epperson v. Arkansas*, 393 U.S. 97 (1968).

RESOURCES

Books

Abraham, Henry J. *Freedom and the Court*, 5th ed. New York: Oxford University Press, 1988.

Alley, Robert S., ed. *The Supreme Court on Church and State*. New York: Oxford University Press, 1988.

Bickel, Alexander. *The Least Dangerous Branch*. Indianapolis: Bobbs-Merrill, 1962.

Bork, Robert. *Slouching Toward Gomorrah: Modern Liberalism and the American Decline.* New York: HarperCollins, 1996.

Chaffee, Zachariah. *Free Speech in the United States*. Cambridge: Harvard University Press, 1954.

Chopper, Jesse. *Judicial Review and the National Political Process*. Chicago: University of Chicago Press, 1980.

Clor, Harry M., ed. *Censorship and Freedom of Expression*. Skokie, IL: Rand McNally, 1971.

Dierenfield, Bruce J. *The Battle over School Prayer: How* Engel v. Vitale *Changed America*. Lawrence, Kansas: University Press of Kansas, 2007.

Ducat, Craig R. *Modes of Constitutional Interpretation*. St. Paul: West Publishing, 1978.

Emerson, Thomas I. *The System of Freedom of Expression*. New York: Vintage Books, 1970.

Etzioni, Amitai. *The Spirit of Community*. New York: Crown Publishers, 1993.

Fortas, Abe. *Concerning Dissent and Civil Disobedience*. New York: NAL, 1977.

MacKinnon, Catharine A. *Only Words*. Cambridge: Harvard University Press, 1993.

Meiklejohn, Alexander. *Free Speech in Relation to Self-Government*. New York: Harper & Row, 1948.

Monsma, Stephen V. *Positive Neutrality: Letting Religious Freedom Ring*. Westport, CT: Greenwood Press, 1993.

Mooney, Christopher Z., ed. *The Public Clash of Private Values: The Politics of Morality Policy*. New York: Chatham House, 2001.

Segers, Mary C., and Jelen, Ted G. *Wall of Separation? Debating the Public Role of Religion*. Lanham, MD: Rowman & Littlefield, 1998.

Shapiro, Martin. *Freedom of Speech: The Supreme Court and Judicial Review*. Englewood Cliffs, NJ: Prentice Hall, 1966.

Tatalovich, Raymond, and Daynes, Byron W., eds. *Moral Controversies in American Politics*, 3rd ed. Armonk, NY: Sharpe, 2005.

Witte, John, Jr. *Religion and the American Constitutional Experiment: Essential Rights and Liberties*. Boulder, CO: Westview, 2000.

Wolfe, Christopher, ed. *The Family, Civil Society, and the State*. Lanham, MD: Rowman & Littlefield, 1998.

Websites

American Civil Liberties Union: **www.aclu.org**

Americans United for Separation of Church and State: **www.au.org**

Christian Coalition of America: **www.cc.org**

The Institute for Communitarian Policy Studies: **www.gwu.edu/~ccps**

The Leonard E. Greenberg Center for the Study of Religion in Public Life, Trinity College: **www.trincoll.edu/depts/csrpl**

Interfaith Alliance: **www.interfaithalliance.org**

James Madison Center for Free Speech: **http://www.jamesmadisoncenter.org**

NARAL Pro-Choice America: **www.naral.org**

National Catholic Educational Association (Public Policy Department): **www.ncea.org/public/index.asp**

National Education Association (Legislative Action Center): **www.nea.org/lac**

National Organization for Women (NOW): **www.now.org**

National Right to Life: **www.nrlc.org**

Glossary

accommodationist Interpretation of the establishment clause that would permit even-handed government assistance to religious belief and practice. *See also* **wall of separation**.

accountable care organizations Organizations of physicians, hospitals, and other providers established under PPACA that are designed to deliver health care effectively and efficiently.

acid rain Precipitation, including snow, that contains heavy concentrations of sulfuric and nitric acids.

ADA *See* **Americans with Disabilities Act**.

Adequate Yearly Progress (AYP) Requirement under the No Child Left Behind Act that each state establish clearly defined goals for student and school performance.

AFDC *See* **Aid to Families with Dependent Children**.

affirmative action Federal policies requiring businesses and educational institutions guilty of past discrimination or in receipt of federal funding to demonstrate by positive action that they attempt to hire and admit minorities and women.

Aid to Families with Dependent Children (AFDC) Primary public assistance entitlement that transferred cash to households with state-determined need; replaced by TANF in 1996.

alternative tax proposals Efforts to supplement or replace the current federal income tax structure with alternatives, especially a flat tax or a value-added tax.

Americans with Disabilities Act of 1990 (ADA) Law that extended to persons with disabilities the kinds of protection granted to minorities and women in the 1964 Civil Rights Act.

amnesty Pardon granted to illegal immigrants for entering the country illegally, including permission to remain in the United States under certain conditions.

antitrust policy Policy aimed at preventing domination of a market by one or a small number of firms or agreements to restrict competition.

asylee Class of immigrants who claim political persecution in their home country based on their ideas or political activities.

AYP *See* **Adequate Yearly Progress**.

baby boom Generation of twenty years beginning in 1946.

balance of power Concept that no one power or coalition of powers will be allowed to gain such dominating power as to be able to dictate terms of the relationships among nations.

Balanced Budget Act of 1997 (BBA) Legislation aimed at eliminating the federal budget deficit through program cuts and revenue enhancements.

Bilingual Education Act of 1974 Provided federal funds to meet the language needs of non–English speaking students.

block grant Money provided by the federal government to state or local units for general purposes instead of specific projects.

boycott The organized attempt to deny patronage to a given business or agency to force it to change its behavior.

Bracero Program Agreement between Mexico and the United States for seasonal importation of Mexican workers from 1951 to 1964. *See* **guest worker**.

***Brown v. Board of Education* (1954)** Landmark decision by the Supreme Court that outlawed "separate but equal" educational facilities.

CAFE (corporate average fuel economy) Fuel economy standard requiring that the automobile industry produce a mix of cars with an average fuel efficiency of 26.5 miles per gallon.

cap and trade Market-based approach to controlling pollution emissions by granting firms permits for a specified level of emissions (cap) and allowing firms to sell or trade permits for any level they do not use up to their caps.

capitalism *See* **market capitalism**.

cash assistance Public assistance provided in the form of direct cash transfer.

categorical grants Money provided by the federal government to the states for a specific project with stipulations on exactly how the money can be used.

categorical programs Programs of social support for which a beneficiary qualifies by having a certain characteristic, for example, being over age sixty-five.

censorship A person or institution with authority to determine to which material society may be safely exposed without endangering public order, morality, or security.

Centers for Medicare and Medicaid Services (CMS) U.S. Department of Health and Human Services administrative entity responsible for administering Medicare, Medicaid, SCHIP, and the Patient Protection and Affordable Care Act.

charter school A tuition-free entity that receives funding from the state and provides educational choice to students and parents.

chlorofluorocarbons Any of several gaseous compounds that contain carbon, chlorine, fluorine, and sometimes hydrogen; major cause of stratospheric ozone depletion.

civic conservatism The idea that social rights should be secured by meeting some social obligation; first embodied in the Family Support Act of 1988.

Civil Rights Act of 1964 Law that forbids discrimination on the basis of race, creed, color, national origin, or gender in employment or places of public accommodation.

Civil Rights Act of 1965 Law that forbids discrimination in voting qualifications or election structures.

Civil Rights Act of 1968 Law that forbids discrimination on the basis of race, creed, color, or national origin in the sale or rental of most housing.

Civil Rights Act of 1991 Law that forbids racial quotas in hiring; makes statistical disparities in the workforce prima facie evidence of employment discrimination; and places burden of proof on employers to show business necessity for hiring qualifications.

class action suit Case in which one party sues on behalf of all people in a similar situation.

classical diplomacy *See* **realism**.

clear and present danger test Freedom of speech protected in the arena of public discussion, unless danger to public order is imminent.

CMS *See* **Centers for Medicare and Medicaid Services**.

Cold War Post–World War II tension between America and its allies and Soviet Union and its allies.

collective goods *See* **public goods**.

collective security Agreement by multiple nations to come to each other's assistance if attacked by another nation.

communitarianism Ideological movement stressing interconnection between rights and responsibilities; policy attention concentrates on local neighborhood and city institutions, community policing, family restoration, character formation, and education reform.

comparable worth Proposed legal guarantee of equal pay between men and women for different jobs requiring equal levels of skill, training, or responsibility.

comparative effectiveness Research studies that compare the relative success of medical treatments, tests, and pharmaceuticals in curing or alleviating various medical conditions. Treatments found to be most effective and least costly should be promoted and covered by public and private insurance.

compelling public interest High standard of proof needed for government to justify in court classifying a group differently from other groups.

conservatism Ideological position favoring individual responsibility, limited government, especially in economic matters, and state responsibility for social programs; usually associated with the Republican Party.

containment American Cold War policy of resisting the expansion of communism.

cost–benefit analysis Compares benefits or outcomes of a program with costs of implementing it.

Cost of Living Adjustment (COLA) A yearly adjustment to benefit levels in many entitlement programs to reflect increases in the cost of living resulting from inflation.

cost-push inflation Cost of goods and services increases even though demand remains constant or decreases.

Council of Economic Advisors (CEA) Panel of respected economists who advise the president on economic policy.

crime rate Usually derived from the FBI Uniform Crime Report (issued annually). In that source, it means the number of criminal acts in a category per 100,000 population.

cross-cutting requirements Case in which a condition on one grant is applied to all programs using federal funds.

crossover sanctions Sanctions applied to one program activity for failure to comply with certain conditions in another program.

Current Population Survey (CPS) The CPS *March Supplement* is the annual, nationally representative survey that documents people's income and is also used to derive the national poverty rate by comparing their incomes to the absolute poverty line.

decriminalization The legalization of victimless crimes or substantial reduction of penalties for their violation.

de facto segregation Educational segregation of races not caused by law or public policy, but by residential choice.

de jure segregation Educational segregation of races caused by state or local law or policy.

deficit spending Occurs when government expenditures exceed revenues in a given fiscal year.

defined benefit Present form of Medicare and Social Security in which level of some income or medical benefits is specified and all recipients meeting specified eligibility criteria are entitled to them.

defined contribution An approach to Medicare and pensions in which a fixed financial contribution for each individual is specified; recipients then receive benefits based on investment return of the funds and any funds they choose to contribute above the specified contribution.

demand-pull inflation Prices go up because the demand for goods and services grows faster than available supplies.

demand-side economics Traditional, Keynesian economic theory that the economy is driven primarily by demand for goods and services.

demography Generational, racial, and residential characteristics of a nation's population.

dependency The extent to which citizens depend on government for basic needs, rather than being able and/or willing to find work to provide for these needs.

depression Prolonged decline in economic activity because of a slump in demand. *See also* **recession**.

deregulation Removal of rules and restrictions on activities by government organizations.

deterrence Preventing an unwanted act from occurring by the threat of punishment of the potential perpetrator. In foreign policy, the possession of sufficient and varied power to survive the best first strike by a potential foe with enough power and willingness to inflict unacceptable damage on such an attacker.

dioxin Any of several heterocyclic hydrocarbons that occur as persistent toxic impurities in herbicides.

diplomacy Negotiations among the representatives of governments to resolve differences. Scholars differ as to whether an understood threat of force should be considered part of diplomacy.

direct costs and benefits Those related to the specific allocation of resources and the policy's impact on its intended population.

direct impact Outcomes related to a policy's impact on its intended population.

direct orders Regulations that prohibit or mandate state and local government actions.

discount rate Interest rate charged by the U.S. Federal Reserve Bank on loans to member banks.

Disparities Unjustified inequalities in the receipt of benefits such as health care and differences in outcomes according to race and ethnicity, income, education, and occupation.

distributive policies Policies that allocate benefits to certain segments of the population.

diversity immigrant Category of immigrant from countries with very low representation in the U.S. population.

donut hole Gap in coverage for prescription drugs under Medicare Part D; patients reaching this level must pay the entire cost of their prescriptions; scheduled to be eliminated under PPACA.

dual eligibles Low income persons covered by both Medicare and Medicaid.

due process of law Second paragraph of the Fourteenth Amendment, referring to the procedures the state must go through in order to take away life, liberty or property; used to apply the procedural part of the Bill of Rights to state criminal proceedings.

earned income tax credit Federal program of cash assistance to low-income working families.

EIC *See* **earned income tax credit**.

Elementary and Secondary Education Act of 1965 (ESEA) First federal legislation providing financial assistance to local schools for textbooks, libraries, and other instructional materials.

elite model Policy process model that focuses on the influence over policy exercised by powerful individuals or groups.

empirical dimension Aspect of policy evaluation referring to the measurable outputs and outcomes of a policy.

Employee Retirement Income Security Act Federal law that regulates and guarantees many private pension plans and self-funded health insurance plans.

employment-based preferences Admission of immigrants based on job skills or abilities.

enterprise zones Geographic areas designated for economic development where government, private, and nonprofit organizations work together to solve problems with tax incentives and other financial help.

entitlement Government benefit programs to which persons have a legal right because they meet program criteria; for example, Medicare and Social Security.

Equal Employment Opportunity Commission (EEOC) Federal agency that implements policy toward ending discrimination by employers or labor unions with twenty-five or more persons.

Equal Rights Amendment (ERA) Proposed constitutional amendment rejected in 1982; would have eradicated most gender-based classifications in law and public policy.

equality of material well-being Concept of proportional equality; the idea that a social group's percentage in the overall population should be equaled by its share of material benefits.

equality of opportunity Right of all individuals to realize the human potential to become whatever their personal abilities allow, free from barriers imposed by society and its institutions.

equality under law Concept that government must treat people as individuals rather than members of groups; when categorizations are made, the burden of proof rests on government to show they express a valid public purpose.

ERA *See* **Equal Rights Amendment**.

ERISA *See* **Employee Retirement Income Security Act**.

ESEA *See* **Elementary and Secondary Education Act**.

establishment clause Clause in the First Amendment forbidding direct government support of religion and prohibiting granting any one sect special status.

EU *See* **European Union**.

European Union (EU) Association of European nations to integrate their economic systems and currency as well as many social policies.

exclusionary rule Constitutional principle that illegally obtained evidence may not be used in court.

externalities *See* **indirect impact**.

Faith-Based and Community Initiative Program of the George W. Bush presidency to encourage government partnerships with faith-based and other community organizations to provide programs of social assistance.

family reunification Immigration policy giving preference to family members of citizens or permanent residents.

fast track authority When president is given authority to negotiate a trade treaty and Congress has to accept or reject it without changes.

Fatah Yasser Arafat's wing of the Palestinian Authority (PA). While the perpetrator of numerous terrorist acts in the past, it occasionally is willing to negotiate with Israel and, hence, is regarded as the comparatively moderate wing of the Palestinian Authority.

Federal Insurance Contributions Act (FICA) Payroll tax on employers and employees to support Social Security and Medicare including old age, survivors, and disability insurance (OASDI).

Federal Reserve Board (Fed) The central banking authority of the United States and the principal agent of monetary policy.

federalism Political system that distributes powers between a central government (national) and constituent units (states); power relationship cannot be changed except by action of both levels.

fee-for-service (FFS) Health care payment system in which each separate consultation, procedure, or device has a separate and specific price for which the patient or insurance company is billed.

feminism Ideology that evaluates policy according to impact on role of women in society.

FICA *See* **Federal Insurance Contributions Act**.

fiscal policy Tax policy, spending policy, and debt policy used as tools to stabilize the economy.

fossil fuel Fuel (coal, oil, or natural gas) formed in the earth from plant or animal remains.

free enterprise Private ownership of the means of production operating through supply and demand.

free exercise clause Clause in the First Amendment that forbids government from impeding the practice of religion.

GATT *See* **General Agreement on Tariffs and Trade**.

Gaza Small strip of land on the southern coast of Palestine that fell from Egyptian to Israeli control in the Six Day War. Israel evicted its settlers and turned the land to Palestinian control in spring 2007.

GDP *See* **gross domestic product**.

General Agreement on Tariffs and Trade (GATT) International agreement to reduce barriers to free trade.

general revenue sharing Transfer of money from one level of government to another with little or no restriction on its use.

geothermal Technology utilizing the heat of the earth's interior to produce steam for electricity.

globalization World economic and industrial system in which the impact of economic and other activities transcends international borders.

government subsidy Policy that supports a particular group or interest, usually with cash payments.

Great Society Considered the period of 1961–1978 during which substantial expansion of the U.S. welfare state occurred.

green card Immigrant permit to work in the United States.

greenhouse gases Carbon dioxide, chlorofluorocarbons, methane, and more than a dozen other gases in concentration in the atmosphere, so called because of their heat-trapping "greenhouse" properties.

gross domestic product (GDP) Measures the value of all goods and services produced in a nation in a single year.

group model Policy process model that emphasizes interest groups that form advocacy coalitions that are active in some policy areas, but not in others.

guest worker Program allowing workers to enter the United States for certain jobs on the promise to return to their home country at the end of the work period. *See* **Bracero Program**.

Hamas Militant wing of the Palestinian Authority (PA) who won control of the PA in a 2007 election and control of Gaza by force. Hamas is explicitly committed to the extermination of Israel and rejects any negotiation with or recognition of that state.

Health Care and Education Reconciliation Act 2010 budget reconciliation act that accompanied and made changes in the health care reform legislation (PPACA).

health savings accounts (HSA) Individual tax-free savings plans and high deductible insurance used to cover medical expenses.

hegemony A situation in which one nation so dominates other nations that it may dictate the terms of the relationship between them without the need to compromise its interests.

historical institutionalism Model of the policy process that stresses how early policy decisions carry large effects through time, so that policies become *path dependent*.

home schooling Form of education in which parents assume complete responsibility for the education of their children.

hostile takeover When a company acquires another company against the wishes of the one being acquired.

HSA *See* **health savings accounts.**

idealism Principle that there are knowable and universal principles of justice over and above the laws and policies of any particular state. These principles should guide foreign policy.

illegal immigrant Immigrant who has entered the United States without proper documents.

immigrant Person who newly arrives in a nation with intent to settle.

impacts (sometimes called outcomes) Actual effects that policy outputs have on society; can be intended or unintended.

implementation Steps taken to put a policy into practice to achieve the policymaker's goals.

income maintenance/income support *See* **public assistance**; **social insurance**.

independent regulatory commission Agency independent of direct presidential or congressional control, designed to regulate a specific sector of the economy.

indexation of benefits *See* **Cost of Living Adjustment**.

indirect costs and benefits Those related to a policy's impact on individuals and groups not intended to be part of the target population.

indirect impact Outcomes related to a policy's impact on individuals and groups other than its intended population; also referred to as externalities or spillover effects.

inflation Rise in price of goods and services while the value of goods and services does not increase.

in-kind assistance Public assistance provided in the form of goods, for example, food or housing.

institutional model This model stresses the opportunities and constraints on policy that are part of the very structure of the American constitutional order.

intended impact Policy consequence anticipated as the policy or program was developed.

intergovernmental relations Relationships between national government and states and local governments, as well as interactions between and among states and local governments.

interstate compact Formal agreement between or among states to address specific issues.

Intifada Arab term referring to a popular uprising involving recurring use of nonmilitary violence to weaken and ultimately destroy Israel.

investor immigrant Immigrant who is granted a *green card* based on investment of $1 million and employment of ten employees or other combinations of investment and employment.

Islamism or Islamist Radical and militant aspects of Islam, not the entire Muslim world.

Jihad Muslim concept whose most frequent use in foreign policy means a "holy war" to defend or advance the faith.

judicial activism Nullification of a law or governmental action by a court using an interpretation of the Constitution on which reasonable persons might disagree.

liberalism Ideological position favoring equality, social responsibility, limited government, especially in matters of personal choice, and federal responsibility for social programs; usually associated with the Democratic Party.

libertarianism Ideology that combines conservative economic agenda with liberal social ideas.

macroeconomic policy Overall government management of the economy.

maintenance of effort State and local governments cannot use federal money to replace their own spending on a program.

managed care System for organizing provision and payment for medical care; characterized by selective contracting, physician gatekeepers, and other procedures for controlling use of health care resources.

market capitalism Private ownership of means of production and trade with unrestricted marketplace.

market failure A concept justifying government intervention into a realm of economic activity when the conditions for the effective operation of free markets are absent or imperfect.

MCT *See* **minimum competency tests.**

means test Determination of minimum income required for receipt of government assistance.

Medicaid A state–federal public assistance program to provide health care for low income persons.

Medicare A federal program of social insurance for the health care needs of elderly and disabled persons.

Medicare Modernization Act (MMA) 2003 legislation that added a prescription benefit to Medicare and created new features to address the program's long-term problems.

Medigap Federally regulated private insurance policies designed to cover medical expenses not covered by Medicare.

merger Action in which two or more firms combine to form one firm.

microeconomic policy Government activities regarding particular firms and businesses.

minimum competency tests (MCTs) Tests required by the states and now utilized by the No Child Left Behind Act to measure student performance; sometimes required for movement to the next school grade or for high school graduation.

***Miranda* rule** Includes (1) the right to remain silent, (2) the right to know that anything said can and will be used against the accused in court, and (3) the right to be represented by counsel, at state expense if necessary.

models of policy making Pictures of the policy process that summarize the primary forces at work in order to reduce complexity to a degree manageable for policy analysis.

monetary policy A macroeconomic tool that seeks to use the supply of money in circulation to impact interest rates and inflation.

money supply A measure of the amount and value of money in circulation, including currency and deposits in banks, credit unions, and savings institutions.

monopoly Situation in which there is an absence of competition, blocked entry into the market, a single seller, or a few sellers who work together to limit competition.

mother's pensions State-level cash assistance to widows with children that became a model for the design of federal assistance in the Social Security Act of 1935.

multiculturalism Educational reform movement with objective to change traditional views of the Western European impact on the Americas; emphasis placed on respecting the diverse and disparate ethnic elements in American society.

multilateralism View that serious foreign policies ought to be implemented only in concert with and presumably with the blessing of one's major allies.

NAFTA *See* **North American Free Trade Agreement**.

national debt Accumulation over time of annual deficits.

national health insurance Health care system in which all citizens have access to health care through guaranteed government-mandated insurance.

nationalization Government ownership of an enterprise.

natural gas Gas from bored wells consisting of a combustible mixture of methane and hydrocarbons used chiefly as a fuel.

naturalization The process by which an immigrant becomes a citizen.

neo-conservatives Ideological group critical of government regulation of business and suspicious of government action to correct past injustices, such as affirmative action; not, however, as opposed to government macroeconomic activity; favor an assertive foreign policy.

New Right Ideological movement often associated with evangelical Christians; directs most attention to social issues, abortion, same-sex marriage, feminism, pornography, and government interference in religious expression.

No Child Left Behind Act (2001) The major education initiative of President George W. Bush.

normative dimension Aspect of policy evaluation referring to values, beliefs, and attitudes of society, of particular groups, and of policy evaluators themselves.

North American Free Trade Agreement (NAFTA) Free trade agreement among United States, Canada, and Mexico.

Nuremberg Principle Principle that the leadership and population of the sovereign nations of the world are morally obligated to disregard and disobey laws and policies to the extent that these laws and policies violate universal principles of justice.

OASDI *See* **Old Age, Survivors, and Disability Insurance**.

obscenity Published material offending fundamental values of a society and containing strong sexual content or egregious violence.

Office of Management and Budget (OMB) Agency in the Executive Office of the President that assists the president in the preparation of the federal budget.

oil depletion allowance Allowed oil companies to deduct part of their gross income from taxable income to allow for the nonrenewability of the oil they produced.

Old Age, Survivors, and Disability Insurance The primary programs constituting Social Security; funded by the Federal Insurance Contributions Act (FICA).

OPEC *See* **Organization of Petroleum Exporting Countries**.

open market operations Tool of monetary policy, used by the Federal Reserve Board, involving the purchase and sale of U.S. Treasury and other federal agency securities.

open society A society in which all perspectives on controversial moral questions are tolerated and may be advocated.

Organization of Petroleum Exporting Countries (OPEC) Organization representing the major oil and natural gas producing nations in the developing world.

outcomes *See* **impacts**.

outputs Observable and measurable results of policy adoption and implementation.

ozone Reactive form of oxygen formed naturally in the atmosphere by a photochemical reaction; a major air pollutant in the lower atmosphere, but a beneficial component of the upper atmosphere.

ozone layer An atmospheric layer at heights of about twenty to thirty miles (thirty-two to forty-eight kilometers) normally characterized by high ozone content that blocks most solar ultraviolet radiation.

Palestine A geographic entity that includes the states of Israel and Jordan as well as the unallocated territories called Gaza and the West Bank. It was part of the Byzantine and Turkish Empires; then a League of Nations and U.N. Mandate under British administration until the 1947 Partition.

partial birth abortion A procedure used in late-stage abortions in which the infant is partially removed from the womb; its skull is penetrated and its brains sucked out, making the head more removable. It is regarded by pro-life forces as virtual infanticide.

partial preemption Situations in which national government requires or permits states to administer policies as long as states meet federal criteria for the program.

path dependency Feature of the historical institutional model that recognizes how actions taken in past policy decisions are difficult to reverse.

Patient Protection and Affordable Care Act (PPACA) Health care reform legislation enacted in March 2010.

pay-for-performance (P4P) programs adopted by CMS giving financial incentives (bonuses) or financial disincentives (payment reductions) to health providers who employ proven, evidence-based medicine measures that improve the quality of care.

PAYGO ("pay-as-you-go") Mechanism to control federal spending; requires that spending for any new program has to be matched by a corresponding tax increase or cuts in other programs.

performance management Ongoing review of program accomplishments and problems, and improving results, through decisions based upon the review, with accountability for performance.

permanent resident Immigrant who has been granted the right to live permanently in the United States.

Personal Responsibility and Work Opportunity Reconciliation Act (PRWORA) Public assistance reform legislation passed in 1996.

plea bargaining Offer by prosecutorial forces to reduce criminal charges to those carrying lighter punishment in return for a guilty plea, thus avoiding the costs and uncertainties of a criminal trial.

pluralist model Model of the policy process that stresses that many groups and individuals influence the American democratic system.

policy *See* **public policy**.

policy advocacy Activity by political, interest, or ideological groups or individuals to advance their preferred policy options on the political agenda.

policy analysis Field of political science principally concerned with describing and investigating how and why policies are proposed, adopted, and implemented.

policy evaluation Process of assessing impacts of a policy, that is, the policy's effects on society compared with the policy's intended goals.

Poor Law England's 1601 codification of several prior statutes into one law placing responsibility for the poor with local authorities, allowing for harsh treatment of the able-bodied if they refused to work and provided care for the dependent poor.

populism A movement mobilizing less educated persons, placing faith in their common sense wisdom, and expressing distrust of elites in general and intellectuals in particular.

poverty line An absolute number, computed as three times the U.S. Department of Agriculture's "thrifty food budget"; serves as the income threshold below which a family is considered to be poor.

power Relationship between two or more actors such that the power wielder can get others to do what the power wielder wants them to do and which they otherwise would not have done.

PPACA *See* **Patient Protection and Affordable Care Act**.

preemption The principle that federal law takes precedence over state law and that the federal government may prohibit state action on an issue.

preemptive war Attack on a state or power that poses an imminent threat without waiting for the other state to strike the first blow.

preferential treatment Policy to use membership in a designated group as one positive factor to be taken into account for employment or admission.

presumption of constitutionality Principle that whenever a law or government action is challenged as being unconstitutional, the burden of proof ought to be with the challenger. Judges should not substitute their choices for those of elected officials.

prior restraint Right of government to suppress something said or written in advance of the utterance; *see* **censorship**.

private goods Goods that can be divided and allocated to some persons, but not others. *See also* **public goods**.

privatization (education) Form of education policy in which the operation of either a single school or an entire district may be contracted to a private firm.

privatization (health or social insurance) Conversion of all or part of a social program, such as Social Security, from public control to control by individual program participants.

program evaluation Evaluation of the specific programs created by public policies.

progressive *See* **liberalism**.

proportional equality *See* **equality of material well-being**.

prorationing Governmental regulations to impose production quotas on private energy companies in order to reduce supply.

prospective payment system Medical care reimbursement methodology based on fixed payments for certain diagnoses, rather than on the cost of care.

PRWORA *See* **Personal Responsibility and Work Opportunity Reconciliation Act**.

public assistance Means-tested and categorical programs providing income and support for low-income persons; for example, TANF and food stamps.

public choice model A model of the policy process that thinks of those active in policymaking as actors attempting to choose options that maximize their self-interest.

public goods Goods that cannot be divided. *See also* **private goods**.

public policy An intentional course of action followed by a government institution or official for resolving an issue of public concern.

quota A specific number or percentage allocated to particular groups in hiring, promotion, or in immigration.

racial preference plan Use of race as one among several factors in selecting from an open applicant pool.

racial profiling Sometime police practice of singling out certain racial groups for more intense scrutiny.

rational–comprehensive model Policy process model that conceives of policymakers taking account of all information and options, then selecting the policy options that best fulfill the policymaker's goals.

realism View that the only legitimate goal of foreign policy is national self-interest.

recession Period where there is a decline in economic activity arising from slump in demand for goods and services. *See also* **depression**.

recidivism Rate at which people who have been punished for past crimes commit more crimes.

redistribution policies Policies that allocate benefits or services to certain parts of the population and tax other parts of the population to generate funds.

refugee Person displaced from home country because of political instability or persecution.

regulatory policies Those policies imposing constraints on individuals and groups.

reserve requirement Amount of money a bank must keep on reserve.

retribution Literally revenge; more generally, punishment to satisfy a sense of justice being served.

risk subsidy Government subsidy that protects businesses or consumers from risks of the marketplace.

Road Map to Peace George W. Bush administration's plan outlining the steps toward a final settlement between Israel and Palestinians.

rogue state Nation-state that exhibits disregard for accepted rules of international conduct.

SCHIP *See* **State Children's Health Insurance Program**.

school choice Allowing parents to send their children to schools outside the school geographic boundary including other public schools, private schools, charter schools, and home schooling.

secular humanism A concept that humankind can control its fate independently of the will of a deity and that improvement of life is the proper goal of human action.

secularization Decline of conventional religion, of regular church attendance, and of belief in traditional religious doctrines, along with restriction of religion to private spheres of life.

self-regulatory policies Regulatory policies that give persons or groups regulated authority to formulate and police the regulations governing them.

sequestration Automatic spending cuts across the board if Congress approves spending levels exceeding targeted budget deficit levels.

service intensity A concept in health care referring to a rising number of procedures per year on the average patient.

sexual harassment Legally forbidden situation in which one person, having power over some aspect of another's life uses the power persistently over time to extort sexual favors or create a hostile working environment.

Sheppard–Towner Act of 1918 Established grants-in-aid from the national government to the states to support a range of child health–related programs, the first modern U.S. national effort to deal with poverty-related issues.

single-payer plan Health care access reform proposal that eliminates all private insurance in favor of a national or state-administered single health insurance program.

social insurance Programs of public insurance with mandatory universal or near-universal participation; for example, Social Security and Medicare.

Social Security Program of social insurance providing minimum levels of income for persons aged sixty-five and over, as well as income for disabled workers and surviving spouses and children of deceased workers.

Social Security Act 1935 legislation (amended numerous times since) creating the most important federal programs of social insurance, especially Social Security.

socialism Public or governmental ownership and control of major means of production, distribution, and exchange.

socialized medicine Government-owned and -operated health care system in which all citizens have access to free or very low cost medical care.

solid waste Material discarded because it has served its purpose or is no longer useful. Sources of solid waste include residential, commercial, institutional, and industrial activities.

sovereignty Final power of a political unit to make and enforce its own laws.

sphere of influence Territories contiguous to the borders of a major power in which it is assumed the major power will be the dominant influence and hostile systems will not be tolerated.

spillover effects *See* **indirect impact**.

SSI *See* **Supplemental Security Income**.

stages of policy development Heuristic simplification of the policy process: (1) problem definition or issues formation, (2) policy demands, (3) agenda formation, (4) policy adoption, (5) implementation, (6) evaluation, and (7) policy redefinition.

State Children's Health Insurance Program (SCHIP) Federal block grant to states to expand health insurance coverage to children in families with incomes above the Medicaid eligibility level.

strip mining Mine worked from the earth's surface by the stripping of overburden; typically a coal or copper mining technique.

sunset laws Statutes requiring a program to be terminated at some specific time unless an evaluation leads to a decision to continue it.

Supplemental Nutrition Assistance Program (SNAP) Formerly the Food Stamp program, provides low-income people money that can be spent only on food.

Supplemental Security Income (SSI) Program of cash assistance to aged or disabled persons with incomes below a federal standard.

supply-side economics Macroeconomic approach that emphasizes tax cuts and tax incentives to business in order to promote economic growth.

TANF *See* **Temporary Assistance to Needy Families**.

Temporary Assistance to Needy Families (TANF) Program of cash assistance to families with incomes below state-determined standards.

terrorism Random violence against civilian or noncombatant populations to compel another power to change its policies by generating widespread anxiety or fear among its people.

Title IX of the Educational Amendment Acts of 1972 Law forbidding educational institutions receiving federal funds to engage in gender discrimination, especially in athletic programs.

trade promotion authority *See* **fast track authority**.

underclass Persons who are persistently poor and have serious educational, family, attitudinal, job-skill, or emotional–psychological barriers to social integration.

undocumented workers Persons who take jobs in the United States without the legal right to do so.

unemployment insurance Social insurance entitlement program to maintain the income of workers in periods of involuntary unemployment.

unfunded mandates Requirements imposed on state and local governments with no national government funding to implement them.

Uniform Crime Report Official national crime statistics issued by the Federal Bureau of Investigation (FBI).

unilateralism Policies undertaken without first obtaining political and material support from most major allies.

unintended impact Consequence not anticipated as the policy or program was developed.

victimless crime Crime in which participants are assumed to be consenting or willing adults.

vouchers for education Form of education financing that allows public tax dollars to be redeemed at either private or public schools for education services.

wall of separation Interpretation of the establishment clause that forbids any government support or assistance to religious belief and practice. *See also* **accommodationist**.

War on Poverty Period of 1964–1972 associated with antipoverty programs' growth and change.

welfare *See* **public assistance**.

welfare state A political system that guarantees a generous minimum standard of life through social services, education, public assistance, social insurance, and employment programs to all citizens as a political right, not as charity.

welfare state capitalism System in which allocation of goods and services is partially planned, but production is in private hands.

West Bank Portion of Palestine that lies between the Jordan River and the 1947 boundaries of Israel. Peace process advocates see this as the major part of the new Palestinian Arab state; however, Israel has not dismantled all the Jewish settlements that sprang up there in the wake of the 1967 war.

white-collar crime Crimes committed by middle-class business executives or professionals within their offices or workplaces, involving financial transactions such as stock fraud, embezzlement, or price fixing.

Wilsonian Idealism *See* **idealism**.

World Trade Organization (WTO) Organization that monitors and settles international trade disputes pursuant to GATT.

workers' compensation Social insurance entitlement program to maintain the income and pay medical bills of workers injured on the job.

WTO *See* **World Trade Organization**.

Index

Note: Page numbers in italic type indicate figures or tables.